PORTUGUESE OCEANIC EXPANSION, 1400–1800

This book presents a unique overview of Portuguese oceanic expansion between 1400 and 1800. The chapters treat a wide range of subjects – economy and society, politics and institutions, cultural configurations and comparative dimensions – and radically update data on and interpretations of the economic and financial trends of the Portuguese empire.

Interregional networks are analyzed in a substantial way. Patterns of settlement, political configurations, ecclesiastical structures, and local powers are put in global context. Language and literature, the arts, and science and technology are revisited with refreshing and innovative approaches. The interaction between Portuguese and local people is studied in different contexts, and the entire imperial and colonial culture of the Portuguese world is looked at synthetically for the first time. In short, this book provides a broad understanding of the Portuguese empire in its first four centuries as a factor in the history of the world and as a major component of European expansion.

Francisco Bethencourt is Charles Boxer Professor, King's College London. He is the author of *O imaginario da magia* and *L'inquisition à l'époque moderne: Espagne, Portugal, Italie, XVe–XIXe siècles* and the editor of *História da expansão Portuguesa* (with Kirti Chaudhuri) and *A memória da Nação* (with Diogo Ramada Curto). From 1982 to 1996 he taught at the Universidade Nova de Lisboa, and he has been a visiting professor at the Universidade de São Paulo and at Brown University. He has been Director of the National Library of Portugal and of the Gulbenkian Foundation Cultural Center in Paris.

Diogo Ramada Curto is Vasco da Gama Professor, European University Institute, Florence. He is the author of *O discurso politico em Portugal* and the editor of *The Jesuits as Cultural Intermediaries*, *La cartografia Europea tra primo rinascimento e fine dell'Illuminismo* (with Angelo Cattaneo), *O tempo de Vasco da Gama*, and *A memória da Nação* (with Francisco Bethencourt). He has been a lecturer, reader, and professor at Universidade Nova de Lisboa and a visiting professor at Yale and Brown universities.

Portuguese Oceanic Expansion, 1400–1800

Edited by

Francisco Bethencourt
King's College London

Diogo Ramada Curto
European University Institute, Florence, Italy

CAMBRIDGE
UNIVERSITY PRESS

CAMBRIDGE UNIVERSITY PRESS
Cambridge, New York, Melbourne, Madrid, Cape Town, Singapore, São Paulo

Cambridge University Press
32 Avenue of the Americas, New York, NY 10013-2473, USA

www.cambridge.org
Information on this title: www.cambridge.org/9780521846448

Published with the cooperation and support of the John Carter Brown Library, an institution for advanced research in history and the humanities, founded in 1846 and located at Brown University in Providence, Rhode Island, since 1901.

First published 2007

Printed in the United States of America

A catalog record for this publication is available from the British Library.

Library of Congress Cataloging in Publication Data

Portuguese oceanic expansion, 1400–1800 / edited by Francisco Bethencourt, Diogo Ramada Curto.
p. cm.
Includes bibliographical references and index.
ISBN-13: 978-0-521-84644-8 (hardback)
ISBN-10: 0-521-84644-7 (hardback)
ISBN-13: 978-0-521-60891-6 (pbk.)
ISBN-10: 0-521-60891-0 (pbk.)
1. Portugal – History – Period of discoveries, 1385–1580. 2. Portugal – History – Modern, 1580– 3. Portugal – Territorial expansion. 4. Portugal – Colonies – History. 5. Portugal – Civilization. I. Bethencourt, Francisco. II. Curto, Diogo Ramada. III. Title.
DP583.P677 2006
325′.34690903–dc22 2006011732

ISBN 978-0-521-84644-8 hardback
ISBN 978-0-521-60891-6 paperback

The publication of this work has been made possible by generous grants to the John Carter Brown Library from

Fundação Luso-Americana para o Desenvolvimento

Fundação Calouste Gulbenkian

Fundação Oriente

Fundação para a Ciência e a Tecnologia

CONTENTS

Contents

CONTRIBUTORS

Luiz Felipe de Alencastro Université de Paris IV Sorbonne

Francisco Bethencourt King's College London

Diogo Ramada Curto European University Institute, Florence

Anthony Disney La Trobe University

Francisco Contente Domingues University of Lisbon

Felipe Fernández-Armesto Tufts University

Michael N. Pearson University of Technology, Sydney

Jorge M. Pedreira Secretário de Estado Adjunto e da Educação, Portugal

Luís de Sousa Rebelo King's College London

A. J. R. Russell-Wood Johns Hopkins University

Isabel dos Guimarães Sá University of Minho

Stuart B. Schwartz Yale University

Luís de Moura Sobral University of Montreal

John K. Thornton Boston University

FOREWORD

Norman Fiering

The year 1998 marked the 500th anniversary of the landing of Vasco da Gama on the west coast of India after rounding the southern tip of Africa and crossing the Indian Ocean. The voyage was the outcome of decades of systematic effort by the Portuguese. Two years later, in 2000, the 500th anniversary of the Portuguese landing in Brazil was recognized internationally. These two events of incomparable importance changed the world forever.

In the mid-1990s, at Brown University, which is a national center for Luso-Brazilian studies, in the aftermath of the international commemorations of Columbus's historic voyages sponsored by the Spanish, we felt a certain responsibility to recognize the much less appreciated Portuguese achievement in that era of European expansion and global encounters.

Brown has a Department of Portuguese and Brazilian Studies, one of the few in the United States; an endowed Vasco da Gama Chair of History; and an unequaled collection of colonial Braziliana at the John Carter Brown Library, an independently funded and administered center for advanced research located on the campus. Representatives of these three different constituencies – specifically Onésimo Almeida, Francisco Bethencourt, Diogo Ramada Curto, and I – met for lunch in 1997 determined to use the Portuguese quincentenaries as a springboard for remedial action.

Our principal goal was to provide the English-speaking academic world with better, more up-to-date intellectual resources for telling the story of the Portuguese expansion in the early modern era. Good scholarly literature on the Portuguese colonial empire was at best scarce (the field has always been a small one in the United States), sometimes dated, and most of the time written in the Portuguese language.

Foreword

We drew up a hypothetical table of contents of a comprehensive collection of essays on the early Portuguese empire, with each essay designed to review a major area of activity in that era and to address the salient questions. We then sought foundation support, first to underwrite the commissioning of these essays and second to bring all of the proposed authors together in Providence over a period of several days for group critiques of each contribution.

Money was forthcoming from several foundations in Portugal, for which we are deeply grateful, and our mini-conference on Portuguese Oceanic Expansion, 1400 to 1800, was held June 11 to 13, 1999. It is a pleasure to note here all who were present at this remarkable gathering, where each paper was intensively scrutinized and recommendations made for revision: Luis Felipe de Alencastro, Brazil; Francisco Bethencourt, Portugal; Diogo Ramada Curto, Portugal; Anthony Disney, Australia; Felipe Fernández-Armesto, United Kingdom; Malyn Newitt, United Kingdom; Michael Pearson, Australia; Jorge Pedreira, Portugal; John Russell-Wood, United States; Isabel dos Guimarães Sá, Portugal; Stuart Schwartz, United States; Luís Moura Sobral, Canada; John Thornton, United States; and George Winius, the Netherlands. Two contributors to the resulting volume of essays were not able to be present at this meeting: Francisco Domingues, Portugal, and Luís de Sousa Rebelo, United Kingdom. In the end, not all of those present ultimately produced an essay for the volume.

Collections such as this typically take a long time to evolve from the initial manuscript stage to printed book – in our case, an embarrassing seven years – and still, despite the luxury of time, the result never quite realizes early dreams of encyclopedic comprehensiveness. Some critics of this volume therefore may be quick to notice what is *not* in it, despite the broad promise of the title. News of such deficiencies will not be a surprise to those who put the book together. We accomplished what we could, given the usual practical limits.

The greatest obstacle to gaining a true understanding of the past is our human tendency to read the present into it. Because Portugal is not a world power at the moment, historians feel free to give it scant attention even when writing about sixteenth- and seventeenth-century Europe. One of the missions of the John Carter Brown Library is to encourage approaches to the era of European expansion between 1400 and 1800 that take fully into account the astonishing initiatives of the Dutch and Portuguese, small countries that were big players at a particular moment. The expansion of Europe was without question the most important phenomenon in modern history, with an impact on every square inch of the globe. The consequences in moral terms were mixed, to say the least, but the sheer scope of the impact cannot be denied. The state of the world today traces back to the era of European expansion with only the slightest effort.

The organization of the study and teaching of history in the United States has in the past one hundred years been biased toward the history of the "great powers" of the past two centuries: England, France, Germany, and Russia. It is a case of history belonging to the victors. Yet anyone viewing the world in about 1600 without knowledge of what was to come would not have the same prejudices as existed around 1900.

The active interest by historians in what is now commonly called the "early modern period," which has the advantage of paying little heed to such traditional continental European categories as "Renaissance" and "Enlightenment," has compelled attention to the actual world situation between 1400 and 1800 and to the European overseas incursions that led to a reshaping of the world (as well as to the transformation of Europe itself).

In such contexts as "early modern" and "European expansion," little Portugal is seen to have played a large role, to have met and conquered tremendous hurdles, and to have been pathbreaking in discoveries and deeds.

In viewing this early modern world and its overseas empires, it has become increasingly apparent how much these empires interacted with one another as economic and political rivals in vast maritime settings such as the Atlantic and the Indian oceans. Historians now speak regularly of an "Atlantic history," which necessitates attention to Brazil and Angola and ultimately to the Portuguese empire as a whole.

Moreover, if history was written backward when the story of the "great powers" became dominant in the curriculum, it may also be written backward again when events at the end of the twentieth century reveal the past in a different light. With Iberia now a full participant in the community of European nations, some periods in Portugal's past can only be seen as temporary digressions away from Europe, and the history of Portugal must be retold as having been integral to European history. As the progeny of Portuguese expansion continue to develop, such as in the case of Brazil, it also becomes more urgent to understand the nature and impact of Portuguese culture around the world. As Brazil grows in economic power and gains in stature in international affairs, the need will persist to understand its past and then by implication the past of the Portuguese empire as a whole.

The importance of the Portuguese empire in the history of mankind may be measured by the extraordinary number of people in different parts of the globe for whom to this day the Portuguese language is their mother tongue. The Lusophone world stretches from Macao to East Timor, to Goa, to Angola and Mozambique, to the Cape Verde islands and the Azores, and

Brazil. Portuguese speakers outnumber nearly all other speakers of European languages – English and Spanish excepted. Goa, on the west coast of India, the virtual capital of the Portuguese Asian empire since 1510, was wrested from the Portuguese by the new nation-state of India only in 1961, after some 450 years of Portuguese rule. The stamp of Portuguese culture upon Goa is indelible, and to this day it remains a unique enclave on the Indian subcontinent.

Avoiding on the one hand a glorified or triumphal Eurocentrism and on the other a vapid, politicized multiculturalism or decentered "world history" that lacks a coherent narrative structure, the objective study of the facts of European expansion recognizes the central dynamic of modern history, but it does not gloss over the negative and profoundly disruptive effects of that expansion. Such a study does not fail to observe as well that in the great global interaction that followed, Europe was itself a huge beneficiary.

The economic integration of humankind, which is so overwhelmingly obvious today, had its beginnings under Portuguese auspices more than 500 years ago. If one is to arrive at a sound knowledge of this process of globalization, the Portuguese case must be closely considered, along with Spanish, Dutch, French, and English territorial and maritime expansion. This volume will make it infinitely easier for students and scholars to confront the Portuguese story.

Director and Librarian Emeritus
The John Carter Brown Library

PREFACE

Francisco Bethencourt and Diogo Ramada Curto

The planning for this volume took place during an extended period of collective work that began as a conference at the John Carter Brown Library in June 1999. At this meeting, we discussed the potential significance of the collection and circulated initial versions of our texts. A second, more extended discussion followed, with revised versions of the chapters and a clearer and more coherent sense of the overall shape of the volume to follow. In some cases, the process of redacting and correcting texts in English led to further delays in a process that at its outset was conceived as being far less lengthy than it turned out to be. However, the structure of the collection was relatively stable from the very beginning, notwithstanding certain lacunae that became difficult to fill.

Our special thanks go to Onésimo Teotónio Almeida of the Department of Portuguese and Brazilian Studies at Brown University, who took the initial planning and organizational stages of the conference upon himself and followed the project through to its completion. We are indebted as well to Professor Philip Benedict for his close reading of one of the essays. Another expression of gratitude goes to Dr. José Blanco of the Fundação Calouste Gulbenkian and to Dr. Rui Machette of the Luso-American Development Foundation (FLAD) for making the conference possible. The final product owes a great debt to Norman Fiering, Director of the John Carter Brown Library until July 2006, for accepting the project at the exemplary institution he oversaw for twenty-three years, for taking a principal role in the discussions of the texts, and for consistently stimulating us in our role as coordinators of the project. He has also played a crucial part in revising the texts, demanding that unclear ideas be made more explicit and correcting successive versions of the papers. His efforts made it possible for two

Portuguese historians to serve as editors of a volume in which the majority of contributors were native English speakers. The publication of this volume would have been inconceivable without his involvement, dedication, and exemplary intellectual activity.

Map 1. Portuguese settlements on the west coast of Africa and on the Atlantic islands.

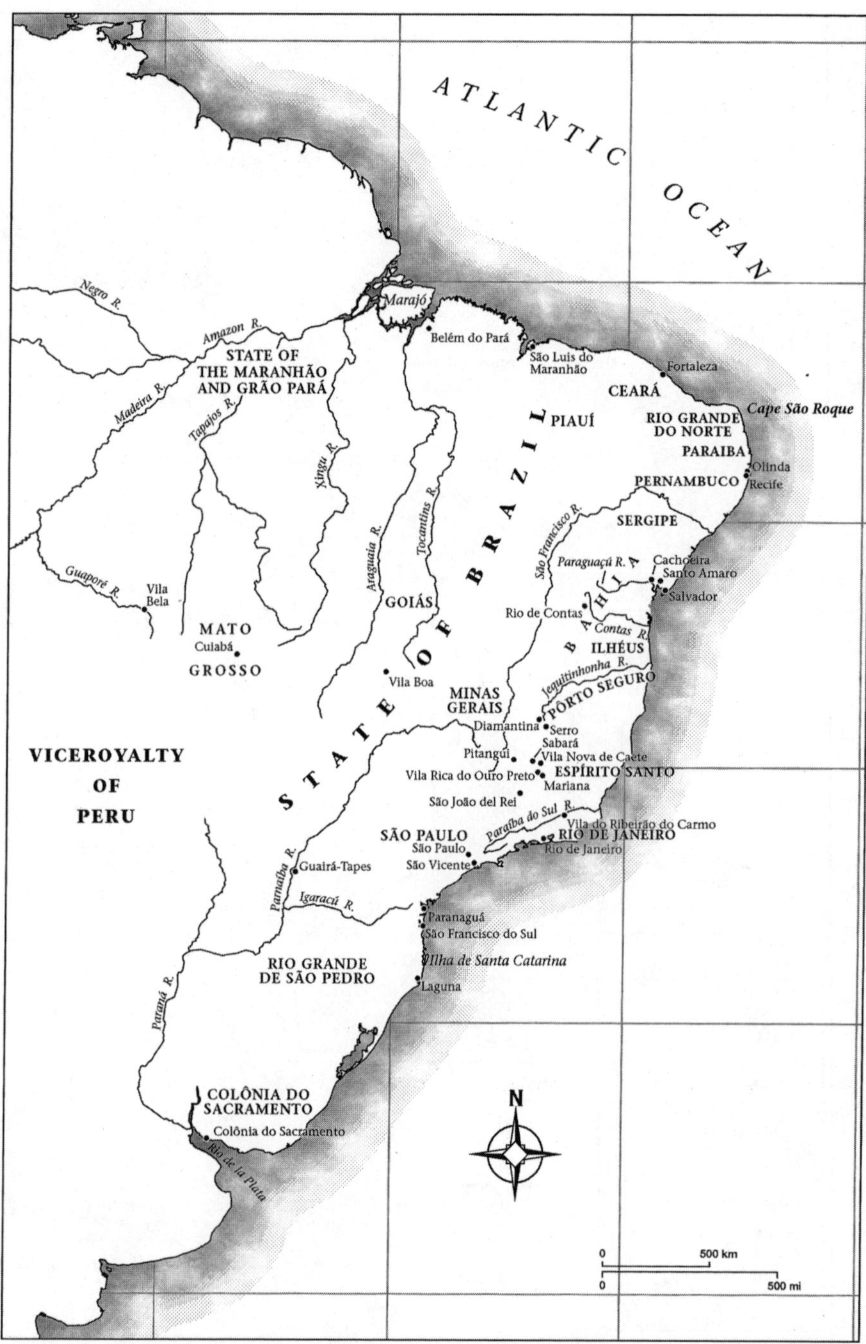

Map 2. Portuguese settlements in Brazil.

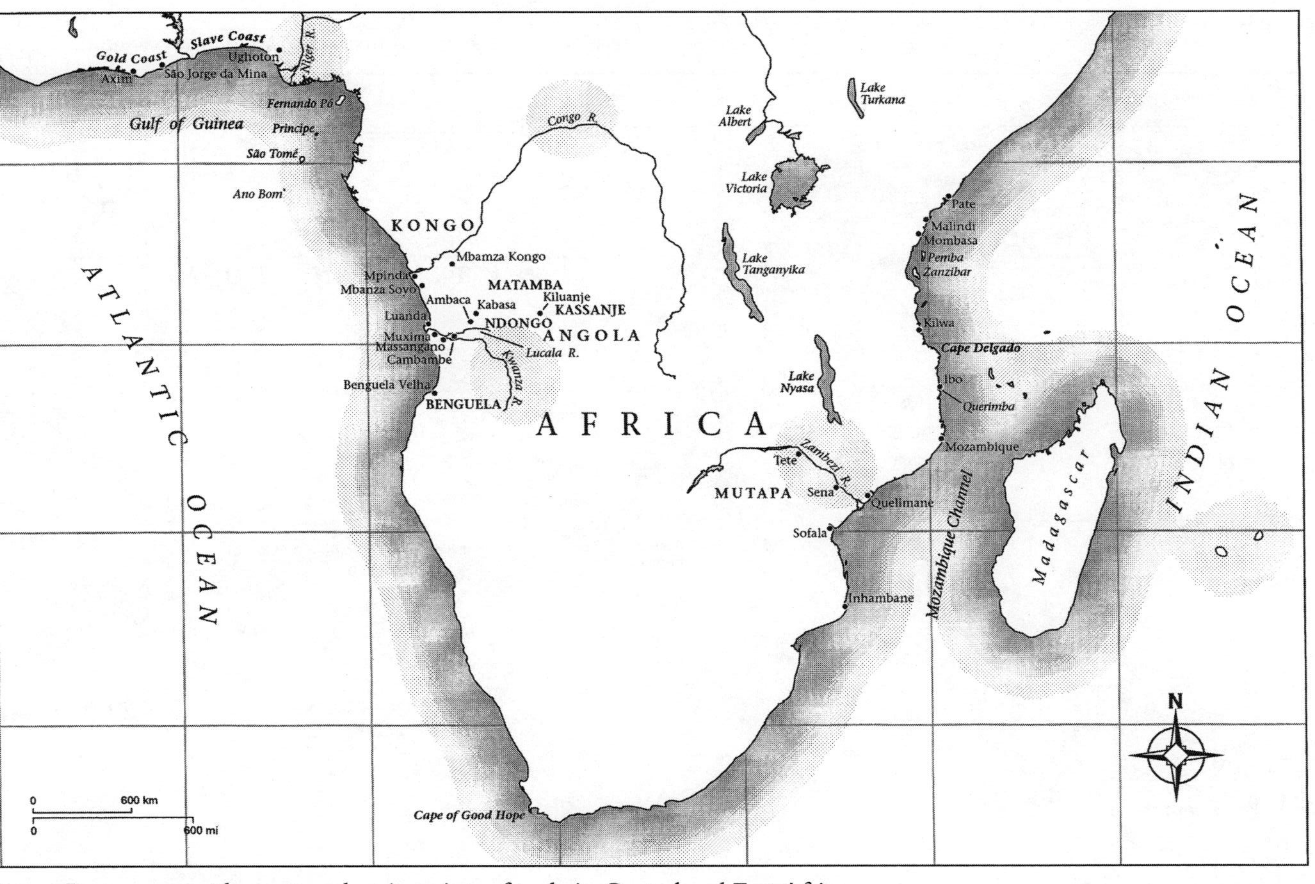

Map 3. Portuguese settlements and main points of trade in Central and East Africa.

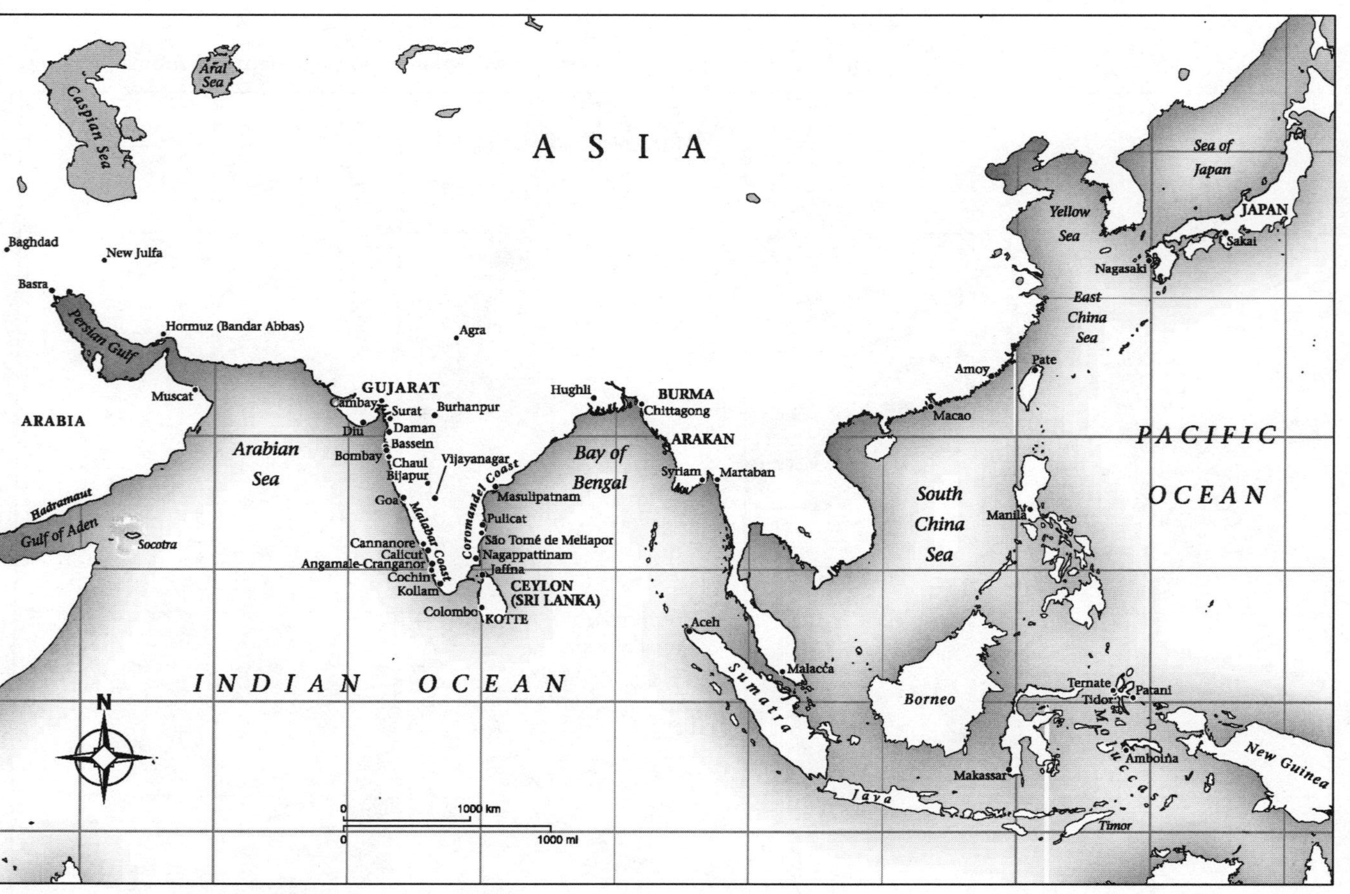

Map 4. Portuguese settlements and main points of trade in Asia.

INTRODUCTION

Francisco Bethencourt and Diogo Ramada Curto

Translated by Neil Safier

The conquest of Ceuta in 1415 was the founding moment of the global Portuguese diaspora. Over the course of the fifteenth century, the Portuguese launched a number of reconnaissance missions throughout the Central and South Atlantic, which led to the discovery of Porto Santo and the Madeira Islands, the Azores, the Cape Verde archipelago, São Tomé and the Príncipe Islands, and the further exploration of the west coast of Africa. The colonization of these Atlantic islands, begun during the 1420s, preceded the establishment of trading posts (*feitorias*) and forts in Morocco, Senegambia, and the Gulf of Guinea. In 1487, seventy years of extensive Portuguese experience with Atlantic currents and wind patterns culminated in Bartolomeu Dias's successful crossing into the Indian Ocean. The way was thus opened for Vasco da Gama's voyage to India (1497–1499), which established the maritime connection between Europe and Asia.

During the sixteenth century, Portuguese expansion continued unabated. In the century's first decades, Portuguese ships surveyed the entire east coast of Africa, the Red Sea, and the Persian Gulf; Hormuz succumbed to their assaults in 1507 and 1515; Goa was conquered in 1510; and Malacca came under Portuguese control in 1511. In the years that followed, the Portuguese reconnoitered Southeast Asia, established a presence on the Molucca Islands, arrived at the mouth of the Pearl River, and sent an ambassador to the emperor of China. From 1520 to 1550, they expanded their presence in Gujarat and along India's west coast with the creation of the "Northern Province." During this period, they also established a presence in Ethiopia and Ceylon (Sri Lanka) and made first contact with the Japanese. Earlier, in the South Atlantic, a voyage to India in the year 1500 under the command of Pedro Álvarez Cabral made landfall on the coast of the territory that would eventually come to be called Brazil.

By the 1520s, the Portuguese had also extended their presence well into northern Africa. Under the command of sharifs from the south, however, Muslims later reconquered Santa Cruz do Cabo de Gué (Agadir) and forced the Portuguese to abandon most of the fortresses that had been built or conquered there (Safi and Azamor in 1541–1542, Alcácer Ceguer and Arzila in 1549–1550). This process ended with the military defeat at Alcazarquibir in 1578, signaling a radical reduction of Portuguese activities in the region.

It was not until the nineteenth century that the Portuguese were able to establish a significant territorial dominion in Senegambia. Up to that point, Portuguese influence in that region and in the Gulf of Guinea had consisted of a network of factories and fortresses engaged in gold and slave trafficking. By the first decades of the seventeenth century, the Portuguese presence, which had been largely negotiated with African powers in the region, began to suffer stiff competition from the English, French, and Dutch, who broke down the Portuguese trading monopoly among West Africa, Europe, and America.

The king of Kongo's conversion by Portuguese missionaries early in the sixteenth century led to an extended period of influence in Central Africa, which in turn made possible more frequent slave traffic to the American continent. The founding of the city of Luanda in 1576 required a transfer of Portuguese regional power to the southwest, thereby increasing the instability of the kingdom of Kongo and its bordering kingdoms. In the seventeenth and eighteenth centuries, a tense but stable situation prevailed in the Kwanza River region and along the coastal zone of Benguela between the Portuguese and the N'gola and Jága peoples. This equilibrium was achieved through a strategy that oscillated between military action and treaty negotiation. The king of Kongo's army, aided by Christian clergy and Portuguese, was decimated by troops from Luanda during the decisive battle at Ambuila in 1665. This episode exemplified the failure of missionary projects in Africa during the *ancien régime*. For the first time, too, political rationale appeared to have overcome religious commitments: Brazilian troops were called in, tipping the military balance and dramatically altering the course of the war in Africa. But Portuguese dominion did not follow immediately on the heels of the kingdom's decline: It was only following the Berlin Conference and the wide diffusion of quinine for the relief of malaria in the last decades of the nineteenth century that the Portuguese were able to occupy large portions of the African interior.

In Mozambique, Portuguese efforts to occupy the interior through military means in the 1570s were thwarted by the spread of disease and the ability of local inhabitants to defend their territory. Nevertheless, the Portuguese were able to establish a network of fortresses that provided support for their various initiatives. The strategy here was to insinuate themselves within the chiefdoms of the Monomotapa confederation, a political structure that was, however, soon to go into decline in the early years of the seventeenth century. From this region, the invaders were able to maintain a hierarchical, if long-distance, relationship with the Estado da Índia. The Portuguese domination of the Zambezi River valley over the course of the seventeenth and eighteenth centuries created one of the few successful European territorial bases on the entire continent, even if genuine territorial occupation of the interior would once again be achieved only in the last few decades of the nineteenth century. The distinctive situation in Mozambique owed much to the miscegenation between the Portuguese and the local chiefdoms, as well as to the preferential trading relationship the area enjoyed in the western Indian Ocean's burgeoning interregional economy.

In Asia, the Estado da Índia was based on a system of key ports through which the Estado sought to control intercontinental, and to some degree interregional, commerce. From the east coast of Africa to Macao, and stretching as far as Nagasaki and Amboina, the Portuguese empire functioned as an interconnected network of port cities that took on diverse institutional and diplomatic features determined by particular economic, political, and cultural interests. In only two cases was there an effort to occupy the Asian interior: the first, along the coastal strip surrounding Daman, Bassein, and Chaul, where the Northern Province was created in the mid-sixteenth century; and the second in Ceylon, where the series of fortresses that the Portuguese established along the coastline allowed for the occupation of a significant portion of the Ceylonese interior in the early seventeenth century.

Although reinforced by missionary work, the basic explanation for the longevity of the Portuguese presence in Asia is to be found in territorial conquest, political control of local populations, and commercial advantages. Nevertheless, there are well-documented cases of extraordinary missionary success outside the boundaries of the empire, especially in southern India (the Pescaria Coast) and Japan, even though the latter was compromised by local political reaction. Meanwhile, the Portuguese were also expanding well beyond the formal frontiers of the empire by establishing mercantile communities in such places as the Bay of Bengal and Southeast Asia. They acquired a surprising level of autonomy by offering their services as mercenaries to various Asian kingdoms, including Pegu and Cambodia, and even came to establish their own fortresses, such as Syriam, at the beginning of the seventeenth century. On occasion, they received explicit support from the Estado da Índia itself. These largely autonomous groups of individuals represent the paradox of Portuguese miscegenation: They spread the traits of Portuguese identity by integrating themselves into native communities.

Although Portuguese power reached its zenith in the Indian Ocean during the first decades of the seventeenth century, competition from the Dutch and the English inevitably reduced its influence in Southeast Asia, the Persian Gulf, the Malabar Coast, and the Bay of Bengal. At the same time, and especially in the 1630s, local potentates, who occasionally teamed up with other European powers, managed to expel the Portuguese from Bengal, Ceylon, Ethiopia, and Japan, in spite of the continuing circulation of Portuguese merchant communities. This confrontation was intensified even further in the eighteenth century, with the definitive occupation of Mombasa by the Omanese empire and the conquest of the Northern Province by the Maratha Confederation. The Portuguese reacted to the latter by conquering the region around Goa in the 1740s, 1750s, and 1760s. These developments confirmed the need to concentrate forces around the capital of the Estado da Índia and prefigured the increasingly peripheral place of the Portuguese empire in Asia as compared with other European powers.

The Brazilian case was the sole example of sustained territorial occupation of a colony by the Portuguese during the long period extending from the sixteenth through the eighteenth centuries. The need to supply the growing sugar economy with the manpower of African slaves linked Brazil to West Africa and structured the entire South Atlantic system. In the sixteenth century, Portuguese settlement of South America progressed slowly, despite crown encouragement through royal privileges for overseas travel and the establishment in the 1530s of "donatory" captaincies, which were huge concessions of land by the king, who delegated with the land various government powers. Three principal factors were responsible for the definition of a first imperial project in South America: the need to counter French projects of colonization; Portuguese attempts to repeat what the Spanish had achieved with the discovery of the Potosí mines; and an interest in finding new sources of income to compensate for the first crisis in India. In 1549, the establishment of a general government (*governo geral*) in Bahia and the arrival of the first Jesuit missionaries provided a fresh impulse for the colony's development. Over time, the power of the donatory captains was reduced, and it was finally eliminated in the eighteenth century by the Marquis of Pombal. At the same time, Indian slavery, justified since the sixteenth century by the idea of defensive war, was limited in practice because of the protection offered the Indians by the Jesuits.

The Society of Jesus came to control a large portion of the indigenous workforce by establishing village settlements (*aldeias*), following a policy that had the support of both the crown and the governors. As a result of this policy, the colonists, hungry for cheap labor, and the Jesuit missionaries, protective of the Indians, frequently found themselves locked in serious conflict. This was especially the case in the poorer regions of Maranhão and Pará, which lacked the financial resources to acquire African slaves, as well as in São Paulo, where Portuguese miscegenation with indigenous populations led early on to a policy of making slaving raids into the interior. Although Jesuit policies certainly contributed to the increased importation of African slaves, the more operative basis for this choice was the resistance of Indians to slave labor and their vulnerability to European diseases. Whatever the case may be, the status of African slaves was never really questioned by the Society of Jesus, as the writings of Padre António Vieira clearly demonstrate. One thing, however, is certain: From the moment that a structure was established to collect and transport African slaves, there was a tendency to exploit this market whenever there was a need for human labor. Over the course of the eighteenth century, this pattern was repeated not only in Brazil but in the Spanish, Dutch, and British American colonies as well.

The stability of the Portuguese system in the South Atlantic was shaken between 1624 and 1654 by the arrival of the Dutch. They first conquered Bahia, which was retaken the very next year by an armada composed of troops from throughout Philip IV's empire. In 1630, they occupied Pernambuco, and in the years that followed they moved into other northern captaincies as well. The incorporation of the two sides of the South Atlantic in the sugar (and tobacco) economy explains the Dutch conquest of São Jorge da Mina (1637), Arguim (1638), and São Tomé and Angola (1641). These moves spurred the first large-scale Portuguese attempt to reconquer the territory the Dutch had captured.

The successful Portuguese expedition to retake Angola and São Tomé in 1648 was led by Salvador Correia de Sá, then governor of Rio de Janeiro, and carried out by troops from Brazil. The interruption of the slave supply signaled the beginning of the decline of Dutch America, further accelerated by the military successes of Brazilians in the region. The expulsion of the Dutch from Brazil in 1654 made it possible for the Portuguese to consolidate their power in the South Atlantic, demonstrating both the deep roots of Portuguese emigration and the Portuguese capacity to recruit troops from among the Indians and African slaves. The success of the campaign against the Dutch in Brazil also transformed military strategies in Angola, with the nomination of Brazilian governors and the transfer of troops from Portuguese America to Africa. This episode demonstrated the relational logic of the Portuguese empire: The losses suffered in Asia were balanced by the victory over the Dutch in the South Atlantic during the same period. This was the first war of the seventeenth century that had been waged between two European powers on different continents, and its results defined the future of both the Portuguese and Dutch empires for decades to come.

In the following decades, the sugar and tobacco economies, in addition to the fishing industry, stimulated Portuguese expansion along the Brazilian coastline and attracted a large number of immigrants from Portugal. With the exception of the expeditions of the *paulistas* (residents of São Paulo), however, the Brazilian interior remained largely unexplored by Europeans until the very end of the seventeenth century. The discovery of gold in the region of Minas Gerais in the 1690s completely transformed this situation, causing a massive migration from Portugal and from other regions within Brazil. The conflict over mining rights between the *paulistas* and those from the metropole (who were allied with groups from other regions in Brazil) led to civil war, ultimately requiring intervention by the government of the southern captaincies. The successful suppression of the *paulistas'* pretensions of exclusivity in the extraction of precious metals encouraged further migration and an expansion of gold and gem mining to other regions, especially in Goiás and Mato Grosso. The expansion of gold and diamond extraction also meant a dramatic leap forward for the Brazilian economy, bringing with it a series of consequences, including the expansion of cattle breeding, the regular use of the immense river system, and the creation of a vast network of roads.

The new economic, demographic, and urban situation also explains the shift in power from the northeast to the south of Brazil, symbolized most concretely by the transfer of the capital of the Estado do Brasil from Salvador da Bahia to Rio de Janeiro in 1763. Encouraged by the Pombaline policy of territorial conquest, the Portuguese were throughout the century able to penetrate deeply into the north using the fluvial networks of the Amazon River and its tributaries. Meanwhile, in the south, the difficulty in defining the borders between Spanish and Portuguese America – the object of two successive treaties in 1750 and 1777 – brought to light the problematic status of indigenous *aldeias*, which had so far been controlled by the Jesuits outside of crown jurisdiction. Ultimately, this situation led in 1759 to the expulsion of the Society of Jesus from Portugal and the rest of the empire. Thus, the greatest moment of global Portuguese expansion occurred in the eighteenth century, with the territorial occupation of the interior of South America. The present-day borders of Brazil by and large owe their contours to this westward expansion. In this context, Pombal's administrative and military reforms provided a more consistent frame in which Portuguese dominion could increase. Despite the poor communication between regions and the appropriation of municipal structures by local notables, the crown managed to establish a certain degree of centralized power over the region.

In Brazil, individuals increasingly assumed a colonial, as opposed to a metropolitan, identity over the course of this complex process of migration and miscegenation, circulation of people and possessions, transfer of investments, and adaptation to diverse locales. Over the course of the eighteenth century, the development of a solid urban network across the country also created a new class of elites, including intellectuals, who established academies and were responsible for the diffusion of new philosophical ideas that often challenged the encrusted interests of a slave-based society. Despite a lack of alliances between captaincies, the emergence of a sense of local autonomy promoted through fiscal and political protests left deep traces of antimetropolitan sentiment throughout Portuguese America, as was apparent in the so-called *Inconfidência Mineira* conspiracy of 1789. Paradoxically, the transfer of the royal court to Brazil in response to the Napoleonic invasion of 1807 breathed new life into this sentiment. The establishment of central authority in Rio de Janeiro, legitimized by the presence of the king himself, led Brazilians to focus more on themselves than on the metropole. The relocation of the crown also brought with it the assimilation of social and behavioral models imported from Lisbon. Meanwhile, the authorization of manufacturing in Brazil and the opening of the ports in 1808 reinvigorated the spirit of autonomy and liberty of the Estado do Brasil, which in turn allowed the consolidation of elite groups that shared its commercial and financial interests. The independence declared by prince Dom Pedro in 1822 received strong and immediate support from these colonial elites.

Contemporary with the Inconfidência Mineira, the 1787 Pintos conspiracy (Conjura dos Pintos) in India showed that local Christian and Hindu elites, active in local politics since the sixteenth century, felt a similar desire for autonomy. These groups, with their long tradition of financial independence, included members of the secular and, after the second half of the eighteenth century, the religious clergy, not to mention large contingents in the armed forces. These elites were pushing for the opening to indigenous soldiers of the artillery corps, a specialized branch of the armed forces reserved for Europeans, an issue that had in large part inspired the conspiracy in the first place. The violent repression of this conspiracy by the Estado da Índia did not deter other revolts over the course of the nineteenth century, nor did it prevent the consolidation of an autonomous spirit that manifested itself most explicitly in the twentieth century before Goa's integration into the Indian Union. The doubly peripheral situation of this elite, in confrontation with both the Portuguese and Indian worlds, goes a long way toward explaining its failure to impose an autonomous solution until the Indian Union decided on military intervention in 1961. A more complex situation is that of Macao, where a community composed of descendants of Sino-Portuguese miscegenation maintained both a strong tradition of autonomy (perhaps the most deeply rooted of the entire empire) as well as surprising political allegiance to Portugal. This attitude can only be explained by Macao's anomalous position as a colony subjected to the daily influences of Chinese power yet situated at the margins of the greater Chinese world.

Portuguese expansion cannot and should not be seen as a cumulative process: It was marked by continuities and discontinuities and by breaches and transformations in the patterns of its activities from the Atlantic to the Indian oceans, from India to the South Atlantic, and from Brazil to Africa. It is possible to speak of successive Portuguese empires, the result of political adaptations to reversals of fortune and to the transfer of people and capital from one region to the other. Studying this process should not therefore be limited only to territories that were controlled by powers authorized or delegated by the crown. There was always a permanent flow of merchants, seamen, and artisans who lived beyond the boundaries of empire and who, in some cases, even ended up serving regimes other than the Portuguese.

The reduced demographic capacities of the metropole – roughly a million people at the beginning of the fifteenth century and nearly three million at the end of the eighteenth – did not prevent constant emigration of the Portuguese, estimated at between one and two thousand people per year for most of the fifteenth century, between two and five thousand per year during the sixteenth, between three and six thousand per year during the seventeenth, and between eight and ten thousand during the eighteenth. These emigrants headed primarily to the Atlantic Islands and to Brazil. The Portuguese presence in Asia always suffered from a demographic scarcity, although this was largely compensated for by a policy of miscegenation with local societies that was put into effect by Afonso de Albuquerque in Goa in 1510. This distinctive characteristic of the Portuguese empire, reproduced in large scale in Brazil and to a much lesser extent in Africa, created colonial societies stratified by complicated "racial" criteria, as was also the case in the Spanish empire. Another specific characteristic of the Iberian empires, as distinguished from the Dutch and British empires, was that religious conversion served as a relatively important factor in the integration of local groups. It should be noted, however, that the use of force mobilized by missionaries to convert these populations (or to maintain them inside Christianity) proved to have a deeply contradictory effect in the long run. The use of local manpower, as mariners, pilots, artisans, soldiers, and clerics, was a characteristic the Portuguese empire shared with other European empires and was especially common in Asia.

Any process of expansion is violent by nature, and its consequences in this regard cannot be ignored. The conveyance of enslaved laborers from Africa, initiated by the Portuguese for the development of Brazil, soon involved the Spanish, English, French, and Dutch colonies in America. This forced relocation of an estimated twelve million individuals resulted in a staggering number of deaths both during the journey and in the first years of their captivity. The imposition of Portuguese dominion in key ports (and surrounding hinterlands) of Africa and Asia meant the destruction of families, communities, and ethnic groups, as well as the unraveling of political and cultural systems. For these reasons, we see our aim in publishing this book as anything but celebratory in nature. Our intention in writing history is to move beyond an ideological appropriation of the past and to deconstruct consciously the successive myths that have been created by various historiographies. The need to rewrite the history of Portuguese expansion stems from our refusal to accept particular ideological or nationalistic perspectives; our objective is to disrupt those encrusted layers of retrograde historiography that are still common today. From our point of view, the debate over historiographical ideas should begin with an acknowledgment of our principal intellectual legacies – examples of which might include studies by Vitorino Magalhães Godinho of the ideal-type of the merchant-knight – and continue through an evaluation both of the new history of European expansion (Spanish, English, Dutch, or French) and the new historiography produced in the former colonial regions. Even today, many of these new studies are carried out within strictly nationalistic frameworks with little effort toward a comparative analysis.

The goal of this collection is to arrive at an understanding of the history of Portuguese expansion during the early modern period from a global perspective. Our approach, conceived by a group of experts in the field, departs in five significant ways from traditional historiography. In the first place, we refuse to treat Portuguese expansion in a compartmentalized fashion, subdivided into continents, regions, and subregions. Without completely disrespecting the specificities associated with local and regional forms of interaction, we find that the academic practice of writing history based upon geographic regions is artificial and undermines a global approach to the process by which successive Portuguese empires were brought into existence. From our point of view, it is impossible to understand what took place in the Estado da Índia if one ignores what was happening in Africa, Brazil, or mainland Portugal itself at the same time. Thus, the development of colonial Brazil needs to be seen as more than an enlargement and definition of territorial boundaries; rather, it should be understood in the context of a bipolar system in the South Atlantic, of which the slave trade was one of the principal and defining features. The job of the historian must be to reconstitute the relationships between regions through a study of the circulation of peoples, goods, and cultural configurations.

Second, we are reluctant to accept an approach that confines itself to periods of short or medium duration, whether this periodization conforms to regnal years or to the local and regional realities being studied. The division of history into arbitrarily defined, isolated chronological slices has come to be practiced today under the pretext of refusing a teleological view of the past. Although appearing to be salutary on the surface, this self-restraint ultimately defeats itself, as it results in a historicism that is unconscious of its own place within that same history. From our perspective, historical inquiry begins as a complex process of confronting an array of possibilities in constant flux. It is impossible to disregard the periods that preceded or followed the objects of one's analyses. Although we acknowledge the importance of local realities and small-scale interconnections, it is not feasible to analyze such a long-lasting process of expansion in piecemeal fashion. Only a global approach grounded in long-term appraisals is capable of defining analytically the models of domination the Portuguese adopted in different social and cultural contexts. Only through this kind of approach is it possible to understand the multiple forms of interaction between the Portuguese and the local and regional power brokers with whom they came into contact, interactions that generated new political relationships, new economic activities, and new financial partnerships.

Third, we cannot accept an approach that confines itself solely to the formal framework of the Portuguese empire without taking into account the circulation of the Portuguese beyond the borders of their political dominion or a model that downplays local political, economic, and cultural conditions. In this collection, we have attempted also to move beyond an anti-Eurocentric rhetoric that features an overly exoticized view of the Portuguese empire. Instead, our approach emphasizes the real ways in which the empire depended for its survival on merchants and local financiers (as in the case of Asia) or on a slave labor force from Africa (as in the case of Brazil). Moreover, we believe the Portuguese empire can only come into clear focus when it is studied in close relation with those Asian, African, and Amerindian networks with which the Portuguese interacted and not just within the context of the actions of other European powers.

Fourth, we reject a historiography that does not question some of the implicit assumptions about European expansion in general and about the

Portuguese empire in particular. We are referring here to a mode of historical thinking that attempts to analyze sources with erudition but ultimately falls short of engaging with the ideological uses to which the colonial and imperial past has recently been put. Our attempt to reach this self-reflective critical position does not correspond to any particular argument or authority held up by particular schools or groups of historians. In principle, the same critical methodology should be used to interpret primary sources, especially those that reflect highly complex forms of knowledge, such as systematic compendia of information on geography, astronomy, languages, forms of political organization, markets, precious metals, currency, and distribution networks. Furthermore, this self-criticism allows us to detect different patterns of reciprocal cultural impact as experienced either by the peoples affected by the Portuguese expansion or by the Portuguese themselves, including economic, social, linguistic, architectural, musical, and artistic exchanges.

Finally, this critical attitude must take into account the development and the degree of institutionalization of the different historiographical traditions that impinge upon the study of Portuguese imperial culture. Any list of these different schools would inevitably be incomplete, but of special note are the traditions established by Jacob van Leur, the inspirational studies of Edward Said, and the decisive contributions of Jan Vansina to the study of African history. One should also mention the successive critique of the ideas of K. N. Panikkar and, more recently, those related to subaltern studies. The developmental models of a global economy, conceptualized by Fernand Braudel, Vitorino Magalhães Godinho, and Immanuel Wallerstein, have inspired new historiographical currents in both Portugal and Brazil that allow scholars to move beyond local particularities and to situate problems in much broader contexts.

In fact, recent Brazilian historiography has demonstrated tremendous vitality and has legitimized the pathbreaking work of such illustrious figures as Capistrano de Abreu, Gilberto Freyre, Sérgio Buarque de Holanda, Caio Prado Júnior, and many others who have followed in their footsteps. It should not be forgotten, too, that the historiography of the Portuguese empire, including Portuguese America, has benefited tremendously from a rich tradition maintained by non-Portuguese historians. In many instances, these historians have been able to break down more nationalistic points of view by bringing into the discussion their own personal experiences of research and debate from centers accustomed to examining world history in a more interdisciplinary framework. Without question, Charles Ralph Boxer leads the list of the non-Portuguese historians who took a profound interest in the Portuguese empire. Successors to Boxer, his heirs within the

Anglo-American world – the so-called Brazilianists as well as others – are well represented in the pages of this collection.

It should by now be clear that, as editors of this volume, we have taken an active position against what we see as several distorted views of the historical realities of the Portuguese empire. One such interpretation, particularly fashionable today, is the idea that the imperial state was a "weak" state. It is true that ever since the nineteenth century, the nationalistic historiographies of the Liberal Monarchy, the First Republic, and the Estado Novo – each with its own respective interpretive shadings – projected an image of a "strong state" within an imaginary imperial past. These schools insisted on a particular kind of political centralization based on a clear division of jurisdictions and hierarchy more typical of contemporary times. It is also true that some of the persistent images and stereotypes of the European expansion tend to identify the Spanish and Portuguese empires with strongly centralized models that were able to impose a Catholic orthodoxy. These images are presented in stark contrast with the more tolerant, representative, liberal imperial model that the British and the Dutch supposedly followed in their respective overseas projects. The view of a strongly centralized Portuguese empire continues to encounter stiff criticism, and it has not been confirmed by textured studies related to the function of imperial institutions, such as the trading posts (*feitorias*), captaincies, municipal chambers (*câmaras*), tribunals, *Misericórdias*, financial institutions (*vedorias da fazenda*), and the general governments (*governos gerais*).

Nevertheless, in the Portuguese case, the assertion of a "weak" model of the colonial empire, instead of helping us to understand the period better, has actually introduced new errors. The example of the Estado da Índia cannot be extended to the other regions of the empire. Moreover, even this example, with its loose fabric organized around urban nodes that controlled scant territory, reveals a reasonable level of political centralization based in Goa. The system of coercive power in the Portuguese empire was not limited to crown institutions but rather included many other forms of legitimate violence and regulation of social problems, such as by the church, which benefited overseas from royal patronage, the *câmaras*, the *Misericórdias*, confraternities, and schools. Whatever one's view of the role of the state in the Portuguese empire, the definition only makes sense in comparative terms, taking into consideration the other cases of European expansion, including the Spanish, French, Dutch, and English cases. Our view of the early modern state cannot be based on current standards but rather on the political theory of the time concerning the organization of empires and the creation of colonies. In the late sixteenth century, for example, Giovanni Botero discussed the advantages and disadvantages of the Portuguese empire, portraying it principally as a territorially discontinuous but centralized state. The exercise of political power, from our point of view, cannot be reduced only to jurisdictional conflicts or to factional clashes among elites.

The "weak" vision of the Portuguese empire has also been associated with an analysis that seeks to reconstitute different local interactions. Although this kind of focus enriches the historiographical landscape, it also runs the risk of diluting the impact of the transfer of European institutions and European forms of political action throughout the empire. Consequently, this approach gives the impression that the imperial structure was fragmentary, which does not correspond with historical reality. The absence of instruments of coercion generally suggests that mechanisms of negotiation were adopted instead, which is to say that peaceful means were used as opposed to more bellicose forms of domination. This interpretation is valid in many different contexts and in fact aptly characterizes many of the situations, from Makassar to Goiás, to which we attribute an imperial meaning. The logic of a supposed weak imperial system is bulwarked, for instance, by the strategy of miscegenation that the Portuguese actively promoted in most parts of their colonies, necessitated by the minimal participation of women in Portuguese migration overseas.

In many contexts, the Portuguese adopted diverse forms of negotiation to compensate for the lack of means to impose their will absolutely. The activities of Portuguese agents and other isolated groups who operated outside the empire's jurisdictional and institutional boundaries make this all too evident. Notwithstanding these characteristics, an interpretative framework that exclusively emphasizes weaknesses, negotiation, and forms of miscegenation privileges a colonial ideology based on Portuguese exceptionalism – an analytical perspective in vogue since the 1950s and associated explicitly with the regime of Antonio de Oliveira Salazar, 1928–1968 (an authoritarian, although incomplete type of Fascism) and the adoption of Gilberto Freyre's Lusotropical theory (praising the specific capacity of the Portuguese to create mixed-race societies). There is no doubt that this retrograde perspective has been reinforced more recently by studies that have emphasized the wide range of possibilities and ambiguities inherent in cross-cultural contact, especially involving ethnic, social, cultural, and artistic *mestizaje*, or hybridity. Here, once again, it is our profound conviction that the real advantages of a new and in some cases deconstructivist discourse can be compromised by glorifying these older ideas about Portuguese (and Spanish) exceptionalism. We have sought to counterbalance these partial perspectives with a more complex framework in which multifarious agents and social groups played critical roles and in which local populations offered creative quotidian resistance in often unspectacular ways. At the same time, the tragic situations in which violence, social control, and exploitation were utilized cannot be discounted or forgotten.

One final distorted view of the Portuguese expansion that we would like to redress stems from a definition of millenarianism that characterizes it as an "imperial ideology." For some time, millenarianism was understood as a peculiarly Portuguese phenomenon and as separate from the other processes of European expansion. More recently, it has been characterized as a particularly Eurasian ideology of imperial expansion. The origin of this kind of approach in Portugal reaches back to the ideological manipulations promoted by the Estado Novo during the commemorations of the Portuguese empire in 1934, 1940, and 1960, a period when expansion was seen as a religious movement. The "generous" propagation of the Catholic faith, in this view, justified past "sacrifices" and glorified past "heroes."

We have come a long way from this kind of ideological interpretation. Any serious approach to Portuguese expansion now acknowledges a plurality of motives. From our perspective, the millenarian thesis advanced today in a "New Age" formulation attempts a deliberate "folklorization" of the Portuguese expansion and functions as an inverted image of the kind of Orientalism projected by Europeans on Asian civilization over the course of the past two centuries. The only serious scholarship on millenarianism as an element in Portuguese expansion, by Jean Aubin, found no more than a few writers influenced by this tradition. By no means was a broad undercurrent of millenarianism or millenarian "ideology" found to have been functioning either in the medium or the long term. No policy of the Portuguese empire was defined or executed as a function of this tradition. If traces of such panic-driven thinking by a people seduced by the idea of a thousand-year period of peace on Earth preceded by the coming of the Antichrist did exist at some point in the empire, such vestiges were located on the margins of the system and never at the center. These threads of millenarianism were not an ideology of expansion but rather religious movements that served as forms of cultural resistance.

This collection is divided into four parts. In Part I, we explore the economy of the Portuguese empire not only by looking at its products and its commercial and financial networks but also by considering the specific societies and markets that the Portuguese entered or attempted to bring into existence. How can we move beyond the idea of economic cyles – of pepper, sugar, or gold – as essential characteristics of the imperial economy? In what way can an empire motivated by mercantilist theory be evaluated in terms of a logic of costs and income? What was the relative impact of the empire as a portion of crown finances, and what was its role in the crown's program of the distribution of privileges? What was the impact of the empire in the Indian Ocean, namely on its sophisticated local merchant communities, the dynamism of which long predated the arrival of Vasco da Gama in Calicut in 1498? What was the particular contribution of the Portuguese to the formation of a slave-based Atlantic economy? And how should we evaluate the Portuguese presence in Africa, especially in the sub-Saharan regions?

By concentrating our attention on these questions, we leave aside, of course, other important subjects. These include: the commercial centers of North Africa, the geostrategic importance of which should be taken into account from the fall of Ceuta in 1415 until the abandonment and transferal of Mazagão during the Pombaline period; the circulation of Japanese silver, from which the Portuguese garnered so many benefits from the midpoint of the sixteenth century until 1639, or the silver deeply cherished by the Macauan Portuguese that had been brought from Spanish America by the so-called Manila Galleon during the period of the union of the Portuguese and Castilian crowns (1580–1640); or the detailed treatment of Southeast Asia, the original supplier of spices to Portugal, whose mercantile networks had been monopolized by the Dutch East India Company throughout the seventeenth century.

To this list of lacunae, we should add the need for a more thorough understanding of informal networks as part of our project to construct a global history. Typically on the margins of a more institutionalized Portuguese presence, these networks showed a distinct capacity for adapting to emerging markets and demonstrated a surprising economic dynamism. In this respect, the case of the Portuguese "Jews" (also known as New Christians, or *cristãos-novos*) in Peru is perhaps the most paradigmatic example, especially if we consider their success in constructing a network of interests from Potosí to Seville and Amsterdam. But it is also necessary to take into account the less spectacular cases of Portuguese groups and even isolated individuals who were active in the Bay of Bengal and Makassar regions.

Part II analyzes the extent to which the colonization process was framed variously by policies conducted by the state, by the church, or by other institutions with European roots, including the forts, trading outposts, municipal chambers, and charitable confraternities. The responses to these questions are organized around a series of models and typologies from which one can observe the variety of actual situations that form part of the Portuguese colonization process. The presence of grand imperial designs or strategies in defining this process appears to have been greatly exaggerated, especially given the decisive role of local configurations and small-scale adaptive strategies developed in the context of daily life. It is nevertheless necessary to examine the large-scale instruments by which imperial policies and goals were rationalized, ordered, and advanced: papal bulls, diplomatic treaties, European traditions of institutional organization, and new techniques of mercantilist exploitation, such as the formation of commercial companies.

Among this panoply of instruments, an important place should be given to military and technological resources of the Europeans. From the armed ship to scientifically designed fortifications, from militarized control of populations to forms of indigenous recruitment, these tools of force served as the most effective means of colonization, and their use was directly involved in the principal internal and external conflicts. If one accepts the idea that the Portuguese empire made a significant contribution to what might be called a "revolution" in military techniques in the early modern period, this participation should not be limited to a particular foundational moment, as represented by the figure of Afonso de Albuquerque, for example, but rather should be thought of as taking place over a much longer period. Equally, the militarization of the Portuguese presence in seventeenth-century Brazil was primarily due to the battles with the Dutch and appears to have intensified years later following the discovery of gold in Minas Gerais in the 1690s, bringing with it an increased need for the Portuguese to protect their mining rights. The imperially ambitious Portuguese state thus appears to define itself in terms of its principal objective, which was to control the revenues that it saw as legitimately its own. Nonetheless, although this objective was proclaimed on several occasions and came packaged as a strong mercantile culture, in practice it never took shape as anything that might be considered a grand strategy.

As Vitorino Magalhães Godinho has shown, in the long sixteenth century the monopolizing and mercantilist state allowed itself to be invaded by the special interests of merchant groups, especially bankers, and by foreign merchants who were represented in Lisbon and in the overseas territories by a wide diversity of agents. Oddly, this false monopoly over commerce was mirrored in the organization of the church: The *padroado régio* – that is, crown control over administrative positions and the ecclesiastical organization of the empire – was challenged by Rome as well as by diverse local and social groups who participated in various institutions connected with the church. It is always tempting to look for conflict and opposition when presented with these forms of control exercised by the crown, the church, or other local political groups or institutions. From the Brazilian *quilombos* (communities of runaway slaves) to the flight from Goa of local populations who feared their orphaned children would be abducted for conversion, it is even possible to construct a typology of forms of resistance. We still do not know, however, whether this conceptual division, based upon a simple opposition between forms of control and forms of resistance, is the best model for understanding the migratory flows and social relations brought about by the process of Portuguese colonization. In fact, we are still far from comprehending fully the motivations and conduct of all Portuguese agents involved in colonization, and it is even more difficult to attempt to reconstruct the role of African slaves and women of different origins in social reproduction. Indeed, we are well aware that the study of women's place in the process of expansion is one of the more significant lacunae of this collection. It is a topic that remains a crucial element in understanding a diverse array of social configurations.

Part III of this volume is dedicated to the study of the cultural developments brought about by, or associated with, the Portuguese expansion. These studies attempt to cover an extremely broad field: perceptions of the initial moments of contact; the study of interactions among the Portuguese; the variety of actions with political and ideological implications and their textual accounts; the most conscious forms of related literary and artistic representations; and scientific ideas and resources, in particular those related to the nautical sciences. In all of these studies, the object is to reconstruct the lived experience of expansion and empire and to show how these experiences were conceptualized and represented between the fifteenth and eighteenth centuries. But did culture, in all of its manifestations, to some degree determine the expansion and the shape of the empire, or did it function as some kind of mirror image? This somewhat inevitable question allows us to deal explicitly with the divisions between those who follow materialist traditions and those who pursue more culturalist interpretations, and the division between historians who prefer social history and those who pursue intellectual history. However this question is answered, the response should retain the ambiguities of doing history.

Perhaps dealing with the cultural aspects of the expansion at the end of a collection of essays that begins by analyzing economic, political, and institutional organization already suggests a relative diminution of the importance of culture and a return to older schemes of global historiography. But it has been our intention to inscribe cultural meaning into specific activities of empire and to study these meanings in concrete situations of interaction or conflict, isolating some of the more explicit vestiges of these interactions related specifically to literary, artistic, or scientific codes. Such a goal suggests a concept of culture that cannot be reduced merely to either an idealist or materialist perspective.

Nevertheless, the variety of cultural meanings suggested by these chapters should not undermine the broader opportunity this book offers to reflect on an assortment of problems related to the global manifestation of Portuguese society and culture. How were colonial domination and exploitation justified, and in what ways did resistance function as an ideological counterpoint to these practices? What kinds of language were used as propaganda for the imperial project, and in what ways were these discourses expressed simultaneously with the critiques, reformist orientations, or decadent views that went along with these same processes of imperial expansion and construction? To what degree were the different forms of communication brought about by these processes (including perceptions, transmissions, and practices of adaptation) reduced to mere projections on the part of those who found themselves in a position to impose their power? To what extent did they lead to the formation of an autonomous sphere of cumulative knowledge?

Part I: Economics and Society

1

THE ECONOMY OF THE PORTUGUESE EMPIRE

Stuart B. Schwartz

Just outside the city of Oporto, at the mouth of the Douro River, stands a fortress named in honor of St. Francis Xavier that because of its shape locals call the "Castelo do Queijo" (The Cheese Castle). Inside, in the principal apartment, hangs a document that explains that the fortress was dedicated in the seventeenth century to the sainted missionary because he had "won so many souls for the Church and so many leagues for Portugal." This union of missionary intent and territorial acquisition was an essential feature of Portuguese expansion as it was in the creation of other empires, and such multiple incentives for empire building must always be kept in mind. But, despite the current interest in empires as venues for cultural display, sexual gratification, and exoticism, the construction of early modern empires rested primarily on economic considerations. Portugal seems almost a classic example of the old mercantilist concept of John Locke that "in a country not furnished with mines there are but two ways of growing rich, either conquest or commerce." Portugal did both. Their Muslim rivals in India later said they had "won an empire as knights and then lost it as peddlers," but in truth they did best of all where they combined conquest and commerce with settlement and production.

The Portuguese empire was a vast, global administrative and economic system that linked continents, peoples, and economic organizations in a network of exchange. This empire had a long history and changed considerably over time. Its spatial focus or core shifted as different products predominated in its trade and production and seemed to create cycles of economic activity: spices, sugar, and gold. The concept of consecutive cycles, however, is misleading, for although each of these commodities had its heyday, their production overlapped, they often remained only regionally predominant, and there were many other products that also contributed to the economy of empire. In fact, one might argue that the commerce of human beings in the slave trade made many of the other activities possible and that emphasis on labor rather than the commodities it produced is more appropriate for understanding how the colonial empire functioned.

Evaluations of the economy of the Portuguese empire generally suffer from four problems. First, the analyses tend to be "Olisipocentric"; that is, their vantage point is Lisbon, and they are made solely in terms of the profit or loss to the metropole. This was justified as a measure of imperial success, but as historians we might wish to ask what the economic arrangements meant to the peoples at the peripheries or who lived in the various subsystems. Surely the view from Bahia, Rio de Janeiro, Cambay, Hormuz, or Malacca differed from that of Portugal. Second, while profit and loss were essential concerns in imperial calculations, the fact that much of this empire was created and functioned in the prestatistical age, coupled with the subsequent loss of documents, makes it difficult to derive a clear picture of the economics of the empire during much of its history. Third, much of the business of this empire was a private matter, conducted by sugar planters, merchants, missionaries, and illegally by officials. In fact, the tension between state-run economic activities and private ones is a constant theme in this history. It is much easier to recover the history of the state's activity than that of private individuals. Finally, although the empire was essentially economic in nature, its real contribution to Portugal was often as much political as economic. The empire became both a prize and a promise, which allowed Portugal a diplomatic latitude and leverage in negotiations that were vital to the political survival of the country. Thus, it is difficult to separate economics from politics or to create a balance sheet that is simply a calculation of profit and loss. This survey therefore seeks to present an overview of the economy of the Portuguese empire that recognizes the political factor, takes into account the various stages of the empire's development, and looks at the economic situation of its component parts.

The Portuguese empire was essentially a maritime system that tied together a series of commercial ports and small settlements. Only in a few places, particularly Brazil, were a settler colony and vast territorial control established. Although the commercial lines of the empire stretched from Macao and Japan to North Africa and Brazil, in fact, the empire after the sixteenth century can be thought of as essentially two great subsystems: an Indian Ocean complex of fortresses, merchant communities, and administrative centers stretching from East Africa to the China coast but centered on Goa and western India; and an Atlantic system dominated by Brazil but including the mercantile trading stations and ports of West and Central Africa as well as the Atlantic islands. In the sixteenth century, the Portuguese wrestled with the problem of establishing control and subordinating the active commercial and economic life of the Asian seas while at the same time, with the exception of West Africa, which was in some ways more like Asia, creating an economy from scratch in the Atlantic. By the eighteenth century, the burgeoning internal economy of Brazil and its centrality in the Portuguese economy created new problems of control for Lisbon.

Over the centuries, different colonies and settlements held pride of place as the leading overseas possession. Following its discovery in 1419, Madeira, because of its sugar economy, held this position in the 1460s and 1470s until the gold and slaves of São Jorge da Mina and São Tomé overtook it after 1480. São Jorge da Mina's gold output crested around 1495 at about 2,800 marks of gold (67,200 milréis, or approximately £89, 600), then fell off for a period, returned to this level in 1532, and thereafter never produced more than 60 percent of that figure. The West African trade remained important, especially because of its connection with Brazilian production and commerce by the end of the sixteenth century, but by 1510, the focus of Portuguese activities had shifted to the Indian Ocean because of the economic potential of trade and plunder in Asia. For most of the sixteenth century, the Estado da Índia was the jewel in Portugal's crown and by far its most successful colonial enterprise. It has been calculated that by 1610 the value of the sea trade with the Estado da Índia (697,000 milréis, or about £188,378) was still ten times greater than that of Brazil (63,000 milréis, or about £17,027), but that ratio was to change drastically in the following three decades.

By the mid-seventeenth century, the roles of Brazil and the Estado da Índia had reversed as a result of a combination of factors. The growing levels of Brazilian sugar production combined with the disastrous inroads of the Dutch in Asia were prominent among them. Corruption, natural catastrophes, and maritime losses also helped to cause an inversion of the roles of the two parts of the empire. Scholars differ on when exactly the reversal took place, but sometime between 1650 and 1680, Brazil and its African supply stations became the unquestioned heart of the empire, and they remained so throughout the eighteenth century. This shift was reflected in the official discourse and perception of the crown. Whereas in the sixteenth century the Portuguese king had styled himself "Lord of the Commerce of Asia" and had never added a mention of Brazil to his titles, in 1650 the heir apparent to the Portuguese throne was given the title "Prince of Brazil," a recognition of the importance that colony had achieved.

Foundations and Origins

The motives behind the early Portuguese expansion into Morocco with the conquest of Ceuta (1415) have been much debated. The potential of Moroccan cities to provide the Portuguese with access to West African gold crossing the Sahara, as well as the fact that areas of Morocco produced a surplus of grains, probably contributed to the original interest in the conquest. For a short while, both Portuguese merchants who established themselves in Ceuta and some of the nobles who acquired positions of command or who raided at will derived profit from the Portuguese presence, but it is unclear whether the crown gained much benefit from these activities. The Portuguese attempted to acquire a number of towns, but it was not until 1456 that they succeeded in conquering Alcácer Ceguer, and not until 1471 that they were in control of Arzila and Tangier. By the end of the fifteenth century, the lack of a clear policy of settlement, persistent misgovernment, and, above all, a shift in the trans-Saharan trade routes in the 1440s away from the towns occupied by the Portuguese undercut the economic viability of Portuguese activity in the region. Moreover, there were periodic droughts and occasional famines such as that which struck the region in 1521.

In economic terms, North Africa became a deficit operation in which the costs of garrisoning and defense probably outweighed the immediate economic benefits. Still, there were other considerations, religious and political. Not only was a Christian presence in the lands of Islam a symbolic act, but Portuguese possession of a string of fortified positions in Morocco such as Azamor and Mazagão did serve to hinder the operation of corsairs, always a problem for ships returning from Brazil and for Mediterranean commerce. It also allowed Portugal to exercise some influence on local politics, although, as in 1578, sometimes with disastrous results. But, in the long run, by the end of the sixteenth century, North Africa was no longer much of an economic consideration for the Portuguese crown. Soldiers whose concerns were mostly military or their own personal aggrandizement administered its *praças*, or urban outposts. In 1532, there were about 5,000 soldiers manning the various Moroccan outposts, and by that time these places were receiving grain from Portugal and Andalusia rather than exporting any surplus to the peninsula. The Portuguese residents in these enclaves did engage in some agriculture and stock raising, but largely for subsistence. By 1540–1550, North Africa had become a military frontier and of secondary importance as attention shifted to India and subsequently to Brazil. In fact, after considerable debate, the outposts of Safi and Azamor (1541) and Arzila and Alcácer Ceguer (1550) were abandoned in recognition of Portugal's limitations given the size and extent of its overseas empire.

Portuguese exploration and settlement of the Azores and Madeira island groups were roughly simultaneous with the North African expansion. The Azores proved to be at a latitude too far north for the cultivation of sugar but suitable for both wine and grains. By the late fifteenth century, it had become a settler colony dedicated to grain production for export. This activity had various effects on the islands themselves, such as deforestation, and eventually also contributed to overpopulation. On Madeira, the tension between those favoring the highly valued luxury commodity sugar and those more interested in the growth of subsistence cereals organized the early economic life of the colony. The excellent agricultural conditions of the island allowed for surplus grain production. Madeira in the mid-fifteenth century could produce over 12,000 bushels a year, or about two-thirds more than it consumed. The export went to Portugal and, after 1460, some to the West African coast. But grains had to compete with sugar. Only about 30,000 hectares on Madeira were arable, and the crown distributed these by charter (*sesmarias*) in the mid-fifteenth century. Climate and soil were favorable for sugar production, and sugar soon flourished on the island with capital introduced by Portuguese and by foreigners – Genoese, Flemings, and others – who not only set up sugar mills (*engenhos*) but also conducted commercial and financial operations. Slaves were brought from the Canary Islands and the African coast, but by the end of the sixteenth century Madeira was confronted with a declining sugar crop and food shortages.

Overall, in the early stages of colonization in North Africa and the Atlantic, an underlying theme seems to have been the recurrent conflict between the multiple goals of the acquisition of precious metals and luxury products, including sugar, and the production of grains to supply the metropolitan markets. This latter goal was only feasible within a relatively restricted radius, given the distances and the technology of transport at the time. The failure of North Africa to fulfill its promise as a grain supplier, the success of the Azores as a cereal producer and later its decline, and the transition of Madeira from wheat production to sugar are all part of the story of the economy of empire in the fifteenth century.

As the Portuguese pushed down the West African coast to Mauritania and then to the Senegambia region, establishing trade forts and contacts, the interplay between subsistence crops and luxury commodities continued. Slaves began to arrive in Portugal by sea in 1441, and grain was being traded for both slaves and gold by the 1450s. West Africa itself supplied no wheat to Portugal, but sorghum, rice, and other grains were available there. Trade in Senegambia was left to private traders, but when gold-producing regions were eventually found, the crown became active in establishing its exclusive control where possible.

Although a variety of products, such as ivory, artworks and handicrafts, and malagueta pepper, were acquired in West Africa, the Portuguese trade in this region began to concentrate on gold and slaves. Raiding coastal settlements had produced the first slaves, but African resistance quickly made this method unproductive. Instead, the Portuguese turned to trade. Some early Portuguese voyages actually created a slave trade by moving captives from one region to another on the African coast, but whatever the case, by the 1480s a regular trade in human beings had been established that moved Africans to Portugal or to the Canary Islands and Madeira, where the developing sugar industries demanded laborers. The Portuguese negotiated with African rulers such as the king of Benin, offering commodities such as brass, textiles, shells, and luxury items and sometimes military assistance in return for trade concessions and access to the pool of potential laborers. The Cape Verde islands and São Tomé were occupied by the Portuguese as an extension of this trade and became way stations in it. In São Tomé, a sugar industry also developed along the lines of the Madeiran precedent but apparently employing larger numbers of slaves.

The trade in slaves was conducted by both the crown, from royal factories at Arguim and after 1481 from El Mina, and private individuals, from various places along the coasts of Mauritania and the Gulf of Guinea. The best estimate of the volume of slaves exported between 1450 and 1530 is about 156,000, with the annual average over 2,200 and possibly as high as 3,800 in the first decades of the sixteenth century when West Central Africa, particularly the kingdom of Kongo, was pulled into the orbit of the slave trade. The trade expanded rapidly in response to European demand. The Portuguese traded effectively in this commerce against African competitors, and their success in this period allowed them to establish a basis of control of the West African coast that would make them the predominant slavers in the Atlantic for the next 150 years (from 1450 to 1600).

Along with this growing commerce in human beings, the Portuguese also finally in 1482 achieved one of their early objectives with the establishment of a trade factory at El Mina, close to the sources of West African gold. Designed to close the gold trade to European rivals and to bully African rulers with access to the gold, the factory at El Mina circumvented dependence on the old trans-Saharan routes of gold supply. The caravel could now outflank the caravan. Slaves, malagueta pepper, and, above all, gold were sent to Lisbon from El Mina, and as early as 1505 Lunardo da Cà Masser reported that 120,000 ducats a year were received by the king of Portugal. Gold shipments from El Mina and smaller amounts from Guiné and the smaller outpost at Axim became an essential part of Portugal's overseas operations and made West Africa a key asset of the empire during the late fifteenth and early sixteenth centuries. After da Gama's voyage of 1497–1499, however, the economic focus of empire shifted dramatically toward the Indian Ocean and the wealth of Asia.

While the Estado da Índia was taking shape beyond the Cape of Good Hope, Portuguese settlers, merchants, and mariners with very little royal interest or support were also establishing a presence on the Brazilian coast. The early occupation of the Brazilian coast emulated the West African model and in many ways was an extension of the earlier experiences on that continent. A series of trading stations were established where *lançados* (castaways or deserters), a few soldiers, and commercial agents bartered with the indigenous peoples for curiosities and for dyewood (*pau brasil*), which proved to be the only profitable item on the coast. The Portuguese never abandoned the search for mineral wealth as well, hoping to recreate El Mina or later to make Brazil "another Peru," but until the great gold strikes of the 1690s, these hopes were generally frustrated. By the 1530s, foreign competition from French merchants and mariners prodded the Portuguese crown to begin a more active program of settlement, creating captaincies using the donatorial form of lordship that had been employed in the Atlantic islands and sponsoring the granting of land to private individuals. Sugar cane was introduced from the Atlantic islands, and by the 1570s that crop was transforming the economy and society of Brazil.

The development of the sugar industry can be measured both by the number of mills (*engenhos*) and by the production of sugar. By 1570, there were 60 *engenhos* in operation along the coast, with the largest numbers concentrated in Pernambuco (23) and Bahia (18). Together these two captaincies accounted for 68 percent of all the *engenhos*. During the next twenty years, the predominance of those two captaincies increased so that by 1585, when the colony had 120 *engenhos*, Pernambuco (66) and Bahia (36) accounted for 85 percent of the total. These captaincies predominated throughout the colonial period, but other captaincies also produced sugar for export. Considerable income was generated in these years of expansion. A royal agent, Domingos Abreu e Brito, who visited Pernambuco in 1591, reported 63 *engenhos* there producing an average of 6,000 arrobas of sugar each, for a total of 378,000 arrobas (1 arroba = 32 lbs., or 14.5 kg). At an average of 800 réis per arroba, this amounted to over 30,240 milréis, which was equivalent to about £39,312. From the 60 *engenhos* in the colony in 1570, there was a considerable growth to 120 *engenhos* in 1583 and then to 192 in 1612. The annual rate of growth had been highest between 1570 and 1585. This expansion seems to have been driven by favorable prices and growing demand in Europe in the last years of the sixteenth century and opening decades of the seventeenth.

Sugar plantations combined both agriculture and processing of the sugar cane into sugar. The mills were complex and expensive factories that demanded considerable inputs of capital. As in Madeira, this came at first from Portuguese merchant and noble investors and from various foreign merchants: Flemings, Germans, and Genoese. Labor was also a problem. The indigenous peoples of the coast were enslaved to work on the *engenhos*, but their resistance, opposition from Jesuit missionaries, and eventually large-scale depopulation resulting from epidemic disease made this source of labor difficult and costly to obtain. Instead, Africans were enslaved. By the last two decades of the sixteenth century, workers arriving from a slave trade from West Africa and, after 1570, from Angola as well were replacing Amerindians in the major sugar regions of Pernambuco and Bahia. This trade at first remained limited to about 1,000 slaves per year but began to expand considerably in later decades. The relationship between the Brazilian economy and Africa became a commonplace, summarized in variations of the refrain "without Angola, no slaves; without slaves no sugar; without sugar, no Brazil."

The Atlantic system that had taken shape in the fifteenth and sixteenth centuries employed programs of colonization and commercial activity. Both royal monopolies and private trade were combined to secure a wide variety of products from gold to grains to dyewood and sugar. During this formative period, the coerced labor of indigenous peoples, and, with increasing importance, the growth of a maritime slave trade, had become a cornerstone of this system and would eventually develop as the essential element that tied the various parts together. In the sixteenth century, however, it was not Brazil and its sugar, or even West Africa with its gold and slaves, but rather Asia and its spices on which the economic hopes of empire rested.

The Estado da Índia

As an economic system, the Estado da Índia was really the articulation of the *carreira da Índia*, the great transoceanic route that linked Lisbon to the Portuguese establishment in Goa on the western Indian coast and to a series of maritime commercial loops that tied various places in Asia to Goa and the carreira. The Portuguese sought to establish a monopoly of trade in the Indian Ocean by eliminating powerful rivals (the Turks, Mamelukes, and Gujaratis) and by controlling trade from a series of *feitorias* (trade stations) and fortresses scattered from Sofala (East Africa) to Hormuz (Persian Gulf), to Cochin (western India), to Malacca (Malaysia), and eventually beyond to Macao (China). The customhouse of the Casa da Índia in Lisbon, the viceroy, and other royal agents in the ports and *feitorias* of the Indian Ocean administered the royal monopoly over pepper, cinnamon, and other spices. During the first half of the sixteenth century, this system provided considerable profits to the crown. But after the original Portuguese penetration and military victories, local trade in the Indian Ocean recovered and found ways to supply the old caravan routes to the Middle East. Continuing Portuguese attempts to choke off this competing trade raised the costs of empire enormously and ultimately became unsuccessful. Policy changed. Rather than eliminate local commerce, the Portuguese sought to control and tax private trade through a system of *cartazes* (licenses) that generated considerable revenues for the Estado da Índia but also allowed the alternate routes for spices to flourish and thus undercut the monopoly of the carreira, which remained the crown's principal concern.

Although a variety of commodities, particularly cinnamon, cloves, and other spices, were sent to Europe around the Cape of Good Hope, pepper made up the bulk in value and volume. The fleet of 1518, for example, carried about 1,000 metric tons of pepper, or 95 percent of the total cargo, and through the sixteenth century pepper constituted the principal commodity of royal commerce. But the great ships of the carreira also carried the goods of private merchants, and while their share of space was only 25–50 percent of the tonnage, the value of their goods was over 90 percent of the total value, and these figures do not take into account contraband. Spices, cloth, jewelry, and other luxury items were carried, but in terms of value, by the 1580s, textiles predominated. This pattern continued well into the seventeenth century.

Ships sailing from Europe carried outbound colonists, soldiers, and officials, some luxury items, and, most importantly, specie to pay for Asian commodities as well as for the military and administrative costs of empire. Table 1.1 lists the decennial figures for tonnage and sailings and arrivals in both directions. It shows a period of great activity between 1531 and 1540 and then a long period of relative stability between the outbound and return voyages. Between 1541 and 1600, about 20 percent more ships sailed for Asia than for Europe. The rate of loss on the eastbound voyages was about 13 percent and somewhat higher, at 17 percent, in the opposite direction. Although the level of activity varied each year, over the course of the seventy years for which we have estimates, between five and six ships annually moved in each direction to maintain the carreira in the sixteenth century.

While the Portuguese monopoly of commerce in the Indian Ocean was a dream never realized because of competition, the private trade conducted by royal officials, soldiers, and private merchants also undercut the crown's

Table 1.1. The Carreira da Índia

Years	Lisbon to Asia		Asia to Lisbon	
	Departures tons (ships)	*Arrivals* tons (ships)*	*Departures tons (ships)*	*Arrivals tons (ships)*
1531–1540	44,660 (80)	42,610 (76)	39,110 (61)	36,410 (57)
1541–1550	40,800 (68)	34,100 (56)	34,550 (58)	30,550 (52)
1551–1560	39,600 (58)	32,500 (46)	33,650 (47)	25,750 (35)
1561–1570	37,030 (50)	35,580 (46)	36,250 (45)	32,150 (40)
1571–1580	42,900 (50)	40,800 (48)	38,250 (42)	35,150 (39)
1581–1590	55,420 (59)	42,870 (45)	48,450 (51)	39,290 (42)
1591–1600	49,200 (43)	42,540 (39)	45,350 (40)	25,000 (22)
1601–1610	77,190 (71)	49,540 (45)	43,390 (36)	32,290 (28)
1611–1620	60,900 (66)	44,060 (47)	40,350 (32)	35,550 (28)
1621–1630	48,000 (60)	31,410 (39)	24,150 (28)	15,050 (19)
1631–1640	20,020 (33)	15,770 (28)	13,710 (21)	9,910 (15)
1641–1650	22,840 (42)	14,280 (28)	16,030 (32)	12,030 (24)
1651–1660	14,320 (35)	18,990 (35)	7,970 (16)	12,030 (24)
1661–1670	8,635 (21)	5,635 (14)	6,070 (14)	4,820 (13)
1671–1680	11,700 (25)	13,900 (29)	10,730 (22)	9,680 (21)
1681–1690	11,650 (19)	11,650 (19)	9,300 (16)	8,600 (15)
1691–1700	14,900 (24)	13,700 (21)	8,950 (14)	7,550 (13)

*Lower figures for arrivals generally indicate losses at sea.

Source: T. Bentley Duncan, "Navigation between Portugal and Asia in the Sixteenth and Seventeenth Centuries," in E. J. Van Kley and C. K. Pullapilly, eds., *Asia and the West* (Notre Dame, IN, 1986).

exclusive control of this trade. After the 1550s, by award or purchase, concessions to royal administrators and private merchants created a system of commercial loops that tied Indonesia, the Bay of Bengal, and other outlying areas to the carreira trade. The crown derived some benefit from customs duties on this trade and from the initial purchase of these routes. It has been estimated that the value of these concessionary voyages, such as Goa to Hormuz or Malacca to São Tomé, was perhaps twice that of the crown's income from the carreira trade in a good year. The route between Macao and Nagasaki, on which the Portuguese carried Chinese silk in return for Japanese silver, or that between Macao and Manila, where Mexican silver was exchanged for the silk destined for consumers in New Spain and Peru as well as in Spain itself, provided great profits, but they were just two of many such circuits in which indigenous "country trade" and Portuguese private trade operated within the Indian Ocean system. In fact, as the historian

James Boyajian has pointed out: "The flowering of Portuguese private trade in Asia and via the Cape was hardly an isolated development. It was part of a vast world of Asia trading in which Portuguese played a secondary role to Gujaratis, Chinese, Javanese, and Japanese."[1]

The concessionary voyages and routes and coastal commerce were then linked to Goa and the carreira by annual convoys and by overland trade. The Portuguese invested heavily in this traffic as well. Each route made its contribution to the apparent apex of the system, which was still the Cape route. Goa received goods from all over Asia: Macao, Bengal, the Moluccas, and Malacca. Between 1580 and 1640, about 75 percent of the total value of goods eventually unloaded in Lisbon in the carreira came from Bijapur, near Goa, and from the more distant regions of Cambay, Gujarat, and Sindh. On each route, local merchants as well as Portuguese traders, many of them New Christians (descendants of converted Jews), collaborated. The latter were squeezed out for the most part in the period 1640–1670 by pressure from the Inquisition, but indigenous Muslim, Hindu, and Christian traders displayed considerable ingenuity and resourcefulness in adapting and exploiting the Portuguese trading system to their own benefit.

What did the empire mean to the Portuguese economy in the early decades of the sixteenth century as the trade from Asia began to have an effect? In 1506, the Asian spices alone constituted over one-quarter of the kingdom's annual income. By 1518–1519 that figure had risen to just under 40 percent. Of the overseas products, the spices of the India trade were by far the largest single item. We should note, however, that the rents and taxes collected in Portugal and the income generated by the Lisbon customhouse continued to be major sources of revenue.

By the close of the sixteenth century, the essential character of the two systems that constituted the Portuguese empire had been defined. Portuguese economic activity within the Estado da Índia was almost exclusively military and commercial, a combination of the use of power and terror, especially in the western Indian Ocean, and clever trading in the Bay of Bengal and beyond Malacca. The economy of the Brazilian colony differed essentially from the empire beyond the Cape of Good Hope. On the Atlantic islands and in Brazil, the Portuguese had invested heavily in production and had organized capital, land, and labor to produce sugar and other commodities. In Asia, such an enterprise was almost never undertaken. There, the Portuguese were willing to allow local populations to produce pepper, spices, silk, and textiles and to trade for these items or to allow their circulation

[1] James C. Boyajian, *Portuguese Trade in Asia under the Hapsburgs, 1580–1640* (Baltimore, 1993), p. 14. Much of the preceding paragraph is drawn from this excellent analysis.

under Portuguese licenses. This is not to say that taxation and land rents were unimportant to the empire in Asia. In some places, such as Sri Lanka (Ceylon), they constituted over 80 percent of the crown's revenue, and by the mid-seventeenth century these sources of income may have represented about one-third of the total. Rarely, however, did the Portuguese enter into the production of the commodities traded. Only in a few places were landed estates (*aforamentos*) developed, the most dramatic being the *prazos* along the Zambezi River in East Africa, where the holders and the institutions were soon "Africanized" as a kind of local ruler. For the most part, the Portuguese were unburdened of the responsibility to organize factors of production, particularly capital or land, and above all the problem of providing or organizing labor was in most places simply not their concern. This was a major economic difference between the two spheres of activity and had broad social implications as well. In the early seventeenth century, Ambrósio Fernandes Brandão, in his *Dialogos das grandezas do Brasil* (Dialogues of the Great Things of Brazil, 1618), noted that in Portugal one could find many men who had returned from India with fortunes, whereas few from Brazil had been able to do so. The difference, he said, was not the level of gain to be had in the two colonial spheres but that the fortunes made in Brazil were in property and fixed assets, whereas those of India were the result of commerce and thus more liquid. Brandão might have gone on to add that the lifestyle and level of consumption in India, where the resident Portuguese used their wealth to impress the local indigenous upper class as well as each other, were far more ostentatious than in Brazil. This conspicuous consumption also contributed to the eventual stagnation of the Estado da Índia.

Crises and Survival in the Seventeenth Century

During the seventeenth century, the role of the Portuguese empire and the context in which it operated changed radically as a result of general changes in the world economy and the emergence of a new political balance in Europe. The disastrous attempt by King Dom Sebastião to expand Portuguese interests in Morocco in 1578 led not only to his death but also to the loss of the throne to the Spanish Hapsburgs for sixty years (1580–1640). Spanish interest in Lisbon as a great Atlantic port and in the India trade lay behind the original intervention, and many noble and merchant families demonstrated considerable support for the Hapsburg cause. In fact, from 1580 to 1620, Portuguese access to Spanish American silver, to markets in the Hapsburg possessions, and to the protection of Spanish arms contributed to the Portuguese economy, a situation aided by the booming production of Brazilian sugar and by strong market prices for that commodity. After 1621, however, the situation drastically changed. First, there was a dramatic recession in the Euro-Atlantic economy from 1622 to 1624, probably caused by overexpansion and the beginning of the Thirty Years War. A renewal of the war with the Dutch, the formation of the Dutch West India Company (1621), which was designed as a commercial weapon against the Spanish Hapsburg dominions, and the increased military and naval demands thus created, placed a great strain on Portugal's resources and its ability to increase production. The Dutch seizure of Northeast Brazil (1630–1654) and the related capture of El Mina (1638) and Luanda (1641–1648) disrupted the slave supply on which the whole Atlantic system rested. This situation and Philip IV's closed mercantilist policies contributed to support for separation from Spain. The "Portuguese Restoration," begun in 1640 by supporters of the Bragança family, initiated a period of military, diplomatic, and economic effort by Portugal that lasted for almost thirty years and exhausted both sides. That the struggle for Portuguese independence from Spain was carried out in the midst of a global struggle to defend its empire against European competitors makes the Portuguese achievement all the more impressive.

Here, the benefits of empire that were not essentially economic can also be seen. In the 1580s, Portuguese opponents of the Hapsburg cause had been able to enlist French and English support by offering concessions in the Brazil trade, and there had even been intimations of territorial concessions or transfers. During negotiations with the Dutch during the 1640s, the lure of colonial trade or the surrender of colonial outposts had been used as bargaining chips. England's support for Portugal after 1642 and especially after the treaty of 1654 was to some extent bought with the promise of trade advantages in Portuguese colonies, and when that relationship was solidified by the marriage of Catherine of Bragança to Charles II in 1661, a major factor in the arrangements was the enormous dowry of 2 million cruzados, much of it raised from taxes on the colonial populations, and the concession of colonial outposts such as Bombay and Tangier. Among the other monarchs of Europe, Portugal by itself counted for little, but Portugal and its global empire always merited some consideration, a fact not lost on the court in Lisbon as well. These commercial arrangements may have been economically disadvantageous to Portugal in the long run but also assured the political independence of the kingdom and enlisted a powerful ally in defense of its sovereignty. This was a benefit that could not be calculated easily on the balance sheet of empire even if such had existed at the time. Moreover, the Atlantic system had also paid directly in men and arms for the survival of the kingdom. Taxation on the sugar industry had been a key element in paying for the war for independence from Spain and in financing the global struggle against the Dutch during which the contribution of colonial forces in the retaking of Pernambuco and Angola had also been major factors. Many of the captains and commanders in the wars of the Restoration had served in Brazil or India.

In the midst of these political events, the sugar economy at the heart of the Atlantic system was altered. Brazil could produce about 22,000 tons by 1630, but lower prices had reduced profit levels by half from those enjoyed in the 1610s. Prices rose again in the 1640s and 1650s, but as they did, foreign competitors in the Caribbean, particularly Barbados, began to produce sugar as well. These developments had two results. With sugar now available from their own colonies, England and France began to restrict Brazilian imports and essentially eliminated Brazilian sugar from those markets. Second, the increased production reduced the price of sugar in the Atlantic market, but at the same time the demand for laborers on the Caribbean plantations drove up the price of slaves. Brazilian planters were caught between the two trends at exactly the moment that the Portuguese state was increasingly taxing sugar to pay for the defense of the empire and the war for independence. Brazil's problem was not production. Even after the Dutch War in 1654, Brazil had the capacity to produce over 1,200,000 arrobas (18,000 tons), more than any competitor. It still had comparative advantages, but international political and economic conditions and their effects on Portugal's fiscal policies combined to create a situation of crisis. Portugal had sought various ways to respond. The Brazil Company was instituted in 1649 to organize the commerce of the colony. Plagued by irregular sailings, contraband, and other problems, it proved relatively successful, sending fleets loaded with the principal colonial products, which now included large quantities of tobacco and hides as well as sugar.

By the 1680s, the economy had reached a low point. The separation from Spain had interrupted and made more difficult the flow of Spanish American silver into the Portuguese economy. Portugal, like the rest of Western Europe, was in a general recession, which led to a devaluation of Portuguese currency in 1688 and to an increased search for new sources of revenue, but the Atlantic system had for the most part survived. The revenues it provided gave the kingdom the strength to maintain its independence and had kept Portugal from going the way of Catalonia or Scotland.

The Estado da Índia had fared much worse over the course of the century. Beyond the Cape of Good Hope, we can note three interrelated processes that affected the nature of the empire. First, the arrival of European rivals, particularly the Dutch and English after 1590, and the subsequent loss of routes, ports, and major outposts such as Malacca (lost in 1641) caused a severe contraction in the operations of the Estado da Índia and in the levels of trade and revenue. Second, at the same time, an Asian riposte to the Portuguese (and European) presence could be seen from the Levant to Japan. The rise in power of the Safavids in Persia, the Moghul expansion in northern India, and the Tokugawa shogunate in Japan created large and powerful states that could not be intimidated, coerced, or cajoled as had been done earlier. These "gunpowder empires" also broke the old division between landed powers and smaller commercial states. The loss of Hormuz (1622) to the Safavids and English and the expulsion of Christians (with the exception of the Dutch) from Japan in 1638–1640 were symptomatic of the contraction of empire that the new powers represented.

In response to both foreign competition and indigenous assertiveness, the Portuguese experimented with new alternatives. The success of Dutch and English trading companies was behind the creation of a short-lived Portuguese East India Company (1628–1633), but it was doomed by high losses at sea and by a shortage of capital, partly because the Inquisition continued to obstruct the participation of New Christians in the effort. The crown increasingly turned to private traders and sold the profitable Asian routes to Goa as concessionary voyages. The levels of income from the carreira itself only began to show serious contraction after mid-century, and partially in response, an attempt was made to integrate the failing Indian Ocean system with the troubled but more successful Atlantic one. Homeward-bound Indiamen began to call with some regularity at Salvador in Brazil, where their silks, pearls, and luxury items were in demand and where, after 1675, they were also allowed to load some sugar for delivery in Lisbon. Eventually, Rio de Janeiro would also be drawn into trade with Goa, and a commerce in tobacco as snuff also flourished between Brazil and Goa.

The carreira experienced its heaviest losses in the mid-seventeenth century, and overall about 20 percent of the tonnage embarked was lost. By 1670, the Estado da Índia as a state enterprise had suffered its worst, but that is not to say that private traders within it did not continue to profit, nor that the thousands of Portuguese scattered from Macao to Siam and Abyssinia as mercenaries, merchants, and missionaries did not continue to have an effect on local societies.

In the global struggle with the Dutch, the Portuguese had essentially lost out in Asia, fought to a standstill in Africa, and had by war and purchase won out in America. The efforts to hold onto Brazil represented recognition that the Atlantic system, despite the pressures to which it was subjected, had become the mainstay of empire in this period. It was now composed primarily of Brazil and West Central Africa. Madeira and the Azores had become producers of wine and grains and were more integrated into the economy and polity of Portugal itself, but the South Atlantic of Brazil and Africa increasingly formed an integrated system of labor and commodity production. Slave import levels were now at about 5,000 a year, and the horrendous mortality and negative rate of natural growth in Brazilian slave society made the slave trade the essential feature of the whole system. The economic life of Angola and other settlements in Africa became almost entirely subordinated to the demands of the slave traffic.

Colony and Metropole: Recovery and Realignment

The two spheres of the empire continued to operate, but after the disasters of the seventeenth century, the economy of the Estado da Índia became a holding operation. There had been some recovery by the 1680s, and when well administered and when costly wars could be avoided, the Estado da Índia could still be a profitable enterprise but one whose stability was under continual threat. The incursions of foreign rivals, which disrupted the old trade circuits, and the loss of the former forts and factories were matched to some extent by losses to local forces, particularly the expansion of the Hindu Marathas between 1739 and 1741, which reduced Portuguese control solely to the area around Goa, Daman, and Diu. Even later Portuguese expansion from the 1740s to the 1760s in the "New Territories" could not restore economic health, which had essentially been destroyed with the loss of both the carreira trade and the country trade in the previous century. Although spices and other Asian products continued to arrive in Lisbon, the Portuguese hung onto a reduced empire in India as a "point of Honor and Religion," as the English governor and council of Bombay observed in 1737.

By the end of the seventeenth century, despite its tribulations, it was clear that Brazil had become the keystone of Portugal's imperial activity. The Brazilian economy in the eighteenth century increased in size and complexity as the colony's territory and population grew and as the nature of its relationship with Portugal and the Atlantic markets changed over time. We can recognize three roughly overlapping chronological divisions. The period from 1689 to 1760 was dominated by the discovery of gold and diamonds and its effects on the shift of free and slave populations southward to the mining zones and away from the areas of coastal agriculture. Between 1760 and 1780, the production of gold began to decline, and export agriculture also experienced a difficult period of low prices and increasing foreign competition. These economic difficulties provided a partial background for the mercantilist measures of the Marquis of Pombal, the energetic dictatorial minister to the king, that were designed to redirect the imperial economy. Although many of Pombal's policies were not immediately successful, changes in the balance of power in Europe after 1780 opened new opportunities for Brazilian products and for an agricultural renaissance that by the 1790s led to a shift in the relative trading positions of the colony and the metropole.

At the end of the seventeenth century, the economy of the Portuguese empire had entered into a period of crisis and uncertainty. Colonial re-exports fell dramatically, and the prices of sugar and tobacco dropped. Although a 20 percent devaluation of the Portuguese currency in 1688 helped to stimulate trade, and the outbreak of wars in 1689, which lasted until 1713, created a new demand for Brazilian and Portuguese products, the unstable nature of the economy in this period contributed directly to the search for new economic programs, of which the Methuen treaty of 1703 was only a part. That treaty, providing as it did lower tariffs on Portuguese wines sent to England in return for an open market in Portugal for English woolens, was really an extension of the English political and economic influence on Portugal established in the seventeenth century. It eventually resulted in great balance-of-trade deficits in England's favor that were paid for by products and specie drawn from Portugal's empire. The availability of gold had made that possible, and the decision by Portugal's wine interests to enter into this agreement undercut a nascent program of manufactures that had begun in the late seventeenth century.

In Asia, East Africa, and Brazil, the search for new sources of specie intensified both under government aegis and in private expeditions, and it is within this context of economic uncertainty and expectations that the discovery of gold in Brazil around 1695 seemed to be so providential. The revelation of large deposits of gold in Minas Gerais, and later, in the 1730s, farther west in Mato Grosso and Goiás, transformed the nature of the Portuguese empire and economic thinking in Lisbon. We have some rough production figures, and the amounts were staggering. Based only on official figures, Minas Gerais alone produced 2.7 metric tons of gold between 1700 and 1710, 5.9 tons from 1711 to 1720, 6.6 tons from 1721 to 1729, and 8.2 tons between 1730 and 1740. These were figures that in a single decade far exceeded all of the gold production of Spanish America up to that time. At its height between 1750 and 1754, Brazilian gold-production levels reached an average of over 3 metric tons per year. Here was the long-awaited "El Dorado" that the Portuguese crown had dreamed of and hoped for in the overseas empire, a golden wave that seemed to drown the production of its other sources in Africa, El Mina, and Monomotapa. Table 1.2 presents the output of the major Brazilian gold-producing areas during the eighteenth

Table 1.2. Brazilian gold production (metric tons)

Years	*Minas gerais*	*Goiás*	*Mato grosso*	*Total*
1700–1710	2.7			2.7
1711–1720	5.9			5.9
1721–1729	6.6		0.73	7.3
1730–1739	8.2	1.4	0.90	10.5
1740–1749	9.0	3.2	1.0	13.2
1750–1759	7.6	4.3	1.0	12.9
1760–1769	6.4	2.3	0.5	9.2
1770–1779	5.3	1.8	0.5	7.6
1780–1789	3.8	0.9	0.4	5.1
1790–1799	3.0	0.7	0.4	4.1

Source: Virgílio Noya Pinto, *O ouro Brasilerio e o comércio Anglo-Português: Uma contribuição aos estudos da economia Atlântica no sécuio XVIII*, 2nd ed. (São Paulo, 1979), 114.

century. It demonstrates the predominant role of Minas Gerais and the crest of production reached in the decade of the 1740s.

The implications of the discovery of gold for the growth of the colony and for the structure of the Portuguese empire were multiple and far-reaching. In Brazil, gold stimulated a tremendous shift of population toward the interior, the abandonment of coastal agriculture, and a new flood of immigration from Portugal. While slave prices had already been rising after 1680 with the opening of the mines, they doubled in the next twenty years. One governor complained that "God has given gold to Brazil in order to punish it," and others lamented the abandonment of coastal agriculture. By 1775, Minas Gerais had over 300,000 people, and over half of them were slaves. This was roughly 20 percent of the population of Brazil as a whole.

As rough mining camps grew into towns, routes of supply and commerce developed. Cattle herds expanded to supply the mines, and small-scale agriculture grew in order to feed the mining areas. Early shortages and famines were eventually overcome, and a diverse, mixed economy eventually developed. Brazil was becoming increasingly less dependent on Portugal, and the vision of empire began to look considerably different from Minas Gerais or Bahia than it did from Lisbon.

Here once again the competing policies of state control and private initiative came into play. Whereas the crown had been satisfied to tax sugar production and commerce and leave its cultivation in private hands, mineral wealth elicited other policies. During this mining boom, the intervention of the state in economic activity was apparent through regulation, control, and enforcement. This kind of attitude was most apparent in the Serro do Frio area, where diamonds were discovered in the 1720s and where strict government control, patrols by companies of dragoons, and a royal monopoly contract were imposed on the mining of the precious stones.

In the midst of the production of so much wealth, contraband was a constant problem. The historian A. J. R. Russell-Wood has pointed out that between 1709 and 1761 over two dozen laws and decrees were passed forbidding Portuguese trade with foreigners or the entry of foreign ships in Brazilian ports.[2] These were essentially a failure. French, Spanish, and English ships found ways of avoiding the prohibitions and of calling at Brazilian ports or making clandestine stops on the coast. The Dutch depended instead on their control of Ouidah and other West African ports for access to Brazilian gold brought by merchants from Bahia. Even worse, British ships often called at Lisbon when the Brazilian fleets arrived in order to pick up gold illegally. Despite attempts at control, colonial mineral wealth flowed into foreign hands illegally or was used to pay for Portugal's balance-of-trade deficit, which was growing because of new demands for luxury items that the access to gold made possible. London alone minted over £8,000,000 of gold coins in the decade from 1713 to 1724. As Adam Smith recognized, Brazilian gold was an essential element in the growth of the British economy. It helped lay the basis for the Industrial Revolution. It did not have similar effects in Portugal, where it provided the Portuguese crown with the resources for pharaonic building projects, such as the palace at Mafra, and for absolutist ambitions. Gold created the false impression that there were resources for any project, no matter how ambitious or expensive.

In truth, gold produced a tremendous amount of revenue for the crown through various taxes and imposts, but administration of the mining areas and royal policies were also very costly. Moreover, the Brazilian El Dorado was somewhat ephemeral, and by the 1760s, as the amount of gold production began to decline, it became increasingly apparent that the image of opulence was deceiving. Finally, it is important to note that at no time did the value of gold outweigh that of agricultural production in the colony. In 1760, when Brazilian exports were valued at 4,800,000 milréis, sugar accounted for half

[2] A. J. R. Russell-Wood, "Colonial Brazil: The Gold Cycle, c. 1690–1750," in Leslie Bethel, ed., *Cambridge History of Latin America*, 10 vols. to date (Cambridge, 1984–), vol. 2, 547–600.

of that figure and gold for 46 percent. Here, once again, the concept of consecutive commodity cycles proved to be misleading.

All during this period, the productive capacity of the colony did not change greatly, and the traditional agricultural exports continued to be the basis of colonial wealth. Not productivity but market opportunities and the irregularities of the fleets to Bahia, Pernambuco, and Rio tended to determine the amount of Brazilian sugar that reached Europe. Brazilian production fluctuated between 1.5 and 2.5 million arrobas (22,000–36,000 tons) in these years. Tobacco had been grown and exported in the seventeenth century to both Portugal and Africa. With the opening of direct trade to the Mina coast after 1645, Brazilian producers began to benefit from this trade. The primary markets for Brazilian tobacco were Portugal and Africa. In 1742, this trade was reorganized in favor of the Brazilian merchants. Only thirty ships a year, twenty-four from Bahia and six from Pernambuco, were allowed to trade directly with the Mina coast, thus securing high prices for Brazilian tobacco on the African coast. By the 1780s, the two markets were receiving roughly equal amounts of Brazilian tobacco, although Portugal re-exported large quantities to other European nations.

Other commodities that reflected the growth of the Brazilian colony were leather and hides, which became regular items in the fleets. Large herds developed in the northeastern interior and on the plains in southern São Paulo (Paraná) and in Rio Grande de São Pedro. Between 1726 and 1734, between 400,000 and 500,000 hides a year went to Rio de Janeiro for export. Livestock herding produced an expansive internal commerce as well as a dried meat (*charque*) industry in southern Brazil. Beginning modestly in 1780, by 1800 about 500,000 arrobas were being sent to the rest of Brazil and exported from the colony. By the beginning of the nineteenth century, the small boats from Rio Grande carrying *charque* and hides made up the majority of vessels entering the port of Rio de Janeiro and were frequent visitors to the ports of the northeast. This development demonstrated how internal economic growth and the development of "colonial" trades were articulated with the broader imperial economy of the Portuguese empire. It demonstrated the growing strength of the Brazilian economy but also its ability to absorb increasing amounts of goods from Portugal and elsewhere in Europe.

For the Brazilian economy, the mid-century period from about 1760 to 1785, roughly coinciding with the rule of the Marquís of Pombal (1755–1777), marked an important turning point, a period of transition whose principal effects would be seen in the last decades of the century. Pombal realized that Brazil had become the cornerstone of the imperial economy and that the key to Portugal's regeneration was the application of mercantilist measures to the Portuguese economy. His goals were to lessen Portugal's economic dependence on England and other European nations while at the same time maintaining the political advantages that accrued to Portugal through alliances and commercial relations, especially with Great Britain. To achieve these ends, he favored various sectors in both the metropole and the colony and fostered contacts between interests on both sides of the Atlantic.

Along with political, administrative, military, and social reforms, Pombal initiated a series of economic and fiscal measures that altered the nature and functioning of the Brazilian economy. Specifically, he instituted *mesas da inspeção* (inspection stations) in the major Brazilian ports (1751) to control the quality of Brazilian agricultural exports and introduced a number of other measures, all designed to stimulate the colonial economy by eliminating or reforming existing problems. These included the elimination of difficult-to-control small-scale merchants trading between Brazil and Portugal (1755), the regulation, and then the abolition, of the fleet system (1765) in order to make commerce with Brazil more efficient, and a series of social measures such as the abolition of slavery in Portugal in order to assure the supply of Africans to Brazil. Perhaps the expulsion of the Jesuits from Portugal and its empire (1759) can also be seen in part as an attempt at economic reform, although the underlying causes of that measure were varied.

Even more important were new policies and innovations that affected traditional sectors of the Brazilian economy, such as agriculture. The creation of large monopoly trading companies such as the Companhia geral do comércio do Grão Pará e Maranhão (1755), designed to develop the economy of northern Brazil through its monopoly of the supply of African slaves and its control of all trade from Europe as well as the export of colonial products such cacao, and the Companhia geral do comércio de Pernambuco e Paraíba (1759), with similar goals for the northeastern captaincies, were cornerstones of Pombaline policy. Pombal might have created such institutions elsewhere in the colony as well, but merchant interests in Bahia and perhaps Rio de Janeiro were strong enough to prevent an attempt to form similar companies for those regions (although the real explanation may be that English interests in those ports were also very strong).

Traditional crops such as sugar needed attention. For sugar's recovery, however, more important than Pombal's actions or policies was the outbreak of war in the 1770s between England and France, which once again opened new opportunities for Brazilian sugar. By the 1770s, however, the Atlantic world looked quite different and Brazil now played a different role in it. Whereas in the 1730s perhaps one-third of all the sugar marketed in the Atlantic (about 2.5 million arrobas) came from Brazil, by 1776, Brazilian exports, at 1.4 million arrobas, had fallen to less than 10 percent of the total. Sugar remained the predominant agricultural activity of the colony, but the colonies of other nations had now surpassed Brazil as sugar producers.

In northern Brazil, Pombal's innovative combination of social reform and economic strategy was even more apparent. Under the aegis of Pombal's brother, Governor Francisco Xavier Mendonça Furtado, former mission villages were secularized and an attempt was made to stimulate the growth of population through the importation of immigrants and the fostering of marriages between indigenous peoples and the Portuguese. The Companhia geral do comércio do Grao Pará e Maranháo continued to develop the export of the *drogas do sertão*, particularly cacao, most of it in Pará, which usually produced over 90 percent of Brazil's export of this crop. Although some cacao was consumed in Portugal, most of it was re-exported to other European consumers. In the captaincy of Maranhão, the Companhia actively developed new crops, cotton and rice, through its importation of African slaves. In the decade of the 1770s, Maranhão produced about 560 tons of cotton per year, far in excess of the tiny combined production of all the other captaincies. In addition, the Companhia also stimulated the cultivation of rice. By the 1770s, Maranhão was exporting large quantities, and cultivation had also begun in Pará. By 1781, Portugal no longer needed to import foreign rice and could depend on the Brazilian colony. The combination of rice and cotton production, much of it based on slave labor in Maranhão, had the effect of transforming the social character of the region. By 1800, Maranhão's population was almost half slave (46 percent), and about 65 percent of its 79,000 people were black or mulatto. Whether we judge the Companhia geral de comércio do Grao Pará e Maranhão successful or not, it clearly had changed the nature of northern Brazil.

Agricultural renovation remained a key to Pombal's policy in Brazil. Rice and cotton were just two of the new agricultural products developed in the colony. Experiments were also made with indigo, hemp, cochineal, and linen. The cultivation of wheat and coffee, which were already being grown in Brazil, was expanded. But for all these efforts and developments, the basic economic situation of the colony within the empire did not change.

Despite his force and imagination, Pombal could not resolve the underlying economic weakness of the empire. With falling gold production and weak markets for its agricultural products (especially after 1763 when peace returned to Europe), the value of Brazil's exports in 1777, despite all of Pombal's measures, was only half of what it had been in 1760. Attempts to eliminate or reduce shipping costs and stimulate commerce were not successful, but they indicate the objectives of Pombal's policies. A royal order of 1766 noted that "agriculture and commerce are the two wellsprings of a people's wealth and finding the latter free and open, there only remains to stimulate the former."

But Pombal's measures had little immediate effect in the colony. Gold production was falling, Caribbean output of tropical products was growing, and unfortunately, war with Spain beginning in 1762 involved Brazil in a long struggle over its southern frontier, which lasted until 1777. From the metropolitan point of view, however, Pombal's economic policies, including his promotion of Portuguese manufactures, produced some benefit. Portugal's exports to England were 34 percent higher and imports 44 percent lower in the period between 1771 and 1775 than they had been between 1751 and 1755. Moreover, the great colonial companies had become vehicles for the import of Portuguese manufactures into the growing Brazilian market. In Brazil, although Pombal's policies were not immediately successful, they had created the conditions, and with the introduction of new crops literally "planted the seeds," for tremendous growth of the Brazilian economy after 1780.

That change was caused not so much by policy as by the international situation. The French Revolution and the Haitian revolt of 1792 disrupted the commerce of the major powers. Portugal was able to fill the gap. Sugar production expanded in old areas and developed in new ones in the south. Sugar made up about 35 percent of all Brazilian exports between 1796 and 1811, and thus it remained the single most important item of colonial commerce, but it was no longer as predominant as it had been in the previous century.

Along with the resurgence of colonial products came the growth of powerful local merchant elites that underlined the changing nature of the empire and potential future difficulties. In Salvador, Rio de Janeiro, and São Paulo, Brazilian merchants were often better able than their metropolitan competitors to control various trades and to finance commercial activities. This provoked concern. An incident in 1770 illustrates the problem. Martinho de Melo e Castro, the overseas minister, in a dispute over privileges in the African slaving ports, wrote in that year that "the capital and its inhabitants should always be favored over the colonies and their inhabitants." Such preoccupations with the relative positions of metropole and colony in overseas trade were paralleled by policies within the colony to maintain royal income and to satisfy imperial needs.

There was also another problem: Brazil itself was growing. Its population had reached over two million by 1800, and the resurgence of colonial products had stimulated an intensification of the slave trade. By the end of the century, as many as 40,000 new Africans a year were arriving. This population had to be fed along with the residents of cities such as Rio de Janeiro.

An active coastal trade in foodstuffs, peasant production for local markets, vast livestock drives, and even some attempts at manufacturing created an internal economy that was linked to exterior commerce and export but also separate from it. By the late eighteenth century, there were both local merchants and foreign commercial agents involved in the Brazil trade who were able to compete with those of Portugal. In a way, Brazil had created a "country trade" similar to that which had existed in the Estado da Índia in the sixteenth century. Although by its nature and that of its population Brazil's internal economy was linked more closely with Portugal than the Asian ones had ever been, the existence of an independent economy recreated a series of control problems for the mother country similar to those faced by the viceroys of Goa in the sixteenth century. Portugal's dependence on Brazil, however, was far greater than it had ever been on Asia, and ultimately it was the colony's economy that determined the relationship. At the beginning of the eighteenth century, Frei António do Rosário, noting the wealth of the Brazilian colony, had written that Brazil was now the "true India and Mina of Portugal" because "India is no longer India."[3] His words proved to be true in ways he did not then anticipate.

The Changing Balance of Colonial Relations

In the period after 1780, the relationship between Portugal and the empire, as well as between Portugal and its dominant ally, England, changed dramatically – a number of times. In general terms, however, this period witnessed the increasing economic strength of Brazil, which in turn weakened the colony's ties with Portugal while at the same time Portugal was becoming increasingly dependent on England.

The balance of trade between Brazil and Portugal and that between Portugal and England reflects in a direct way the changing relationship among the three areas. Although accurate statistics are lacking for the mid-eighteenth century, it appears that Portugal at that time maintained a positive balance of trade with its colonies but had a negative balance, importing more than it exported, with the other nations of Europe. This situation began to change in the late 1770s as the demand increased for colonial products that Portugal could supply to other European nations, and it intensified in the 1790s because of the conjuncture of political events and economic situations created by the upheaval of the French Revolution and its aftermath.

[3] *Frutas do Brasil numa nova e ascética monarquia* (Lisbon, 1702), p. iii.

Brazilian colonial agricultural production boomed in the 1790s as a result of the disruption of Caribbean production caused by the Haitian revolution and the Napoleonic Wars. Portugal was in a position to re-export large quantities of valued American products to England and other European nations. Brazilian sugar, which had filled only about 5 percent of the Atlantic market in the 1770s, now supplied about 15 percent. Brazilian cotton shipments from Portugal to England doubled between the 1780s and 1790s, totaling almost 8,000,000 pounds a year by weight, and by the decade of 1800, perhaps a quarter of Manchester cotton goods were made with Brazilian cotton. By the first half of the decade of the 1790s, Portugal was exporting to England goods valued over a million pounds sterling more than what England was returning. By 1795, Portugal exported to England almost twice as much as it had in 1776. During the period from 1796 to 1806, Portugal's exports had a spectacular annual growth rate of 4 percent.

Clearly, Portugal's economic relationship with England was being altered in this period, a fact of some concern in England itself. Now it was England rather than Portugal that had to send gold to make up the deficit in its balance of trade. Part of England's concern must have been that although trade with Great Britain was still almost 40 percent of Portugal's total exports, the small Iberian country was now also engaged in commerce with the United States, Italy, France, and the Baltic states. Meanwhile, by 1800, contraband trade with England may have been rapidly expanding in Brazil and, if so, that suggests a lower demand in Brazil for imports from Portugal. Between 1796 and 1807, Portugal showed a positive balance of trade with Brazil in only three years, and in 1807 alone Portugal had a deficit of over 6,620,000 milréis, about 60 percent over the total of its exports (10,348,602 milréis) to the colony. These figures make it clear that Brazil had finally assumed a dominant position within the Portuguese colonial system. Brazil received almost 80 percent of all the goods that Portugal sent to its colonies, and over 80 percent of the goods received by Portugal from the colonies originated in Brazil. In 1816, goods from Brazil were valued at over four times those received in Portugal from Asia. Moreover, with its growing population, Brazil had become a major market for a resurgence of Portuguese manufactured goods, which by the first decade of the nineteenth century made up over one-third of the exports to Brazil. It was clear that Brazil had now become not only the most important colony of Portugal but the very heart of the Portuguese empire, overshadowing the metropole itself.

The changing relationship between Portugal and its principal colony may not have been viewed as a crisis in Lisbon because it was made possible by Portugal's positive relationship with its European trading partners. Its ability to re-export the products of its colonies gave Portugal a decided edge in its commerce. Still, that advantage implied Portugal's dependence on its colony, and this relationship was not overlooked by metropolitan administrators or by leading colonial intellectuals and interest groups. Colonial policies such as the *alvará*, or edict, of 1785 that banned textile production in the colony, were a sign that the colonial pact would be jealously maintained despite the changes in the economic balance between colony and metropole and despite the upheavals in the Atlantic colonies of England and France. Although suggestions for improvements and reforms came from the Lisbon Academy of Sciences and from high colonial officials, there was virtually no serious thought given in Portugal to any alteration of the mercantilist colonial system. In Brazil, however, there were those who could conceive of other political and economic alternatives, the bonds that maintained the colonial system began to erode, and these changes in attitude along with the course of political events eventually led to the independence of Brazil in 1822.

Despite the fact that Portugal continued to hold colonies in Africa and Asia after that date, the economic heart of the empire had been lost. Portugal was forced to confront its future without the vast resources of empire, or at least with far more modest ones. What remains impressive about the Portuguese colonial enterprise is not that it was eventually lost but that Portugal held it for so long. Four centuries of empire had their effects. Whatever its economic benefits, the empire imbued Portugal with a sense of greatness and throughout its history enabled its rulers to elicit consideration from its friends and rivals that helped to determine the nation's course.

BIBLIOGRAPHICAL ESSAY

The following is an introductory bibliography that features titles in English along with some of the classic works in Portuguese and other languages. Charles R. Boxer, *The Portuguese Seaborne Empire, 1415–1825* (London,1969); A. J. R. Russell-Wood, *A World on the Move: The Portuguese in Africa, Asia, and America, 1415–1808* (New York, 1992); and Baily Diffie and George Winius, *Foundations of the Portuguese Empire, 1415–1580* (Minneapolis, 1977) are the best introductions for English-speaking readers. On the economic motives for imperial expansion, see Manuel Nunes Dias, *O capitalismo monárquico português* (2 vols., Coimbra, 1963) and Vitorino Magalhães Godinho, *A economia dos descobrimentos henriquenos* (Lisbon, 1962). João Lucio de Azevedo, *Epocas de Portugal económico,* 2nd ed. (Lisbon, 1947) is a classic statement that emphasizes cycles of colonial commerce. There are many chapters of Francisco Bethencourt and Kirti Chaudhuri, *História da expansão portuguesa* (5 vols., Lisbon, 1998–1999) that summarize the current state of knowledge on the economy of the empire. All students must start with Vitorino Magalhães Godinho, *L'économie de l'empire portugais aux xv et xvi siècles* (Paris, 1969), which has been updated and revised in a Portuguese translation as *Os descobrimentos e a economia mundial* (4 vols., Lisbon, 1984). For the Atlantic, the magisterial work of Frédéric Mauro, *Le Portugal et l'Atlantique* (Paris, 1960) remains the basic starting point.

North Africa and the Atlantic Islands

On North Africa, see Vitorino Magalhães Godinho, *História económica e social da expanção portuguesa* (Lisbon, 1947), which provides a detailed study of the economic potential of the region. His other works just mentioned are also fundamental on the origins of Portugal's overseas expansion and the North African episode. David Lopes, "Os portugueses em Marrocos," in *História de Portugal*, Damião Peres, ed. (Oporto, 1931–1932), vols. 3 and 4, provides a basic historical outline. António Dias Farinha, *História de Mazagão durante o período filipino* (Lisbon, 1970) offers a case history of one of the fortified towns, and Otília Rodrigues Fontoura, *Portugal em Marrocos na época de D. João III* (Funchal, 1998) examines the settlements as a whole.

T. Bentley Duncan, *The Atlantic Islands* (Chicago, 1972) provides an introduction to their history but the more recent researches of Alberto Vieira, such as *Os escravos no Arquipelago da Madeira* (Funchal, 1991) and *Portugal y Las Islas del Atlantico* (Madrid, 1992), and the Braudelian study by José Manuel Azevedo e Silva, *A Madeira e a construção do mundo atlántico* (2 vols., Funchal, 1995), are now essential on that island's economy. On the Azores, Maria Olímpia Gil, *O arquipélago dos Açores no século xvii* (Castelo Branco, 1979) is a fine monograph.

West and Southwest Africa

On early contacts in West Africa, see John Thornton, *Africa and Africans in the Making of the Atlantic World* (Cambridge, 1992). A fundamental source on the slave trade is Ivana Elbl, "The Volume of the Early Atlantic Slave Trade, 1450–1521," *Journal of African History*, 38 (1997), pp. 31–75, which incorporates and analyzes all earlier estimates. On El Mina, see John Vogt, *Portuguese Rule on the Gold Coast, 1469–1682* (Athens, GA, 1979), and the exhaustive study by J. Bato'ora Ballong-Wen-Mewuda, *São Jorge da Mina, 1482–1637* (2 vols., Lisbon-Paris, 1993). The later history of the slave trade and the Portuguese in Africa has produced its own extensive historiography. Walter Rodney, *A History of the Upper Guinea Coast,* (New York, 1970) contains much useful information of an economic nature. On the slave trade, the works of Pierre Verger, *Flux et reflux de la traite des negres entre le golfe de Benin et Bahia de Todos os Santos* (Paris, 1968) and Joseph Miller, *Way of Death* (Madison, WI, 1988), are particularly useful.

The Estado da Índia

The literature on the Estado da Índia is vast; that specifically on its economic structures is less so. An excellent starting point is M. N. Pearson, *The New Cambridge History of India: The Portuguese in India* (Cambridge, 1987) and Sanjay Subrahmanyam, *The Portuguese Empire in Asia, 1500–1700* (London, 1993). Also important are Subrahmanyam's monographs, such as *The Political Economy of Commerce: Southern India, 1500–1650* (Cambridge, 1990), and *Improvising Empire: Portuguese Trade and Settlement in the Bay of Bengal* (Delhi, 1990). The work of Luís Felipe Thomaz, *De Ceuta a Timor* (Lisbon, 1994) and his collaboration with Sanjay Subrahmanyam, "Evolution of Empire: The Portuguese in the Indian Ocean during the Sixteenth Century," in *The Political Economy of Merchant Empires*, J. Tracy, ed. (Cambridge, 1991) are essential reading. Two excellent analyses of the economy of empire in the seventeenth century are James Boyajian, *The Portuguese in Asia under the Hapsburgs, 1580–1640* (Baltimore, 1993) and A. R. Disney, *Twilight of the Pepper Empire* (Cambridge, MA, 1978). Disney's essay, "The Portuguese Empire in India, 1550–1650," in *Indo-Portuguese History: Sources and Problems*, J. Correia-Afonso, ed. (Bombay, 1981), pp. 148–162, suggests an approach that takes local conditions into more consideration. There are good regional studies from the various parts of the Estado da Índia. For two examples, Mozambique is particularly well served by E. A. Alpers, *Ivory and Slaves in East Central Africa* (London, 1975), Malyn M. Newitt, *Portuguese Settlement on the Zambesi* (New York, 1973), and by Allen Isaacman, *Mozambique: The Africanization of a European Institution, the Zambesi Prazos* (Madison, WI, 1972). Sri Lanka, where collection of ground rents was important, is analyzed by Tikiri Abeyasinghe, *Portuguese Rule in Ceylon, 1594–1612* (Colombo, 1966), C. R. de Silva, *The Portuguese in Ceylon, 1617–1638* (Colombo, 1972), as well as George Winius, *The Fatal History of Portuguese Ceylon* (Cambridge, MA, 1971). On the Portuguese in China, see George Bryan de Sousa, *The Survival of Empire: Portuguese Trade and Society in China and the South China Sea, 1630–1754* (Cambridge, 1991). A fine example of indigenous response to the Portuguese imperial system is Michael N. Pearson, *Merchants and Rulers in Gujarat* (Berkeley, 1976). Dauril Alden, *The Making of an Enterprise: The Society of Jesus in Portugal, Its Empire, and Beyond* (Stanford, 1996) covers the Jesuit economic activities within the empire. On the complex problem of the finances of empire, V. Magalhães Godinho, *Les finances de l'état portugais des Indes orientales (1517–1635)* (Paris, 1982), is a beginning. The carreira da Índia has generated an extensive literature, but the recent calculations of T. Bentley Duncan, "Navigation between Portugal and Asia in the Sixteenth and Seventeenth Centuries," in E. J. Van Kley and C. K. Pullapilly, eds., *Asia and the West* (Notre Dame, 1986), have forced a rethinking of that trade. The economy of the Estado da Índia in the eighteenth century as a whole has been neglected, but a survey is provided by António da Silva Rego, *O ultramar portugues no século XVIII* (Lisbon, 1970).

Brazil

The basic outlines of the Brazilian economy are presented in the chapters by H. B. Johnson, "Portuguese Settlement, 1500–1580," pp. 1-39; Stuart B. Schwartz, "Plantations and Peripheries, c. 1580–c. 1750," pp. 67–144; A. J. R. Russell-Wood, "The Gold Cycle, c. 1690–1750," pp. 190–243; and Dauril Alden, "Late Colonial Brazil, 1750–1808," pp. 284–343, all of which appear in *Colonial Brazil*, Leslie Bethel, ed. (Cambridge, 1987). On sugar, there is Stuart B. Schwartz, *Sugar Plantations in the Formation of Brazilian Society: Bahia, 1550–1830* (Cambridge, 1985); on tobacco, Jean Baptiste Nardi, *O fumo brasileiro no período colonial* (São Paulo, 1996); on gold, Virgilio Noya Pinto, *O ouro brasileiro e o comércio anglo-português* (São Paulo, 1979), which provides production figures; and Kenneth Maxwell, *Conflicts and Conspiracies: Brazil and Portugal, 1750–1808* (Cambridge, 1973) puts them in a political context. The integration of the Atlantic and Indian Ocean systems is discussed in José Roberto do Amaral Lapa, *A Bahia e a carreira da India* (São Paulo, 1968). Fernando Novais, *Portugal e Brasil na crise do Antigo Regime* (São Paulo, 1979) and José Jobson de Andrade Arruda, *Brasil no comércio colonial* (São Paulo, 1980) and his "Colonies as Mercantile Investments: The Luso-Brazilian Empire, 1500–1808," in *The Political Economy of Merchant Empires*, J. Tracy, ed. (Cambridge, 1991), pp. 360–420, provide theoretical and formal analyses of the late colonial economy. On the changes in imperial structure at the end of the eighteenth and beginning of the nineteenth century, see Valentim Alexandre, *Os sentidos do império: Questão nacional e questão colonial na crise do antigo regime português* (Oporto, 1998); and Jorge Miguel Viana Pedreira, *Estrutura industrial e mercado colonial: Portugal e Brasil (1780–1830)* (Lisbon, 1994). These changes are also the subject of the contributions in José Luís Cardoso, *A economia política e os dilemmas do imperio luso-brasileiro* (Lisbon, 2001). A good recent study on the late colonial commerce is João Fragoso, *Homens da grossa aventura: Acumulação e hierarquia na praça mercantil do Rio de Janeiro, c. 1790–1840* (Rio de Janeiro, 1992). There is a rapidly growing literature on the development of the internal economy. See Stuart B. Schwartz, "Peasants and Slavery: Feeding Brazil in the Late Colonial Period," in *Slaves, Peasants, and Rebels: Reconsidering Brazilian Slavery*, Stuart B. Schwartz, ed. (Champaign, 1992), pp. 65–102; Guillermo Palacios, *Cultivadores libres, Estado y crisis de la esclavitud en Brasil en la época de la Revolución industrial* (Mexico City, 1998); and João Fragoso and Manolo Florentino, *Arcaísmo como projeto: mercado atlântico, sociedad agrária e elite mercantil no Rio de Janeiro, c. 1790–c. 1840* (Rio de Janeiro, 1993).

Portugal and Its Empire

Finally, on the economy of the metropolis itself within the empire, Vitorino Magalhães Godinho, "Portugal and Her empire, 1680–1720," *The New Cambridge Modern History* VI (Cambridge, 1970), pp. 509–540; Carl Hanson, *Economy and Society in Baroque Portugal, 1668–1703* (Minneapolis, 1981), and his essay, "The European Renovation and the Luso-Atlantic Economy, 1560–1715," *Luso-Brazilian Review*, 4:4 (1983), pp. 475–530, present good overviews. Leonor Freire Costa, *Império e grupos mercantis* (Lisbon, 2002) and her *O transporte no Atlântico e a Companhia Geral do Comércio do Brasil (1580–1663)* (2 vols., Lisbon, 2003) deal with the role of merchants and the state. Nuno Gonçalo Freitas Monteiro, *O crepúsculo dos grandes (1750–1832)* deals with the nobility. An overview of the Portuguese economy in the eighteenth century is found in Albert Silbert, *Le Portugal Méditerranéen à la fin de l'ancien regime*, 3 vols. (Lisbon, 1978). On the effect of the English connection, Jorge Borges de Macedo, *Problemas de história da indústria portuguesa no século xviii* (Lisbon, 1963), is essential reading as is S. Sideri, *Trade and Power: Informal Colonialism in Anglo-Portuguese Relations* (Rotterdam, 1970) and H. E. S. Fisher, *The Portugal Trade: A Study of Anglo-Portuguese Commerce, 1700–1770* (London, 1971).

2

COSTS AND FINANCIAL TRENDS IN THE PORTUGUESE EMPIRE, 1415–1822

Jorge M. Pedreira

The Costs and Benefits of Empire

These days, when the issue of the costs and financial trends of colonial empires is examined, the inquiry tends to be guided, often in a subliminal way, by the intent of drawing up a balance sheet of imperial ventures. In spite of the fact that it is seldom uttered in these terms, the underlying question directing the research often is: All in all, did empires pay off; were they worth having?[1] Ascertaining gains and losses, in both the short and the long runs, is the object of many surveys even though, in the end, most of them leave their intended assignment partly unfulfilled.

There was a time, however, when such an endeavor would have appeared to be a futile exercise, and the suggestion that, after all, colonies might not have been profitable for the mother countries would have seemed wholly preposterous. Why then would several European states engage in the strenuous enterprise of securing control over distant territories and trade routes, and why would they fight war after war to obtain this control and to cling to it? If such competition prevailed for centuries and colonial empires persisted for so long, surely it was because they yielded some returns, probably handsome ones. It was also argued that the evidence of the surplus extracted by the European imperial states from their colonies, and of the extensive exploitation to which the imperial states submitted them, lies in

[1] Patrick K. O'Brien and Leandro Prados de la Escosura, eds., *The Costs and Benefits of European Imperialism from the Conquest of Ceuta, 1415, to the Treaty of Lusaka, 1974*, *Revista de Historia Económica* 16 (1998), no. 1.

the present state of poverty or backwardness of the regions that were once the object of imperial rule.[2]

These views have been challenged for some decades. Economic historians have repeatedly downgraded the contribution of the overseas world in general and of colonies in particular to the development of Europe.[3] Some scholars have gone so far as to argue that imperial powers might have suffered some economic damage in their drive for overseas expansion and that they would have been better off had they invested the resources they used for empire building in other enterprises. But if that is the case, the question remains why that drive was so persistent. Perhaps the primary motives were not economic after all or, as some have pointed out, not without a hint of political sarcasm, it is not unusual that governments embark on unfruitful pursuits, especially when they lack the analytical tools to determine their profitability accurately. At any rate, a broadly deleterious undertaking can still be beneficial for those who have the power to decide – the ruling minority and their allies. The possibility must thus be allowed that for the European powers the balance sheet of their imperial ventures may be negative after all. Notwithstanding, the following question must be raised: Did the political and social protagonists of the time (the government, the royal officials, the nobility, the intelligentsia, and the merchants) conceive of overseas empires, even in their financial dimensions, strictly in terms of costs and benefits? Were they even influenced by these notions in the course of their actions? And if this was not the case, does it make much sense to focus our inquiry on problems those social agents themselves did not contemplate?

Whatever the answer to this last question, the fact is that, in one way or another, either by challenging government policies or by offering advice to the rulers, different social agents at various times expressed their doubts about the utility (and sometimes the legitimacy) of empires. This alone, irrespective of all other economic considerations, should be enough for us to take the question of the costs and benefits of empire as a serious historical problem. Of course, the matter is far too complex to be translated into the simple language of balance sheets. The very notion of cost is debatable and varies according to the unit of analysis: Costs for the state were not the same as costs for society at large, and ultimately costs for the state often constituted

2 See, for instance, Andre Gunder Frank, *Capitalism and Underdevelopment in Latin America: Historical Studies of Chile and Brazil* (New York, 1969); Walter Rodney, *How Europe Underdeveloped Africa* (London, 1972).

3 Patrick K. O'Brien, "European Economic Development: The Contribution of the Periphery," *The Economic History Review* 35 (1982), no. 1, pp. 1–18.

benefits for society (and in this sense may be seen as investments). Furthermore, an adequate cost–benefit matrix is virtually impossible to calculate, and we have no way of knowing what the result would have been if the resources devoted to empire building and management had been diverted to other economic purposes.

This is not the place to enter into a thorough discussion of this topic. What has just been said must suffice to back the assertion that the profitability of empires cannot be taken for granted and that, whenever possible, returns must be measured against costs, something researchers did not do for a long time. But even from a strictly financial perspective, the determination of the balance sheet cannot provide the only focus for inquiry, for this would unduly restrict the scope of research. We also need to elucidate the origins and workings of empires, their persistence as well as the changes they went through over time. Were we to come to the conclusion that empires were unfruitful pursuits, we would then be faced with the more formidable job of explaining their persistence. Thus, if we wish to draw significant conclusions, we must look into the details of financial structures, the ways in which revenues were raised and expenditures made, and the relations and interaction among the various agents who formed the financial configurations. This is precisely what this chapter will try to do for the Portuguese empire.

The study of the financial workings of the Portuguese empire during four centuries, from the beginning of overseas expansion with the conquest of Ceuta (1415) to the successful secession of Brazil (1822), presents special problems. These arise from the fact that over such a long time many changes are bound to take place, and a dominant pattern may be hard to identify, especially because of the particular rhythms of the Portuguese empire. Characteristically, the empire evolved by way of developing new structures without completely destroying the old ones. These part concurrent, part consecutive structures operated in quite different geographical settings (from Morocco to the Atlantic islands and from both coasts of Africa to India, the Far East, and Brazil) and in different institutional frameworks (plunder, conquest, trading posts and monopolies, and plantation and mining settlements). A wide variety of resources and ways of extracting and expending them was always present, with quite disparate social and economic implications. The system of social exchange, which clustered around imperial financial resources and institutions, adapted to these circumstances. Furthermore, the balance sheets for the different parts of the empire showed different results at different moments in time. The manipulation of aggregate figures, assuming the empire persisted through time as a unit, may then be questionable, unless of course we can maintain that it presented itself in this way to contemporaneous agents and observers. But then again, the views on the empire also changed according to social and historical contexts.

All of these considerations render the analysis more complex and make the costs and benefits (in financial terms, this means expenditure and income) of the Portuguese imperial enterprise more difficult to assess. Beyond the balance between revenues and expenses, we must also consider the extent of the financial significance of the empire for Portuguese government and society. These two issues are analytically independent, although usually intertwined. Despite such complications, we shall proceed by drawing a general picture to frame the subsequent analysis.

Major Financial Trends

The financial importance of the empire and its constituent parts certainly changed over time. It is impossible to know for certain what its significance was in the earlier stages, during the fifteenth century. It all began with the conquest of Ceuta in 1415, which, according to one source, cost the best part of 280,000 dobras, some 33 million réis, or about £8,901. Three years later, the expenses for the defense operation against the siege to which Ceuta was subjected reached 85,000 dobras (around 10 million réis). For perspective, this expense may be compared with other extraordinary disbursements of the crown, such as the marriage and dowry of the princess Isabel to the Duke of Burgundy, which amounted to a quarter of a million dobras. Later expeditions in Morocco never rivaled such expenditures. The ill-fated assault on Tangier in 1437 required 57,000 dobras, the campaigns for the capture of Alcácer Ceguer and Arzila, which in turn mobilized some 22,000 or 23,000 men, cost a little over 100,000 dobras each, and various expeditions to relieve these strongholds from sieges and attacks from the mid-fifteenth century to 1481 came to more than 150,000. On the whole, it has been estimated that Moroccan ventures represented about one-fourth of all extraordinary expenses made between 1441 and 1481. As far as ordinary charges were concerned, payments to officials and soldiers in the North African fortresses added up to 4.3 million réis (about £1,162) in 1478, which may be weighed against an anticipated total expenditure of the crown of some 40 million réis, or a little over 10 percent.[4]

[4] Jorge Faro, *Receitas e despesas da fazenda real de 1384 a 1481 subsídios documentais* (Lisbon, 1965), pp. 226–227; Vitorino Magalhães Godinho, "Finanças públicas e estrutura do Estado," in his *Ensaios II – Sobre história de Portugal*, 2nd ed. (Lisbon, 1978; 1st ed., 1968), p. 61.

In the early phase, Moroccan fort-towns were a financial liability and could only be sustained by the transfer of revenue from the kingdom.[5] Ceuta was isolated for a long time, and although the seaport formed a base for trade and privateering, the crown was unable to obtain any money from it and had to make the arrangements for the population to be supplied with foodstuffs. As early as 1423–1424, King João I signed a contract with some Portuguese and Genoese merchants for the supply of Mediterranean corn to sustain the town.[6] Later, factors were established in the Moroccan fortresses to conduct trade on behalf of the crown. There was an active commerce, carried forward by caravans of Muslim, Christian, and Jewish merchants, on which the state certainly made some profits. But this took some time to become established, and meanwhile the towns, although they might have fulfilled some other strategic goals, did not produce any income for the crown. Expenses, on the other hand, were always heavy. In 1502, for instance, the Cortes (the estates assembly) voted a subsidy of 20 million réis for the fortification of the North African strongholds.[7]

The other imperial undertakings in the fifteenth century had a smaller impact on the financial structure of the kingdom. Until 1443, voyages of trade and plundering along the coast of Africa were open to all those interested, provided they paid a duty of one-fifth on the merchandise they brought to Portuguese ports (a duty from which the expeditions organized by the households of princes Henry and Pedro were exempt). In 1449, the factory at Arguim was chartered for ten years to a trading company, which enjoyed a monopoly of trade.[8] From 1469 to 1475, the Guinea trade (with the exception of Arguim) was leased to a Portuguese entrepreneur for a yearly sum of 200,000 réis. His privilege was later extended to the fort of Arguim and to the trade in malagueta pepper (which had originally been excluded from the lease) for the payment of another 200,000 réis. The crown expected to receive 400,000 réis a year from these contracts, which formed the most valuable concession of the time. This figure may be compared with the total revenue of taxes and customs duties to be collected in Portugal in 1473, which amounted to 47 million réis. In that same year, an overall state expenditure of 37 million réis was anticipated.[9]

[5] Vitorino Magalhães Godinho, *A economia dos descobrimentos Henriquinos* (Lisbon, 1962), p. 121.

[6] Virgínia Rau, *A Casa dos Contos*, Supplement to *Revista Portuguesa de História* (Coimbra, 1951), p. 99.

[7] Godinho, "Finanças públicas," p. 61.

[8] Godinho, *A economia dos descobrimentos Henriquinos*, p. 190.

[9] Faro, *Receitas e despesas*, pp. 85–86.

There were, of course, other sources of colonial revenue at the time, but it is impossible to calculate their financial contribution accurately. To a large extent, the proceeds of the customs of Lisbon and the Algarve also originated in the overseas trade. However, it may be said that the fiscal value of the empire was not yet paramount. At the same time, costs for the crown were also low because it left a large part of the initiative to private merchants and merchant societies, and in any case an expedition to Guinea might cost no more than 2,000 to 2,500 dobras, much less than any campaign in Morocco.[10]

In the last two decades of the fifteenth century, this situation was to change dramatically. From then on, the empire became very important in financial terms. The permanent establishment of the Portuguese at El Mina (on the Gold Coast), opening a new, more immediate route to the gold of Sudan, made all the difference, and it played a major role in the financial growth of the empire. Before the turn of the sixteenth century, receipts coming from the gold trade of El Mina were already in excess of 100,000 cruzados a year (some 40 million réis), as much as 70 percent of the state revenue collected in Portugal proper.[11] The returns from the trade of Guinea, which developed around slaves and malagueta pepper, must be added to this revenue. According to one source, the trade was chartered for 40,000 cruzados a year to the great Florentine merchant Bartolomeo Marchione. This price may seem excessive in view of the fact that the receipts it generated ten years later did not match one-tenth of the proceeds of the gold of El Mina. Irrespective of the doubts concerning its total value, the receipts provided by the trade from Guinea must come into the final assessment. The same goes for the crown's share of the sugar produced in Madeira, which must have amounted to some 20,000 cruzados, and for the income transferred from the other Atlantic islands (the Azores and Cape Verde), up to 5,000 cruzados. All in all, in a conservative estimate (or we should say a learned conjecture), the empire generated directly some 140,000 cruzados (55 million réis), which was somewhat less than the 170,000 cruzados coming from the kingdom of Portugal itself. In sum, at the end of the fifteenth century, as much as 45 percent of the total revenue of the Portuguese state came from the empire.

The preeminence of the empire in the structure of Portuguese finances was strengthened after the beginning of the sixteenth century, when new sources of income were found, such as the monopoly on dyewood from Brazil and, most of all, the pepper trade from Asia. By 1506, the empire

[10] Ibid., p. 72.

[11] Godinho, "Finanças públicas," p. 56.

supplied in one way or another about 60 percent of the crown's computed receipts (see Table 2.1). At that time, spices imported from the East were already more important as income providers than the gold shipments from El Mina (135,000 to 120,000 cruzados), but both still supplied less than the revenue raised in the kingdom itself (197,000 cruzados, of which 24,000 came from the Lisbon customs). The financial role of the spice trade was further enhanced in the following decades. In 1518–1519, it produced some 300,000 cruzados (120 million réis), more than the kingdom (285,000 cruzados) and much more than the gold imports, which had not grown at all. The Asian empire and the *carreira da Índia* (the trading route to the East Indies) now retained a crucial position in the structure of the Portuguese royal finances.

This vital position, which the empire as a whole and especially the Eastern empire had assumed, pertained not merely to its capacity as a generator of funds but also to the substantial share the dominions held in the overall expenditures of the state. The cost of building, sustaining, and defending the empire figured prominently among the extraordinary expenses made between 1522 and 1542, with some 1.3 million cruzados out of a total of 3.7 million. This amount represented the aggregate value of the cost of the squadrons for the protection of the Brazilian shores and the Grain Coast (160,000 cruzados), of bolstering the northern Moroccan strongholds and evacuating the southern fort-towns of Safi and Azamor (400,000 cruzados), which were considered untenable after the surrounding Moorish communities became hostile, and of reinforcing the armadas for the East Indies in order to expand the foothold in the Indian Ocean, to punish the local antagonistic rulers and to face the Turkish threat (800,000 cruzados). Once again, the Eastern empire and the spice trade played the dominant role, as they also did in the new phenomenon of state indebtedness, but they still did not match the value of the dowries and marriages of the royal family and of princely gifts, which amounted to 1.6 million cruzados, or 640 million réis.[12]

The outfitting and operating expenses of the Indies fleets (among which must be included losses at sea experienced between 1522 and 1555 in the amount of 3 million cruzados on the East Indies route and in excess of 350,000 cruzados on the Flanders route) and the cost of marketing the spices in Flanders (namely the administration of the trading factory at Antwerp) were largely accountable for the spectacular growth of the floating debt of the Portuguese monarchy.[13] The transaction costs of the East Indies trade (never purely commercial in nature) were charged to the

[12] Ibid., p. 62.

[13] Ibid., pp. 61–63.

Table 2.1. Sources of royal income (sixteenth–eighteenth centuries)

	1506		1518–1519		1588		1607		1619		1681		1716		1766	
Sources of Income	*value*	*%*	*value*	*%*	*value*	*%*	*value*	*%*	*value*	*%*	*value*	*%*	*value*	*%*	*value*	*%*
Kingdom	65.7	36.3	96.0	33.5	471.9	42.5	661.0	45.9	711.8	45.7	1,120.5	70.2	2,577.0	65.4	2,922.1	45.5
Customs					20.2	1.8	186.5	13.0	170.0	10.9	269.9	16.9	200.0	5.1	233.8	3.6
Lisbon customhouse	9.1	5.0	15.7	5.5	105.0	9.5					341.5	21.4	700.0	17.8	737.1	11.5
India trade	51.3	28.3	117.6	41.0	191.8	17.3	234.4	16.3	234.4	15.1	112.1	7.0	60.0	1.5	39.8	0.6
Tobacco											290.1	18.2	760.0	19.3	1,189.4	18.5
North Africa					1.0	0.1	3.9	0.3	1.2	0.1						
Madeira	10.3	5.7	19.6	6.8	24.2	2.2	21.4	1.5	24.2	1.6	25.4	1.6				
Azores	1.0	0.5	6.9	2.4	30.0	2.7	40.0	2.8	30.0	1.9	29.4	1.8				
Cape Verde and Guinea	5.3	2.9			16.7	1.5	16.4	1.1	14.0	0.9						
El Mina	45.6	25.2	47.0	16.4	40.0	3.6	9.9	0.7	10.0	0.6						
São Tomé					7.8	0.7	5.5	0.4	14.0	0.9						
Angola					11.0	1.0	25.0	1.7	26.0	1.7	18.0	1.1			31.1	0.5
Brazil	1.9	1.0			26.8	2.4	66.0	4.6	78.4	5.0			545.0	13.8	2,241.5	34.9
Brazilwood	1.9	1.0			13.6	1.2	24.0	1.7	24.0	1.5					164.0	2.6
Gold and diamonds													345.0	8.8	1,786.4	27.8
Eastern empire					288.9	26.0	355.6	24.7	412.5	26.5						
Total empire	64.0	35.4	73.5	25.6	446.4	40.2	543.7	37.8	610.3	39.2	72.8	4.6	545.0	13.8	2,272.6	35.4
Total empire and trade	115.3	63.7	191.1	66.6	638.2	57.5	778.1	54.1	844.7	54.3	475.0	29.8	1,365.0	34.6	3,501.7	54.5
Total	181.1	100.0	287.1	100.0	1,110.1	100.0	1,439.1	100.0	1,556.5	100.0	1,595.4	100.0	3,942.0	100.0	6,423.9	100.0

Values in million réis.

Sources: Vitorino Magalhães Godinho, "Finanças públicase e strutura do Estado," in Godinho, *Ensaios II – Sobre história de Portugal* (1st ed., 1968; 2nd ed., Lisbon, 1978); Fernando Tomaz, "As finanças do Estado Pombalino, 1762–1777," in *Estudos e ensaios: Em homenagem a Vitorino Magalhães Godinho* (Lisbon, 1988), pp. 355–388; Carl A. Hanson, *Economy and Society in Baroque Portugal, 1668–1703* (Minneapolis, 1981); António Manuel Hespanha, *História de Portugal*, vol. 4: *O antigo regime*, ed. José Mattoso (Lisbon, 1993).

Table 2.2. The financial balance of the Estado da Índia

Year	*Revenues*	*Expenditures*	*Balance*
1571	258.4	229.3	29.1
1574	278.5	235.6	42.9
1581	263.0	242.8	20.2
1588	303.1	259.9	43.2
1607	355.6	235.7	119.9
1610	390.6	257.0	133.6
1620	324.7	318.4	6.3
1630	240.6	288.1	−47.5
1634	355.6	334.6	21.0
1680	219.5	136.4	83.1
1687	239.8	260.6	−20.8

Values in million réis.

Sources: Francisco Bethencourt, "O Estado da Índia," in Francisco Bethencourt and Kirti Chauduri, eds., *História da expansão Portuguesa* (Lisbon, 1998), vol. 2, p. 296; Artur Teodoro de Matos, *O orçamento do Estado da Índia, 1571* (Lisbon, 1999).

state.[14] Furthermore, the Eastern empire, the so-called Estado da Índia, although it ordinarily yielded a net surplus, was very demanding in financial terms (see Table 2.2).

To meet these requirements, the royal treasury resorted to credit and accepted bills of exchange drawn on leading European financial marketplaces, namely Antwerp and Medina del Campo. Indebtedness grew at an impressive pace after 1522 (when gold remittances from El Mina were faltering). In 1534, outstanding bills totaled 400,000 cruzados, and in 1543 this sum had already reached 1.9 million. Interest rates of 20 and 25 percent could not help but aggravate the rise of the royal debt. The yearly interest paid on the bills of exchange became much heavier than the annuities remunerating the holders of the *padrões de juro* (the bonds of the funded debt), and they almost devoured the net profit of the spice trade for the crown. To put a stop to the escalating short-term debt obligations, the crown shut down the Portuguese factory in Antwerp in 1549 and in 1560 consolidated the outstanding bills of exchange, which were converted to royal bonds paying interest of just 5 percent. In the meantime, the funded debt, which had been inaugurated in 1500, when the king was contemplating an expedition in Morocco, had

[14] Anthony R. Disney, *The Twilight of the Pepper Empire: Portuguese Trade in Southwest India in the Early Seventeenth Century* (Cambridge, MA, 1978), p. 41.

also increased, but at a much slower rate (interest paid grew from 100,000 to 117,000 cruzados in the same period). There were times, however, when the royal treasury found it hard to honor its commitments.[15]

Despite these and other worries, the financial significance of the empire did not diminish in the decades following. On the contrary, in 1588, the empire returned some 640 million réis, equivalent to 57 percent of the royal income. Duties and profits on the Asian trade reached 191.8 million réis, and the Estado da Índia supplied another 288 million. El Mina, now clearly on the decline, contributed some 40 million, the Azores 30 million, and Brazil (including the monopoly on brazilwood) no more than 26.8 million réis as yet (see Table 2.1). Five years later, the financial resources of the empire were still growing. According to an assessment made at that time, the spice trade was expected to supply the state with more than 350 million réis.[16] Such an increase must be explained by the fact that this estimate was based on the price of the contract for six and not just four carracks, as had been the case in 1588. Therefore, even without the receipts from the Estado da Índia, which in all probability were rising as well, the empire exceeded the kingdom as a provider of funds for the crown.

The end of the sixteenth century must have marked the first crest. To be sure, in 1607 imperial revenue reached about 56 percent of the government budget, but at the same time colonial expenditures were on a rising tide. By then, the Portuguese had surrendered their monopoly of the sea route to the East Indies. Only two or three carracks arrived each year, carrying no more than 10,000 quintals of pepper (compared with a minimum of 16,000 in 1588 and more than 20,000 in the next few years). This would produce 234 million réis for the crown, much less than in 1593 and far below the rather optimistic estimate put forward by the secretary of state, Luís de Figueiredo Falcão, who anticipated revenue of more than 422 million réis on the basis of the arrival of five ships with 20,000 quintals of pepper.[17] In 1608–1609, it was reckoned that, if the galleons expected to come from India failed to return, it would be virtually impossible to raise the money for the fleet of the following year.[18] On its own account, the Estado da Índia paid more than 355 million réis in taxes, duties, and trading profits, and the Atlantic

[15] Godinho, "Finanças públicas," p. 60.

[16] Francisco Carneiro, *Relação de todas as rendas da coroa deste reyno de Portugal* (1593), ed. Francisco Mendes da Luz (Coimbra, 1949).

[17] Luís de Figueiredo Falcão, *Livro em que se contém toda a fazenda e real património de Portugal, Índia e ilhas adjacentes* (1607), 2nd ed. (Lisbon, 1859); Vitorino Magalhães Godinho, *Os descobrimentos e a economia mundial*, 2nd ed. (Lisbon, 1981–1983), vol. 3, pp. 75–76.

[18] António de Oliveira, *Poder e oposição política em Portugal no período Filipino, 1580–1640* (Lisbon, 1990), p. 79.

empire also grew more important, although Brazil's own contribution did not exceed 42 million réis, or 63 million once the dyewood monopoly is included (see Tables 2.1 and 2.3).

However, the cost of sustaining the empire against the fierce competition of the new maritime powers now proved much heavier. After 1591, this competition started to take its toll. In 1607, aside from the eastern empire, the Atlantic islands, and Angola, the dominions did not record profits in their financial administration. A commentary on the finances of the kingdom of Portugal offered in 1608 singled out three major articles of ordinary expenditure: the armada of the Indies and the funding of the pepper trade; the sustenance of El Mina and the African outposts in general; and the squadrons for the protection of the coasts.[19] These costs were to become heavier in the following decades.

Trading conditions may have eased off temporarily in the beginning of the seventeenth century. The Twelve Years Truce between the Hapsburg monarchy and the United Provinces (1609–1621) fostered a moderate recovery, although the Dutch did not refrain from assailing the Portuguese outposts in the East. It is apparent that by 1619 the empire had become a financial burden, even if it still matched the contribution of the mother country to the royal treasury. Even the spice trade barely covered the administrative expenses and transaction costs (and it would surely show a loss if the general protection costs were included). The Estado da Índia spent its entire ordinary surplus on fortifications, armadas, and military requirements; and all other possessions, once again with the exception of the Atlantic islands and Angola, recorded deficits on their balance sheets. The crown disbursed 83 million réis to sustain the Moroccan strongholds (which produced only 1.2 million réis) and a further 36 million réis in the fortification of the African bastions, and it could not, within the empire, find the means of covering these charges.

Under such circumstances, extraordinary expenses became permanent and grew especially burdensome, requiring expedient financial solutions. Fresh resources had to be procured, either by way of credit or by more forceful means. Money was raised by borrowing from merchants and bankers and by issuing annuities (*padrões de juro*) more regularly and in larger quantities. Short-term indebtedness specifically originating in the kingdom of Portugal (since 1580 one of the crowns of the Hispanic monarchy) and its imperial conquests never ran out of control as it had done in the first half of the sixteenth century, but the crown would now also resort to forced loans and extraordinary taxes. In 1604, for instance, the New Christians, both in the

[19] Ibid., p. 99.

kingdom and in the empire, were persuaded to offer a generous indemnity against the promise of a general pardon. The most prominent members of the community, who were more business-oriented, expected this money to be spent in reasserting the Portuguese monopoly in the East. And in fact it was, although the first share of more than 300,000 cruzados (120 million réis), paid in 1605, was diverted to the central government in Spain and to the war in Flanders, even if the two empires, the Spanish and the Portuguese, were supposed to be kept separate. All in all, until 1610, more than 70 percent of the subsidy found its way to the carreira da Índia.[20] In 1609, the government turned to the Lisbon business community, which was coerced into making a contribution of 120 million réis for the outfitting of the squadron designated to defend El Mina against the Dutch. However, before 1621, when the truce with the United Provinces was broken, extraordinary receipts did not count for much in the final financial balance. From 1609 to 1620, some 371.2 million réis were acquired in this way; that is, 31 million annually on average, which was the equivalent of just 2 percent of the total ordinary income.[21] In the ensuing years, the proportion of revenues gained by exceptional means was bound to increase.

In fact, between 1619 and 1631, special tributes and requisitions produced more than 233,000 cruzados a year (about 116.5 million réis), or 7 to 8 percent of the ordinary receipts. The largest share of the money thus obtained was consumed in the defense of India and Brazil and for the protection of the maritime trade. Metropolitan revenues were increased by as much as 50 percent in the ten years after 1621.[22] The Portuguese empire in this period between 1580 and 1640 when the Iberian crowns were united, had come under constant attack from the enemies of Spanish monarchy. In 1605, the Moluccas were lost to the Dutch, who in the following decades, between 1638 and 1658, also seized the fortresses of Ceylon. In 1622, the English assisted the Persians in forcing the Portuguese out of Hormuz, which was one of the major trading posts of the Estado da Índia. Two years later, Brazil became the target, and Bahia was taken by an expedition from the Netherlands (although it was promptly recovered). The Dutch West India Company then began to attack Pernambuco, finally founding a settlement there, which lasted for almost twenty years.

[20] James Boyajian, *Portuguese Trade in Asia under the Habsburgs, 1580–1640* (Baltimore, 1993), pp. 92–94.

[21] António Manuel Hespanha, *História de Portugal*, vol. 4: *O antigo regime*, ed. José Mattoso (Lisbon, 1993), p. 225.

[22] I. A. A. Thompson, *Crown and Cortes: Government, Institutions and Representation in Early Modern Castile* (Aldershot, 1993), p. 48.

El Mina (1637) and Malacca, Angola, and São Tomé (1641) were soon to follow.

In the meantime, buccaneers captured or sunk an unprecedented number of Portuguese ships engaged in the Atlantic and the Eastern trade. In the 1620s, as much as 35 percent of the galleons that set sail to India and 32 percent of those returning to Lisbon never reached their destinations.[23] Of course, some of these losses were caused by bad weather, excessive lading, or poor navigation, but most were caused by the systematic assault of privateers and other vessels launched from England and the Netherlands. On the route to Brazil, damages were equally staggering, extending to more than 120 ships in 1633–1634 and more than 230 in 1647–1648.[24] Colonial territories needed permanent military assistance. The common but very expensive *socorros* (relief expeditions) for India and Brazil and the reinforcement of armadas for the protection of both the seaboard settlements and the ocean trade made huge demands on the royal treasury. It has been estimated that, between 1630 and 1636, the war of resistance against the Dutch in Northeast Brazil cost the central government some 1.5 million cruzados. As much as another 2 million cruzados in *local* taxes, both ordinary and extraordinary, which in part belonged to the crown, ceased to be transferred to Lisbon or Madrid and were used for the same purpose.[25] In the same period, more than 500,000 cruzados in cash subsidies were dispatched from Lisbon to Goa.[26] In a very rough balance, this kind of expenditure corresponded to 120 million réis a year, more than 10 percent of the total ordinary revenue of the kingdom (without the empire and the overseas trade).

Such demands could only be met by exceptional means. New issues of bonds and forced contributions (subsidies or donations, as they were euphemistically termed) became more and more frequent. In 1631, for example, a loan of 500,000 cruzados was requested (supposedly to be repaid in five years) for the preparation of an armada of some fifty galleons for the recapture of Pernambuco.[27] Specific tributes (at both the local and the national levels) were levied and new monopolies institutionalized (for instance, the salt monopoly of Brazil was specially created in 1631 to sustain the war expenditure). All this fed public discontent and even raised doubts about the

[23] T. Bentley Duncan, "Navigation between Portugal and Asia in the Sixteenth and Seventeenth Centuries," in E. J. van Kley and C. K. Pullapilly, eds., *Asia and the West: Encounters and Exchanges from the Age of the Explorations* (Notre Dame, IN, 1986).

[24] Evaldo Cabral de Mello, *Olinda Restaurada: Guerra e Açúcar no nordeste, 1630–1654*, 2nd ed. (Rio de Janeiro, 1998), pp. 449–450.

[25] Ibid.

[26] Disney, *The Twilight of the Pepper Empire*, p. 62.

[27] Oliveira, *Poder e oposição*, p. 118.

wisdom of clinging to the Indian conquests at a time when the perpetual financial distress of the Hapsburg monarchy and the parallel increase of fiscal pressure from that direction became almost intolerable.

Of the innumerable suggestions and proposals addressed to the king on financial matters (the favorite topic of the *arbitristas*, or advice givers), the government under the Spanish prime minister the Count-Duke Olivares eagerly supported the idea of fighting the enemies with their own weapons, the chartered company. A Portuguese East India Company would enjoy the monopoly of trade but would also be responsible for the costs of protection. Yet, although it looked good on paper, the company could not perform its intended function. It never really interested the business community, either in Lisbon or abroad, leaving the crown and the Lisbon municipal council as the main suppliers of the initial investment and working capital. The company was bound to be a short-lived enterprise, operating only between 1628 and 1633.

In subsequent years, Brazil replaced India on the government's priority list. The 1630s were a disastrous decade for trade to the East, with an average of only 1.4 ships arriving in Lisbon each year.[28] From then on, the goal of defending Brazil was pursued even at the cost of escalating the fiscal burden in Portugal to the point of alienating significant political support.[29] The vice-regal institutions were restored in 1633 in order to secure a fixed revenue of 500,000 cruzados for the defense of the colony.[30]

After the Restoration of the independence of Portugal in 1640, the new government resorted to an institutional solution similar to the one undertaken by Olivares. To defend trade with Brazil against the Netherlands, who had taken Pernambuco through the agency of the Dutch West India Company and were raiding Portuguese ships through the vehicle of the Zeeland corsairs, a new company would be formed. This time, however, in view of the severe shortage of public funds, capital had to come from private chests, and particularly from the merchants of Lisbon. Following a scheme that had been tried in previous years, when some entrepreneurs undertook the protection of the fleets on their own account in return for the exclusive privilege of providing food and ammunition to Brazil, the General Company for the Trade of Brazil (Companhia Geral do Comércio do Brasil) was founded in 1649. It was given the assignment of organizing and carrying out that protection, for which it would be granted the monopoly of supplying salt, olive oil, flour, and dried codfish to the Brazilian domains. The crown,

[28] Duncan, "Navigation between Portugal and Asia," p. 22.

[29] Oliveira, *Poder e oposição*, p. 146.

[30] Thompson, *Crown and Cortes*, p. 43.

responding to the inadequacy of its own financial resources, privatized the defense of the trade with Brazil and in the process put the familiar tool of monopoly to good service.

The General Company, although it faced strong opposition and working difficulties (and could never fulfill its obligations), proved instrumental in the ultimate restoration of Portuguese sovereignty in Northeast Brazil and the demise of Dutch Recife.[31] This war of restoration had already begun in Brazil, at the initiative of local Portuguese settlers, which is why, in a very rough estimate, the crown contributed directly only 15 or 20 percent of the 400 million réis spent from 1645 to 1653.[32] To a large extent, Brazil paid for its own restitution to Portugal (such was the case of Pernambuco), and local initiatives even helped to recapture other territories (for instance, Angola). In view of the financial condition of the mother country, it could hardly have been otherwise.

After the Restoration of Portugal to independence, the financial problems of the government grew even more acute. The war was no longer exclusively waged at sea or in the colonies; it had to be fought in the mother country as well. The defense of the empire had to share scarce financial resources with the protection of the home territory. Furthermore, in securing the support of Great Britain and in ratifying the terms of peace with the United Provinces, the government accepted additional commitments, namely an indemnity of 4 million cruzados to the Dutch (of which 500,000 was to be paid by Brazil) and another 2 million for the dowry of the future queen of England.[33] This meant that in the following decades, both in the colonies and in the metropole, the fiscal burden was heavy indeed, and it also meant that the overseas territories had to fund their own defense because the transfers of money could not be as great as in the past.

The financial value of the empire declined in the second half of the seventeenth century. New taxes were levied, such as the so-called military subsidy of the *décima* (a one-tenth income tax, later reduced to 4.5 percent), others were increased (for instance, the *real d'água*, the excise on meat and wine), and money manipulation became more frequent. These and other financial requisitions, although also sustained by the dominions, fell primarily on the kingdom. Moreover, the receipts from the spice trade and the

[31] Leonor Freire Costa, "Pernambuco na história da Companhia Geral do Comércio do Brasil," in Manuel Correia de Andrade et al., eds., *Tempo dos flamengos e outros tempos* (Recife, 1999), pp. 267–301.

[32] Cabral de Mello, *Olinda Restaurada*, p. 205.

[33] Carl A. Hanson, *Economy and Society in Baroque Portugal, 1668–1703* (Minneapolis, 1981), p. 144; Cabral de Mello, *Olinda Restaurada*, p. 205.

Estado da Índia, now reduced to a fraction of its former territory, endured a substantial decline, and those from Brazil, although on an upward trend, were still too modest and unstable to compensate for the losses in the East. The average number of ships arriving in Lisbon from Asia, after a brief recovery in the 1640s, decreased to 1.6 per year in the 1650s and to 1.3 in the 1660s, and the annual tonnage fell to 812 and 482 tons respectively, during the same period (from the 3,500 recorded in 1611–1620).[34] By that time, trading profits accruing to the crown and customs duties probably did not top an average of 60 million réis per year, or around 3 percent of the total royal revenue (a decline from 15 percent in 1619).

By 1680, Portuguese trade had been transformed. The Cape route to India became linked with Brazil, as ships stopped at Bahia on their way to Goa or, more commonly, when returning from the East. Diamonds and cotton textiles (in part to be used in the slave trade) were now the major staples, soon to be supplemented with the export of Brazilian tobacco to Asia, which eventually fell under government control. References to customs duties on tobacco in the Estado da Índia may be traced as far back as 1623, when a contract for Goa was settled for 1.5 million réis a year.[35] In 1634, this amount had grown to 10 million réis (6.8 percent of the revenues of the district of Goa), and it reached 8.3 million réis in Bassein, almost one-fourth of the local income.[36] At that time, these duties supplied no more than 7 percent of the revenue collected in the Estado da Índia, but this proportion was increasing fast, and it had risen to 20 percent in 1687.[37] Tobacco trade from Brazil had become one of the mainstays of the Estado da Índia, but for the government in Lisbon its significance did not compensate for the persistent decline of the traffic on the Cape route.

To be sure, the crown still earned something from the tariffs and commercial profits on the eastern trade, but the rhythms of business were highly irregular. Sometimes, as was the case in 1672, merchandise disembarked from three ships arriving from Goa could be valued at 4 million cruzados.[38] But it could just as well happen that the galleons from Asia had to load sugar and tobacco in Bahia to complete their cargo before continuing on to Lisbon. Therefore, it may be estimated that in the 1680s the revenue from

[34] Duncan, "Navigation between Portugal and Asia," p. 22.

[35] Francisco Bethencourt, "O Estado da Índia," in Francisco Bethencourt and Kirti Chaudhuri, eds., *História da expansão Portuguesa* (Lisbon, 1998), vol. 2, p. 299.

[36] Vitorino Magalhães Godinho, *Les finances de l'etat Portugais des Indes Orientales, 1517–1635: Matériaux pour une étude structurale et conjoncturelle* (Paris, 1982), p. 66.

[37] Bethencourt, "O Estado da Índia," pp. 298–300.

[38] Vitorino Magalhães Godinho, "Portugal, as frotas do açúcar e as frotas do ouro," in his *Ensaios II – Sobre história de Portugal*, 2nd ed. (Lisbon, 1978), p. 313.

the East Indies trade did not exceed the same 3 percent of the crown's total receipts. The eastern empire's financial significance quite obviously withered. The Casa da Índia (the customhouse for the Indies trade) collected 62 million réis (slightly over half the amount it obtained in 1619), and another 50 million came from the *consulado* duties.[39] As for the Estado da Índia, proceeds declined from a maximum of 350–400 million réis to 220–240 million in the 1680s, and this revenue need not be brought into the picture, for even though there was usually a net surplus (for instance, 83 million réis in 1680), it was generally drained by local extraordinary expenses. In any case, from 1684 to 1687, the accounts showed an average deficit of 20 million réis.[40]

The stature that Asian trade and empire had held for so long in the financial structure was not immediately taken over by the Atlantic empire. As previously seen, the war against the Dutch comprehensively disturbed the financial mechanisms in Brazil, forcing the government to introduce new exactions (namely a new tax on sugar) and to use up all available funds to meet the costs of defense.[41] In the process, extraordinary revenues and expenditures usually became more important than the ordinary budget, and the distinction between royal and municipal receipts and in some instances even receipts from donatory grantees was temporarily blurred. In the 1660s, the contracts for the collection of the tithe, the main ordinary royal tax in Brazil, regularly totaled 70 million réis.[42] This indicated impressive growth since the beginning of the century, but it was a long way from making up for the demise of the eastern sources of income.

Nevertheless, Brazil supported the Portuguese financial system in quite a different way. It supplied commodities that could be converted into royal monopolies and then rented out to private capitalists. The monopoly on brazilwood, established almost immediately after the discovery in 1500, was leased in 1679 for just 12 million réis. But the exclusive rights over tobacco trade and distribution, which generated 290 million réis in 1680, were on the way to becoming the most coveted of business concerns.[43] In addition, Brazil supplied ample financial resources by indirect means, because the goods imported into Portugal (mainly sugar) paid regular customs duties. Although the price of sugar in Lisbon decreased by more than 40 percent in the twenty years before 1689 (the competition from the Caribbean and the general

39 Hanson, *Economy and Society.*

40 Ibid., p. 212; Bethencourt, "O Estado da Índia," p. 296.

41 Vitorino Guimarães, *As finanças na guerra da Restauração, 1640–1658*, offprint from *Revista Militar* (Lisbon, 1941), p. 62.

42 Frédéric Mauro, *Le Portugal, le Brésil et l'Atlantique au XVIIe siècle, 1570–1670* (Paris, 1983).

43 Godinho, "Finanças públicas"; Hespanha, *O antigo regime*; Hanson, *Economy and Society*, p. 155.

European crisis were to blame), duties on imports from Brazil still made up a sizable proportion of customs revenues. Tariffs amounted to 395 million réis in 1681 (505 million including the *consulado* duties), the customs of Lisbon generating the major portion (270 million in addition to the *consulado*, or just under 350 million). In a conservative estimate, it may be assumed that, despite the crisis, at the very least, one-third of this sum originated in the Brazilian trade. In this way, even if the direct financial contribution of the empire declined in the late seventeenth century (and it certainly did, by some 20–25 percent), it remained an essential part of the fiscal structure and, in more peaceful times, it proved much less costly to defend.

At the turn of the eighteenth century, the invaluable financial role of the empire was restored. Trade in sugar and tobacco expanded once again, and a new asset became available that in time would dominate Portuguese colonial exploration and the financial system. Gold was first unearthed in 1680 in Paranaguá, and in the next year 22 kilograms were collected by the crown by way of the *quinto*, the one-fifth tax on mining activities (a fiscal rule that had been in place since 1603). Then, after 1692, the really rich veins were found, and almost immediately gold started to be remitted to Portugal. It was not easy to deploy a system that could secure for the state a significant share of the gold extracted without also raising administrative costs to impossible and irrational levels. In the early days, more was being obtained from the confiscation of gold from smugglers who were attempting to evade the tax than from the regular payment of the tax itself. In 1702–1704, the *quinto* yielded some 16.5 kg, whereas confiscation amounted to 43.8 kg.[44] Remittances also fluctuated sharply at that time. Before 1714, the quantities collected in Minas Gerais could range from 6 to 49 kg (that is, from 2 million to 16 million réis in value) per year. After 1713, a minimum quota of 30 arrobas (or 441 kg) was established that had to be handed over each year by the gold explorers in the district of Minas Gerais.

The government established foundries and mints in the mining districts and engaged a number of inspection officials to try to stop gold from being smuggled. This certainly produced some results, but administrative and overhead expenses grew high. In 1733, after leaving office, a former governor estimated that the mint cost almost 65 million réis each year to operate.[45] Furthermore, increasing fiscal pressure was met with dogged local resistance. From time to time, the administration had to bargain with the local

[44] Virgílio Noya Pinto, *O ouro Brasileiro e o comércio Anglo-Português: Uma contribuição aos estudos da economia Atlântica no século XVIII*, 2nd ed. (São Paulo, 1979), p. 60.

[45] Manuel da Silveira Soares Cardozo, "Os quintos do ouro em Minas Gerais (1731–1732)," in *Congresso do Mundo Português*, vol. 10 (Lisbon, 1940), p. 128, n. 53.

population over the modes of implementation of the fiscal regime, but this did not prevent occasional riots. More than once, the government altered the system in an effort to extract more revenues from gold production in Brazil and to fight tax evasion more effectively, and there was controversy in the administration over the best system to be adopted. From 1714 to 1724, the fixed quota was kept in force (in Minas Gerais it was reduced from 30 to 25 arrobas and then exceptionally rose to 52 arrobas in 1722–1723). After a brief return to the simple regime of the fifth, a new system was introduced that taxed the number of slaves employed in gold extraction rather than the gold extracted (1735–1749), which seems to have been the most effective scheme. From then on, the fiscal organization combined the one-fifth tax and the minimum quota (which was established at 100 arrobas for the Minas Gerais district).

No matter what the system, the amounts collected by the crown never even approached one-fifth of the actual known production.[46] Yet, despite the persistence of massive smuggling and fiscal prevarication, which was virtually ineradicable, gold became one of the major sources of income for the Portuguese crown. In 1716, the one-fifth tax returned 345 million réis (almost 9 percent of the state's budget for that year), and in the coming decades it became even more important. The value of gold remitted from Minas Gerais on the account of the royal treasury amounted to 150 million réis until 1717; it then dropped to 120 million in 1718–1721 but more than doubled to 250 million in 1722–1723. In the next few years, growth proceeded at this impressive pace, and between 1725 and 1728 remittances exceeded 560 million réis. In 1729–1730, this trend was interrupted by a crisis, which gave way to a period of instability marked by sharp fluctuations. During this period, which lasted until 1736, the value of shipments averaged some 500 million réis, but it soon rose above 600 million, a level that was sustained until mid-century.[47] Minas Gerais was by far the more important source of Brazilian gold, but remittances from other regions (Goiás, Mato Grosso, and Bahia) were not at all negligible, amounting to between one-fourth and one-third of those from Minas Gerais.[48]

The invaluable contribution that gold made to the Portuguese financial system in the first half of the eighteenth century may also be shown by the growth of other fiscal revenues from the mining districts. Contracts

[46] Michel Morineau, *Incroyables gazettes et fabuleux métaux: Les retours de trésors Américains d'après les gazettes Hollandaises, XVIe–XVIIIe siècles* (Cambridge, MA, 1985), p. 141.

[47] Pinto, *O ouro Brasileiro*, pp. 72–73; see also Kenneth Maxwell, *Conflicts and Conspiracies: Brazil and Portugal, 1750–1808* (Cambridge, 1973), pp. 252–254.

[48] Pinto, *O ouro Brasileiro*, pp. 72–73; Morineau, *Incroyables gazettes*, pp. 146–148.

for the collection of the tithe and for the collection of the taxes imposed on circulation, the *portagem* (toll) and the *entradas* (entries), were sold for increasing prices. In Minas Gerais, the receipts obtained in this way were very substantial indeed. They rose from just over 100 million réis before 1720 to more than 150 million in the 1720s, to 200 million in the early 1730s, next to around 250 million, and consistently approached 300 million after 1740.[49] Although most of these funds were spent locally to sustain the fiscal organization, the administration, the church, and the military, they helped to reinforce government control and ultimately rendered possible the very construction of Brazil. In the process, they also helped the royal treasury to meet some of its more pressing commitments.

As important as it was, gold was certainly not the only colonial resource that generated substantial revenues for the state. Trade with the East had long ago lost its crucial role, and this clearly showed in the annual receipts of the Casa da Índia, which remained stagnant at 60 million réis. But Brazil supplied other commodities that sustained an active commerce with the metropole and in this way produced significant fiscal returns. The duties on the fleets and the monopoly on brazilwood, for instance, amounted to 200 million réis in 1716, which was almost 60 percent of the proceeds of the one-fifth tax on gold. Then, in the 1730s the precious metal was joined by precious stones. The government tried immediately to keep the extraction of diamonds under control so that prices did not fall inordinately as a result of excessive supply. The strategy followed the same basic rules prescribed for gold extraction, but soon a monopoly was established and the familiar system of contracts was adopted. For their privilege, the contractors paid a head tax on slaves employed in the diamond district, which could not exceed 600 persons. The crown received some 140 million réis from this tax, which was less than 10 percent of the gross receipts from diamond extraction.[50]

Long-established Brazilian exports, such as hides and sugar, also contributed substantially to the government revenues from customs tariffs (duties paid in the customs of Lisbon alone amounted to 20 percent of the royal budget in 1716).[51] Although sugar prices fell after 1703 (following a decade of improvement), exports benefited from the disruption caused by the War of the Spanish Succession. Soon, however, Brazilian planters had to deal with increasing competition, declining prices, and the rising cost of slave labor, which resulted from the massive demand created by the gold rush.

49 Maxwell, *Conflicts and Conspiracies*, pp. 246–248; Pinto, *O ouro Brasileiro*, pp. 76–79.

50 Pinto, *O ouro Brasileiro.*

51 João Lúcio de Azevedo, *Épocas de Portugal económico*, 3rd ed. (Lisbon, 1973; 1st ed., 1928), p. 463.

Accordingly, exports declined, but sugar continued to play a prominent part as a source of public income. It was now, however, surpassed by tobacco.

In the eighteenth century, tobacco further strengthened its position as one of the most important resources for the Portuguese crown. In 1716, the charter-holders of the monopoly on the distribution of tobacco paid the state 560 million réis, and a further 200 million was collected in the form of customs duties. Tobacco also helped support the trade with the East Indies and sustained the direct communication between Bahia and the Gold Coast, where most of the slaves for the local plantations were obtained. The financial role of tobacco was further enhanced in the last third of the century. After 1763, the monopoly on the tobacco trade produced between 800 million and 1 billion réis a year, or 16 to 19 percent of the total receipts of the royal treasury.[52] Customs tariffs added an average of 140 million réis to this figure, raising the percentage by approximately 3 percent. This is to say that about one-fifth of the Portuguese public revenue derived in one way or another from the tobacco trade.

In the last third of the eighteenth century, revenues from the empire achieved an overwhelming importance, although characterized by irregularity. Remittances of gold as payment of the *quinto* became erratic in the 1760s and started to wane by the end of the decade. Between 1762 and 1768, the annual average amounted to 790 million réis, or 15 percent of the aggregate revenues. Between 1769 and 1776, these numbers were down to 460 million and 8.6 percent, respectively. The proceeds from the contracts on the extraction and sale of diamonds were even more irregular, reaching 440 million réis a year in 1766–1770 but no more than 190 million between 1771 and 1776. Notwithstanding, these fluctuations did not diminish the financial role of the empire. Customs duties on sugar could reach 560 million réis, more than 40 percent of all tariffs collected in Lisbon, or 8.7 percent of the royal income. The monopolies on the supply of salt to Brazil and on brazilwood provided more than 150 million réis (or 3 percent). Finally, there were direct financial transfers from the colonies. Brazil paid a donation for the reconstruction of Lisbon after the earthquake of 1755, much in the same way it had once paid a tax to support the settlement of the peace indemnity owed to the Netherlands and the expenses of Catherine of Braganza's marriage to Charles II of England. Altogether, this meant that Brazil alone generated nearly 40 percent of the royal income.[53] If we also assigned to Brazil a share of the monopoly on the distribution of tobacco in Portugal

[52] Fernando Tomaz, "As finanças do estado Pombalino, 1762–1777," in *Estudos e ensaios: Em homenagem a Vitorino Magalhães Godinho* (Lisbon, 1988), pp. 355–388.

[53] Ibid.

(and it must be stressed that most of this commodity came from Brazil), the extent of that contribution would be even more impressive.

Colonial territories on other continents made additional contributions. The eastern trade, even though its golden age was long gone, still produced valuable receipts, some 150 million réis each year, which for the most part proceeded from tariffs paid in the Casa da Índia. The contract for the supply of tobacco snuff from Bahia to India returned another 60 to 80 million *réis*, but this sum was spent to sustain the Estado da Índia and suitably the contractors were local merchants.[54] At any rate, this sum was not even included in the budget of the metropole. As for the African dominions, the only significant source of income, the contract for the collection of duties on the export of slaves and ivory from Angola, grew in importance during the eighteenth century, and the bid price increased, exceeding 90 million réis in the 1760s.[55] All in all, at that time, the empire, excluding its share in the monopoly on tobacco, supplied some 42 percent of the royal revenues.

Even if the 1760s and early 1770s are usually known as a period of crisis, originating from the fall of gold remittances from Brazil, this period must have marked the high point of the financial contribution of the empire, proving that the regulation of that contribution owed more to rent-seeking mechanisms, to the ability to monopolize resources and opportunities, than to the government's capacity for collecting customs duties and other taxes. In the next few decades, although accurate figures are lacking, the available records indicate that direct transfers from the colonies (monopolies on brazilwood, diamonds, and salt, the *quinto* on gold, and other taxes paid in the dominions but inscribed in the central government's budget) suffered a steep decline, although the Brazilian economy was undergoing an agricultural renaissance. In 1797–1798, such direct transfers were down to one-fourth of the average numbers from 1762 to 1776.[56] However, this could have been partly offset by the growth of customs revenues.

After the American War of Independence, and most of all after the European wars that arose from the French Revolution, Portugal benefited from the problems that befell other colonial powers and its overseas trade prospered. In one way or another, the empire supplied almost 65 percent of customs duties. In addition to direct trade, which formed 40 percent of

[54] Celsa Pinto, *Trade and Finance in Portuguese India: A Study of the Portuguese Country Trade* (New Delhi, 1994), appendix 17, pp. 290–292.

[55] Joseph C. Miller, *Way of Death: Merchant Capitalism and the Angolan Slave Trade, 1730–1830* (London, 1988), pp. 555–557.

[56] Fernando Dores Costa, *Crise financeira, dívida pública e capitalistas, 1796–1807* (Lisbon, 1992), p. 26.

total trade, it supplied half the exports to foreign nations and was responsible for one-fourth of the imports from abroad, which were re-exported to the dominions. Nonetheless, at the turn of the nineteenth century, the contribution of the empire to the financial structure probably did not go beyond 25–27 percent (once again excluding any possible participation from the tobacco contract). This share was almost entirely formed by customs duties. This was, of course, a major shift from previous times, when trading profits, freight, and monopolies formed the bulk of the financial contribution of the empire.

The fact that the state could no longer draw revenue directly out of colonial trading resources, be they from the pepper trade or gold and diamond extraction, stood as an important restriction on its ability to secure receipts from the empire. Customs tariffs could not be raised without endangering trade and encouraging contraband, which was a permanent concern for financial authorities.[57] Even in a time of undisputed commercial prosperity, the crown could not obtain as much from the empire as it had in the mid-eighteenth century. Yet trade with Brazil formed a very important basis for the generation of royal income. The collapse of the old colonial system after the invasion of Portugal by Napoleon's troops in 1807 and the relocation of the court to Rio de Janeiro could only exacerbate the financial strain, which the dramatic rise in diplomatic and military expenditures had induced. In 1817 and 1821, customs duties were down to 77 percent of the value in 1800–1802, and although changes in prices may attenuate this decline, troubles in the trade with Brazil certainly worsened the fiscal crisis.[58] Furthermore, the lengthened sojourn of the king and court in Brazil meant that money transfers had changed direction, something that was strongly resented in Portugal and provided one of the motives for the first Portuguese liberal revolution, in 1820. In trying to reassert the authority of Portugal over Brazil and to redress the financial balance, the revolutionaries finally alienated the support of the Brazilian elites and precipitated the secession of the former colony in 1822.

In this way, a whole era of Portuguese history came to an end. For the first time in four hundred years, the empire became virtually insignificant to Portugal from an economic or financial point of view. Throughout those

[57] Ernest Pijning, *Controlling Contraband: Mentality, Economy and Society in Eighteenth-Century Rio de Janeiro* (Baltimore, 1997); Jorge M. Pedreira, "From Growth to Collapse: The Breakdown of the Old Colonial System, Portugal and Brazil, 1750–1830," *The Hispanic American Historical Review* 80 (2000), no. 4, pp. 853–860.

[58] Luís Espinha da Silveira, "Aspectos da evolução das finanças públicas Portuguesas, 1800–1827," *Análise Social* 23 (1987), no. 97, p. 528; Jorge M. Pedreira, *Estrutura industrial e mercado colonial: Portugal e Brasil, 1780–1830* (Lisbon, 1994), p. 364.

four centuries, despite the changes in the geographic and institutional settings and the inevitable fluctuations, the colonies and colonial endeavors had played a paramount role in generating and consuming resources for the Portuguese crown and society. But then the empire was reduced to a few scattered strongholds along the coast of Africa – in Guinea, Angola, and Mozambique – which incidentally had closer economic ties with Brazil through the slave trade than with the metropole – and to the poor remnants of the Estado da Índia. When the secession became apparent, a few voices came forward calling for the making of a new Brazil in Africa, but only in the last years of the nineteenth century did the empire (and a very different empire it was) regain some economic relevance.

The Financial System of the Portuguese Empire

Having sketched the broad financial trends of the Portuguese early modern empire over the four centuries of its existence, we now move on to a more comparative and analytical approach. First, it must be noted that the structure of the financial apparatus of the Portuguese monarchy is quite exceptional in the context of early modern Europe. A thorough comparative analysis, which is beyond the purpose of this chapter, would certainly show that the empire played a much more crucial role for Portugal than did the empires of the other European powers for their respective countries. Spain provides the most obvious basis for comparison, and it can easily be confirmed that even at the time of the massive inflow of gold and silver from Mexico and Peru, the American empire did not play the same pivotal role that the Portuguese colonies performed. In 1554, the Spanish colonies supplied 11 percent of the crown's total income, and in 1576–1600 this proportion increased to a maximum of 25 percent. By 1600–1625, it was down to 15 percent, and it rose again in 1726–1750 to a new peak of 19 percent.[59] It should be emphasized that in Portugal the empire repeatedly provided more than half the government's financial resources. These figures must obviously be handled with caution, since systems of classification may diverge (i.e., the criteria for the inclusion and exclusion of income sources may not always be the same). Nonetheless, they definitely evince a contrast between Portugal and Spain and display the peculiarity of the Portuguese financial structure.

[59] John H. Elliott, *The Old World and the New*, 2nd ed. (Cambridge, 1992), pp. 85–87; Bartolomé Yun-Casalilla, "The American Empire and the Spanish Economy: An Institutional and Regional Perspective," in O'Brien and Prados, *The Costs and Benefits of European Imperialism*, p. 126.

This singularity was already perceived in the sixteenth century. Jean Bodin, when he considered the different ways in which a state could obtain its revenues, explicitly pinpointed Portugal after the voyages to the Gold Coast and the discovery of the sea route to the East Indies as the example of a state that relied on a colonial trading empire for its financial resources.[60] This could appear as an alternative to the evolution toward a true state fiscal system. In fact, in the earlier period, colonial revenues could absolve the government from the need to build a vast fiscal bureaucracy and from having to enter into negotiations with powerful and privileged social groups, the only method that might enable it to draw on domestic wealth and income. According to Magalhães Godinho, this is precisely what happened when the crown allowed the *sisas*, a tax on sales, to be settled through the payment of an annual sum predetermined on the basis of an assessment carried out for each municipal council.[61] In the early seventeenth century, the author of a set of recommendations on policy matters estimated that the *sisas* would produce 800 million réis, instead of just 200 million, if this system was replaced by the direct collection of taxes by the fiscal administration.[62] However, the system did not change. This episode can be seen as an indication of the way in which the monarchy disengaged from the development of an extensive fiscal apparatus in the mother country once the alternative provided by the receipts from the empire had fully materialized. In time, however, a fiscal apparatus had to be built in the colonies, and sometimes this proved to be rather costly.

In the case of Portugal, the dependence of the public financial structure on an imperial base, early as it was, may be interpreted as the development of an "entrepreneurial domain state" as opposed to a "fiscal state."[63] The procurement, either by means of direct seizure or through trade and navigation, of resources and opportunities on which to build rent-seeking mechanisms (monopolies, privileges, and tributes) was surely critical both for the relative importance of the colonial revenues and for the pattern of social exchange that developed around those mechanisms. To depict the development of the Portuguese royal finances in the fifteenth century as a transition from a seigneurial to a mercantile system is in fact deceptive.

[60] Jean Bodin, *Les six livres de la république* (1576), reimp. (Paris, 1986), bk. 3, chap. 6; Richard Bonney, ed., *Economic Systems and State Finance* (Oxford, 1995), pp. 167–168.

[61] Godinho, "Finanças públicas," pp. 63–64; João Cordeiro Pereira, "A receita do estado Português no ano de 1526: Um orçamento desconhecido," in *Estudos de História de Portugal: Homenagem a A. H. Oliveira Marques*, vol. 2 (Lisbon, 1983), pp. 15–55.

[62] Diogo Ramada Curto, *A cultura política em Portugal, 1578–1642: Comportamentos, ritos e negócios* (Lisbon, 1994), p. 443.

[63] Bonney, *Economic Systems and State Finance*, pp. 458–460.

Contrary to a pervasive notion, the development of trade was not necessarily opposed to seigneurial institutions. It could, conversely, be the very object of such institutions. Trade was seen not only as a possible source of wealth but as wealth in and of itself, and therefore it could be subject to appropriation and turned into a possession. In this manner, it could easily become incorporated in seigneurial social relations.[64]

In the early stages of the Portuguese empire, well into the sixteenth century, rulers did not simply promote trading monopolies or colonial exploration as business ventures. They could and often did grant commercial privileges and monopolies as they would other seigneurial rights over their own patrimonial possessions. Trade was the object of royal donations and endowments. Prince Henry, the so-called Navigator, was awarded important trading privileges, such as the monopoly of navigation south of Cape Bojador, and King Afonso V conferred exclusive rights to the Guinea trades upon his son, Prince João, making him their *donatário* (donatory or grantee).[65] Newly acquired territories could be given in much the same way. The early colonization of Madeira and Brazil advanced on the basis of an institutional model of proprietary settlement, which was reminiscent of the "typical royal grant of lordship in late medieval Portugal".[66] Thus, new resources could be allocated in old ways. This is not to state that commercialization, which paralleled Portuguese expansion, did not shift the structures of society, for it certainly did. But it is equally important to keep in mind that the structures of trade were themselves poured into preexisting frameworks and social institutions.

These last remarks, of course, go a long way toward elucidating the character of the Portuguese polity in the early phase of expansion. However, it is not enough simply to ascertain the distinctive bearing that colonial revenues had on state building in Portugal. To understand the nature of this emerging state, we must go beyond the assessment of the impact of aggregate figures and look into the financial structure in a more discriminating manner. In the preceding section, we mentioned different sources of imperial revenue and ultimately referred to the process that resulted in the substitution of fiscal revenues for the returns from direct participation in trade, but other variations, both in time and space, were equally important.

[64] Jorge M. Pedreira, "Mercadores e formas de mercantilização," in Diogo Ramada Curto, ed., *O tempo de Vasco da Gama* (Lisbon, 1998), p. 177.

[65] Ibid., p. 177.

[66] H. B. Johnson, "Portuguese Settlement, 1500–1580," in Leslie Bethell, ed., *Colonial Brazil* (Cambridge, 1987), p. 13.

In Brazil, for instance, until the war with the Dutch, revenues came from two major sources: the monopoly on brazilwood and the tithes. The crown collected the tithes because the king had become the lord of the religious-military orders and, as far as the church was concerned, Brazil belonged to the Order of Christ, to which the royal patronage had been granted. In one way or another, sugar provided the bulk of the royal income, and when the war made huge demands on the treasury, the crown turned once more to sugar for the extraordinary receipts. This was before the gold rush, which of course turned taxes on gold into the primary source of revenue and favored the enforcement of duties on circulation as well. In the process, the nature of the financial apparatus changed, requiring facilities such as the minting houses and a large bureaucracy to collect the one-fifth tax and to see that smuggling was kept to a minimum and that smugglers were brought to justice. On the other hand, the collection of the taxes on circulation, as well as the tithes, were leased to private capitalists, usually local merchants, sugar-mill owners, or merchant firms.

In the East, the picture was quite different. Among the many ports and fortresses that made up the Estado da Índia, there were very diverse structures. Customs (sometimes with specific institutions for the collection of duties on horses and foodstuffs), trading licenses, commercial voyages, local monopolies (for instance, on opium, indigo, or palm-wine), tolls, and land rents formed the most significant types of state revenues. The relative importance of each of these sources varied in time and from one fortress to another.[67] The tax on horses was very profitable in Goa, for example; land rents counted for more in Bassein, Daman, and the district of Goa; trading privileges were particularly fruitful in Malacca. Generally, customs generated the larger share of receipts, even though duties were usually much lower than those collected in Portugal.

These financial mechanisms, of course, supposed that the Portuguese authorities exerted some kind of territorial control, which allowed them to set up a fiscal administration that taxed both long-distance and local trade. There were, however, other receipts that resulted exclusively from the direct application of power. The Portuguese authorities in the East, from Kilwa and Hormuz to Kanara and Ceylon, dictated the payment of tribute from the local political units, especially when they had presented some resistance to their rule. Kilwa was punished for disregarding this duty, and in Hormuz the tribute initially fixed at 15,000 sheraffins a year in 1515 increased to 25,000 in 1519 and then, as a retaliation for attempted rebellions, was raised to 60,000 in 1523 and to 100,000 in 1529 (although until 1542, less than

[67] Godinho, *Les finances de l'etat Portugais des Indes Orientales.*

40,000 was actually obtained).[68] Sometimes, the Portuguese simply turned existing relations to their own advantage, replacing more powerful local rulers in the collection of the tribute. This is what happened in Kanara, where the tribute exacted on small principalities formed one of the largest sources of income for the state.

Besides this kind of tribute, the Portuguese also raised revenue from selling protection to ships navigating in the Indian Ocean. Using their superior firepower at sea, they deployed a financial device for extracting resources from intra-Asian trade, a protection rent, which became a significant source of income for the Estado da Índia.[69] This imposition was not only a means of compensating for the heavy financial burden of underwriting the armadas in the East but also one of the established financial expedients for extracting a surplus from regional maritime trade. Because of such methods, it has been claimed that the Portuguese in the East were less interested in trade itself than in preying on it, which is a manifest overstatement.[70] Still, this practice certainly created the opportunity for the abuse of local authorities, even at the lower ranks of the administration. Complaints over this abuse (in addition to accusations of corruption and general thievery) were plentiful, which offers another argument for the presentation of the Estado da Índia as a basically predatory system.

To be sure, the state established some standards of financial control. Officials, such as factors, treasurers, customs agents, and other clerks, were required to keep a regularly updated register of all their receipts and expenditures (whether merchandise, cash, or bills of exchange) and were obliged to render a general accounting of their activities at the end of their terms. As a result, some were occasionally incarcerated for malfeasance, and even the odd captain or viceroy could be banned or arrested. This was not enough, however, to deter self-remuneration by royal officials, a widespread practice that the government could not help but be aware of but to which it often turned a blind eye. Such actions became a form of social negotiation built into the financial system itself.

We have now been led to the last two questions that must be addressed: the pattern of colonial expenditures and the nature of the social agents (and of their interactions and relations with the administration and the crown) who clustered around the financial system of the empire. In fact, for the purpose of drawing the profile of the Portuguese early modern polity and

68 Ibid.

69 Frederic C. Lane, *Venice and History* (Baltimore, 1966).

70 Niels Steensgaard, *Carracks, Caravans and Companies: The Structural Crisis in the European–Asian Trade of the Early Seventeenth Century* (Copenhagen, 1973).

assessing the status of the empire within that polity, the ways in which the government allocated resources are no less revealing than the structure of revenues. This is a matter that the literature on the subject often overlooks. As a result, it is easier to follow minutely over long periods of time the changes in the sources of the royal income than it is to determine in detail the composition of expenditures. In the preceding section, while ascertaining the major financial trends of the Portuguese empire, more attention was paid to revenues than to expenditures. This omission must now be redressed.

The classifications we use here for the purpose of determining the patterns of expenditure have to be akin to those used at the time by the institutions themselves. In the first place, expenditures must be broken into two primary categories: ordinary and extraordinary. As previously seen, ordinary budgets were usually balanced or even showed a surplus, either in the kingdom itself or in the empire at large (for instance, in the Estado da Índia). However, extraordinary charges, mainly caused by the cost of warfare, introduced major deficits that could not be met by regular means and that forced governments to resort to equally extraordinary financial procedures (requests, subsidies, forced loans, and ultimately government indebtedness). A second criterion for classification should allow us to distinguish between resources devoted to the military, the church, and the political and civil administration, for either regular or exceptional expenditures. In addition, general payments in the form of interest due on the funded or floating debt and the different kinds of pensions (*moradias*, *tenças*, etc.) had to be made.

Unfortunately, current research and available sources do not allow us to follow the course of expenditures with the same detail with which we have observed the vicissitudes of revenues. Thus, a close examination of the 1607 budget (with only some references to other sources) will have to do. It was a terrible time for the empire, which was under continuous attack from the Dutch and the English. Extraordinary military expenditures were very high, but as far as regular costs were concerned, in Brazil it was the civil administration, not the military, that accounted for the largest share of the payments. In fact, local government and the judicial and fiscal organization, incipient though they still were, cost some 22 million réis, more than half the total budget. The church consumed almost 20 percent, which was of course the compensation the king paid for receiving the proceeds of the tithe. Finally, military expenses amounted to 11 million réis, a little over one-fourth of total expenditures (Table 2.3). This showed that, to a large extent, the defense of Brazil relied on the local population and local resources.

In the Estado da Índia, the pattern of expenditures was quite different. It is not surprising that military costs, particularly paying for the armadas

Table 2.3. Brazil – financial structure 1607

	Expenditures						
	Church		*Civilian*		*Military*		
Captaincies	*value*	*%*	*value*	*%*	*value*	*%*	*Total*
Pernambuco	1,517.3	8.1	11,090.4	58.9	6,211.9	33.0	18,819.6
Itamaracá	105.0	1.6	6,211.9	94.0	293.7	4.4	6,610.6
Parahiba	351.3	44.5	293.7	37.2	144.0	18.3	788.9
Sergipe	100.0	22.7	144.0	32.7	196.0	44.5	440.0
Rio Grande	249.7	45.8	196.0	35.9	100.0	18.3	545.7
Bahia	5,032.0	56.2	100.0	1.1	3,820.6	42.7	8,952.6
Espírito Santo	65.0	1.6	3,820.6	94.4	160.0	4.0	4,045.6
Ilhéus	40.0	20.0	160.0	80.0	–	–	200.0
Porto Seguro	40.0	100.0	–	–	–	–	40.0
Rio de Janeiro	305.0	75.3	–	–	100.0	24.7	405.0
São Vicente and São Amaro	242.0	59.6	100.0	24.6	64.2	15.8	406.2
Total	8,047.2	19.5	22,116.6	53.6	11,090.4	26.9	41,254.2
Revenue							42,000.0

Values in thousands of réis.

Source: Luis de Figueiredo Falcão, *Livro em que se contém toda a fazenda e real património de Portugal, India e ilhas adjacentes* (1607), 2nd ed. (Lisbon, 1859).

and the wages of the fortress captains, took some 40 percent of an ordinary budget of 235 million réis (the same proportion as in 1571). The church, mainly the Jesuit congregations, received another 20 percent, and the rest was spent in the government, the civil administration, and other public activities (which in 1571 accounted for 48 percent of expenditures). The vice-royalty consumed a large proportion of the resources devoted to civilian endeavors (12.3 percent), which were distributed among the fiscal bureaucracy (5.1 percent), health and poor relief (4.9 percent), and the administration of justice (3.7 percent). But there were other important state concerns in shipbuilding and manufacturing (4.4 percent) and in trading ventures and trading posts, or factories (2.5 percent). Living side by side with powerful neighbors, the Estado da Índia had to expend a sizable proportion of its budget on diplomatic affairs: Gifts sometimes worked as a substitute for tribute, allowing the Portuguese to settle and trade in some areas, and in these cases they had to pay their dues (Table 2.4).

The expense for pensions inscribed in the budget of the Estado da Índia was not very significant. Frequently, the payment of pensions, the interest on bonds, and some of the civil servants' wages were assigned to particular

Table 2.4. Estado da Índia – structure of expenditures

	1571		*1574*		*1607*	
Expenditure	*value*	%	*value*	%	*value*	%
Military	93,422.2	40.7	89,206.9	37.2	95,955.7	40.7
Church	12,705.9	5.5	17,709.2	7.4	47,617.0	20.2
Civilian	110,143.8	48.0	102,853.8	42.8	85,404.0	36.2
Government and administration	21,705.6	9.5	22,931.2	9.6	28,910.9	12.3
Justice	6,129.1	2.7	3,801.9	1.6	8,699.3	3.7
Finance	10,292.0	4.5	7,560.6	3.1	12,008.5	5.1
Trade and factories	7,447.2	3.2	5,293.6	2.2	6,000.3	2.5
Diplomacy	4,550.3	2.0	5,781.8	2.4	5,152.6	2.2
Shipbuilding and manufacturing	45,523.6	19.9	40,409.0	16.8	10,398.5	4.4
Pensions	6,436.8	2.8	6,542.1	2.7	2,702.3	1.1
Health and poor relief	8,059.3	3.5	10,533.6	4.4	11,531.5	4.9
Extraordinary	12,995.0	5.7	30,285.0	12.6	6,760.7	2.9
Total	229,266.8	100.0	240,055.0	100.0	235,737.4	100.0

Sources: Luis de Figueiredo Falcão, *Livro em que se contém toda a fazenda e real património de Portugal, India e ilhas adjacentes* (1607), 2nd ed. (Lisbon, 1859); Vitorino Magalhães Godinho, *Les finances de l'etat Portugais des Indes Orientales (1517–1635): Matériaux pour une étude Structurale et conjoncturelle* (Paris, 1982); Artur Teodoro de Matos, *O orçamento do Estado da Índia, 1571* (Lisbon, 1999).

sources of income. For instance, the receipts of the Casa da Índia or the customs of Lisbon were partly consigned to the payment of *padrões de juro* or *tenças*, which in fact had been originally issued as an advance or an allowance on those revenues. This system operated as a kind of mortgage, which in time might compromise any chances for the development of an effective financial policy. Furthermore, the expedient of revenue assignment made the aggregate royal income little more than a fiction.

Other constraints on the management of public finance were also present. Obstacles to calculation (Arabic notation was not in use in official budgets until the end of the sixteenth century, and double-entry bookkeeping was not introduced before the middle of the eighteenth century) and the lack of a competent fiscal administration certainly hampered the state's ability to raise revenues and to keep expenses under control. Despite the peculiarities of the Portuguese financial system, there was no specific financial theory under which it operated. Most authors writing on fiscal matters tried to offer advice on new ways of increasing the royal income, not on managing that income. Some worried about population growth and the need to develop agriculture or manufacturing, but they might easily fall into fiscalism, that is, into trying to expand the crown's revenues even if the resources from which those revenues came remained unchanged. In such a case, financial affluence became detached from economic development, and the management of the fiscal apparatus and the different roles played by the social agents who moved in and around that apparatus would capture center stage.

It can be said that financial policy consisted to a large extent in the management of these roles. One expression of the controversy over this management is the criticism aimed at the officials of the royal treasury and the trading posts for their incompetence and the praise of merchants and their role. This argument runs from Albuquerque, the celebrated governor and conqueror of the Portuguese East Indies, to Duarte Gomes Solis, a New Christian merchant and adviser to Philip IV.[71] Another similar expression were the allegations of corruption, extortion, and embezzlement directed against the administration in general, which became immortalized in the pen of Diogo do Couto.[72] Conversely, arguments in favor of the administration and against the private contractors of royal monopolies and revenue collection were also articulated. The factor of Cochin, Francisco Costa, portrayed the system of contracts and that of direct management of the pepper monopoly by the crown as absolute opposites (which they were not, for there was always some measure of private participation), only to commend direct management and of course, the role of royal officials.[73] This same position was argued by the *arbitrista* Baltasar de Faria Severim with respect to the collection of revenues in the kingdom.[74] More than 150 years later, disapproval of the great capitalists who held the contract for the tobacco monopoly was still quite common.

[71] José Luís Cardoso, *Pensar a economia em Portugal: Digressões históricas* (Lisbon, 1997), p. 21; António Borges Coelho, "O mercantilista Português Duarte Gomes Solis, 1561/2–ca. 1630," *Portugaliae Historica*, 2nd series, 1 (1991), p. 226; Duarte Gomes Solis, *Alegación en favor de la Compañia de la India Oriental, y comercios ultramarinos, que de nuevo se instituyó en Portugal* (Madrid or Lisbon, 1628), new ed. by Moses Bensabat Amzalak (Lisbon, 1955), pp. 42–43.

[72] George Winius, *The Black Legend of Portuguese India: Diogo do Couto, His Contemporaries, and the Soldado Prático* (New Delhi, 1985).

[73] Curto, *A cultura política em Portugal*, pp. 398–407.

[74] Diogo Ramada Curto, "A economia política no tempo do alvitrismo," in José Luís Cardoso, ed., *Contribuições para a história do pensamento económico em Portugal* (Lisbon, 1988); Curto, *A cultura política em Portugal*, pp. 443–445.

The problem was that a complex system of social exchange developed around the financial resources elicited by the crown and around the institutional apparatus it created to extract and manage those resources. This system was based on the monopolization by the crown of some assets and the means of obtaining them, and therefore on the rent-seeking institutions and attitudes it promoted. The more the crown tried to monopolize income-producing endeavors, the more it became dependent on an administration that had to be paid from the returns of those endeavors. In a prevailing political culture in which a system of patrimonial and personal rewards headed by the crown played a central role (see Diogo Ramada Curto, Chapter 10, this volume), the administration might as well have been directly remunerated for its participation in the exploitation of resources under royal monopoly. This could be done overtly and legally, by way of the formal concession of trading rights and privileges to all ranks of royal officials, both civilian and military, or illegally, by way of corruption, embezzlement, and smuggling. The extent of knowledge about, and the degree of tolerance of, these illegal practices varied, but government inaction virtually amounted to the endorsement of such ways.

On the other hand, the crown could opt to lease the monopolies to private entrepreneurs and capitalists. This would excuse it from developing the necessary institutions and a bureaucracy, but it would also sizably reduce the rent generated by the very process of monopolization. This problem led to a complex relationship between the monarchy and its chief contractors, both parties trying to obtain more from the contract than what was involved in the contract itself. The monarchy tried to extract additional funds from the contractors on more favorable terms. At the same time, the contractors took advantage of the needs of the crown and tried to extend the terms of their contracts and to obtain other rewards in the form of social distinctions, often symbolic in character.[75]

The intricacies of this system of social exchange also appear in the military aspects of the process of empire building. Once extraordinary expenses are taken into account, military costs are surely the most important ones. Part of a soldier's pay could take the form of a right to participate in a small way in the business ventures reserved for the crown, but the military still had to be armed, fed, and clothed by the state. Furthermore, their service to the king, as well as the service of other royal officials, had to be rewarded with more than simply wages. They secured rights to honorific distinctions and royal

[75] Fernando Dores Costa, "Capitalistas e serviços: Empréstimos, contratos e mercês no final do século XVIII," *Análise Social* 27 (1992), nos. 116–117, pp. 441–460.

pensions that individually were not very significant but on the whole placed a heavy burden on the treasury. This system produced a vicious spiral: The more the empire expanded, the greater the military strain and the larger the number of soldiers and officials who could claim a pension for their service. The expenditures for royal pensions grew at a much faster pace than for wages in the second half of the sixteenth century and even outweighed wages in 1588.[76]

Finally, this leads us back to the question of the nature of costs. Pensions and wages were, of course, a cost for the crown, but they formed the revenue of civil and military servants and their families. The system of social exchange that clustered around the crown's finances operated as a gigantic mechanism of allocation of the resources centrally extracted by the monarchy both in the kingdom and in the empire. Therefore, as we have already noted, costs for the state were not the same as costs for the society at large. This is not to say that society did not have to bear the costs of empire building; it certainly did. Besides the distortions that the empire may have inserted into the system of resource allocation, deaths in shipwrecks, in battles, and from tropical diseases numbered in the thousands. This should suffice to show that, although it may have profited from the oceanic expansion in various ways, Portuguese society also paid its dues.

BIBLIOGRAPHICAL ESSAY

Readers who are not familiar with the Portuguese language will find it difficult to gain access to the literature on the financial structure and dynamics of the Portuguese empire in the early modern period. In fact, the pivotal contribution for the study of this topic has been provided by the works of Vitorino Magalhães Godinho, of which unfortunately only a very minor part, and not the most significant, is available in English; see "Portugal and Her Empire," in J. S. Bromley, ed., *The New Cambridge Modern History*, vol. 6 (Cambridge, 1970) pp. 509–534. In an illuminating essay, Godinho was the first to point out the vital importance of maritime trade and imperial sources of income to the structure of Portuguese public finance and the early modern state; see "Finanças públicas e estrutura do Estado," in *Ensaios II – Sobre história de Portugal*, 2nd ed. (Lisbon, 1978; 1st ed., 1968), of which an earlier French version referring only to the sixteenth century was published as "Les finances publiques et la structure de l'état Portugais au xvie siècle," *Revista de Economia* 14 (1962), pp. 105–115. He was also the first to make extensive use of quantitative sources (budgets, official accounts, etc.) and to offer an

[76] Godinho, "Finanças públicas," p. 69.

exhaustive exploration of the financial workings of the Portuguese eastern empire (see *Les finances de l'etat Portugais des Indes Orientales, 1517–1635: Matériaux pour une étude structurale et conjoncturelle*, which was first published in Paris in 1982 but had been available to the public since 1959). His books on the economy of the Portuguese empire as a whole also offer major insights on the financial question, namely on the marketing operations of the state and on the relationship between the state and the private merchants and merchant societies: *A economia dos descobrimentos Henriquinos* (Lisbon, 1962) and *L'économie de l'empire Portugais, XVe–XVIe siècles* (Paris, 1968), greatly enlarged for the Portuguese version, *Os descobrimentos e a economia mundial*, 2nd ed. (4 vols., Lisbon, 1981–1983). Moreover, they depict the broad rhythms of the imperial economy on which the financial system depended. For a brief survey of the general economic consequences of the empire that also deals with the financial question, see also Jorge M. Pedreira, "'To Have and Have Not': The Economic Consequences of Empire: Portugal, 1415–1822," in P. K. O'Brien and Leandro Prados, eds., *The Costs and Benefits of European Imperialism from the Conquest of Ceuta, 1415, to the Treaty of Lusaka, 1974, Revista de Historia Económica* 16 (1998), no. 1, pp. 93–122.

The work of Vitorino Magalhães Godinho, in this respect as in many others, is as yet unsurpassed. Most of the newer contributions are merely additions to the general framework he established. João Cordeiro Pereira was one of the first to follow in his footsteps; see "A receita do Estado Português no ano de 1526: Um orçamento desconhecido," in *Estudos de história de Portugal: Homenagem a A. H. Oliveira Marques*, vol. 2 (Lisbon, 1983), pp. 15–55, and "O orçamento do Estado Português no ano de 1527," *Nova História – Século XVI* 1 (1984), pp. 27–65. In his studies on the Portuguese early modern system of government, António Manuel Hespanha also deals with financial issues; see his *As vésperas do Leviathan: Instituições e poder político: Portugal, século XVII*, 2nd ed. (Coimbra, 1991), and *O antigo regime*, vol. 4 of *História de Portugal*, ed. José Mattoso (Lisbon, 1993), particularly pp. 203–239. These essays have amplified our knowledge of the Portuguese financial system (disclosing more quantitative sources and in the case of Hespanha's latter study focusing on the ideological conditions as well as the ethical and religious constraints), but they did not change the overall picture Godinho has drawn. They also do not add much to our relatively scanty knowledge of the composition of government expenditures as compared with our data on public receipts (an imbalance that is also present in Godinho's work). David Justino has explored the workings of the financial techniques and mechanisms and particularly the public debt in his *História da bolsa de Lisboa* (Lisbon, 1994). Anyway, the empire holds only a marginal position as a topic for inquiry in the essays by Cordeiro Pereira, Hespanha, and Justino.

Financial matters, on the other hand, have formed a focal point for research in the context of the analysis of the tensions within the Iberian union between 1580 and 1640. António de Oliveira examined this issue in his *Poder e oposição política em Portugal no período Filipino, 1580–1640* (Lisbon, 1990), and I. A. A. Thompson's excellent "The Reign of Philip IV," in his *Crown and Cortes: Government, Institutions and Representation in Early Modern Castile* (Aldershot, 1993), allows us to set the problem in the broader context of the Spanish monarchy. For the late seventeenth century, English-speaking readers can find a valuable summary on this theme in the chapters on public finance and the overseas trade in Carl A. Hanson's *Economy and Society in Baroque Portugal, 1668–1703* (Minneapolis, 1981), a book that otherwise displays major limitations in the characterization of Portuguese early modern society.

Inquiry on Portuguese state finances in the first half of the eighteenth century has focused almost exclusively on the question of the gold remittances from Brazil, so we have to move to the second half of the century to find a more general approach. The financial system of the government of Pombal has been thoroughly documented in a study by Fernando Tomaz, "As finanças do Estado pombalino, 1762–1777," in *Estudos e ensaios: Em homenagem a Vitorino Magalhães Godinho* (Lisbon, 1988). The financial tensions of the late eighteenth and early nineteenth centuries are also well known thanks to the statistical information provided by Luís Espinha da Silveira in his "Aspectos da evolução das finanças públicas Portuguesas, 1800–1827," *Análise Social* 23 (1987), no. 97, pp. 505–529, and most of all to the study of Fernando Dores Costa, *Crise financeira, dívida pública e capitalistas, 1796–1807* (Lisbon, 1992). However, none of these works are focused on the empire.

As far as the empire is concerned, the attempt to systematize the available information offered by J. M. Azevedo e Silva in *A Madeira e a construção do mundo Atlântico (séculos XV–XVIII)* (2 vols., Funchal, 1995), and which has been reproduced in other works such as Francisco Bethencourt and Kirti Chauduri, eds., *História da expansão Portuguesa*, vol. 1 (Lisbon, 1998), p. 400, presents more shortcomings than those it intends to solve. (For instance, it classifies the receipts of the Casa da Índia, meaning the receipts from the eastern trade, as income originating in the kingdom and not in the empire.) Studies of a regional scope have been more successful. In this respect, the eastern empire has attracted most of the interest. In the wake of Godinho's early essay, Artur Teodoro de Matos has consistently supplied more statistical information; see his "The Financial Situation of the State of India during the Philippine Period, 1581–1635," in *Indo-Portuguese History: Old Issues,*

New Questions, ed. T. R. de Sousa (New Delhi, 1985), and *O orçamento do Estado da Índia, 1571* (Lisbon, 1999). However, as far as analytical procedures are concerned, very few advances can be acknowledged, since not even a simple classification of the receipts and expenses of the Estado da Índia is presented. The general financial data have also been compiled in Sanjay Subrahmanyam's *The Portuguese Empire in Asia, 1500–1700* (London, 1993), and by Francisco Bethencourt in *História da expansão Portuguesa*, vol. 2, pp. 294–303. The crisis of the seventeenth century has been examined in Anthony Disney's *The Twilight of the Pepper Empire: Portuguese Trade in Southwest India in the Early Seventeenth Century* (Cambridge, MA, 1978) and James Boyajian's *Portuguese Trade in Asia under the Habsburgs, 1580–1640* (Baltimore, 1993). The circumstances of the Eastern empire during the eighteenth century are almost entirely ignored, except for the latter part of the century; see Celsa Pinto, *Trade and Finance in Portuguese India: A Study of the Portuguese Country Trade* (New Delhi, 1994).

The financial structure of the African and Brazilian dominions has drawn comparatively less interest in the literature. General studies on El Mina deal with financial issues; see John Vogt, *Portuguese Rule on the Gold Coast, 1469–1682* (Athens, GA, 1979), and J. Bato'ora Balong-wen-mewuda, *São Jorge da Mina, 1482–1637* (2 vols., Paris, 1993). Joseph Miller also addresses the question in the context of his examination of the fiscal workings of the Angolan slave trade in his *Way of Death: Merchant Capitalism and the Angolan Slave Trade, 1730–1830* (London, 1988).

On the other hand, the essays collected in the volume *Colonial Brazil*, edited by Leslie Bethell (Cambridge, 1987), generally neglect the financial issues. Frédéric Mauro's *Le Portugal, le Brésil et l'Atlantique au XVIIe siècle, 1570–1670* (Paris, 1983), offers an overview of the financial workings within the empire. He also provides some statistical information on Brazil, but the data are sparse and the time series are incomplete. Evaldo Cabral de Mello, for his part, has stressed the fiscal scope of the war with the Dutch in Pernambuco in his *Olinda Restaurada: Guerra e Açúcar no nordeste, 1630–1654*, 2nd ed. (Rio de Janeiro, 1998). The age of gold and diamond exploration has invited a large share of scholarly attention. After the early work of Charles Boxer in *The Golden Age of Brazil, 1695–1750: Growing Pains of a Colonial Society* (Berkeley, CA, 1964) and beyond the references in Kenneth Maxwell's *Conflicts and Conspiracies: Brazil and Portugal, 1750–1808* (Cambridge, 1973), the period has been thoroughly investigated by Virgílio Noya Pinto in *O ouro Brasileiro e o comércio Anglo-Português: Uma contribuição aos estudos da economia Atlântica no século XVIII*, 2nd ed. (São Paulo, 1979) and by Michel Morineau in *Incroyables gazettes et fabuleux métaux: Les retours de trésors Américains d'après* *les gazettes Hollandaises XVIe–XVIIIe siècles* (Cambridge, 1985). Some references on the contribution of Brazil to the receipts of the Portuguese crown in the context of the collapse of the old colonial system can also be found in Jorge M. Pedreira's *Estrutura industrial e mercado colonial: Portugal e Brasil, 1780–1830* (Lisbon, 1994) and "From Growth to Collapse: The Breakdown of the Old Colonial System, Portugal and Brazil, 1750–1830," *The Hispanic American Historical Review* 80 (2000), no. 4, pp. 839–865.

The examination of ideological concepts, representations, and political propositions on financial issues can be found, other than in the abovementioned essay by A. M. Hespanha, in Diogo Ramada Curto's "A economia política no tempo do alvitrismo," in *Contribuições para a história do pensamento económico em Portugal*, edited by José Luís Cardoso (Lisbon, 1988), and *A cultura política em Portugal, 1578–1642: Comportamentos, ritos e negócios* (2 vols., Lisbon, 1994), and in the works of José Luís Cardoso, who has conducted a very consistent inquiry into Portuguese economic thought. Most of the references to the early modern period and the empire are to be found in his *Pensar a economia em Portugal: Digressões históricas* (Lisbon, 1997); unfortunately for the English-speaking reader, only fleeting allusions can be traced in *A History of Portuguese Economic Thought* (London, 1998), which he co-wrote with António Almodovar. For the individual case of a Portuguese Jewish merchant and adviser to Philip IV, see António Borges Coelho, "O mercantilista Português Duarte Gomes Solis, 1561/2–ca. 1630," *Portugaliae Historica*, 2nd series, 1 (1991), pp. 183–257.

The issue of the social configurations that developed around the financial institutions and resources of the empire are still to be fully investigated. The nature of the agents and their attitudes must be directly addressed. The problem of corruption, which has been used to depict the Portuguese empire in the East as an essentially predatory system, for instance by Niels Steensgaard in his *Carracks, Caravans and Companies: The Structural Crisis in the European–Asian Trade of the Early Seventeenth Century* (Copenhagen, 1973), has not come under close scrutiny, but see George Winius's *The Black Legend of Portuguese India: Diogo do Couto, His Contemporaries, and the Soldado Prático* (New Delhi, 1985).

The role of merchants, bankers, and tax farmers has been studied by James Boyajian in *Portuguese Bankers in the Court of Spain, 1626–1650* (New Brunswick NJ, 1983) and by David Grant Smith in *The Mercantile Class of Portugal and Brazil in the Seventeenth Century: A Socioeconomic Study of the Merchants of Lisbon and Bahia* (Ann Arbor, MI, 1985). In an insightful essay, Fernando Dores Costa has elucidated fundamental aspects of the relationship between this type of social agent and the crown; see his "Capitalistas e serviços: Empréstimos, contratos e mercês no final do século XVIII," *Análise*

Social 27(1992), nos. 116–117, pp. 441–460. In this same vein, Jorge M. Pedreira's "Mercadores e formas de mercantilização," in *O Tempo de Vasco da Gama*, edited by Diogo Ramada Curto (Lisbon, 1998), pp. 157–178, explores this system of social exchange and pursues Godinho's former suggestions on these matters. Finally, Richard Bonney's comparative analysis and the system of classification he conceived in his *Economic Systems and State Finance* (Oxford, 1995) are most useful in positioning the Portuguese state and empire in the broader setting of early modern Europe.

3

MARKETS AND MERCHANT COMMUNITIES IN THE INDIAN OCEAN: LOCATING THE PORTUGUESE

Michael N. Pearson

Markets and merchant communities are obviously closely related because merchants operate in markets or travel from one market to another. A market is most succinctly defined as a place where goods can be exchanged by specialists (that is, merchants of various sorts) or can be purchased by consumers. However, in the real world it is not merely a two-way process with an exchange between a producer and a merchant and then between the merchant and a consumer. Rather, there are layers of different kinds of merchants, and goods may be exchanged, transported, and exchanged again many times before they reach a consumer. A quantity of nutmeg grown in eastern Indonesia would pass through several markets, and be owned by several merchants, before it ended up in a stall or shop in Europe or China, where it would be sold to a cook or an apothecary.

The important Dutch governor J. P. Coen well described the complexity of the trade that the Dutch East India Company hoped to enter, as indeed they did:

> Piece goods from Gujarat we can barter for pepper and gold on the coast of Sumatra, rials [silver currency] and cottons from the [Coromandel] coast for pepper in Bantam, sandalwood, pepper and rials we can barter for Chinese goods and Chinese gold; we can extract silver from Japan with Chinese goods, piece goods from the Coromandel coast in exchange for spices, other goods and rials, rials from Arabia for spices and various other trifles – one thing leads to the other.[1]

In this chapter, the focus will be on those markets where the Portuguese operated or whose activities affected the Portuguese. Consequently, a host

[1] Quoted in Niels Steensgaard, *The Asian Trade Revolution of the Seventeenth Century: The East India Companies and the Decline of the Caravan Trade* (Chicago, 1974), p. 407.

of large and small markets in the interior of India or China, or in Central Asia, will not be discussed. Our main focus will be on the great port cities strung along the littoral because this was where Portuguese attention was focused. I will first provide an overview so that we can locate the Portuguese in the context in which they were forced to operate. Then I will specify the changes that occurred as a result of the activities of the Portuguese.

In a discussion of port cities, there are two variables to take into account. Some ports were autonomous political entities, whereas others were ruled from distant capitals of landed empires. Some were pure emporia, existing only to exchange products brought in from far inland or overseas, whereas others had productive hinterlands, and in some cases major manufacturing enterprises within their walls.

A merchant is a person who exchanges one good for another or buys a good for money with the intention of selling it to someone else. It would be tedious and pointless to merely list a confusing array of merchants in each port city. Rather, I will concentrate on the main communities and attempt to describe the role of merchant communities in general rather than specific terms. Some merchants were permanently located in a particular marketplace, although the goods they dealt with could come from far away. Others traveled widely, chaffering their way all around the shores of the Indian Ocean.

Much trade was done by humble people (that is, peddlers), for we are increasingly aware that most trade was coastal and consisted of bulk, low value goods. Nevertheless, there were also merchants who were very far from being humble peddlers. Such magnates have been described by Sanjay Subrahmanyam as "portfolio capitalists," people who spread their investments into many areas, including banking, shipping, and trade in a host of commodities.[2] These merchant princes, many of them Muslim at this time, overlapped with rulers and nobles, who also traded. None of these were humble men at all. The Europeans wrote in awe of the great Jain merchant Virji Vorah in Surat, reputedly the richest man in the world and who could have bought and sold the northern European trading companies with ease. Virji Vorah, who died in 1665, engaged in every imaginable enterprise. He was a banker, a ship owner, and a trader in indigo, pepper, and many other products. He engaged in both retail and wholesale trade and lent money to the Moghul nobility. He also lent money to the Europeans and used his power quite unscrupulously.

[2] Sanjay Subrahmanyam and C. A. Bayly, "Portfolio Capitalists and the Political Economy of Early Modern India," in Sanjay Subrahmanyam, ed., *Merchants, Markets and the State in Early Modern India* (Delhi, 1990), pp. 242–265.

Most of these wealthy men did not travel themselves but rather had agents spread around the great port cities of the littoral and also far inland. Virji Vorah had agents in Calicut, Agra, Burhanpur, and all over the interior of Gujarat, as well as agents or connections at all the great emporia around the Indian Ocean littoral. Networks of other Gujarati traders, especially the Hindu merchant group known as *banias*, extended even beyond this to the Philippines and even to Russia. These agents often would all be members of the same community. Sometimes they were even related to the central figure.

This raises the matter of merchant communities. The point here is that ethnicity, kinship, and religion were vital in trading matters. The much-quoted account of the Armenian merchant Hovhannes has provided us with a typical case. He was by no means a peddler but rather an agent of larger Armenian merchants in the Armenian suburb of New Julfa in Isfahan in Iran, and later Agra in India. However, Hovhannes's importance for us is that he operated as a member of a very dispersed community. His journal describes his travels over the period 1682 to 1693. During this time, he visited and traded in Bandar Abbas and Surat, and then in Agra, where he spent most of a year. From there he went to Tibet, then back to India, to Patna, and then to Bengal. Everywhere he went he had contact with, and assistance from, other members of the far-flung Armenian merchant community. Hovhannes may well have had written advice on where to trade, and what to trade in, for a seventeenth-century Armenian merchant's manual gave details on prices, commodities, and merchants for all the places Hovhannes visited.[3]

The markets of most concern for us, where most merchant communities were to be found, were the great port cities, or emporia, ringed around the coast. It is true that inland markets were also important, if only because they handled the initial exchange of the commodities to be traded, for there was little "industrial" production on the coasts. Yet the Portuguese knew little of these inland markets, and indeed this ignorance, a product of the largely maritime nature of their empire, at least in the sixteenth century, affected Portuguese success very greatly. For example, they had several forts on the Malabar Coast of India, their aim being to take over the trade in pepper. However, the pepper was grown inland, where Portuguese influence was slight. Failure to control the initial sale of the pepper, being instead reliant on intermediaries, prejudiced importantly the success of Portugal's attempts

[3] Levon Khatchikian, "The Ledger of the Merchant Hovhannes Joughayetsi," in Sanjay Subrahmanyam, ed., *Merchant Networks in the Early Modern World* (Aldershot, 1996), pp. 125–158.

to monopolize the pepper trade. In contrast, the Dutch from the mid-seventeenth century on did control the production areas for the fine spices in the Molucca islands and as a result were able to get much closer to a monopoly.

Turning now to the major port cities cum markets of the Indian Ocean area, we will present a sketch of the situation in 1500 and then note what changes occurred over the next two centuries or so.

The important point to be made here is that long-distance trade, with an integrated series of markets and active merchant communities, existed long before the arrival of Vasco da Gama at Calicut in 1498. Europeans extended trade between Asia and Europe; they did not create it. As European merchants themselves noted, when they got to Asia they were at no particular advantage. A merchant from Florence in western India in 1510 wrote,

> We believe ourselves to be the most astute men that one can encounter, and the people here surpass us in everything. And there are Muslim merchants worth 400,000 to 500,000 ducats. And they can do better calculations by memory than we can do with the pen. And they mock us, and it seems to me that they are superior to us in countless things, save with sword in hand, which they cannot resist.[4]

Where then were the major markets in the Indian Ocean area in 1500? We should begin in East Africa. In the far south, Sofala provided gold and ivory from the far interior. The gold was mined or washed in the inland Mutapa state in present-day Zimbabwe and brought to the coast to be exchanged for cloth and other manufactures from India and the Middle East. To the north, Kilwa had been the great emporium on the coast between roughly 1250 and 1330, from which time date a great mosque and palace, the latter having been the largest roofed stone building south of the Sahara until modern times. By 1500, the greatest port city was Mombasa, an important center for the exchange of ivory and gold from the south with manufactures from the west and north. Malindi was a smaller center at this time, but Mogadishu was another major port, thanks to its proximity to the Red Sea and Hadramaut. All of these ports on the Swahili Coast were autonomous politically and indeed engaged in much competition and even conflict with each other. None of them were important centers of production; rather, they acted as outlets for export goods from the interior, especially gold and ivory. Exports were exchanged for cloths and other manufactured goods from India and the Middle East. Indeed, extensive Chinese porcelain remains

[4] Quoted in Sanjay Subrahmanyam, *The Political Economy of Commerce: Southern India, 1500–1650* (Cambridge, 1990), p. 7.

have been found on the coast and far inland. Yet here and elsewhere the major products traded were humble bulk goods carried along the coast in myriad small dhows: lumber (mangrove poles), cheap cloth, food, and even water.

The next important markets were Aden, near the mouth of the Red Sea, and Hormuz, located to control the entrance to the Persian/Arabian Gulf. Both these great markets were independent of any exterior political authority at this time. They acted as major centers for the exchange of Middle Eastern and even European goods for products from all over the Indian Ocean area. Among the more important products were cloths and spices. Located on barren foreshores and deficient even in water, let alone food, neither had any major productive role. Rather, they were hinges linking areas to the north with those to the south and east.

As we move across the Arabian Sea to the west coast of India, we begin to find variations on this pattern. The great ports of Gujarat were certainly important centers of exchange, but they were located on the maritime fringe of important production centers for such products as indigo, saltpeter, and especially a vast variety of cotton cloths. Indeed, some of the manufacturing process was done in these very port cities. In 1500, the greatest port was Cambay, at the head of the Gulf of Cambay. This, like many other ports within and around the gulf, was not an independent city-state; rather, in 1500 it was part of the important Muslim sultanate of Gujarat and from 1572 was absorbed in the mighty Moghul empire. Here were huge volumes of trade, skillful merchants, and a very well articulated network of production and exchange and credit. For such ports (that is, those with productive interiors), connections with the land were obviously crucial, as compared with, say, Aden and Hormuz, which, being dependent on the exchange of products from all over the Indian Ocean but not from their interiors, were less concerned about what happened directly inland from them.

The ports farther down India's west coast were less important, in part because the interior was less productive. The next major group of port cities was in Malabar, now the Indian state of Kerala. The dominant port here was Calicut, ruled by a powerful and independent ruler, the Samudri raja or *zamorin*, and not only a market for a host of "foreign" goods but also a great collection and distribution center for the pepper that was harvested in abundance in the interior. Nevertheless, Calicut, unlike several of the ports of Gujarat, was not a center for manufacturing. It was a place where goods from both near and far were available, with those from nearby, especially pepper, undergoing little value-added processing in the town itself. In Sri Lanka, then called Ceylon, the major market was at Colombo, where cinnamon was available, brought from the interior.

Around 1500, the major ports in the Bay of Bengal were, on the Coromandel Coast, Pulicat, which drew on production, especially textiles, from the great Hindu kingdom of Vijayanagar but was little affected by it politically. In Bengal, the most important port was Chittagong, which similarly was little controlled from the political center of Gaur. Leaving aside the minor ports of Arakan and Burma, the next major port of which we need to take account was Malacca, located along the coast above modern Singapore. This great market was of equal importance with Cambay, Calicut, Aden, and Hormuz. It was an independent sultanate and unlike all the others had risen to prominence only during the fifteenth century. In this great exchange center were to be found products from all over the Indian Ocean and far beyond: Chinese silks and porcelains, Indonesian spices, textiles from India, and a host of European products. Malacca functioned as a pure exchange center: Local products, let alone local manufactures, were of very slight account. It was the great hinge in Indian Ocean trade at this time, connecting up what could be called the "larger" Indian Ocean, which would include the South China Sea on one side and the Mediterranean on the other.

Moving to the South China Sea, China's greatest ports around 1500 were Canton as well as Amoy in Fukien province. These two areas provided imports for the vast internal Chinese market and served as entrepôt for exports such as silks and porcelain. Both were much more than mere centers for exchange. Canton profited from its proximity to markets to the south and indeed earlier in the fifteenth century had a copious direct trade with southern India. Amoy was closer to China's major export market, Japan. In both areas, trade was affected to an extent by state attempts to restrict the Chinese from trading overseas, although these attempts could often be ignored. It appears that Amoy was slightly less constricted by a Confucian disdain for trade and merchants than was Canton. Finally, Japan from the late fifteenth century until about 1580 was wracked by civil war, and trade suffered. There was, however, considerable trade with northern China.

What of the major merchants located in these markets? We are often told that the trade of the Indian Ocean in the fifteenth century was Muslim: The ocean was a "Muslim lake." To be sure, there is much truth in this. Islam had spread from the heartland of the Red Sea all around the Indian Ocean over water. One would predict that coastal people would most likely be converted first, and indeed this was the case. By the fifteenth century, it was not Muslim Arabs from the Red Sea and Egypt who dominated Indian Ocean trade and its markets, except perhaps for Calicut; rather, it was local converts, from such coastal areas as Gujarat and Bengal, and Middle Eastern Muslims, who often had migrated to the Indian Ocean area.

A brief tour around the markets that we have just listed will make these differentiations clearer. On the East African coast, the coastal trade was carried on by local people, the Swahili, who had been quite early converts to Islam. Much of the overseas long-distance trade was handled by Muslims from the Hadramaut and Yemen, and they were important people in the Swahili port cities; indeed, many of the rulers were descended from, or married to, merchants from further north. However, there also was a sizable Hindu presence, men from Gujarat who came in with the seasons and, unlike the Muslims, did not settle for a period of time. Hindus were also to be found, this time often settled, in the great market of Aden, and indeed further into the Red Sea, but obviously this area was dominated by Muslims, in this case Arabs. In Hormuz were to be found a great variety of traders: some Europeans and Hindus, as well as Muslims from various areas, but the majority of them local (that is, Persians). In Gujarat, the interior trade and the domestic markets were largely controlled by Hindus and Jains, but they also engaged in oceanic trade. However, more important were a bewildering variety of Muslims: local Persians, still some Arabs, plus others from Bengal. Both here and in Calicut it seems that the long-distance trade was handled mostly by "foreign" Muslims, who were able to draw on far-flung family connections, whereas local converts were more likely to engage in coastal and inland trade. Around the corner, on the Coromandel Coast, we find a larger role for Hindu traders, especially *klings*, who were south Indian Hindus. Bengal, however, had an important Persian merchant community. Malacca, as the greatest market, had the greatest variety of merchants: all sorts of Muslims, Hindus from both Coromandel and Gujarat, plus local people from the Malay world, most of them now Muslim, and of course Chinese traders, who in turn dominated trade in Amoy and Canton. In Japan, until reunification late in the sixteenth century, merchants seem to have profited from the absence of a strong central authority. In the trading port of Sakai, for example, guild leaders administered the city. They even had a military role.

All of these Asian port cities, but especially those that were independent of any interior power, such as Kilwa, Mombasa, Aden, Hormuz, Calicut, and Malacca, prospered not by compulsion but by providing facilities for trade freely undertaken by a vast array of merchants. What the rulers provided was opportunities, fair treatment, and an infrastructure within which trade could take place. They ensured low and relatively equitable customs duties, and a certain law and order, but did little else. Visiting merchants (to call them "foreign" in this era before the modern state would be anachronistic) enjoyed considerable juridical autonomy and typically lived in defined areas with their fellows and handled most of their legal and commercial matters themselves. Officials concerned with trade were instructed to encourage and welcome visitors. In short, visiting merchants wanted and got a level playing field.

State revenue in these independent cities did not come from land revenue because these were territorially very small states; rather, it came from commodity taxes, taxes on professions and the various communities, and especially from taxes on trade, and from the rulers' own participation in trade. In the latter case, however, it was unusual for rulers to use their position to give themselves particular advantages. On reflection, this is not a surprise, for such an attempt would simply lead the merchants to take their trade elsewhere. The initiative was very much with the merchants.

These merchant groupings, based on community, acted relatively autonomously. In Malacca at the time of the Portuguese conquest in 1511, four merchant communities were dominant, each of them living autonomous lives with their own headmen, called *shahbandars*, and governing themselves with little or no reference to the ruler, the sultan, who provided facilities, law and order, and fair dealing in return for customs duties. The first of these four groups were Gujaratis. Many were residents, but some one thousand merchants from Gujarat visited each year. The other main groups were other merchants from the west, namely from India, and especially *klings* from Coromandel, Malays from Indonesia and as far east as the Spice Islands and the Philippines, and then the East Asians, mostly from southern China but also from Japan and Okinawa. Similarly, in the great Gujarati ports, different merchant communities had recognized leaders, although their autonomy here was less because they were located not in an independent port city but in a city that was part of a major landed state. In Calicut, there was a clear distinction, and considerable autonomy, for Gujarati Hindu merchants, foreign Muslims from various places of origin (the most important being those from the Red Sea and Cairo, known as *pardesi*), and local Muslims, known as Mapillas. These heads usually settled any points of contention within the group on their own, or perhaps after taking advice from some sort of council of more senior members of the community. Disputes between members of two groups were settled by negotiation between the respective heads. It was very rare indeed for the political authority, agents of the sultan of Malacca or of the Samudri raja of Calicut, to be involved even in criminal cases, and they were almost never involved in commercial disputes.

What was the basis of these merchant communities? Specialty was important. Thus, in major markets one would find communities based on trade in gold, silk cloth, or pots, just as even today in many parts of Asia and in the past in Europe all the traders or shops dealing in a particular commodity are grouped. Religion was probably equally important. Armenians, of course, practiced a particular form of Christianity. Jews had their own faith. Larger trading groups were internally divided – Hindus most obviously by caste, as were Jains. As to the major dispersed trading communities in the Indian Ocean, namely Muslims, it is well known that merchants and religious specialists worked hand in hand in the period under discussion. Indeed, a trader could well adhere to a particular *sufi* (Muslim devotional) order, and a religious specialist would trade on his own behalf. Islam spread along the trade routes of the Indian Ocean and was expanding vigorously in Indonesia at this time. Many of the major Muslim merchant communities were based on adherence to a particular form of Islam. These merchant groups are sometimes called *natios* (a word deriving from the Mediterranean that can be used to refer to Asian merchant communities), but certainly the difference between the various groups in this premodern and prenational age was not nationality: These people did not carry passports and knew little or nothing of frontiers between sovereign states, as the travels of our Armenian merchant make clear.

What changes occurred in the two centuries after the arrival of the Portuguese in the Indian Ocean? In the broadest sense, what we are describing in this chapter are the effects of the creation of a world economy on markets and merchant communities in the greater Indian Ocean area. It is not a matter of the current phenomenon of "globalization," of a tightly integrated worldwide market. Nevertheless, from 1500 to about 1750 we see the beginnings of increased contact through most of the world as a consequence of the introduction of the Americas into global exchange. The most obvious example is the flow of American silver across the Atlantic in Spanish ships and then through the Mediterranean or via the Cape of Good Hope to the Indian Ocean or the other flow from Acapulco across the Pacific to Manila on the famous Manila galleon, and so on to China. All of the Europeans in Asia up to the mid-eighteenth century used this bullion to buy Asian goods. This dependence is also why the Dutch East India Company engaged in the country trade, meaning the intra-Asian trade, thus generating profits in the Indian Ocean that at the end of the chain could be used to buy Asian goods for Europe. This massive increase in the supply of bullion had some impact on the economies of the Indian Ocean. It meant, for example, that ambitious rulers, especially in Moghul India, could now demand their taxation on the produce of the land, the land revenue, in cash rather than kind. Hence the Indian countryside was monetized, and markets spread to many remote villages.

There were other global connections as well. Diseases spread to and from the Americas and to and from the Indian Ocean. More benignly, many new crops came into the Indian Ocean from the Americas, such as tobacco, chilies, pineapples, sweet potatoes, corn, avocados, and guavas. There are even examples of intercontinental competition impacting deleteriously on Indian Ocean producers. In the seventeenth century, indigo and sugar, both major cash crops in India and elsewhere, were undercut by cheaper similar products from the Americas. Later, cloves from Zanzibar similarly were undercut. Some merchant networks now spread even farther than before: Portuguese traders in the Indian Ocean area had connections going all the way to the Americas.

Nevertheless, we should not make too much of this wider aspect. The opening of the Americas had some effect, but perhaps not a major one, on the Asian littoral at this time. The vast majority of markets were initially little affected; most merchant communities similarly continued as before. As we have stressed, the vast bulk of exchange involved humble necessity goods traded over quite short distances by either land or sea. This was not the start of a new era dominated by European power; it is continuity, not change, that we find in the areas with which we are concerned. The changes in markets that did occur were usually a result of changes in the land routes that fed the markets for, as we have noted, some of these port cities were as dependent on land connections as on maritime ones. Thus, as we look at change over time, we will certainly want to examine the impact of the Portuguese, and later the Dutch and English, on markets and merchant communities in the Indian Ocean, yet we will be scrupulous not to attribute all change to their presence.

Although the nature of the products traded is not our primary concern, in fact this changed little over these two centuries. Europeans funneled into the Indian Ocean hordes of American bullion, but bullion had been available, albeit in smaller quantities, for many centuries. In any case, much bullion also came from Japan at this time, and probably more bullion from America came into the Indian Ocean via the Red Sea, handled by Asian traders, than was brought around the Cape of Good Hope by Europeans. Similarly, although the Spanish brought much American bullion across the Pacific to Manila on the famed Manila galleon, subsequently this bullion was carried by Chinese traders to China. Europeans bought Asian products with this bullion but produced no new demand for any new product from Asia. Sometimes European demand, say for a particular type of cloth, changed production patterns, but we must also remember that for all of this period the trade to Europe from the Indian Ocean was far inferior to that within the Indian Ocean; thus maybe nine-tenths of all spices distributed were consumed within Asia.

The Portuguese goal in the Indian Ocean was to monopolize trade in spices and control, direct, and levy customs duties on all other trade. In East

Africa, several changes occurred in markets and merchant communities as a result of the Portuguese presence. In the south, Sofala was taken by the Portuguese and declined thereafter. It had been the great export center for gold from the inland Mutapa state. The Portuguese tried to monopolize this product; much "smuggling" by local Swahili traders resulted, and they of course stayed away from Sofala. However, Portugal's main focus in the area was Mozambique, and this indeed became an important military center and a port of call for large Portuguese ships (*naus*) on the *carreira da Índia* between Lisbon and India, but it was less successful as a market. In the north, Mombasa was taken in the 1590s, and Malindi had been turned into a client port early on. As regards merchant communities, the main aim of the Portuguese was to take over trade from Muslims, and especially those from the heartland of the faith, the Red Sea area. On the East African coast, they failed in this aim; especially in the north, the main traders continued to be Muslims. As for the local Muslims, the coastal Swahili people, by and large, were unaffected by Portuguese policies. The coast was long and complex, and they were able to continue to trade, although sometimes their focus shifted to new markets far from the partial and faltering centers of Portuguese power. Pate, Lamu, and Angoche rose, whereas Sofala fell.

When we move to the southern shores of the Middle East, we find a rather different situation. In terms of markets, there was one major, but temporary, change as a result of the activities of the Portuguese. For a few decades, they were able, by and large, to monopolize the trade in pepper and spices, and this meant that markets that dealt in these commodities – Aden, Jiddah, Basra on the Persian/Arabian Gulf, Cairo and Alexandria, and Aleppo on the Mediterranean – suffered, as did the Muslim traders who had dominated this trade. However, the Portuguese monopoly had been largely broken by mid-century, and these markets revived as a result. Aden suffered more than most, and indeed even after it was taken by the Ottoman Turks in 1538 it continued to decline, while a major new market, the port of Mocha inside the Red Sea, rose to prominence. Moving along the Hadramaut coast, there seems to have been little change in the predominantly coastal trade of this region. However, this was not the case for Hormuz. This port city and major market, controlling the mouth of the Persian/Arabian Gulf, was taken by the Portuguese in 1515. The intention was to block the spice trade up the Gulf and thereby overland to the eastern Mediterranean. However, the Portuguese needed to conciliate the shah of Iran as a counterweight to their main enemy, the Ottoman Turks, and they allowed some pepper to continue to pass through and into the Persian/Arabian Gulf. Through the sixteenth century, Hormuz provided much revenue for the Estado da Índia, but it was no longer a major market populated by very diverse merchant communities. Many of them seem to have moved to Basra or to the Persian port of Bandar Abbas.

In Sindh, the major port was Lahari Bandar, favored by private Portuguese traders and Muslim merchants. The greatest markets, and the most dominant merchant communities, were to be found in Gujarat. Changes here were rather slight. This, however, does not apply completely to the first port city we come across as we move south and east. From late in the fifteenth century, Diu had become a great market, dominated by Turks. Large trading ships called here to collect Gujarati products and those from further east in exchange for goods from the Middle East and Europe. The capture of Diu was a central aim of the Portuguese and was achieved in 1535. As a consequence, the Muslim merchants left. Diu now became really just a place where Indian Ocean ships were forced to call in and pay customs duties. Like Hormuz, it provided much revenue for the Portuguese state, but its role as a market declined.

In the rest of Gujarat, Hindus and Jains dominated the internal economy, but the main sea traders were Muslims. The effect of the Portuguese on the activities of these people was slight. For the Portuguese, Gujarati goods from Cambay and other ports were vital to make up the cargoes for Portugal, especially the large private cargoes sent home on the great *naus*, which were overwhelmingly cloths from Gujarat. This, however, made up only a very small addition to the total trade of Gujarat. By the end of the century, Surat was the greatest market in India, in the Indian Ocean, and indeed maybe in the whole world.

Along most of the west coast of India, coastal trade was dominant, with small local ships carrying goods to the major nodes, of which Surat and Goa were the most important. As one example, the area of Kanara was a rice surplus region that provided food to other areas up and down the coast and indeed as far as Hormuz. The next major market that we must note is the Portuguese capital of Goa. Goa was analogous to other exchange markets in that it drew very little from its hinterland. Rather, like Diu, its vaunted sixteenth-century prosperity was a direct result of Portuguese policies. Goa was the focus of their military-economic attempt to centralize Indian Ocean trade in their ports. The result was that Goa rose from being a relatively minor port to a major exchange center, based on coercion. Within the Portuguese system, Goa was most important as their capital and as the place where private traders could collect cargoes for their trade both within Asia and also to Europe on the state-owned or licensed *naus*. Yet although Goa had the advantage of military backing from the Estado da Índia, as a market it ranked far behind the great ports in Gujarat. At its height in the late sixteenth century, Goa's trade was worth at most one-tenth that of all the ports of Gujarat, and Surat alone far out-traded Goa. As the Estado da Índia declined in the next century, the gap widened: Surat alone around 1640 had four times the trade of Goa.

In one important respect, Goa and the other Portuguese port cities were, with regard to merchant communities, atypical in that unlike others in the Indian Ocean world they hosted no important Muslim groups. This was the result of Portuguese antipathy toward Muslims in general and Turks in particular. Goa was ruled by the Portuguese, but its internal economy was dominated by a caste of Saraswat Brahmins and its main financiers were *banias* from Gujarat.

The Kerala, or Malabar, Coast was the second great area of concern to the Portuguese because this is where they got pepper, and the *naus* for Portugal usually sailed from Cochin. There were several major changes in this area as a result of the Portuguese presence. Calicut, which in 1500 was the greatest market by far and dominated by Muslims from the Red Sea and Cairo, the *pardesi* Muslims, declined as a result of Portuguese attacks. These foreign Muslims moved out to safer areas. The local Muslims, local converts called Mapillas, stayed perforce and continued to try to trade in pepper outside of the Portuguese monopoly system. Cochin became a Portuguese puppet town and a center of their trade in pepper. The town included a large *casado* population, but trade other than that to Portugal was dominated by Gujarati merchant groups and locally by Malabar Hindu groups.

The Bay of Bengal was an area where the official Portuguese writ ran lightly. The most important port had been Pulicat, and during the sixteenth century the Portuguese dominated this and the neighboring port of São Tomé, especially the very lucrative trade to Malacca. Consequently, local traders moved further north to Masulipatnam, which became the greatest market in the whole Bay of Bengal. This is yet another sign of the way local merchants could simply avoid and evade the Portuguese, in this case by moving from Pulicat to Masulipatnam, in others from Diu to Surat, Hormuz to Bandar Abbas, or Sofala to Mombasa. Masulipatnam drew on an extensive and productive hinterland in the sultanate of Golconda. Here the main merchant communities, apart from the Portuguese, were Hindu groups such as the *klings* and *chettis*, Muslims such as the *chulias*, and also yet again some Gujaratis and Persian Muslims. Further north in Bengal, the main market was Chittagong and later Hughli. Whereas the local economy was controlled by indigenous Bengali traders, long-distance trade was often dominated by people from outside. Thus trade to the major market of Malacca was undertaken by *kling* merchants based in Malacca and the pepper trade by Persians.

Now we reach one of the greatest port cities, Malacca. It will be remembered that there were four major merchant communities in Malacca at the time of Albuquerque's conquest in 1511. Portuguese control affected them considerably. Their attempts to centralize and tax trade led to an exodus, especially of the Gujaratis, who moved off to more welcoming ports. In particular, the decline of Malacca led to the rise of Aceh, in northern Sumatra, which during the century became a major center for trade, especially pepper from the east and Indian products from the west.

One of Portugal's greatest successes was its entry into East Asian trade. The Portuguese were able to acquire a foothold in Macao in 1557. In the last few decades of the sixteenth century and into the next, Portugal controlled a very valuable trade that linked southern China and Japan, especially at the port of Nagasaki. Japan at this time was a major exporter of silver, and there was an insatiable demand for this metal in China. Official Chinese restrictions on trade with Japan meant that the Portuguese state was able to contract out virtually monopolistic voyages between Macao and Japan. This trade was immensely profitable for the Estado da Índia and was achieved without the use of force. It declined only when other Europeans arrived to compete with them in Japan and vanished when the Portuguese were excluded completely from the Japan market in 1639.

How then should we sum up changes in markets and merchant communities in the sixteenth century as a result of the Portuguese presence? The key word must be continuity. Most things did not change. Markets and trade remained controlled, at the most fundamental level, by the monsoons. The major markets needed to be located either adjacent to major production areas, as in Gujarat and southern China, or at choke points, such as Aden, Malacca, and Hormuz. The goods traded in these markets changed little. The great mass of the trade remained coastal trade in humble port markets strung all along the Asian littoral. For the dominant merchant communities, variety remained the key. A host of traders, both peddlers and princes, crossed the oceans. The only change was the arrival of a quite large group of Europeans, who joined and participated in the intricate warp and woof of Asian trade at this time, operating with no particular advantage compared with the Armenians, the Jews, the Shirazis, the *chettis*, or the *banias*.

What the official Portuguese did was temporarily to divert trade in spices from the Red Sea and Persian/Arabian Gulf to the Cape of Good Hope; markets in the first two areas were detrimentally affected for a time. In areas controlled more or less tightly by the Portuguese, which were only on the west coast of India, Muslim traders faced formidable opposition and moved away. Other communities were little affected. With regard to markets, at least four formerly important ones declined once they were taken over by the Portuguese: Sofala, Hormuz, Diu, and Malacca. To be sure, Hormuz and Diu had large surpluses from customs duties, but these resulted not from their roles as markets but from Portugal's coercive trade-control system. Calicut, although not taken over, was badly damaged by Portuguese attacks. The only success was Goa, which prospered thanks to concentrated Portuguese efforts; but we must remember that its trade was, as noted, only one-tenth that from Gujarat's ports. In any case, Goa's success was entirely dependent on the success of Portuguese trade-control policies, and once these were challenged and rendered nugatory by the arrival of the Dutch, Goa fell into decline, as did Diu. In southern China, the Portuguese were used by local authorities as middlemen in the important trade with Japan. Canton's trade expanded considerably as a result, although it is to be noted that Portugal's role was on the sufferance of the Chinese authorities.

We have yet to discuss the number of Portuguese engaged in private trade all along the East African and Asian littoral. They made up a loosely integrated new merchant community in the area that was distinguished by religion and, to an extent, ethnicity. The latter, however, declined in importance as intermarriage with local people produced a *mestiço* population that increasingly merged into local societies.

We can somewhat arbitrarily see four sorts of Portuguese engaged in private trade. First were officials and clerics, who were part of the "official" presence but also traded on their own behalf. Second were *casados*, people who had typically come out to Asia as soldiers (*soldados*) and then left military service and settled down as private, usually married, residents in Portuguese-ruled areas. Third were a few substantial merchants, or agents of European trading firms, who had never been in state service. Fourth were known as *solteiros*, who had left Portuguese areas and lived in other littoral areas. These categories are not completely discrete; thus some *casados* settled in areas not controlled by the Estado da Índia.

For the first group, it is sufficient to note that virtually all officials traded on their own behalf. Many governors returned home with vast fortunes derived from their trading activities. Among the clerics, the Jesuits were particularly successful in making large profits from trade and from investment in land. Some officials were given the right to undertake monopolistic voyages, say from Diu to Mombasa or Goa to Macao to Nagasaki. Many officials sold these rights to others.

In the major Portuguese settlements, such as Mozambique, Diu, Goa, Malacca, and Macao, *casados* played a major economic role, albeit one usually outranked by native competitors such as Chinese in Macao and Indians in Goa and Diu. *Casados* owned shops and competed for government revenue contracts. Their goods made up a substantial part of the goods carried on the huge convoys from Gujarat to Goa and to Cochin. In all these port cities, the *casados* interacted closely with indigenous traders, merchants, and financiers. In Goa, many of the best government contracts were held by Saraswat Brahmins, and Gujaratis provided financing to both the Estado da Índia and the *casados*. In Diu, the dominance of the city's economy by Gujaratis meant that the Estado da Índia had to treat them with some delicacy and, for example, moderate the more excessive demands of the religious orders when these were offensive to the indigenous population. Chinese controlled most of the trade and commerce of Macao, as noted.

The *casados* were mostly small traders, making small investments and small profits. Our third group, private merchants, were much bigger traders and much more cosmopolitan, coming not only from Iberia but also from south Germany, Venice, Holland, England, and France. James Boyajian claims that most of them were New Christians. Be that as it may (and I think he exaggerates here), he has shown that between 1580 and 1640 about 90 percent of cargoes by value going back to Portugal on the carreira were privately owned, and it seems that most of these goods, in which cotton cloths predominated, were owned by big merchants. Others bought at auction the major government contracts, such as that for customs duties. The biggest contract, however, was for pepper, which later in the sixteenth century was often sold to European bankers, who in turn sent out agents to supervise collection in Cochin and Goa.

Ferdinand Cron was one such agent. His career has been studied by several scholars, most recently by Pius Malekandathil.[5] A native of Augsburg, Cron lived in Goa from 1587 to 1624. He was an agent for the great German banking houses of Welser and Fugger and also handled affairs for various Portuguese notables living in Portugal. However, he also owned land and traded on his own behalf. Other private merchants settled as far afield as Macao but maintained contact with other agents in Goa and also in Europe and increasingly Brazil. Some of these merchants were thus connected into very extended networks indeed.

All three of these groups operated within the Portuguese Estado da Índia, and many of them owed what success they achieved to its policies. Thus, the convoys to Gujarat were directed and protected by the Estado da Índia, and the various contracts were issued by it. The *solteiro* (also called *lançado*) category is quite different. They were people who for various reasons chose to leave Portuguese areas and settle elsewhere. Some left because they were New Christians and were subject to persecution in Portuguese areas; others

[5] Pius Malekandathil, *The Germans, the Portuguese and India* (Munster, 1999), pp. 97–111.

saw better occupational or trading opportunities elsewhere. Many of them worked as military specialists and were to be found in all the major Asian states. Most, however, were traders, both large and small. These people, as Rene Barendse has pointed out, were in precisely the same situation as all the other merchant communities that we have delineated, which he prefers to call *natios*.[6] They should be seen as constituting communities on the same bases as Jews, Armenians, Shirazis, or people from Jiddah. On the Swahili Coast and in the southern interior around 1600, the *solteiros* numbered perhaps some hundreds of people, some based in the Portuguese port of Mombasa to be sure but others located in other port city markets up and down the coast and especially in several ports in the Lamu archipelago.

Such was the case all over the Asian littoral. In the great port city of Cambay, some one hundred or so private Portuguese settled, usually marrying local women. They formed part of a very heterogeneous mosaic of merchants. In the Bay of Bengal, hundreds of Portuguese settled, married, and merged into the fabric of peddler trade. In 1600, it was claimed that there were over 600 of them in Hughli alone. Others operated farther east: Makassar had a sizable *solteiro* population at that time, as did Arakan, although there most of them were mercenary soldiers rather than traders.

By the middle of the seventeenth century, the Portuguese official position in the Indian Ocean area was in ruins. Dutch and English companies had replaced them in the trade to Europe. Most of the Estado da Índia's major forts – Malacca, Cochin, Colombo, and Hormuz – had been lost, usually to the Dutch. On the East African coast, the Estado da Índia retained toeholds only in Mozambique, and in Mombasa until the 1690s. Elsewhere it kept only Timor and Macao and on the west coast of India Goa, Daman, and Diu. The Portuguese had been expelled from Japan in 1639 and replaced in the China trade by the northern Europeans. In part, the Estado da Índia now moved from being a maritime entity to a land-based one, as the northern provinces of Bassein (until lost to the rising Indian power, the Marathas, in 1739) and Daman became flourishing agriculture-based areas where many Portuguese did well. The great businessmen, many of them not Portuguese anyway, left as the decline began. The private Portuguese traders, the *casados* and the *solteiros*, continued to trade as they had done in the sixteenth century. They were to be found all around the Bay of Bengal, on the west coast of India, and along the Swahili Coast. Thus, while the state declined, autonomous Portuguese individuals continued to operate. Beginning later in the eighteenth century, the British empire in India expanded. These

[6] Rene Barendse, *The Arabian Seas: The Indian Ocean World of the Seventeenth Century* (Armonk, NY, 2002), pp. 87–125.

individual Portuguese operated within its entrails, serving as middlemen, petty traders, and facilitators for the dominant British.

My aim in this chapter has been to locate the Portuguese in the Indian Ocean mercantile milieu in which they operated. Once the major markets and merchant communities have been identified, it becomes possible to specify the extent to which they were affected by Portuguese policies. However, I have tried to "disaggregate" the Portuguese, to identify different kinds of involvement by different groups within the broad rubric of the "Portuguese." This reveals complex patterns of interaction with various merchants and markets around the littoral of the Indian Ocean. The official Estado da Índia, for example, had very different priorities regarding Gujarat or the Bay of Bengal as compared with the *casados*, who simply wanted to get on and make a living. The general conclusion is that unofficial Portuguese, the *casados* and *solteiros,* merged into existing networks and markets and competed more or less successfully with existing traders. On the other hand, the Estado da Índia tried to implement quite ruthless monopoly policies but predictably failed to achieve its aims because of the resilience and skill of Asian traders.

BIBLIOGRAPHICAL ESSAY

The literature relating to this chapter is rather scattered, and not surprisingly a lot of it is in Portuguese. I have concentrated on English-language materials in this essay. Much information has to be dug out of standard works on the Indian Ocean and on the early European presence in the area. All of the books listed here contain extensive footnotes and bibliographies to guide the reader to further publications. The works of V. M. Godinho are still fundamental: *Les finances de l'état Portugais des Indes Orientales, 1517–1635* (Paris, 1982); *Mito e mercadoria, utopia e prática de navegar, séculos XIII–XVIII* (Lisbon, 1990); and especially the second edition of *Os descobrimentos e a economia mundial* (4 vols., Lisbon, 1981–1983). The *Cambridge Economic History of India*, vol. 1 (Cambridge, 1982), edited by Irfan Habin and Tapan Raychaudhuri, contains several chapters of interest, especially Ashin Das Gupta's "Indian Merchants and the Trade in the Indian Ocean." His book on Surat's merchants, *Indian Merchants and the Decline of Surat, c. 1700–1750* (Wiesbaden, 1979, repr. New Delhi, 1994), is the best description of the merchants of one particular port city that we have. Several of his articles are also reprinted in his book *Merchants of Maritime India, 1500–1800* (Aldershot, 1994). Two books by K. N. Chaudhuri contain good information on merchants and port cities: *Asia before Europe: Economy and Civilisation of the Indian Ocean from the Rise of Islam to 1750* (Cambridge, 1990); and *Trade and*

Civilisation in the Indian Ocean: An Economic History from the Rise of Islam to 1750 (Cambridge, 1985). Pius Malekandathil has written a very good book on an important port city: *Portuguese Cochin and the Maritime Trade of India, 1500–1663* (New Delhi, 2001). Two useful overviews edited by Sanjay Subrahmanyam are *Merchants, Markets and the State in Early Modern India* (Delhi, 1990) and *Merchant Networks in the Early Modern World* (Aldershot, 1996). Both include useful introductions followed by a series of reprinted articles, many of which are relevant to the Indian Ocean area. In the first of these books, the relevant articles are by Subrahmanyam, Brennig, Prakash, Arasaratnam, and Bayly with Subrahmanyam, and in the second volume are articles by Wang, Subrahmanyam, Khatchikian, and Arasaratnam. Rene Barendse published a brilliant book on the Arabian Seas in the second half of the seventeenth century that includes masses of information relevant to our topic, *The Arabian Seas, 1640–1700* (Leiden, 1998). A revised American edition is called *The Arabian Seas: The Indian Ocean World of the Seventeenth Century* (Armonk, NY, 2002). Reference must also be made to Barendse's short overview, "Trade and State in the Arabian Seas: A Survey from the Fifteenth to the Eighteenth Century," *Journal of World History*, 11 (2000), pp. 173–225. For the early modern period, the standard text on the Indian Ocean is Ashin Das Gupta and M. N. Pearson, eds., *India and the Indian Ocean, 1500–1800* (Calcutta, 1987, 2nd ed. Delhi, 1999). An attempt at a broad overview is Michael Pearson's *The Indian Ocean* (London, 2003). There is also a valuable collection of studies in Denys Lombard and Jean Aubin, eds., *Marchands et hommes d'affairs Asiatiques dans l'Océan Indien et la Mer de Chine 13ᵉ–20ᵉ siècles* (Paris, 1988), now available in English as *Asian Merchants and Businessmen in the Indian Ocean and the China Sea* (New Delhi, 2000). An equally useful collection is Roderich Ptak and Dietmar Rothermund, eds., *Emporia, Commodities and Entrepreneurs in Asian Maritime Trade, c. 1400–1750* (Stuttgart, 1991). Patricia Risso has written a very valuable overview of the role of Muslim merchants: *Merchants and Faith: Muslim Commerce and Culture in the Indian Ocean* (Boulder, CO, 1995). A study by Claude Markovits of Indian merchants under British rule still has useful ideas for those working on an earlier period; see his *The Global World of Indian Merchants, 1750–1947: Traders of Sind from Bukhara to Panama* (Cambridge, 2000).

Many books dealing primarily with the arrival of Europeans in the Indian Ocean include much material of use for us. James D. Tracy's two edited volumes, *The Rise of Merchant Empires: Long-Distance Trade in the Early Modern World, 1350–1750* (Cambridge, 1990) and *The Political Economy of Merchant Empires: State Power and World Trade, 1350–1750* (Cambridge, 1991), contain useful chapters by, in the former, Steensgaard, Habib, and Wang, and in the latter by Pearson, Subrahmanyam and Thomaz, and Chaudhuri. On the

Swahili Coast, see M. N. Pearson, *Port Cities and Intruders: The Swahili Coast, India, and Portugal in the Early Modern Era* (Baltimore, 1998). For overviews of the role of the early Europeans, all of which pay considerable attention to what was happening to their Asian interlocutors, see the now somewhat dated collection edited by Blair B. Kling and M. N. Pearson, which put forward an overly sanguine view of early Asian–European relations: *The Age of Partnership: Europeans in Asia before Dominion* (Honolulu, HI, 1979). For the Portuguese, see Sanjay Subrahmanyam, *The Portuguese Empire in Asia, 1500–1700: A Political and Economic History* (London, 1993); M. N. Pearson, *The Portuguese in India* (Cambridge, 1987); and especially the numerous fundamental studies of Luis Filipe F. R. Thomaz, which relate especially to Southeast Asia and Malacca; see his *De Ceuta a Timor*, 2nd ed. (Lisbon, 1998). The first section of Om Prakash's *European Commercial Enterprise in Pre-colonial India* (Cambridge, 1998) is an intelligent overview. For major and relatively successful reform efforts in the late seventeenth century, see Glenn Ames's important study, *Renascent Empire? Pedro II and the Quest for Stability in Portuguese Monsoon Asia ca. 1640–1682* (Amsterdam, 1999). A. J. R. Russell-Wood has provided an excellent overview of connections between the far-flung parts of the Portuguese empire in his *A World on the Move: The Portuguese in Africa, Asia, and America, 1415–1808* (New York, 1992). Our knowledge of nonofficial trade has been greatly extended by James C. Boyajian's *Portuguese Trade in Asia under the Habsburgs, 1580–1640* (Baltimore, 1993). Pius Malekandathil's *The Germans, the Portuguese and India* (Munster, 1999) highlights the German presence and includes a useful overview of the career of Ferdinand Cron. For the English and Dutch, see the rest of Prakash's *European Commercial Enterprise*, cited earlier, and Holden Furber's classic *Rival Empires of Trade in the Orient, 1600–1800* (Minneapolis, 1976). Niels Steensgaard's *The Asian Trade Revolution of the Seventeenth Century: The East India Companies and the Decline of the Caravan Trade* (Chicago, 1974) is a seminal work that has provoked much controversy. Sinnappah Arasaratnam has written a series of important books on the Coromandel Coast of India and merchants in the Indian Ocean in general: *Maritime Commerce and English Power: Southeast India, 1750–1800* (Aldershot, 1996); *Maritime India in the Seventeenth Century* (Delhi, 1994); and *Merchants, Companies and Commerce on the Coromandel Coast, 1650–1740* (Delhi, 1986). Two classic books on the Malay world are J. C. Van Leur's *Indonesian Trade and Society: Essays in Asian Social and Economic History* (The Hague, 1955) and M. A. P. Meilink-Roelofsz's *Asian Trade and European Influence in the Indonesian Archipelago between 1500 and about 1630* (The Hague, 1962). Much more modern is Anthony Reid's two-volume *Southeast Asia in the Age of Commerce, 1450–1680* (2 vols., New Haven, CT, 1988–1993). On East Asia, see George

Bryan Souza's *The Survival of Empire: Portuguese Trade and Society in China and the South China Sea, 1630–1754* (Cambridge, 1986), and for an excellent overview, although now a little dated, see a review article by John E. Wills, Jr., that discusses the literature available at the time he wrote: "Maritime Asia, 1500–1800: The Interactive Emergence of European Domination," *American Historical Review* 98 (1993), pp. 83–105.

4

THE ECONOMIC NETWORK OF PORTUGAL'S ATLANTIC WORLD

Luiz Felipe de Alencastro

Translated by Marguerite Itamar Harrison

Portugal's longest-lasting sphere of influence as a colonial power occurred in the Atlantic, where it also amassed its greatest expanse of territory and concentrated its most important influence overseas.[1] From Senegambia to the Gulf of Guinea and Angola to Brazil, a complex of exchanges and economic activities, predominantly based in slave trade and slavery, encompassed and transformed the Portuguese Atlantic. Hence, a study of this region must consider the evolution of the main territorial enclaves under Lisbon's control – in the Upper Guinea, the Gulf of Guinea, Central Africa, and South America – and its interaction over several issues: cycles of agricultural production, mercantile exchange between the colonies and the kingdom, and intercolonial trade. Factors influencing territorial occupation should also be taken into account: "factories" in West Africa; the constant pillaging by colonial war and trade in Angola; native and foreign sources of labor in Portuguese America; land, river, and sea transportation; the dynamics of sugar production; cattle breeding; the advent of gold mining; and the interregional division of labor in eighteenth-century Brazil.

The Formation of the Portuguese Atlantic

Upper Guinea

In Upper Guinea, natives navigated the Senegal, Cacheu, and Gambia rivers to transport inland goods to the coast. A network of trade within the Niger

[1] Parts of this chapter are based on my book *O trato dos viventes: Formação do Brasil no Atlântico Sul, séculos XVI e XVII* (São Paulo, 2000).

basin extended outward from the Senegal River, forming a mercantile system of fluvial and land routes that connected Senegambia with the Gulf of Guinea. Whites and mulattoes of Portuguese origin, called *lançados* or *tangomaus*, traveled the rivers of Upper Guinea exchanging local and foreign goods. The *lançados*, including adventurers, deportees, and Jewish exiles, expanded Portuguese dealings in the inland.[2] Increasingly, sub-Saharan societies came to recognize the mercantile value of the slave, a fact that underscored an essential difference between precolonial Africa and America. In African areas where such preconditions did not exist, commercial exchanges proved to be more problematic for the Portuguese.

By the end of the sixteenth century, royal officers, merchants, and missionaries had come to fear these West African areas as a breeding ground for disease and a target for privateers. Gradually, the Cape Verdean archipelago and Upper Guinea were left out in favor of ports in the Gulf of Guinea and Central Africa, where Angola was given a governor (1571) and turned into a new diocese alongside the Kongo kingdom (1596). Although they also exported wax, ivory, and furs, the main activity of the Portuguese in Cacheu and Bissau was slave trading. In the seventeenth century, this trade was directed toward Spanish America and the Atlantic offshore islands; by the second half of the eighteenth century, it was reoriented toward the northern part of Portuguese America. There is evidence of an important trade in local textiles (*panos da Costa*) woven from Cape Verdean cotton exported to the African continent. Between 1756 and 1777, this Cape Verdean cloth paid for 23 percent of the 20,000 slaves exported from Cacheu and Bissau to Pará and Maranhão, Brazil.[3] Further activities were also developed by the Portuguese in the Gulf of Guinea.

Gulf of Guinea and São Tomé: A Laboratory for Tropical Slavery

In 1471, when King Afonso V initiated maritime trade with gold prospectors on the Volta River, the Akan, he achieved one of the original goals of the 1415 conquest of Ceuta: to break the Muslim monopoly on the transportation of Guinean gold across the Sahara. The fortress of São Jorge da Mina, later known as El Mina, was built in 1482, east of the Cape of Three Points, on the Gulf of Guinea. Guinean gold required neither European penetration of the hinterland nor processing onsite (as would later be the

[2] Jean Boulègue, *Les Luso-Africains de Sénégambie XVIe–XIXe siècles* (Lisbon, 1989); Philip D. Curtin, *Economic Change in Precolonial Africa – Senegambia in the Era of Slave Trade* (2 vols., Madison, WI, 1975).

[3] Antonio Carreira, *Os Portugueses nos rios de Guiné, 1500–1900* (Lisbon, 1984), pp. 65–66.

case in Minas Gerais, Brazil) and was worth twice as much once it reached Europe.

Yet, Lisbon also set up commercial arrangements that shared European, Asian, and African merchandise in a coastal exchange. Slaves purchased from the Portuguese by the Akan at the trading post of El Mina were used as carriers and miners, as well as for other activities. From 1482, when the fortress was built, to the beginning of regular slave trade to Brazil in the mid-sixteenth century, the Portuguese at El Mina sold approximately 30,000 individuals from the Slave Coast and the Congo basin.[4] All ships in the area dropped anchor at São Tomé, occupied in 1484 as a trading base in the Gulf of Guinea. There were two harbors linking the African continent and the island: El Mina, and Mpinda at the mouth of the Congo River.

Methods developed on Cape Verde Madeira, and São Tomé to introduce Portuguese and Luso-African forms of slavery and sugar plantations in the tropics were transferred on a large scale to Portuguese America. Techniques of farming, raising acclimatized cattle, trading and controlling slaves, developing a labor force of both free and enslaved men familiar with the colonial system and immune to tropical diseases, and appropriate dietary and medicinal practices were later to be implemented in Brazil. Thus, aside from direct migration from Portugal, the Atlantic islands created a Luso-tropical vector for the expansion and adaptation of the Portuguese in America.[5]

The slave diet, consisting of American and African products, was an important element in the economic system that linked Luso-African ports to enclaves in Portuguese America. In Central Africa, in addition to American products such as sweet potatoes and maize, manioc flour was the staple food of slaves, soldiers, seafarers, rivermen, and all others involved in the South Atlantic system. Given the absence of natural pests, manioc culture became widespread, and today it is harvested from south of the Sahara to southern Angola and Mozambique, emerging as the most important primary source for calories in Africans' diet. In the reverse direction, the banana and African sorghum were transplanted to Portuguese America in this exchange of foods, diseases, peoples, and colonial practices across the South Atlantic. In the first decades of the eighteenth century, *bandeirantes* (slave raiders) from São Paulo who forged westward introduced the banana into Mato Grosso. From that point on, the banana joined the native rice crop in becoming the staple diet of the Indians of Brazil's midwest.

[4] J. B. Ballong-Wen-Mewuda, *São Jorge da Mina, 1482–1637* (2 vols., Paris, 1993).

[5] C. A. Garcia, "A Ilha de São Tomé como centro experimental do comportamento do luso nos trópicos," *Studia* 19 (1966), pp. 209–221.

In the mid-sixteenth century, colonists of São Tomé began to trade with Benin and El Mina. Later, Mpinda emerged as the leading port for exports in Central Africa, attracting Congo's markets to the Atlantic system. Slaves, ivory, and copper became trade goods along the coast.[6] São Tomé re-exported to Portuguese America slaves more resistant to diseases, already able to talk in the "São Tomé tongue," a generic Luso-African language, and sometimes trained on sugar plantations. Nevertheless, in the last quarter of the sixteenth century, several slave insurrections arose in São Tomé, disrupting sugar production and slave trade activities.

With the falling demand for slaves in Portugal itself and in Madeira, Cape Verde, and São Tomé, the slave trade took on a transatlantic configuration. The deportation of Africans to Brazilian ports reached new heights in the first decades of the seventeenth century, when the shift resulting in the alliance between the Portuguese and some factions of Jága warriors unleashed a massive plundering of the peoples of Angola and Central Africa.

Angola and the Iberian-American Market

By acquiring a monopoly of the *asientos* (royal contracts for supplying African slaves to Spanish America) during the period when Portugal and Spain were under the same crown, Portuguese slave traders, shipowners, and well-to-do merchants gained control over the Hispanic-American slave trade. Through business transactions from the Court of Madrid to the overseas ports on the periphery, cosmopolitan investors were able to engage in the trade of Angolan slaves.[7]

A series of financial and merchant operations made by Antonio Fernandez de Elvas – the purchase of the *asiento* and the acquisition of the *contrato* (the royal contract for collecting taxes) for Cape Verde and Angola (1615–1622) – corresponded with a shift in Portuguese investment from the Indian Ocean to the Atlantic, a move sparked by the Anglo-Dutch offensive in Asia, the end of the pepper cycle, and the economic crisis in Portuguese India.[8] Leaving the Guinean ports, considered too exposed to European rivals, Elvas concentrated his activities on the coast of Angola, consolidating the trade and routes that would gain predominance in the following decades. Driven by the demands of the *asiento*, Portuguese military initiatives enlarged the

[6] Jan Vansina, *Kingdoms of the Savannahs* (Madison, WI, 1975).

[7] Enriqueta Vila Vilar, *Hispano-America y el comercio de esclavos – Los Asientos Portugueses* (Seville, 1977).

[8] James C. Boyajian, *Portuguese Bankers at the Court of Spain, 1626–1640* (New Brunswick, NJ, 1983); Boyajian, *Portuguese Trade in Asia under the Habsburgs, 1580–1640* (Baltimore, 1993).

occupation of Central Africa, an expanse of territory under direct European control as in no other African region. A line of fortresses and trading posts guided inland exchanges toward Luanda and Benguela, allowing territorial bases in Central Africa that ensured Portugal's dominion in the South Atlantic for several centuries.

The overlap between the colonial plundering and overseas trade reached an unparalleled intensity in the Angolan territory. In truth, pillage and trade complemented one another. As was noticed in 1782 by a Luso-Brazilian expert in Angola, when imported merchandise became devalued or locals blocked routes and the exchange of goods, pillage and military raids helped to generate a new cycle of demand for Portuguese and Brazilian goods in the inland markets of Central Africa.[9]

In the first half of the seventeenth century, a time of diminishing royal revenue and increasing military expenses overseas, investments of the private *asientista* (contractor) sector helped to expand Portugal's dominion over Central Africa. After the Restoration (1640) and the subsequent war against Spain, Portuguese resources, including trade exchanges, naval equipment, and the infrastructure generated by *asientista* funds formerly invested in the South Atlantic, were transferred to the slave-trading system connected with Brazil. Faced with the rising need for coerced labor in Brazil's sugar production, Portuguese, Luso-Africans, and Luso-Brazilians together established the largest slave market in the Atlantic. Those macroeconomic factors stimulated the expansion of the African slave trade and restrained the use of Indian coerced labor in Portuguese America.

Native states structured around commercial dealings involving the inland and the coast emerged in West and Central Africa. The kingdom of Ndongo, next to Luanda, collapsed under European attacks.[10] The kingdoms of Matamba and Kassanje, however, located in the Angolan hinterland, were strengthened throughout the seventeenth century by the Atlantic slave trade. During the following century, the kingdom of Dahomey took advantage of European rivalries along the coast to affirm its independence and to profit from slave trade with the Europeans. In Portuguese America, nothing of the sort occurred. Indian tribes did not go through social change aimed at involving themselves in the slave trade. Moreover, capital investment in schemes related to indigenous slaves proved incompatible with the colonial system. Such ventures collided with a dynamic sphere of commercial capital

9 Elias Alexandre da Silva Correa, *História de Angola* (1782) (2 vols., Lisbon, 1937), vol. 2, p. 15.

10 Beatrix Heintze, "Das Ende des unbhängigen States Ndongo (Angola) – Neue Chronologie und Reinterpretation 1617–1630," *Paideuma* 27 (1981), pp. 197–273.

(invested in the African slave trade), with the crown's fiscal system (linked to the African slave trade), with imperial politics (based on the complementary exploitation of Portuguese America and Portuguese Africa), and, finally, with missionary activities and the crown's ideological apparatus (promoting the evangelization of the Indians, not their enslavement). In fact, the contingencies of the Indian policy of Portugal appear more clearly in the Amazon basin.

The Amazon Basin and the Estado do Brasil

In 1621 the crown divided Portuguese America into two political entities, the Estado do Grão-Pará e Maranhão (including North captaincies as well as the Amazon basin) and the Estado do Brasil. The economics of resource extraction in the Amazon region encompassing the Estado do Grão-Pará e Maranhão was quite peculiar. Because of the maritime conditions created by the Guyana currents, it was easier to travel from Maranhão to Lisbon than from Maranhão to Bahia or Rio de Janeiro. These geographical facts also helped shape the Amazon area's distinct administrative and economic character, as contrasted with the Estado do Brasil.

In view of these differences, it seems more appropriate to compare the Portuguese Amazon with French and English Canada in the seventeenth and eighteenth centuries or even to the Missouri River valley and the Rocky Mountains in the first decades of the nineteenth century, following the transfer of Louisiana to the United States. Much like the North American fur trade, the process of extracting natural resources from the Amazon forest was based on inelastic demand. From the start, Amazonian collectors, rivermen, and itinerant traders lived in constant debt to merchants who furnished them with goods and services on credit. Any increase in supply would mean a decrease in export prices, which in turn affected the Amazon market.

Grão-Pará and Maranhão exported cloves collected from the forest as well as small amounts of cultivated cacao and tobacco in the seventeenth century. Additional products later joined the bounty: parsley, indigo, and other vegetable derivatives such as *copaíba* balsam, which was used both as a dye and as a medicine. One major difference distinguishing the expansion of Canada from that of the Amazon region lay in the latter's exploitation of Indian coerced labor. Amazonian natives were used not only to collect forest products and harvest but also as rowers for the canoes that served as the region's primary means of transportation.[11] The few data available

[11] Roberta M. Delson, "Inland Navigation in Colonial Brazil: Using Canoes on the Amazon," *International Journal of Maritime History* 7 (1995), no. 1, pp. 1–28.

show a high mortality among Indians used as rowers by settlers, traders, missionaries, and royal troops. Hoping to eliminate the conflict between the Jesuits and the local authorities and colonists over the control of the Indians, the crown created the Companhia do Estanco do Maranhão (1679). This trading company was to develop the exports from Maranhão and supply African slaves to the colonists.

Beset by difficulties, the Companhia got off to a shaky start when trade in the Portuguese Atlantic plummeted as a result of a recession in the European economy. In consequence, the company was able to enforce its monopoly over the exports of Maranhão but could not fulfill its agreement for supplying Africans to the colonists. Conceived by the Jesuit Antonio Vieira, the charter called for another significant stipulation: By a royal order of 1680, the enslavement of Indians was to be curtailed. Intervention by the crown thus operated in two complementary ways: It allowed the African slave trade into the region and narrowed the ability of colonists to make use of the natives' labor. The second part of the project, the constraints on access to Indian labor, was implemented, but the first part (the African slave trade) was not put into practice, provoking protests against the Companhia's monopoly. After a colonists' revolt in 1684, the crown increasingly relied on the help of Jesuits. In 1686, a new law gave the Jesuits control over the natives.[12]

Jesuit missions in the Amazon experienced a period of economic and demographic growth following the commercial recovery in colonial and world markets in the first half of the eighteenth century. However, the Jesuits' wealth and, especially, their influence over the Indians, motivated envy and anger among colonists and local authorities and led to their downfall. In 1759, the crown expelled the Society of Jesus from overseas colonies, as well as from Portugal itself, and confiscated all of its assets.[13] At the same time, the crown organized a major operation – this time a successful one – in order to incorporate the Amazon region into Portugal's Atlantic network. Royal decrees definitively prohibited indigenous enslavement and at the same time promoted new agricultural business ventures. Fiscal subsidies sustained the two northern captaincies. Furthermore, a new trading company – the Companhia Geral do Grão-Pará e do Maranhão (CGGPM) – began to enforce its commercial monopoly while promoting the Atlantic

[12] Mathias C. Kiemen, *The Indian Policy of Portugal in the Amazon Region, 1614–1693* (New York, 1973).

[13] Dauril Alden, "Economic Aspects of the Expulsion of the Jesuits from Brazil: A Preliminary Report," in H. H. Keith and S. F. Edwards, eds., *Conflict and Continuity in Brazilian Society* (Columbia, SC, 1969), pp. 15–45.

slave trade. Africans from Angola and Upper Guinea were regularly sold to the planters of the Amazonian coast from 1755 to 1778.[14]

The significance of these measures was made clear by the sequence of three royal decrees elaborated by the Marquis of Pombal and signed by King José I on June 6 and 7, 1755. The first decree granted freedom to the Indians, the second transferred the control of the villages administered by the Jesuits to royal authorities, and the third established the CGGPM. To link the Amazonian economy with Portugal, the authorities first had to connect it with the African slave trade, a decisive factor for integration into the Atlantic market. Receiving also the government of Cacheu from the crown, the CGGPM was able to incorporate Upper Guinea into the Portuguese American slave trade. From 1756 to 1801, approximately 38,000 Africans from that region entered Amazonian ports. Rice transplanted from the Carolinas and coffee from the French Caribbean, along with cotton and cacao, began to be grown in the region, which, in the last decades of the eighteenth century, became one of the chief areas of economic recovery for Portuguese America.[15] Similar to the influence of the Caribbean in the north Amazon, Brazil was attracted by the Rio de la Plata system in the South.

Southern Brazil and the Rio de la Plata Region

Two economic ties connected the Rio de la Plata basin and Lower Peru with Brazil in the first half of the seventeenth century. The first was the *peruleiro* network linking Rio de Janeiro with Buenos Aires, which was characteristically sea-based, related to the African slave trade, and spurred by the smuggling of silver from Potosí. The second link, between São Paulo and Paraguay, was land-based and depended on the capture and use of Indian slaves in São Paulo's regional economy.

São Paulo, a peripheral region in the Atlantic system, developed as the provider of food staples to the rest of the colony, foreshadowing a similar situation that would propel the agriculture of Minas Gerais at the end of the eighteenth century. Towns in the north of Brazil and even as far as Angola imported *paulista* manioc flour and wheat flour, maize, beans, cured meats, lard, sausages, quince paste, crude fabrics, and cotton jackets resistant to natives' arrows. Iberian troops sent to the northern captaincies during the

[14] Manuel Nunes Dias, *A Companhia Geral do Grão-Pará e Maranhão (1755–1778)* (Belém, 1970).

[15] Antonio Carreira, *As Companhias Pombalinas de Grão-Pará e Maranhão, e Pernambuco e Paraíba* (Lisbon, 1983).

war against the Dutch occupation (1630–1654) relied also on food staples exported from São Paulo. European goods such as salt, fabrics, spices, wine, tools, and gunpowder traveled in the reverse direction, through Santos to São Paulo, always carried by Indians. This constant transportation of merchandise, materials, and goods accelerated the use of Indian slaves on *paulista* routes as well as in agriculture.[16] It might be assumed that the number of Indians captured and put in captivity in the period 1625–1650 surpassed the number of Africans introduced to Dutch and Portuguese Brazil during the same period. On a global scale, the number of slaves from sub-Saharan Africa imported to Western markets (that is, to the Iberian Peninsula, Atlantic islands, and the Americas) adds up to fewer than 150,000 individuals during this quarter century.[17] Therefore, slave raids by *bandeirantes* during the years 1627–1640, concentrated in the region of the Guairá-Tapes and involving the capture of close to 100,000 Indians, constituted one of the most rapacious enslavement operations in modern history.

Data elaborated by Stuart Schwartz point to a sharp increase in the average cost paid for Africans in Bahia during the second quarter of the seventeenth century. Other figures, gathered by Joseph Miller, demonstrate that from 1640 to 1650 the difference separating the price of slaves in Angola and the price in Brazil reached the highest level recorded in the century.[18] Finally, the most noticeable increase in the capture of Indians by the *bandeiras paulista* (slave raiders from São Paulo) occurred precisely during the period in which a halt in the Atlantic slave trade caused the price of Africans to double in Portuguese America.

Reflecting the differences between the *peruleiros* from Rio de Janeiro and the São Paulo Indian raiders, a new geographical pattern emerged in the South Atlantic. Steered toward the Tropic of Capricorn, the subequatorial seafaring routes drew Rio de Janeiro into a maritime economy. Indian-hunting expeditions were abandoned in favor of naval projects, the African

[16] John M. Monteiro, "From Indian to Slave: Forced Native Labor and Colonial Society in São Paulo during the Seventeenth Century," *Slavery and Abolition* 9 (1988), pp. 105–127; Monteiro, *Negros da terra – Índios e bandeirantes nas origens de São Paulo* (São Paulo, 1994).

[17] Herbert S. Klein, *The Atlantic Slave Trade – New Approaches to the Americas* (Cambridge, 1999), pp. 210–211; D. Eltis, Stephen D. Behrendt, and David Richardson, *The Volume of the Transatlantic Slave Trade: The Participation of National Groups in Europe and the Americas*, unpublished paper, 1999, discussed in Luiz Felipe de Alencastro, *O trato dos viventes*, appendix 7.

[18] S. B. Schwartz, *Sugar Plantations in the Formation of Brazilian Society: Bahia, 1550–1835* (Cambridge, 1985); Joseph C. Miller, "Slave Prices in the Portuguese Southern Atlantic, 1600–1830," in Paul E. Lovejoy, ed., *Africans in Bondage* (Madison, WI, 1986), pp. 43–77.

slave trade, and exchanges with the Plata region. Political consequences arose from the divergence between the sea-based, African slave-related, intercolonial network initiated by settlers from Rio de Janeiro and the undertakings of the *paulistas*, which were oriented toward the inland and the Indians and which tended to be anti-Portugal and anti-Jesuit. In fact, the Indian-slave economy encouraged the sense of autonomy that flourished along the São Paulo plateau.

Gradually, the port of Rio de Janeiro attained a hegemonic position in Brazil. Detached from the Serra do Mar mountain range, Rio de Janeiro assumed a maritime role as early as the seventeenth century, a position underscored a century later when it came to serve as the port city for Minas Gerais and as the capital of the viceroyalty (1763). Rio's dominance as a port would facilitate the territorial administration of the national government after independence (1822). In the nineteenth century, two-thirds of Brazil's foreign trade would pass through the capital of the Brazilian empire.

Several important events took place in the second half of the seventeenth century during the Rio de Janeiro offensive to amass African slaves and Peruvian silver from the ancillary regions of Angola and the Rio de la Plata.[19] The first event involved the joint Portugal–Rio de Janeiro expedition to retake Angola from the Dutch in 1648. The second, the settlement of Laguna in 1674, was followed by the creation of the diocese of Rio de Janeiro in 1676, with a jurisdiction that extended as far as the mouth of the Rio de la Plata. The third event was related to the 1680 establishment of the Colônia do Sacramento next to Montevideo.

The mining of precious metals in Minas Gerais created a high demand for slaves and led to the abandonment of the Colônia do Sacramento. Nevertheless, as gold reserves declined in Minas Gerais in the last quarter of the eighteenth century, Rio de Janeiro slave traders reestablished the Luanda–Rio de Janeiro–Buenos Aires commercial triangle.

The Brazil–Angola Complex

Three main maritime routes articulate Angola and Brazil during the seventeenth century: to Recife (a 35-day voyage from Luanda), to Bahia (a 40-day voyage), and to Rio de Janeiro (a 50-day voyage). In the first quarter of the century, alongside contraband Peruvian silver, the Brazilian product at the center of this trade was manioc flour. Contemporary writers mentioned these exchanges, which may be termed a "manioc cycle"

[19] C. R. Boxer, *Salvador de Sá and the Struggle for Brazil and Angola, 1602–1686* (Westport, CT, 1975).

and reached its peak during the years 1590–1630. The pervasiveness of American products in the slaves' diet, manioc flour in particular, lowered freight costs to Brazil and African ports and contributed to the Africans' adaptation to Luso-Brazilian slavery.

South American products transplanted to Africa also reinforced local crops and increased the incursions of the captors and slave traders. The addition of maize and manioc flour as staples of the Jága troops' diet made it possible for these slave-hunting groups to expand their areas of capture. Both manioc and maize were also cultivated by the Jesuits and colonists on plantations in Angola in the second quarter of the seventeenth century. The export of cowrie (*zimbo*) from Bahia, in Brazil, had an even greater supportive effect on Luso-Brazilian commerce in Central Africa. Because shipments of Brazilian cowries to Africa followed a uniquely bilateral course, this commercial venture gained great significance in the South Atlantic. Since it was supplied out of Salvador or Rio de Janeiro without being taxed (with the consequence that we cannot accurately analyze the quantities exported), Bahian cowrie money escaped Portuguese control. Still, an important document from 1782 credits the weight of the cowries from Bahia in the Angolan trade.[20]

Cowrie money from Bahia, as well as manioc flour from Rio de Janeiro and even Bahian tobacco, penetrated African markets without competition from other exporters. The trade in Brazilian sugar cane liquor (called *jeribita* in Angola and *cachaça* in Brazil) was quite different. Exported from Bahia, Pernambuco, and Rio de Janeiro, *jeribita* competed with Portuguese and European wines and spirits sold in Central Africa beginning in the last decades of the seventeenth century. Thus, following pressure from wine and spirits exporters from Portugal, the crown prohibited the imports of Brazilian rum into Angola in 1679. Nevertheless, ten years later, accepting the demands of Luso-Brazilian *jeribita* producers, merchants, and slave traders from both sides of the South Atlantic, the crown again allowed this bilateral trade.[21]

Usually ignored or underestimated by historians of Brazil, the production of *cachaça* represents a particular instance of the overall transformations motivated by the "General Crisis," the economic crisis of the seventeenth century. As is well known, one of the solutions for overcoming the crisis in the West was the manufacture and marketing of new distilled alcoholic

[20] da Silva Correa, *História de Angola*, vol. 1, pp. 136–137.

[21] José C. Curto, *Alcohol and Slaves: The Lusobrazilian Commerce in Alcoholic Beverages with West-Central Africa (Mpinda, Luanda and Benguela) during the Atlantic Slave Trade, c. 1480–1830*, Ph.D. thesis, University of California, Los Angeles, 1988.

beverages.[22] In the sugarcane economy, the manufacture of *cachaça* increased slaveowners' profits while expanding the exploitation of slave labor. Exported to Central Africa, *jeribita* transferred the cost of slave reproduction from Brazil to the families and villages of Africa. *Jeribita*'s conquering of the African market rendered further profits to sugar mill owners, lowered maritime transportation costs, and assured Luso-Brazilian participation in the slave trade in Central Africa.

Based on the statistical analysis of a series of sugar mills in Bahia over the period from 1716 to 1816, Stuart Schwartz estimates that molasses and its derivative, *cachaça*, represented between 7 and 17 percent of the mills' annual income. In fact, these by-products increased sugar mill owners' gross profits by approximately 25 percent.[23] This was a significant percentage, especially during periods when sugar prices fell, as was the case during the years 1660–1690, precisely at the time that *jeribita* started to be exported to the Angolan market. An index taking into account *jeribita* prices – and not merely those of white sugar – would demonstrate that sugar mill owners must have continued to pay relatively low prices for African slaves during the second half of the seventeenth century. On a macroeconomic level, it is therefore important to take into account the advantages of *jeribita* production in the overall scope of Brazil's foreign trade.

Spanish exports of wine and spirits had traditionally prevented Portuguese liquor from dominating the Angolan market. By contrast, Brazilian *jeribita* was able to eliminate competitive products from Spain. A new market configuration altered distribution of Portuguese and Brazilian alcoholic beverages abroad. In the Northern Hemisphere, the sale of Portuguese wines to England stabilized trade between England and Portugal during the last decades of the seventeenth century, while in the Southern Hemisphere, *cachaça* improved exchanges involving Angola and Brazil and reduced imports of Spanish wines into Central Africa.[24] By 1800, when Europeans traded slaves from northern Angola and from the Congo to the

[22] Fernand Braudel, *Civilisation matérielle, économie et capitalisme XVème–XVIIIè siècles* (3 vols., Paris, 1979), vol. 1, pp. 194–213; I. Wallerstein, *The Modern World-System*, vol. 2 (New York, 1980), pp. 140–141; John J. McCusker, *Rum and the American Revolution: The Rum Trade and the Balance of Payments of the Thirteen Continental Colonies, 1650–1775* (New York, 1989), pp. 55–60. With regard to the global economic crisis of the seventeenth century, sometimes referred to as the "General Crisis," see Geoffrey Parker and Lesley M. Smith, eds., *The General Crisis of the Seventeenth Century* (London, 1978).

[23] Schwartz, *Sugar Plantations*, pp. 145–146 and 185–189, graphic p. 167.

[24] J. V. Serrão, "O quadro econômico, configurações estruturais e tendências de evolução," in J. Mattoso, *História de Portugal*, vol. 4 (Lisbon, 1994), pp. 80–81 and table 1.

Caribbean – where the price of slaves was double that recorded in Brazil – the sale of *jeribita*, considered by the natives to be "the most precious drink," provided the continuity of Portuguese and Luso-Brazilian exchanges in the region. José Curto estimates that in the period 1710–1830, Brazilian rum purchased 25 percent of the slaves exported from Central Africa to Portuguese America.[25]

In the same way that *jeribita* helped Luso-Brazilians obtain a share of the Central African market, the tobacco trade helped colonists to penetrate the Gulf of Guinea. Tobacco was cultivated primarily in Bahia, Pernambuco, and Maranhão, and to a lesser degree in Rio de Janeiro and Minas Gerais. The crown had monopolized the tobacco trade since 1634. In general, the Portuguese market absorbed one-fifth to one-quarter of Brazilian tobacco exports to Europe in the seventeenth century. Portugal then re-exported the remaining tobacco to other European and Asian markets, an enterprise that would become more significant in the eighteenth century.[26] As with the *jeribita* exported to Central Africa, this trade was characterized by the bilateral relations linking Bahia and the Slave Coast. In a total of 1,410 voyages from Bahia and Pernambuco, 8,131,000 arrobas (a measure of weight equivalent to 14.7 kg) of tobacco were exported to the Slave Coast in the eighteenth century. About 575,000 slaves from that region were brought into Bahia and Pernambuco during the same period. Together, Brazilian exports of *jeribita* and tobacco were used to purchase 48 percent of the 2,027,000 slaves that arrived in Portuguese America between 1701 and 1810.[27] Considering also the exports of horses, leather, manioc flour, maize, sugar, and dried and cured meats and fish, as well as the contraband of gold and diamonds, it is possible to conclude that more than half of the Africans introduced into Portuguese

[25] José Curto, personal communication.

[26] Jean-Baptiste Nardi, *O fumo Brasileiro no período colonial* (São Paulo, 1996), pp. 115, 125, 150, 163, 366–369; Catherine Lugar, "The Portuguese Tobacco Trade and Tobacco Growers of Bahia in the Late Colonial Period," in Susan Socolow, ed., *The Atlantic Staple Trade: The Economics of Trade*, vol. 2 (Brookfield, VT, 1996). The trade of Brazilian tobacco in Portuguese India is studied in Francisco Bethencourt, "O Estado da Índia," in F. Bethencourt and K. Chaudhuri, eds., *Historia da Expansão Portuguesa* (Lisbon, 1998), vol. 2, pp. 284–314.

[27] José Ribeiro Júnior, *Colonização e monopólio no Nordeste Brasileiro* (São Paulo, 1976), pp. 130–131; Pierre Verger, *Flux et reflux de la traite de nègres entre le golfe de Bénin et Bahia de Todos os Santos, du XVIIe au XIXe siècle* (Paris, 1968); Patrick Manning, "The Slave Trade in the Bight of Benin, 1640–1890," in H. Gemery and J. Hogendorn, *The Uncommon Market* (New York, 1979), table 4.5, p. 138; Eltis, Behrendt, and Richardson, *The Volume of the Transatlantic Slave Trade.*

America in the eighteenth century were eventually purchased with Brazilian goods.[28]

This explanation must take into account the primary system of navigation in the South Atlantic. It is known that the Saint Helen anticyclone creates a wind pattern at the junction of the Benguela and subequatorial currents that benefited the bilateral trade between Brazil and Angola.

Data covering the period 1736–1770 show that the majority of ships docking at Luanda were primarily of Brazilian origin: 41 percent coming from Rio de Janeiro, 22 percent from Pernambuco, 22 percent from Bahia, and only 15 percent from Lisbon.[29] Most of these ships returned directly to Brazilian harbors. In fact, unlike other African cargo, such as ivory and precious metals, live merchandise (i.e., slaves) could not endure a stopover in Lisbon and had to arrive promptly at its Brazilian destination. As mentioned earlier, most Africans sent to Bahia from the Slave Coast were part of this bilateral trade pattern. Consequently, two types of complementary, though distinct, routes of exchange came into being: Brazil–Portugal and Brazil–Africa. This bilateral system did not correspond to the triangle trade route, which Herbert Klein quite correctly referred to as "the myth of the so-called triangle trade."[30]

There were striking differences concerning the commercial dealings involving Bahia and trading posts at the Gulf of Guinea, on the one hand, and the trade that linked Angola and the rest of Brazil, especially Pernambuco and Rio de Janeiro, on the other. Portuguese economic politics in Angola deserve special attention. Whereas other slave-trading powers concentrated their activities on coastal posts, where trade was made with the local natives, Portugal went across a large territory in Angola and became the only European power to undertake official, large-scale military operations to hunt for slaves. Although these expeditions did not capture a large number of the slaves exported from Angola, their role was important in securing slave trade networks and opening new markets in the hinterland. With economic and military support from its American colonists, Lisbon assumed control of Central Africa and won the largest market of slaves of

[28] The trade of Brazilian horses to Angola and its impact on warfare in Angola were first studied on Roquinaldo A. Ferreira, *Transforming Atlantic Slaving: Trade, Warfare and Territorial Control in Angola, 1650–1800*, Ph. D. thesis, University of California, Los Angeles, 2003, pp. 183–236.

[29] C. Medeiros Dos Santos, "Relações de Angola com o Rio de Janeiro 1736–1808," *Estudos Históricos* 12 (1973), pp. 7–68, table 1, completed in Curto, *Alcohol and Slaves*, table IX, p. 109.

[30] Klein, *The Atlantic Slave Trade – New Approaches*, pp. 96–97.

Africa, which they exploited to consolidate greater holdings on the other side of the Portuguese Atlantic. Thus, the continuous destruction of Angola explains the simultaneous construction of Brazil.

The Occupation of Portuguese Africa

By the mid-seventeenth century, troops from Brazil – acclimatized to the tropical environment and battle-hardened in warfare against the Indians, Dutch, and runaway slaves who built their own fortified communities known as *quilombos* – were dispatched to Angola to help the Portuguese settlers there overcome African resistance and broaden the slave trade.[31] At least ten military expeditions recruited and equipped in Brazil crossed the South Atlantic to Luanda and Benguela up to the mid-eighteenth century. Periodic shipments of horses and individual soldiers from Brazil also strengthened Portuguese power in Central Africa. Still, the hostility of the natives and the epidemiological environment restricted the Portuguese territorial occupation and evangelization of Angola.

The crown's reasons for opting to establish trading posts and "factories" rather than pursuing the goal of territorial occupation and direct control were clearly spelled out in the debate over the journey to *contra costa* (the opposite coast), referring to the land route through Angola and Mozambique. From the end of the sixteenth century, the opening of land communications through the two coasts of southern Africa had been discussed in Lisbon. In 1696, the Overseas Council made an important decision on the matter. Because gold and ivory from East Africa were worth far more in India's markets, to which they were usually exported, than in Portugal, a trade route between Angola and Mozambique would have no economic advantages. The transportation of these goods to Lisbon through African hinterlands and along Atlantic routes would yield little profit and would undermine Portuguese trade in the Indian Ocean.

This decision closed the expansionist cycle in Central Africa unleashed by the reconquest of Angola led by Salvador de Sá in 1648. With regard to the establishment of a way from Angola to Mozambique, it is important not to interpret Lisbon's plans concerning this journey as so many lost opportunities to establish Portuguese domination in the entire southern Africa

[31] Questions related to economic and military issues on the Dutch War in Brazil are studied in Evaldo Cabral de Mello, *Olinda Restaurada – Guerra e Açúcar no nordeste, 1630–1654*, 2nd ed. (Rio de Janeiro, 1998).

area. Contrary to what Oliveira Martins has argued, we must be wary of attributing this inaction to a Portuguese failure to anticipate rival European actions. For that matter, neither should the scant number of Portuguese settlers be held to blame, nor the negative effects of the slave trade, as Jaime Cortesão has stated.[32] For all practical purposes, the colonial settlement of southern Africa was not essential to the overseas politics of the Portuguese crown, which favored commercial considerations over the broadening of its conquests. The arrival of imperialism at the end of the nineteenth century radically changed the pattern of colonial politics. Territories of uncertain dominion gained economic importance after the Industrial Revolution and the unification of the United States market at the end of the Civil War. These events paved the way for the "Second European Expansion," which characterizes the period 1870–1950. Hence, it is important to examine why Portuguese America became significantly extended and populated prior to this period.

The Repeopling of Portuguese America

Battles on overseas fronts during the Thirty Years War (called "The First World War" by Charles Boxer) exposed the vulnerability of the Portuguese on both sides of the South Atlantic, where natives turned to alliances with the Dutch invaders. Therefore, the Dutch retreat from Angola (1648) and Brazil (1654) instigated a wave of Portuguese and Luso-Brazilian retaliation against autonomous local communities. In Central Africa, the kingdom of Matamba and the kingdom of Kongo (at the Battle of Mbwila, 1665) were raided by Portuguese and Luso-Brazilian troops. At the same time, hostile Indian tribes and the African-Brazilian Quilombo de Palmares were destroyed in Brazil.[33]

At its beginning, the expansion of African slave labor in Portuguese America was irregular, and colonists as well as the authorities relied largely on Indian coerced labor. Nevertheless, in the mid-seventeenth century, the Overseas Council acknowledged that, following their demographic decline, the Indian communities were no longer able to sustain new economic activities. The constant flow of slaves from Africa, mainly from Angola, implied that the native communities no longer served as a potential reserve of enslaved labor to the colonists. Thus, Indians became an obstacle to the expansion of frontier agriculture and cattle ranches, opening the way to

[32] Jaime Cortesão, *O Ultramar Português depois da Restauração* (Lisbon, 1971), pp. 16 and 294.

[33] R. K. Kent, "Palmares: An African State in Brazil," *Journal of African History*, 6 (1965) no. 2, pp. 161–175.

offensives that aimed at their extermination. In this sense, the so-called Guerra dos Bárbaros (the War of the Barbarians) – a string of conflicts that decimated the natives on the cattle-breeding frontiers of North Brazil (1651–1704) – represented a break in the history of Portuguese America.[34] The politics of repeopling that spurred these conflicts relied on the introduction of Europeans and Africans to Portuguese America and in turn led to the decline of Indian communities squeezed to decimation by the unification of colonial outposts.[35]

The Cattle against the Indians

In fact, the process of repeopling expanded as the economic territory – previously restricted to the cane-growing coast – came to incorporate the backlands, where acclimatized cattle, originally imported from Cape Verde, were grazed. For the first time, the Portuguese promoted large-scale animal husbandry overseas. The results were of considerable importance.

Cattle ranches were as responsible as the Indian hunters for the devastation of native communities. Cattle herds introduced into Sergipe at the end of the sixteenth century multiplied and by mid-century were already an indispensable element in the sugar-producing economy and became a source of Luso-Dutch disputes in Portuguese America. By the end of the seventeenth century, cattle drovers had penetrated along the banks of the São Francisco River inland and toward Piauí and Maranhão. Another point of departure for South American internal migrations was the Plata estuary, where cattle herds and droving routes became established. In the following decades, cattle from these areas were sold in Minas Gerais. The convergence of the herds from the north, northeast, and south at the Minas Gerais marketplace led ultimately to the establishment of Brazil's current territorial borders. This process led to the colonial unification of the three major South American river basins: the Uruguay River, the São Francisco River, and the Amazon River.[36]

[34] Pedro Puntoni, *A Guerra dos Bárbaros – Povos indígenas e a colonização do sertão nordeste do Brasil, 1650–1720* (São Paulo, 2002).

[35] The process of colonial repeopling is discussed by A. M. Stevens-Arroyo, "The Inter-Atlantic Paradigm – The Failure of Spanish Medieval Colonization of the Canary and Caribbean Islands," *Comparative Studies in Society and History* 35 (1993), no. 3, pp. 515–543.

[36] Capistrano de Abreu, *Capítulos de História Colonial, 1500–1800* (Chapters of Brazil's Colonial History, 1500–1800), translated from the Portuguese, with a preface by Fernando A. Novais and an introduction by Stuart Schwartz (New York, 1997), chap. 9, pp. 91–165.

In addition to extending Brazil's territory, cattle breeding had an even more profound impact on Luso-Brazilian society. Meat from Brazil's interior improved the alimentary diet on coastal plantations and sugar mills, making it possible for the planters to concentrate the work of their slaves and their use of land on agricultural exports. Cattle ranches were also drawn into the Atlantic sphere by the increase in tobacco exports beginning in 1680 because bundles of tobacco shipped overseas (30,400 bundles in 1686) were wrapped in rawhide. At the same time, exports of leather soared.[37]

Rural ventures stimulated other forms of economic activity unrelated to slavery. African slaves may have been significant to individual ranchers, but the tenuous availability of mercantile capital, the nature of the production process, and the absence of masters' direct control greatly reduced the impact of the slave system in cattle areas. A distinct social class grew from the ranks of cowboys paid to manage the ranches and steer the cattle herds. Enslaved or free, those inland cowboys (*curraleiros*) had little to do with the slaves in the fields or with the farmhands who were dependent on sugar plantation masters. In time, these cattlemen would become one of the chief vehicles of economic expansion and the repeopling of Brazil.

Brazil's Gold at the Center of the Portuguese Atlantic

The Portuguese did not directly mine gold in El Mina, in Monomotapa, or in the Far East. The situation would be different, however, in Brazil. Brazilian gold mines were located deep in the interior of the country, so their discovery created new migrations and trade networks, thereby weakening the governing mechanisms of the empire. As they changed the distribution of factors of production, the gold mines reshaped the colonial territory.[38]

At first, the crown tried to channel the production of gold directly to the Atlantic ports in the hope of controlling the changes taking place in the hinterland. When the Caminho Novo (New Road) was built from Rio de Janeiro to Minas Gerais in 1701, the direct trade involving the gold region and Bahia was first prohibited but then later permitted again. In 1704, the connection between Minas Gerais and Espírito Santo was interrupted. In 1710, the crown established a system of territorial customs on all roads

[37] Dauril Alden, "Price Movements in Brazil before, during, and after the Gold Boom, with Special Reference to the Salvador Market, 1670–1769," in Lyman Johnson and Enrique Tandeter, eds., *Eighteenth-Century Price Movements in Latin America* (Albuquerque, NM, 1989).

[38] Mafalda P. Zemella, *Abastecimento da capitania de Minas Gerais no século XVIII* (São Paulo, 1990).

leading to Minas Gerais. This system consisted of *registros*, or tax-collection posts, through which *entradas*, or entry taxes, were collected. However, because of the 1711 victory of the Portuguese from the metropole (called *emboabas*, i.e., "foreigners") over the *paulistas* then established in the mining area, expansion to the west resumed. In 1720, royal decrees attempted to hinder migrations from Portugal to Minas Gerais. In 1725, gold deposits were discovered in Goiás, but communications through Goiás and Minas Gerais or Maranhão were soon interrupted (in 1730). Finally, in 1733, a moratorium was declared on all new roads to Minas Gerais. Geopolitical and fiscal factors would eventually bring about a reversal in Portuguese America's policies.

Unable to prevent the expansion of mining activities in the interior, the crown began to develop an interregional division of labor. These policies aimed at consolidating territorial occupation to secure new boundaries for Portuguese America during Luso-Spanish negotiations for the Treaty of Madrid (1750). The captaincy of Mato Grosso was established in 1748 in a region that still belonged to Spain. The land and fluvial route linking Mato Grosso to Belém, stretching 5,000 km along the rivers Madeira and Guaporé, was initially created in 1742 in defiance of royal law but was subsequently encouraged by the crown. African slaves introduced into Mato Grosso from Belém were exempt from entry fees in order to stimulate trade relations between the two captaincies (1752). For the same reasons, Belém do Pará was given exclusive rights to sell sea salt to the captaincy of Mato Grosso.[39]

Another important factor in the territorial occupation was the interregional market for mules. It was Luís Antonio de Sousa (the Morgado de Mateus), governor of São Paulo from 1765 to 1775, who was primarily responsible for new regulations governing the mule trade. Effectively, Sousa imposed territorial boundaries on the breeding of mules: The animals could only be sold in Minas Gerais if they had arrived at the markets of São Paulo (primarily Sorocaba) from the ranches of the region that is now Rio Grande do Sul. In a 1768 letter to the court, Sousa summarized his reasons for this policy. First, Minas Gerais already had an economic specialization, taking profits from gold activities, and did not require further income from the breeding of mules. Second, it was more advantageous for São Paulo to stimulate the interregional trade and the merchant capital, relying on the *entradas* (taxes imposed on the circulation of goods) rather than *dízimos* (tithe taxes imposed on regional products). Third, the sale of

[39] David M. Davidson, "How the Brazilian West Was Won: Free-lance and State on the Mato Grosso Frontier, 1737–1808," in Dauril Alden, ed., *Colonial Roots of Modern Brazil* (Los Angeles, 1983).

mules from the south would aid in unifying Portuguese America's economy and encourage settlement of the fields of the south, which bordered Spanish territories. These initiatives later received the support of the court.[40] The policies of the Morgado de Mateus took advantage of the sellers' market in Minas Gerais, prohibiting local breeding of an essential element of transportation, the mule, a nonreproductive hybrid animal. The deterritorialization of the mule's reproduction helps us understand the economic and geopolitical advantages of the deterritorialization of the reproduction of slaves – that is, the Atlantic slave trade. Because they had to buy slaves in Portuguese Africa, Luso-Brazilian colonists engaged in economic and regional specialization, increased the profits of the merchants and the crown's fiscal revenue, and spurred the expansion of the colonial settlements on both sides of the South Atlantic.

In order to control the territories received from Spain following the *uti possidetis* ("as you possess") ruling in the Treaty of Madrid, the crown stimulated an interregional division of labor centered in the mines. In the eighteenth century, tax-collection posts (*registros*) were established throughout Portuguese America, outlining the territorial and administrative bases of the coming Brazilian nation. From Viamão on the southern border, to Alcobaça in Pará in the Amazon basin, and from Cuiabá in the west up to Paraty on the Atlantic coast, at least 138 *registros* constellate the continental exchanges existing around the gold and diamond mines.

Markets created around the mine areas of Minas Gerais, Goiás, and Mato Grosso transformed Portuguese America's archipelago of economic enclaves into a unified territory. Therefore, the "gold cycle" was essentially different from the preceding "brazilwood cycle" and "sugar cane cycle." In fact, continuous access to the African slave market allowed the simultaneous preservation of old agricultural areas along the coast and the development of new economic regions in the interior. The intensification of the slave trade, however, served to increase the autonomy of Luso-Brazilian maritime commerce as distinct from direct exchanges with Portugal.

The Marquis de Pombal attempted to redress this balance by creating commercial companies predominantly funded by metropolitan investors. As mentioned earlier, the Companhia Geral do Grão-Pará e Maranhão, created in 1755 and active until 1788, was intended to transform an economy based on gathered products and forestry into an agricultural economy that would

[40] Dauril Alden, *Royal Government in Colonial Brazil; with Special Reference to the Administration of the Marquis of Lavradio, Viceroy, 1769–1779* (Berkeley, CA, 1968); Heloisa L. Belotto, *Autoridade e conflito no Brasil Colonial: O govêrno de Morgado de Mateus em São Paulo* (São Paulo, 1979).

link the Portuguese Amazon region with the Atlantic. The Companhia Geral de Pernambuco e Paraíba (1759–1786) encompassed the two named captaincies in addition to surrounding captaincies and the São Francisco River backlands. Consequently, all of Portuguese America north of the São Francisco River fell under the jurisdiction of the two chartered companies focused on the slave trade. Contrary to similar companies organized by the English, the Dutch, or the French, the intent of the Marquis de Pombal's ventures was not to link new mercantile routes overseas with existing commercial activity in the metropole; rather, they attempted to reintroduce the metropolitan interests in Portuguese areas conquered by the Luso-Brazilian trade.

The Marquis de Pombal's intervention had an impact as well – in a more original manner – on another portion of the market devoted to colonial labor: the administration of the Indians. Following the expulsion of the Jesuits, the Law Code (*Directorio*) compiled in 1757 for the administration of Amazon Indians (which in 1758 was extended to all native tribes throughout Brazil) deemed Indian labor to be complementary to African slave labor. Royal administrators attempted to direct Indian labor into auxiliary sectors of the Atlantic trade, including food production, transportation, and public works, such as the construction and maintenance of roads.[41] For the same reason, African slave labor was channeled to areas more directly related to the export market. Despite these efforts, the Marquis de Pombal was unable to impose his monopolistic trade system on Bahia and Rio de Janeiro. Bahia developed its own bilateral exchanges with the Slave Coast, whereas Rio de Janeiro penetrated more forcibly into the Angolan market, notably through the port of Benguela. In the second half of the eighteenth century, the mercantile area around this port was distinct from Luanda and closely tied to Rio de Janeiro.[42]

The increase of the slave trade, especially with Angola, promoted gold exploration in Brazil but also an expansion of the repeopling, an interregional division of labor, and the reinvigoration of agriculture for export. In the last quarter of the eighteenth century, the decline in the mining of gold and diamonds was followed by a diversification of exports and the reestablishment of agrarian activities along the coast. From 1790, Rio de Janeiro's mercantile pole, through exports of Brazilian goods and the re-exports of European commodities, attracted the slave trade from Eastern Africa, thus

[41] Colin Maclachland, "The Indian Directorate: Forced Acculturation in Portuguese America, 1757–1799," *The Americas* 28 (1972), no. 4, pp. 357–387.

[42] Joseph C. Miller, *Way of Death – Merchant Capitalism and the Angolan Slave Trade, 1730–1830* (Madison, WI, 1988).

bringing about an "Atlanticization" of Mozambique, which until then had been tied to exchanges within the Indian Ocean. It is worth noting that from 1780 to 1810, the renewal of the slave trade from Brazil to the Plata (some 2,500 or 3,000 individuals transported annually) supplied Lisbon with the silver that fueled Portuguese trade in Asia.[43]

In this light, it becomes possible to comment on the "quadrangular commerce," in the words of Sandro Sideri, encompassing commercial relations connecting England with Portugal, Portugal with Brazil, and Brazil with Angola.[44] There are conclusions to be drawn from an analysis of five series that evolved during the eighteenth century: first, the number of slaves imported to Brazil; second, gold exported from Brazil to Portugal; third, Portuguese exports to England; fourth, English exports to Portugal; and fifth, the trade balance between England and Portugal. Broadly speaking, until the decade of 1751–1760, English exports to Portugal closely followed the rise in Brazilian gold shipments to Lisbon, promoting an analogous development in the trade balance that was advantageous to England. From 1761 to 1770 and onward, gold shipments declined while Portugal developed its manufacturing capacity, expanded its agricultural exports from the colonies, and diversified its foreign trade, especially with respect to Asia. Hindered by the American Revolution and the Napoleonic Wars, England was able to rekindle its trade with Portugal only after the 1808–1810 royal laws and treaties, which opened up the again predominantly agricultural Brazilian economy to British trade.[45]

The disruption of trade and production areas in North America and the West Indies, caused by the War of Independence, Napoleon's Continental system, the Embargo Act, and the War of 1812, as well as the revolution in Saint-Domingue and the political troubles in Spanish America, facilitated Brazilian exports of sugar, tobacco, rice, cotton, cacao, and leather. Simultaneously, in the hills surrounding Rio de Janeiro, a new crop – coffee – started

[43] Manolo G. Florentino, *Em Costas Negras, uma história do tráfico Atlântico de escravos entre a África e o Rio de Janeiro, séculos XVIII e XIX* (São Paulo, 1997); Rudy Bauss, "Rio Grande do Sul in the Portuguese Empire: The Formative Years, 1777–1808," in Socolow, *The Atlantic Staple Trade*, vol. 2, pp. 519–535.

[44] S. Sideri, *Trade and Power: Informal Colonialism in Anglo-Portuguese Relations* (Rotterdam, 1970).

[45] Philip D. Curtin, *The Atlantic Slave Trade – A Census* (Madison, WI, 1969), table 62, p. 207; José C. Curto, "A Quantitative Reassessment of the Legal Portuguese Slave Trade from Luanda, Angola, 1710–1830," *African Economic History* 20 (1992), pp. 1–25; Sideri, *Trade and Power*, table I; Fernando A. Novais, *Portugal e Brasil na crise do antigo sistema colonial, 1777–1808* (São Paulo, 1979), tables 26 and 27; Virgilio Noya Pinto, *O ouro Brasileiro e o comércio Anglo-Português* (São Paulo, 1979); Michel Morineau, *Incroyables gazettes et fabuleux métaux* (Paris, 1985).

to be cultivated and by 1830 had become the main export item of the new country.

Clearly, the Brazilian economy entered a new stage at the end of the eighteenth century. The economic development stimulated by the cultivation of new crops (cacao, rice, and coffee) and the opening of Brazilian harbors to foreign trade in 1808 brought about external exchanges with broader markets. Moreover, the transfer of the royal family and the court from Lisbon (1808–1821) converted Rio de Janeiro into the capital of the Portuguese empire, enlarging its political and economic roles. At the same time, England strengthened its influence in the Atlantic, with Liverpool substituting for Lisbon as the dominant player in the Portuguese American economy. The independence of Brazil (1822) was to follow.[46] This is the standard and almost canonic periodization followed by the Brazilian historiography.

Yet we must play down the significance of 1808 as a watershed in Brazilian history to subsume it into the long-term patterns that embodied the Portuguese Atlantic. Indeed, two other important events taking place in 1808 – the abolition of the slave trade by both the United States and England – left Brazil as the main importer of African slaves into the New World. Fostered by the supply of Asian and European bartering goods for use in African markets and by the growing external demand for tropical commodities, the slave trade connecting Brazil with Portuguese Africa remained active as legal commerce until 1831 and illegally until 1850. Up to the end, the share of this traffic in external exchanges remained substantial: In the years between 1841 and 1849, the value of Africans introduced into Brazil amounted to 41 percent of the value of the country's exports.[47]

Therefore, the comparison of economic growth cycles leads to an important issue concerning the slave trade, the central economic factor of the Portuguese Atlantic: At the beginning of each productive stage, more Africans arrived in Portuguese America than anywhere else on the American continent. Such was the case between 1575 and 1625, an impressive period in sugar production; in the period 1701–1720, at the beginning of the gold cycle; and, finally, between 1780 and 1810, a period of agricultural resurgence and

[46] Economic and political issues of the ending of the Portuguese colonial system in Brazil are debated by Jorge M. V. Pedreira, "From Growth to Collapse: Portugal, Brazil, and the Breakdown of the Old Colonial System, 1750–1830," and by José Jobson de Andrade Arruda, "Decadence or Crisis in the Luso-Brazilian Empire: A New Model of Colonization in the Eighteenth Century," *The Hispanic American Historical Review* 80 (2000), no. 4, pp. 839–864 and 865–880, respectively.

[47] L. F. de Alencastro, "Bahia, Rio de Janeiro, et le nouvel ordre colonial, 1808–1860," in Jeanne Chase, ed., *Géographie du capital marchand aux Amériques, 1760–1860* (Paris, 1987), table 5, p. 149.

economic diversification. Each new productive phase in the Brazilian economy engendered a significant rise in the number of slaves imported into the country. In other words, there is a single economic cycle in Brazil in the modern period: the slave trade cycle, which spanned several centuries. All the other cycles – those of sugar, tobacco, gold, diamonds, and coffee – derived from a slave trade cycle extending over the long period from 1550 to 1850.

BIBLIOGRAPHICAL ESSAY

Interpretive studies of the Portuguese Atlantic can be found in C. R. Boxer's *Salvador de Sá and the Struggle for Brazil and Angola, 1602–1686* (Westport, CT, 1975), a seminal work on Salvador de Sá, the main architect of the Portuguese Atlantic; Bailey Diffie and George D. Winius's *Foundations of the Portuguese Empire, 1415–1580* (Minneapolis, 1977), a useful work on the first period of the Portuguese empire; Frédéric Mauro's *Le Portugal et l'Atlantique au XVIIe siècle, 1570–1670, étude économique* (Paris, 1960), reissued in Portuguese as *Portugal, o Brasil e o Atlântico, 1570–1670* (Lisbon, 1989), a thorough and influential approach to the subject; Caio Prado, Jr.'s *The Colonial Background of Modern Brazil* (originally published in Portuguese in 1942) (Berkeley, CA, 1967), a classical book on the Brazilian past; Bailey W. Diffie's *A History of Colonial Brazil, 1500–1792* (Malabar, FL, 1987), on the origins and growth of colonial Brazil; A. J. R. Russell-Wood's *A World on the Move: The Portuguese in Africa, Asia and America, 1415–1808* (New York, 1992), focusing on issues emphasized by more recent scholarship; Vitorino Magalhães Godinho's "Portugal and Her Empire, 1680–1720," in J. S. Bromley (ed.), *New Cambridge Modern History*, vol. 6 (New York, 1978), pp. 509–540; Fernando A. Novais's *Portugal e Brasil na crise do antigo sistema colonial 1777–1808* (São Paulo, 1979), an influential book; J. J. de Andrade Arruda's "Colonies as Mercantile Investments: The Luso-Brazilian Empire, 1500–1808," in James Tracy (ed.), *The Political Economy of Merchant Empires: State Power and World Trade, 1350–1750* (New York, 1991), pp. 360–420, a useful synthesis.

Issues on the Dutch–Portuguese conflict in Brazil are discussed in Charles R. Boxer's *The Dutch in Brazil, 1624–1654* (Oxford, 1957), and in Evaldo Cabral de Mello's *Olinda Restaurada – Guerra e Açúcar no nordeste, 1630–1654*, 2nd ed. (Rio de Janeiro, 1998). Cabral de Mello, a major Brazilian historian, also wrote *O negócio do Brasil – Portugal, os países baixos e o Nordeste, 1641–1669* (Rio de Janeiro, 1998), studying the Luso–Dutch negotiations on Brazil. Jonathan Israel's *Dutch Primacy in World Trade, 1585–1740* (Oxford, 1992), is a work by an author who has done substantial research on the economic rivalry between the Iberian powers and the Dutch. On military careers, see also David Tengwall's "A Study in Military Leadership – The *sargento-mor* in the Portuguese Atlantic Empire," *The Americas* 40 (1983), no. 1, pp. 73–94. The trade networks between South Brazil and the river Plata basin are examined in Alice P. Canabrava's *O comércio Português no Rio da Prata, 1580–1640* (originally published in 1943) (São Paulo, 1984), and in Zacarías Moutoukias's *Contrabando y control colonial en el siglo XVII: Buenos Aires, el Atlántico y el espacio peruano* (Buenos Aires, 1988). The Portuguese trade in Hispanic America is also analyzed in Harry E. Cross's "Commerce and Orthodoxy – A Spanish Response to Portuguese Commercial Penetration in the Viceroyalty of Peru, 1580–1640," *The Americas* 35 (1978), no. 2, pp. 151–167, and in Lewis Hanke's "The Portuguese in Spanish America with Special Reference to the Villa Imperial de Potosi," *Revista de Historia de America* 51 (1961), pp. 1–48.

On the economic relations among England, Portugal, and the Portuguese empire, Sandro Sideri's *Trade and Power: Informal Colonialism in Anglo-Portuguese Relations* (Rotterdam, 1970) is useful for understanding the issues of the eighteenth century; see also H. E. S. Fisher's *The Portuguese Trade: A Study of Anglo-Portuguese Commerce, 1700–1770* (London, 1971), and more specifically, Alan K. Manchester's *British Pre-eminence in Brazil, Its Rise and Decline: A Study in European Expansion* (New York, 1964), Carl A. Hanson's *Economy and Society in Baroque Portugal, 1668–1703* (Minneapolis, 1981), C. R. Boxer's *The Portuguese Seaborne Empire, 1415–1825* (London, 1977), and Vitorino Magalhães Godinho's *Ensaios*, vol. 2, 2nd ed. (Lisbon, 1978).

The sugar economics and society in the Brazilian northeast are studied in Stuart B. Schwartz's *Sugar Plantations in the Formation of Brazilian Society: Bahia, 1550–1835* (Cambridge, 1985). Tobacco is studied in Catherine Lugar's "The Portuguese Tobacco Trade and Tobacco Growers of Bahia in the Late Colonial Period," in Susan Socolow (ed.), *The Atlantic Staple Trade: The Economics of Trade*, vol. 2 (Brookfield, VT, 1996). Useful, especially on the economics of manioc flour, is B. J. Barickman's *A Bahian Counterpoint: Sugar, Tobacco, Cassava and Slavery in the Reconcavo, 1780–1860* (Stanford, CA, 1998). Gilberto Freyre's *The Masters and the Slaves: Casa-Grande & Senzala: A Study in the Development of Brazilian Civilization* (New York, 1964), originally published in Portuguese (1933), is the classical and influential study of life under domestic slavery in the plantation house.

On the Brazilian gold economics in the eighteenth century, see Charles R. Boxer's *The Golden Age of Brazil: Growing Pains of a Colonial Society, 1695–1750* (New York, 1995). The break created in Brazil's economics by gold exploitation is analyzed in Celso Furtado's *The Economic Growth of Brazil: A Survey from Colonial to Modern Times* (Berkeley, CA, 1963), and Virgílio Noya Pinto's *O ouro Brasileiro e o comércio Anglo-Português* (São Paulo, 1979), whose conclusions are reviewed and completed in Michel Morineau's *Incroyables gazettes et fabuleux métaux (XVIe–XVIIIe siècles)* (London and Paris, 1985). New evidence based on the chemical analysis of Brazilian gold and monetary circulation in France is presented in Cécile Morrisson, Christian Morrisson, and Jean-Noel Barrandon's *Or du Brésil monnaie et croissance en France au XVIIIe siècle* (Paris, 1999). On shipbuilding and trade between Brazil and Portuguese India, see José R. de Amaral Lapa's *A Bahia e a Carreira da Índia* (São Paulo, 1968).

The reforms of the Pombaline period are studied in Kenneth Maxwell's "Pombal and the Nationalization of the Luso-Brazilian Economy," *Hispanic American Historical Review* 48 (1968), no. 4, pp. 608–631, and his *Pombal: Paradox of the Enlightenment* (New York, 1995). Another valuable study on the same subject is Dauril Alden's *Royal Government in Colonial Brazil; with Special Reference to the Administration of the Marquis of Lavradio, Viceroy, 1769–1779* (Berkeley, CA, 1968). For more specific analyses of the conflict with the Jesuits see Dauril Alden's "Economic Aspects of the Expulsion of the Jesuits from Brazil – A Preliminary Report," in Henry H. Keith and S. F. Edwards (eds.), *Conflict and Continuity in Brazilian Society* (Columbia, SC, 1969), pp. 24–65. Kenneth Maxwell's *Conflicts and Conspiracies: Brazil and Portugal, 1750–1808* (New York, 1973), is an essential work on the political background of Brazilian independence. The economic issues on the ending of the colonial system in Brazil are studied and debated in Fernando A. Novais's *Portugal e Brasil na crise do antigo sistema colonial* (São Paulo, 1979), José Jobson de Arruda's *O Brasil no comércio colonial* (São Paulo, 1980), Valentim Alexandre's *Os sentidos do império: Questão nacional e questão colonial na crise do Antigo Regime Português* (Oporto, 1993), and Jorge M. V. Pedreira's *Estrutura industrial e mercado colonial: Portugal e Brasil (1780–1830)* (Lisbon, 1994).

On Portugal and Africa, useful information is found in James Duffy's *Portuguese Africa* (Cambridge, MA, 1968). The role of the *lançados* and the Portuguese trade in Senegambia are analyzed in Jean Boulègue's *Les Luso-Africains de Sénégambie XVIe–XIXe siècles* (Lisbon, 1989), John Vogt's *Portuguese Rule in the Gold Coast, 1469–1682* (Athens, GA, 1979), and Robert Garfield's *A History of São Tomé Island, 1470–1655: The Key to Guinea* (Lewiston, NY, 1992). David Birmingham's *Trade and Conflict in Angola – The Mbundu and Their Neighbours under the Influence of the Portuguese, 1483–1790* (London, 1966), is an important work on the slave trade and the colonial wars in Angola. Joseph C. Miller' *Way of Death – Merchant Capitalism and the Angolan Slave Trade, 1730–1830* (Madison, WI, 1988), is a major study on Angola and the South Atlantic. On seventeenth-century Angola, an important work is Beatrix Heintze's *Studien zur geschichte Angolas im 16. und 17. jahrhundert: Ein lesebuch* (Cologne, 1996). See also Adriano Parreira's

Economia e sociedade em Angola na época da rainha Jinga (Lisbon, 1990). Phyllis M. Martin's *The External Trade of the Loango Coast, 1576–1870 – The Effects of Changing Commercial Relations on the Vili Kingdom of Loango* (Oxford, 1972) examines an African state on the northern boundaries of Angola and the consequences of Dutch–Portuguese conflicts in the area. For the Dutch–Portuguese rivalry in the slave trade, see J. M. Postma's *The Dutch in the Atlantic Slave Trade, 1600–1815* (New York, 1990). On the Portuguese Atlantic contact with Central African states and native peoples, see Anne Hilton's *The Kingdom of Kongo* (Oxford, 1985), and John K. Thornton's *The Kingdom of Congo – Civil War and Transition, 1641–1718* (Madison, WI, 1983), and his *Africa and Africans in the Making of the Atlantic World, 1400–1800*, 2nd ed. (Cambridge, 1998).

On the Atlantic islands, see Thomas Bentley Duncan's *Atlantic Islands: Madeira, the Azores, and the Cape Verdes in Seventeenth-Century Commerce and Navigation* (Chicago, 1972), a global study covering a decisive period; Felipe Fernández-Armesto's *The Canary Islands after the Conquest: The Making of a Colonial Society in the Early Sixteenth Century* (Oxford, 1982), focusing on the transition from Portuguese to Spanish domination in the Canary Islands; Alberto Vieira's *O comércio inter-insular nos séculos XV e XVI, Madeira, Açores e Canárias* (Funchal, 1987), by one of the main historians of Madeira; João Marinho dos Santos's *Os Açores nos séculos XV e XVI* (2 vols., Ponta Delgada, 1989); and José Manuel Azevedo e Silva's *A Madeira e a construção do mundo Atlântico (séculos XV–XVII)* (2 vols., Funchal, 1995).

The beginning of the Atlantic slave trade and slavery within Portugal are studied in A. C. de C. M. Saunders's *A Social History of Black Slaves and Freedmen in Portugal, 1441–1555* (London, 1982); Charles R. Boxer's *Portuguese Society in the Tropics – The Municipal Councils of Goa, Macao, Bahia and Luanda, 1510–1800* (Madison, WI, 1950), a pioneering work on the main colonial cities; and José Honório Rodrigues' *Brazil and Africa* (Berkeley, CA, 1965), on relations and trade between Portuguese Africa and Brazil. The slave trade in the seventeenth century is debated and analyzed in David Eltis's *The Rise of African Slavery in the Americas* (Cambridge and New York, 2000). Pierre Verger's *Bahia and the West Coast Trade (1549–1851)* (Ibadan, 1964) and also his *Flux et reflux de la traite de nègres entre le golfe de Bénin et Bahia de Todos os Santos, du XVIIe au XIXe siècle* (Paris, 1968), emphasize the bilateral trade between Bahia and the Gulf of Benin. Corcino Medeiros Dos Santos's "Relações de Angola com o Rio de Janeiro 1736–1808," *Estudos Históricos* 12 (1973), pp. 7–68, provides evidence about the bilateral trade between Luanda and Brazilian ports. Robert E. Conrad's *World of Sorrow: The African Slave Trade to Brazil* (Baton Rouge, 1986) and Leslie Bethell's *The Abolition of the Brazilian Slave Trade – Britain, Brazil and the Slave Trade Question,*

1807–1869 (New York, 1970), discuss the debate on the legal and illegal slave trade in Brazil, a subject studied in a comparative perspective in David Eltis's significant book *Economic Growth and the Ending of the Transatlantic Slave Trade* (Oxford, 1987). Herbert S. Klein's *The Atlantic Slave Trade – New Approaches to the Americas* (Cambridge, 1999) provides a study of recent research on the slave trade. Katia M. de Queirós Mattoso's *To Be a Slave in Brazil, 1550–1888* (New Brunswick, NJ, 1986), is a useful book on Brazilian slavery. The role of the slave trade in the Portuguese Atlantic is analyzed in Luiz Felipe de Alencastro's "The Apprenticeship of Colonization," in Barbara L. Solow (ed.), *Slavery and the Rise of the Atlantic System* (Cambridge and New York, 1991), pp. 151–176.

On the Portuguese and the South American Indians, see Alexander Marchant's *From Barter to Slavery: The Economic Relations of Portuguese and Indians in the Settlement of Brazil, 1500–1580* (Gloucester, MA, 1966), and Mathias C. Kiemen's *The Indian Policy of Portugal in the Amazon Region, 1614–1693* (New York, 1973). John Hemming's *Red Gold* (London, 1978), covering the period 1500–1760, and his *Amazon Frontier* (London, 1987), covering 1760 to 1910, present a complete study of European contact with native peoples in Portuguese America. On the Jesuit Antonio Vieira and his Indian policy, see Charles R. Boxer's *A Great Luso-Brazilian Figure: Padre Antonio Vieira* (London, 1957). See also Stuart B. Schwartz's "Indian Labor and New World Plantations – European Demands and Indian Response in Northeastern Brazil," *American Historical Review* 1 (1983), pp. 43–79, and Robin M. Wright, with the collaboration of Manuela Carneiro Da Cunha, "Destruction, Resistance and Transformation – Southern, Coastal, and Northern Brazil, 1580–1890," in Frank Salomon and Stuart B. Schwartz (eds.), *The Cambridge History of the Native Peoples of the Americas*, vol. 3, part 2 (Cambridge, 1999), pp. 287–381. On *bandeirantes* and Indians, see Richard M. Morse (ed.), *The Bandeirantes: The Historical Role of the Brazilian Pathfinders* (New York, 1965). Alida Metcalf's *Family and Frontier in Colonial Brazil: Santana de Parnaíba, 1500–1822* (Stanford, CA, 1992), and John M. Monteiro's "From Indian to Slave: Forced Native Labor and Colonial Society in São Paulo during the Seventeenth Century," *Slavery and Abolition* 9 (1988), pp. 105–127, and his *Negros da terra – Índios e bandeirantes nas origens de São Paulo* (São Paulo, 1994). See also Sérgio Buarque De Holanda's *Caminhos e fronteiras*, 3rd ed. (São Paulo, 1994), on the material life of the *paulistas*. The impact of colonization on nature is treated in Warren Dean's *With Broadaxe and Firebrand: The Destruction of the Brazilian Atlantic Forest* (Berkeley, CA, 1995), an original and daring work. On Indian wars and the cattle-breeding frontiers, Capistrano de Abreu's *Chapters of Brazil's Colonial History, 1500–1800* (Oxford, 1997), first published in Brazil (1907), is still useful.

Collective Works include Dauril Alden (ed.), *Colonial Roots of Modern Brazil* (Berkeley, CA, 1973); Dauril Alden and Warren Dean (eds.), *Essays Concerning the Socio-economic History of Brazil and Portuguese India* (Gainesville, FL, 1977); Leslie Bethell (ed.), *Colonial Brazil*, seven interpretive essays previously published as part of volumes 1 and 2 of the *Cambridge History of Latin America* (Cambridge, 1984, 1987); and Manuela Carneiro da Cunha (ed.), *História dos índios no Brasil* (São Paulo, 1992), focusing on recent research on the ethnohistory of native peoples in Brazil. See also Maria Beatriz Nizza da Silva (ed.), "O Império Luso-Brasileiro, 1750–1822," in Joel Serrão and A. H. de Oliveira Marques (eds.), *Nova história da expansão Portuguesa*, vol. 3 (Lisbon, 1986). Volumes 1–3 of F. Bethencourt and Kirti Chaudhuri (eds.), *História da expansão Portuguesa* (5 vols., Lisbon, 1998), include essays on the fifteenth through the nineteenth centuries.

Bibliographic information on colonial Brazil is collected in Charles R. Boxer's "Some Reflections on the Historiography of Colonial Brazil, 1950–1970," in Dauril Alden (ed.), *Colonial Roots of Modern Brazil* (Berkeley, CA, 1973), pp. 3–15, Robert Conrad's *Brazilian Slavery: An Annotated Research Bibliography* (Boston, 1977), Francis A. Dutra's *A Guide to the History of Brazil, 1500–1822: The Literature in English* (Santa Barbara, CA, 1980), A. J. R. Russell-Wood's "United States Scholarly Contributions to the Historiography of Colonial Brazil," *Hispanic American Historical Review* 65 (1985), no. 4, pp. 683–723, and Rubens Borba de Moraes's *Bibliographia Brasiliana: Rare Books about Brazil Published from 1504 to 1900 and Works by Brazilian Authors of the Colonial Period* (2 vols., Los Angeles, 1983). Other references can be found in Joel Serrão (ed.), *Dicionário de história de Portugal* (4 vols., Lisbon, 1963–1971), Robert M. Levine's *Historical Dictionary of Brazil* (Metuchen, NJ, 1979), Adriano Parreira's *Dicionário glossográfico e toponímico da documentação sobre Angola – séculos XV–XVII* (Lisbon, 1990), Douglas L. Wheeler's *Historical Dictionary of Portugal* (London, 1993), Maria Beatriz Nizza da Silva (ed.), *Dicionário da história da colonização Portuguesa no Brasil* (Lisbon, 1994), Luís de Albuquerque (ed.), *Dicionário de história dos descobrimentos Portugueses* (2 vols., Lisbon, 1994), and Ronaldo Vainfas (ed.), *Dicionário do Brasil colonial, 1500–1808* (São Paulo, 2000).

Documents and works are collected in Bradford E. Burns (ed.), *A Documentary History of Brazil* (New York, 1966), Robert E. Conrad's *Children of God's Fire: A Documentary History of Black Slavery in Brazil* (University Park, PA, 1994), António Sérgio (ed.), *Antologia dos economistas Portugueses – século XVII* (Lisbon, 1974), and Beatrix Heintze's *Fontes para a história de Angola do século XVII* (2 vols., Stuttgart, 1985–1988).

5

THE PORTUGUESE IN AFRICA

John K. Thornton

Portuguese expansion into Africa began from three fronts: the continuing war against the Muslims in the Iberian Peninsula that spilled across the Strait of Gibraltar; the exploration of the seas to the west of Portugal and the discovery of the Atlantic islands; and the search for Prester John and a route to his lands, as well as developing trade in more prosaic commodities such as gold and slaves. The fronts were interdependent: the exploitation of the Atlantic islands might help to finance the wars in North Africa, and an alliance with Prester John was a way to find support behind the Muslim powers of northern Africa. Success on one front might privilege it over the others for a time.

Chronologically, the war against the Muslims came first. Although the Muslims had effectively been expelled as early as 1249 from what would end up being Portuguese territory, it was not until the capture of Ceuta in 1415 that the Portuguese crown was able to carry the war beyond the Iberian Peninsula and onto African soil. The Castilians had invaded North Africa earlier, taking Tetuán in 1399 and holding it for a few years, but Portuguese efforts in Morocco were far more sustained and extensive. Although the Portuguese benefited from internal dissensions among North African leaders and thus could expand south along the Moroccan coast, the rise of the Sa'adid monarchy in 1511, with its spirited leadership of holy men, eventually drove them from most of their positions after the fall of Agadir in 1541. The subsequent evacuation of most of the other posts followed in the next few years, culminating at the battle of Alcazarquibir, where D. Sebastião's quixotic and unsuccessful attempt to restore Portuguese fortunes was crushed in 1578.

The Western Crusades that matched Castile, Aragon, and Portugal against the Muslims of Iberia and North Africa were also connected with the larger effort of Western Christendom against Muslims in general that since the eleventh century had produced the Crusades to Jerusalem. With the fall of the last Crusader kingdoms in Syria (Acre in 1291) came the demand for renewed war as well as a recognition that it would be more difficult. Christian Ethiopia had also been involved in the Crusading struggle, at least indirectly. The Solomid dynasty, which had come to power in Ethiopia in 1270, developed an aggressive policy against Muslims. It was often at odds with the rulers of Egypt, who controlled the patriarch of the Coptic (and Ethiopian) church and had a policy of seeking alliances with Christian Europe. In 1306, an embassy from Ethiopia arrived in Europe seeking to contact the "king of the Spains." For Iberians, this embassy permanently rooted in their minds the idea that the mysterious Prester John, whose twelfth-century letter had set much of Europe to speculation, was in fact the ruler of Ethiopia. With the end of the Crusader kingdoms in 1291, the Ethiopians needed to connect with another power, and probably Catalan commercial involvement in the upper Nile area made "the Spains" a likely possibility. The potential of the alliance was enhanced by a proposed double dynastic marriage between Ethiopia and Aragon in 1428, even though it never materialized. Iberian monarchs in general tended to form alliances through marriage, and Portugal, in turn, was connected with Aragon, sometimes through mutual hostility toward Castile and sometimes through marriage politics. The possibility of a sea route to Prester John thus helped to stimulate Portuguese exploration of the Atlantic as indeed the chronicle of Zurara contends that it did.

However, the initial Portuguese expansion into the Atlantic was more connected with the old exploration of the so-called Mar Pequeña, the stretch of the Atlantic that lay directly off the Iberian and Moroccan coasts. The earliest European efforts in this area, led by the Genoese Lanzarotto Malocello, were accidental offshoots of the new commerce between the Mediterranean and Northern Europe. Official Portuguese involvement in the developing trade of the Mar Pequeña began with its sponsorship of an Italian exploration expedition in 1341. Armed and prepared to raid or to trade, this expedition visited the Canaries as well as other islands, probably Madeira and possibly even the Azores, and it created a precedent for Portuguese claims in the Canaries, colonization of the uninhabited Atlantic islands, and eventually its expansion on the African coast.

Shipping in the Mar Pequeña also led Portugal to pursue a second long-held goal, the discovery of a sea route to the gold-producing centers of West Africa. Catalan interests had been deeply involved in this trade, for maps produced by Catalan cartographers showed a deep knowledge of the geography of the western Sudan (as they did of Prester John's domains in

Ethiopia), including a "River of Gold" (the Senegal). The first attempt to reach this gold-producing area by sea was also Catalan: Jaume Ferrer's unsuccessful expedition of 1346.

Ultimately, it was this expansion into the Atlantic that brought the other fronts together on the African coast. Dreams of alliance with Ethiopia or the final defeat of the Muslims in Andalucia or Morocco were bounded and limited by the familiar and difficult conditions that these wars had faced since the eleventh century. Radical notions of outflanking the Muslims in the west or the east had to await the more prosaic development of advancements in shipping. Portuguese military operations in Morocco and the Canaries, and the colonization of the farther islands in the fifteenth century, put Portuguese shipping into the Mar Pequeña in quantity. More ships, more knowledge, and eventually the discovery of what navigators called the "Little Wheel," a system of currents that connected the African coast, the Atlantic islands, and the European mainland, was the crucial breakthrough. Once discovered, the Little Wheel allowed European ships to overcome the greatest of the nautical difficulties that prevented them from visiting Africa.

In 1434, Gil Eanes led the first Portuguese ship beyond Cape Bojador and returned. It was obvious that a round trip to more distant points on the African coast was possible, including commerce with the Catalan cartographer's "River of Gold."

The Portuguese ships that began visiting West African waters in 1444 carried with them a heritage of raiding and trading born out of their war in North Africa and the commercial and military life of the Mar Pequeña in the fourteenth and fifteenth centuries. The ships came heavily armed and prepared to attack any unprepared people they might find, but if there was enough resistance they were also prepared to trade. The first visitors to the Canaries found the inhabitants unprepared and subjected them to raiding. Even when Canarians managed to greet the visitors with arms at the ready, they faced a certain disadvantage in that they made no watercraft and could only engage Europeans on the land. As a result, although many of the Portuguese came and left peacefully after trading, the raiding, and eventually conquering, faction prevailed where access to the coast was easy.

In West Africa, the raiding phase started first because, like the Canarians, West Africans were at first completely unprepared to confront the ocean-going ships off their coast. But unlike the Canarians, West Africans did make watercraft – if not ocean-going craft, then at least large craft, well suited for navigating the tricky coastal waters and estuaries of their region, where larger Portuguese ships could not venture. They soon showed that they could defeat Europeans even on the water, and especially on the land. At times, they were able to carry their victories even to the ships themselves, and in a series of military-naval victories from 1445 to 1452, they forced the Portuguese to rethink their approach to Africa. Therefore, in 1456, the crown dispatched Diogo Gomes, a nobleman of the royal household, to negotiate a peace agreement with the various powers of the African coast and to arrange for secure and peaceful trade to follow. The suspicion bred by a decade of hostility made Gomes's mission difficult, and he was forced to deal slowly, so that it was 1462 before Portugal could be said to have negotiated commercial access to all the lands between the Senegal and the Gambia rivers.

In light of the radical plan of outflanking the Muslims that the Portuguese sometimes invoked, their expansion on the Atlantic coast may be judged to be fairly slow. This is because whatever the will of the Portuguese crown might have been, such expeditions were not financially prudent. Prince Henry the Navigator sponsored the early fifteenth-century voyages in the Mar Pequeña, and impecunious members of the Portuguese lower nobility or merchants, rather than the crown, led most of the early travel in the Atlantic. These men were seeking glory and fortune to improve their lot and were willing to take risks to get it. Usually the crown permitted and protected these early voyages, giving them wide legal and fiscal leeway to explore new areas, try markets, or make conquests. However, once the explorers discovered profitable and safe markets or made conquests, the crown's tendency was to introduce regulation or even to appropriate the rights of the former holders and regrant them to favorites.

Thus, expansion in West Africa halted during the early years of trade primarily because the crown was generous with access to the markets. As long as this was true, there was little incentive to take the risks associated with the exploration of new stretches of the African coast, even if they were fairly accessible by ship. Sure and predictable profits from known markets were usually preferable to the risks of exploration. But when the crown demanded monopolization of the trade of the region, the less favored groups sought to locate markets farther afield. The exploration of the Gulf of Guinea in the 1470s was the response of the next group of lesser noble, merchant adventurers. It led to the discovery of sea routes to the much richer gold fields of modern Ghana, contact with the kingdom of Benin, and the locating of the uninhabited islands of the Gulf of Guinea (São Tomé, Príncipe, and Ano Bom) as potential bases. Unlike their predecessors on the Senegambian coast, those who ventured this far south never tried any hostile action against the Africans they met but established peaceful relations from the very beginning.

At the same time, the crown intervened early and forcefully when the pioneers discovered markets on the coast of modern Ghana where gold could be purchased in quantity. In 1482, Diogo de Azambuja was dispatched to build the fort of São Jorge da Mina, whose role was to protect gold exports and prevent incursions by other Europeans who had been drawn there by the lure of gold.

That same year, and for the first time, the Portuguese crown decided to invest in more speculative explorations that would address the older, more strategic concerns of the war with Islam. Acting on advice brought back by earlier visitors to Benin, and making a false connection between the Christian cross and the cross-shaped emblems worn by emissaries from the nearby kingdom of Ogané (probably the Igala kingdom) to Benin, the royal advisers decided on the basis of consulting Ptolemy's geography (as revised by recent voyages) that the lands of Prester John were just a short voyage from Benin. Consequently, Diogo Cão was ordered to explore this route and was fitted out at royal expense.

But the crown's first venture into exploration was disappointing. Instead of tending east toward Ethiopia as the cartographers of the court had imagined, the coast turned sharply south at Cameroon and continued more or less south for nearly 4,000 kilometers. Diogo Cão's ships managed to reach what they thought may have been the end of the continent, but his voyage also revealed a radically different geography. Follow-up voyages by Cão and by Bartolomeu Dias (1488) reaffirmed this geography even as they confirmed that the African continent did indeed end at the Cape of Good Hope.

Given that the sea route to the Indies was not likely to prove easy, the crown began to seek Prester John by overland routes. Even before Dias returned from his voyage, Pero da Covilhã was sent in 1487, in disguise, across the Mediterranean to Egypt with the idea of learning as much about "the Indies" (including information about Prester John) as possible. Covilhã and Afonso de Paiva traveled to Egypt, and from there Covilhã passed through Arabia and ultimately to Calicut in India, where he gathered substantial details about the Indian Ocean spice trade, the gold trade of East Africa (he claimed he had visited the gold-exporting emporium of Sofala on the Mozambique coast), and the general geography of India and East Africa. He may have been able to communicate this information back to Portugal (he certainly did send letters back), but when he learned that his companion had not reached Ethiopia, he set out in that direction, eventually reaching the court of the Negus. However, he was unable to report to Portugal on this contact and was not permitted to leave. A proposed Luso-Ethiopian alliance therefore was forced to wait for the final oceanic connection to be made.

Cão's voyages, though disappointing in the matter of linking Portugal with Ethiopia by sea, did have the redeeming feature of bringing Portugal into contact with the powerful Central African kingdom of Kongo. Kongo not only demonstrated potential for being a profitable market, but its king, Nzinga a Nkuwu, expressed a willingness to adopt Christianity (he was baptized as João I in 1491). As Kongo evolved firmly into a Christian ally of Portugal in the first part of the sixteenth century, the Portuguese continued to hope that a river route up the Congo River might link Kongo's northern frontier with the southern territories of Ethiopia, and indeed maps as late as Pigafetta's of 1591 continued on this optimistic note, showing for at least another century the two Christian powers lying just a short distance apart.

Portugal's relationship with all the kingdoms met in Africa in the period following Diogo Gomes's missions to Senegambia was fixed by its earliest experiences on the African coast. Portugal made no attempts to conquer or to attack coastal positions but always sought diplomatic contacts. At the same time, however, the Portuguese discovered that some of the devices of European warfare of the late Middle Ages could be helpful in Africa. It was not that in Atlantic Africa, at least, Portugal had a military superiority that allowed them to win battles; the Senegambians had shown that was impossible. Rather, they learned that they might be able to serve as special-purpose mercenaries in African armies and in this way earn wealth and trading advantages that they could not seize on their own.

The idea of mercenary service was not easily applied, however. In 1488, Bemoim, a disappointed pretender to the throne of Jolof in modern Senegal, appealed to Portugal to give him military assistance, and subsequently a mission was dispatched to place him on the throne. The mission failed, however, when Bemoim and the leader of the expedition quarreled and Bemoim was killed.

In Kongo, the mercenary strategy worked better because it was more limited. In 1491, Portuguese armed forces cooperated with those of Kongo to put down a rebellion in one of its provinces that lay along the Congo River. The situation of the rebels made it possible for Portuguese sailors to support the attack from the river and deploy bombards, while Portuguese armor and armor-piercing weapons (such as crossbows and muskets) proved helpful to the military efforts of Kongo. Other military missions followed, being used in various ways by the Kongo rulers in 1509 and 1512. King Afonso Mvemba a Nzinga (1509–1542), the Christian ruler of Kongo, gave considerable favors to these soldiers, allowing them trading advantages and giving them grants of income and shares in the spoils of war.

Similar relationships developed between Portugal and the kingdom of Benin in modern Nigeria a bit later. Although the details are less well known, and perhaps were less officially supported, Portuguese mercenaries were serving in Benin armies in the early sixteenth century, and the king of Benin was even using a captured Portuguese bombard in 1516. Even more shadowy and less formal relationships continued along other parts of the African coast, such as Sierra Leone, where mid-sixteenth-century reports mention private Portuguese, often gunners, in the service of various African lords, no doubt in exchange for concessions of trade and grants of income.

Finally, the fort at El Mina provided another outlet for Portuguese military activity. The primary mission of the fort was gold trading, and indeed its most significant role in African politics, at least by the early sixteenth century, was as a mediator of disputes and local wars that interrupted the flow of gold. But the Portuguese crown was concerned that the fort was unable to prevent other Europeans from trading along the same coast. Increasingly they sought to enlist the aid of the many rulers of small states situated along the coast to assist them in expelling foreign traders, although few rulers were interested in providing this support for its own sake. Portuguese did, however, manage to provide soldiers to ambitious Africans, and together they sought to exert a sort of commercial hegemony in the area. These attempts set them at odds with other African rulers, and the mid-sixteenth century saw occasional wars conducted by Portugal and its allies against other states, who sometimes had the assistance of English traders. For all this, however, there was no change of sovereignty, for neither Portugal nor its allies were able to conquer the neighboring areas or stifle trade with foreigners.

In the late fifteenth and early sixteenth centuries, the slave trade began to emerge as one of the most important commercial mainstays of the Portuguese trade with Africa. Initially, it had been through raids that Portuguese had acquired slaves – but African naval superiority in the waters close to shore had ended this phase as it did Portugal's attempts at military dominance by the 1460s. Thereafter, slaves were overwhelmingly acquired only by trade with African sellers. A great irony in this was that the people imported into Portugal from Africa numbered only a few hundred during the time of the raids, mostly drawn from poor fishermen and peasants who lived along the Senegambian coast, but once peaceful trade was established, the number of slave imports shot up to the thousands, roughly 5,000 per year at the start of the sixteenth century and steadily growing. The supply of slaves made it possible for Portugal to acquire the manpower it needed to settle the offshore islands of the Cape Verde group and the São Tomé–Príncipe group, and even to export them to Portugal, to Spain, to the Spanish possessions in the Canaries, and then, after 1502, to the Spanish possessions in the New World. African slaves working on São Tomé would eventually make that small island Europe's most important producer of sugar for a few years in the mid-sixteenth century, and they would make the Spanish colony of Hispaniola appear as a "New Guinea" to the Italian visitor Girolamo Benzoni in 1545.

At times, the Portuguese acquired these slaves by purchase from African middlemen or state authorities, and these enslaved people had often been captured at some other point in Africa. Occasionally, however, when African states employed Portuguese soldiers as mercenaries, the slaves may have been directly captured by Europeans, at least when they served as a component in African armies. This probably happened in Benin in the 1520s; it certainly happened in Kongo, where joint Kongo–Portuguese armies participated in wars and brought back hundreds of captives, many of whom were subsequently turned over to the Portuguese as their pay.

The development of trade with Kongo and other parts of the Gulf of Guinea, the first mercenary activities, and the beginnings of settlement on São Tomé provided Portuguese merchants and the crown with lower-risk options and hence delayed for a time the further exploitation of Cão's and Dias's discoveries with regard to the geography of Africa and the possibility of a sea route to the Indian Ocean. Increasingly, however, toward the end of the century, these early pioneering ventures were once again choked off – São Tomé, successfully settled by Álvaro de Caminha, became a royal possession in 1499. But it was no longer on private initiative that exploration was being undertaken. In 1497, nine years after Dias's voyages, the crown dispatched another royal expedition, this one led by Vasco da Gama, to make the link to "the Indies."

Contrary to expectations, when da Gama's fleet arrived in the Indian Ocean, it did not head straight for the land of Prester John. Possibly inspired by details from Pero da Covilhã's communications from Egypt, da Gama sought instead the gold-trading port of Sofala. When he reached Kilwa in modern Tanzania in 1498, his interest was in searching out local Christians said to inhabit the east coast of Africa. The result was that in spite of Prester John's role in inspiring strategic thinking, Portugal's first contacts in East Africa were not with the fairly isolated Ethiopian state but with a region connected with the larger Indian Ocean economy.

Portuguese contact on the Indian Ocean side of Africa was quite different from that in West Africa. Whereas in West Africa the Portuguese had found it impossible to use their ships and guns to defeat African opponents and in fact lost badly in the confrontations in the shallow waters of the coast, in East Africa they found large coastal cities that were vulnerable to sea-based attack. Not only could cities such as Sofala, Mombasa, and Kilwa be stormed successfully, they also lay at the head of lucrative trade routes both to the African interior and to the Indian Ocean. The Portuguese forged an alliance with Malindi from the time that da Gama arrived in 1498, and initially sought to dominate Kilwa, demanding tribute and then storming the city in 1502, and finally, in 1505, building a fortress there and garrisoning it.

In the north, they reduced Mombasa's influence on behalf of Malindi, their ally, and Kilwa, their subject, by periodically attacking and destroying the town, first in 1505 and again in 1528. In fact, much of Portuguese policy in East Africa in the first half of the sixteenth century was predicated upon their ability to plunder any town or settlement that achieved some concentration of wealth.

However, the Portuguese wanted to go beyond the destructive policy of plunder and create a controlled trading system of rule. They initially believed that Kilwa was the key to the gold trade of Sofala, but upon discovering that Kilwa's former domination of the coast, witnessed by its substantial and rich architecture, was no longer effective, they decided to occupy Sofala itself. By 1512, they abandoned their position at Kilwa altogether in favor of Sofala when the local politics also proved costly to manage to their favor. In 1505, they built a fortified trading post at Sofala but did not attack the town or interfere with the ruler. Unfortunately for the Portuguese intruders, however, it turned out that even Sofala was not a gold-mining center but drew its supplies from the vast interior kingdom of Karanga, ruled by the Mwene Mutapa. The gold reached the sea through many ports, and soon, as a result of the Portuguese presence, Sofala and Kilwa received none, whereas other posts flourished. The Portuguese then attempted to control these smaller ports and the Zambezi valley, first by developing Mozambique Island as a secure port for the larger region in 1507 and then by using it as a base for continued raiding in the Zambezi valley. But at the same time, private Portuguese traders established themselves in the region in trading posts and market towns from Inhambane in the south to Quelimane in the north.

The attempts to occupy and garrison key towns were part of a larger Portuguese plan for the Indian Ocean that gradually unfolded in the early sixteenth century, culminating in the system put in place by Afonso de Albuquerque by 1515. Portugal would dominate shipping by force and require all the existing merchants and shippers to obtain licenses. It would also obtain special privileges for the Portuguese shippers themselves in the ports of the whole region. When the island of Socotra was captured in 1507 as part of this plan, the Portuguese at last renewed the search for Prester John, this time through Indian Ocean positions. The king sent João Gomes as ambassador, and like Covilhã before him, Gomes arrived and was received with honor in Ethiopia, but he was not allowed to leave the country.

The development of a close relationship with Ethiopia was slow. The program for a grand Christian alliance belonged ultimately to Mediterranean powers such as Aragon, and, moreover, the crusading concepts of earlier times had largely been abandoned, at least in the traditional crusading grounds of the Levant, except for ideological purposes when it was needed. The trade in the Indian Ocean and the gold of Sofala proved more useful and acceptable, and as a result the Portuguese crown took few steps to invigorate the mission to Ethiopia that since 1482 had driven them ultimately to India.

In 1512, the Ethiopians sent their own ambassador to the Portuguese governor in India. When he reached Portugal, the crown eventually responded by sending a return embassy, which arrived in 1520, remaining in Ethiopia until 1526. On the whole, the mission was not very successful, but it did establish formal relations, and a few Portuguese remained behind in Ethiopia. These relations were suddenly to become critically important, however. The year after the Portuguese embassy retired, Ethiopia's long-time Muslim enemy, the sultanate of Adal, fell under the control of Ahmad Grañ, a charismatic Islamic holy man. Grañ's forces from Adal were reinforced by Somalis who flocked to his leadership and by Turkish soldiers from the Ottoman empire, who having recently occupied Egypt and the coast of Arabia (1516) provided musketeers and artillery to their host. Within a few years, the Ethiopian army was humbled, and Grañ's forces swept through the land, destroying churches and slaughtering people.

Galadewos, king of Ethiopia at this time, sent a desperate mission to Portugal, offering, among other things, the submission of the Ethiopian church to Rome, at least according to the ambassador, João Bermudes, a minor Portuguese member of the earlier mission, who arrived in Portugal declaring that the pope had named him patriarch of Ethiopia. Portuguese assistance was forthcoming, and an expeditionary force under Cristovão da Gama arrived at the Red Sea coast of Ethiopia in 1541. Thus, Portugal's relations with Ethiopia were not unlike those it had with many countries of Atlantic Africa, serving as mercenaries in hopes of commercial reward, booty, or political advantage. Luck favored the new combined army. After an initial setback in 1542, in which many Portuguese were killed and their artillery lost, they managed to kill Grañ in action against the allied forces, and upon his death the Islamic movement broke up, giving the Ethiopians the opportunity to counterattack.

The Portuguese, although diminished in numbers, remained in the country as a special fighting force, as directed by the king of Portugal, and in time married into the Ethiopian elite. Bermudes's claim to be head of the Ethiopian church, denounced by the king of Portugal as fraudulent in 1546, was ended when the new Coptic patriarch and the new bishop of Ethiopia (called the *abuna*) removed Bermudes in 1550.

Thus, by the middle of the sixteenth century, Portugal had established stable relations all around the coast of Africa. During this period, as a long-range consequence of their initial defeats on the African coast in the 1450s, the Portuguese had not been conquerors except for the two towns on the East African coast, first Kilwa and then Mombasa. They had established more permanent bases on offshore islands: Arguim on the desert coast of the Sahara, the Cape Verde islands off the coast of Senegambia, São Tomé and Príncipe off the Gulf of Guinea and serving both West and Central Africa, and on Mozambique Island for the southeast African coast. Official factories, flourishing more or less on the sufferance of African rulers, were to be found near the mouth of the Senegal, around the "Rivers of Guinea" in modern Guinea-Bissau, at El Mina on the Gold Coast, sometimes in Benin, and at Mpinda in Kongo. Portuguese mercenaries were in the service of the kings of Ethiopia and Kongo with official crown sanction.

Outside of the zone of official presence, however, there was a large unofficial zone of private Portuguese who were functioning as merchants, settlers, or mercenaries. All were closely tied to African authorities, more closely so than those in officially sanctioned factories or missions. Most had substantially divided loyalties politically, and virtually all were hostile to Portuguese taxation policies and notions of crown control.

In the entire process of expansion, the crown had played a careful cat-and-mouse game about taxation and control. On the one hand, it had encouraged expansion through tax breaks and grants of authority to pioneering people, mostly from the lower strata of the aristocracy but with a healthy strain of commoners mixed in (or foreigners, often of non-noble origins, such as Flemings and especially Italians). On the other hand, once the risks of exploration, development of markets, and the winning of political favor had been passed, the crown wished to tighten control, gather more taxes, and give authority to its own agents, typically from higher up the social strata.

In areas where the crown had full control, such as the islands off the African coast, this process was fairly straightforward. A pioneer of lower social origins took the risks and effected colonization – the Italian Antonio da Noli, for example, in Cape Verde, and the Portuguese Álvaro de Caminha in São Tomé – but once colonization was established, the original grants were challenged, either because of problems of inheritance or because grantholders held effective political control weakly, or in response to pressure from the local powers, and eventually the challenges led the crown to intervene and administer the territory directly. To manage the administration, the crown appointed captains or governors. Often the captains – appointed for a short period of time – were members of the aristocracy looking for a career that would ultimately lead them back to Portugal and greater wealth.

It was a different story, however, in those areas where the crown had less control. Technically, where there was a factory or a mission, the crown also appointed an authority, often with the title of captain (occasionally governor), over the whole Portuguese community, the activities of which were then to be controlled and the liability to taxation met. In the military missions, such as those to Kongo or Ethiopia, there was to be a "Captain of the Portuguese," who coordinated military activities as well as managing the taxation of returns that the soldiers might receive.

Beyond these areas, there were places all along the African coast, such as Sierra Leone, for example, or along the coast of southeast Africa, where Portuguese had gone to settle without permission or direction. In Guinea and Sierra Leone, these people were often called *lançados*; in Central Africa, those who had settled outside the official Kongo mission, especially in the lands of its rival kingdom of Ndongo, were called *pombeiros*. In southeast Africa, a whole string of accidental settlements could be found that were populated by the survivors of shipwrecks on the dangerous coast of Natal. In most of these areas, the resident Portuguese were merchants, but in the same areas, they managed to parlay their skills into official positions in an African state and perhaps into local wealth in slaveholding or through connections (often by marriage) with other powerful people in Africa.

In all the areas that fell beyond close crown control, there was a struggle between crown and settler in which the settler had an important ally – independent African rulers who valued their services. In Kongo, for example, there was a constant struggle throughout the whole first half of the sixteenth century between the crowns of Kongo and Portugal over the powers and authority of the captain of the Portuguese, and often the Kongo ruler sided with his own unofficial Portuguese clients among the Portuguese community against the captains appointed by Lisbon. In 1553, this struggle reached a point where Lisbon had to relent – the king of Kongo appointed the captain of the Portuguese there. Likewise, in Ethiopia, the command of the military mission was strongly contested when its original commander was killed in action in 1542. The issue ultimately came to a head in a dispute over which flag the soldiers should fly when marching out to do battle – the Portuguese or the Ethiopian one. Not surprisingly, it was the Ethiopians and those Portuguese who put their support behind the mulatto soldier Aires Diniz who won on this count.

Elsewhere, there was little hope of Lisbon gaining control because the Portuguese had never lived under the command of a Portuguese leader, and in the absence of an official mission to that area, they never would. Not surprisingly, to bring such communities under control was a constant goal of the crown, and that policy governed most of the Portuguese activity in the period that followed. Although the degree to which the crown was willing to spend its treasure and risk its troops to subordinate renegade Portuguese varied from time to time, and other motives beyond this fairly parochial one were evident as well, it was an important theme in virtually all actions of Portugal in Africa after 1550.

It may not be surprising that the impetuous King Sebastião would be the most vigorous partisan of taking strong military action to increase crown authority, but the policy continued after his reign under the Spanish monarchs, too. In any case, it was in the reign of Portugal's most romantic and disastrous king that the seeds of Portugal's land-based empire in Africa were sown.

In all the crown's efforts at empire, the Jesuit Order proved to be an important element supporting this policy. The Order was formed in 1540, and in 1548 the first missionaries were sent to Kongo, already a Christian country. While serving as missionaries, the Jesuits also meddled in Kongo's politics, especially involving themselves with the locally established Portuguese community. The Portuguese of Kongo played a role in spoiling the Jesuits' relationships with King Diogo until the priests abandoned the mission in 1555. For their part, the Jesuits tried various means to overthrow Diogo, whom they regarded as a renegade pagan for his opposition to their plans.

The most successful Jesuit venture was in Angola. The roots of Portuguese expansion in Angola lay in their early relationship with Kongo, with its military mission increasingly independent of the Portuguese crown by the mid-sixteenth century. At the same time, however, the rivalry between Kongo and Ndongo had given the Portuguese crown additional opportunities in the region. As early as 1518, Ndongo had sent embassies to Portugal, and although attempts had been made to establish a Portuguese mission there to rival that of Kongo, first in 1520–1526 and then again under Paulo Dias de Novais in 1560–1564, both failed. The first attempt failed because Kongo was only a lukewarm supporter, although Kongo's King Afonso was prepared to take the Portuguese from Ndongo into his own service; the second failed probably because of hostility from an informal but influential Portuguese colony in Ndongo that believed a formal relationship would be detrimental to their status in Ndongo. A Jesuit also accompanied the second mission and remained as a semi-prisoner when Dias de Novais retired in 1564.

In 1571, Sebastião tried again to establish formal ties with Ndongo, again entrusting the mission to Paulo Dias de Novais. More Jesuits, anxious to restore their fortunes in Central Africa, accompanied him. Kongo was distracted by the invasion of the "Jágas," a group of uncertain origin who had forced King Álvaro I to flee his capital and ask for a Portuguese military mission from São Tomé to restore him to the throne. This mission, under

Francisco de Gouveia Sottomaior, arrived in Kongo in 1570 with orders to restore the king but also to build a fort and to concentrate the Portuguese who were living there under his own authority. Although he may have tried to do this, in fact, when he left in 1574, he had restored Álvaro but the Portuguese community had not been brought under undisputed crown control. As a part of the price for rescuing Álvaro, however, Sottomaior also obtained permission for Portugal to land and take up a position on Luanda Island, a maneuver that would be undertaken by Dias de Novais. Luanda, the best natural harbor in Atlantic Africa, was on a semiarid coast but was in easy reach of the Kwanza River, where Portuguese vessels could operate.

Dias de Novais's instructions, however, called for more than a military mission. Instead he was to build a colony along the coast south of Luanda and, if possible, to conquer regions elsewhere. Among his many duties were the construction of several strongholds and the colonization of a number of Portuguese families. Finally, he was also to concentrate commerce in his hands and place the whole Portuguese community in Ndongo under his authority. Whatever his instructions may have said, Dias de Novais functioned for a few years like the head of a military mission, offering his services to the king of Ndongo and in fact taking his army inland to the capital of Ndongo to serve more fully. There, however, the impact of his royal authority frightened the earlier Portuguese community, who had been avoiding taxation and control for some years, trading through contacts in São Tomé. They managed to convince the king of Ndongo that Dias de Novais meant to use his troops to win power over the kingdom and, in 1579, King Ngola Kiluanji ordered an attack on Dias de Novais and his men.

Although much was lost, Dias de Novais and a group of followers managed to fight their way back to Luanda, where they called on Kongo to support them. The Kongolese army, including many of the Portuguese who had resided there for years, invaded Ndongo, in part in respect for their debt to Portugal for rescuing them from the Jágas and in part to extend Kongo's authority over Ndongo and the regions to the south. However that may be, the attack failed, and the overextended Kongo army was forced to withdraw by 1580, leaving Dias de Novais hanging onto a few fortified positions around Luanda.

Fortunately for Dias de Novais, his luck had not run out. Ndongo was temporarily exhausted by the war with Kongo and could not force him from the coast. At the same time, Dias de Novais found that a number of local rulers, anxious to escape from Ndongo's power, were prepared to ally with him and in this way to expand his army. In addition, many thousands of Kongolese soldiers served as mercenaries in the Portuguese army. By the mid-1580s, Portuguese-led forces, composed of a core of Portuguese infantry and some thousand locally recruited soldiers under their own commanders, had driven Ndongo back to the highlands behind Luanda and, moreover, were actually beginning steps to invade the region. They founded forts at Massangano and Cambambe along the Kwanza River, where Portuguese naval forces allowed both resupply and artillery support. However, in a cataclysmic battle on the Lucala River at Christmas 1590, the Portuguese and their allies were utterly defeated by an Ndongo army and forced once again to retreat. Many of their allies abandoned them, and although Portugal was not likely to be driven out of Africa by force, it was also not likely to make a major conquest. A treaty of 1599 between Portugal and Ndongo settled borders that kept Portugal out of the highlands but made its fort at Massangano the secure base for potential further expansion.

In the early seventeenth century, the new colony of Angola began to emerge. When Dias de Novais the pioneer died in 1591, the crown, following a familiar pattern, found that he had not fulfilled the terms of his grant and resumed its title over the region, placing the fledgling colony under a royal governor serving for a term. The colony itself was in fact a tiny area surrounded by the lands of neighboring *sobas*, as the local rulers were called. The *sobas* had submitted to Portuguese rule, but because they supplied the bulk of the troops to the army, their loyalty needed to be won and held and could not be commanded. Individual settlers and Jesuit priests often collected the tribute that *sobas* paid themselves and took on responsibility for mediating Portuguese affairs with them. As long as Ndongo remained a threat, and as long as Portuguese depended on the *sobas* to defend them, real government authority would be lacking.

The impasse was slowly broken, first by recruiting soldiers from among slaves to serve in the Portuguese army under Portuguese commanders or by enlisting African mercenary troops whose loyalty could be better controlled, but more importantly through the steadily advancing alliance with the Imbangala. This group was a series of militarized bands, as much like robber gangs as real armies, but fearsome, for they were alleged to be cannibals and recruited their members from young males, often only children. They pillaged and destroyed the northern edge of Angola's great central highlands, and by 1600, Portuguese from Angola were traveling there to buy the hundreds and thousands of people they took captive and to serve informally with their bands.

In the first years of the seventeenth century, individual Portuguese settlers made alliances with these bands as they raided ever closer to the Portuguese posts on the Kwanza. Governor Luís Mendes de Vasconcelos, who arrived in 1617, had orders to stop this practice, but within two years he had formed a major alliance with three bands, which he transported across the Kwanza to make war on Ndongo. The alliance was a remarkable military success, for the invasion not only stunned Ndongo, forcing King Ngola Mbandi to flee the heartland and take refuge on islands in the Kwanza River, but eventually provoked a succession dispute in the devastated country when the despondent king committed suicide in 1624. Portugal was able to champion the cause of one of the pretenders, Ngola Hari, against the dead king's sister, Njinga Mbandi, and thus Portugal gained a large African army to augment their own and the Imbangala mercenaries. Queen Njinga was only able to protect herself by making her own alliances with the rootless and opportunistic Imbangala and by moving still further east to build a base in Matamba, whose lands she conquered in 1631–1635.

The Imbangala period (roughly 1615 to 1665) had a tremendous impact on the Portuguese presence in Angola. They were able to go on the offensive, and, moreover, tens of thousands of people were captured and enslaved in the wars. From 1615 to 1640, slaves captured by this alliance formed as much as 85 or even 90 percent of the slaves brought to Brazil and the Spanish Caribbean (under arrangements sponsored through the union of the two crowns from 1580 to 1640). Although there were some substantial territorial conquests in the earlier part of this period, much of the military weight was simply to punish rebellion and to conduct raids against enemies rather than to annex lands. Portuguese Angola's survival and wealth were assured.

Meanwhile, the era of D. Sebastião produced a second attempt at colonial expansion along the Zambezi River, which was much less successful than the Angolan adventure but produced a second significant colony of Portugal in Africa. As in Kongo and Angola, the first efforts were made with Jesuits. A Jesuit priest, António da Silveira, was dispatched to seek a diplomatic alliance with (and the Christian conversion of) the king of Karanga in 1560 but was murdered in the court of Karanga, possibly by Muslim traders who feared the consequences of such an alliance. In any case, the murder of the priest was the immediate justification for a Portuguese expedition under Francisco Barreto in 1570, almost at the same time as Paulo Dias de Novais was obtaining the donation of Angola. Barreto took more than 1,000 soldiers with him, reinforced by 700 more a few years later, one of Portugal's largest expeditions in the Indian Ocean.

The complex expedition of Barreto, and his successor, Diogo Homem, after Barreto's death, continued until 1575, when the last troops, badly defeated on several occasions, returned to Mozambique. They had failed to conquer Karanga or to seize the gold mines of the region, but they had succeeded in getting formal recognition of the Zambezi valley market towns of Sena and Tete and the immediate region surrounding them as Portuguese possessions. As was the case elsewhere in Africa, this colonization actually allowed the crown to obtain fuller control over an informal community of Portuguese who resided in the valley towns. However, unlike Angola, the crown did not have nearly the local power over the Portuguese community or its African subjects and allies. The governor resided in Mozambique, and his agents were never fully obeyed in the Zambezi.

The situation in the area was complicated considerably by the invasion of bodies of Maravi, sometimes styled "Zimbas" in contemporary sources, from north of the Zambezi, whose lifestyle and fighting techniques were similar to those of the Imbangala in Angola. These invasions, which began in the 1560s (Barreto had fought against one such group, led by Mongas, in 1571), had become stronger south of the Zambezi in the last years of the sixteenth and the early seventeenth centuries. Like the Imbangala, they, too, could be recruited to fight for the Portuguese, although also like the Imbangala they frequently followed their own course.

Portuguese residents in Sena, Tete, and subsequently in the market town of Masapa in the highlands exercised considerable local authority and took their own initiatives in many matters. In 1607, Diogo Simões Madeira, a powerful Tete trader, was able to raise a substantial army of Portuguese and local allies and intervened in the civil war that disturbed the Karanga kingdom. The Mwene Mutapa, or king of Karanga, Gatse Rusere, granted him control of all the mines in the country in exchange for his support against the rebellion, although in fact this brought little revenue because the mines were small and locally worked. Over the following decades, Madeira and his allies campaigned for Gatse Rusere all over Karanga.

In any case, the Portuguese crown sent Nuno Álvares Pereira as an official governor to administer the lands and mines that had been conquered or granted to Madeira in 1609, although, in the end, neither he nor his successors were able to win new conquests without Madeira's support or the cooperation of Gatse Rusere. The rivalries between the royal appointees and the settlers would cripple attempts to build a centrally administered colony.

A second civil war in Karanga, starting in 1628 and complicated by renewed invasions from across the Zambezi by Maravi, brought more Portuguese success. Dominicans, serving in the same capacity as had Jesuits in Angola, managed to put Mavura, a puppet ruler, on the throne of Karanga but were unable to beat down resistance, effectively splitting the state. At this point, in 1632, the Portuguese crown sent in another governor, Diogo de Sousa de Meneses, whose campaign was successful in defeating the rebel Mwene Mutapa and ensuring the rule of Mavura. For the next half century, Karanga was more or less under Portuguese control, although it was control that was held in a complex alliance between old Portuguese settlers and their African allies from the Zambezi, Dominican priests, and the Portuguese crown that sought to use these conquests in their interests. But at no time did it approach the royal control of Angola.

Portugal also made plans to extend its influence in West Africa, for example, by attempting to concentrate Portuguese traders and residents in a royally controlled settlement in Guinea in 1590, although both resident Portuguese and the local authorities opposed it. In the end, although a factory was established, a real colony was not. Another attempt to create a colony in Sierra Leone, discussed in Lisbon in the first decade of the seventeenth century, never came to anything, although the Jesuit mission there, so often the precursor to colonization, was quite successful. By the 1620s, there were several Christian kingdoms among the petty states of the area around Sierra Leone, and their religion attracted missionaries, if not conquerors, for much of the rest of the century.

The Portuguese were also active in Ethiopia, through the Jesuits who fell under Portuguese patronage. The Portuguese soldiers of the first mission, left in Ethiopia by the crown, abandoned any loyalty to Portugal and were soon absorbed into the Ethiopian population, although they seem to have kept their allegiance to the Catholic faith. To strengthen the faith and to bring the whole of the Ethiopian church to Rome, the Jesuits, led by Andrea da Oviedo, arrived in Ethiopia in 1557. Their task was to reconcile the Ethiopian church to Rome, and they relied on some vague promises made by King Galadewos that they would join the Catholic communion and abandon their more ancient allegiance to the patriarch of Alexandria. Because the Muslim Ottomans had reduced the capacities of the Alexandrine patriarchs, it was more and more difficult for Ethiopia to obtain the requisite spiritual leaders, and the role of the *abuna*, an Egyptian sent by the patriarch to lead the Ethiopian church on a lifetime appointment, was restricted. Thus, transferring allegiance to Rome might make sense.

The Jesuits, however, were not seeking to effect a reconciliation. They were quite confident that they knew the whole theological truth and were less than willing to accommodate Ethiopian practices. Long and arcane debates ensued, which if they did nothing else, forced the Ethiopian church to reexamine its doctrine and to meet the intellectual and spiritual challenge of the Jesuits. Jesuits enjoyed imperial support, in part at least, because Ethiopian rulers hoped that more military aid would be forthcoming from Portugal. Jesuits were granted lands at Fremona in the north of the country, where they served the descendants of the original Portuguese force and made a few converts among the nobility. As it happened, however, the crown of Portugal was reluctant to send troops so far away to a country that was no longer seriously threatened by Muslims. Ethiopia's greatest threat came from the invasion of the Oromo in the late sixteenth and the seventeenth centuries, but these Oromo practiced a traditional religion and were capable of becoming Muslims or Christians, depending on their situation.

In 1607, Susenyos, an emperor with strong Catholic leanings, came to the throne. Over the course of the following years, he favored the Catholics among his subjects, eventually declaring himself in favor of making the whole country Catholic in 1622. Jesuits, led by the new bishop, Alfonso Mendes, a Spaniard appointed by the papacy, sought to replace the original clergy with priests of their own making and to alter the liturgy completely. But these changes were not just theological, sweeping as they were. The Catholics were also a political faction, and their enemies capitalized on popular discontent with the religious changes to spark civil war. Soon even loyal followers of the emperor had turned against him, and after ten years of civil war Susenyos abdicated in favor of his son Fasiladas, who in turn promptly restricted the Jesuits and restored the old faith. After another twenty years, the Jesuits were effectively eliminated from the country, and by 1700 there were no more Catholics among the laity.

Portugal would scarcely have benefited even if the Jesuits had been successful, because they were foreign, but Susenyos hoped that military support from Portugal would allow him to carry off his reform. But this sort of adventure was well beyond Portugal's means.

After the middle of the seventeenth century, Portuguese expansion can be said to have ended, although the growth of the possessions of individual Portuguese settlers in the Zambezi valley continued, but with scarcely any metropolitan control. The Dutch began to encroach on Portuguese domains, especially after the formation in 1622 of the West India Company, which occupied posts on the Gold Coast, captured El Mina in 1637, and occupied Angola from 1641 to 1648. They and the English also raided Portuguese coastal holdings in East Africa as well. In East Africa, the Omanis, throwing off Portuguese rule in the late seventeenth century, soon began naval campaigns along the coast, eventually driving out the Portuguese.

In Angola, the round of wars that had begun with the attempt of the Portuguese to use their military allies, the Imbangala, to put a puppet on the throne of Ndongo evolved into a larger war between the pro-Portuguese king, Ngola Hari, and his legitimist rival, Queen Njinga. Although Njinga was driven out from much of Ndongo in 1628–1635, she managed to use a rebuilt kingdom in Matamba as a base to carry on a war against her rival. At the same time, Portuguese attempts to use their Imbangala allies to invade Kongo in 1622 led Kongo's king, Pedro II, to write to the States

General of the Netherlands and invite them to participate in a land and sea invasion of Angola with the aim of driving out the Portuguese. After a false start in 1624, the Dutch did manage a successful capture of Luanda and made an alliance not only with Kongo but with Njinga against the Portuguese. However, the Dutch were overextended and did relatively little to assist either of their allies against the entrenched Portuguese, who had retreated inland to Massangano. It was only when the Portuguese received reinforcements that Njinga and the Dutch made a concerted war against the Portuguese, capturing nearly all their positions in campaigns in 1647–1648. When a second relief expedition, led by Salvador de Sá, arrived from Brazil in 1648, the Dutch hastily capitulated and Njinga's forces were driven back. Njinga was forced to sue for peace in 1654, and when the treaty was finally ratified in 1656, this major phase of the Angolan wars came to an end.

In signing peace with Njinga, however, the Portuguese effectively abandoned the claims of their ally Ngola Hari and his descendants to the throne of Ndongo. Bitterness about this led Felipe III Ngola Hari to rebel against Portugal in 1680, and a long campaign finally captured his capital and extinguished his kingdom, which then was placed under more direct Portuguese control. At that point, effective Portuguese intervention in African affairs was over in Angola. Some minor wars took place later, of course, in the highlands south of the main colony behind the Portuguese outlying post of Benguela, for example, and Portuguese forces occasionally took long expeditionary marches into the interior, as they did in the 1720s. Likewise, Portugal still sought to gain control of trade routes and posts for fiscal reasons in the eighteenth century, constructing a fort at Encoge in 1759 for that purpose and conducting fairly extensive campaigns (mostly punitive raids rather than those aimed at conquest) to support this. But these military operations did not extend Portuguese authority in any significant way.

During the eighteenth century, the slave trade gradually became the most important item of commerce for all Europeans coming out of Africa. In Angola, which had been the leading exporter of slaves in the early seventeenth century through Portuguese warfare, the supply of slaves continued even when the wars came to an end: Angola was exporting 5,000 to 6,000 slaves per year as its wars drew to a close in the mid-seventeenth century, but the numbers grew dramatically in the eighteenth century, reaching nearly 12,000 yearly by 1740 and almost 19,000 annually by the end of the eighteenth century. Portuguese shippers, although losing the near monopoly in exports of slaves in the seventeenth century, continued to be the sole suppliers of Brazil, which was itself one of the primary users of slaves in the Atlantic world.

In the east, Portuguese trajectories followed those of Angola. When Changamire, the ruler of the state of Rozvi in the Zimbabwe highlands, launched a campaign against the Portuguese positions in the highlands in 1693, Portuguese traders and their allies were swept away from the Karanga kingdom. As a result, all that Portugal had to show for its seventeenth-century expansion against the Karanga kingdom were the poorly controlled positions in the Zambezi valley and the coastal port of Sofala. The Zambezi dependencies, unlike those in Angola, gradually fell into the hands of the local settlers and their mixed-race descendants. Although the Zambezi dependencies claimed to be Portuguese and were so noted in Portuguese administration, the crown itself effectively controlled only Sofala and Mozambique in the region. It would take major wars to bring the Zambezi under Portuguese colonial control again in the scramble period of the late nineteenth century.

Portugal was far more deeply involved in Africa for far longer than any other European country. Only the Dutch, whose positions around the Cape of Good Hope in South Africa eventually expanded across the continent, could rival them. Portuguese success in Africa was largely a result of shrewdly recognizing their shortcomings and inabilities and capitalizing on their knowledge of the region. Their skillful use of allies, recognition of the strengths and weaknesses of African states, and their mercantile skills all gave them a privileged position that they were able to maintain even as their military and naval power weakened in the face of competition from European rivals.

BIBLIOGRAPHICAL ESSAY

In the public eye, Portuguese expansion is widely regarded through the romantic lens that also views Columbus's voyages as the fifteenth-century equivalent of the exploration of space. This old-fashioned notion of the search for truth and bold adventurers has been largely refuted by Portuguese historians since the 1940s, who followed the lead of Duarte Leite and Vitorino Magalhães Godinho in pointing out the complex and largely prosaic motives that drove Portugal into the Atlantic and to Africa.

A good general work on Portuguese history with excellent coverage of the expansion is José Mattoso (ed.), *História de Portugal* (8 vols., Lisbon, 1992–1994). The most valuable specialized work on Portuguese expansion is Vitorino Magalhães Godinho's *Os Portugueses e a economia mundial* (2 vols., Lisbon, 1981). For specifically African aspects, see John Thornton's *Africa and Africans in the Making of the Atlantic World, 1400–1800*, 2nd ed. (Cambridge, 1998), and also his "Early Kongo–Portuguese-Kongo Relations,

1483–1575: A New Interpretation," *History in Africa* 8 (1981), pp. 183–204, for interpretations that underlie this one and go well beyond Kongo and São Tomé.

A good introduction to the history of the African countries, as well as an overview of Portuguese activities in the light of African history, can be found in contributions by Marian Malowist, Jan Vansina, J. E. Inikori, Boubacar Barry, Eike Haberland, and A. I. Salim in Bethwell Ogot (ed.), *General History of Africa*, vol. 5 (Berkeley, CA, 1992).

Primary source material has been published in many places, and one of the best for West and Central Africa is António Brásio (ed.), *Monumenta missionaria Africana*, 2 series: 1st series, Central Africa and Lower Guinea (15 vols., Lisbon, 1952–1988); 2nd series, Senegambia and Upper Guinea (5 vols., Lisbon, 1958–1985).

For southeast Africa, George Theal's classic collection *Records of South-Eastern Africa* (9 vols., Cape Town, 1964 [originally published 1898–1903]) is augmented by A. da Silva Rego, T. W. Baxter, and E. E. Burke (eds.), *Documents on the Portuguese in Mozambique and Central Africa* (8 vols., Lisbon, 1962–1975). A useful collection of documents on the East African coast is G. S. P. Freeman-Grenville (ed.), *The East African Coast: Select Documents from the First to the Earlier Nineteenth Century* (Oxford, 1962).

The basic collection of documents on the Portuguese in Ethiopia is C. Beccari's *Rerum Aethiopicanum scriptores Occidentales* (15 vols., Rome, 1903–1917), although some more recent editions of some works are superior. The introductions and notes of editions of some of these works also give an overview of the role of the Portuguese; see especially Charles Beckingham and G. W. B. Huntingford's edition and translation of Francisco Alvares's *The Prester John of the Indies* (London, 1961).

A solid work on the Portuguese on the Gold Coast and nearby areas is J. Bato'ora Ballong-Wen-Mewuda's *São Jorge da Mina, 1482–1637: La vie d'un comptoir Portugais en Afrique occidentale* (Lisbon, 1993), which advances on John Vogt's *Portuguese Rule on the Gold Coast, 1482–1637* (Athens, GA, 1979). P. E. H. Hair and A. Teixeira da Mota's *East of Mina: Afro-European Relations on the Gold Coast in the 1550s and 1560s* (Madison, WI, 1988) and Hair's own *The Founding of the Castelo de São Jorge da Mina: An Analysis of the Sources* (Madison, WI, 1994) both provide a wealth of detail on the earliest Portuguese activities. Alan Ryder provides important information on Benin in *Benin and the Europeans* (Evanston, IL, 1969).

For the story of Angola, the narrative tale is told in detail in Graziano Saccardo's *Congo e Angola con la storia del'antica missione dei Cappuccini* (3 vols., Venice, 1982–1983). David Birmingham's older *Trade and Conquest in Angola* (Oxford, 1966) is still valuable. An important collection of studies is found in Beatrix Heintze's *Studien zur Geschichte Angolas im 16. und 17. jahrhundert* (Cologne, 1996).

For East Africa, the general narrative is still well told by Justus Strandes in *The Portuguese Period in East Africa* (Nairobi, 1961), originally published in 1899. The issue of Portuguese colonization in the Zambezi valley was extensively discussed in M. D. Newitt's *A History of Mozambique* (Bloomington, IN, 1995), which summarizes earlier literature by himself and also Allen Isaacman's *Mozambique* (Madison, WI, 1975). Politics in the African countries are reviewed in S. I. G. Mudenge's *A Political History of Munhumutapa c. 1400–1902* (Madison, WI, 1988) and H. H. K. Bhila's *Trade and Politics in a Shona Kingdom* (Harlow, 1982).

No history of the Jesuit Order and its role in colonization can now do without Dauril Alden's *The Making of an Enterprise: The Society of Jesus in Portugal, Its Empire, and Beyond, 1540–1750* (Stanford, CA, 1996). A useful survey of Christian missions in general and especially those of Portugal is found in Adrian Hastings's *The Church in Africa, 1450–1950* (Oxford, 1994). The Jesuit mission to Ethiopia is well discussed in Girma Beshah and Merid Aregay's *The Question of the Union of Churches in Luso-Ethiopian Relations* (Lisbon, 1964). See also the valuable general survey by Adrian Hastings cited earlier.

Part II: Politics and Institutions

6

PATTERNS OF SETTLEMENT IN THE PORTUGUESE EMPIRE, 1400–1800

A. J. R. Russell-Wood

December 20, 1999, marked the formal cession of Macao, Portugal's last vestige of a colonial empire, to the People's Republic of China. This was the final step in a steady process of attrition. The period from 1580 to 1690 saw Portuguese sea routes threatened by the Dutch, English, and French and settlements besieged, attacked, and even occupied by Europeans: by the French in the Maranhão; by the Dutch in Indonesia, on the Malabar Coast, in Angola, in the Gulf of Guinea, and in Northeast Brazil; and by the English in the Persian Gulf. There were also losses to native rulers: Hormuz fell to the Persians in 1622; in India, the Marathas ousted the Portuguese from Bassein and the Província do Norte in 1737–1740; and Omani Arabs expelled the Portuguese from Muscat in 1650 and expelled them from city-states in East Africa and took Mombasa in 1698. The independence of Brazil in 1822 marked the end of the Portuguese American empire.

A century and a half later, Portugal could not remain immune to anti-imperial sentiments, the force of nationalism in India, and colonial wars in Africa. The Portuguese were ousted from Goa in 1961, and the 1970s saw the decolonization of Portuguese Africa and adjacent islands: Angola, Mozambique, Guinea-Bissau, Cape Verde, São Tomé, and Príncipe. By 2000, a global empire that in its heyday had extended from Macao to Mato Grosso was reduced to continental Portugal and the archipelagos of the Azores and Madeira, which became autonomous regions of the republic in accordance with the 1976 constitution. This relentless attrition makes all the more remarkable the endurance of a Portuguese presence throughout the world at the dawn of the twenty-first century. This can be measured in the number of people of Portuguese birth or descent, the prevalence of the Portuguese language as the third most spoken European language in the world today (in Portugal, Brazil, Madeira, the Azores, Cape Verde,

Angola, Guinea-Bissau, São Tomé, Príncipe, Mozambique, East Timor, and still vestiges in Goa and Macao), and the legacy of a Portuguese cultural tradition spanning, in some cases, more than five hundred years. This chapter examines the genesis and development of Portuguese settlement in Africa, Asia, and America between 1400 and 1800.

Two points must be made at the outset. Historians have to be alert to the temptation to see events within Portugal and domestic policies through the prism of empire, with resulting distortions and de-emphasis of domestic conditions. Second, although my focus is on overseas settlements, during the same period there was not only an ebb and flow of Portuguese between the mother country and other European nations but also substantial settlements of Portuguese in Flanders, France, Italy, Germany, and in Seville and London. There were also diasporic communities of displaced Portuguese Jews. This exodus was sufficiently serious to warrant a law in 1660 prohibiting persons from leaving Portugal without royal permission and a passport issued by the crown and forbidding remittances of money from Portugal to such emigrants. That expatriate communities of Portuguese are prominent in Paris and other European cities today is but the continuation of a centuries-long tradition.

Overseas Settlement in the Context of National Goals

With regard to Portuguese crown policy on overseas settlement, a distinction must be drawn between an "ideology of expansion" and those imperial objectives attainable only through settlement. The answer given by a convict (*degredado*) in the fleet of Vasco da Gama when asked, on disembarking in Calicut on May 21, 1498, why the Portuguese had come so far – that they had come to "seek Christians and spices" – has been given primacy in the balance sheet of motivations for overseas expansion. In fact, there was no single overarching factor. One or more of the following were present: political, economic, commercial, and religious objectives; comparative military advantage; scientific curiosity; and adventure. At different periods and for specific regions, one or more predominated. Settlement was not a prerequisite for evangelization. But a physical presence – a critical mass of Portuguese – as measured by settlements was highly desirable to the furtherance of crown policies in three respects.

First was the commercial, namely, for better access to sources of commodities for sale on the European market and, ideally, to control the flow of these commodities; to create and control sources of production of raw materials (such as sugar or cotton); to gain access to routes of precious metals or spices or, even better, control their sources; and, finally, to create areas under Portuguese control to provide security for the accumulation, dispatch, and receipt of commodities for import or export. Commerce could not be micromanaged by a bureaucracy in Lisbon, by crown representatives in Goa, Salvador, and Rio de Janeiro, or by factors in trading posts. It required individuals or groups to make contacts and establish local networks, which were the preconditions for the creation of wide-ranging commercial webs. Equally important was denial to competitors, European or indigenous, of access to these same facilities or opportunities.

Second, a prerequisite for this complex and sometimes protracted process to occur was a physical presence over time and in such numbers as could only be achieved by settlement. Pursuit of comparative commercial advantage also demanded a military presence in sufficient numbers to protect metropolitan commercial interests. Although this could be accomplished in part by dispatch from Portugal of soldiers and by (in some regions) technological superiority, this was expensive, made exceptional demands on a limited human resource pool, and could be undermined by desertion. Overseas settlements provided not only an administrative context for garrisons but a social context for soldiers. Oft expressed by kings was the hope that settlements would bring stability, that stability would encourage population growth, and that, through natural reproduction and immigration, there would be created sufficient numbers of able-bodied men to serve overseas as troops-of-the-line and in militia companies.

Third, in an age when possession was nine-tenths of the law, settlements not only ensured a comparative commercial and military advantage but sent the clear message that the Portuguese were there to stay. Papal bulls notwithstanding, exploration, conquest, possession, and settlement validated assertions of sovereignty. Evidence of settlement was a legitimizing instrument for political purposes. Settlements, and not only those on the peripheries of empire, reinforced, and were expressions of, a Portuguese crown presence. This was as important in challenging counterclaims by European rivals as in dissuading indigenous leaders from ousting the Portuguese interlopers.

Portugal's engagement overseas had predictable negative consequences for the metropole. It siphoned off able-bodied men to the point of causing sexual imbalance, demographic collapse, and labor shortages, jeopardized the agricultural basis of the nation's economy, and disrupted a social fabric based on village communities. Such generalizations demand a note of caution. The impact on Portugal was not uniform for several reasons. First, there were variants in family structures in Portugal: Whereas the Minho was characterized by a population whose majority lived inland and consisted of extended families, families in the Algarve were more likely to be nuclear and dependent on the sea for their subsistence. Second, cities and towns were less affected than rural areas, and, in the latter, there were also regional variants depending on the period under discussion. Third, adverse demographic and economic repercussions on the mother country were not always exclusively attributable to overseas settlement. In the case of Africa and Asia, the numbers of Portuguese settlers at any time between the sixteenth and eighteenth centuries were modest in comparison with the large numbers of males sent to the Estado da Índia as soldiers or bureaucrats, whose absences or deaths were disruptive to family life and to the rural economy in the mother country. The sixteenth century saw a population increase in Portugal from about 1 million to 1.2 million. The case can be made that this was attributable to a desire to compensate for males who were absent and that the introduction of maize into Portugal permitted the expansion of the agricultural sector of the economy. In terms of the impact of overseas settlement exclusively, this was most keenly felt in the fifteenth and sixteenth centuries with emigration to the Atlantic islands of Madeira and the Azores and in the seventeenth and eighteenth centuries with emigration to Brazil. In the latter case especially, the fact that nephews, brothers, and male relatives joined other members of the family who had migrated earlier could result in more extended family networks overseas.

Overseas settlements taxed an overextended imperial system of governance. Generally accepted prior to the nineteenth century was the "doctrine of the two spheres": namely, that treaties between European powers did not necessarily apply overseas and, conversely, that European powers could enter into treaties whose applicability was exclusively extra-European. European rivalries were played out on African, Asian, and American stages. Commerce spurred inter-European hostilities on land and sea. Quite apart from the decisions of individuals, it was in the best interests of the Portuguese crown to have settlements overseas, provided that these were self-sustaining and not a drain on the metropolitan exchequer and, preferably, revenue-generating.

Parameters of Settlement

Papal bulls and binational treaties in the fifteenth century established rights of domain of Spain and Portugal, respectively, and recognized the concept of spheres of influence. By the Treaty of Alcáçovas (1479; ratified 1480), Portugal recognized Spain's right to the Canary Islands. Spain acquiesced to Portuguese claims to the archipelagos of Madeira, the Azores, and Cape

Verde and to lands in Africa "discovered and to be discovered." The concept of global demarcation was expressed in the bull *Inter caetera* (1493). The Treaty of Tordesillas (1494) extended the line of demarcation to 370 leagues west of the Cape Verde islands. This gave Portugal the right to establish settlements east of this longitudinal line running roughly from Marajó Island in northern Brazil to the mouth of the Paraná River; in practice, from today's Pará in northern Brazil eastward across Africa and India to the Moluccas in Indonesia. With some exceptions, Brazil being an egregious example, Portugal adhered to this ruling. In the Brazilian case, the Treaty of Madrid (1750) recognized Portuguese territorial transgressions and acknowledged what were substantially to become the oft-disputed boundaries of an independent Brazil. Portuguese kings had no grand plan for overseas settlements, nor, even in region-specific cases, was there a coherent or sustained policy for settlement. Instead there was experimentation with different models, false starts, and even an ad hoc quality to settlement and colonization. The crown, corporate groups, and individuals, but not chartered companies as was the case with the Dutch, English, and French, were all involved in overseas settlement.

Even with a papal imprimatur and a binational treaty for Portuguese settlements in prescribed regions of the world, and crown policies promoting such settlement, there were constraints. Madeira, the Azores, Cape Verde, São Tomé, and Príncipe were uninhabited prior to the arrival of the Portuguese. These were islands where the Portuguese could freely create their world. But the royal will was tempered, thwarted, or strengthened by local conditions in Africa, Asia, and America. Generally, these fell into two categories: sociopolitical and natural. Preexisting local conditions, indigenous reactions to Portuguese intrusion, and how the Portuguese responded were critical to determining the nature of Portuguese settlement. In continental Africa the Portuguese encountered a gamut of polities, including empires and city-states, of leadership (kings, sultans, and "big men"), of social hierarchies, and of religions ranging from Islam to fetishistic cults. In Africa, they also found a sophisticated knowledge of metallurgy and of crop and animal husbandry, with established trading patterns in West and Central Africa and in East Africa a dense network of local commerce and maritime trade to the Red Sea, the Persian Gulf, and the west coast of India. In South, Southeast and East Asia, the Portuguese came into contact with major empires, sophisticated forms of governance, powerful local leaders, established religions, technological skills, long-established labor practices, interlocking systems of local and oceanic trade, and societies with profound ethnic distinctions and complex divisions and hierarchies. By way of contrast, in America the Portuguese encountered Stone Age peoples whose governance, mores, hierarchies, and religious practices were as unrecognizable as they were baffling and disturbing to Europeans.

At various times and places, and as the result of tactics running the full range of the proverbial carrot-and-stick approaches, the Portuguese acquired sovereignty or suzerainty over non-European territories and peoples. Some territories were effectively Portuguese protectorates: Kongo in the early sixteenth century and Hormuz with the Shah being maintained in office. Sometimes the Portuguese were granted extraterritorial rights for unfortified settlements as occurred (ca. 1557) in Macao. In El Mina (São Jorge da Mina) (1482) and Diu (1535), they were authorized to build forts. Early sixteenth-century Morocco set a successful precedent for the practice of having tributary kings or sultans. Some rulers, as in the case of the sultan of Malindi, swore allegiance and became puppet rulers. Others became client kings. Sometimes a Portuguese presence was the result of conquest, as in Ceuta (1415), Goa (1510), Malacca (1511), and Hormuz (1515).

There was a crucial difference between Portuguese Asia and Portuguese America with respect to settlement. In the former, the Portuguese existed on the sufferance of indigenous leaders, and Portuguese policymaking and actions could not occur in isolation from indigenous considerations and prevailing circumstances. A Portuguese presence could be tolerated or terminated at the whim of a local ruler. In some cases, the Portuguese could establish a base for settlement only because factionalism and dissent among the local rulers made it impossible for them to present a united front against the intruders. At other times, the Portuguese exploited local rivalries, such as between the sultans of Mombasa and Malindi or the king of Calicut and the raja of Cochin. In Brazil and Angola, settlement was marked by ongoing hostilities with indigenous peoples. But it was in Brazil, where the Portuguese faced no political, religious, or social constraints imposed by local rulers or mores, that they had a virtual carte blanche to act independently of local peoples. Nowhere were dispossession (from the indigenous perspective) and indigenous mortality resulting from the Portuguese presence to be more pronounced than in Brazil. Preexisting indigenous political, social, economic, and religious contexts explain why Portuguese settlement evolved very differently in each hemisphere.

Geography of Settlement

Portuguese overseas settlement was the fruit of crown intention and individual initiative, but it was also framed by natural forces that imposed their own rhythms on the administration, commerce, and settlement of empire.

As befitted a seaborne empire, wind systems and currents played a role in patterns of settlement: The trade winds of the Atlantic imposed a different order of constraints than did the monsoonal systems of the Arabian Sea, the Indian Ocean, and the many seas extending eastward to the Sea of Japan and the Timor Sea. Trade winds and currents of the Atlantic made some locations more desirable than others for settlement and influenced the chronology and effectiveness of communications and trade between settlements and with Lisbon.

Let us take one example. Atlantic gyres effectively divided the east–west coast (from the mouth of the Amazon River to Cape São Roque) of Brazil from the north–south coast (from Cape São Roque to Rio de La Plata), making for two Brazils. East of the Cape of Good Hope were monsoonal systems, each with its own characteristics and chronology, to which the Portuguese had to accommodate if they were to travel and establish settlements on the coasts of the Arabian Sea to the west and, to the east, the numerous seas of Indonesia, the East China Sea, and the Sea of Japan. Rivers were also critical to Portuguese settlement, especially in Brazil. In the far north were the Amazon-Madeira-Guaporé and the Araguaia-Tocantins river systems and tributaries and, to the south, the Paraguay-Paraná-La Plata hydrographic system. To these could be added the rivers São Francisco, Paraíba do Sul, Jacuí, Doce, Jequitinhonha, Rio de Contas, Paraguaçú, and Parnaíba, with varying degrees of navigability and access to the interior and on whose banks settlements were established. In Africa, rivers played a less important role in terms of settlement, with the exception of the Kwanza in Angola and the Zambezi. In Asia, there was a virtual absence of Portuguese riverine settlements, but Goa, Hughli, and Macao bore testimony to the importance of estuarine settlement in the pursuit of what has been referred to as "emporia trade."

Climate and epidemiological considerations made some regions unattractive for European settlement. The fact that the resident Portuguese populations in Mozambique and Angola were small, despite the strategic importance of the former and potential riches of the latter, was attributable to the well-deserved reputation each had as a death trap for Europeans. Contemporary reports spoke highly of Ceylon as a desirable area for settlement and also of certain regions of Brazil.

There is a strong psychological component to emigration and the decision to settle overseas. Added to other constraints imposed on the Portuguese when it came to settling overseas was fear of unlimited space. To any European, the *pampas*, the Australian outback, or the Great American Desert could be intimidating. In Portuguese, the word for such regions was *sertão* and, to better capture their infinite and unbounded quality, Portuguese used the plural form *sertões*. These terms were applied to southeast Africa, the interior of Angola, and the vast expanses in Brazil from the Maranhão and Ceará to Minas Gerais. In Brazil, *sertão* came to be associated by the Portuguese with climatic excess, topographic disorder, and chaos. The land itself was demonized. The Portuguese perception of the land was inalienable from how they viewed the indigenous population: barbarous, cannibalistic, subhuman, immoral, no better than beasts, and impervious to outside civilizing influences. Such lands were shunned for settlement by the Portuguese. In his description (1635) of the environs of Daman, António Bocarro used *sertão* in the context of Portuguese jurisdiction over lands inhabited by "Gentiles and Moors who have a virulent hatred for our holy Catholic faith" ("gentios e mouros, que tem grande ódio à nossa sancta fé catholica") or in reference to lands bordering territories of rulers hostile to the Portuguese. Here it was the religious beliefs of the inhabitants or lands vulnerable to attack that he was describing. There is no indication that the vast interior regions of India inspired fear in the Portuguese. In 1800, the boundaries of much of Portuguese America and Portuguese Africa were still states of mind and geopolitical pretensions rather than surveyed, mapped, or mathematically defined areas.

Emigration was a necessary prerequisite to overseas settlement by Europeans. From the fifteenth through the eighteenth centuries, Portuguese overseas settlement was the result of migration by sea. In the absence of reliable figures, the Portuguese historian Vitorino Magalhães Godinho has postulated the following numbers for emigration from Portugal: fifteenth century: 50,000; 1500–1580: 280,000; 1580–1640: 360,000; 1640–1700: 150,000; 1700–1760: 600,000. In short, between 1 million and 1.5 million persons emigrated from Portugal between 1415 and 1760.

Although the focus here is on overseas emigration from Portugal, it cannot be overemphasized that there were numerous examples of settlements established by Portuguese departing from places other than the mother country: of Madeirenses and Azoreans settling in Brazil; of settlements on the African mainland formed by persons from the Cape Verde archipelago; and of persons of Portuguese descent moving from the west coast of India to southeast Africa, Mozambique, and the Zambezi valley. In the Gulf of Guinea and in Mozambique, there were small communities of Brazilians; and in the Bay of Bengal, there were informal settlements of Portuguese traders and former soldiers (*casados*) who had moved there from Goa and other crown-approved settlements on the Malabar Coast. In these cases, regardless of whether the migration was from Portugal to Africa, Brazil, or Asia, or between areas over which the Portuguese claimed or exercised jurisdiction, migration was by sea. This was also the case for Brazil in the late seventeenth and eighteenth centuries. But Brazil was unique in the Portuguese empire in that, in addition to large numbers of migrants arriving by sea during this period, there was concurrently a massive internal migration by river and overland. This applied not only to persons of Portuguese birth and descent but also to persons of African birth and descent in an internal interregional slave trade attributable to the demand for labor in the extractive industries and opportunities for agricultural ventures with the emergence of new markets.

These factors – treaties setting lines of demarcation, local sociopolitical conditions, the degree of Portuguese success in establishing a foothold and by what means (by conquest, negotiation, or cession), and natural and psychological considerations – contributed to the geography of settlement in the Portuguese empire in at least five ways. The most obvious was propinquity to the sea. Not only was this a seaborne empire, in terms of the importance of the maritime umbilical, but this was also a littoral empire, featuring island settlements, Brazilian port cities, West and East Africa, India and Indonesia, Macao, and Nagasaki. Exceptions can be counted on one hand: in Brazil, sixteenth-century São Paulo and eighteenth-century settlements in the interior spurred by gold fever; and the meager Portuguese presence – rather than significant settlement – in Angola and southeast Africa, and trading settlements on the Zambezi. In Brazil, by 1808, the greatest concentration of urban population was still in port cities, and clustered around Salvador and its Recôncavo, the Várzea of Pernambuco, and Rio de Janeiro and the Baixada fluminense.

A second characteristic was that, especially in Africa and the Estado da Índia, Portuguese settlements lacked a hinterland under Portuguese control: Malacca and Macao were two flagrant examples. This highlights the fact that it was the exception for Portuguese to have control over extensive contiguous territories, and the norm was enclave settlement. Brazil was the most significant exception: Angola and Mozambique were two further exceptions. But even these were illusory. Royal government in the hinterland of southeast Africa, in the interior of Angola, or in the *sertão* of Brazil was absent, problematical, or sporadic. In Angola, it was essentially a few forts and garrisons. Only in Brazil was there present the combination of extensive territorial holdings, soil and climatic conditions conducive to the cultivation of crops, the potential for open-range ranching, access to labor, and reasonably healthy conditions. Territorial size and the absence of constraints such as were imposed by sultans, city-states, or kings meant that only in Brazil did there exist extensive core–periphery relationships, development of secondary centers with their own peripheries, and the potential for interperipheral commercial exchange independent of centers. This market-driven dynamic led to new settlements and changing relationships between centers, their immediate surrounding areas, and more distant hinterlands. In 1711, the Tuscan-born Jesuit André João Antonil made the perceptive observation that the mule trade linked the south of Brazil with the central regions and that the movement of cattle on the hoof and their drovers provided a link between different regions of the colony. Local conditions did not permit this kind of long-distance exchange elsewhere in the Portuguese empire.

The Portuguese empire was characterized by a pattern of discrete settlements that were widely dispersed and often isolated from each other by very substantial distances. Viable transportation was by sea rather than by land in virtually all instances. But dependence on current and wind systems could, in and of itself, result in seasonal isolation. This characteristic was not limited to coastal settlements. In Brazil, Angola, Mozambique, the Província do Norte in India, and Ceylon, where the Portuguese had access to larger areas of contiguous land, there were few clusters of settlement. At first blush, an exception was the creation between 1711 and 1718 of mining townships in the captaincy-general of São Paulo e Minas Gerais in Brazil. Closer scrutiny shows that although the towns of Vila Rica, Vila do Carmo, Sabará, São João del Rei, and São José del Rei were settlement nuclei, as a group these mining settlements stood alone. This was also the case with settlements in Goiás (Vila Boa) and Mato Grosso (Cuiabá and Vila Bela). In Minas Gerais, Goiás, and Mato Grosso, there were also small mining camps (*arraiais*) initially. But, in fact, these reinforce the notion of the archipelagic quality of settlement in Brazil: islands of settlement separated by distance and physical barriers. Communities along drover roads and on fluvial arteries played predominantly a service role (inns, stabling, fodder, foodstuffs, provisions, and trade) rather than being important as settlements. This characteristic also applied to trading posts on the Zambezi River. In 1800, much of Portuguese Africa and America, not only on the peripheries but in the vast interstices between settlements, was still unknown and unsettled by Europeans.

Fourth, only in Brazil were there substantial changes in the pattern of settlement distribution over three hundred years. These changes were attributable, in part, to the potential of the land (i.e., the incentive for mobility created by its sheer vastness) but also to the fact that only in Brazil did Portuguese claims to sovereignty go substantially unchallenged. There were few constraints on Portuguese settlement other than distance, inhospitable terrain, drought, and Amerindians. In the late sixteenth and seventeenth centuries, there were thrusts to the far north and far south, leading to settlement initially northward to Ceará and subsequently to Maranhão and Pará and southward to Paraná. These population moves continued in the eighteenth century, notably to Santa Catarina and Rio Grande de São Pedro in the south. Between 1700 and 1750 there was a massive relocation of people from coastal areas as far removed as the captaincies of Maranhão and Grão Pará and São Paulo but also from the interior of Pará, Maranhão, Ceará, Piauí, Pernambuco, Bahia, and São Paulo. There was no comparable voluntary population shift elsewhere in the Portuguese empire or a multiphase establishment of settlements extending over two centuries. From the early seventeenth century through the mid-eighteenth century alone, the settlement continuum can be gauged by the following (incomplete) list of new towns: in the north, São Luís do Maranhão (French, 1612; Portuguese, 1615), Belém do Pará (1616), and Fortaleza (1699); in the south, Vila de Nossa Senhora do Rosário de Paranaguá (between 1646 and 1649), São Francisco do Sul (between 1658 and 1660), Colônia do Sacramento (1680), Laguna (1714), Desterro (ca. 1726), and Rio Grande de São Pedro (ca. 1747); and, in the interior, Ribeirão do Carmo, Vila Rica do Ouro Prêto, and Nossa Senhora da Conceição do Sabará in 1711, São João del Rei in 1713, Vila Nova da Rainha de Caeté and Vila do Príncipe in 1714, Pitanguí in 1715, and São José del Rei in 1718, all in Minas Gerais; in Bahia, Jacobina (1721), Nossa Senhora do Livramento (1724), and Nossa Senhora do Bom Sucesso (1730); Vila Real do Senhor Bom Jesus de Cuiabá (1727) and Vila Bela da Santíssima Trindade (1752) in Mato Grosso; and Vila Boa (1739) in Goiás.

Finally, there was a marked contrast between settlement patterns in the Atlantic area and even in southeast Africa on the one hand and Portuguese settlements on the shores of the Arabian Sea, in India, and reaching out to Japan. There was a markedly rural dimension – be this smallholdings or plantations – to Portuguese settlement in the Atlantic islands (Madeira, Pôrto Santo, the Azores, and Cape Verde), in São Tomé and Príncipe, and in Brazil. In all cases, the prospect of free land for cultivation was a major incentive to settlers. Exports reflected this rural dimension: sugar, wines, sweet grapes, and vegetable dyes and resins from Madeira; from the Azores, much the same, plus wheat; maize and orchil from Cape Verde; sugar from São Tomé; and sugar, hides, flour, cacao, cotton, coffee, rice, and wood products from Brazil. By way of contrast, commerce and financial gain, but not land or agriculture, was the prime incentive for Portuguese settlement in the Estado da Índia. Portuguese settlement east of the Cape of Good Hope was in an urban context: Regardless of whether these were forts, towns, or cities, in all cases the commercial and trading component was at the fore. In East Africa, there was a cluster between Sofala and Pate; and in India a further concentration from Diu south to Cochin, extending to Jaffna and Colombo in Ceylon (Sri Lanka). Although numbers of Portuguese in East African settlements remained few, it was in settlements on the west coast of India that there were concentrated the greatest numbers of Portuguese overseas in the sixteenth century.

The greatest human contrast between Portuguese Asia and Portuguese Brazil concerned Portuguese women. East of the Cape of Good Hope there were few women of Portuguese birth either as emigrants or settlers; some settlements counted one or two, or even none. In contrast, although outnumbered by Portuguese males, in Brazil and the Atlantic islands Portuguese-born women and their female offspring were present in sufficient numbers for there to be families who could count Portuguese descent on both sides over several generations. One result was that in Brazil there was less assimilation of Portuguese males into, or accommodation with, the societies and cultures of their female partners or wives than occurred in Africa and Asia.

Promoting Settlement

The Portuguese crown had a mixed record in promoting emigration and overseas settlement. This will be examined from two perspectives. The first is primarily bureaucratic, namely how – through decrees and appointments – the crown sought to create contexts conducive to settlement; second, how individuals were encouraged or coerced into emigration with a view toward settlement. A starting point is a survey of royal instructions (*regimentos*) and decrees (*alvarás*) that show how settlement was envisaged initially by the crown and how responsibility for settlement was delegated to lords-proprietor (*donatários*). *Cartas de doação e de mercê* and *forais* were documents over the royal signature setting out terms by which the crown ceded to individuals jurisdiction over overseas territories and granted specific rights, privileges, and benefices. Such royal favors carried the obligation of accepting responsibility for settlement. Donatorial captaincies were the preferred instruments for settlement in the first phase (Madeira, Pôrto Santo, the Azores, São Tomé, Cape Verde) of Portuguese expansion in the fifteenth century and in the second, sixteenth-century phase (Brazil and Angola). Between 1534 and 1536, Dom João III divided regions of Brazil from the mouth of the Amazon in the far north to São Vicente in the south into fifteen grants and allocated these to twelve lords donatory (*donatários*). Each was responsible for levying and collecting taxes, appointing judicial officials, establishing towns and villages, promoting agriculture and cultivation of land, and making land grants (*sesmarias*) to suitably qualified individuals. Undercapitalization, poor selection of lords-proprietor, bickering settlers, and hostile Amerindians contributed to the failure of captaincies in Brazil and the imposition of royal government in 1549. This did not deter the crown from continuing the donatory system in Angola, Sierra Leone, and even in Brazil after 1549. For the next 150 years, the Portuguese crown sought to regain the lands and jurisdictions it had conceded.

Preconditions for successful settlement were security, community, and opportunity. The crown sought to promote the first by introducing royal government. Governors and later viceroys were created for the Estado da Índia and for Brazil. Their responsibilities included creation of a secure physical environment for future settlers. Through "treaties of peace and friendship," Portuguese envoys, governors, or viceroys sought the compliance of local leaders, but the Portuguese did not shy away from warfare to obtain a strategic location. The uninhabited islands of the Atlantic presented no challenge. In Brazil, initially friendly relations with Amerindian peoples rapidly deteriorated, leading to hostilities and vigorous campaigns in the late sixteenth century, notably during the governorship of Mem de Sá (1557–1572), against native peoples.

The crown also sought to create living space – towns and villages where Portuguese could settle, establish their communities, and multiply. By 1550 in India, a Portuguese presence had been consolidated and Portuguese institutions introduced. Cities such as Goa, Bassein, Chaul, Daman, Cochin, Colombo, and even São Tomé de Meliapor exhibited some of the characteristics to which the Portuguese had become accustomed. There were opportunities for self-advancement socially and financially, servants, and sexual access to indigenous women. In Portuguese America, the establishment of Salvador in 1549 represented an extraordinary crown initiative. Prompted by the failure of the donatory system, the crown underwrote the costs of dispatching a fleet of six vessels, appointed a governor-general, and created the basis for royal government with public officials, including the all-important crown judge (*ouvidor*) and treasury commissioner. The spiritual dimension was entrusted to six Jesuits under Manuel da Nóbrega. The fleet included 320 persons of distinction (*pessoas destacadas*), soldiers, artisans in the building trades, and a workforce of convicts. The city was built, royal government established, defensive measures taken, and a capital created for Portuguese America. In 1551, the bishopric of Salvador was created. The city and environs attracted potential settlers. In 1584, Fernão Cardim, S. J., put the population at 3,000 Portuguese, 8,000 Amerindians converted to Christianity, and 3,000–4,000 African slaves. This bold and decisive initiative by Dom João III sent the message to European challengers that Portugal was in Brazil to stay. Over the next two centuries, as potential colonists moved away from the first nuclei of settlement, the crown created municipalities not only as instruments of governance but also to provide matrices conducive to stability, collective identity, and settlement. The crown also promoted construction of forts and trading posts in Africa and Asia.

In the Portuguese seaborne empire, other than in the extractive industries in Brazil, opportunity usually took the form of agriculture or trade. Efforts to promote settlement in Morocco in the fifteenth century included exemptions, concessions of lands by terms of *cartas de doação*, and *rendas em dinheiro*, but bore little fruit. For Madeira, the Azores, São Tomé, Príncipe, and especially Brazil, the crown strongly promoted settlement with an agricultural basis. Incentives came in the form of *sesmarias* (land grants), exemptions (as on payment of taxes for a specified period), and immunities such as from foreclosure for debt. In sixteenth-century Asia, commerce presented the greatest opportunity, and success depended largely on individual initiative. Not surprisingly for a crown whose attitudes toward overseas holdings were framed in the context of mercantilism and metropolitan control of commerce, the crown placed obstacles in the way of unbridled individual initiatives and especially when these might impinge negatively on royal monopolies and the metropolitan economy. In keeping with the notion that colonies should not be a drain on the mother country but should be revenue-generating, crown support for agriculture took the form of privileges, concessions, and exemptions rather than disbursements from the exchequer.

There were few instances of crown-sponsored emigration. When they did occur, these reflected royal concern to establish a stable Portuguese physical presence, provide incentives for settlement, especially on the peripheries of the empire, and create demographic nuclei for military and political reasons. Sponsored voluntary migration – of which there were also few examples – took two forms: first, dispatch of young women of marriageable age, known as "orphans of the king," to East Africa, India, and Brazil in the hope that they would contract marriages and anchor an otherwise volatile male population. The numbers were too small, however, to make a significant contribution. The crown also underwrote the passages of family groups to strategically sensitive areas. In the seventeenth century, there were proposals for sponsored emigration to and settlement of Mozambique, but either this did not come to fruition or the yield was slight. Sponsored relocation of homesteaders from the Azores to Santa Catarina in southern Brazil in the mid-eighteenth century was more successful.

In addition to voluntary sponsored emigration, there was coerced emigration from Portugal from the fifteenth century through 1800. This included lepers, New Christians, gypsies, vagabonds, and convicts. Convicted felons of both sexes were exiled to Morocco, São Tomé, Cape Verde, Angola, Brazil, East Africa, and India. Males performed hard labor or were impressed for garrison duty. The crown used convicts to further a multiple agenda: for military service, to gain commercial or political intelligence, and as instruments for settlement. Governors from Angola to Brazil complained that such undesirables and felons were highly disruptive and bemoaned the fact that the crown renounced any further responsibility for them once they left Portugal, provided no funds for their rehabilitation or occupational training, and gave little direction to governors as to how to regulate this human flotsam and jetsam on their arrival in the colonies.

Migrants and Settlers

When thinking of Portuguese settlement beyond Europe, the first question that comes to mind is: What were the push and pull factors that led Portuguese to leave the mother country? At the individual level, push factors were the law of primogeniture, inadequate quality and extent of land to provide a viable living, physical hardship, impressment for military service, dissatisfaction with prevailing conditions (financial, domestic, religious, or political), famine, plague, and disruption caused by war. The pull factors were free land, opportunity, and the lure of financial and social advancement. In the balance sheet of factors leading to individual decisions to settle overseas, we can be sure of one thing: There was no shortage of information, misinformation, and disinformation. Many potential settlers may have been functionally illiterate, but a cornucopia of information was available by word of mouth from returning soldiers and seamen, artisans, traders, priests, and friars. There must have been few villagers in Portugal who had not experienced the departure of a neighbor or relative or whose native sons had not sent news home. Portuguese in the cities and countryside of Portugal would have been familiar with major sea routes (*carreira da Índia*, *carreira do Brasil*, *carreira da África*) and with Portuguese settlements in the Estado da Índia. Such was the interlocking nature of the Portuguese Atlantic world that news of Africa and Brazil was readily available. So strong was the sense of identity shared by persons from the same village or rural community in Portugal or the Atlantic islands that there was chain emigration. This explains, for example, the strong Minho roots of families in eighteenth-century Minas Gerais.

Emigration was characterized less by patterns than by trends. This fluidity was apparent in the demography of emigration, waxing and waning in intensity at different periods and for different regions, with varying rhythms of acceleration and stagnation. Broadly speaking, major trends were: 1450–1500, a strong move from Portugal to Madeira and significantly less to the

Azores; 1500–1550, accelerated migration to the Azores and a more steady increase to Madeira; 1500–1600, constant and progressive emigration from Portugal to India, initially to the west coast and then to Ceylon and points further east; 1530s–1600, steady emigration to Brazil but less than to the Estado da Índia; and 1560s–1700, steady emigration from Madeira and the Azores, primarily to Brazil. The seventeenth century saw declining emigration from Portugal to India and a shift to Brazil, which thereafter eclipsed Asia as the destination of choice for emigrants from Portugal, Madeira, and the Azores. Portuguese emigration to North Africa and to West and Central West Africa was small in any period, although Mozambique did attract settlers over the sixteenth century. There was dispersion beyond port cities: from Mozambique up the Zambezi valley to the trading settlements of Sena and Tete; from Goa or Cochin to other coastal areas of western India; and to Coromandel, Ceylon (Sri Lanka), the Bay of Bengal, Indonesia, and Macao. In sixteenth-century Brazil, there was rare and tentative movement beyond the coast, notably with the establishment in 1554 of São Paulo de Piratininga, but increasingly wider dispersion in the seventeenth and eighteenth centuries.

Most Portuguese emigrants came from the north of Portugal, especially the provinces of Entre Douro e Minho and Beira and from Estremadura. The Algarve and Alentejo were underrepresented. Emigration from Portugal to Madeira and the Azores was predominantly by couples and by families. For all other destinations, emigration was pronouncedly male, although married women accompanying their husbands and even single women were on vessels to India and Brazil in the sixteenth century. The number of white women did increase in the seventeenth century, but even for early eighteenth-century Brazil, Portuguese kings, viceroys, and governors bemoaned the dearth of white women of marriageable age. In Macao and in East or West Africa, a white woman was a rarity. In 1636, there was one white woman in Macao. One ramification was a very low rate of natural increase in the Portuguese empire other than by interracial sexual liaisons.

Finally, the fact that Brazil today is second only to Nigeria in having the world's largest population of persons of African descent underlines the extent of a slave trade that saw the forced resettlement in Portuguese America of between 2.5 and 4 million slaves prior to 1800. An important ramification was that rare was the settlement in colonial Brazil in which whites were not a demographic minority. It is also well to remember that, prior to 1500, as many as 100,000 Africans may have been forcibly relocated to Cape Verde, to São Tomé and Príncipe, and to Europe. There was also the trade in slaves from Mozambique and ports in East Africa across the Arabian Sea to

India. Persons of African descent became an integral part of the population of Portuguese cities and forts of the Estado da Índia, as well as in Brazil and Portugal.

Chronology of Settlement

If the conquest of Ceuta in 1415 set the tone for a military campaign seen as a continuation of the *reconquista* for Portuguese settlement in Morocco, it was during the reigns of Dom Afonso V, "the African" (1438–1481), and Dom Manuel I, "the Fortunate" (1495–1521), that an aggressive policy was pursued toward Morocco both militarily, in terms of the construction of forts, and commercially. Heavy expenditures led Dom João III (1521–1557) to abandon some garrisons, and by 1550 the Portuguese presence was limited to Ceuta, Tangier, and Mazagão. The disaster of Alcazarquibir in 1578 sounded the death knell to a further significant Portuguese presence. More important in terms of settlement was the discovery and colonization of the archipelagos of Madeira (in the 1430s) and the Azores (in the 1440s). Efforts to promote settlement in Cape Verde (in the 1460s) evoked minimal response, but there was a trickle of Portuguese settlers to São Tomé (in the 1490s) and Príncipe. Even by 1570, the islands of Fernando Pó and Ano Bom, also in the Gulf of Guinea, had attracted few settlers. Although the Portuguese moved down the African coast at the rate of a degree of latitude each year in the fifteenth century, there was little settlement on the African continent other than in trading posts and forts (Arguim, ca. 1455; El Mina, 1482; Axim, 1490s). The sixteenth century saw the growth of Portuguese settlements in the Atlantic islands: In the Azores, towns (*vilas*) were established, Angra do Heroísmo and Ponta Delgada were accorded the status of a city (*cidade*), and Angra was made a diocese in 1534. In Cape Verde, Ribeira Grande on the island of Santiago was made a diocese in 1533. In the Gulf of Guinea, São Tomé was made a town in the 1520s and accorded the status of a city and made a bishopric in 1534. Settlement growth on the islands was not paralleled by Portuguese settlement on the mainland of West or Central Africa, where failure marked Portuguese initiatives. In Kongo, despite an auspicious reception of the Portuguese in the 1480s and 1490s and unbridled enthusiasm shown by the royal family and elites for things Portuguese and Christianity, this did not result in Portuguese settlement. Relations deteriorated as the impact of the slave trade became increasingly oppressive. Further south, in that part of Kongo that came to be termed Angola, by the mid-sixteenth century there was a small settlement of Portuguese, but only after the return of Paulo Dias de Novais with 700 people in 1575 did prospects for settlement appear promising. Novais was unable to fulfill clearly stipulated terms of his 1571 charter, which included settlement of 100 families, the establishment of chartered towns, settling of 400 able-bodied men, and construction of three forts and also churches. São Paulo de Luanda was established in 1576 by Novais and, in an atmosphere of vigorous military action, forts were built at Massangano (1583), Muxima (1599), Cambambe (1604), and Ambaca (1617–1618) in the basin of the Kwanza River. The construction of a fort in 1617 on the coast to the south was the forerunner of the future city of São Felipe de Benguela.

The voyage (1497–1499) of Vasco da Gama that inaugurated the Cape route to India opened up a new area for Portuguese settlement. In southeast Africa, the Portuguese built fortified trading stations (Sofala, 1505) and forts, established small communities in Pemba and Pate, and created a strategically significant settlement in Mozambique. They had settlements in Hormuz and Muscat on the Persian Gulf. Within the sixteenth century, in rapid order, settlements were established in Gujarat (Diu and Daman), on the west coast of India (Bombay, Goa, Cannanore, Calicut, Cranganor, and Cochin), in Sri Lanka (Colombo and Jaffna), on the Coromandel Coast and northern Bay of Bengal (Hughli), and in present-day Indonesia from Malacca (1511) to Timor, Tidor, and Amboina. About 1557, Macao was founded, and in 1570 a Portuguese presence was established in the small fishing village of Nagasaki. In addition to these settlements, there were pockets of Portuguese scattered across Asia from the Levant to China. By 1600, the pattern for Portuguese settlement in Africa and the Estado da Índia was set and there was no significant new settlement after that date. Indeed, on the contrary, there was attrition.

Already in the early sixteenth century there had been a trickle of Portuguese to Brazil and the establishment of small settlements. The introduction of the donatory system stimulated settlement, notably in Pernambuco and São Vicente. The second half of the sixteenth century saw increasing settlement on the coast and the establishment of Rio de Janeiro (1565). Both Angola and Northeast Brazil came under Dutch attack in the seventeenth century, in the latter case resulting in a quarter-century of occupation, but – unlike settlements in the Estado da Índia – the Portuguese regained the lost territory. As the seventeenth century progressed, Brazil exerted ever greater appeal for settlers. Many factors contributed to this shift: a swifter and less hazardous voyage; better prospects for settlers; greater potential for occupational diversity; growing urban centers with concomitant opportunities; and, above all, the emergence of a major sugar industry, which recovered from the Dutch occupation and thrived, generating opportunities in related industries and increasing demand for skilled as well as field labor. In the early part of the century, Rio de Janeiro emerged as a major focus of settlement. With the defeat of the French by a Spanish-Portuguese joint force at the battle of Guaxenduba (1614) and capture of São Luís (1615) by the Portuguese, São Luis do Maranhão grew as an increasingly important Portuguese settlement. The seventeenth century saw the consolidation of already established settlements and the creation of new settlements in the far north (Rio Grande do Norte, Ceará, Maranhão, and Pará) and south of Rio de Janeiro. Gold strikes radically altered the settlement map of Brazil. Between the 1690s and 1750s, a series of strikes resulted in new towns being established in Minas Gerais, Goiás, and Mato Grosso but also in São Paulo, in Bahia, and in other captaincies not directly associated with gold and diamond extraction. The ebb and flow of peoples – reflecting the latest rumors of fabulous strikes, the demand for foodstuffs, and a developing network of trails – saw new settlements in Pernambuco, Bahia, Espírito Santo, and in central-southern Brazil during the first half of the eighteenth century. Some existed for only a few months. Even towns fell victim to the unpredictability of an industry based on a wasting asset such as gold: The population of Vila Rica do Ouro Prêto dropped from some 20,000 in the 1740s to 7,000 in 1804. Although *paulistas* in the seventeenth century had demonstrated the importance of rivers for travel, only in the eighteenth century was the potential of fluvial transportation of people and commodities fully exploited. Settlement in Mato Grosso especially was attributable to a network of rivers reaching from near the town of São Paulo to the far west of Brazil. Only in the 1740s and 1750s were the southernmost regions of Brazil to be settled: Santa Catarina and, more successfully, Rio Grande de São Pedro. Whereas there was contraction in the Estado da Índia, in eighteenth-century Brazil there was a momentum reflected in demographic growth, new and more dispersed settlements, and new captaincies-general and subordinate captaincies.

Structures of Settlement

Forts

One of the lasting legacies of the Portuguese empire is military architecture: the massive fortresses of Arzila (1509) and Mazagão (enlarged and strengthened in the 1540s) in Morocco, São Jorge da Mina, Fort Jesus in Mombasa, Hormuz, Mozambique, Cannanore and Diu, the complex military fortifications of Muscat, and smaller forts such as those at Cacheu and Bahrein (1559–1560). A report from 1619 referred to some 54 fortresses, forts, castles, and bastions in the Estado da Índia. Although their purpose was primarily military, in Morocco and elsewhere fortresses and forts often provided protection for a civilian population. In addition to dependents of military personnel, in Morocco there were especially active merchant communities. Mazagão counted a community of Portuguese *fidalgos* (nobles), *infantes* (infantry soldiers), artillerymen, families and servants of *fronteiros* (frontiersmen), and widows and orphans. The construction of São Jorge da Mina (1482), as in the case of the fortress at Mozambique, was prompted by the desire to protect commercial interests, but these military garrisons came to house civilian populations. The influx of 100 artisans in the construction phase of São Jorge da Mina created a nucleus for the creation of a civilian population, but its location did not make it attractive to Portuguese traders or Portuguese women. Unlike Mazagão and other forts, São Jorge da Mina never housed a large Portuguese community. The granting of municipal status to São Jorge da Mina (before 1486) and to Mazagão (1541) was indicative either of crown hopes that this would encourage settlement or, in the case of Mazagão, recognition of a stable Portuguese community. In Brazil, forts were constructed, especially in the late sixteenth and seventeenth centuries, for the defense of port cities (e.g., the major forts of Santo António da Barra and São Marcelo and a half dozen smaller forts for Salvador) or river bars (Santa Cruz de Itamaracá defending the Igaraçú River), whose function was exclusively military. The most magnificent fort of Portuguese America was Forte da Beira (1776–1783) in Mato Grosso. These forts had no civilian component but existed purely for defensive purposes. This was also the case for the fortress of Santiago in Funchal (begun 1614) and the magnificent fortress of São Filipe (begun in 1592 and renamed São João Baptista after the Restoration in 1640) in Angra do Heroísmo.

There were also Portuguese settlements, especially in the Estado da Índia, that were synonymous with a fortress. Chaul provides an excellent example. The extended walls of Chaul, heavily defended with enormous towers and bastions, housed a Portuguese settlement further protected by the magnificent fortress known as Chaul de Cima. In the 1630s, some 200 Portuguese *casados* and 50 locals who had converted to Christianity lived within its walls in two-story houses of stone and lime. Also within the walls were six churches, the cathedral, the *Misericórdia*, a royal hospital, the Jesuit College, and Dominican, Augustinian, and Franciscan churches and their respective religious communities. The walls drew a clear line of demarcation between the Portuguese city and the indigenous city of Chaul. The demarcation was even clearer in Mozambique, where the Portuguese fort was on an island. In the early seventeenth century, this housed a garrison of 300. But, unlike Chaul, the Portuguese settlement was extramural, albeit within the walls of the fort. In the 1630s, this comprised some 70 *casados*, their families, and servants, living in stone and lime houses with farms and an abundance of pine trees. Within the fortress was one church, but religious and social life was extramural. The settlement housed the *Sé* (principal church of a diocese), the Jesuit and Dominican churches, the *Misericórdia*, and a hospital. In Mozambique, as in all more important settlements, there were crown officials, magistrates, and fiscal officers. These were settlements in the full sense of the word, with municipal charters. They should not be confused with exclusively military enclaves or trading posts (*feitorias*) such as Arguim or a fortified trading post such as at Safim in Morocco (1491), which so gained in importance that in 1516 construction began on the major fort known as Castelo do Mar.

Cities and Towns

Portuguese kings saw the conferral of municipal charters as being at the heart of crown policy for settlement overseas. Charters were granted in recognition of existing Portuguese communities and to stimulate the genesis and growth of towns. There is a policy continuum from the fifteenth century in Madeira and the Azores, to the Estado da Índia and Brazil in the sixteenth century, to the mining towns of Brazil in the early and mid-eighteenth century, and to the creation of towns in the south of Brazil later in the eighteenth century. Donataries, governors, and viceroys were exhorted to establish urban settlements. Not only did these reflect crown authority, but their physical layout was such as to reflect their counterparts in Portugal and to compensate for the possible sense of alienation from kith and kin left behind in Europe by Portuguese who had made the critical decision to live and die overseas. In addition to the civil dimension, there was a strong religious component to such settlements, reflected in churches and chapels and calculated to provide spiritual reassurance. To be a *vizinho*, or resident of a town or city, carried special privileges. Dom Manuel designated Goa as a "royal city," and his subsequent instructions (1518) to the incoming governor of the Estado da Índia show how the crown promoted settlement by married persons in an identifiably Portuguese city by deploying a gamut of nonmonetary instruments available only to a monarch. Married Portuguese males who settled in Goa enjoyed the following privileges and exemptions: freedom to trade and to import any commodity, provided such trade was not with enemies of the faith or of Portugal; eligibility for public office, as on the municipal council (*Senado da Câmara*); exemption – except at times of crisis when every able-bodied man or boy was required for defense – from gubernatorial edicts requiring public service; immunity from liability for forfeiture of properties or possessions in legal sentencing, except for treason and other specific charges; and house arrest – rather than jail – pending sentencing in civil cases. A further decree allocated lands to Portuguese already or about to be married and who were willing to settle in Goa. In short, married Portuguese in Goa enjoyed many of the same privileges as did citizens of Lisbon, Oporto, and Évora. Although there were fewer towns and cities in the Portuguese overseas empire even by 1800 than in the Spanish empire by 1550, urban settlement was a crucial component in the creation and existence of the Portuguese overseas empire.

Major cities of the Portuguese empire owed their genesis to a combination of perceived needs: comparative military advantage or defense; commercial centers; magnets for settlement; and as part of a Portuguese imperial presence. They developed into multifunctional centers: commercial, religious, social, military, and administrative. Goa, Salvador, and Rio de Janeiro fulfilled these roles concurrently. The occupations of the populace were varied – a mix of artisans, traders, priests, and slaves – and there was a less pronounced gender imbalance than elsewhere among the population of Portuguese birth or descent.

There were also urban settlements that developed less because of crown initiative than because of individual or collective initiative and special circumstances. The best example is Macao. This owed its creation primarily to the acumen of Portuguese entrepreneurs. Commerce was the raison d'être of Macao. Merchants dominated the *Senado da Câmara*, and the *Câmara* – not the crown-appointed governor – negotiated with the Chinese viceroy in Canton and with other Asian leaders. Although the city had a Portuguese imprint, the population was diverse. There were few Portuguese women. A Chinese magistrate had jurisdiction over the Chinese population. Nagasaki was another special case. Like Macao, there had been a prior small indigenous community, but the fact that there was a Portuguese presence owed much to Jesuit initiative.

What singles out Portuguese towns in Angola and makes Macao unique in the Estado da Índia is that the norm for Portuguese settlements east of the Cape of Good Hope was to be within or contiguous to already established towns or cities. Urban settlement reflected a variety of approaches by Portuguese toward preexisting non-European communities. Conquest or possession through military intervention would carry an unexpungeable legacy of antagonism toward the interlopers. In East Africa and throughout Asia, indigenous cities and towns carried highly visible religious and secular markers of multicultural and multiethnic communities – mosques, temples, the palace of a king or sultan, noble residences, port facilities, and markets – and spatial allocation reflecting caste, occupational, and ethnic differences.

There was a strong sense by both locals and Portuguese as to what constituted indigenous space and Portuguese space. This could be a tacit, but unwritten, understanding, or it might be explicit. Often construction of a Portuguese fort was the first step (followed by the construction of churches, a *Misericórdia*, and a town hall) in the creation of a Portuguese settlement distinct from any preexisting or contiguous indigenous town. In his description of Bassein, Bocarro opens with the words: "Baçaim he huma cidade de Portuguezes" ("Bassein is a city of Portuguese"). Indeed, this was the case in that there was no contiguous indigenous town, and all Portuguese military, secular, and religious institutions were intramural. But, in addition to 400 Portuguese, "the majority nobles," Bocarro notes the presence of some 200 "prêtos christãos" ("black Christians"). In Cochin, the construction in 1505 of a fort anchored the future Portuguese settlement as distinct from the indigenous city. The Portuguese referred to the latter as Cochim de cima, the current Mattancherry district, whereas the Portuguese settlement, which was later accorded the status of a city, corresponded to today's Fort Cochin. Such a distinction was not unusual among European settlements overseas. In eighteenth-century Calcutta under the British, there was a "black town" and a "white town."

In Brazil, the Portuguese faced no such constraints on the establishment or subsequent development of settlements. Despite the absence of politically imposed constraints, in Brazil the Portuguese themselves elected to establish settlements on the coast. Given the presence of superb sheltered harbors along the coast, this was understandable. In the sixteenth and seventeenth centuries, urban settlement in Brazil was synonymous with ports, and ports were synonymous with commerce and crown and ecclesiastical government. In fact, the only cities (*cidades*) in the colony prior to the elevation of São Paulo (1712) and Vila do Ribeirão do Carmo (1745, and renamed Mariana) to city status were on the Atlantic seaboard. But towns were also established away from the coast in response to soil and climatic factors or to the potential for the extractive industries. Two groups of townships can be taken as examples of such settlements. The first was the cluster of towns (Cachoeira, Santo Amaro, Maragogipe, and São Francisco do Conde) established in the Recôncavo of Bahia (i.e., the lands around the Bay of All Saints), whose soil, rainfall, and climate made it eminently suitable for cultivation of sugar and tobacco, where slave labor was readily available, and where rivers provided easy transportation. Gold was the stimulus for mining encampments that later were granted municipal status in Minas Gerais, Bahia, Mato Grosso, and Goiás. An urban cluster comparable to the Bahian Recôncavo was in the future captaincy of Minas Gerais: Vila do Ribeirão do Carmo, Vila Rica do Ouro Prêto, Vila de Nossa Senhora da Conceição do Sabará, São

João del Rei, Vila Nova da Rainha de Caeté, and São José del Rei. All were granted municipal status within the span of seven years, and all were within a three-day ride from Vila Rica. These townships of Bahia and Minas Gerais have a further feature in common. Sugar cultivation and gold mining are labor-intensive, and in no other region of colonial Brazil was there such an overwhelming majority of persons of African descent. Other facets of the Brazilian colonial economy – cattle raising, fishing, tobacco, and cotton – did not stimulate the creation of townships as did sugar and gold.

Agriculture provided the organizing principle for the bulk of Portuguese settlers in the Portuguese empire other than in Asia, where individual commercial interests predominated. This was not surprising given the predominantly agricultural composition of the population of Portugal, Madeira, and the Azores, which provided the settlers of empire. Settlements in Madeira, the Azores, and Cape Verde were agricultural. Fifteenth-century *cartas de doação*, which were royal charters issued to lords-propietor, emphasized the distribution of land for smallholdings and farms. Novais's charter (1571) for Angola focused on cultivation of the land, as did instructions (1666) to Tristão da Cunha as he took up his appointment as governor and captain-general of Angola. These instructions dwelt on reallocation of noncultivated lands and how failure to improve such lands within five years would result in forfeiture. Even for India, royal decrees of 1519 ordered equitable division and distribution of arable lands, titles of ownership, and that such lands be hereditary. Instructions (1530s) to lords-proprietor in Brazil emphasized promotion of agriculture and distribution of lands as central to settlement. Instructions (*regimento*, 1548) to the first governor had specific clauses relating to land distribution and promotion of cane cultivation. The importance of sugar cane as an export crop and the importance of sugar in the social and political formation of colonial Brazil were enormous. From this *regimento* it is apparent that the king saw sugar mills not only as commercial ventures but as nodes for settlement. One clause stipulated that construction of a sugar mill also imposed the responsibility for building a *casa forte* ("strong house") to protect settlers. Justifiably, one can point to the plantations of Pernambuco and Bahia as landed estates that were akin to small villages, often populated by between 30 and 100 slaves (and only exceptionally reaching 150 or 200) but with a numerically sparse Portuguese presence. Their importance to the colonial economy and the social and political prestige enjoyed by the larger owners (known as *senhores de engenho*) did not make such landed estates significant in terms of settlement but in terms of maximizing the potential of the land. The same can be said for São Tomé, precursor of the monocultural American plantation based on slave labor. Of greater importance as loci for settlement in the Atlantic islands and Brazil were rural smallholdings. This rural peasantry – paying rent or owning plots of land – was more characteristic of settlement in Brazil than plantation owners and cattle ranchers. In the context of settlement in the Portuguese empire, smallholdings and farms were more prevalent than the great landed estates and occupied more settlers of Portuguese birth or descent.

The riches associated with "Golden Goa" and the wealth gained by some Portuguese through commerce have resulted in underestimating the degree to which Portuguese in the Estado da Índia engaged in agriculture. In the early sixteenth century, the Portuguese on Mozambique Island already had farms on the mainland. There were small communities of Portuguese in Zanzibar and Pemba cultivating rice, millet, oranges, and citrus fruits. Contemporary illustrations – by António Bocarro or António de Moniz Carneiro – of forts and towns in the seventeenth-century Estado da Índia show that there was little space available within forts for cultivation. Outside of the forts, houses in such Portuguese enclave settlements might have walled vegetable gardens or orchards. Bocarro noted that the Portuguese on Mozambique Island had houses "with large gardens with many trees, especially pines." Within the walls of Daman there was cultivation of fruit trees. As was common in India, Portuguese *casados* (married settlers) of Daman were granted tribute from villages. While visiting Daman in 1673, the French traveler Dellon observed that "the leading inhabitants have villages to which they go to spend the harvest season." But in northern India in the Província do Norte (110 kilometers of coast between Bombay and Daman and extending, at most, 40 kilometers inland), in and around Bassein (conceded to Portugal in 1531) Portuguese *fidalgos* (nobles) and persons of means established estates. Some were absentee landlords, often resident in Goa, until a 1559 gubernatorial order required all owners of land in Bassein to reside there on penalty of forfeiture. This agriculture-based community of Portuguese, many of whom were wealthy and prominent socially and who built manorial houses, was the closest equivalent in the Estado da Índia to the *lavradores de cana* (sugar cane farmers) and the wealthier *senhores de engenho* (plantation owners) of Brazil.

Three types of settlements require brief reference. The first were settlements of Portuguese outside the administrative sphere of influence of royal government. Some such settlers were persons unwelcome in Portugal or its overseas settlements: convicts, New Christians, renegade clerics, deserters, and fugitives from justice. Such were scattered throughout the *sertão* of southeast Africa and Brazil. To these were added traders and merchants, some of whom were wealthy entrepreneurs and influential with local rulers in East and West Asia. There were sixteenth-century reports of

Portuguese communities in Ethiopia, in Basra, Baghdad, and Lar in Persia, in Martaban in Burma, and in Tenasserim and Surat. They were in Patane (Sri Lanka), scattered along the Coromandel Coast and around the Bay of Bengal, in Arakan, Pegu, and in Patani and Pahang in the Malay Peninsula, and as far as coastal China. There were also Portuguese communities in Lima, Cartagena, Mexico, the Spanish Caribbean, and later in Manila. The establishment of the Inquisition in 1560 in Goa led Jews and New Christians to move later to towns under Dutch or English control, where there was religious freedom. With the transfer of Bombay to the English East India Company, there was a further move of New Christians to Bombay.

Two other forms of settlement in the Portuguese-influenced world were unique to Brazil. One was the creation, by the Jesuits initially in the 1550s and later by other religious orders, of settlements (*aldeias*) to be populated by Amerindians for the express purpose of catechizing them and converting them to Christianity. Such villages were under the strict control of the Jesuit fathers, who imposed codes of behavior, labor, allocation of time, and worship, and oversaw agricultural production. Some villages were wiped out by disease, notably smallpox, others by attacks by slave traders. In addition to the missionary dimension and the potential of such Amerindians as labor, Portuguese were not oblivious to the fact that the Amerindians' skills as trackers and archers could be invaluable in the case of attacks on Portuguese settlements, towns, and cities. An appreciation of the magnitude of such settlements can be gauged by the following: In 1600, there were 50,000 Amerindians in 150 Jesuit *aldeias* on or near the coast between São Paulo and Northeast Brazil; and in the early 1740s, 50,000 Amerindians lived in *aldeias* in Grão Pará, which numbered 63 by 1750 and were administered by various other religious orders besides the Jesuits. During the 1750s, such villages were secularized. Some became towns with municipal councils made up of settlers rather than Amerindians. Another form of settlement was created by runaway slaves of African birth or descent. These were known as *mocambos* or *quilombos*. Some comprised as few as five to ten persons. Others counted a population in the hundreds. Some were transitory, others more permanent. For much of the seventeenth century, a federation of a dozen or more *quilombos*, known collectively as Palmares, existed in what is now the state of Alagoas. That the population of these villages numbered in the thousands is certain, but estimates as high as 20,000 appear exaggerated. Eighteenth-century *quilombos* in Minas Gerais were also substantial settlements: Ambrósio, destroyed in 1746, counted a population estimated at 10,000, and Quilombo Grande numbered about 1,000 when attacked in 1759. What is most notable about such settlements by persons of African descent in Brazil was their size, their longevity, the evidence of political leadership and social organization, and crop cultivation. Names of villages and towns in Brazil today reflect their genesis as *aldeias* or *quilombos*.

Conclusion

There were certain features that made Portuguese overseas settlement distinctive. Some were inherent to the mother country: a small pool of potential emigrants and future settlers; limited financial resources to promote settlement; and the absence of a sustained crown policy for settlement. The last was a boon and a bane. Its absence permitted flexibility and adaptability in responding to opportunities, to local shifts of power, and to changing military situations. This absence was tacit acknowledgment that no single policy could have been devised for a far-flung empire in which discrete parts demanded individual measures. The downside was that, especially in the allocation of scarce financial and human resources, there was the tendency to respond to individual crises or to local pressure groups instead of a more equitable allocation of resources in accordance with long-term strategic planning. The chronology and the spatial distribution of Portuguese settlements also distinguished them from those of other European nations overseas. Portugal was actively engaged in an ongoing process of establishing overseas settlements over the four centuries under discussion. As regards spatial positioning, as of the 1530s, the Portuguese were establishing settlements concurrently – and with emphasis on the word "concurrently" – in Africa, Asia, and America. To a greater degree than those of other European nations, Portuguese settlements overseas were often so dispersed as to constitute a network of isolated settlements – ranging from trading factories to cities – rather than nuclei of intensive settlement.

Portuguese settlers in Africa, Asia, and America constituted a racial, ethnic, religious, linguistic, and demographic minority. In the Estado da Índia, they intruded into societies with well-established leadership, hierarchies, mores, and religions, complex and extensive networks of commerce, and that were polyglot and multicultural. The fact that Portuguese were able to establish settlements east of the Cape of Good Hope was often attributable to the fact that they were regarded as yet one more group with commercial interests in what were polyglot, multiethnic, and polycultural societies. In East Africa and Asia, religion more than political allegiances or ethnic and racial differences was the stumbling block to the integration of Portuguese into indigenous societies but also to the integration of non-Europeans into Portuguese communities. In Brazil, neither the Amerindians as the autochthonous inhabitants, nor Africans imported by the Portuguese as slaves, played any role in any decision-making process concerning Portuguese settlements. In Brazil, legally established settlements, towns, and cities were Portuguese creations. They were built neither on preexisting Amerindian villages nor on sites captured by war or obtained through negotiation. Nor were they Portuguese counterpoints to already existing indigenous towns. There were no parallel indigenous and European settlements. Settlements were not divided between Portuguese and indigenous space. In settlements in Brazil, civil authority, architecture, institutions, buildings, and the allocation of space were incontrovertibly Portuguese. Yet it was probably in Brazil that persons of African descent and, in specific cases (e.g., São Paulo and Belém), of Amerindian descent, had more freedom to circulate unconstrainedly throughout towns and cities. In Brazil, there was no sense of a "white town" and a "black or native American town," and there was no systematic allocation of space by race, religion, or legal status as slave or free. Miscegenation was prevalent in all Portuguese overseas settlements (with the exception of the Azores) and was attributable to the chronic imbalance between Portuguese males and females. In Macao and Portuguese settlements in West and East Africa, white women were virtually absent. In Brazil and Africa, miscegenation and concubinage were rampant. In Asia, the Portuguese entered established societies that had been pluricultural and multiethnic for centuries. In Brazil, the arrival of the Portuguese, subsequent colonization, and forced immigration from Africa led to settlements that rapidly became pluricultural and multiethnic.

In many cases, settlers of Portuguese descent and of the Catholic faith shared the territory under their immediate control or influence with Flemish, as in the Azores, with New Christians, as in Brazil and India, and with non-Christians and non-Europeans. Be it in Africa, Asia, or America, settlements bore the hallmark of being Portuguese and identified themselves and were identified by other Europeans and indigenous peoples as being Portuguese. What is remarkable is that even today cities and towns in Brazil, in Asia, and in Africa continue to bear a Portuguese imprint even where a Portuguese physical presence is minimal and the Portuguese language is no longer spoken. It is ironic that one of the first nation-states in Europe – if this term is interpreted in the sense of having territorial integrity, a single predominant religion, ethnic and racial homogeneity, and a national language – should have created settlements around the world that were characterized by cultural, ethnic, and racial diversity and in many of which the Portuguese language and Catholicism were in competition with non-European languages and belief systems. Could it be that, overseas, this led to greater resilience and to an enhanced sense of self-identity as Portuguese?

European kingdoms that had established a degree of political unity were at the fore in reaching beyond Europe and establishing settlements overseas: Portugal and Spain in the fifteenth and sixteenth centuries; and France and England in the seventeenth and eighteenth centuries. To these can be added the settlements established by the Dutch East and West India Companies, the English East India Company, and French trading companies. Danes and Swedes also established settlements overseas, but to a lesser degree. These were not the first Europeans to establish extra-European colonies or trading posts. Already there had been Norse settlements in Iceland and Greenland and on the North American continent, and Venetians and Genoese established trading colonies in the Levant, Africa, and Asia. But, between 1450 and 1800, it was the Portuguese, French, English, and Dutch who established settlements in Africa, Asia, and America, and it was Spaniards who created an empire in the Americas and particularly on the Pacific rim and in the Philippines. European settlements overseas were conceived as, or became part of, greater imperial designs that, in some cases, led to colonies on more than one continent. Such settlements resulted – to varying degrees – in territorial dispossession (from an indigenous perspective) and imposition by Europeans of domain over the polities, commerce, societies, and cultures already well established before the arrival of the Europeans. Although this intrusion severely encroached on, or even eroded and eradicated, the cultures, social organization, values, and belief systems of many of those with whom the Europeans came into contact, nowhere would dispossession be so rampant as among autochthonous peoples of the Americas.

Nationalistic histories, coupled with a fragmented – oceanically, geographically, or chronologically – historiography of European overseas empires, have distracted attention away from the very basic tenet that European states did have shared objectives in establishing overseas settlements and from the fact that differences between these objectives are often more of detail than of substance. In all cases, Europeans were intruders. Other than in the Americas, where European diseases, horses, armor, and weapons were decisive, a sustained European presence was as often the fruit of negotiation, diplomacy, or perceived comparative advantage or sufferance by indigenous leaders as of warfare. Initial settlements were dependent on non-Europeans for labor, building materials, foodstuffs, and the critically important interpreters. In Asia especially, to this list would soon be added access to indigenous production and distribution networks, and even transportation and capital. Europeans overseas relied heavily on non-Europeans for military service. Despite ambiguity or opposition to marriages between Europeans and local women, these couples and their progeny were important as potential settlers in newly acquired or disputed territories.

Certain features of Portuguese settlement overseas were characteristically Portuguese. But to use nationality as the criterion for describing such overseas settlements is to give too much emphasis to an identifying label that did not possess in the early modern period the importance subsequently ascribed to it. There are more potentially rewarding avenues for comparative studies of settlements established by Europeans overseas. One is to compare settlements on the basis of the different preexisting human, political, social, cultural, and physical environments at the time of initial European settlement and how, subsequently, indigenous peoples and Europeans rejected each other, accommodated each other, and coexisted. The other is to select settlements for comparative study on the basis of prevailing economies, commerce, societies, and cultures. Such research agendas encompass the European component without being Eurocentric and recognize the important contribution by non-Europeans to such settlements. This approach also recognizes that settlements were made up of expatriate Europeans whose decision to emigrate and settle overseas implicitly acknowledged that they would live out their lives in multicultural environments and die far from the lands of their birth.

BIBLIOGRAPHICAL ESSAY

The challenge facing a potential reader interested in the history of settlements in the Portuguese empire is that there is no single monograph that embraces the period 1400–1800 and is a comprehensive survey of settlements from Mozambique to Nagasaki and the Moluccas or in those places whose shores were washed by the Atlantic. My purpose here is initially to suggest general works on this empire and then move to published primary and secondary sources on which I have drawn for this chapter. These are organized according to the themes treated in the chapter. Initially, there are references to secondary sources on those papal bulls and treaties that had a bearing on the general territorial areas in which Portuguese established settlements and suggested readings on emigration. The next batch of suggested readings focuses on settlement. These are arranged geographically: the Atlantic islands, Africa, India, Southeast and East Asia, and Brazil. Because a cross-cultural dimension is inherent in any discussion of settlement, the reader may like to pursue some suggested readings. The final section directly addresses types of settlements: garrisons and their civilian populations; and cities and towns. I conclude with a discussion of readings on topics as varied as Amerindian mission villages, runaway slave communities, and even sugar plantations, which, in some cases, were the institutional progenitors of urban centers. The conclusion suggests a few works that place Portuguese settlement in the early modern period in a comparative framework.

To establish a context for Portuguese overseas settlement, Charles Boxer's *The Portuguese Seaborne Empire, 1415–1825* (London, 1969) is fundamental. His *Four Centuries of Portuguese Expansion, 1415–1825* (Johannesburg, 1963) provides an effective synthesis. See also A. J. R. Russell-Wood, *The Portuguese Empire, 1415–1808: A World on the Move* (Baltimore, 1998), and M. D. D. Newitt, *A History of Portuguese Overseas Expansion, 1400–1668* (New York, 2005). Reflecting the best of recent scholarship are essays in Francisco Bethencourt and Kirti Chaudhuri, eds., *História da expansão portuguesa*, vols. 1–3 (Lisbon, 1998). These are required reading for all aspects of Portuguese settlement overseas. Meticulously researched, highly interpretative, and still invaluable is Vitorino Magalhães Godinho's *História económica e social da expansão portuguesa* (Lisbon, 1947). Bailey W. Diffie and George D. Winius's *Foundations of the Portuguese Empire, 1415–1580* (Minneapolis, 1977) is more limited in scope, covering the Atlantic world up to 1500 and then focusing primarily on the Estado da Índia to 1580. Very readable and concise is A. H. de Oliveira Marques's *History of Portugal, Vol. 1: From Lusitania to Empire* (New York, 1972).

This chapter is based on a wealth of published sources in Portuguese. Vitorino Magalhães Godinho's *Documentos sôbre a expansão portuguesa* (3 vols., Lisbon, 1945) is indispensable. Portuguese policies and their implementation in India can be gleaned from the *Cartas de Afonso de Albuquerque seguidas de documentos que as elucidam* (7 vols., Lisbon, 1884–1935). For the Estado da Índia especially, seminal texts for the sixteenth century are: João de Barros, *Ásia* (4 vols., Lisbon, 1945–1946); Gaspar Correia, *Lendas da Índia* (2 vols., Lisbon, 1858–1860); and Fernão Lopes de Castanheda, *História do descobrimento e conquista da Índia pelos portugueses* (2 vols., Oporto, 1979). Diogo do Couto's *Da Ásia* (Lisbon, 1788) has details of forts and cities. This last work should be complemented by Luís de Figueiredo Falcão's *Livro em que se contem toda a fazenda & real patrimonio dos reinos de Portugal, Índia & ilhas adjacentes* (Lisbon, 1859). An important descriptive and iconographic source is António Bocarro's *Livro das plantas de tôdas as fortalezas, cidades e povoações do Estado da Índia Oriental*, illustrated by Pedro Barreto Resende. Originally written in 1635, it appears in *Arquivo Português Oriental*, Nova edição, Tomo IV, vol. 2, Parts 1–3 (Bastorá, 1937–1940); see also the derivative 1639 report by António de Mariz Carneiro, *Descrição da fortaleza de Sofala e das mais da Índia* (Lisbon, 1990).

The best source on papal bulls remains Charles-Martial de Witte's *Les bulles pontificales et l'expansion portugaise au XVe siècle* (Louvain, 1958). *Do Tratado de Tordesilhas (1494) ao Tratado de Madrid (1750)*, edited by Maria Helena Carvalho dos Santos (Lisbon, 1997), has a wide-ranging series of essays, some directly on the ramifications for settlement. See also Luís Ferrand de Almeida's *A diplomacia portuguesa e os límites meridionais do Brasil (1493–1700)* (Coimbra, 1957). A useful introduction to royal instructions concerning settlement is António da Silva Rego's *Portuguese Colonization in the Sixteenth Century: A Study of the Royal Ordinances (Regimentos)* (Johannesburg, 1959). The most thorough monograph on captaincies is António Vasconcelos de Saldanha's *As capitanias: O regime senhorial na expansão ultramarina portuguesa* (Funchal, 1992). For land grants in Brazil, Brasil Bandecchi's *Origem do latifúndio no Brasil* (São Paulo, 1963) can be profitably consulted.

Portuguese emigration has not received the attention it deserves. A starting point is Vitorino Magalhães Godinho's "L'émigration portugaise (xve–xxe siècles): Une constante structurelle et les réponses aux changements du monde," *Revista de História Econômica e Social* 1 (1978), pp. 5–32. On convicts and "orphans of the king," see Timothy J. Coates's *Convicts and Orphans: Forced and State-Sponsored Colonizers in the Portuguese Empire, 1550–1755* (Stanford, CA, 2001); and Maria Augusta Lima Cruz's "Exiles and Renegades in Early Sixteenth Century Portuguese Asia," in *Indian Economic and Social History Review* 33(1986), pp. 249–262. Fascinating details of the Jewish diaspora are contained in James C. Boyajian's *Portuguese Trade in Asia under the Habsburgs, 1580–1640* (Baltimore, 1993). There is extensive literature on New Christians in Brazil: Relevant to our subject are Arnold Wiznitzer's *Jews in Colonial Brazil* (New York, 1960) and José Gonçalves Salvador's *Os cristãos-novos e o comércio do Atlântico meridional (com enfoque nas capitanias do sul, 1530–1680* (São Paulo, 1978). A brilliant and comprehensive study of a major part of the slave trade is Joseph C. Miller's *Way of Death: Merchant Capitalism and the Angolan Slave Trade, 1730–1830* (Madison, WI, 1988). This can be read in conjunction with *To Be a Slave in Brazil, 1550–1888*, by Katia M. de Queirós Mattoso (New Brunswick, NJ, 1986).

There is geographical imbalance in the historiography on settlement. For Madeira, the reader may turn to the seminal article by Maria Luís Rocha Pinto and Teresa Maria Ferreira Rodrigues, "Aspectos do povoamento das ilhas da Madeira e Pôrto Santo nos séculos XV e XVI," in *Actas: III Colóquio Internacional de História da Madeira* (Funchal, 1993), pp. 403–471, and Alberto Iria's *O Algarve e a Ilha da Madeira no século XV* (Lisbon, 1974). For Morocco, there are useful studies for the fifteenth and sixteenth centuries. See David

Lopes's *História de Arzila durante o domínio português* (Coimbra, 1925), and two works by António Dias Farinha: *História de Mazagão durante o período filipino* (Lisbon, 1970) and *Portugal e Marrocos no século XV* (2 vols., Lisbon, 1997). David Birmingham's *Trade and Conflict in Angola: The Mbundu and Their Neighbours under the Influence of the Portuguese, 1483–1790* (Oxford, 1966) is a clearly written narrative history. For East Africa, see Eric Axelson's *South-East Africa, 1488–1530* (London, 1940) and *Portuguese in South-East Africa, 1600–1700* (Johannesburg, 1964), and his "Portuguese Settlement in the Interior of South East Africa in the Seventeenth Century," in *Congresso Internacional de História dos Descobrimentos*, vol. 5 (Lisbon, 1961), pp. 1–17. Useful also is Alexandre Lobato's *A expansão portuguesa em Moçambique de 1498–1530*, vols. 1–3 (Lisbon, 1954, 1960). Malyn D. D. Newitt's *Portuguese Settlement on the Zambesi: Exploration, Land Tenure and Colonial Rule in East Africa* (New York, 1973) and *A History of Mozambique* (London, 1995) are excellent; see also Michael N. Pearson's revisionist *Port Cities and Intruders: The Swahili Coast, India, and Portugal in the Early Modern Era* (Baltimore, 1998). Pearson also provides an introduction to settlement in India in *The Portuguese in India* (Cambridge, 1987). For Asia, although subtitled "A Political and Economic History," Sanjay Subrahmanyam's *The Portuguese Empire in Asia, 1500–1700* (London, 1993) contains a wealth of detailed information on settlement.

For Brazil, a starting point is the essay by H. B. Johnson, "The Portuguese Settlement of Brazil, 1500–1580," in Leslie Bethell, ed., *The Cambridge History of Latin America, vol. 1: Colonial Latin America* (Cambridge, 1984), pp. 249–286. Demography is discussed by Maria Luiza Marcílio in volume 2, pp. 37–63, and Chapters 12–15 in the same volume, on economic and social structures, hold much pertinent information. These essays have been collected in *Colonial Brazil* (Cambridge, 1987), edited by Leslie Bethell. Caio Prado Júnior's *The Colonial Background of Modern Brazil* (Berkeley, CA, 1969) contains an interesting section on population and settlement, and Charles Boxer's *The Golden Age of Brazil, 1695–1750* (Berkeley, CA, 1962) also discusses settlement. John Hemming's *Red Gold: The Conquest of the Brazilian Indians, 1500–1760* (Cambridge, MA, 1978) and *Amazon Frontier: The Defeat of the Brazilian Indians* (Cambridge, MA, 1987) discuss Portuguese reactions to and interaction with Amerindians. More specifically on Amerindian cultures are essays in Manuela Carneiro da Cunha, ed., *História dos Índios no Brasil*, 2nd ed. (São Paulo, 1992), and the fascinating and revisionist essays in Colin McEwan, Cristiana Barreto, and Eduardo Neves, eds., *Unknown Amazon: Culture in Nature* (London, 2001). Readers familiar with Portuguese may turn to volumes 6, 7, and 8, titled *O império Luso-Brasileiro*, in the series *Nova história da expansão portuguesa*, directed by Joel Serrão and A. H. de Oliveira Marques (Lisbon, 1986, 1991, 1992).

A thread running through my chapter is the cross-cultural dimension to Portuguese settlements. Three sources may profitably be read because of the insights they provide: Ivana Elbl's "Cross-Cultural Trade and Diplomacy: Portuguese Relations with West Africa, 1441–1521," *Journal of World History* 3 (1992), pp. 165–204; Teotónio R. de Souza's *Goa medieval: A cidade e o interior no século XVII* (Lisbon, 1994); and the stimulating essays in Stuart B. Schwartz, ed., *Implicit Understandings: Observing, Reporting, and Reflecting on the Encounters between Europeans and Other Peoples in the Early Modern Era* (Cambridge, 1984).

There is growing scholarly interest in structures of settlement. The Portuguese empire is blessed with a rich iconography, an important source for studies of settlement patterns. Highly recommended is Luís Silveira's *Iconografia das cidades portuguesas do Ultramar* (3 vols., Lisbon, 1960). Absolutely fundamental to an understanding of the military dimension to Portuguese settlement is Rafael Moreira, ed., *História das fortificações portuguesas no mundo* (Lisbon, 1989), especially the essay by Renata Malcher de Araújo on "Engenharia militar e urbanismo." A region-specific work on this topic is A.W. Lawrence's *Trade Castles and Forts of West Africa* (London, 1963). In neither case is the social dimension at the fore. This is remedied in part by António Dias Farinha for Morocco in his *História* discussed earlier and by C. R. Boxer and Carlos de Azevedo in their *Fort Jesus and the Portuguese in Mombasa, 1593–1729* (London, 1960). The most comprehensive study of a trading station is J. Bato'ora Ballong-Wen-Mewuda's *São Jorge da Mina, 1482–1637* (2 vols., Lisbon and Paris, 1993).

The structure and the evolution of urban centers in the Portuguese empire have received an enormous stimulus in recent years by the initiatives of the Portuguese architect Walter Rossa. Highly recommended is his bilingual (Portuguese/English) *Cidades Indo-Portuguesas/Indo-Portuguese Cities* (Lisbon, 1997), which combines historical maps and plans with twentieth-century photographs and a clearly written text to support the proposition that "nothing outlasts the urban and territorial structures of a culture, not even language." After a stimulating introduction, the author examines in detail Cochin, Goa, Chaul, Bassein, Diu, and Daman. A wonderful complement is *Os espaços de um império: Estudos* (Oporto, 1999), essays accompanying an exhibit of the same name that examines urban space in the Portuguese Estado da Índia from Mozambique to Nagasaki and Timor. Available on CD-ROM are reproductions of maps of urban nuclei in Portugal, the Atlantic islands, Africa, Asia, and Brazil (*Imagens do arquivo virtual de cartografia urbana portuguesa* at http://urban.iscte.pt).

For Brazil there is a rich body of literature penned by Brazilian scholars from different disciplines. General surveys include Aroldo de Azevedo's *Vilas e cidades do Brasil Colonial: Ensaio de geografia urbana retrospectiva, Boletim no. 208, Geografia no. 11* (São Paulo, 1956); Nelson Omegna's *A cidade colonial* (Rio de Janeiro, 1961); and Nestor Goulart Reis Filho's *Evolucão urbana do Brasil, 1500–1720* (São Paulo, 1968). Paulo F. Santos addressed the issue of medieval irregularity and Renaissance orthogonal design and attempted a typology of cities in his essay "Formação de cidades no Brasil colonial," in *Actas: V Colóquio Internacional de Estudos Luso-Brasileiros*, vol. 5 (Coimbra, 1963), pp. 7–116, which has been reprinted with the same title and illustrations by the Universidade Federal do Rio de Janeiro (Rio de Janeiro, 2001). The construction of Salvador has been described by Pedro Calmon in his *História da fundação da Bahia* (Salvador, 1949) and with more emphasis on its evolution and social aspects in Thales de Azevedo's *Povoamento da cidade do Salvador*, 2nd ed. (São Paulo, 1955). More recent monographs have focused on urban space: Américo Simas et al., *Evolução física de Salvador, 1549–1800* (Salvador, 1998); and António Risério's *Uma história da Cidade da Bahia* (Salvador, 2000; 2nd ed. Rio de Janeiro, 2004). Gilberto Ferrez, *As cidades do Salvador e Rio de Janeiro no século XVIII* (Rio de Janeiro, 1963), brings a comparative iconographic and scholarly dimension. The literature in English is sparser. A good introduction is the highly interpretive essay by Richard M. Morse, "Brazil's Urban Development: Colony and Empire," *Journal of Urban History* 1 (November 1974), pp. 39–72. Ports are discussed in A. J. R. Russell-Wood's "Ports of Colonial Brazil," in Alan K. Karras and J. R. McNeill, eds., *Atlantic American Societies from Columbus through Abolition, 1492–1888* (London, 1992), pp. 174–211. Roberta M. Delson opens new perspectives for the study of urbanization in her essay "Planners and Reformers: Urban Architects of Late Eighteenth-Century Brazil," *Eighteenth-Century Studies* 10 (1976), pp. 40–51, and in her monograph *New Towns for Colonial Brazil: Spatial and Social Planning of the Eighteenth Century* (Syracuse, NY, 1979).

Stuart B. Schwartz's wide-ranging *Sugar Plantations in the Formation of Brazilian Society, 1550–1835* (Cambridge, 1985) demonstrates how some plantations had many of the attributes of a small village. On Jesuit villages in the context of Brazilian settlement, see João Lúcio de Azevedo's *Os Jesuítas no Grão-Pará: Suas missões e a colonização*, 2nd ed. (Coimbra, 1930), and the two books by John Hemming already noted. There is a growing body of literature on *quilombos* in Portuguese; English-language readers are referred to the seminal essay by R. K. Kent, "Palmares: An African State in Brazil," *Journal of African History* 6 (1965), pp. 161–175, and the article by Stuart B. Schwartz reprinted in his *Slaves, Peasants, and Rebels: Reconsidering Brazilian Slavery* (Urbana, IL, 1992).

For a comparative dimension to settlement, see Joyce Lorimer, ed., *Settlement Patterns in Early Modern Colonization, 16th–18th Centuries* (Aldershot/Brookfield, VT, 1998); A. J. R. Russell-Wood, ed., *Local Government in European Overseas Empires, 1450–1800* (2 vols., Aldershot/Brookfield, VT, 1999); and Russell-Wood's *Government and Governance of European Empires, 1450–1800* (2 vols., Aldershot/Brookfield, VT, 2000).

7

POLITICAL CONFIGURATIONS AND LOCAL POWERS

Francisco Bethencourt

From 1415 to 1822, the Portuguese empire had a variable geometry that was based on distant, discontinuous, and fragmented territories. The changing configuration of the empire reveals permanent movements of expansion, retreat, and compensation between continents, and its maintenance required an interregional mobilization of resources, strong military assistance, common political ground, and an ethnic identity shared by the Portuguese communities. The underlying question addressed in this chapter is how this empire was kept together despite the challenges of local and regional powers, not to mention the threat of other expanding European powers. Although political action and political organization are not sufficient in themselves to explain the perpetuation of this empire, these issues are nonetheless crucial in approaching the subject.

To begin, I reject the nationalistic perspective of a highly centralized empire.[1] This anachronistic approach prevents us from understanding the realities on the ground, where decisions made by the crown's central agencies did not shape real action and were constantly opposed by local initiatives and political responses to daily challenges. Nationalistic historiography, which continues to prevail in all countries of the world, does not allow us to understand the real interaction among the colonists, the local population, and the regional powers. Any historian who is influenced by this perspective becomes trapped within his own national references, reproducing the discourse of legitimizing the state that was traditionally assigned to the profession. An empire is always improvised, formed by an ambiguous balance

[1] The extreme case is Joaquim Veríssimo Serrão's *História de Portugal* (12 vols., Lisbon, 1978–1990); a liberal and republican version of nationalistic historiography is provided in A. H. de Oliveira Marques's useful *History of Portugal*, 2nd ed. (New York, 1976).

among central strategies, local initiatives, and political possibilities that are framed by opposing powers. An empire is built on conquest, negotiation, and compromise with different organizational cultures and peoples. These crucial aspects are avoided by the nationalistic approach, which confuses serious study with epic feeling and state propaganda.

However, neither do I share the postmodern perspective of a weak and headless empire.[2] This vision minimizes the position of the crown in the empire, instead exaggerating the importance of local powers and ducking the main issue: how this discontinuous empire managed to stay together for centuries. Ironically, the ideological consequences of this horizontal and loose political perspective reinforce the nationalistic approach: If the state was so weak, then the only power capable of sustaining the Portuguese communities overseas would have been the Catholic Church. This leads us straight back to Salazar's commemorations of the discoveries from the 1930s to the 1960s, which emphasized the importance of missionary work as a justification for the Portuguese expansion. It was exactly this kind of ideological trap that serious historiography, starting with Vitorino Magalhães Godinho,[3] tried to escape. As in other similar cases, the Portuguese expansion was the result of a combination of economic, social, and religious motivations, and it is pointless to renew a fifty-year-old dispute. The important issue is to consider how these motivations mingled, coexisted, and shifted in relative importance over time. Identifying the proper place of religion in empire building, for instance, means questioning the role played by the Catholic Church under the royal patronage. If we consider that the Catholic Church was part of the imperial state, we then have to probe further into the constant clash between "religious reason" and "political reason," which explains some of the conflicts that took place inside royal institutions.

[2] A good example of the direct transition from a nationalistic to a postmodern approach is Luís Filipe Thomaz's "A estrutura política e administrativa do Estado da Índia no século XVI," in Luis de Albuquerque and Inácio Guerreiro (eds.), *II Seminário Internacional de História Indo-Portuguesa* (Lisbon, 1985), pp. 511–541; a different case of transition from a Marxist to a postmodern approach, although with shared results, is António Manuel Hespanha's "Os poderes num império oceânico" (with Maria Catarina Santos), in José Mattoso (ed.), *História de Portugal, vol. 4: Antigo regime* (ed. António Manuel Hespanha) (Lisbon, 1993); Hespanha, "A constituição do império Português: Revisão de alguns enviesamentos correntes," in João Fragoso, Maria Fernanda Bicalho, and Maria de Fátima Gouveia (eds.), *O antigo regime nos trópicos: A dinâmica imperial Portuguesa (séculos XVI–XVIII)* (Rio de Janeiro, 2001), pp. 163–188.

[3] Vitorino Magalhães Godinho, *A economia dos descobrimentos Henriquinos* (Lisbon, 1962), excluded from the official publications to commemorate the centenary of Prince Henry the Navigator, is crucial for understanding the challenge to Salazar's historiography, which insisted on the predominant role of religion in the Portuguese expansion.

In turn, the postmodern perspective emphasizes local and regional approaches. The outcome is either a fragmented vision or a projection of questionable results based on a particular case, such as the Estado da Índia, onto the whole of the empire.[4] Despite all the advantages of local studies, we need a comparative global approach to show the transfer of institutions and the circulation of people, as well as the differences among the various territories of the empire. Postmodern studies' prejudice against the concepts of state and empire as outdated tools simultaneously dismisses the political theory of the sixteenth and seventeenth centuries. Instead, we should go back to the teachings of Marc Bloch and Lucien Febvre,[5] who sustained a balance between the theoretical developments of their time and the theoretical framework of the historical periods they studied. The theories of state in Niccolo Machiavelli[6] and Jean Bodin[7] are well known, but the reflections of Giovanni Botero[8] and Tommaso Campanella[9] are even more relevant for the Spanish and Portuguese empires.

My own definition of the "nebula of power" that maintained the Portuguese empire in a permanent yet unstable balance among local, regional, and central crown agencies, competing with each other but allowing royal tutelage of the system, was suggested by the systematic analysis of political action in different territories.[10] The problem is not only one of rejecting anachronistic nineteenth-century concepts of state and empire but also of recovering previous concepts and identifying a system that was less hierarchical and less centralized, whose logic of functioning was very different from that of modern states.

My understanding of the imperial state does not identify it with the crown. Rather, it involves the Catholic Church (with its different powers:

4 Ronaldo Vainfas, "Império," in Vainfas (ed.), *Dicionário do Brasil colonial (1500–1808)* (Rio de Janeiro, 2000).

5 Marc Bloch, *Mélanges historiques* (2 vols., Paris, 1963) (mainly the chapters on comparative studies); Bloch, *Apologie pour l'histoire ou métier de l'historien*, 5th ed. (Paris, 1964); Lucien Febvre, *Pour une histoire à part entière* (Paris, 1962) (mainly the study on the genesis of the word "civilization").

6 Niccolo Machiavelli, *Opere* (2 vols. published, Turin, 1997–1999).

7 Jean Bodin, *The Six Books of a Commoneale* (ed. K. D. MacRae, based on the English translation by Richard Knolles published in London in 1606) (Cambridge, MA, 1962).

8 Giovanni Botero, *Delle cause della grandeza delle città* (Rome, 1588); Botero, *La ragion di stato* (1st ed. 1589), ed. Chiara Continisio (Rome, 1997); Botero, *Relationi universali*, 2nd ed. (Vicenza, 1595).

9 Tommaso Campanella, *Monarchie d'Espagne et monarchie de France* (ed. Germana Ernst) (Paris, 1997); Campanella, *De politica*, ed. Antimo Cesare (Naples, 2001).

10 See my chapters in Francisco Bethencourt and Kirti Chaudhuri (eds.), *História da expansão Portuguesa*, vols. 1–3 (Lisbon, 1998).

archbishops, bishops, cathedral chapterhouses, principals of religious orders, and beneficiaries of local churches, and all nominated with the intervention or agreement of the king), the Inquisition, the municipal councils, the *Misericórdias* (confraternities protected by the king, which played a major role in the transmission and execution of wills), and the crown agencies operating at different levels (Casa da Índia, Overseas Council, viceroys, governors, judges, captains, financial supervisors, and commercial agents). That is to say, it includes all formal mechanisms that maintained "firm control over people" (as Botero would put it), exercised the legitimate monopoly of violence, and regulated social conflicts.[11]

This complex system, which operated through the transfer, adaptation, and integration of local institutions, was quite decentralized, consisting of a strong base, an adaptable intermediate level, and a competitive, quarrelsome, fragile regional top level, not to mention the different types of local political affiliations and associations. The system shows the constant presence of the crown in all spheres of organizational culture, distributing privileges, legitimizing nominations, ratifying decisions, and establishing judicial and financial control. In my view, the "nebula of power" that defined the Portuguese empire was kept together by the king, who used competition and hierarchical anomy to maintain his own power at a distance. It is this "nebula of powers" in different continents, as well as the experience of different forms of political action, that I attempt to analyze in this chapter.

Estado da Índia

It was through the creation of trading posts (*feitorias*) that the Portuguese first established themselves in India. Although the system originally met with little success when initiated on Vasco da Gama's first voyage in 1498, it was eventually made viable in 1500 with the subsequent voyage under the command of Pedro Álvares Cabral.[12] Political discord among the small maritime states along the Malabar Coast allowed the Portuguese to establish

[11] An approach inspired by Botero, *La ragion di stato*, p. 7; Max Weber, *Economy and Society: An Outline of Interpretative Sociology*, ed. Guenther Roth and Claus Wittich, translated from German (2 vols., Berkeley, CA, 1978); Niklas Luhmann, *Trust and Power*, translated from the German, with an introduction by Gianfranco Poggi (Chichester, 1979).

[12] João de Barros, *Asia: Primeira década*, ed. António Baião (Coimbra, 1932), Book V, Chapters 8, 9, and 10, particularly pp. 198, 202, and 210. After two failed attempts in Calicut in 1498 and 1500, Cabral managed in his voyage to establish a trading post in Cochin, run by Gonçalo Gil Barbosa. The voyage of João da Nova in 1501 led to the establishment of another trading post in Cannanore, run by the agents of two private merchants, Dom Álvaro, the Duke of Bragança's brother, and Bartolomeo Marchionni, from Florence. For

a permanent presence in Cochin and Cannanore. The unique nature of the Portuguese presence in these areas was expressed by the construction of forts in authorized places, built under the pretext that they would guarantee the safety both of the Portuguese king's agents and of their commercial interests. In both the coastal towns, the forts – founded respectively in 1503 and 1505 – were first built of wood and then later of stone, and successive building programs soon transformed them into key defensive structures along the entire coast.[13] Despite these successes, the Portuguese still faced difficulties. Their second attempt at establishing a trading post in Calicut, during Cabral's voyage, culminated in the local population attacking the position, plundering the building, and murdering dozens of Portuguese. These events at Calicut were not unique, and similar conflicts were to occur following the first Portuguese contacts in Kollam and Malacca. Such experiences would lead the Portuguese to subordinate commercial strategy to political and military strategy, as demonstrated in the conquests of Hormuz (1507–1515), Goa (1510), and Malacca (1511).

During the sixteenth century, the Portuguese Estado da Índia evolved by implementing a broad range of political solutions that came in response to practical situations encountered in the field. The case of Cochin is significant, as it provides an example of the Portuguese capacity for adaptation. The fort there guarded the entrance to the port in such a manner that the Portuguese were able not only to control maritime activities but also to dominate the local population, even if they did not have direct jurisdiction over them. The relationship between the Portuguese and the local authorities in Cochin was unique. Freed from Calicut's suzerainty by the Portuguese, the raja was treated as a brother by the Portuguese king, although, in practical terms, his status was similar to that of a vassal.[14] Nonetheless, during the first years of the Portuguese presence in India, the raja did try to interfere in Portuguese politics that affected the region, such as the conflict between Viceroy Francisco de Almeida and his successor, Governor Afonso de Albuquerque.[15] However, the peace agreement of 1513 (ratified by King Manuel) between the Portuguese governor and the ruler of Calicut made the raja

more on this case, see references in Marco Spallanzani, *Mercanti Fiorenti nell'Asia Portoghese (1500–1525)* (Florence, 1997), pp. 49–51.

[13] Rafael Moreira (dir.), *A arquitectura militar na expansão Portuguesa* (Lisbon, 1994), pp. 140–142; José Manuel Correia, *Os Portugueses no Malabar (1498–1580)* (Lisbon, 1997), pp. 48–51.

[14] *Cartas de Afonso de Albuquerque seguidas de documentos que as elucidam*, ed. Raimundo António de Bulhão Pato, vol. 3 (Lisbon, 1903), pp. 38–40 and 73–76.

[15] *Comentários do grande Afonso de Albuquerque*, ed. António Baião, vol. 1 (Coimbra, 1922), Part II, Chapter 6, pp. 280–281; *Cartas de Afonso de Albuquerque*, vol. 4, pp. 42–45.

completely dependent on the Portuguese, despite his futile protests.[16] In compensation, the raja continued to receive ritual gifts and funds from the Portuguese, mainly in the form of periodic allowances (*tenças*) to the local authorities that exceeded the normal payments of customs rights.[17] Indeed, the fort at Cochin remained the seat of government in the Estado da Índia for over thirty years, largely because it became the main center for the export of pepper from India to Europe. Although the capital of the Estado da Índia was transferred to Goa in 1530, the convoy (*carreira da Índia*) continued to sail to Cochin, and the city was still used as an alternative port until 1611, with the governor sometimes wintering there.[18]

The kingdom of Hormuz was in a peculiar situation. The majority of the ports or forts in the Persian Gulf under the kingdom's domain were devastated by the acts of war inflicted by Afonso de Albuquerque's fleet in 1507, prior to his conquest of the capital in that same year. Nevertheless, the king of Hormuz was maintained in power, albeit subject to an agreement stipulating his obligations to the Portuguese king. Dissent among the captains of the fleet then forced Afonso de Albuquerque to withdraw and led to the suspension of the agreement, which only later was enforced with a new military expedition in 1515.[19] After that date, the kingdom of Hormuz operated formally as an independent state but was in reality a vassal of the Portuguese crown. The model adopted in Cochin was reproduced in Hormuz with the creation of a fort/trading post, but the military conquest meant that the king had to pay heavy annual tribute to his conquerors. This reflected the impossibility of maintaining direct Portuguese control in a region completely dominated by Islam and in which the Portuguese navy could only impose itself within the context of permanent conflicts between the Safavid and Ottoman empires. Yet, tenuous as this arrangement was, it was only challenged by the arrival of the ships of the English East India Company (EIC) in the Persian Gulf during the early seventeenth century. Hormuz fell in 1622 to a coalition of British and Persian forces, where the latter were eager to eradicate the "anomaly" at the outer reaches of their

[16] *Cartas de Afonso de Albuquerque*, vol. 2, pp. 111–115 and 448–452; vol. 3, pp. 38–40 and 73–76; vol. 4, pp. 71–73 and 177–188.

[17] *Cartas de Afonso de Albuquerque*, vol. 4, pp. 42–45; Diogo do Couto, *Da Asia: Década décima* (Lisbon, 1788), Book IV, Chapter 13; Panduronga Pissurlencar, *Regimento das fortalezas da India* (Bastorá-Goa, 1951), pp. 217–219.

[18] A. R. Disney, *Twilight of.the Pepper Empire: Portuguese Trade in Southwest India in the Early Seventeenth Century* (Cambridge, MA, 1978); Catarina Madeira Santos, *"Goa é a chave de toda a India": Perfil político da capital do Estado da Índia (1505–1570)* (Lisbon, 1999).

[19] *Comentários do grande Afonso de Albuquerque*, vol. 1, Part I, Chapters 19–52, and Part IV, Chapters 30–42.

empire. Despite this setback, the Portuguese remained in the Persian Gulf until the eighteenth century. First, they controlled the old dependent forts of Hormuz on the southern border, with the capital in Muscat, until those forts were conquered by the imam of Oman in 1650; then they maintained a trading post in Kung and commercial agents in Basra and Muscat. Evidently, this presence was subject to constant negotiations and treaties, such as those agreed with the Persian authorities in 1690.[20]

The first case of direct Portuguese governance came in Goa, where Portuguese authority extended beyond the city to its surrounding area. This control was made possible by a policy of mixed marriages and an alliance with the Hindu community against the Muslim community, which was largely eliminated or removed from Goa after the conquest.[21] The balance of power in this regional context, characterized by political fragmentation and competition among the surrounding states, made it possible for the Portuguese to establish the city as its central nucleus of power in the Estado da Índia. Nevertheless, the Portuguese had to engage in a complicated game of tactical alliances in order to avoid unfavorable coalitions.[22]

Most of the institutions set up in Goa were transferred directly from Europe. The political examples were the municipality (*câmara*), established immediately after the conquest, the captain of the city, the governor of the state and his respective council (1530), and the *tribunal da relação*, a court of appeal that supervised the governor's main decisions (1544). Financially, there was the crown treasury, divided between the *vedoria da fazenda* (which controlled the contracts under royal monopoly and the customs), the Casa dos Contos (the accounting agency), and the Matrícula Geral (responsible for the registration of all the Portuguese soldiers). Religious institutions were represented by the head of the bishopric (1534), later elevated to an archbishopric (1557), the Inquisition tribunal, with jurisdiction over "heresies" (1560), and the Mesa da Consciência e Ordens, a council designed to advise the governor on religious matters and military orders (1570). Finally, there was the *tribunal da chancelaria* (1586), the Conselho dos Três Estados, a council with representatives of the three social orders (created by the end of the sixteenth

[20] *Comentários do grande capitão Rui Freire de Andrade*, ed. José Gervasio Leite (Lisbon, 1940); Roberto Gulbenkian, *Estudos históricos, vol. II: Relações entre Portugal, Irão e Medio Oriente* (Lisbon, 1995); Júlio Firmino Júdice Biker (ed.), *Colecção de tratados e concertos de pazes que o Estado da Índia Portuguesa fez com os reis e senhores com quem teve relações nas partes da Asia e Africa Oriental desde o principio da conquista até o fim do século XVIII*, vol. 4 (Lisbon, 1884), pp. 216–218, 230–288.

[21] *Comentários do grande Afonso de Albuquerque*, Part III, Chapters 4–5.

[22] *Comentários do grande Afonso de Albuquerque*, Part III, Chapters 6–8, 53–54, and Part IV, Chapters 14–19, 21–23, 27–28; Biker, *Colecção de tratados*, vol. 1 (Lisbon, 1881).

century), and the *tribunal da bula da cruzada* (1593),[23] an agency established with the pope's permission to sell indulgences and use the profits for the "crusade" against Muslims.

The Portuguese generally respected prior native ownership of the land, native village structures, and the preexisting system of imposing and collecting taxes. Meanwhile, new offices composed of missionaries – such as the Pai dos Cristãos (Father of Christians), generally a Jesuit who was the patron of the recently converted[24] – were rapidly formed to push ahead with the proselytizing process. The Portuguese also adopted a strategy of converting the local elites, who benefited by gaining greater access both to public positions and to the Portuguese matrimonial market. This strategy produced a new social situation that favored the entrenchment of the Estado da Índia.[25]

The relative political homogenization in Goa, which was accompanied by a degree of ethnic miscegenation, was unique within the entire Estado da Índia. Equally, the systematic destruction of Hindu temples, carried out in Goa in the 1540s and 1550s, had no parallel in any of the other territories, in this case because of local socioethnic and political conditions. The conquest of Goa made it possible to concentrate power at all levels, a process that was spurred on by the city's geopolitical and religious positions. The situation was radically different in Malacca, where these conditions did not exist. Instead, the Portuguese maintained Malacca's commercial position by protecting the maritime traffic and managing to establish a certain degree of control over the Strait of Malacca, access to the China Sea, and maritime connections to Southeast Asia, namely the spice trade of the Moluccas and the Banda Islands, as well as the sandalwood trade from Timor. But the Portuguese were not able to build a chain of forts in this region as they had done on the Malabar Coast. In order to maintain their position in this hostile environment, they were forced to negotiate a succession of accords and alliances with the neighboring kingdoms and with the various ethnic groups that made up the population of Malacca. The fundamental difference between the political structures in Goa and Malacca was that in the latter

[23] Carlos Renato Gonçalves Pereira, *História da administração da justiça no Estado da Índia* (2 vols., Lisbon, 1964–1965); Santos, "Goa é a chave de toda a India." As referred to in Bethencourt and Chaudhuri, *História da expansão Portuguesa*, vol. 1, pp. 355–357 and 359–360 and vol. 2, pp. 304–307 and 347–350, some of these institutions were either replaced or adopted other forms over the years.

[24] José Wicki (ed.), *O livro do "Pais dos Cristãos"* (Lisbon, 1969).

[25] On this process, see Bethencourt and Chaudhuri, *História da expansão Portuguesa*, vol. 1, pp. 369–386, and Caio Boschi, in Bethencourt and Chaudhuri, *História da expansão Portuguesa*, vol. 2, pp. 388–452, and vol. 3, pp. 294–392.

case the representatives of the mercantile communities were involved in city governance after the conquest, a significant fact that expressed the temporary impossibility of direct and exclusive rule.[26] Some of the traditional local roles, such as the the chief of ethnic communitties (*xabandar dos gentios*) or the *tumungo*, who was responsible for justice and finances, continued as in the past, albeit under Portuguese administration, but Portuguese institutions took control of the government of the city. Examples of these institutions include the captain and the city council, which was established later, around 1552.

The situation in Diu was complicated by the fact that the Portuguese only occupied the city after the territory had been ceded to them – under pressure from Moghul troops in 1535 – by Sultan Badur, the Lord of Gujarat.[27] This delicate situation continued even though Portuguese possession of the city had been guaranteed by their victory in two important sieges: the first in 1538, when the Gujarati allied themselves with the Turks;[28] and the second in 1546.[29] The Portuguese had coveted Diu since their first voyages to India, and the city would be transformed into one of the key strategic points in the Estado da Índia, maintaining its enormous capacity to attract commerce, as confirmed by the port's continuing large customs receipts up until the 1620s.[30] Political control of the city was eased by the creation further south of the *Província do Norte* (Northern Province), which consisted of the territories structured around the ports or forts of Daman, Bassein, and Chaul. Diplomatic negotiation with the local powers, which faced military coercion and periods of war brought by the expansion of the Moghul empire, helped the Portuguese occupation of these territories between 1521

26 *Comentários do grande Afonso de Albuquerque*, Part III, Chapters 32–33; Luís Filipe Thomaz, *De Ceuta a Timor* (Lisbon, 1994), pp. 487–512, 531–534.

27 Biker, *Colecção de tratados*, vol. 1, pp. 63–71.

28 Biker, *Colecção de tratados*, vol. 1, pp. 79–80; Diogo do Couto, *Da Asia: Década quinta*, Part I, Books III–V.

29 do Couto, *Da Asia: Década Sexta*, Part I, Books I–IV; *História quinhentista (inédita) do Segundo cerco de Dio, ilustrada com a correspondência original, também inédita, de D. João de Castro, D. João de Mascarenhas e outros*, ed. Antonio Baião (Coimbra, 1927).

30 Vitorino Magalhães Godinho, *Les finances de l'etat Portugais des Indes Orientales (1557–1635)* (Paris, 1982); Artur Teodoro de Matos, *O Estado da Índia nos anos de 1581–1588: Estrutura administrativa e económica. Elementos para o seu estudo* (Ponta Delgada, 1982); Matos, "The Financial Situation of the State of India during the Philippine Period (1580–1635)," in Teotónio de Souza (ed.), *Indo-Portuguese History: Old Issues, New Questions* (New Delhi, 1984); Glenn Joseph Ames, "The Estado da Índia, 1663–1677: Priorities and Strategies in Europe and the East," *Studia* 49 (1989) pp. 283–300; Francisco Bethencourt, "O Estado da Índia," in Bethencourt and Chaudhuri, *História da expansão Portuguesa*, vol. 2, pp. 284–314, especially pp. 294–303.

and 1559. Moreover, the presence of Portuguese administrative institutions in Diu, such as the captain, the agent of the royal treasury (*vedor da fazenda*), and the municipal council (a late arrival, as in Malacca) was also a defining characteristic of the city. Unlike Goa, a policy of broad and systematic religious conversion was not introduced in Diu. Alongside Ceylon and the Zambezi River valley, the administrative situation in the Northern Province was the most complicated in the Estado da Índia because of the extension of the hinterland, which covered over 2,800 square kilometers, and land concessions of villages to the Portuguese *fidalgos* (nobles) as a reward for services rendered. These concessions were made on the condition that the *fidalgos* would supply military aid when requested, a system that had originated in the Bassein region of Muslim India, where the existing concessionaires had been replaced by Portuguese *fidalgos* following the second siege of Diu. These *fidalgos* were given estates on the basis of a "three-generation land lease" under well-defined terms of succession,[31] a practice that was common in Portugal. However, in the Northern Province, it was designed to secure tax revenue, not landholding, the distinguishing features from Portuguese tradition being that the *foreiro* (tenant) had military duties and benefited from tax exemptions.

The Portuguese role in the Moluccas is equally complicated because the establishment of trading forts in Ternate and Tidor meant that the Portuguese were caught up in the middle of constant local conflicts. The Portuguese managed to establish their position by gaining support from one of the kings involved in these conflicts, whose survival came to depend on European military aid. This led to unexpected situations, naturally manipulated by the Portuguese captains, as in the case of the king of Ternate, who entrusted his kingdom to the Portuguese king in 1564, declaring himself a feudal vassal who would maintain direct control over the territory.[32] Clearly, this declaration of vassalage was legally more complex than the one extorted from the king of Hormuz in the first conquest because it was presented as a goodwill gesture by the king, his son, and the nobility. The Portuguese objective was to secure ties of political subordination because they were isolated in the forts and depended on local leaders to manage the population and guarantee that their ships could load the desired merchandise. The status and efficacy of the Portuguese presence was the product of their capacity to manage conflicts and to hold power in an unstable political situation. In fact, the vulnerability of the Portuguese military presence was obvious in the Moluccas from the frequent local uprisings that ultimately led to the

[31] Thomaz, *De Ceuta a Timor*, pp. 235–239.

[32] Biker, *Colecção de tratados*, vol. 1, pp. 157–160.

surrender of the captain of Ternate in 1575.[33] The eviction of the Portuguese was followed by Castilian incursions from the Philippines and by the arrival of the Dutch, who subsequently occupied Ambon and the Moluccas in 1605. The reconquest of the Moluccas in 1606 – the work of an expedition organized by Pedro de Acuña, then governor of the Philippines, involving thirty-six ships and around 4,000 sailors and soldiers – was short-lived and only emphasized the new balance of power between Manila and Malacca. In fact, the captain of Malacca was able to send only three Portuguese ships to join the expedition.[34] In general, the European presence in the Far East after the 1580s cannot be understood without a study of the Castilian influence via Manila.[35]

The case of Ceylon is one of the most interesting. The Portuguese established themselves in Colombo using their usual model: building first a crown trading post and then a fort (in 1518). Their military presence on the island was increased throughout the sixteenth century and the early seventeenth century as they built a chain of forts along the coast (Galle, Kalutara, Negombo, Mannar, Jaffna, Trincomalee, and Batticaloa) that allowed the Portuguese to monopolize the cinnamon supply. In this case, a practical relationship of suzerainty was established with the king of Kotte, the main power on the island, enabling control over the hinterland to be enforced. This suzerainty was strengthened through the religious conversion of the king, Dom João Dharmapala (1551–1597), who bequeathed his kingdom in 1580 to the king of Portugal, Cardinal Dom Henrique.[36] Following his conversion, the king of Kotte had only limited power, so his gesture was merely an artificial offering of something he had already lost, as he was already living under Portuguese protection and had little influence in the territory. The gesture was, however, used by the Portuguese as a means of legitimizing the politics of territorial dominion, a rare event in the Estado da Índia. With the death of Dom João Dharmapala, the *korales* (crown representatives in the provinces) were summoned by the

[33] Vitorino Magalhaes Godinho, *Os descobrimentos e a economia mundial*, 2nd ed., vol. 3 (Lisbon, 1982), pp. 158–164; Manuel Lobato, "The Moluccan Archipelago and Eastern Indonesia in the Second Half of the 16th Century in the Light of Portuguese and Spanish Accounts," in Francis Dutra and João Camilo dos Santos (eds.), *The Portuguese and the Pacific* (Santa Barbara, 1995), pp. 38–63.

[34] Bartolomé Leonardo de Argensola, *Conquista de Islas Malucas* (1st ed. 1609) (Madrid, 1992); Antonio de Morga, *The Philippine Islands, Molucas, Siam, Cambodia, Japan and China, at the Close of the 16th Century* (1st ed. 1609), translated from Spanish (London, 1868).

[35] Pierre Chaunu, *Les Philippines et le Pacifique des Ibériques (16ᵉ, 17ᵉ et 18ᵉ siècles)* (Paris, 1960).

[36] Biker, *Colecção de tratados*, vol. 1, pp. 180–184.

captain-general to an assembly in Colombo, where they swore oaths of loyalty to the Portuguese king in exchange for a Portuguese commitment to respect their laws, rights, and traditions.[37] This political scheme evolved relatively well between 1597 and 1630 but was followed by a decline triggered by the defeat of Dom Constantino de Sá's troops by the forces of the kingdom of Kandy in August 1630, which literally wiped out the expedition, killing the captains and the governor. Kandy's resistance to Portuguese power was also significantly reinforced by the Dutch, who went on to conquer all the Portuguese forts between 1637 and 1658.[38]

The organization of Portuguese control over Ceylon was based on the aforementioned network of forts, governed from the dominant position of Colombo and underlined by the senior position of the captain-general. The power structures were undoubtedly identical to those in the other domains of the Estado da Índia, consisting merely of a municipal council in Colombo. In the first decades of the seventeenth century, Portuguese dominion of the hinterland covered hundreds of villages, while still respecting the preexisting institutions, especially the local powers and the traditional means of collecting taxes. However, some Portuguese did benefit, even during Dom João Dharmapala's time, from the concession of villages and their rents.[39] This policy of land concessions was further developed by the financial superintendent (*vedor da fazenda*) sent by the king in 1607, who created a register of all the villages, showing their borders, charters, and donations. This register included the conditions governing the granting of village concessions for a period of three generations to the Portuguese, Modeliares, Araches, and Lascarins born on the land, "according to the merits of each person," and with the possibility of female succession. In return, the grantees had to supply soldiers and guns in the event of war. The villages of the Chalias that ensured the supply of cinnamon were exempt from such concessions and maintained their traditional taxes. These concessions were subsequently approved by the viceroy and ratified by the king.[40] In some respects, it

[37] João Ribeiro, *Fatalidade histórica da ilha de Ceilão* (ms. 1685, 1st ed. 1836) (Lisbon, 1989), Chapter 9.

[38] George Davidson Winius, *The Fatal History of Portuguese Ceylon* (Cambridge, MA, 1971); Chandra Richard de Silva, *The Portuguese in Ceylon, 1617–1638* (Colombo, 1972); Tikiri Abeyasinghe, *Jaffna under the Portuguese* (Colombo, 1986); Jorge Manuel Flores, *Os Portugueses e o mar de Ceilão: Trato, diplomacia e Guerra (1498–1543)* (Lisbon, 1998); Flores, *Quinhentos anos de relaçoes entre Portugal eo Sri Lanka* (Lisbon, 2001).

[39] J. H. da Cunha Rivara, *Arquivo Portugues-Oriental* (1st ed. 1857–1876, reprinted New Delhi, 1992), fasc. 6, p. 1.

[40] M. A. Hedwig Fitzler, ed., *Os tombos de Ceiláo da Secçã ultramarina de Biblioteca Naciorial* (Lisbon, 1927).

could be said that the feudal type of territorial occupation in the Northern Province was adopted in Ceylon, no doubt because local traditions were similar, although female succession was a unique feature. The closest comparison, therefore, is to the one that flourished in the Zambezi River valley, as we will see.

The diverse situations briefly outlined relate to the Portuguese dominions in Asia that were directly or indirectly governed by the Estado da Índia. However, there were some very specific cases that either partially or completely escaped the Estado da Índia's control. The first is Macao. It is known that Portuguese merchants first came into contact with China immediately after the conquest of Malacca, via Canton and the Pearl River. Moreover, the embassy of Tomé Pires (1516) followed the same route.[41] Yet it was not until the 1550s that reports record the settlement of a Portuguese mercantile community – the origin of Macao – at the mouth of the Pearl River. This community had a fluid relationship with Malacca, its strategic rearguard, without in fact acquiring a clearly defined status. The settlement only gained strategic importance in the 1560s and 1570s, after the passage to Japan became important for the economy of the Estado da Índia. In turn, this route only made sense following the reestablishment of the traditional commerce between Japan and China based on the exchange of Chinese silk for Japanese silver. In 1586, Macao was granted the status of a municipal council identical to that of Évora. The traditional self-government of the merchant community shifted to control by the municipal council, although the temporary presence of the captain of the fleet to Japan introduced a sense of hierarchy and dependence on Goa. It was only in 1623 that the governor of the Estado da Índia started appointing a permanent captain in Macao, partly as the result of external influence, since the Dutch had attempted to conquer the colony in the previous year. In any case, Portuguese power in Macao was only possible through constant negotiation with the Chinese authorities in Canton, who defined the rules of the port's operation and kept the city under surveillance until the middle of the nineteenth century.[42]

[41] Armando Cortesão, *The Summa Oriental of Tomé Pires and the Book of Francisco Rodrigues* (2 vols., London, 1944); Rui Manuel Loureiro, *O manuscrito de Lisboa da "Suma Oriental" de Tomé Pires* (Macao, 1996).

[42] Eduardo Brazão, *Apontamentos para a história das relações diplomáticas de Portugal com a China, 1516–1753* (Lisbon, 1949); Charles Boxer, *Estudos para a História de Macau, séculos XVI–XVIII*, a collection of essays translated from the English, vol. 1 (Lisbon, 1991); Boxer, *O grande navio de Amacau* (translated from English) (Lisbon, 1989); Fok Kai Cheong, *Estudos sobre a instalação dos Portugueses em Macau* (Lisbon, 1996).

The arrival of English troops in 1808, under the pretext of protecting the colony against a French attack, revealed this dependence on China, as the English were forced to leave because of opposition from the Cantonese authorities.[43] The existence of Macao clearly depended to a large extent on the interest that the Chinese had in maintaining an open port for maritime traffic. Thus, the survival of Macao was the result not of central political action but of local negotiation and convergent interests. In this perspective, the community of Portuguese merchants sought institutional support from the Estado da Índia as a way of reinforcing their political position. As such, the creation of the port stemmed from the spontaneous initiative of a group of merchants and not from a specific strategy of the Estado da Índia. The community settled and was able to exploit the multiple opportunities for trade, especially with Japan until the prohibition in 1639 and then with Makassar and other ports in Southeast Asia.[44] These permanent establishments would prove to be extremely important in the long run, even though their status came only from recognition by the local authorities and the fact that they had at best a fluid hierarchical connection to the government of the Estado da Índia. The main question was how such establishments on the peripheries of the empire could be maintained.

The remaining cases of Portuguese settlement in the Far East are more specific since their existence either did not lead to recognition from the Estado da Índia or eluded regularized political status for a long time. Although the Portuguese had been in the Solor and Timor islands since 1514, no captain of the islands was appointed for decades. In any case, following the arrival of the Dutch in 1613, the Portuguese presence was rather fragile, mainly consisting of Dominican missionaries who negotiated with local powers. The sandalwood trade permitted a constant connection between Timor and Macao, but the administrative structures proved to be ineffective without the presence of captains and with the abuse and usurpation of power by local merchants. The appointment of Captain Antonio Coelho Guerreiro in 1701 was crucial in enforcing changes. He managed, albeit temporarily, to bring the local authorities under the control of the military structures and imposed regular taxes that were to be paid to the crown.[45] However, the transfer of the capital to Dili did not significantly alter the status of the region until the end of the nineteenth century. Solor

[43] Biker, *Colecção de tratados*, vol. 11, pp. 98–245.

[44] George Bryan Souza, *The Survival of Empire: Portuguese Trade and Society in China and the South China Sea, 1630–1754* (Cambridge, 1986).

[45] Artur Teodoro de Matos, *Timor Português, 1515–1769: Contribuição para a sua história* (Lisbon, 1974); Thomaz, *De Ceuta a Timor*, pp. 593–597.

and Timor continued to be a kind of protectorate whose federal structure was based on the people's diplomatic acceptance (more in theory than in practice) of Portuguese sovereignty.[46]

The most exceptional cases of the Portuguese presence are concentrated in the Bay of Bengal, a region of rich maritime commerce that consistently rejected any external governance. Portuguese communities had existed on the Coromandel Coast since the 1510s, first at Pulicat and in the following decade at Nagappattinam and São Tomé de Meliapor. These communities had been established by private traders – deserters, fugitives, and merchants – who roamed at will and negotiated their right to reside in the ports of different states (such as the Vijayanagar empire), from which they could trade and avoid the control of the Estado da Índia. Nonetheless, the Portuguese governors in Goa displayed great flexibility in dealing with these communities, appointing a captain and a *feitor* (factor) for the Coromandel Coast. In the 1540s, these posts also serviced the needs of Nagappattinam and Meliapor, where magistrates (*ouvidores*) were also appointed. Despite these posts, the Estado da Índia had no jurisdiction in that region, and the appointments only helped to reinforce the existing Portuguese communities. The *casados* (literally, married people, meaning settlers or converted natives integrated into the Portuguese environment) themselves had installed the medieval model of a city council with its own elected members, a structure only officially recognized by the Estado da Índia in 1607 in São Tomé de Meliapor and in 1643 in Nagappattinam.[47] In both cases, the organization of the charitable institutions (*Misericórdias*) participated in the structure of the Estado da Índia by reporting legacies of deceased persons to the Goa *Misericórdia*, the accepted hierarchical superior and legal agent in the proceedings and execution of wills in Portugal.[48] São Tomé de Meliapor also benefited from the creation of a diocese in 1606, one year before the recognition of the municipal council.[49] The fluctuations observed in the population of the Coromandel communities were linked to the political and economic state of the region, affected by the decline of Vijayanagar and the emergence of Golconda. In this, São Tomé de Meliapor took advantage of its closeness to Pulicat, while Nagappattinam benefited from its proximity to Ceylon. Pulicat was of great importance until the decade of 1560, when São Tomé

[46] Thomaz, *De Ceuta a Timor*, p. 227.

[47] Sanjay Subrahmanyam, *Improvising Empire: Portuguese Trade and Settlement in the Bay of Bengal, 1500–1700* (Oxford, 1990).

[48] Isabel dos Guimarães Sá, *Quando o rico se faz pobre: Misericórdias, caridade e poder no império Português, 1500–1800* (Lisbon, 1997), especially pp. 168–171.

[49] Fortunato de Almeida, *História da Igreja em Portugal* (1st ed., 1930), vol. 2 (Oporto, 1968), pp. 40, 709–710.

de Meliapor took over, maintaining its position until the first decades of the seventeenth century. Nagappattinam, which proved to be the most active Portuguese community on the coast in the beginning of the seventeenth century, ultimately shared the same fate as Jaffna, its main trade partner, as the Dutch conquered both towns in 1658.

The constant activity of the Portuguese in the region is confirmed by the founding of another community further south, in Porto Novo (in the 1590s). This community, which specialized in regional trade, gained another dimension after the fall of Nagappattinam in 1658, taking in the refugees and inheriting and expanding the other town's trade connections. Vigilance was the key word in Porto Novo, and this community survived the attentions of its main competitor, the Dutch East India Company, which established a trading post there in 1680 after a failed first attempt in 1643. In fact, documents record the activity of Portuguese shipowners and merchants until the end of the seventeenth century. The problem in this case is to know to what extent the local Portuguese communities really controlled the ports where they settled, a relevant issue regarding Nagappattinam and Meliapor. Certainly, during times of prosperity, the Coromandel communities took advantage of the system of granting voyage concessions created by the Portuguese king, who sold or granted access privileges between the diverse ports in Asia. This led to expeditions from São Tomé de Meliapor to Malacca and Pegu, and from Nagappattinam to Martaban, Mergui, Ujang Selang, Trang, Kedah, Malacca, Pipli, Satgeon, and Chittagong.

The other communities in the Bay of Bengal require further study. It is known that there were Portuguese communities in Masulipatnam, Satgeon, Chittagong, Hughli, and Pipli, that they had their own captains, and that they participated actively in trade with the Bay of Bengal, Malacca, and the western Indian Ocean, namely Hormuz. Satgeon went into decline when the port silted up during the 1560s and 1570s, while Chittagong in turn declined at the end of the sixteenth century.[50] In contrast, Hughli and its extremely active Portuguese community dominated regional commerce in the first decades of the seventeenth century. The Portuguese visibly controlled the city until it was conquered by Moghul troops in 1632, and although some Portuguese returned and settled there again, the community never had the same impact as before. The most significant military initiative in the Bay of Bengal, however, involved Filipe de Brito Nicote and Salvador Ribeiro, who commanded a group of Portuguese mercenaries who served the king of Arakan. They managed to create a trading post and build a fort in the port of Syriam, which operated from 1599 until their final defeat in

[50] Subrahmanyam, *Improvising Empire.*

1613, supplying rice to Malacca despite constant attacks from the regional landlords. During this period, Aires Saldanha, the viceroy of the Estado da Índia, received Filipe de Brito Nicote, who offered the fort he had built to the king of Portugal. The viceroy, in return, made him captain of the fort and captain-general of the conquests of the Pegu kingdom, promising military and diplomatic assistance.[51]

These Portuguese communities – and other, farther-flung ones in Manila, Makassar, and Bantam – cannot be characterized as border communities because they thrived in territories that were completely alien to the Estado da Índia. Instead, they came under the jurisdiction of governments that had established a variety of different relationships with the Portuguese empire as allies, neutrals, or enemies. These Portuguese outposts were similar to those of other ethnic mercantile communities operating in the Indian Ocean (Gujarati, Tamil, or Javanese), which were independent and self-ruling within the free-trade environment traditionally accepted in the area. The difference lay in the Portuguese communities' use of military force to reinforce their commercial position and in the special nature of the Estado da Índia as the general manager of maritime commerce throughout the Indian Ocean, a role it played for most of the sixteenth century. The Portuguese communities, who wanted recognition and political and military support from the Portuguese authorities as a way of securing their own negotiating power with local authorities, exploited this last feature in the Bay of Bengal. Although the communities consisted of men who had fled the Estado da Índia, they could still have interests convergent with those of the Portuguese authorities. These autonomous communities sought suitable links by rendering commercial and economic services, such as support to the concession-ship voyages or supplies to the Portuguese forts. The Estado da Índia proved to be surprisingly flexible in its handling of these "renegade" settlements, as they could provide access to a range of markets and complete the network of interregional commerce. This explains the military support that the Estado da Índia gave to the Portuguese operating outside its normal jurisdiction, as in the case of Filipe de Brito Nicote, one of the few who could be considered a *fronteiro* (frontiersman) in the Iberian tradition. It is equally inappropriate to speak of *lançados* (men who abandoned their roots and went to live as natives) in this region because the status of the Portuguese there was not identical to that of settlers in Senegambia or Guinea.

The adaptable attitude of the viceroys toward the Portuguese communities in the Bay of Bengal was defined at the highest institutional level. Even

[51] Maria Ana Marques Guedes, *Interferência e integração dos Portugueses na Birmânia, 1580–1630* (Lisbon, 1994), pp. 125–148; Pissurlencar, *Regimento das fortalezas da India*, pp. 515–522.

the Inquisition received orders from the king and the General Inquisitor to assume a friendly stance toward those "renegades" who wished to rejoin the Catholic faith. In return, the autonomous communities needed the Estado da Índia to probate wills and benefit from royal protection if they returned to Portugal. It is thus not surprising to find that some members of the local elites that lived outside the Estado's jurisdiction had obtained the status of captain or even become members of a military order. It is also of note that three posts, the captains of Nagappattinam, Hughli, and Pipli, were auctioned by the Estado da Índia in 1614, which was the biggest if not the only such auction recorded.[52] Whereas the last two captaincies had very low pay, the same cannot be said of the captaincy of Nagappattinam. Clearly, the Estado da Índia saw its sphere of influence increase or decrease according to the actions of the Portuguese living beyond its frontiers. The arrival of the Dutch, and later the English, would be a major blow to this trade network.

The importance of the world of the *casados* in India has not been sufficiently stressed by the historiography. The strategy of the Portuguese authorities after the conquest of Goa in 1510 was to encourage marriage with women from the local elites, a practice that was widespread not only in the territories controlled by the Portuguese but also in the peripheries of the empire. This strategy also involved the conversion, integration, and mobilization of natives for war because of the small number of Portuguese in Asia. The participation of these converted natives in municipal councils, and in village and regional power structures, was a result of a strategy of alliance between the Portuguese and the local elites whose main purpose was to increase human resources within the fragile and vulnerable empire. The Estado da Índia, a highly militarized state since its creation, needed constant recruitment of manpower, which was the role played by the *casados* in many forts and regions of the Estado da Índia, especially in the Northern Province and in Ceylon. It is curious that this distinctive feature of the Estado da Índia as a highly militarized state has escaped the most recent analysis of the military history of Portugal and its empire.[53]

Obviously, the degree of collaboration or conflict between the Portuguese and the local powers played an important role in the process of Portuguese expansion. The resistance of the sultanate of Aceh to Portuguese control

[52] Sanjay Subramanyam, *The Portuguese Empire in Asia, 1500–1700: A Political and Economic History* (London, 1993), p. 155.

[53] Manuel Themudo Barata and Nuno Severiano Teixeira (eds.), *Nova história militar de Portugal*, vol. 2, ed. António Manuel Hespanha (Lisbon, 2004). It is a pity that the volume did not analyze the seventeenth-century Estado da Índia, including the long war against the Dutch.

over the Strait of Malacca and over maritime commerce in the region had an influence on the crisis of the Portuguese empire in Asia at the beginning of the 1570s.[54] Aceh's alliance with the sultanate of Johor led to several blockades of the Strait of Malacca and attacks on Malacca, carried out with Dutch assistance in the early seventeenth century.[55] In turn, the new phase of expansion of the Safavid rulers of Iran under Shah Abbas explains the capture of Hormuz – with English help – in 1622.[56] The expansion of the Omani empire led to the conquest of Muscat in 1650, followed by a maritime presence on the west coast of India and the Swahili Coast. This eventually led to the conquest of Mombasa in 1698[57] and the exclusion of the Portuguese from the entire area except Mozambique. Likewise, the emergence of the Ikeri kingdom on the Kanara Coast led to the occupation of the Portuguese forts of Onor, Barcelor, Cambolin, and Mangalore in the mid-1650s, while the organization of the Maratha Confederation in India led to the occupation of most Northern Province territories in 1737–1740, even threatening the existence of Goa.[58] The new Portuguese strategy was to concentrate its military forces in the region of Goa, which led to the creation of a territory measuring 3,600 square kilometers. This expansion, largely resulting from the new conquests between 1741 and 1788,[59] was a major change, moving away from the dispersed empire of the past. This restructuring was also imposed by the new balance of political power in India in that the territorial concentration of the Portuguese Estado da Índia was the direct reaction to new local resistance and to the competition from other European empires.[60]

54 Vitorino Magalhães Godinho, *Ensaios*, vol. 2 (Lisbon, 1968); Luís Filipe Thomaz, "A crise de 1565–1575 na história do Estado da Índia," *Mare Liberum* 9 (1995), pp. 481–519.

55 Denys Lombard, *Le Carrefour Javanais: Essai d'histoire global* (3 vols., Paris, 1992); Paulo Jorge de Sousa Pinto, *Portugueses e malaios: Malaca e os sultanatos de Johor e Achém, 1575–1619* (Lisbon, 1997); Jorge Santos Alves, *O dominio do Norte de Samatra: A história dos sultanatos de Samudera-Pacém e de Achém e das suas relações com os Portugueses (1500–1580)* (Lisbon, 1999).

56 Charles Boxer, "Anglo-Portuguese Rivalry in the Persian Gulf, 1615–1630," in Boxer, *Chapters in Anglo-Portuguese Relations* (Watford, 1935); Neil Steensgard, *Carracks, Caravans and Companies: The Structural Crisis in the European-Asian Trade in the Early 17th Century* (Copenhagen, 1972).

57 Charles Ralph Boxer and Carlos de Azevedo, *A fortaleza de Jesus e os Portugueses em Mombaça* (Lisbon, 1960); Eric Axelson, *Portuguese in South-east Africa, 1600–1700* (Johannesburg, 1960).

58 Alexandre Lobato, *Relações Luso-maratas, 1658–1737* (Lisbon, 1965).

59 Maria de Jesus dos Mártires Lopes, *Goa setecentista: Tradição e modernidade, 1750–1800* (Lisbon, 1996).

60 Ibid.

In Mozambique, the Portuguese-dominated territories remained under the jurisdiction of the Estado da Índia until the establishment of an independent administrative unit in 1752. Earlier records include an anonymous document from 1582 that describes the Portuguese forts at Sofala and on Mozambique Island, which were designed to control the trade of gold and ivory from the confederation of Monomotapa to western India, especially Gujarat. Besides these forts, a captain in Malindi, where the Portuguese had a trading post, usually patrolled the coast with a fleet. Every year, another fleet loaded with commodities, including textiles from Cambay, sailed from Goa to Mozambique.[61] Yet, by 1635, according to the description by Antonio Bocarro, the situation was already completely different. Records show that there were forts – almost all built of adobe and some privately built – in Quelimane, Chipangura, Matuca, Tete, Luanza, Dambarare, Massapa, Matafuna, Chipirivi, and Mavura (some inside the Monomotapa confederation) that were designed to protect the Portuguese presence in local markets and mines. In a rare instance of administrative decentralization, almost all the captains, including the one at Sena, where there was no fort at that time, were appointed by the captain of Mozambique Island. In some cases, the captains were even members of the court of the Monomotapa ruler, juggling the interests of the Portuguese and local political powers. In fact, the captain of Mozambique Island paid a regular annual tribute of 15,000–16,000 cruzados to the ruler so that the Portuguese could trade freely throughout the territory. Apart from the two forts built in the sixteenth century, respectively on Mozambique Island and in Sofala, a key fort was also founded during the early 1590s further north, in Mombasa, its purpose being to collect tributes from landowners and taxes on coastal trade. Around 1630, a Portuguese royal customs office opened north of Mombasa, in the kingdom of Pate. Based on an agreement with the local ruler, this was designed to increase control over maritime trade on the Swahili Coast.[62]

In the meantime, Portuguese penetration into the interior regions of Mozambique had suffered the effects of population migrations from Central and East Africa. The key expeditions to reconnoiter and conquer the mines in Monomotapa, such as those led by Francisco Barreto in 1569, Nuno Álvares Pereira in 1609, and Diogo Simões Madeira in 1614, ended in fiasco because of local resistance and malaria. However, during the seventeenth

[61] Francisco Paulo Mendes da Luz (ed.), *Livro das cidades e fortalezas que a Coroa de Portugal tem nas partes da India, e das capitanias e mais cargos que nelas ha, e da importancia deles* (Lisbon, 1960).

[62] Antonio Bocarro, *Livro das plantas de todas as fortalezas, cidades e povoações do Estado da Índia Oriental*, ed. Isabel Cid (3 vols., Lisbon, 1992), especially vol. 2, pp. 9–43.

century, the Portuguese exerted a strong influence in the already declining Monomotapa confederation, obtaining a treaty of vassalage in 1629. In spite of their small number, the Portuguese managed to be part of the system of chieftaincies in the Zambezi valley, acting as local lords with or without the official status of captain recognized by the Portuguese authorities. Moreover, although their presence was stronger in Sena, Tete, and Quelimane, they had more influence on the population of Tonga, where they married women from the elite class, mobilized the workforce, and organized private armies.[63] Consequently, there was an interdependence between the Afro-Portuguese colonists and the African population that laid the foundations of the mixed system of regional feudalism and land concession for a period of three generations, later formalized by the Portuguese authorities. This system started in the late sixteenth century with the expulsion of the Muslim community, who had organized a rudimentary urban network, and was firmly in place in the seventeenth century, reaching full maturity in the eighteenth. The system of land grants (*prazos*) in the Zambezi valley was not radically different from the one in the Northern Province and Ceylon, although the concession in Africa was granted to women and passed on through matrilineal succession.[64] The contracts drawn up from 1575 to 1675 between the captain-general of Mozambique and the viceroy of Goa were a unique feature of the Portuguese administration in the region, as they granted the former trade privileges and the right to appoint captains, magistrates, and administrators of the region.[65]

This system mixed selling official posts (*venda de ofícios*) with electing captains (as practiced by the small Portuguese communities that settled near the local market and mines), who were then recognized by the captain of Mozambique. The elimination of privileged contracts between the crown and the captain of Mozambique in 1675 introduced a new dynamic to the six captaincies and jurisdictions created in the Sena River area at the end of the sixteenth century (Sofala, Quelimane, Sena, Tete, Manica, and Mokaranga). Their relative autonomy was underlined by the creation in 1709 of the post of lieutenant-general, a figure who was responsible for making all the

[63] Malyn Newitt, *A History of Mozambique* (Bloomington, IN, 1995), especially pp. 53–104.

[64] I will not reproduce here the historiographical debate about the nature of the *prazos*. On this issue, see Alexandre Lobato, *Colonização senhorial da Zambézia e outros estudos* (Lisbon, 1962); Giuseppe Papagno, *Colonialismo e feudalismo: La questione dei Prazos da Coroa nel Mozambico alla fine del secolo XIX* (Turin, 1971); Allen Isaacman, *Mozambique: The Africanisation of a European Institution, the Zambezi Prazos, 1750–1902* (Madison, WI, 1972); Malyn Newitt, *Portuguese Settlement on the Zambesi* (Harlow, 1973); and Thomaz, *De Ceuta a Timor*, p. 239.

[65] Newitt, *A History of Mozambique*, pp. 110–119.

various administrative appointments in the area. The creation of a separate government of Mozambique in 1752 was followed by the establishment of free trade (1755); payment in money to those who held public office (1757); financial reform, part of a program covering the entire empire (1761); and the organization of local administration, with new councils created in the 1760s. Despite these measures, the traditional ties between the Estado da Índia and the region were not disrupted, as confirmed by the constant migration of Indians and descendants of Portuguese to Mozambique.[66]

Charles Boxer rightly considered the municipal council and the *Misericórdia* to be the two pillars of the Portuguese empire.[67] The latter institution, a kind of confraternity that had no equivalent in the Spanish empire, brought advantages in establishing solidarity, socialization, and mutual support among the local elites throughout the territories, even those in areas that lay beyond the empire's jurisdiction.[68] The municipal council had been introduced into the Atlantic islands (Madeira and the Azores) as early as the fifteenth century, acknowledging their established position within Portugal's political life and their capacity to represent the local oligarchy within the framework of the empire. Introduced during the sixteenth century and based on the *Regimento dos oficiais das cidades, vilas e lugares destes reinos* (1504), and the chapters of *Ordenações Manuelinas* (1512–1513, Book I, Chapters 45–54), the municipal councils were entrusted with numerous responsibilities. These included local government, safety, the health and hygiene of urban centers, determining prices and salaries, levying taxes, establishing rules for building, distributing and leasing land, making provisions for war, creating defensive structures, and regulating holidays and religious processions. In addition, the crown agents – usually the magistrate (*corregedor* or *ouvidor*) – were frequently responsible for defining the electoral list, which was an important tool in determining who among the urban oligarchy had the right to vote and also validated the election of councilmen by lots. The number of councilmen who served varied according to the status of each municipality. Thus, for example, the Goa council initially had ten members with the right to vote: one *fidalgo*, two noblemen, two common judges, one city attorney, and four representatives of the craft guilds. In addition, the council included the secretary, the price maker, the treasurer, the judge for

[66] Fritz Hoppe, *A Africa Oriental Portuguesa no tempo do Marques de Pombal, 1750–1777* (Lisbon, 1970); Réné Pélissier, *A história de Moçambique, Formação e oposição, 1854–1918*, translated from the French (2 vols., Lisbon, 1994); Newitt, *A History of Mozambique*, pp. 119–126.

[67] Charles Ralph Boxer, *Portuguese Society in the Tropics: The Municipal Councils of Goa, Macao, Bahia and Luanda, 1510–1800* (Madison, WI, 1965).

[68] Sá, *Quando o rico se faz pobre*; see also her chapters in Bethencourt and Chaudhuri, *História da expansão Portuguesa*, vol. 1, pp. 360–368; vol. 2, pp. 350–360; vol. 3, pp. 280–289.

the orphans, the standard bearer, the porter, the accountant, and the works supervisor. The privileges of the council members were defined according to the models of Lisbon, Oporto, and Évora, cities whose specific status was recognized by the king. Thus, the Lisbon council included the representatives of the guilds, while Oporto council members enjoyed the privilege of being transported by mules. However, all these models shared identical judicial immunities, such as exemption from military service, privileges comparable with those enjoyed by the king's knights, and the authority to correspond directly with the king. Apart from the Goa council, set up immediately after the conquest of 1510, it took some time before municipalities were established in the Estado da Índia, and the decrees stipulating privileges were issued later still. Goa's status, attributed in 1516, was similar to that of Lisbon, but instead of a house of twenty-four representatives of the craft guilds, it operated as a house of twelve, and Macao was granted the same status as the city of Évora in 1586.

The empire imposed certain rules in specific cases, such as the compulsory presence of the captain of the Goa fort, a royal appointee who had a double vote, at the meetings of the city council. Furthermore, in 1688, a royal decree abolished the triennial lottery of elections in Goa, requesting instead that the list of candidates be handed over to the viceroy for scrutiny. Since its very beginning, the Goa council had assumed a primacy in relation to other municipal councils of the Estado da Índia, sending agents to the king and conducting full assembly meetings in times of political crisis that involved members from other councils. King João IV recognized this informal status in the mid-1650s when he declared that Goa would send representatives to the royal parliament, Cortes, as did Salvador da Bahia, then the capital of Brazil.

In Macao, the city council played a different role, intervening directly in governmental affairs until 1623, when the king first appointed a city captain. Even after the regular appointment of a captain, the *procurador* (city attorney) continued to accumulate responsibilities as treasurer until 1738 and as the city's representative when dealing with the Chinese authorities, who eventually awarded him the title of junior mandarin. In the meantime, the secretary of Macao's city council took on the post of *alferes* (lieutenant), first elected for a period of six years rather than three and then, after 1630, appointed to a lifetime term, making the position part of private patrimony.

The specificity of the municipalities in the Estado da Índia is also evident in the social composition of the councils as a result of intermarriages between the Portuguese and the local elites. Access to city councils was restricted to "Old Christians" (*cristãos velhos de nação e geração*) as imposed by royal decrees dated 1689, a criterion that was most embarrassing in Macao because the

Portuguese community there was mostly composed of merchants, some of them "New Christians," meaning of Jewish origin. Meanwhile, Goan society had long seen mixtures between the local elite, the Portuguese newcomers (nobles, royal officials, and merchants), the superior Brahmin castes that traditionally dominated the priesthood, the administration, and educational positions, and the Chardos, a kind of rural aristocracy. All of these groups had some influence on the composition of the council. In general, the municipal councils functioned as autonomous powers that limited the action of the captains and the viceroy, although there were often tactical alliances according to the whims of the crown.[69]

The Estado da Índia was, then, a political and administrative power delegated by the king. It was made up of the governor, who was assisted by his council and "exported" institutions and had its headquarters in Goa. The territories governed by the Estado da Índia were structured by intermediary powers such as captains, magistrates, agents of the royal treasury, and the municipal councils. The fleets were also governed by delegated power, their captains' authority being similar to that of fort-captains, and they sometimes commanded a larger number of men than those found in the strongholds. At a lower level, there were many local institutions, such as the rural communities (*gancarias*) of Goa or the villages of the Northern Province, which retained the traditional structures and mechanisms for collecting taxes. Then, given the precarious situation of the peripheral territories, the missionaries often held informal power, as in the case of the settlements in Japan or in the Solor and Timor islands. In conquered territories such as Hormuz or Malacca, geopolitical conditions required the continuance of a local power under vassalage or the continuance of representative structures from the mercantile community. However, in other cases, such as Ceylon, the Moluccas, or the Northern Province, the Portuguese presence forced the kings to bequeath their territories to the Portuguese, make declarations of vassalage, or cede territory in exchange for accepting local rules and traditions. Finally, in situations where the local powers supported the construction of trading forts (Cochin, Cannanore, and Kollam), there was an obvious maintenance of the status of sovereignty and vassalage.

In Mozambique, the capacity of Portuguese "renegades" to integrate into the border regions' local system of chieftainships through negotiations with local powers and Portuguese captains led to a form of seigneurial dominance similar to that of the Northern Province and Ceylon, albeit each with its own particular elements. Portuguese communities that wanted to benefit

[69] For more on this, see the chapters in Bethencourt and Chaudhuri, *História da expansão Portuguesa*, vol. 1, pp. 353–360; vol. 2, pp. 343–350; vol. 3, pp. 270–280.

from free trade settled in areas that lay beyond imperial control but still maintained an ambiguous relationship with the Estado da Índia, based on their shared interests. These peripheral locations either claimed or rejected – depending on the situation – connections with the Estado da Índia while maintaining a clear relationship with the crown representatives. Although the royal trading posts were sometimes a way of settling in an area and later led to the construction of forts, in other cases they maintained their exclusively peaceful purposes and were commonly found in regions where there was a reduced Portuguese presence, such as Martaban, Pacem, Basra, Kung, and Surat.

There is thus a need to replace the hierarchical vision of the Asian empire with one that is multifaceted and polarized in both space and time. In a sense, the Estado da Índia could be described as a "nebula of power" whose formal hierarchy demonstrated tremendous fluidity, with different and constantly overlapping levels of decision making. As a result, political action varied according to distance and conjuncture, which gave rise to a range of potential situations. Negotiation was the key word for proposed activities in both the internal and external spheres. From this point of view, the importance of local powers and local traditional institutions was more pronounced than historians have previously claimed. Ultimately, the position of the Portuguese depended on the nature of the relationship established with the local peoples and on the involvement of native intermediaries, especially in matters of war and finance.

The model of centralized power delegated by the king that was applied from the very start of the Portuguese expansion in Asia was the product of having to govern from afar rather than from past experience in other areas of the empire. As a matter of fact, the first Portuguese expansion – the fifteenth-century moves into the Central Atlantic and Western Africa – had involved a far less centralized organization of power. Although the expansion to Asia began almost a century after the conquest of Ceuta, the new model of imperial power created in Asia was subsequently exported to Brazil and other regions of the empire, replacing the seigneurial/feudal structures that had been established at the very beginning of the expansion. The experience in India, where this centralized model proved its efficiency, led to its export, although it had to undergo a long transitional period in the South Atlantic. In Brazil, despite the territorial differences, a similar structure of a nebula of power controlled by a strict hierarchical relationship between the king and the governor was ultimately established in the long run. The rule of a three-year term of office was observed in all hierarchical positions, thereby enabling the king to affirm his power. Instituting either formal or informal reciprocal control between the governor and the *tribunal da relação* (court of appeal), the governor and the captains, the captain and the agent of the royal treasury (in some cases the same person), and the city council and the captain or even the governor often led to obstructions in the decision-making process and to serious management difficulties. However, it did guarantee royal control over the whole system. The resulting power structure allowed relative freedom to those at the intermediary level, those who actually ensured that the entire system functioned properly: the captains, city councilors, and agents of the royal treasury. The scarcity of material and human resources required intense contact between the different levels of administration and the local structures, a practice that guaranteed some flexibility in the system.

Despite the mechanism of inspections (*residência*), the Portuguese viceroys in India and the governors of Brazil shared similar difficulties of hierarchical control over the captains. Yet, in Brazil, the problem was magnified by the sheer scale of the occupied territory and the absence of any serious indigenous military threat. Excluding the conflicts in the south, the zone of the missions and the River Plate, peace with the Spanish empire was the rule in Brazil. But the Estado da Índia model also incorporated forms of exercising and extending crown power as a commercial enterprise, means that had been tried in other regions. There was nothing original about trading posts/forts – the nucleus of the system – as they had already been used on the African coast (namely in Arguim and El Mina), inspired by the previous experiences of the Venetians and especially of the Genoese in the Mediterranean. But Asia, with its dense population and diverse political structures, called for some innovations resulting from the proximity between trading forts and local centers of power. These innovations were characterized by power sharing with the local authorities in a somewhat two-headed system. It is this density of relatively stable local political structures that also explains the good understanding between the various Portuguese communities scattered around the periphery of the Asian empire and the government of the Estado da Índia. Whether for economic, social, or political and military reasons, the different colonial mercantile Portuguese communities (or republics) could not afford to alienate themselves from the government at Goa.

The Dutch and British Empires

The Dutch empire in seventeenth-century Asia clearly benefited from the experience of the Portuguese empire. The conquest of the Portuguese forts in Ambon and the Moluccas in 1605 was merely the first step toward a political presence in Asia. This was then consolidated by the capture of Jakarta in 1619, reconstructed, fortified, and named Batavia, the conquest of Malacca in 1641, and the progressive occupation of a part of Java. The Dutch strategy of establishing themselves in the vulnerable areas of the Portuguese empire revealed both the Estado da Índia's weak defensive structure and the Dutch capacity to assess the areas that would bring the most lucrative market for trade in Europe. The periphery of the Portuguese empire thus became the center of the Dutch empire. This demonstrates that the competition between European maritime empires was organized around the geography of the spice trade markets from the very beginning, while also including wood, silk, porcelain, and precious metals, and later tea and other stimulating beverages. The connection to intercontinental trade meant that the distribution network had to be reorganized but also implied, in some cases, that production required the same process. The Dutch copied from the Portuguese the tactic of occupying places of strategic commercial and military importance, although they reversed it, progressing from east to west as they took over the main Portuguese forts and trading posts in Ceylon and the Bay of Bengal (not to mention Cochin in Malabar) between 1637 and 1663. There were also similarities in strategy and even in methods, such as the use of both military and diplomatic means to conquer the markets and impose commercial monopolies, the use of interregional commerce, the broad maintenance of local systems of territorial occupation and tax collecting, plundering local populations, and piracy. However, this resemblance should not lead to the conclusion that the two power structures were identical.[70]

Indeed, the Dutch case involved a commercial company with stockholders – the Verenigde Oostindische Compagnie (VOC) – that was oriented toward making a financial profit. The organization of the Dutch cargo ships emphasized efficiency and demanded competence from the officials and crew on board, all of whom carried out specialized functions under the command of the captain. Yet despite the strong hierarchical discipline, the administrative network in the field – which was accountable to the council of directors (Heren XVII) that represented the six regional chambers of stockholders in the Netherlands – was charged with numerous transgressions,

[70] This is one of the points where I diverge radically with Sanjay Subramanyam, *The Portuguese Empire in Asia*, pp. 212–215, who discards the differences among the diverse European empires in Asia in an article written in collaboration with Luís Filipe Thomaz, "Evolution of Empire: The Portuguese in the Indian Ocean during the 17th Century," in James Tracy (ed.), *The Political Economy of Merchant Empires: State Power and World Trade, 1350–1750* (Cambridge, 1991), pp. 298–331. My position, based on the comparative study of the organizational cultures of the different empires, can be found in "Competição entre impérios Europeus," in Bethencourt and Chaudhuri, *História da expansão Portuguesa*, vol. 2, pp. 361–382.

notably widespread corruption. Although it is clear that, as with the Portuguese, there were examples of waste and the maintenance of posts that were losing money, the economic logic was more important in the decision-making process.

The motivation and behavior of those who migrated varied enormously. Whereas almost all Portuguese settlements included numerous examples of *casados* (settlers of Portuguese descent or natives who converted to Christianity, integrated into the Portuguese political structure), Dutch European settlements were practically confined to Java and (after 1652) South Africa, with no such widespread practice of interethnic marriages until a late date. Furthermore, the dispersion of Portuguese communities to the peripheries of the empire, with an ambiguous relationship with the government of the Estado da Índia, had no parallel in the Dutch case. This does not mean that there were no "renegades," Dutch employees or soldiers (not to mention the numerous foreign employees of the VOC) that served other powers; merely that these people did not create new mercantile communities. A commercial company governed by business logic literally excluded the possibility of recognizing "free" trading posts. In the case of the Portuguese empire in Asia, the existence of these "free" trading posts in the peripheral areas changed the nature of the administration and reinforced a permanent interchange between public and private interests.

The VOC's superior economic potential is demonstrated by a few simple figures: In 1608, the company already had 40 ships and 500 employees in Asia, with an average of 12 ships per year sent from Europe. By 1688, company growth had reached a peak (maintained until 1720) of about 7,500 soldiers, 2,400 sailors and craftsmen, and 700 administrative and commercial employees in the Asian territories under direct company control, not to mention hundreds of trading post employees who were not under military control. The number of ships sailing to Asia reached 24 per year, employing about 6,000 staff, while Asian interregional commerce involved 80 ships and 4,000 employees. In total, this amounts to about 22,000 VOC employees during the period.[71] In contrast, Portuguese figures reveal an average of 6 ships per year sailing to India at the height of Portuguese power in the first quarter of the seventeenth century, although the actual tonnage shipped would need to be compared. Over 100 small ships were involved in interregional trade and defensive missions in Asia. In turn, the number of the Estado da Índia's military and civilian employees never exceeded 9,000,

[71] Charles R. Boxer, *The Dutch Seaborne Empire, 1600–1800* (1st edition, 1965, reprinted London, 1990), p. 77; Jonathan I. Israel, *The Dutch Republic: Its Rise, Greatness and Fall, 1407–1806* (Oxford, 1995), pp. 939–943.

which may be subdivided into no more than 6,000 in the forts and 3,000 working on the carreira da Índia and in interregional commerce.[72] The difference in economic potential revealed by the mobilization of capital and the capacity for investment is certainly dramatic, but the differences do not end there.

The apex of Portuguese political power – the governorship – was dominated by the titled aristocracy, who negotiated new titles and privileges with the king and secured the captaincies of forts for family members and clients. Yet the *cursus honorum* or standard career of this imperial elite did change over time. During the sixteenth and early seventeenth centuries, most of this warrior aristocracy had acquired their experience in North Africa. Later appointees started their careers in the War of Independence against Castile (1641–1668) or the War of the Spanish Succession (1703–1713).[73] In turn, the fort-captains enjoyed broad autonomy of action, despite the mechanisms for control at the disposal of the governor and the financial superintendent (*vedor da fazenda*). Finally, as shown, the captains sometimes had special contracts with the crown that entitled them to commercial privileges. In short, the Estado da Índia functioned as a crown enterprise that made many people wealthy, particularly the aristocrats who had access to the main posts, although the three-year appointment system was a way of controlling the rotation of elites and renewing the system. Yet the benefits also extended to the shipowners, merchants, contractors, and tenants who managed the customs, large business interests, and ecclesiastical revenues. As is also known, the royal monopoly over the spice trade established the rules for concessions and reserved certain areas for strict control that, despite potentially changing over time, never hindered private trade.

The VOC, as a private company, strictly prohibited its employees from running their own businesses, and its administrative structure adopted a logic entirely different from the one used by the Estado da Índia. The governors-general appointed to Batavia were never chosen from the nobility but were of lower- or middle-class origins and made their careers in India as company employees, generally as military commanders or administrative

[72] Data from 1574 on salaried workers of the crown in the empire can be found in Bethencourt and Chaudhuri, *História da expansão Portuguesa*, vol. 1, pp. 404–406. The increase in the number of employees in the first decades of the seventeenth century can be reconstituted from the following studies and printed sources: Vitorino Magalhães Godinho, *Mito e mercadoria, utopia e pratica de navegar, séculos XIII–XVIII* (Lisbon, 1990), pp. 338, 345, and 365; Godinho, *Les finances de l'etat Portugais des Indes Orientales*; and Bocarro, *Livro das plantas*.

[73] See the results of my research in Bethencourt and Chaudhuri, *História da expansão Portuguesa*, vol. 1, pp. 283, 329–335; vol. 3, pp. 242–249.

heads. They included an elite group with many years of service, such as Joan Maetsuyker (governor-general from 1653 to 1678), who had served in Asia since 1636; Rijklof Van Goens (governor-general from 1678 to 1681), who had been a military commander in Asia since 1657; Cornelis Speelman (governor-general from 1681 to 1684), a military officer in Asia since 1663; and Joannes Camphuys (governor-general from 1684 to 1691), who had arrived in Asia in 1659.[74] These governors-general and the governors of the various territories could not make any decisions without the approval of a council composed of individuals who were responsible for trade, finances, justice, and the military and naval forces. The governors were obliged to follow the directives of the Heren XVII and transmit their decisions to be ratified by that council. There was, nevertheless, a certain flexibility in the system. One example is Jan Pieterszoon Coen's conquest of Jakarta in order to set up an operational base that was vital to the VOC, even if his decision violated the Heren XVII's policy, which insisted on gaining concessions through diplomacy.

In the first quarter of the seventeenth century, the EIC started its activities in the area by creating trading posts in Bantam (Java), Ambon (Indonesia), Surat (Gulf of Cambay), Masulipatnam (Gulf of Bengal), Ayuthia (Siam), Patani (Malay Peninsula), and Hirado (Japan). However, in 1623, it decided to abandon the last three ports, concentrate its commercial activities elsewhere, and reduce investment in interregional trade. With time, its activities in the Gulf of Bengal increased, as it set up new posts in Hughli, Madras, and Calcutta. Based on the textile trade to Southeast Asia and Europe, the region soon became one of the company's favorites, and in 1676 the English gained access to Chinese markets by setting up a post in Amoy, later replaced by another in the Canton region in 1699.

Although the English case is similar to that of the Dutch, during its first century of activity, the EIC lacked the capital that the VOC could muster. It was this funding that enabled the VOC to maintain a larger permanent fleet and more armed forces in Asia than any of its European competitors. Dutch superiority over the English in other aspects was also obvious in this period. The English attack on Dutch trading posts and ships off the coast of Java in 1618 ended in a defeat that led to a treaty (1619) between the two companies, forcing the EIC to contribute to the cost of protecting shipping in exchange for access to one-third of the spice production. Another conflict broke out in 1623, this time over access to spices in the Moluccas, where English agents at the Ambon post were massacred. Finally, in 1682, the English trading post at Bantam was closed down by the Dutch, who went

[74] Israel, *The Dutch Republic*, p. 946.

on to take control of Makassar, the English mainstay in the region. None of these defeats, however, prevented the EIC from returning to its main – or alternative – ports of activity. The naval capacity of the English in Asia remained relatively reduced until the end of the seventeenth century, despite their defeat of the Portuguese in the Strait of Surat in 1615. However, it was that victory that gained the English the esteem of the Grand Moghul and allowed them to establish a trading post in the port, a decisive element in the defeat of the Portuguese at Hormuz in 1622.

The English were fundamentally concentrated in the Gulf of Cambay, the Persian Gulf, the Gulf of Bengal, and Southeast Asia, and their presence was confined to genuine trading posts that involved no exercise of political or territorial control. This situation changed slightly when the Portuguese ceded Bombay in 1665, part of the dowry when Catherine of Bragança married Charles II. This generous act, stipulated in the treaty of 1661 between Portugal and England, led to the Portuguese possession being turned over to the EIC three years later, and this new territorial base enabled the EIC to test a different model of dominion on the west coast of India. Grounded both in religious tolerance (as already exercised by the Dutch in their territories) and growing military potential, this policy contrasted with traditional Portuguese rule, which constantly subordinated economic and political logic to religious reasoning, a practice that was disadvantageous to the Estado da Índia vis-à-vis the local population. The development of naval power also enabled the EIC to expand to other parts of India despite defeats by the Moghuls in the Strait of Surat between 1686 and 1689, among others. A new military policy also emerged during this period, with the fortification and defense of trading posts, so that by the beginning of the eighteenth century, the EIC had a solid position in maritime trade, with establishments in Basra, Gombroon, Surat, Bombay, Madras, Calcutta, and Bantam.[75]

I will not discuss here the nature of the careers and the social origin of the administrators and governors, which would reveal certain specific features of the two companies. It can, however, be said that the main difference between the EIC and the VOC is attributable mostly to the meager military investment made by the English during most of the seventeenth century, a fact that explains the EIC's practice of establishing trading posts without

[75] Kirti N. Chaudhuri, *The East India Company: The Study of an Early Joint-Stock Company, 1600–1640* (London, 1965); Chaudhuri, *The Trading World of Asia and the English East India Company, 1660–1760* (Cambridge, 1978); P. J. Marshall, "The English in Asia to 1700," in W. M. Roger Louis (ed.), *The Oxford History of the British Empire, vol. 1: The Origins of Empire, The British Overseas Enterprises to the Close of the 17th Century*, ed. Nicolas Canny (Oxford, 1998), pp. 164–185.

territorial occupation. This policy ensured that the British had enormous strategic and tactical flexibility. Thus, the EIC's large- or small-scale participation in interregional commerce varied according to the possibilities and short-term needs. After the concentrated efforts made in 1623, this participation almost disappeared, only to reemerge at the end of the seventeenth century. In this last period, major investment in the Gulf of Bengal and the coast of China enabled the EIC to keep up with consumption trends in Europe, which imposed a shift in intercontinental trade from spices to textiles and to stimulating beverages, principally tea and coffee. Faced with the rise of English naval power during the seventeenth century and its dominance in the eighteenth, the VOC's position began to be eroded. Its huge administrative and military investments in Java and Ceylon restricted the flexibility required to invest in new markets. In parallel, there was the progressive increase of the EIC's capital: In 1708, this stood at £3.2 million, divided among some 3,000 stockholders, plus public bonds; by 1744, its capital had reached £6 million. At this time, twenty to thirty large-tonnage ships were sent each year to Asia, and annual sales reached £1.2 to 2 million. The superiority that the English gained over the Dutch after the 1720s was the result of the progressive increase in economic and political power and led to the military policy that Clive developed in the 1750s, which strengthened Madras's position in 1756 and enabled the conquest of Calcutta in 1757.[76]

When the English finally decided to conquer territories, the idea came from the local governors, not from the administration in London. This decision was made at a time when the Moghul empire was declining, the Maratha Confederation in India was in a state of disorganization, there was growing French expansion in the region, and the emergence of peripheral native powers threatened English control of the main markets.[77] The decline of the great Islamic empires in Asia during the eighteenth century can be partly explained by their inability to control such peripheral powers, a phenomenon that is also evident in North Africa and the Middle East. The competition between the English and the French empires in India completes the explanation of why the British opted for territorial conquest. This must also be linked to the Seven Years War (1756–1763), where the British won

[76] Chaudhuri, *The Trading World of Asia*, quoted; Philip Lawson, *The East India Company: A History* (London, 1993).

[77] Henry Dodwell, *Dupleix and Clive: The Beginning of Empire* (London, 1968); Pierre Pluchon, *Histoire de la colonisation Française: Le premier empire colonial: Des origines à la Restauration* (Paris, 1991); C. A. Bayly, *Indian Society and the Making of the British Empire* (Cambridge, 1988).

control of colonial regions because of their naval supremacy.[78] The EIC's administrative system in Asia was radically altered when its nature changed from being predominantly a commercial enterprise to a company that was responsible for territorial governance. Although the implementation and military defense of this system were massively financed by Indian merchants and bankers, the situation required increasing intervention by the English government from the 1760s until the complete takeover of the empire in India in 1813.[79] In sum, the character of the English presence in Asia underwent considerable changes. However, it would be meaningless to continue the comparison with the Portuguese empire.

The Portuguese Estado da Índia had been constructed according to a specific logic implemented by the Portuguese crown: as a commercial enterprise linked to private interests by way of contracts and concessions, with a strong component of redistributing revenue among the various levels of the administration. The Portuguese attempts to copy the English and Dutch model of commercial companies with stockholders, as tried in 1628, failed owing to the lack of commitment from private investors.[80] Conversely, the Portuguese maritime empire, which had emerged from 200 years of transfers, adaptations, and re-creations of political and commercial structures, could not act as a model for English overseas policies, which featured the organizational culture of private companies and differences in the political, military, and financial contexts that characterized the territorial conquest of India.

The Atlantic Expansion

The main difference between the Portuguese empire in Asia and the Portuguese empire in the Atlantic is that the latter was never under the control of a single governmental structure. The general governmental principle was, however, implemented in Brazil, albeit with a different logic derived from

[78] Paul M. Kennedy, *The Rise and Fall of British Naval Mastery* (1st ed., 1976; London, 1986), Chapters 3 and 4; C. A. Bayly, *Imperial Meridian: The British Empire and the World, 1780–1830* (London, 1989), Chapters 1 and 2; P. J. Marshall, "The British in Asia: Trade to Dominion, 1700–1765," in P. J. Marshall, *The Eighteenth Century*, vol. 2 in *The Oxford History of the British Empire*, pp. 487–507.

[79] Rajt Kanta Ray, "Indian Society and the Establishment of British Supremacy, 1765–1818," in P. J. Marshall, *The Oxford History of the British Empire*, vol. 2, pp. 508–529; H. V. Bowen, "British India, 1765–1813: The Metropolitan Context," in P. J. Marshall, *The Oxford History of the British Empire*, vol. 2, pp. 520–551.

[80] Anthony R. Disney, *Twilight of the Pepper Empire: Portuguese Trade in Southwest India in the Early 17th Century* (Cambridge, MA, 1978).

prior experience of the donatory-captaincy system, which had never been instituted in Asia. In fact, it was the system of trading posts and captaincies that had been adapted to the Asian context after the first experience in the Atlantic. The different types of political control in the Atlantic followed a certain logical (if not chronological) sequence, as some – the dispersed government by captaincy, the trading posts/forts, and the donatory-captaincy, which remained in place in certain regions until the eighteenth century – had been implemented in the fifteenth century. Some of the models of territorial control resulted from the first experiences in the Atlantic, especially control of the coasts from the islands, such as the relationship between Madeira and North Africa or between the Cape Verde islands and Guinea, but these appeared to be less pertinent in the Indian context. In comparison, the need for negotiated solutions was more obvious in Asia than in the Atlantic because of the different complexities of local urban, political, and military powers. The transfer of European power structures to the South Atlantic was easier, especially in Brazil and – to a lesser degree – in Angola because of the different forms of resistance shown by the local peoples. Whatever the local constraints might have been, there was unquestionably a reciprocal transfer of experiences between the Portuguese dominions in the Indian Ocean and the South Atlantic. For this reason, there is a need to analyze the diverse schemes that were tried out in the Atlantic.

Each Portuguese fort in North Africa was commanded by a captain, who played a fundamentally military role but also had judicial and fiscal control over the population. The exercise of this type of power was responsible for the constant conflicts with the hostile Muslim population in surrounding areas. This military option, implemented after the Portuguese conquest of Ceuta in 1415, was repeated following the conquests of Alcácer Ceguer (1458), Arzila and Tangier (1471), Santa Cruz do Cabo de Gué (or Agadir, 1505), Mogador (or Essaouira, 1506), Safi (in 1508, but under Portuguese influence since 1481), Azemmour (in 1513, under Portuguese influence since 1486), and Mazagão (now El Jadida, 1514). Although the initial strategy of conquering inland territories was supported by the identification of the captains with medieval Hispanic frontier warriors (*fronteiros*), the fundamental objective was to create a network of fortified ports that would control maritime movement both within the region and to the South Atlantic. This power structure remained in place for over 200 years, even though the Portuguese presence in North Africa was considerably reduced between 1541 and 1550 with the loss of Agadir and the withdrawal from Mogador, Safi, Azemmour, Alcácer Ceguer, and Arzila. This came after the rise of the sharif of Souss, who would conquer the kingdom of Fez in 1549 and establish a new dynasty.

The captains of the various Portuguese forts were appointed by the king and were accountable only to him.[81] The practice of a three-year appointment to the various administrative posts had been in place since the second phase of the conquests and would successively be applied to the entire Portuguese empire. Although these captains initially had identical status before the king, Mazagão's resistance to a lengthy siege in 1562 led to the title being upgraded to "governor" two years later. Despite the constant conflicts and skirmishes, there is no evidence of any attempt to create a centralized government ruling the region's forts, which would have permitted coordinated action. The absence of any such central leadership is perhaps explained by the proximity to Portugal and to Madeira, which acted as a military backup. Another explanation is that certain families, such as the Meneses and the Carvalhos, who continuously inherited the posts, ended up controlling the forts for a long time.

As noted earlier, North Africa offered the nobility a world of experience and military training, a stage in the *cursus honorum* that ultimately led to their appointment to the most important posts in India and Brazil.[82] The disastrous attempt at territorial conquest led by King Sebastião in 1578 stemmed from the idea that the Christian reconquest of Iberia should extend to North Africa. But equally important was that the rise of a new economic complex in the South Atlantic, shaped by trade with Brazil, was threatened by European and Berber pirates. Significantly, the Portuguese had already developed a strategy to create a network of forts in Morocco, the objective being to control the main coastal ports, maritime navigation, and access to the inland markets. Although this strategy failed because of the relative homogeneity of the powers facing the Portuguese, it was temporarily successful when transferred to the Malabar Coast, where the dispersion of local powers offered ideal conditions for implementation. Except for the brief moments of peace with the local powers, the North African forts survived only with support from southern Iberia and through contraband with the hinterland. In religious terms, the population of the forts was relatively

[81] David Lopes, "A expansão em Marrocos," in Antonio Baião, Hernani Cidade, and Manuel Murias (eds.), *História da expansão Portuguesa no mundo* (Lisbon, 1937), vol. 1, Part I, pp. 131–210; Charles-André Julien, *Histoire de l'Afrique du Nord – Tunesie, Algérie, Marroc*, 2nd ed. (2 vols., Paris, 1953); Robert Ricard, *Études sur l'histoire des Portuguais au Maroc* (Coimbra, 1955); António Dias Farinha, *História de Mazagão durante o periodo Filipino* (Lisbon, 1970); Farinha, *Portugal e Marrocos no século XV* (2 vols., Lisbon, 1997); Farinha, "Norte de Africa," in Bethencourt and Chaudhuri, *História da expansão Portuguesa*, vol. 1, pp. 118–136.

[82] See F. Bethencourt, chapters in Bethencourt and Chaudhuri, *História da expansão Portuguesa*, vol. 1, pp. 342–345; vol. 2, pp. 329–335.

homogenous because captured Muslims were immediately converted and often sold as slaves to Portugal, while the Jewish communities maintained their identity for some time, in contrast to the policy of exclusion adopted on the mainland after 1496.[83] The same exceptional situation would also be found in certain Portuguese forts in Asia for diplomatic and commercial reasons.

The exploration of the African coast was followed by the establishment of trading posts, a policy that was begun during the seigneurial rule of Prince Henry, who had been granted the rights to explore the area and who worked with private interests under his patronage until his death in 1460. A contract between King Afonso V and the Lisbon merchant Fernão Gomes in 1468 stipulated that the latter had to explore 100 leagues of coastline per year and pay an annual rent of 200,000 réis in exchange for the monopoly of trade in Guinea. This contract, extended until 1474,[84] was responsible for the exploration of the Gulf of Guinea and the islands of Fernando Pó, São Tomé, Príncipe, and Ano Bom.

This model of a normally temporary charter for commerce, granted by the crown as a trade monopoly, was also applied in Brazil. In 1502, King Manuel signed a three-year contract with a trading company that gave it the monopoly of commerce (mainly of brazilwood) in exchange for exploring 300 leagues of coast, setting up and maintaining a trading post, and the payment of an annual rent of 4,000 cruzados. The contract stipulated that there would be no payment of royalties on goods for the first year of activity but one-sixth of the revenues in the second year and one-quarter in the third.[85] The success of this contract led, in 1504, to the royal grant of São João Island (known afterward as the island of Fernando Noronha) to Fernão de Loronha, a businessman, Lisbon resident, and knight of the king's household. Under this two-generation agreement, Loronha had to populate the territory and pay the king a tithe and one-quarter of the revenues, with the exception of drugs, dyes, and spices, because the crown held the monopoly of trade in these goods. In fact, this system was a variation on the donatory-captaincy model developed in the Atlantic islands (including

[83] José Alberto Rodrigues da Silva Tavim, *Os Judeus na expansão Portuguesa em Marrocos durante o século XVI: Origens e actividades duma comunidade* (Braga, 1997).

[84] Damião Peres, *História dos descobrimentos Portugueses* (1st ed., 1943; Oporto, 1992), pp. 116–120 and 166–168.

[85] Duarte Leite, "O mais antigo mapa do Brasil," in Carlos Malheiro Dias (ed.), *História da Colonização Portuguesa do Brasil*, vol. 2 (Oporto, 1923), pp. 255, 278; Antonio Baião, "O comércio do pau brasil," in Dias, *História da colonização Portuguesa*, vol. 2, pp. 324–330. The terms of this contract, usually summarized this way, are probably exaggerated because of the crossed reading of two letters written by merchants not involved in the transaction.

Cape Verde) during the fifteenth century. However, as will be shown, the trading posts/forts built by private traders would revert to the crown at the end of such contracts. In the Gulf of Guinea, some crown trading posts had no fortification whatsoever, such as that at Guato in the kingdom of Benin, established in 1486, which served the slave trade.[86]

In Brazil, the southern trading fort at Cabo Frio (in a region then known as São Vicente) was established in 1504 under the terms of the royal contract mentioned earlier. It operated for many years until it was superseded by another on the island of Itamaracá (in the northern region of Pernambuco), which was probably established in 1516 during Cristovão Jacques's first voyage.[87] This *fidalgo* of the king's household was appointed governor of "parts of Brazil" in 1526 and spent two years leading naval operations against the French ships that roamed the coast. Once again, the status of governor had more to do with naval command, coastal control, and trading post protection than with European colonization. In fact, there are contemporary references to the captains of trading posts/forts,[88] a sign of the ambiguous status of local power structures. The same ambiguity is found in the appointment of Martim Afonso de Sousa as captain-major of an expedition that set out in 1530 to explore the entire coast from the Amazon to the River Plate, founding São Vicente and Piratininga (the first attempt) and capturing several French vessels. The same period also saw the creation of the post of captain of Pernambuco, clearly indicating the dual nature of the position as commander of both a naval force and a trading fort. The official documents stated that Martim Afonso de Sousa was to become the captain-major of the lands he found and discovered, to have military, administrative, and judicial power over the inhabitants, to distribute land to be cultivated, and to appoint officials.[89] This hybrid of captain and donatory – a juridical system that was successfully used in the Atlantic islands during the fifteenth century – precedes the introduction of the donatory-captaincy system in Brazil in 1534–1536. Before we analyze this new model of political power in

[86] Avelino Teixeira da Mota, *Guiné Portuguesa*, vol. 2 (Lisbon, 1954), p. 13.

[87] Carlos Malheiro Dias, "A expedição de 1503," in Dias, *História da colonização Portuguesa*, vol. 2, pp. 291–297; Jorge Couto, *A construção do Brasil* (Lisbon, 1995), p. 201.

[88] F. M. Esteves Pereira, "O descobrimento do Rio da Prata," in Dias, *História da colonização Portuguesa*, vol. 2, pp. 351–390; Antonio Baião and C. Malheiro Dias, "A expedição de Cristovam Jacques," in Dias, *História da colonização Portuguesa*, vol. 3, pp. 549–1594.

[89] Jordão de Freitas, "A expedição de Martim Afonso de Sousa," in Dias, *História da colonização Portuguesa*, vol. 3, pp. 97–164; Jaime Cortesão, *A fundação de São Paulo, capital geografica do Brasil* (Rio de Janeiro, 1955); Cortesão, *História do Brasil nos velhos mapas*, vol. 1 (Rio de Janeiro, 1965); *Diario da navegação de Pêro Lopes de Sousa (1530–1532)*, ed. A. Teixeira da Mota and Jorge Morais Barbosa (Lisbon, 1968).

the area, the trading posts and their role in different contexts need to be reexamined.

The trading forts along the western coast of Africa and the Gulf of Guinea were set up first in Arguim (founded in the mid-fifteenth century and gradually fortified),[90] then in São Jorge da Mina (1482), Axim (1503), Sama (1526), and Accra (destroyed by the local peoples in 1570).[91] Despite suffering as the region's gold trade declined in the late sixteenth century, they still played an important role in the slave trade. The early seventeenth-century Dutch occupation of Portuguese trading posts in Gabon, Cape Lobo Gonçalves, Fernando Pó, Rio d'El Rey, Calabar, and Rio Real[92] was merely a prelude for future action, as they went on to conquer the forts of El Mina (1637), Arguim (1638), and Axim (1642), which meant that the Portuguese had lost their monopoly over maritime commerce in the region. By the end of the seventeenth century, there were already fourteen European forts (seven Dutch, five British, one Brandenburg, and one Danish) on the Mina Coast, as well as numerous nonfortified trading posts, eight of which were owned by the English Royal African Company alone.[93] In similar fashion, despite the existing fortifications in Cacheu since 1588 and in other areas of Rio Grande de Buba since the beginning of the seventeenth century, the Portuguese on the Guinea Coast were unable to keep the English at bay. The latter established their presence during the seventeenth century by building a fort on St. James Island (at the mouth of the Gambia River) and installing two minor fortifications on Bence Island (Sierra Leone) and York Island (in the Sherbro River), not to mention the trading posts of Barra Kunda, Buruko, Sangrigoe, Furbroh, Rufisque, Portudal, and Joal. This network of forts was ultimately taken in the late seventeenth century by the French, who thereafter controlled a large part of the trade in Senegambia.[94]

The king of Portugal consequently decided in 1680 to build another trading post/fort on the Gulf of Guinea at São João Baptista de Ajudá (Ouidah), although the structure was not completed until forty years later. In the meantime, the Portuguese presence in Guinea was reinforced by the construction of a fort in Bissau (1687), which proved to be a highly complex issue. Preceded by the creation of short-lived trading companies – the

[90] Théodore Monod, *L'île d'Arguin (Mauritanie): Essai Historique* (Lisbon, 1983).

[91] Avelino Teixeira da Mota, *Guiné Portuguesa*, vol. 2, pp. 12–27; Vitorino Magalhães Godinho, *Os descobrimentos e a economia mundial*, 2nd ed., vol. 1 (Lisbon, 1989), pp. 168–176.

[92] José Joaquim Lopes de Lima, *Ensaios sobre a estatistica das possessões Portuguesas na Africa Ocidental e Oriental, na Asia Ocidental, na China e na Oceania*, vol. 2 (Lisbon, 1844), pp. xi–xii.

[93] K. G. Davies, *The Royal African Company* (1st ed., 1957; New York, 1970), p. 246.

[94] Ibid., pp. 213–221, 263, 270–274.

Cacheu and Rios da Guiné in 1676, Cape Verde and Cacheu in 1680 – it must be related to the *asiento* contracts for the slave trade to Spanish America and the appointment of a captain in the region in 1696. However, the creation of the post of captain in Bissau caused a jurisdictional conflict with the government of Santiago (Cape Verde) because Guinea depended on the Cape Verde administration, a situation that continued until 1879.[95] In the other trading posts/forts, the status of captain of North Africa was transferred with the same principle of military control over the administrative (fiscal and legal) structure. The captain was appointed by the king and was accountable only to him, not to any level of regional hierarchy. With the exception of São Jorge da Mina, which was granted the status of a city in 1486 by King João II, the Portuguese communities and native intermediaries that settled in the forts and their surroundings were not important enough to justify the development of complex organizational structures by the Portuguese authorities. Once again, we are faced with relatively dispersed power structures that depended on occasional assistance from the strongest forts.

The power structures of the Portuguese empire in this area of the Gulf of Guinea and its rivers were shaped by the ambiguous status of the trading posts and forts established along the coast. It was ambiguous because, unlike the forts in North Africa, the Portuguese presence in this region depended on negotiations and agreements with local powers. These agreements were often obtained through paying tribute, rarely mentioned as such in Portuguese documents, which chose instead to refer to the regular "gifts" sent by the ambassadors to local powers and regional neighbors. The case of São João Baptista de Ajudá is significant. The records kept by Father Vicente Ferreira Pires on the kingdom of Dahomey in 1800 include references to the precious gifts that the African king received from those responsible for European trading posts and forts on such occasions as the "big tradition" (celebration of the new king) or the "tradition" (the annual festivals of winter and summer solstices). At the time, gifts sent by the governor of São João Baptista de Ajudá were accurately calculated in Portuguese currency – 400,000 réis – a significant amount that ipso facto indicates a type of tribute. In fact, Father Pires, who spent six years in Dahomey as an apostolic ambassador of the Portuguese crown, appointed under the *padroado régio* (the royal patronage of the church), carefully documents the protocol involved

[95] Teixeira da Mota, *Guiné Portuguesa*, vol. 2, pp. 9–56; and Zelinda Cohen, "Administração das ilhas de Cabo Verde e o seu distrito no segundo século da colonização (1560–1640)," in Maria Emilia Madeira Santos (ed.), *História Geral de Cabo Verde*, vol. 2 (Lisbon, 1995), pp. 189–224.

in the "gift" ritual, whereby the European potentates came first, followed by the African potentates, demonstrating a clear political ranking.[96]

This region does reveal the application of the Madeira model, where the offshore fort, a stronghold of European colonizers, was used to support the forts in North Africa. Thus, the trading forts on Guinea's rivers depended on support from Cape Verde, while the trading forts in the Gulf of Guinea benefited from the rearguard support of the islands of São Tomé and Príncipe.[97] There was, in fact, a Portuguese model of colonizing the uninhabited Atlantic islands. First, the land was cleared and then used for agriculture: sugar cane in Madeira and São Tomé, cattle breeding and cereal production in the Azores. In addition, the islands were also used as commercial depots, namely the slave trade in Cape Verde and a seaport in the Azores for fleets returning from the Indies.[98] Both these functions strengthened logistic and military support to Portuguese vessels and to the coastal settlements.

The Portuguese tried to export the model of naval control from offshore to the Indian Ocean when they conquered Socotra in 1507 but soon abandoned this idea because of the radical difference in the context. They created settlements on the Malabar Coast and the Persian Gulf but did not manage to establish any on the Red Sea or the Swahili Coast north of Mombasa. Essentially, it was a hopeless and unsound idea to attempt to maintain a military force on an already inhabited island. Constant efforts would have been required to control the native population, which neither produced an agricultural surplus nor had any traditional trade with the mainland. Such problems explain why orders were given to destroy the fort and leave Socotra in 1511. The Madeira model would never again be used in the process of expansion in Asia.

Although the Portuguese king had taken upon himself the responsibility for undertaking the voyages of discovery, the crown granted territories colonized in the Central and South Atlantic to the donatory-captains under predetermined conditions. In practice, the latter could – to a certain extent – exercise military, judicial, and fiscal power over their respective territories in

[96] I have followed the summary produced by José Joaquim Lopes de Lima in his *Ensaios sobre a estatistica*, vol. 2, pp. 89–100, which coincides with the original report, a manuscript I consulted at the Biblioteca da Ajuda.

[97] On the number of Africans reaching these islands from the coast, see Isabel Castro Henriques's *São Tomé e Principe: A invenção de uma sociedade* (Lisbon, 2000).

[98] Rui Carita, *História da Madeira* (3 vols., Funchal, 1989–1991); João Marinho dos Santos, *Os Açores nos séculos XV e XVI* (2 vols., Ponta Delgada, 1989); Avelino de Freitas de Meneses, *Os Açores nas encruzilhadas de Setecentos (1740–1770)* (2 vols., Ponta Delgada, 1993–1995).

return for assuming responsibility for organizing the settlement process and distributing the land to be cultivated. From 1433 until his death in 1460, Prince Henry, the first to benefit from the donatory-captaincy system, held seigneurial control over Madeira and the Azores, although he delegated this power.

This feudal vassalage form of granting power in overseas territories was not unlike some medieval practices in Europe and stemmed from the need to find capital to invest in equipment, ships, and human resources that exceeded the crown's financial capacities. The donatory-captaincy system thus played a dual role: assuming both the delegation of powers traditionally held by the king and responsibility for colonizing the territories granted. Eventually the donatories, who usually remained in Portugal, developed an administrative program similar to that of the king, appointing captains to territories, setting up municipalities, and defining appropriate forms of taxation. They also authorized the establishment of ecclesiastical structures, initially under the control of the Order of Christ, which was delegated the royal patronage of religious structures overseas at the same time as the territorial grant was made to Prince Henry, who was the governor of that military order. One of the distinctive elements of the donatory-captaincy system was that the grant could be handed down. Nonetheless, some factors, such as King Manuel's circumstantial succession to the Atlantic islands or the death of a captain with no heir (as in Angola), led the crown to reassume control over several territories. The inheritability of the donation was logically followed by that of the captains that the donatories appointed, a situation that explains the dynasties of captains in the Atlantic islands even after the crown had again assumed direct authority there. The powers of the donatories had already been reduced at the judicial and fiscal levels during the reign of João II, when *corregedores*, accountants, and tax collectors were appointed to Madeira and the Azores, enabling the crown to take definite control of all customs posts.[99]

Used in the Atlantic islands throughout the fifteenth century, this donatory-captaincy system was applied to Brazil in 1534–1536. The king divided the coast into fifteen partitions of land, each of which was about fifty leagues in latitude, distributing them among twelve beneficiaries (nobles

99 Paulo Merêa, "A solução tradicional da colonização do Brasil," in Dias, *História da colonização Portuguesa*, vol. 3, pp. 165–188; Charles Verlinden, "La position de Madère dans l'ensemble des possessions insulaires Portugaises sous l'infant D. Fernando (1460–1470)," in *Actas do I Coloquio Internacional de História da Madeira,* vol. 1 (Funchal, 1989); António de Vasconcelos Saldanha, *As capitanias: O regime senhorial na expansão Portuguesa* (Funchal, 1992); Francisco Bethencourt, "As capitanias," in Bethencourt and Chaudhuri, *História da expansão Portuguesa*, vol. 1, pp. 341–352.

and crown servants) who were to colonize, cultivate, and explore the territories. The donation of Pernambuco to Duarte Coelho (March 10, 1534) is revealing, as he was given legal land rights *de juro e herdade*, for himself and his successors. He also enjoyed civil and criminal jurisdiction, except in cases of heresy, treason, sodomy, and money counterfeiting. Furthermore, he could appoint magistrates (*ouvidores*), institute townships, establish the list of electors, ratify the election of judges and officials to the municipal councils, and appoint public and judicial notaries. He also received rents, privileges, and tributes from the *alcaidarias-mores* (castle governors) of villages and towns, as well as rents from the watermills, salt mines, and sugar mills that he licensed. Finally, as the landlord and apart from paying the tithe to the Order of Christ, he had the right to keep a tax-exempt property of ten leagues of latitude (about fifty kilometers) calculated from the coastline. If the captain did not wish to keep this land, it could be rented or leased. In return, Duarte Coelho was obliged to distribute the remaining uncultivated land without payment of any tribute or rights (except for the tithe) and excluding family members from any of the benefits accrued from this land. Moreover, the captain received half the tithe from the fishing revenue, one-tenth of the rents and rights belonging to the king, and one-twentieth of the proceeds from the brazilwood contract.[100] Having undergone some adaptations from the model of donatory-captains used in the Atlantic islands, the situation in Brazil had a less restricted form of succession. Because the position was exempt from the *Lei Mental*, which defined the criteria of inheritance, women, illegitimate children, or collateral relatives could all inherit the donation, keeping broad privileges of jurisdiction (excluding the royal *corregedor*) and control over large territories. Indeed, the status of the donatory grew in importance and became more flexible because of the responsibilities of colonization and the risks involved in investing in an inhabited and distant region.

The transfer of this political model did not work out entirely as expected. In some captaincies, the settlements were destroyed by antagonistic natives, while some donataries or their appointed captains were killed or fled, leading to the abandonment of European colonization. The most successful captaincies were Pernambuco and São Vicente, thanks to political alliances formed with local powers and the practice of miscegenation with the natives. In other cases, the problems faced could variously be attributed to the absence of the donatories themselves, to certain transactions forbidden by

[100] Oliveira Lima, "A Nova Lusitânia," in Dias, *História da colonização Portuguesa*, vol. 3, pp. 287–323 (especially pp. 309–313, with the transcription of the concession and charter).

the charters but allowed in practice by the king, and to the absence of a system for mutual assistance in a region located far from Portugal.

Consequently, in 1549, it was decided to create a general government, which would be based in Bahia, one of the abandoned captaincies. This introduced the dynamics of vertical control into a fifteen-year-old power structure that was based on purely horizontal power relations between the donatories. Although the donatory-captaincy system was not abolished – the crown inherited those abandoned or left heirless, as in Rio Grande in 1582 and Maranhão and Pará in 1612 – the general government imposed itself and soon reduced the privileges by introducing royally appointed judges and tax collectors. These officials were accountable to the senior judge (*ouvidor geral*) and treasurer (*vedor da fazenda*) of Bahia, while the new system made the crown administration directly responsible for the defense of inheritable captaincies. The implementation of new centralized organizations in Salvador, such as the high court (*tribunal da relação*) in 1609, was important in this process. This institution gained jurisdiction as a court of appeal over all of Brazil and was empowered to ratify (or veto) legal acts instituted by the governor-general, the donatory-captains, and the municipal councils. The chancellor of the high court also substituted for the governor in the event of the latter's absence or death and served as the judge for the knights of the military orders. In parallel, the magistrates (*desembargadores*) of the high court participated in the state council, intervened in the choice of the judicial employees in the captaincies, and inspected the senior state administrators at the end of their mandate.[101]

Regional organizations were set up at the same time, such as the courts (*ouvidoria*) for the southern captaincies (1609) and for Maranhão (1619), which extended the crown's administrative control over all the captaincies. With the expulsion of the Dutch from Pernambuco in 1654, that former donatory-captaincy also came under the crown's direct authority. This loss of Pernambuco as an autonomous captaincy was perhaps the biggest blow to the donatory institution after the creation of the general government in 1549, even though inheritable captaincies continued to be created in Brazil to encourage the settlement of peripheral areas in Maranhão and Pará such as Tapuipera (1633), Caeté (1633), Cametá (1636), Cabo do Norte (1637), Marajó (1665), and Xingu (1685). In other cases, inheritable captaincies were granted as a means of rewarding services. This happened with the grant of Correia de Sá in Rio Grande de São Pedro, a territory measuring 75 leagues (about 375 kilometers) of longitude north of the River Plate,

[101] Stuart Schwartz, *Sovereignty and Society in Colonial Brazil* (Berkeley, CA, 1973).

which was ceded in 1676 but restored to the crown in 1727. Ultimately, by the mid-eighteenth century, all the inheritable captaincies had been returned to crown control.[102]

With the discovery of gold in Minas Gerais in the 1690s, Brazil posed a huge new administrative challenge for the crown. The gold rush stimulated European colonization of the interior, and new captaincies were soon created: São Paulo and Minas Gerais in 1707 (separated in 1720), Goiás and Mato Grosso (both created in 1748), and Santa Clara and Rio Grande do Sul (both created in 1760, subordinated to Rio de Janeiro). The intermediate administrative level became so dense owing to this new colonization that twenty-four districts and more than a hundred townships (thirty-six in São Paulo alone) could be counted in Brazil by the end of the eighteenth century. The installation of a new high court in Rio de Janeiro in 1751, followed by the transfer of the capital from Salvador to Rio in 1763, revealed the relocation of the economic and social axis from the northeast to the south of Brazil throughout the eighteenth century. Although these processes may suggest a linear, centralized administration, that would be far from accurate. The fact that the crown unsuccessfully attempted to make several regional divisions demonstrates how difficult it was to establish administrative control over such a vast colony. In 1572, one year after an attempt to reorganize the Estado da Índia, the crown decided to divide Brazil into two states. One state, whose capital was in Salvador, had jurisdiction over the northern captaincies of Ilheus, Bahia, Pernambuco, Itamaraca, and Paraíba; the second, whose capital was Rio de Janeiro, held jurisdiction over the southern captaincies, including Porto Seguro, Espírito Santo, São Tomé, Santo Amaro, São Vicente, and Santa Ana. This scheme survived for just four years, as it proved impossible to mobilize a military force against the resistance of the natives whose territories were being occupied and because of the colonists' attempts to capture Indian slaves for labor. Another effort to separate the southern captaincies was made in 1607, this time as a favor to the former governor, Francisco de Sousa, who promised to discover and exploit gold mines and precious stones. This undertaking also failed to last more than four years. In fact, the only long-lasting administrative hold came in the northern

[102] Francisco Adolfo Varnhagen, *História geral do Brasil*, 4th ed. (5 vols., São Paulo, 1948–1953); Rodolfo Garcia, *Ensaio sobre a história politica e administrativa do Brasil, 1500–1810*, 2nd ed. (Rio de Janeiro, 1975); Frédéric Mauro (ed.), *O império Luso-Brasileiro, 1620–1750*, in Joel Serrão and A. H. de Oliveira Marques (eds.), *Nova história da expansão Portuguesa*, vol. 7 (Lisbon, 1991); Maria Beatriz Nizza da Silva (ed.), *Dicionário de história da colonização Portuguesa do Brasil* (Lisbon, 1994); Francisco Bethencourt, "O complexo Atlântico" and "A América Portuguesa," in Bethencourt and Chaudhuri, *História da expansão Portuguesa*, vol. 2, pp. 315–342, and vol. 3, pp. 228–249, respectively.

captaincies of Pará, Maranhão, and Ceará, created in the early seventeenth century after the French had been expelled from São Luís do Maranhão. The Atlantic winds and sea currents had delayed colonization of this region, as they hindered navigation to the most populated European captaincies (Pernambuco, Bahia, and São Vicente), but it did ease direct communication with Portugal. This led to the creation of the state of Maranhão and Pará in 1621 (which also suffered various vicissitudes until it was integrated into the state of Brazil in 1772), along with the subaltern captaincies of Rio Negro and Piauí.[103]

The crown's administrative centralization should be viewed in relative terms since the captaincies enjoyed considerable autonomy in relation to the governor, who could impose his authority only in matters of defense. It was during the war against the Dutch (1625–1654) that the first battalions (*terços*) of regular troops were organized, along with mercenary troops (composed of Portuguese, "assimilated" Indians, and mulattoes) that had been used to overcome Indian resistance. Much later, the military reorganization introduced by the Count of Lippe in Portugal at the beginning of the Seven Years War was extended to Brazil when the Marquis of Lavradio was appointed viceroy in 1769.[104] The sporadic warfare between the southern captaincies and the Castilian empire from 1753 to 1801 accounts for the formation of local auxiliary groups and their conversion into military companies in 1796. Not enough emphasis has been given to their role in shaping a colonial identity that transcended regional consciousness. Although the vision of Brazil as a single political entity was developed in the crown's central organs, especially the overseas council, there is no indication of a global political consciousness among the colonial elite, which was restricted to each captaincy until the court arrived in Brazil in 1808. The real process of centralization began from that date, with the transfer of key crown agencies, the opening of ports to international trade, the freedom to develop industries, the development of a far-reaching bureaucracy, and the diffusion of the social model of court society.

Confirmation of this may be found in a review of the various mutinies that occurred in São Paulo, Rio de Janeiro, São Luís, Vila Rica, Mariana,

[103] Sérgio Buarque de Holanda (ed.), *História geral da civilização Brasileira*, 8th ed., vols. 1 and 2 (Rio de Janeiro, 1989–1993).

[104] Dauril Alden, *Royal Government in Colonial Brazil, with Special Reference to the Administration of the Marquis of Lavradio, Viceroy, 1769–1779* (Berkeley, CA, 1968); and Pedro Puntoni, "L'art de la guerre dans le contexte de l'expansion de la frontière de l'Amérique Portugaise, de 1550 à 1700," in François Crouzet, Denis Rolland, and Philippe Bonnichon (eds.), *Pour l'Histoire du Brésil: Hommage à Katia de Queirós Mattoso* (Paris, 2000), pp. 157–169.

Ouro Preto, and other locations, with colonists opposing the Jesuits and gold prospectors opposing crown tax collectors. These conflicts occurred over a period of 200 years in specific places (in some cases in an entire region), and no records mention any request for help from other captaincies. The Emboabas War (1707–1709) between *paulistas* (residents of São Paulo) and those born in Portugal (allied with the Bahians and other colonists from various parts of Brazil) for the right to exploit gold in Minas Gerais can be characterized as an internal conflict that brought different colonial settlements into opposition. The Mazombos unrest, which brought the mill owners of Olinda into conflict with the merchants in Recife (1710–1712), also pitted debtors against creditors over the decision to create a new municipal council in Recife, which had previously been under the jurisdiction of Olinda. The conflict eventually extended to the whole region, but it did not spread beyond the border of the captaincy. Similarly, the Inconfidência Mineira of 1789, a project of rebellion targeting the excessive royal taxes on gold production, did not affect other captaincies apart from Rio. The later conspiracies – in Rio de Janeiro (1794) and Salvador de Bahia (1798) – failed to achieve the same social and political impact because of the panic among the colonial elites generated by the slave revolt in Haiti in 1791.

The position as governor of Brazil – coveted by the same titled nobility that had, until the late seventeenth century, preferred an appointment in India – became important because of the war against the Dutch and, above all, when gold was discovered. Pedro de Vasconcelos e Sousa, Count of Castelo Melhor, appointed governor in 1711, was followed as governor of Brazil by twelve counts and four marquises. In some cases, as in India, the title was granted at the same time as the beneficiary was appointed to the post. The logic behind this simultaneous nomination and promotion to the ranks of the nobility was to reward services rendered to the king, with examples including the Marquis of Angeja in 1714 (previously the Count of Vila Verde), the Count of Cunha in 1760, and the Count of Azambuja in 1763. The title of viceroy – first conferred in Brazil on Jorge de Mascarenhas in 1640, followed by Vasco Mascarenhas in 1663 – was only renewed in 1714 with the appointment of Pedro António de Noronha and became systematic after the appointment of Vasco Fernandes César de Meneses in 1720. Holding the governorship became the culmination of a career, as had previously also happened in India. The government of major captaincies, whose hierarchy was defined by the political and military status or the amount of wealth they controlled, also drew the attention of titled nobility, as can be seen in Pernambuco, Rio de Janeiro, Minas Gerais, Maranhão, São Paulo, Goiás, and Mato Grosso. Because the appointment of captains was under strict royal jurisdiction, enabling the crown to maintain direct contact with this level of power, it was difficult to establish a chain of hierarchy that the governor controlled. Instead, the crown preferred to create dispersed powers that competed with one another to ensure its own central authority, as had also been the case in India.[105]

Although the Portuguese Atlantic empire had never been a formal centralized power, from the very start the colonists were aware of the bilateral relation between Brazil and Africa, stimulated by the economic dependence on the slave trade. Political awareness of this relationship was to be developed by the crown's central agencies, such as the Overseas Council. The capture of Luanda from the Dutch in 1648 by troops recruited in Rio under the command of Salvador Correia de Sá demonstrates the practical regional awareness of an Atlantic geographical complex. The political elite in Brazil knew that the most effective way of breaking down Dutch resistance in northern Brazil was to block the supply of slaves arriving from Angola. The crown's strategy of appointing two Pernambuco war veterans as governors of Angola – João Fernandes Vieira (1658–1661) and André Vidal de Negreiros (1661–1666), both of whom embarked for Africa with troops recruited in Brazil – is another clear example of the bilateral relationship. Besides, as Luiz Felipe de Alencastro has insisted, the political and military culture of these governors was geometrically opposite that of their predecessors, as they were used to fighting against both the natives and the Dutch. This certainly explains the increase in the number of conflicts between the Portuguese who had settled in Angola and the kingdom of Kongo, culminating in the battle of Ambuila (1665), which changed the balance of power between Europeans and natives in this region of Africa.[106]

In spite of King Manuel's inheritance, the leasing and granting of land continued in the Atlantic islands for some time. Thus, São Tomé Island was leased until 1522, the captaincy of Ribeira Grande (Cape Verde) until 1572, the captaincy of Praia (also Cape Verde) until the 1580s, and the island of Príncipe until 1773. The captaincy of Angola was granted to Paulo Dias de Novais in 1571 after the first mission under his leadership and with the help of the Jesuits in 1560–1565. In a fashion similar to the land charters in Brazil, this concession brought the donatory 35 leagues (about 175 kilometers) of latitude on the coast south of the Kwanza River. Of this, he could choose

[105] For a better explanation of this analysis, see Bethencourt, "A América Portuguesa," pp. 228–249.

[106] António de Oliveira Cadornega, *História geral das guerras Angolanas* (3 vols., Lisbon, 1972); Charles R. Boxer, *Salvador de Sá and the Struggle for Brazil and Angola, 1602–1686* (London, 1952); Luiz Felipe de Alencastro, *O trato dos viventes: Formação do Brasil no Atlântico Sul, séculos XVI e XVII* (São Paulo, 2000).

20 leagues (about 100 kilometers) to be tax exempt, except for the tithe payable to the Order of Christ, and this land could then be divided into four or five lots to be cultivated or rented. The concession was made on the condition that if the grant was not used for a period of fifteen years, the land would automatically return to the crown. The donatory would have civil and criminal jurisdiction, was empowered to appoint an *ouvidor*, judges, public notaries, and officials, and was free from the control of the royal *corregedor*. He could build towns, grant charters, and establish *alcaidarias-mores*, as well as enjoying exclusive rights over mills, salt pits, and fisheries. Moreover, he received one-third of the rents and privileges of the captaincy, had exclusive rights to the shellfish industry (the trading currency in Kongo), and could export forty-eight slaves per year. In return, he was obliged to keep a galleon, two caravels, and five *bergantins* (small fast ships), set up an army of 400 men for twenty months in the captaincy, build three forts in ten years between the Zuenza and the Kwanza rivers, settle 100 families in six years, and build a church in honor of Saint Sebastian. By the time Paulo Dias de Novais died in 1589, his territorial control had extended to Massangano, where a fort had been built, supported by a municipal council and a captain, and regular slave trafficking to Brazil and Spanish America had been established. Owing to his lack of successors and the fragile military situation in the territory, Philip II decided three years later to integrate the captaincy into crown possessions. Thereafter, the colony was administered by a governor-general and by a network of fort captains appointed by the king. The expansion of the colony met strong resistance and only progressed in the second half of the seventeenth century through alliances and military actions. Even so, it was only at the end of the nineteenth century that the interior was occupied, under pressure from the Berlin Conference and because of the discovery of quinine. A systematic offensive strategy was launched (continuing until the 1910s), a network of communication was created, the number of colonists increased, and the administrative system gained some consistency.[107]

The first municipal councils in Madeira and the Azores were created in the mid-fifteenth century by their donatory, Prince Henry, who granted privileges to the inhabitants of the first urban nucleus. This implied a regular division of the areas of jurisdiction and the spread of the institution to new colonial territories, namely the Cape Verde archipelago, the islands of

[107] Ralph Delgado, *História de Angola* (4 vols., Luanda, n.d.); *Monumenta missionaria Africana: Africa Ocidental (1570–1599)*, ed. António Brásio, vol. 3 (Lisbon, 1953), pp. 383–388, 391–396, 401–403; René Pélissier, *Les Guerres Grises: Résistance et révoltes en Angola (1845–1941)* (Orgeval, 1978).

São Tomé and Príncipe, Angola, and Brazil. The members of the municipal councils in the Atlantic islands were elected annually, with the smallest municipalities consisting of just a councilman, a judge, and an attorney. In larger communities, with the exception of the attorney, the number of members doubled and two representatives of the craft guilds were added. The municipal council of Salvador, created at the same time as the general government, only received a status equivalent to the city council of Oporto in 1646, after Rio (1642) but before São Luís de Maranhão and Belém in Pará (1655). It comprised only three councilmen, two civil judges, and an attorney. The four representatives of the craft guilds were only integrated into the council in 1641, despite the fact that the king had stipulated eighty years before that they should be elected and included. They would be definitively excluded in 1713 after the Maneta revolt. Like Goa within the Estado da Índia, Salvador played the leading role among the municipal councils in Brazil until the end of the seventeenth century. A royal decree of 1693, which decentralized royal power, allowed governors to establish towns in the interior regions and to acknowledge foundations set up by the captains. This facilitated the creation of municipal councils in Brazil. However, we can only speak of a real network of cities and towns in Portuguese America that had the capacity to organize the colonial space following the discovery of gold and the colonization of the interior of Brazil, that is, after the mid-eighteenth century.[108]

The importance of municipal councils in the Atlantic complex can be analyzed by looking at instances of political intervention. Examples include São Tomé, where the council had governmental privileges in the absence of a captain, as defined in the royal decree of 1548, and Luanda, where the council dismissed and expelled governors, a fate shared by Francisco de Almeida (1593) and Tristão da Cunha (1667).[109] In Brazil, the unique conditions of the colonization process meant that certain council functions had to be reinforced, such as their jurisdiction over urban occupation and organization, the distribution and sale of common land, and control over agriculture in that land. The amount of land to be distributed in this colony was far more important than in any other region of the empire, and the impact of council intervention in the crucial issue of the creation and reorganization of founding elites was correspondingly far greater, as shown by

[108] See the analysis and bibliography of the chapters on the municipal councils in Bethencourt and Chaudhuri, *História da expansão Portuguesa*, vol. 1, pp. 353–360; vol. 2, pp. 343–350; and vol. 3, pp. 270–280.

[109] Carlos Agostinho das Neves, *São Tomé e Príncipe na segunda metade do século XVIII* (Lisbon, 1989); Boxer, *Portuguese Society in the Tropics*, p. 115.

São Paulo.[110] In this case, the municipal council not only controlled the distribution of land and organized the rural suburbs, which later became towns, but also played a decisive role in regulating access to the indigenous labor market. When the city expelled the Jesuits in 1640, following a typical urban mutiny against the order regulating access to indigenous labor, the municipal council leased the Jesuit-created indigenous villages to colonists, although the situation did not last long because of the intervention of the governor.

From the very start, Brazil was the stage for conflict between Portuguese settlers born in the colony and emigrants actually born in Portugal (*reinóis*). Royal decrees from 1643 to 1747 granted the former group easier access to the municipal council, except in the case of São Luis do Maranhão. The social origin of the local oligarchies varied but did not follow the "blood purity" (*limpeza de sangue*) and noble origin required by royal legislation. This had a precedent in São Tomé in 1520, when King Manuel allowed the mulattoes that were "men of fortune or married" to serve on the council, an exception that was also extended in 1546 on the island of Santiago (Cape Verde), where "mulattos and blacks" could be council members.[111]

The sugar aristocracy in Brazil controlled the municipal council and the *Misericórdias* of Salvador, Olinda, and other main centers in the northern territories, except for Recife, where a merchant elite managed to create its own municipal council in 1710.[112] In other cases, such as Rio de Janeiro, the land-based aristocracy succeeded in keeping the merchants – who were accused of being of Jewish origin – out of the municipal council, despite the positions adopted by successive governors. The powerful pressure that the merchants exerted against the old local oligarchy in the late seventeenth and early eighteenth centuries,[113] might have contributed to the Inquisition's violent repression between 1707 and 1714,[114] when some 130 New Christians accused of being Jews were sent for trial in Lisbon. The repression had a particularly strong impact in Rio de Janeiro because several social strata – including landowners, sugar mill owners, merchants, judges, lawyers, doctors, students, soldiers, and craftsmen – were involved. The Inquisition's

110 John Manuel Monteiro, *Negros da Terra: Índios e bandeirantes nas origens de São Paulo* (São Paulo, 1994), pp. 110–111.

111 *Monumenta missionaria Africana*, ed. António Brásio, 1st series, vol. 1 (Lisbon, 1952), pp. 500–501; 2nd series, vol. 2 (Lisbon, 1963), pp. 386–387.

112 Evaldo Cabral de Mello, *A fronda dos mazombos, Nobres contra mascates, Pernambuco, 1666–1715* (São Paulo, 1995).

113 Maria Fernanda Baptista Bicalho, *A cidade e o império: O Rio de Janeiro no século XVIII* (Rio de Janeiro, 2003).

114 Arnold Wiznitzer, *Jews in Colonial Brazil* (New York, 1960), Chapter 7.

intervention led to a decline in the city's financial resources, which might have encouraged the French sack of Rio by Duguay-Trouin in 1711. A similar assumption can be made about the Inquisitor's visit to Salvador one hundred years earlier (1618–1620),[115] which led numerous New Christians to flee to Lima, weakening the financial structure of the city and easing the Dutch conquest in 1624.

Conflicts between factions in cities were also common, as were those between the captains and the governors. As in the Estado da Índia, it is possible to speak of a nebula of power with overlapping competences to confirm top-level decisions, a situation that enabled the king to control the political game at a distance. In Brazil, the municipal councils had less political weight than in the Estado da Índia because of the vast scale of the territories that composed the captaincies. However, the density of the network in the eighteenth century brought about identical structures, which were assimilated by the local elites and contributed to the maintenance of political unity after independence.

Comparative Perspectives

A comparison between the Portuguese empire and those of other European nations in the Atlantic area reveals the different times of operation and the individual forms of action when faced with a common context. In sub-Saharan Africa, malaria, the established indigenous populations, and complex state organizations hindered European colonization until the nineteenth century. The European presence was restricted to the trading posts and stout forts on the coast, obtained through negotiations with local powers that demanded, in most cases, the payment of tribute. The presence of the Portuguese in certain inland regions of Angola, Kongo, and Mozambique can be considered an exception, but during the seventeenth century, settlements grew without assuming complete political and administrative control. Between the fifteenth and the nineteenth centuries, 12 million slaves were traded from Africa to the American continent to supply labor for mines and sugar cane, tobacco, and cotton plantations. Apart from the gold and ivory, this trade was the reason behind the European commercial presence

115 Rodolfo Garcia (ed.), "Livro das denunciações que se fizerão na visitação do Santo Oficio à cidade de Salvador da Bahia de Todos os Santos do Estado do Brasil no ano de 1618," *Annaes da Biblioteca Nacional do Rio de Janeiro* 49 (1927), pp. 75–198; Eduardo de Oliveira França and Sónia Siqueira (eds.), "Segunda visita do Santo Oficio às partes do Brasil pelo Inquisidor e visitador Marcos Teixeira: Livro das confissões e ratificações da Bahia, 1618–1620," *Anais do Museu Paulista* 17 (1963).

in Africa. The slaves were supplied by middlemen (some of them former slaves) and the local powers. In the Gulf of Guinea, the conflict between the European powers established on the coastline turned out to be beneficial to the Dutch and the English, who managed to control access to the slave markets during the seventeenth and eighteenth centuries. The Portuguese did, however, maintain their position in Angola (and later in Mozambique), from which they continued to supply Brazil and the Plate River area. Yet even in this domain, Portuguese attempts to create new companies based on the Northern European model never lasted long. Instead, the trade was carried out by private entrepreneurs under crown protection.

The West-Indische Compagnie (WIC), created in 1621 along the lines of the VOC (Verenigde Oost-Indisches Compagnie), took control of Dutch shipping and trade in America and West Africa. This company had five regional city councils representing the stockholders, which appointed the nineteen members of the senior administrative council. The WIC shares were more dispersed than those of the VOC and had already reached a value of 7 million guilders – a larger investment than the VOC's – one year after the company started up. However, the administrative council had an oligarchic character and was connected with the ruling class from the beginning. The early years of the WIC's activity were its "golden years," as they succeeded in seizing 547 loaded Portuguese ships between 1623 and 1638 and 249 more ships during 1647–1648.[116] In 1628, they achieved the resounding success of intercepting the Spanish treasure fleet at the Cuban port of Matanzas, giving the stockholders an enormous dividend of 75 percent of their share value the following year. The company also gradually took over the Brazil trade, seizing Pernambuco in 1630 and then the northern captaincies, but this period of economic, cultural, and political success – associated with the government of Johann Maurits van Nassau-Siegen – ended with the revolt of the Portuguese colonists and the final expulsion of the Dutch in 1654. The company managed to survive with supplies from Africa and the transfer of sugar cane production to the Antilles after conquering Curaçao in 1634, yet the European economic crisis in the 1670s, which caused the price of sugar to plummet, accelerated the company's decline and led to the dissolution of the WIC in 1674. The new company that was subsequently set up concentrated mainly on the slave trade and the transport of sugar cane from Curaçao.[117]

[116] Frédéric Mauro, *Le Portugal et l'Atlantic au XVIIe siècle, 1570–1670: Etude économique* (Paris, 1960), p. 449.

[117] Boxer, *The Dutch Seaborne Empire, 1600–1800.*

Political Configurations and Local Powers

Any comparison between the Portuguese and the Spanish empires in America is biased by their radically different contexts. The Castilians arriving in Mexico and Peru found urbanized societies with complex state structures that controlled a large variety of subordinated populations who helped the new conquistadores. These Amerindian states had forms of tax collection and systems to exploit the mineral resources that were used, in many cases, by the Castilians. In contrast, the Portuguese found seminomadic inhabitants with limited agricultural activities, few state organizations, a dispersed population, and the absence of any fiscal system. The Spanish initially controlled the native population through the institutionalized *encomienda* (the distribution of the workforce among the conquistadores), whereas the Portuguese controlled territories by means of land distribution based on the medieval *sesmaria*, which in the Brazilian context excluded natives.

The type of political control was also different. The Castilian domain never instituted donatory-captaincies, and the crown had direct control of the territories almost from the beginning. The political and administrative structure of the Castilian empire was comparatively more hierarchical and more influenced by the military nature of the conquest (recalling the initial role of the *adelantados de Indias*, the military adventurers in search of conquest and reward), without the "nebula of power" that so characterized the Portuguese empire. Moreover, in contrast with the Portuguese case, the Castilian viceroys intervened in the appointment of captains. Ten courts of appeal were set up in the Castilian empire between 1511 and 1565, enjoying a vast range of powers compared with the court of appeal in Bahia, which was not created until 1609. Again, the Brazilian municipal councils consisted of elected members, and there was no sale of offices, as widely practiced in Spanish America. This is not to say that there were no cases of patrimonial offices at some levels of the administration, such as the governor-general's secretary. However, they did not have the character of a public sale, a fact that further emphasizes the redistributive function of the Portuguese empire, based as it was on the concession of grants, commercial privileges, and lease contracts. The Brazilian municipal councils had more autonomy than those of Spanish America, where the *corregidor* presided over the sessions of the *cabildo* (municipal council). A major element that distinguished Spanish municipal councils in America from their Portuguese counterparts was that the Spanish endorsed the creation of councils made up of indigenous peoples. This excluded the Spanish, mulattoes, and Africans, following the political idea of the coexistence between two republics and in view of the fact that the Spanish had found preexisting representational forms among the local people. Nothing comparable could be observed in the Brazilian territory. Administrative divisions in Spanish America were already dense by the end of the seventeenth century, with thirty-seven provinces in the two viceroyalties of New Spain (created in 1535) and Peru (1543), which confirms the specialization of functions and defining careers. The practice of the *residencia* (an inspection process) was systematically observed in the Spanish empire at all administrative levels, starting with the viceroy, who was obliged to leave a *memoria de gobierno*, a report by the governor on his activities, for the benefit of his successor.[118]

The best comparison regarding the social and cultural context of colonial societies is between the Portuguese empire and the British empire in North America, although there was a higher population density of indigenous peoples in the latter, despite the impact of epidemics caused by the Europeans. In British America, there were political forms of native confederation for defensive purposes that did not exist in Brazil, at least not of the same dimension. The British empire had also been built up through the transfer of institutions from the metropole, but the presence of the crown had been distant and indirect for most of the seventeenth century. The license given to mercantile companies, aristocrats, or emigrant groups made it possible for them to maintain loose ties with the legitimate claims of the British monarchy, but at the same time allowed the colonists to create autonomous political structures. These included the local and provincial assemblies of landowners, who distributed land and organized tribunals in both Chesapeake and New England. In some cases, the colonists elected their governors, with the choice later being ratified by the crown. Whereas colonization in the South was based on tobacco plantations that required servants and slaves, colonization in the North was based on agriculture, cattle breeding, fishing, fur trading, lumber, and naval supplies. New England established important trade links with England and other British colonies in America because it supplied food and the ships needed for transport. New England also had types of autonomous political representation that avoided the empire's control for years, for example in Rhode Island, because of the religious convictions of the colonists. In Massachusetts, there was a movement to set up villages for converted indigenous people in the mid-seventeenth century, a phenomenon that should be compared to the Jesuit villages in Brazil. In fact, the British crown only began to impose its authority in the late seventeenth century, by means of administrative reorganization and the direct appointment of governors. In this first phase, the British possessions in the Caribbean were the most profitable because of tobacco

118 Manuel Lucena Salmoral (ed.), *História de Iberoamerica, vol. 2: História moderna* (Madrid, 1990); Francisco Bethencourt, "Competição entre impérios Europeus," in Bethencourt and Chaudhuri, *História da expansão Portuguesa*, vol. 2, pp. 361–382.

and sugar production. The import of servant labor, mainly from Ireland, followed by the massive importation of slaves, justified the rise in the legislative power of each regional colonial assembly. Crown intervention was indirectly established through the introduction of the Navigation Acts of 1651 and 1660, which required that all exports from the colonies be sent to England and excluded transport by other countries. Although the slave trade was opened up to international commerce in 1698, the monopoly of commerce with the metropole was maintained, which in fact was the same policy as in the Portuguese empire.[119]

During the eighteenth century, the British crown made an effort to tax the colonists for the cost of protecting the transport of goods, for the development of naval power, and for other defense expenses. It also reinforced councils that were invested with the competence to ratify colonial legislation. Apart from this political and military intervention, which accounted for the successive victories against the Dutch and the French, a superiority consolidated during the Seven Years War (1756–1763), the power of the colonial assemblies and the elected governors was greater than that of the administration, which was dependent on the king. In addition, contrary to the captaincies in Brazil, the political status of each colony varied. The British colonies in America had a precocious sense of individual identity that developed among colonists because of the easy political relations with London and the strong business ties between the different colonies. This had no parallel in the captaincies of Brazil.

This sense of common interests was decisive in the growing political consciousness that was so well expressed in the American War of Independence (1776–1783). The American Revolution was imbued with a radicalism that had no counterpart in the Brazilian declaration of independence fifty years later.[120] The locally promulgated declaration by the prince regent of the

[119] James Horn, "Tobacco Colonies: The Shaping of English Society in Seventeenth Century Chesapeake," in Louis, *The Oxford History of the British Empire*, vol. 1, pp. 170–192; Virginia DeJohn Anderson, "New England in the Seventeenth Century," in Louis, *The Oxford History of the British Empire*, vol. 1, pp. 193–217; Hilary McD. Beckles, "The Hub of Empire: The Caribbean and Britain in the Seventeenth Century," in Louis, *The Oxford History of the British Empire*, vol. 1, pp. 218–249.

[120] Nicholas Canny and Anthony Pagden (eds.), *Colonial Identity in the Atlantic World, 1500–1800* (Princeton, NJ, 1987); Jack P. Greene, *Pursuits of Happiness: The Social Development of Early Modern British Colonies and the Formation of American Culture* (Chapel Hill, NC, 1988); Gordon S. Wood, *The Radicalism of the American Revolution* (New York, 1991); David Hancock, *Citizens of the World: London Merchants and the Integration of the British Atlantic Community, 1735–1785* (Cambridge, 1995); Ian K. Steele, "The Anointed, the Appointed and the Elected: Governance of the British Empire, 1689–1789," in Louis, *The Oxford History of the British Empire*, vol. 2, p. 127.

Portuguese crown led to the creation of an empire in Brazil that lasted until 1889. Although this was responsible for the emergence of a new bureaucratic elite and political governance, there was a certain continuity in the power structure set up by the Brazilian colonial elite. In this case, we could talk about an "interiorization" of the metropole by the colonial elite,[121] even if the country followed a completely independent path after its liberation from the old European grip. Yet the Portuguese legacy was surprisingly strong in one significant domain: respect for the frontiers established throughout the eighteenth century. Despite its enormous territory and the traditional autonomy of its different regions, namely the captaincies of the north, Brazil did not fragment after independence, in contrast to Spanish America. In Brazil, the less centralized state and the weakness of the regional elites, too widely dispersed across large territories, helped to create a sense of common interest and cultural identity in the face of the neighboring countries. This pattern is not alien to a previous feature found in the Portuguese empire: a permanent tension between the central agencies of the crown and the regional and local colonial powers, whose divergent interests were never sufficiently strong for them to break away from the mother country and follow their own autonomous purposes. The independence of Brazil reveals the change of scale in the colony, where the social density and complexity of the elites allowed the pursuit of their own interests, in turn implying the creation of a new state.

BIBLIOGRAPHICAL ESSAY

Few studies in English are available on the political configurations of the Portuguese empire. The global approaches proposed in Charles Ralph Boxer's *The Portuguese Seaborne Empire, 1415–1825* (London, 1969) or Bailey Diffie and George D. Winius's *Foundations of the Portuguese Empire, 1415–1580* (Minneapolis, 1977) are still useful. Boxer's groundbreaking study *Portuguese Society in the Tropics: The Municipal Councils of Goa, Macao, Bahia and Luanda, 1510–1800* (Madison, WI, 1965) stressed the idea that municipalities and *misericórdias* were the two pillars of the Portuguese empire. This approach inspired A. J. R. Russell-Wood's *Fidalgos and Philanthropists: The Santa Casa da Misericórdia of Bahia, 1550–1755* (Berkeley, 1968). Russell-Wood recently

[121] Maria Odila Silva Dias, "A interiorização da metrópole, 1808–1853," in Carlos Guilherme Mota (ed.), *1822 – dimensões*, 2nd ed. (São Paulo, 1986); Iara Lis Carvalho de Souza, *Pátria Coroada: O Brasil como corpo político autónomo, 1780–1830* (São Paulo, 1998).

organized two books of essays from a comparative perspective: *Local Government in European Overseas Empires, 1450–1800* (2 vols., Aldershot, 1999); and *Government and Governance of European Empires* (2 vols., Aldershot, 2000). The historical background of the donatory-captaincies in Brazil has been studied by Harold B. Johnson in *From Reconquest to Empire: The Iberian Background to Latin American History* (New York, 1970). The first important study of a Portuguese tribunal in the empire is by Stuart Schwartz, *Sovereignty and Society in Colonial Brazil: The High Court of Bahia and Its Judges, 1609–1751* (Berkeley, CA, 1973). Dauril Alden's *Royal Government in Colonial Brazil, with Special Reference to the Administration of the Marquis of Lavradio, Viceroy, 1769–1779* (Berkeley, CA, 1968) solidly approaches the institutional framework during a period of change. Sound insights on administrative and political organization in Africa are provided in Malyn Newitt's *A History of Mozambique* (Bloomington, IN, 1995). Unfortunately, Sanjai Subrahmanyam's *The Portuguese Empire in Asia, 1500–1700: A Political and Economic History* (London, 1993) contains too many mistakes to be useful on matters of political organization. There are two crucial works in French by Vitorino Magalhães Godinho, who changed the historiography of the Portuguese empire by integrating it into world history: *L'économie de l'empire Portugais aux XVe et XVIe siècle* (Paris, 1969) (a Portuguese revised edition was published in four volumes in Lisbon in 1981–1983); and *Les finances de l'etat Portugais des Indes Orientales, 1557–1635: Matériaux pour une etude structurale et conjoncturelle* (Paris, 1982). Despite focusing on economic history, these volumes provide crucial perspectives on the social history of organizations, such as the systematic leasing of the royal monopoly to merchants and the emergence of the social figure of the "merchant-knight." The publication of financial sources provided researchers with important material for understanding the extension of the crown administration in the Estado da Índia. There has been an explosion of Portuguese studies since the mid-1980s. Only a few cover the field of political configurations, although many have useful references. Study of the captaincies has been renewed by António Vasconcelos de Saldanha in *As capitanias e o regime senhorial na expansão ultramarina Portuguesa* (Funchal, 1992). He has also written a global study of the diplomacy of the Estado da Índia: *Iustum imperium: Dos tratados como fundamento do império dos Portugueses no Oriente. Estudo de história do direito internacional e do direito Português* (Lisbon, 1997). The new histories of the Portuguese expansion offer useful insights on political configurations, even if they mostly present a compartmentalized view of different territories of the empire: see A. H. de Oliveira Marques and Joel Serrão (eds.), *Nova história da expansão Portuguesa* (8 vols. published to date, Lisbon, 1986–2005) (the volume on nineteenth-century Africa organized by Jill Dias and Valentim Alexandre being particularly good); A. H. de Oliveira Marques (ed.), *Historia dos Portugueses no Extremo Oriente* (5 vols. Lisbon, 1998–2001); and Francisco Bethencourt and Kirti Chaudhuri (eds.), *História da expansão Portuguesa* (5 vols. Lisbon, 1998–1999).

8

ECCLESIASTICAL STRUCTURES AND RELIGIOUS ACTION

Isabel dos Guimarães Sá

At the beginning of the Portuguese expansion, with the conquest of Ceuta in 1415, the method used to convert other peoples to the Christian religion was not unlike the method applied by the crusaders toward Muslims: It consisted basically of building churches on the ruins of destroyed mosques. This overlaying of religious spaces serves well as a metaphor for the belief that a shift in religion will naturally follow the occupation of space by military conquest. Because the enemies were Muslims, whose religion punished apostasy with death and condemned Christian missionaries to the same fate, occupation of territory was the only means of gaining new spaces in which Christianity could flourish. Space, but not souls: The fight against Muslims was considered in itself to be a *serviço de Deus* (a service to God); that is, one of the ways to enable eternal salvation.

The Portuguese came into contact with non-Muslim "others" for the first time during the 1440s on the coast of Guinea, but a long time would pass before they would have the will to convert and would develop adequate tools for efficient missions. It was not until the fourth decade of the sixteenth century that Europeans were able to aim seriously at transforming other individuals into Christians. At that time, they began to send effective bodies of missionaries, organized in religious orders, ready to discover the best way to convert other peoples to Christianity: learning their language and their mores, and making themselves revered, obeyed, and, if possible, loved.

The reorganization of the Roman Catholic Church brought about by the Council of Trent (1545–1563) would transform missionary action into one of the main duties of Catholicism. Whereas the Spanish had only pagans to convert in the Americas and the Philippines, the Portuguese encountered Muslims on both coasts of Africa, in several parts of India, and in Southeast

Asia. This led eventually to the persistence of the religious ideals of the Crusades in the Portuguese empire, although by the end of the sixteenth century the Portuguese had abandoned their ambition to convert Muslims and concentrated their efforts on peoples of other religions. The variety of systems of beliefs the Portuguese had to deal with was enormous and compelled them to acquire knowledge of other religions: from the Amerindian and African ones to the Chinese Taoist sects and the Buddhists in Japan. They also faced a wide variety of religions in confined areas, India being the most famous case, where Hinduism was perhaps the dominant belief system.

Before the Jesuits and other religious orders began to undertake missionary work on a large scale from the 1540s onward, efforts to Christianize were inconsistent. We are led to suspect that, despite stated ambitions to convert other peoples, the Portuguese arrived in new places with just enough priests to minister to the passengers on their ships. In India, for instance, the only religious order regularly established before the Jesuits were the Franciscans, who specialized in poor populations of the Fishery Coast. These were massively converted in 1536 and 1537. The Franciscans were also the only religious order before the arrival of the Jesuits in 1542 to establish houses where the brothers could live together communally in places such as Cochin, Goa, and Chaul. Missions from other religious orders did not enjoy lasting success before the Jesuits stimulated a competition among the different orders for influence in areas around the world.

In the long run, military violence alone could not ensure domination. This was especially true for a small country with relatively few people to export, such as metropolitan Portugal. In order to transform territorial occupation into hegemony, colonial powers had to transform other peoples' cultures. From the sixteenth to the eighteenth centuries, at least, the most effective way to do this was to use religion. It gave the recipients a new master narrative, conveniently mirrored in existing social and political structures. Native and imported populations were integrated into the church by baptism and acquired new clothes and new names and were encouraged to adopt monogamous marriages in order to follow a model of family identical to that of the colonizers. The evangelization task progressed without ever threatening seriously the colonial enterprise or the slave system.

As Charles Boxer noted in his impressive *The Church Militant and Iberian Expansion*, papal bulls issued from 1452 to 1456 legitimized African slavery, and the voices raised against the slave trade were few and mainly from Spanish ecclesiastics. The only Portuguese author who condemned it openly was a Dominican, Fernando de Oliveira, whose book, *Arte da guerra do mar* (Art of Sea Warfare), published in 1555, had little impact. As in the Spanish empire, but unlike the Dutch or the English, who made relatively little effort to evangelize until the nineteenth century, the will to integrate colonized peoples into the Catholic Church was an essential element of the colonial enterprise of the Portuguese. It cannot be understood separately from the economic and political motivations of expansion.

The *Padroado Régio* and the Military Orders

In the Portuguese empire, as with the Spanish, the crown was in charge of the administration of ecclesiastical affairs. This prerogative, known as the *padroado régio* (royal patronage), entitled Portuguese kings to propose the creation of new bishoprics in the empire and to nominate bishops, who would later be subject to papal confirmation. In return, kings were responsible for the funding of religious activities and religious institutions, such as building churches, paying stipends to the secular clergy, or underwriting the religious orders that were established overseas. To raise this money, the crown received the ecclesiastical tax, the *dízimo*, normally exacted by the church. Not only did the crown enjoy the control of the church in their empire, but they also held a monopoly of religious action, and missionaries had to abide by Portuguese rules. Even if such missionaries were not Portuguese, they had to affiliate with Portuguese branches of religious orders, or they had to acknowledge Portuguese authority, namely by departing from Lisbon aboard Portuguese ships.

The Portuguese *padroado* preceded its Spanish counterpart by nearly fifty years. In 1433, the Portuguese king D. Duarte was already granting spiritual jurisdiction over the Madeira Islands to the Order of Christ, and in 1455 the bull *Romanus pontifex* recognized the crown's rights to rule spiritual matters in the newly discovered territories. The Spaniards began their efforts in papal court in order to obtain the same prerogatives in the 1480s in the context of the fight against Spanish Muslims and the colonization of the Canary Islands. Only in 1508 did Julius II grant the bull *Universalis ecclesiae*, which enabled the Castilian crown to rule spiritual matters in the Americas.

How did the Portuguese rulers gain this degree of control over church affairs? In order to answer this question, we have to go back to the Reconquest in the Iberian Peninsula. War against the Muslims was regarded as sacred. Knights who participated in it joined military religious orders, which were entrusted with the conquest of new territories and often were rewarded with vast tracts of land in frontier areas. Their members were expected to obey vows of chastity, poverty, and obedience. There were four such orders in Portugal – Santiago, Avis, Hospital, and Christ – all of them created to fight Islam in the context of the Crusades. In the long run, the Avis dynasty appropriated rulership and control of those powerful institutions. Two processes concurred to bring about this outcome: their "nationalization" and "royalization." By the former, they came under Portuguese control after losing their ties with the main branches, which were situated outside the realm. The Order of Christ replaced (or succeeded) the Order of the Temple, suppressed by the pope, and the orders of both Avis and Santiago were freed from Castilian control (Avis was a branch of the Order of Calatrava). The Hospitallers were the exception, remaining international, but they were of secondary importance. Only the orders of Avis, Santiago, and Christ are of major concern. By "royalization," we mean the process by which their leadership tended to be increasingly granted to men of the royal family, either legitimate or illegitimate sons of kings, and even, albeit more rarely, to their nephews. Both of these processes can be traced back to the fourteenth century and reached a peak in 1550, when King João III merged the leadership of the three orders in his person, an arrangement that Pope Julius III institutionalized the following year.

One of these military orders in particular was granted important privileges concerning "spiritual action" in the newly discovered and conquered Portuguese territories: the Order of Christ. This occurred mainly in the period when Henry the Navigator was its governor and used the Order of Christ to back up his exploratory activities in the Atlantic and West Africa. The town of Tomar, the location of the headquarters of the Order of Christ, was to have through its *vigairaria* (district church) authorization to direct the spiritual well-being of the new territories, without recourse to episcopal authority. Naturally, with such prerogatives, the Order of Christ was soon to overshadow the two other existing military orders. It became increasingly wealthy, especially after 1500, when Manuel I began a significant political and economic investment in the Order of Christ, to which the pope granted a vast amount of ecclesiastical property, resulting in a spectacular increase in the number of members.

The control of the *vigairaria* of Tomar over the religious structures of the new territories soon had to give place to new bishoprics as the empire expanded. Its role as spiritual headquarters would cease when the first bishopric with metropolitan status was created overseas in Funchal in 1514. This diocese was assigned religious control over the territories between Cape Bojador and India until 1551. It lost this prerogative when the need to form new dioceses in distant territories arose.

Although the Portuguese crown never lost control of the religious institutions inside its empire, it is true that after the middle of the seventeenth century it could not ensure the monopoly of religious action. The downfall of the *padroado* occurred between the 1620s and 1640s. The Congregation of Propaganda Fide was created in 1622, by which the pope took specific action to encourage missionary activity instead of delegating it to the Iberian imperial nations as before. He thus broke the traditional religious monopoly of the two empires. This meant that not all the religious orders acting in them would be national or obey national authority. The 1630s proved to be the most damaging to Portuguese religious activity. Jesuits and other missionaries were violently expelled from Ethiopia and Japan. In other areas, European competitors of the Portuguese increased their military activity, as was the case in Malacca, which Portugal lost to the Dutch in 1641. After the Portuguese expelled the French Capuchin mission from Maranhão in 1615 and the Dutch from Pernambuco in 1654, Brazil remained the Portuguese colony where the religious monopoly of the *padroado* was most efficient.

The Dioceses of the Empire

The formation of bishoprics followed the evolution of the empire. After the foundation of the diocese of Funchal, the next wave of new bishoprics was created in 1533–1534: Angra (Azores), Santiago (Cape Verde), São Tomé, and Goa. The increasing importance of Brazil led to the creation of the See of Bahia in 1551. Then the patriarchy of Ethiopia followed in 1555, and two new dioceses were dismembered from Goa, one in Cochin and the other in Malacca, both in 1557. Later in the century, the dioceses of Macao (1575) and of Funai in Japan (1588) were created. In mainland Africa, the first diocese was created in 1596, the bishopric of Congo-Angola.

The main shift in spiritual authority was the elevation of Goa to metropolitan status in 1558, with jurisdiction over all the Indian Ocean and East Asia. The second major restructuring of authority occurred in 1676, when Bahia was elevated to the metropolitan see of Brazil. The following year, it would aggregate under its authority the Diocese of Angola, thus confirming the close ties between the two areas, linked by the slave trade. The Portuguese empire would thus have two religious centers, one in the Indian Ocean and the other in the Atlantic. Goa would have jurisdiction over the bishoprics of Cochin, Malacca, Macao, Japan (Funai), Meliapor (founded in 1600), the prelacy of Mozambique (1612), and the last bishoprics to be created by the Portuguese in the East, Nanqing and Beijing (both founded in 1690). Bahia aggregated under its authority the newly created dioceses of Rio de Janeiro and Olinda (both founded in 1676), Maranhão (created in 1677), Angola (placed under its authority in 1677), Sao Tomé (incorporated in 1679), and during the eighteenth century the dioceses of Pará (1719) and Mariana, Sao Paulo, and Goiás (all founded in 1745) followed. The structure of the dioceses was thus closely related to the administrative organization of the empire. There was the Atlantic triangle and the Estado da Índia, although Macao came to enjoy a certain autonomy because of its distance from Goa, its religious importance as the last Portuguese territorial outpost in eastern Asia, and as the crossroads of the arrival and departure of missionaries to China and Japan. As such, it had a special link with the bishoprics created in either Japan or China.

Also in the Estado da Índia, the diocese of Angamale-Cranganor became a special case. It was constituted in the area where the only existing Christian community in India before the arrival of the Portuguese was located. After some years of contact, there were problems because the Portuguese considered such a community impure by Catholic standards. At first, nothing could be done because the pope recognized the authority of the patriarch of Armenia as legitimate. A campaign was initiated to submit these Christians to the *padroado*, and the fight was won when the Synod of Angamale (1599) condemned some of the doctrinal propositions of the Malabar Christians. The diocese was elevated to metropolitan status in 1608, although it never had any bishopric under its authority. This peculiar situation derived from the fact that the nomination of the first archbishop, the Catalan Jesuit Francisco Ros, created tensions among his colleagues because he was not Portuguese. He had been appointed precisely because he knew Syriac, and his see was elevated to metropolitan status in order to give him autonomy from Goa.

The actual presence of Portuguese bishops varied. Bishops tended to be absent from their assigned dioceses until the Council of Trent insisted upon the permanent residence of bishops in their dioceses. But, even if the Council set a standard, bishops could be difficult to replace in certain areas, or unexpected difficulties would keep a see vacant for several years, as was the case when an appointed bishop died on the way to his diocese. There were other complications as well. It was impossible to obtain papal confirmation for nominee bishops between 1640 and 1668, during the Restoration War, because the popes were pressured not to do so by the Spaniards.

Bishops from the secular clergy were rare, and the religious orders tended to monopolize the spiritual command of certain dioceses, such as the Franciscans in Cape Verde, the Augustinians in São Tomé, and the Dominicans in Mozambique in the seventeenth century. Jesuits avoided being named bishops, an office they did not consider their vocation, except in areas where they sought supremacy in missionary activity, such as Ethiopia, Macao (although not in the eighteenth century), Angamale-Cranganor, and Japan. Nevertheless, most dioceses in the empire had bishops from a great variety of alternating religious orders: Franciscans (several branches), Dominicans, and Augustinians most frequently; Carmelites, friars of the Order of Christ, and secular clergy tended to be fewer; and Benedictines and Cistercians very rarely assumed this role. Bishops also tended to concentrate on their urban functions, which consisted mainly of caring for the Portuguese colonists or creole population, and were less concerned with missionary activities. In contrast to the prolific Jesuits, and to a lesser extent Dominicans and Franciscans, not many bishops were linked with printing activities or were the authors of religious literature. One of the few exceptions was the Franciscan Gaspar de Leão, bishop of Goa from 1560 to 1567 and 1571 to 1576. He was the sponsor of the second printing press to be installed in Goa and was the author of a treatise on the conversion of Gentiles and Muslims entitled *Desengano de Perdidos*.

Synods were few in the Portuguese empire and accordingly only a small number of printed synodal constitutions survive to this day: Angra (1559), Funchal (1578), one in Goa (1567), one in Angamale (also known as Diamper, in 1599), and one in Bahia, published as late as 1707. The only archbishopric where synodal activity was significant was Goa, where four other synods took place (in 1575, 1585, 1592, and 1606), although the results were not published at the time. Bishops in the Portuguese empire limited themselves to diocesan visitations, rarely venturing out to the wilderness (except for the Amazonian expeditions of two bishops of Pará, D. Frei João de S. José Queirós and D. Frei Caetano Brandão in the 1760s and 1780s). Episcopal seminaries were also few; instead, Jesuit schools for the training of their members and the education of the local elites were created everywhere in the empire, but the formation of a native clergy was severely limited by racial prejudice. The secular clergy suffered from an ill reputation for ignorance, greed, and loose behavior, and the Jesuits (and even other religious orders sometimes no less guilty of the same accusations) did not hesitate to profit from their moral advantage.

Historians have also confirmed the scarcity of parish clergy in all the areas of the empire and their lack of high moral and intellectual qualities. The *padroado* suffered from the same ills as the other elements of the Portuguese empire. The kings failed to give ecclesiastical institutions their fair share of royal revenues and often paid them late. More than that, bishops also became royal officers, who were often asked to gather extra monies for the military defense of the empire, as was the case in Asia when Portuguese territories were under attack during the seventeenth century. For instance, D. João Ribeiro Gaio, bishop of Malacca, took charge of the defense of the city during the siege of 1587.

Religious Orders

Secular priests under direct supervision of bishops could not alone, because of their relatively small number, have provided adequate spiritual service to such large new territories. Recruitment of ecclesiastics relied heavily upon religious orders whose members, as distinguished from secular priests, lived according to a rule and inside the walls of a monastery. Although not always setting evangelization as their main task, many of the existing and new religious orders in Portugal expanded to the new territories. Some expanded modestly, as did those of medieval origin, such as the Benedictines, who went only to Brazil, where they founded monasteries with rural estates similar to the ones they had in northern Portugal.

The most suitable for overseas export were no doubt the mendicant orders, whose friars, unlike the monks of the monastic orders, enjoyed greater mobility and had since their beginning included evangelization among their goals. Before the Jesuits made their entrance in the 1540s, Franciscans and Dominicans had already arrived in Asia, although there were few places where they arrived before the Jesuits. Only the Fishery Coast, Ceylon, and East Africa can be quoted as examples of pre-Jesuit missionary activity. There were areas where they obtained the monopoly of religious action from the pope, as was the case with the Franciscans in Ceylon. Nevertheless, time would show that the only areas to be indoctrinated exclusively by a religious order other than the Jesuits were the islands of Solor and Timor. There, the Dominicans were the only missionaries as well as being strong political agents, ensuring a Portuguese presence in the area as the Jesuits did in Japan. Other religious orders would be influential in other Asian areas, such as the Augustinians in Bengal and Pegu (southern Burma) and the Franciscans in Ceylon and southern India. Carmelites, Theatines, and other smaller religious orders (often non-Portuguese) arrived during the seventeenth century in the Portuguese territories, although their presence was not significant when compared with the Jesuits and the two main mendicant orders, the Franciscans and the Dominicans.

It would not be an exaggeration to say that the Jesuits were engaged in a permanent rivalry with the Dominicans and the Franciscans. The rate of founding new monasteries intensified after the appearance of the Jesuits, who set the stage for a fight for areas of influence that would go on for the next 200 years. China and Japan were perhaps the areas where such competition was most fierce because it involved not only rivalries between the mendicant orders and the Jesuits but also Luso-Spanish frictions during the period of dynastic union. The Franciscans and Dominicans who threatened the Jesuits' monopoly over religious affairs arrived from the Philippines, which was under the Spanish *patronato*. The attempts of the Franciscans and Augustinians in Manila to create convents in Macao during the 1580s, which failed, can also be viewed as attempts to challenge both the Portuguese *padroado* and the Jesuits' monopoly over the missions in Japan and China.

The Portuguese empire was the first field of evangelization of the Jesuits (the order was scarcely two years old when Xavier departed for India), preceding by some twenty years their service in the Spanish and French empires. Among all the religious orders that were engaged in evangelization, historiography has stressed the Jesuits' success in Portuguese colonies. Nevertheless, we do not know to what extent the self-production of sources by this order is responsible for a distortive effect that leaves other orders, albeit themselves not lacking in literary production, largely in the Jesuits' shadow. Even so, we could argue that, even if the main competitors, the Franciscans and Dominicans, cannot be ignored, the efficacy of Jesuit propaganda was sufficient to create an image of success that the reality of missionary work would in many cases deny.

Several reasons may be cited to explain why the Jesuits came to appear to be the most successful religious order that engaged in missionary activity in the Portuguese empire. This "success" was the result of an effective combination of organizational devices, political pragmatism, and economic independence.

With regard to organization, the Jesuits possessed like no other religious order the requisites for successful missionary activity. Unlike other regular clergy, they could make free use of their time: They were not limited by the demands of the cloister and did not need to comply with canonical hours. As soldiers of Christ, they were trained to obey orders without questioning them.

Also, an abundant network of colleges and Jesuit residences, both in Portugal and overseas, made sure that each missionary was given adequate doctrinal and theological training. Also, the Jesuits would do everything in their power to acquire the tools necessary to convert populations. The initial use of interpreters was soon replaced by the learning of local languages, and in Brazil they even adopted a general language for the indoctrination of the Amerindians. In Goa, Macao, and Japan, Jesuit headquarters were equipped with printing presses for the publication of books, either in Portuguese or in local languages, which would help them in their doctrinal work. The other religious orders might eventually follow these strategies but never all of them simultaneously and never on the same scale. Also, the Jesuits organized the promotion or public relations of their order in a way that made their missionary efforts the best-publicized in Europe. To start with, they were an international organization: Their members were recruited throughout Catholic Europe, and obviously they intended for their efforts to become known as widely as possible. The so-called annual letters or relations, sent by virtually all missions, could be published in Europe within a short time after their arrival and were carefully edited to serve propaganda functions. The Jesuits were so well organized that such reports could even be published at the same time in different cities. If some letters were not considered sufficiently important to be published, they could still serve as vehicles of updated information to the central authorities of the order.

None of this would have sufficed if the Jesuits had not proved to be good politicians: They managed to remain close to power, especially to the monarchs and their representatives, either as confessors or as educators. They could also adopt low-profile strategies, performing services and collaborating with other local institutions, apparently without self-interest. They would preach at local churches, serve as confessors to the powerful, administer extreme unction to the dying, and care for the sick and wounded on board ship, in hospitals, or in their homes. In brief, they would do anything that might give them local prominence, even tasks the order was not originally intended to perform, such as the responsibility for parishes, the nomination for bishoprics, or the administration of hospitals. The most famous hospital administered by the Jesuits was the Royal Hospital of Goa, under their administration since 1591, but in India they would also specialize in hospitals for the newly converted. With few exceptions, such as the controversy over the enslavement of native Brazilians, the Jesuits never took official stands against royal and colonial institutions. They always presented themselves as loyal servants of the king, although, in practice, they gained effective control of some areas of missionary work. This was the case in Japan, where the Jesuits were largely responsible for the presence of Portuguese merchants. This was also what happened in Brazil, where they gained authority over villages of converted Amerindians. In the 1720s, for instance, Jesuits did not allow diocesan visitations to Brazilian missions.

If the Jesuits hesitated before they contradicted established political power, they did not do so when it came to ensuring economic independence. The order developed means of self-sufficiency and became largely autonomous from the *padroado régio*, whose payments tended to be postponed and devaluated. In Brazil, the Jesuits became owners of large estates, either raising cattle or, after the beginning of the seventeenth century, becoming involved in the sugar plantation economy. In urban environments, they owned a large number of houses, which provided them with rents. In India, they received tributes from villages they owned as the result of a major transfer of lands from indigenous control to their hands, after the temples to which such lands belonged were destroyed and the property subsequently appropriated. Income from lands in India financed a number of missions, even as far away as China or Japan. In the latter, Jesuits were largely responsible for the development of the silk trade, and the Japanese converts also supported local churches.

The success of the Society of Jesus as an institution cannot be mistaken with the efficiency of their religious action. Recent historiography has emphasized the limits of the conversion work they undertook. In Brazil, as demonstrated by Charlotte de Castelnau l'Estoile, the missionaries who actually lived among the Indians in villages were just a small proportion of the Jesuits living in Brazil and the most subaltern members of the order; they complained bitterly about their "barren vineyard." Ines Zupanov analyzed the way in which theological disputes could mask professional rivalries, distinctions of social background, and nationalism by studying the history of the competition between Gonçalves Fernandes Trancoso and Roberto da Nobili in the Indian mission of Madurai. This conflict went as far as Rome, where the papacy was to have the final word over the acceptance of Nobili's adaptive methods of conversion, which his partner so strongly opposed. True, the Portuguese empire could not do without the Jesuits from their appearance in 1540 until virtually the beginning of the eighteenth century. Nevertheless, as an institution that could be singled out for its "otherness," the Jesuits were always (even before their expulsion) easy targets for criticism, especially from less successful competitors. In the long run, this process of "othering" would cause their ruin, and the crown, other religious orders, and even segments of the population were happy to see the Jesuits expelled from metropolitan Portugal and its colonies after 1759. After the expulsion, missionary and teaching activities in the empire were disorganized, and efforts had to be made to replace the Jesuits; in Goa, there was a serious attempt to form a native clergy that would attend to the numerous parishes the Jesuits had left unattended.

The Inquisition

Another institution created in metropolitan Portugal to be exported to its empire was the Inquisition. The Portuguese Inquisition, created by the pope in 1536 at the request of João III, persecuted mainly crypto-Judaism. Persecution of converted Muslims was confined mainly to the second half of the sixteenth century. The Inquisition was slow to expand overseas: Only in the 1560s, after a strong controversy both locally and in Portugal, was it introduced to Goa, where it acted mostly against converted Jews that had sought refuge both there and in Cochin following the persecutions in metropolitan Portugal. The Goan Inquisition had a reputation for cruelty and persecuted a higher number of individuals than any other metropolitan branch. By the second half of the seventeenth century, persecution of New Christians gave way to the persecution of local converted populations under suspicion of sustaining Hindu cults. The Inquisition was also used against European rivals. One of them was the French doctor Charles Dellon, who was accused of heresy and incarcerated for several years. He wrote an account, published in Leiden in 1678, which was to be a major contribution to the "black legend" of Portuguese India. It not only enjoyed tremendous success in Protestant Europe but also was one of the first writings against the Inquisition to be published in Catholic Europe. The work appeared in four French editions before 1700.

The Inquisition was never established in Brazil, in contrast to Spanish America, where it was established in Lima (1570), Mexico (1571), and Cartagena (1610). This does not mean that the Inquisition did not make its presence felt in Brazil, however. The territory was under permanent surveillance. The accused were sent to Lisbon for trial and sentencing, and several detection systems for deviant behavior were installed. The first such devices were inquisitorial visitations, in which inspection teams from the Lisbon Inquisition would be sent to Brazil. The first covered the areas of Bahia and Pernambuco and took place between 1591 and 1595. There were similar visitations in this decade to the Azores, Madeira, and Angola. Other inquisitorial visitations in Brazil followed in the seventeenth and eighteenth centuries, one between 1618 and 1620 in Bahia and the other in Grão-Pará from 1763 to 1769.

After 1637, such visits were interrupted because of the financial crisis brought about by the Restoration War (1640–1668). Also, a network of alternative control was put in place to monitor the colony's orthodoxy, which made such visitations by the metropolitan Inquisition superfluous. Among them was the development of an ecclesiastical justice system independent from the Inquisition, where bishops organized diocesan visitations that paid due attention to deviant behavior. Last but not least, the Jesuits were eager to help in persecuting offenders, often acting as representatives of the Lisbon Inquisition (*comissários*). The Inquisition in Brazil, although directed at religious orthodoxy, was not as harsh on crypto-Judaism as its Goan counterpart and was soon to have "sexual offenses" perpetrated by Old Christians as its main target. Sodomy, fornication, and bigamy (considered to be inspired by the devil) were the main crimes prosecuted. Nevertheless, although many of the accused were sent to Portugal for trial, the colony was spared from harsh inquisitorial action because the latter might threaten the political stability of a territory that supplied high tax profits to the crown.

The Inquisition of Goa was suppressed by Pombal in 1774, then reopened by Queen Mary I when the former prime minister of José I fell into disgrace (1778), but it was closed definitely in 1812 as a result of pressure from the English. Nevertheless, in the years immediately before its first closure in 1774, it lived up to its reputation for harshness and cruelty, increasing the number of convicts and public executions, with low-caste Christians from India accused of idolatry (*gentilidade*) as the main victims.

Confraternities and Religious Life

Confraternities revealed and reflected the adherence of the local populations to Catholicism. They were an expression of the religiosity of the laity, linking formal ecclesiastical structures with communities of believers. They encouraged the practice of everyday religious observance and made sure that the events in the ritual calendar were duly celebrated. Confraternities proved to be the most efficient religious institutions at the local level: They organized processions; catered for the building of churches and maintenance of religious equipment; assured the payment of priests for the regular cure of souls; and provided the locals with a sense of social importance through membership. In the mining area of Minas Gerais, for instance, they were for a long time the only religious institutions available. The religious orders had been forbidden in the territory because the crown was not willing to lose any profits drawn off by pious legacies or tax exemptions. In Northeast Brazil, the chapels of the sugar mills would have similar functions, providing spiritual services both to slavemasters and to their workers.

Private arrangements and associations created through the initiative of local populations, even if under the auspices of the religious orders, could be more important than parishes. Confraternities allowed the populations to compensate for the inefficient religious structures set up by the *padroado régio*. Even when parishes existed, the tendency was to give them to the care of religious orders, which would sometimes compete ferociously for their control. In the hinterland of Goa, for instance, the crown divided the territory among different religious orders, ascribing specific groups of parishes to the Jesuits, Franciscans, secular priests, Dominicans, and Augustinians.

Confraternities were ever present in the empire, just as they were in metropolitan Portugal: Strictly hierarchical and discriminating in their requirements for membership, confraternities existed to match virtually any social situation, and the number of confraternities to which a person was able to belong was a sign of distinction. From the *Misericórdias* to the Third Orders, limited strictly to local white elites, one could find confraternities for everyone. More than ensuring the celebration of weekly masses or the receiving of sacraments, they made the religious cult a part of life in any Portuguese colony.

Confraternities were not always the spontaneous gathering of locals in associations; they were often promoted by the religious orders, and, as such, they could be arenas for competition among them. More than just a means of improving devotion, confraternities could also be used by religious orders to channel eventual inheritances into the hands of a sponsoring order. Religious orders needed confraternities because members would bequeath masses and assign property to pay for them. In Goa, the main enemies of the local *Misericórdia* were confraternities sponsored by the existing religious orders, especially the Jesuits, who became the *Misericórdia*'s main opponent.

In Brazil, confraternities were particularly important to the African population, both slaves and freedmen. They provided a means by which some autonomy for the black and mulatto populations in relation to the white colonists could be negotiated. In fact, whites were ever present as part of black confraternities, sometimes as members of the boards of directors and at other times as patrons. Brazilian confraternities would even have regular denominations based on race: The Santo Sacramento would be for whites, the Nossa Senhora das Mercês for mulattoes, and the Rosary ones for the blacks. Brazilian confraternities could group individuals of African origin according to their color (blacks and mulattoes tended to go to separate confraternities) and even ethnic origin, although this was not always the case because in areas such as Minas Gerais, brotherhoods for nonwhites did not make such distinctions. For ethnic and religious minorities, confraternities could serve as powerful devices for social integration: They incorporated New Christians in both Brazil and India (Cochin and Goa). In the latter, they were especially sought after as integrative devices when the establishment of the Inquisition in 1560 started to persecute the New Christian community.

The world of confraternities was strictly hierarchical. For instance, in Brazil, the Santíssimo Sacramento confraternities, which admitted whites, prepared the main altar for the Corpus Christi celebration, while other confraternities prepared the secondary altars. Even cults included distinctions. In Brazil, white colonists would pay blacks and mulattoes to take their places and whip themselves in penitent processions during Lent. In a hierarchical world, no wonder such confraternities tended to be in conflict over protocols, and public disorders between them verged on the ridiculous. A confraternity might refuse to participate in a procession if the place to which it had been assigned was judged inferior; another might even compare the quality of the wax it used in its candles with the wax used by another brotherhood.

Women and Religion

Religion in the empire was a male-controlled business like much of every aspect of colonial life. The few women either of Portuguese birth or with Portuguese ancestry living in the different parts of the empire were urged to enter the marriage market. The lack of white brides was real, but there was never a consistent policy to make them available in the colonies, probably because there were plenty of nonwhite women with whom to create marital relationships. Also, for inheritance reasons, most parents in the colonies wished to place their daughters in convents and did so by sending them to Portugal. Convents for women in the colonies were few and founded late: The policy of the crown was to delay their establishment as much as possible. Only three convents were founded in the seventeenth century: Santa Monica in Goa in 1606, the barefoot Carmelites of Macao in 1633, and the Poor Clares of the Desterro in Bahia in 1677. In the Spanish empire, by the 1620s, there were already thirty-six convents for women, fifteen of those located in Mexico City. The contrast is striking, and it can be partially explained by the reluctance of the crown to found new female convents overseas, despite the willingness of the municipal authorities to safeguard the honor of widows and orphaned girls in the cloister.

Female convents were not established in Asia in the following century. In the second third of the eighteenth century, however, five more convents were created in Brazil: three in Bahia (Lapa, Mercês, and Soledade) and two in Rio de Janeiro (Ajuda and Santa Teresa).

The alternative to placing women in convents was the *recolhimentos*, which allowed the cloistering of women according to monastic rules without the necessity of their taking vows. The *recolhimentos* were convenient because they permitted women to reenter the marriage market. Because the crown was not so restrictive about their foundation, they were founded in higher numbers than convents, but equally slowly.

We can expect a low participation of women from the Portuguese colonial groups in the public activities of confraternities, although there are few studies on the subject. Such women were not welcome outside the domestic sphere, although they were expected to attend Mass at church. Even so, women of high status would travel to churches in coaches and litters that concealed them from public exposure. As for devotional activities organized by confraternities, we find white women as honorary members (mostly through widowhood) of elite confraternities, such as the *Misericórdias*, rather than as active participants. Nevertheless, in Brazil, white women of high status could enter the Third Orders as members (and not just as representatives of a deceased husband or father) and participate actively in their devotional life.

Strategies and Methods of Evangelization

The Church of Rome took upon itself the goal of converting to Christianity virtually every people on Earth. In consequence, the number and variety of potential Catholics was immense, and different strategies were necessary for success. The indoctrination effort was especially strong and coherent after the Council of Trent. Earlier, war with the Muslims precluded conversion by peaceful means, and the church lacked the tools to indoctrinate local populations. Hence, the first conversions by the Portuguese were little more than baptisms, either of single individuals or of people in large numbers, the so-called mass baptisms. More than that, such conversions were often the result of diplomatic efforts by the representatives of the Portuguese king in the newly discovered territories; they were not the result of any organized initiative on the part of ecclesiastics.

The case of Africa is a good example of conversions on a limited scale, where cultural misunderstandings on both sides prevailed. Efforts to convert the natives took place mainly during the reign of João II, with the baptism of the kings of Kongo, or with the rearing of African-born children in Portugal in the Lóios convent of Lisbon (of the Order of Saint John the Evangelist). Later missions to the west coast of Africa did not last long, and we can sense a tension between the exigencies of the slave trade and the Christian faith. We can even suspect that conversion of the king of Kongo, D. Afonso, in 1491 was due to his interests in the slave trade and that the guns and horses he acquired from the Portuguese contributed to his supremacy over other African peoples in the area.

The adoption of Portuguese habits accompanied conversion: The local king and his relatives at a baptismal ceremony would be renamed after the Portuguese king and his family. A new ritual practice, which included the granting of Portuguese noble titles and the Order of Christ to the native king's entourage, would last well into the eighteenth century. The king of Kongo would give the habit of the Order of Christ to his subjects, but this would mean nothing except the use of crosses on dress and other attire. Similarly, the king was elected, but his authority was confirmed by a coronation officiated over by a Catholic priest.

Advantages in the slave trade, the opportunity to acquire guns, and increased authority through the adoption of Portuguese civil and religious rituals, often misunderstood, are among the benefits to native rulers that might explain such "spontaneous" conversions in times when organized religious action on the part of the Portuguese was scarce. But, even as the empire further developed, missionaries faced difficulties establishing themselves in Africa. Climate and disease, for example, were major obstacles, causing high mortality among them.

Religious investment in black slaves would begin not in Africa but upon their arrival in Brazil. For practical reasons, it was easier to Christianize them in a territory entirely controlled by the Portuguese, where the effects of African cultural resistance to conversion could be suppressed. In Bahia, for instance, slaves would be baptized on arrival near the port in the lower part of the city, in the church of the Conceição da Praia, after death had taken its heaviest toll during the crossing of the Atlantic, thus reducing the potential "wastage" of evangelization efforts.

In East Africa, the Jesuits also had a tenuous presence. In fact, their missions did not last long on either of the African coasts: They withdrew from Cape Verde and Guinea and were chased from Ethiopia. Only the missions in Mombasa and Mozambique were to last, owing to the transit of ships en route to India and Macao that used those ports, but the effort lacked enthusiasm. The presence in Africa of missionaries from other religious orders would also be tenuous. They existed but were irregular, and the number of missionaries in the field was ridiculously small because of the previously mentioned climatic and cultural obstacles.

In India, missionaries tended initially to baptize a large number of locals without indoctrination, preferably from the lower castes and untouchables. The religious orders that were more prone to turn first to the poor for converts were no doubt the mendicants, especially the Franciscans. They proselytized among fishermen and other low-caste strata on the Fishery Coast because such groups complemented their ideology of poverty. Often this strategy engendered conflict with the authorities, as was the case with the Franciscan martyrs in Japan in 1597, who made the mistake of failing to secure authorization before beginning their mission. On the whole, missionaries tended to be respectful of hierarchies and sometimes were eager to take advantage of them: The principle *cujus regis ejus religio* (the religion of the people follows the religion of the prince) was implicit in many conversions because it was expected that after the conversion of the local potentate his subjects would follow. Winning local powers to the Christian faith was an inevitable strategy in territories where military conquest was impossible for the Portuguese, as was the case in Japan and China but also in Ethiopia and Tibet. Nevertheless, this policy did not preclude the Jesuits from investing in the indoctrination of common people. They devoted themselves to the indoctrination and the maintenance of cult routines, to the translation of religious books, to preaching, and to the creation of confraternities that allowed local converts to organize devotion and replace the insufficient numbers of resident missionaries or the nonexistence of parishes.

Francis Xavier became known for his mass conversions in many parts of the Asian continent during his ten years of travel there (1542–1552). It is not likely that those neophytes were seriously indoctrinated before and after baptism. The top-down policy was no doubt attempted in Ethiopia, India, Japan, and also China. In the latter, all efforts were made to convert the emperor, especially during the times of Adam Schall von Bell, who enjoyed a prominent position in the emperor's court between 1645 and 1661. Such efforts were a continuation of the Jesuits' cultivated ability to become close to people in high circles and to exert influence on them, as they had done also in Catholic courts in Europe from the beginnings of the order in the 1540s. But if in Japan the feudal system ensured that the conversion of *daimyos* was followed by the conversion of their subjects, in China it proved to be different because the mandarins were little more than administrative pieces in the imperial machine, lacking power to determine the conversion of the populations under their authority. Recent scholarship also demonstrates that the Jesuits not only created missions in many areas of the Chinese empire but also created very large Christian communities, and there were hundreds of thousands of conversions.

In east India, conversion would oscillate between force and peaceful indoctrination. For a brief moment, Vasco da Gama and his men did not recognize the Hindu religion as distinct from Christianity, thinking that Hindu temples were Christian churches. Some years of tolerance followed even after this misunderstanding vanished, but things would change after the 1540s. In the 1550s and 1560s, the Portuguese destroyed hundreds of Hindu temples and some mosques in the Goa area and appropriated their revenues, but the ideal solution was to induce the new converts to destroy them themselves, encouraged by the missionaries, as was done in Japan. Another strategy was to indoctrinate children, judged the best means of making a deep impression. In India, one tactic was to give privileges to those who converted, such as exemption from paying certain taxes (*dízimos*) to the Portuguese, or to give preference in awarding contracts for the exploitation of land. In the area of Goa, the office of Pai dos Cristãos ("Father of Christians") was created, a Portuguese ecclesiastic whose responsibility it was to see to the well-being of the converted, who were frequently expelled or ostracized by their communities. The office would also see to it that the privileges enjoyed by new converts would be respected. The Jesuits controlled this office in the region from 1557 to 1759.

Another strategy for conversion would be the creation of local confraternities especially designed for the natives. These institutions allowed for the maintenance of cult duties with a minimum of Jesuit priests, delegating devotional practices to chosen converts as well as creating a sense of community among the neophytes. Many of these institutions also performed charitable practices, and in China and Japan they were mostly Marian or even imitations of the Portuguese *Misericórdias*. The Jesuits also organized them in India, sometimes accompanied by a hospital for the converts, and introduced them in the Amerindian villages they established. They also had special confraternities for students boarding in their colleges or for the newly converted in both Goa and Bahia, which would stage spectacular processions, especially on the occasion of collective baptisms, and also theater plays.

In Brazil, Padre Manuel da Nóbrega favored military dominance over the Amerindians as a precondition of any efforts at conversion. This policy, elaborated in 1556 and 1557, was radically opposed to the position of the Spanish Dominican Bartolomé de Las Casas, who advocated the absence of violence in religious proselytism. Nóbrega's policy seems to have been a response to the disappointments he had experienced as a missionary, which had revealed to him the inner difficulties of making the natives truly understand the Christian faith. José de Anchieta, another Jesuit missionary, also supported the forced grouping of Amerindians in villages. But even in Asia, some missionaries were convinced that successful conversion was necessarily a long process that might take generations to accomplish if the Christian religion was to be fully incorporated. It was implicit in their efforts, as in the case of the destruction of Hindu temples, that initial violence would lead to peaceful evangelization efforts that would succeed in the long run. Two recurrent metaphors in the writing of missionaries, "conquest" and "sowing" of souls, illustrate slightly different attitudes toward evangelization: Whereas the former is mainly a military metaphor, the second implies continuing efforts that would lead to successful conversion.

In the Far East, the missionaries had to adapt to an environment that was not under the hegemony of the Portuguese. No wonder that the strategy of the missions was adaptation, also called dissimulation by its detractors, because the Jesuit Alessandro Valignano "invented" it between 1579 and 1582. In Japan, where the Jesuits were the first to embark upon evangelization, they had to adapt to other mores, dress, and manners. It has to be said that the most famous men willing to give up European ways of living – albeit only in appearance – were not Portuguese but the Bavarian Adam Schall, the Flemish Ferdinand Verbiest, or the Italians Alessandro Valignano, Matteo Ricci, Michele Ruggieri, and Roberto de Nobili. Nevertheless, it would be advisable to relate such a strategy with peripheral spaces not integrated in the Portuguese or any other European empire. Moreover, it would be an exaggeration to say that such men were the first Europeans to leave Eurocentrism behind. They were still engaged in cultural or religious imperialism on behalf of Catholic Europe, and if they tried to understand and adapt to other cultures, they often judged them negatively compared with European values. Of course, the adaptive few faced resistance from orthodoxy and could develop their strategy only because they were in peripheral areas where there was little immediate supervision from the center. The number and quality of their opponents in Europe, both inside and outside the Jesuit Order, is a measure of the novelty of their attitude. Both in China and Japan, the missionaries consciously changed their clothes, shaved their beards, adopted local hairdos, and even dropped their liturgical rituals. In China, they carefully imitated the dress and manners of the Chinese elites who they thought were the most important to be converted, and they adopted Chinese names of honor. The Italian Jesuit Roberto de Nobili (b. 1577–d. 1657) adopted a similar strategy in Madurai (on the southwest coast of India). He presented himself as an Italian Brahmin who had renounced the world, thus traveling barefoot, eating a vegetarian meal a day, and dressing poorly. Although he was accused by some of his fellow Jesuits of mixing pagan rites with Christianity and of having accepted the caste system in 1623, the pope approved his methods of conversion.

Adriano Prosperi has related such missionaries to Italian court culture and to the civilization of manners in Europe. Italian Jesuits were used to "dissimulation" in their home courts and transferred the practice in order to overcome difficulties in converting the Japanese and the Chinese. Certainly they could not be won over by force as was the case in Brazil, where Amerindians were sufficiently powerless to be grouped in villages at the will of the missionaries. It is questionable, however, that dissimulation was the monopoly of Italian courts.

Missionaries were accepted in China for reasons that had little to do with the Catholic faith: Their scientific knowledge became highly appreciated, whether related to clockworks, mapmaking, or astronomy. In 1781, after the Jesuits had already been chased from Macao (1762) and when evangelization had been forbidden in China, the emperor still wanted a Portuguese man of science by his side to fill the See of Beijing. Thus, the "bishop of Peking" was sent as quickly as possible in the hope that he might secure the precarious statute of Macao with concise instructions on how to perform his mission.

The proof that the Jesuits were far too innovative when compared with other missionaries is the rites controversy, which followed shortly after the Jesuits lost the monopoly on evangelization of China to other religious orders in the early 1630s. These other orders soon questioned the adaptation of doctrine and ritual that had been developing since the times of Matteo Ricci and Ruggieri, and the pope condemned the Jesuits' methods after a debate that lasted approximately a century. This debate, which developed between 1645 and 1742, when the pope at last condemned these Jesuit approaches to conversion definitely, contradicted the acceptance of Nobili's methods in 1623 and would undermine the possibility of successful missionary work in China.

The evangelization of Japan had started in 1549, thirty-three years before that of China, and Japan was where Valignano in the early 1580s had first developed the idea of adapting to the local culture. He was opposed by colleagues less prone to give up their lifestyles and religious principles, but in spite of such controversies, missions in Japan were so successful as to convince the Jesuits and the European Catholic world that a conversion of all the Japanese was imminent. In the beginning, they had every reason to be optimistic: The existence of a single language in Japan made indoctrination easier than in areas where there were many, and converts, although numbers are uncertain, were in the hundreds of thousands. Nevertheless, time would show otherwise. Between 1587 and 1639, a set of prohibitions of the Christian faith was introduced, followed by the martyrdom of both Japanese Christians and European missionaries. In the end, Christianity was almost completely eliminated in Japan.

Indirectly, it was the Jesuits, as the avant-garde of the European penetration of Japan, who made available the means to unify the islands under a centralized power. The guns that were essential to the process of unification were introduced into Japan as a result of the commercial relations the Jesuits helped to develop. But to a unified Japan, the very existence of Catholics in their midst was unthinkable because it suggested submission to a foreign religious power. When the Japanese came into contact with Europeans who traded without proselytizing, such as the Dutch, the fate of the presence of the Catholics was sealed. The same was to occur much later in China, when the rites controversy convinced the emperor K'ang-hsi (1654–1722) that Catholicism was impractical in China.

Conclusion

The Portuguese would eventually succeed in converting, at least superficially, most of the natives and the imported populations in the territories over which they exercised colonial rule for several centuries. This is true for Brazil and for colonies in Africa, Goa, and East Timor. From the sixteenth to the eighteenth century, European rivals who visited Portuguese colonies, Protestants as well as Catholics, often made comments in their travel accounts about the questionable behavior of slaves in church, the lack of integrity of the clergy, both secular and regular, and the "idolatry" of the religious rites they witnessed. None of these comments were innocent of biases generated by the competition among European nations for the amassing of territories overseas. A French traveler, Pouchot de Chantassin, observed black slave women attending a Mass in the Cape Verde islands with naked breasts. Van Braam Houckgeest, a Dutchman, in the late 1780s described in ironic detail a puppet show inside a church in Macao during Holy Week designed to represent the ascension of Christ in the presence of his Holy Mother. Even if we know these descriptions were influenced by the imperial ambitions of their authors, they also draw attention to one characteristic of the evangelization carried out by the Portuguese that was also common to the Spanish empire, namely its exteriority. No doubt the exteriority of the Catholic faith in general, even if allowing for the existence of "fake" Christians among the newly converted, made it more accessible to peoples whose culture also relied heavily on highly visible public ritual.

We should not overestimate the importance of insufficient orthodoxy or the superficiality of conversion to Catholicism. Never in colonial times was there the assumption that Christianized natives would have the same rights as the colonizers or experience spirituality in the same way. Conversion did not imply equality; if converted "pagans" were to be equal in their afterlife, the same could not be said of the earthly one. Never before the second half of the eighteenth century was there any serious or successful effort to give the newly converted the same access to colonial institutions as whites. They could not enter religious orders, be admitted as members to elite confraternities, or attain most administrative offices in the imperial structure on the same standing as the European-born or those of European origin. They were barred from the priesthood, and even when Valignano, the Neapolitan Jesuit, tried to enforce his policy of transforming some converted Japanese into Jesuit missionaries, he was severely opposed by his peers. Native clergy were not numerous in any of the places ruled by the Portuguese before the regime of the Marquis de Pombal. There was always an ambiguous and contradictory relationship concerning the formation of native ecclesiastics among the Portuguese authorities.

One of the arguments of the Congregation of the Propaganda Fide against the Portuguese *padroado* was precisely the lack of a significant body of native priests, and the new institution had precisely the formation of local clergy as one of its main goals. Yet in spite of this accusation, there were more native ecclesiastics in the Portuguese empire than in Spanish America, although they tended to become secular priests rather than friars because the various religious orders were always reluctant to admit nonwhites. But the truth is that regular efforts to recruit nonwhite clergy were irregular over time in most Portuguese colonies. Even if some natives from the East African coast, from the African islands of Cape Verde and São Tomé, and from Goa or Japan were ordained priests, their existence was always controversial among the Portuguese authorities; more than that, they managed only exceptionally to escape subaltern roles in the ecclesiastical hierarchy.

Conversion was often harmed by bitter rivalry among religious orders. National issues could be at stake, but most often each religious order fought for the supremacy of its missions in a given area. The Jesuits opposed the influence of other orders and even opposed their peers from the Spanish empire in converting the Japanese, even if the Order was transnational in theory. In Brazil, even while trying to protect the Amerindians from the greed of the colonizers who enslaved them, the Jesuits would not recognize the same humanity in black slaves because the missionaries were just as involved in the plantation economy as other colonists.

Today, scholars are prone to emphasize opposition and resistance to conversion in contrast to the thousands of letters sent to Europe by missionaries that publicized endless triumphs and good hopes for the conversion of other peoples. Even in these letters, we come across, albeit rarely, testimonies to the idea that most subjects of evangelization associated religious action with the desire of the missionaries to dominate them. It happened for instance in Japan, where the persecutions of Christians were motivated by fears of imminent military invasions by the troops of the Spanish emperor. Even if religious sources rarely mention the matter of resistance to Catholicism, the many narratives of treason and martyrdom prove that evangelization did not take place without opposition. Rebellion could be violent and fatal to the missionaries who fell victim to violence. Nevertheless, the martyrdom of missionaries was more symbolic capital from which the Catholic Church was eager to profit. Religious orders gave abundant publicity to the suffering of their missionaries, and the prestige of the faraway missions was such as to ensure a regular flow of recruits to the most distant missions. The times when religious proselytism would outrightly be accused of imperialism were still to come.

BIBLIOGRAPHICAL ESSAY

Ecclesiastical Structures

As a general reference, Fortunato de Almeida's *História da Igreja em Portugal* (4 vols., Oporto, 1967–1971) offers general and usually extremely concise information on facts related to ecclesiastic institutions. Padre António Lopes's *Dioceses fundadas nos territórios ultramarinos e padroado português a partir de Lisboa com seus respectivos bispos (e substitutos no governo das dioceses)* (Lisbon, 1994) offers the most accurate list of dioceses and their bishops.

On the Military Orders, "Padroado Régio," and the Formation of Dioceses

A general survey, although in Portuguese, can be found in Francisco Bethencourt's "A Igreja," in Francisco Bethencourt and Kirti Chaudhuri, eds., *História da Expansão Portuguesa*, vol. 1 (Lisbon, 1998), pp. 369–386. Works in English are nearly confined to those authored by Francis Dutra: "Evolution of the Portuguese Order of Santiago, 1492–1600," *Mediterranean Studies* 4 (1994), pp. 63–72; "Membership in the Order of Christ in the Sixteenth Century: Problems and Perspectives," *Santa Barbara Portuguese Studies* 1 (1994), pp. 228–239; and "The Order of Santiago and the Estado da Índia, 1498–1750," in Francis Dutra and João Camilo dos Santos, eds., *The Portuguese in the Pacific* (Santa Barbara, 1995), pp. 287–304. Charles-Martial de Witte, O. S. B., published all the papal bulls that granted the *padroado* in "Les bulles pontificales et l'expansion portugaise au XVe siècle," *Revue d'Histoire Ecclésiastique* 48 (1953), pp. 683–718; 49 (1954), pp. 438–461; 51 (1956), pp. 413–453, 809–836; and 53 (1958), pp. 5–46, 443–471. See also António Joaquim Dias Dinis, O. F. M., "A prelazia 'Nullius Diocesis' de Tomar e o ultramar Português até 1460," *Anais da Academia Portuguesa de História,* 2nd series, 20 (1971), pp. 233–270.

On Confraternities and Devotional Life

On the Portuguese *misericórdias* in general, see Isabel dos Guimarães Sá's *Quando o Rico se faz pobre: Misericórdias, caridade e poder no império Português, 1500–1800* (Lisbon, 1997). For Goa, see Leopoldo da Rocha's *As confrarias de Goa (séculos XVI–XX): Conspecto histórico-jurídico* (Lisbon, 1973). For Brazil, see Mariza de Carvalho Soares's *Devotos de Cor: Identidade étnica, religiosidade, e escravidão no Rio de Janeiro, séc. XVIII* (Rio de Janeiro, 2000); Luiz Mott's "Cotidiano e vivência religiosa: Entre a Capela e o Calundu," in Laura de

Mello e Souza, ed., *História da vida privada no Brasil*, vol. 1 (Sao Paulo, 1997); Caio César Boschi's *Os leigos e o poder: Irmandades leigas e política colonizadora em Minas Gerais* (Sao Paulo, 1986); Patricia A. Mulvey's "Black Brothers and Sisters: Membership in Black Lay Brotherhoods of Colonial Brazil," *Luso-Brazilian Review* 17 (1980), pp. 253–279; and A. J. R. Russell-Wood's "Black and Mulatto Brotherhoods in Colonial Brazil: A Study in Collective Behaviour," *The Hispanic American Historical Review* 54 (1974), pp. 567–602. On Women and religious action, see Leila Mezan Algranti's *Honradas e devotas: Mulheres na Colônia: Condição feminina nos conventos e recolhimentos do sudeste do Brasil, 1750–1822* (Rio de Janeiro, 1993) and the proceedings of the conference *O rosto feminino da expansão Portuguesa: Congresso Internacional* (2 vols., Lisbon, 1995). On the Inquisition in general, see Francisco Bethencourt's *História das Inquisições: Portugal, Espanha e Itália* (Lisbon, 1994). For Goa, see Ana Cannas da Cunha's *A Inquisição no Estado da Índia: Origens (1539–1560)* (Lisbon, 1995); Maria de Jesus dos Mártires Lopes's "A Inquisição de Goa na segunda metade do século XVIII: Contributo para a sua história," *Studia* 48 (1989), pp. 237–262; António Baião's *A Inquisição de Goa: Tentativa de história e sua origem, estabelecimento, evolução e extinção* (2 vols., Lisbon and Coimbra, 1939–1949). For Brazil, see Ronaldo Vainfas's *Trópicos dos pecados: Moral, sexualidade e Inquisição no Brasil*, 2nd ed. (Rio de Janeiro, 1997 [1989]) and his *A heresia dos Indios: Catolicismo e rebeldia no Brasil colonial* (Sao Paulo, 1995); Caio César Boschi's "As visitas diocesanas e a Inquisição na Colônia," *Revista Brasileira de História* 7 (1987), pp. 151–184; and José Veiga Torres's "Da repressão religiosa para a promoção social: A Inquisição como instância legitimadora da promoção social da burguesia comercial," *Revista Crítica de Ciências Sociais* 40 (1994), pp. 109–135.

Religious Action

General

C. R. Boxer's *The Church Militant and Iberian Expansion* (Baltimore, 1978) is still highly readable and can be used as a starting point on religious action. Works by Adriano Prosperi are always useful, such as "The Missionary," in Rosario Villari, ed., *Baroque Personae* (Chicago, 1995), and *Tribunali della coscienza: Inquisitori, confessori, missionari* (Turin, 1996). Luís Filipe Thomaz offers a general interpretation of evangelization in "Descobrimentos e evangelização: Da cruzada à missão Pacífica," *Congresso Internacional de História: Missionação Portuguesa e encontro de culturas: Actas*, vol. 1 (Braga, 1993), pp. 81–129. See also chapters on religious expansion by F. Bethencourt (vol. 1, pp. 369–386), Caio Boschi (vol. 2, pp. 388–455 and vol. 3, pp. 294–395), and Diogo Ramada Curto (vol. 2, pp. 458–531) in Francisco Bethencourt and K. Chaudhuri, eds., *História da expansão Portuguesa* (Lisbon, 1998), as well as the crucial survey by José Pedro Paiva, "Pastoral e evangelização," in João Francisco Marques and António Camões Gouveia, eds., *História religiosa de Portugal* (Lisbon, 2000), vol. 2, pp. 239–313. A. J. R. Russell-Wood's *A World on the Move: The Portuguese in Africa, Asia and America, 1415–1808* (New York, 1992) also offers good insights into the intercontinental mobility of missionaries. On the Jesuits, the most comprehensive work is Dauril Alden's *The Making of an Enterprise: The Society of Jesus in Portugal, Its Empire and Beyond, 1540–1750* (Stanford, CA, 1996), although works by area can provide a better understanding of the specificities and the fragile nature of mission work.

Missions by Area

Africa remains the most understudied continent with regard to missionary work. As a general work, there is João Paulo Costa's "As missões cristãs em Africa," in Luís Albuquerque, ed., *Portugal no mundo*, vol. 3 (Lisbon, 1989), pp. 88–103. A recent thorough study of the Jesuit mission in Ethiopia can be found in Hervé Pennec's *Des Jésuites au Royaume du Prête Jean (Éthiopie)* (Paris, 2003). On Congo, see António Custódio Gonçalves's "As influências do Cristianismo na organização política do Reino do Congo," *Congresso Internacional Bartolomeu Dias e a sua época: Actas*, vol. 5 (Oporto, 1989), pp. 523–539, and António Brásio's "Informação do Reino do Congo de Frei Raimundo de Dicomano," *Studia* 34 (1972), pp. 19–42. On Cape Verde, see Nuno da Silva Gonçalves, *Os Jesuítas e a Missão de Cabo Verde (1604–1642)* (Lisbon, 1996). On India, there is an impressive array of printed sources edited by Joseph Wicki, G. Schurhammer, and A. da Silva Rêgo about missionary work there. They have also written numerous historical works that are very informative but offer a Jesuit perspective. See especially Schurhammer's biography of St. Francis Xavier (G. Schurhammer, S. J., *Francis Xavier: His Life, His Times, India (1543–1545)* (4 vols., Rome, 1977). Recent scholarship has elaborated new approaches to missionary work. Among them stands the work of Ines G. Zupanov, who offers an excellent analysis of the subtleties of competition among Jesuits in the mission of Madurai in her *Disputed Mission: Jesuit Experiments and Brahmanical Knowledge in Seventeenth-Century India* (New Delhi, 1999); see also, by the same author, "The Prophetic and the Miraculous in Portuguese Asia: A Hagiographical View of Colonial Culture," in Sanjay Subrahmanyam, ed., *Sinners and Saints: The Successors of Vasco da Gama* (Delhi, 1998), pp. 135–161, and also Joan-Pau Rubiés, *Travel and Ethnology in the Renaissance: South India through European Eyes, 1250–1650* (Cambridge, 2000). Other works are: E. R. Hambye, "Goa," in R. Aubert, ed., *Dictionnaire d'histoire et de géographie ecclésiastiques*, vol. 21 (Paris, 1986), pp. 282–338; Michel Chandeigne, ed., *Goa – 1510–1685: L'Inde Portugaise, apostolique et commerciale* (Paris, 1996); Teotónio R. de Souza and Charles J. Borges, eds., *Jesuits in India in Historical Perspective* (Macao, 1992); Teotónio R. de Souza, *Essays in Goan History* (New Delhi, 1989); Maria de Jesus dos Mártires Lopes, *Goa Setecentista: Tradição e Modernidade, 1750–1800* (Lisbon, 1996); João Paulo A. de Oliveira e Costa and Victor Luís Gaspar Rodrigues, *Portugal y Oriente: El proyeto Indiano del Rey Juan* (Madrid, 1992); and Chandra Richard De Silva, "Beyond the Cape: The Portuguese Encounter with the Peoples of South Asia," in Stuart Schwartz, ed., *Implicit Understandings: Observing, Reporting, and Reflecting on the Encounters between Europeans and Other Peoples in the Early Modern Era* (Cambridge, 1994), pp. 295–322. On Brazil, Charlotte de Castelnau-L'Estoile's *Les ouvrier d'une vigne stérile: Les Jésuites et la conversion des Indiens du Brésil, 1580–1620* (Paris, 2000) is one of the most fascinating books ever written about the Jesuits in Brazil. Luís Felipe de Alencastro's "A interacção Europeia com as sociedades Brasileiras entre os séculos XVI e XVIII," in *Brasil, nas vésperas do mundo moderno* (Lisbon, 1992), pp. 97–119, is also useful. See also Geraldo J. Amadeu Coelho Dias's "Os Beneditinos Portugueses e a missão," *Bracara Augusta* 38 (1984), pp. 3–24; Laura de Mello e Souza's *O diabo e a Terra de Santa Cruz: Feitiçaria e religiosidade popular no Brasil colonial* (Sao Paulo, 1986); Harold Johnson and Maria Beatriz N. da Silva's "O império Luso-Brasileiro, 1500–1620," in Joel Serrão and A. H. de Oliveira Marques, eds., *Nova história da expansão Portuguesa,* vol. 6 (Lisbon, 1992); and Frédéric Mauro, ed., "O Império Luso-Brasileiro, 1620–1750," in Joel Serrão and A. H. de Oliveira Marques, eds., *Nova história da expansão Portuguesa,* vol. 7 (Lisbon, 1991). On Japan and China, Michael Cooper, S. J., in his *Rodrigues the Interpreter: An Early Jesuit in Japan and China* (New York, 1974), presents an excellent introduction to missionary life in the Far East. Jorge Manuel dos Santos Alves offers a general survey in Portuguese on this area in "Cristianização e organização eclesiástica," in A. H. de Oliveira Marques, ed., *História dos Portugueses no Extremo-Oriente,* vol. 1, part I, "Em torno de Macau" (Lisbon, 1998), pp. 301–347. The crucial work for understanding the Jesuits in Japan and their subsequent expulsion is George Elison's *Deus Destroyed: The Image of Christianity in Early Modern Japan* (Cambridge, MA, 1973). Léon Bourdon's book *La Compagnie de Jésus et le Japon, 1547–1570* (Paris, 1993) has also kept its usefulness. See also Armando Martins Janeira's *O Impacto Português sobre a civilização Japonesa,* 2nd ed. (Lisbon, 1988); Roberto Matos Carneiro and A. Teodoro de Matos, eds., *O século Cristão do Japão: Actas do Colóquio Internacional comemorativo dos 450 anos de amizade Portugal-Japão (1543–1993)* (Lisbon, 1994); João Paulo A. de Oliveira e Costa, *A descoberta da civilização Japonesa pelos Portugueses* (Lisbon, 1995); João Paulo de Oliveira e Costa, "Em torno da criação do bispado do Japão," in *As Relações entre a India Portuguesa, a Asia do Sueste e o Extremo Oriente: Actas do VI Seminário Internacional de História Indo-Portuguesa* (Lisbon, 1993), pp. 141–171; and Ana Maria Prosérpio Leitão, "Os primórdios das rivalidades entre Franciscanos e Jesuítas no Japão em finais do século XVI: A questão da vinda de outras congregações religiosas," in *Congresso Internacional de História: Missionação Portuguesa e encontro de culturas: Actas*, vol. 2 (Braga, 1993), pp. 343–358. In spite of its still being unpublished, the best work on China is no doubt Liam M. Brockey's Ph.D. dissertation *The Harvest of the Vine: The Jesuit Missionary Enterprise in China, 1579–1710* (Brown University, Providence, RI, 2002). For a focus on religious orders other than the Society of Jesus, see Pascale Girard, *Les religieux Occidentaux en Chine à l'époque moderne: Essai d'annalyse textuelle comparée* (Paris, 2000). See also the interesting chapters by Willard J. Peterson, "What to Wear? Observation and Participation by Jesuit Missionaries in Late Ming Society," and Ann Waltner, "Demerits and Deadly Sins: Jesuit Moral Tracts in Late Ming China," both in Stuart Schwartz, ed., *Implicit Understandings: Observing, Reporting, and Reflecting on the Encounters between Europeans and Other Peoples in the Early Modern Era* (Cambridge, 1994), respectively on pp. 403–421 and pp. 422–448.

Quoted Printed Sources

See also Claude Michel Pouchot de Chantassin's *Relation du voyage et retour des Indes Orientales pendant les années 1690 & 1691* (Paris, 1693); Charles Dellon's *Relation de l'Inquisition de Goa* (Leiden, 1687); André Everard Van Braam Houckgeest's *Voyage de l'Ambassade de la Compagnie des Indes Orientales Hollandaises, vers l'empereur de la Chine, dans les années 1794 & 1795*, vol. 2 (Philadelphia, 1797), pp. 283–290; D. Gaspar de Leão's *Desengano de perdidos* (orig. publ. 1573), ed. Eugenio Asensio (Coimbra, 1958); and Gonçalo Fernandes Trancoso, S. J., *Tratado sobre o Hinduísmo* (Maduré, 1616), ed. Joseph Wicki (Lisbon, 1973).

Part III: The Cultural World

9

PORTUGUESE EXPANSION, 1400–1800: ENCOUNTERS, NEGOTIATIONS, AND INTERACTIONS

Anthony Disney

Initial Encounters

It is uncertain exactly when Portuguese voyages of exploration along the Saharan coast began; nor do we know precisely who was responsible for them. Fishermen, out to exploit the rich fisheries off Atlantic Morocco, and corsairs, cruising in search of Muslim shipping to prey upon, were both active on the fringes of the region in the early fifteenth century, but it is likely that many of their exploits went unrecorded. The first voyages of which we have reasonably detailed accounts were those conducted under the patronage of Prince Henry, a son of King João I. They commenced soon after the Portuguese capture of Ceuta and quickly developed into regular events.[1]

By about 1420, Henry's ships had passed Cape Noun, 150 kilometers beyond Agadir, and so entered waters not previously frequented, even by Muslim shipping. From that point onward, as they sailed progressively further into the unknown, Portuguese expeditions experienced an extraordinary series of first encounters with peoples previously unfamiliar to Europeans – first along the coasts of Atlantic Africa and later in East Africa, Monsoon Asia, and the Americas. The encounters usually took place at port cities but otherwise on islands and open beaches. They were creative moments in history, initiating entirely new relationships between peoples. Often they brought in their wake profound changes, particularly to weaker, more vulnerable "discovered" societies.

[1] For the early Henrican voyages, see A. H. de Oliveira Marques, ed., *Nova história da expansão Portuguesa, vol. 2: A expansão quatrocentista* (Lisbon, 1998), chap. 2; and Peter Russell, *Prince Henry 'the Navigator': A Life* (New Haven, CT, 2000), chap. 5.

The earliest descriptions of Portuguese first encounters on the African coast occur in the pages of the fifteenth-century chronicler Gomes Eanes de Zurara. At first, he explains, as the Portuguese sailed southward, they found no sign of any human presence on the desert shores they were coasting. Then, on a voyage in 1435, footprints of men and camels were seen, and the following year an actual first encounter took place. Two young Portuguese had been sent inland on horseback from a point where their captain, Afonso Gonçalves Baldaia, had anchored his ship. Their instructions were to search for inhabitants. After riding some distance along a river, they came across a band of men. These were probably Sanhaja, a people of Berber origin. Immediately the two Portuguese attacked, putting the band to flight. Zurara speculates that the tribesmen must surely have been amazed at the sudden appearance of their attackers – strange young men of unusual color and features, mounted, and bearing unfamiliar arms.[2]

Almost a decade later, in 1444, Dinis Dias, sailing in the vicinity of Cape Verde, made the first recorded European sighting of black Africans in their own country. The people concerned were Jolofs, whom Zurara affirms had never before seen a sailing ship. He claims they were unable to make up their minds whether Dias's caravel was a kind of fish, an enormous bird, or even an apparition. Eventually, a curious group approached in a dugout canoe – but quickly fled on discovering that the mysterious object contained men.

This incident must have constituted one of the earliest "ethnographic moments" in the history of European expansion – a landmark first encounter between indigenous people and a shipload of white intruders. Such moments were to be repeated many times during the next three and a half centuries, in the course of Portuguese and other European global voyaging. As in this case, the appearance of Europeans was often greeted with intense curiosity by those being "discovered." Initially, this was usually a strikingly relaxed and unfearful kind of curiosity, although liable to turn swiftly to alarm and then hostility as the newcomers' intentions became more suspect.

From the Portuguese point of view, first encounters were elements in a process of reconnaissance. As such, they served first and foremost as information-gathering exercises. By making contact with unfamiliar peoples, the Portuguese could acquire new knowledge – and the thirst for such knowledge, so characteristic of the European Renaissance mentality, undoubtedly played a role in the Portuguese urge to voyage ever further into the unknown. But the Portuguese were also well aware that new knowledge

[2] C. R. Beazley and Edgar Prestage, eds., *The Chronicle of the Discovery and Conquest of Guinea, Written by Gomes Eannes de Azurara* (London, 1896–1899), vol. 1, pp. 34–38.

could be turned to material advantage. Voyaging was costly and was seldom undertaken without at least some prospect of profit. Initial encounters for the Portuguese were perceived as openings to explore new and previously unexploited business opportunities that might indeed be high risk but could with luck prove lucrative. It was therefore always a priority to find out as quickly as possible whether pursuing a long-term relationship with a newly contacted people was likely to be materially fruitful. If a case looked promising – that is, if it appeared probable that the benefits gained would outweigh the costs and risks incurred – the Portuguese would then usually seek to establish a more permanent presence.

In the fifteenth and sixteenth centuries, repeated contacts of this kind occurred between the Portuguese and non-Europeans in many disparate parts of the globe. Consequently, it was often Portuguese who undertook the first European observations of other peoples and places, and it was through Portuguese eyes that many images of others were first conveyed to Europe. Conversely, the images of Europe and Europeans first formed by other peoples in the early centuries of expansion were frequently based primarily on observations of the Portuguese.

When in 1498 Vasco da Gama, sailing via the Cape of Good Hope and the coast of East Africa, finally reached Asia by sea, his first encounter with Indians in India took place at the southwestern port city of Calicut, in present-day Kerala. The moment is vividly recounted by a Portuguese eyewitness, usually identified as Álvaro Velho, a scribe accompanying the expedition.[3] The circumstances of this first encounter differed from those with coastal West Africans, for India had been known in Europe, albeit somewhat vaguely, since classical times, and a trickle of European travelers had continued to visit the subcontinent using the overland routes ever since. Also, King João II of Portugal had sent a secret intelligence mission overland to India in the 1480s. It is possible, although not certain, that members of the da Gama expedition had been briefed from its report.[4]

In any event, on his arrival in Calicut, da Gama sought an audience with the local ruler with a view toward establishing diplomatic and commercial relations. In this he was fairly successful, but as an information-seeking exercise his expedition was hardly a triumph. It is true that he was able

[3] The journal usually ascribed to Velho is translated into English in E. G. Ravenstein, trans. and ed., *A Journal of the First Voyage of Vasco da Gama, 1497–1499* (London, 1898).

[4] The agent was an Arabic-speaking Portuguese courtier called Pero de Covilhã. He did not return to Portugal but is known to have visited the port cities of the Kerala Coast in southwest India. Covilhã's report may have been brought back to João II through other agents but has never been located by researchers. See Marques, *Nova história da expansão Portuguesa*, vol. 2, pp. 109–110.

to observe quite accurately the physical environment, and also the appearance and some of the manifest customs, of the people he encountered. He also came to appreciate, in a general sense, that Indian culture and society were rich and complex, but he acquired little understanding even of their essentials, let alone their subtleties. Despite the existence of medieval reports to the contrary, da Gama had apparently left Portugal assuming that India was inhabited mainly by Christians, with a Muslim minority – and he and his companions maintained this belief throughout their three-month stay in Calicut. The so-called Velho journal vividly describes how, soon after the expedition's arrival, the leaders were taken to a Hindu temple. This they promptly identified as a church – even though they were puzzled by what seemed to be grotesque representations of saints painted on its walls. The journal also includes a brief survey of various Asian states, reporting optimistically that most of them were inhabited and ruled by Christians. This was the situation made known to King Manuel on the expedition's return to Lisbon – and it was initially accepted by him as accurate.[5]

Conversely, at the first encounter of Indians and seaborne Portuguese in 1499, the Indians tried to locate the newcomers within the range of their own previous experience. The Portuguese were therefore identified as just another group of Near Eastern Muslims – a type of "Western" foreigner that was already well known in the Kerala ports. Local people flocked to see the visitors but were puzzled by their unusual dress and their inability to speak or understand Arabic.[6] Each side was therefore highly inquisitive about the other, but each was inclined to interpret that other within a frame of reference that was comfortably familiar.

Two years later, Pedro Álvares Cabral chanced on the coast of Brazil, and another first encounter occurred. The Portuguese, of course, had never before set eyes on Brazilian Amerindians – nor had the Tupiniquins of what is now southern Bahia seen or heard of Europeans. Pero Vâz de Caminha, an eyewitness aboard Cabral's fleet, described the encounter and

[5] The journal reports Coromandel, Ceylon, Sumatra, Siam, Tenasserim, Malacca, and Pegu all had Christian inhabitants and rulers but that Bengal had mainly Muslim inhabitants and a Muslim ruler. See Ravenstein, trans., *A Journal of the First Voyage of Vasco da Gama*, pp. 96–102. For a discussion of the Portuguese identification of Hindus as "deviant" Christians in 1499, see Sanjay Subrahmanyam, *The Career and Legend of Vasco da Gama* (Cambridge, 1997), pp. 128–133, 151–154; and Joan-Pau Rubiés, *Travel and Ethnology in the Renaissance: South Asia through European Eyes, 1250–1625* (Cambridge, 2000), pp. 165–166.

[6] Fernão Lopes de Castanheda, *História do descobrimento e conquista da Índia pelos Portugueses*, 2nd ed. (Oporto, 1979), vol. 1, p. 41 (liv.1, chap. 15).

gave first impressions of the strangers.[7] No direct communication occurred, but presents of hats were offered by the Portuguese and accepted at a distance by the Tupiniquins, who gave in exchange a feathered headdress. From the start, the dark skins and nakedness of the Tupiniquins particularly intrigued the Portuguese. The following day, two Amerindian men picked up by a watering party were brought aboard the flagship, where their casual nakedness again drew comment. They showed little fear of unfamiliar surroundings, displayed no sensitivity to rank, and, in an astonishing display of casualness, after refusing food, promptly lay down on the deck and went to sleep. In the following days, the Portuguese, as they saw more of both male and female Tupiniquins, found themselves fascinated by these Indians' unself-consciousness, charmed by their physical beauty, and touched by their seeming naivete. They also convinced themselves that such a people would both readily accept Christianity and make excellent laborers.

Instances of this kind suggest a number of generalizations about first encounters. Typically, these encounters were vivid experiences – exciting, unpredictable, and with an element of risk. Usually those present were acutely aware of the drama of the occasion and were stirred by intense curiosity. For the Portuguese, that curiosity sprang partly from a simple desire to learn about unfamiliar and mysterious peoples. But it was also animated by an underlying determination to obtain accurate and useful information on the basis of which cost/benefit analyses could be made to determine what kinds of relationships should be sought with the newly encountered in the future. In the early West African stages of expansion, profit was especially sought through the traditional pursuits of plundering and slave raiding. Later, the emphasis almost invariably switched to trading, and – in some instances – to settling. To clear the way for slave trading, as early as 1448 Prince Henry forbade slave raiding by anyone voyaging to West Africa south of Cape Bojador.[8]

Obtaining information at first encounters was often handicapped by difficulties of communication, particularly in Africa beyond where Arabic was understood and in Brazil. When Vasco da Gama put in at various points in southern Africa during his first voyage of 1497–1498, he could communicate with the local Khoisan and Bantu only through sign language. Later, Cabral experienced the same difficulty in Brazil. On such occasions, much depended on what could be seen rather than heard.

[7] There are several published editions of Caminha's letter extant, one of the most reliable being in Joaquim Romero Magalhães and Susanna Münch Miranda, eds., *Os primeiros 14 documentos relativos à armada de Pedro Álvares Cabral* (Lisbon, 1999), pp. 95–121.

[8] L. F. F. R. Thomaz, *De Ceuta a Timor* (Lisbon, 1994), p. 124.

In managing a first encounter, assessing the ability and will of native inhabitants to offer resistance was always a priority. Accordingly, one of the first observations Caminha made of the Tupiniquins was that they carried bows and arrows.[9] These they were persuaded by signs to lay down before any further contact proceeded. Only after this did the Portuguese move on to the next stage, attracting the Amerindians by offering gifts, then taking fuller note of their appearance, dress, body decoration, and demeanor.

Learning how newly encountered natives organized the material bases of their lives and, furthermore, comprehending their social order, beliefs, and values, were necessarily gradual processes that required time. Along the way, European preconceptions sometimes contributed to oversimplifications, misunderstandings, and the creation of distorted stereotypes. Early in the expansion, there was a Portuguese tendency to view all peoples within the context of the global struggle between Christianity and Islam. More broadly, African, Asian, and Amerindian societies were expected to possess more or less familiar hierarchies, with grades of status from kings to the lowliest of commoners, as in Europe. In religious terms, the Portuguese categorized newly encountered peoples according to whether they professed Islam, Judaism, or some form of Christianity – that is, whether they were people of "the Book," who possessed a biblical tradition, or merely *gentios* (idolaters). When this formula was applied to the population of India and it had become obvious that Hindus were not in fact deviant Christians, they were logically labeled *gentios*.[10] In this way, they fitted into a medieval European view of the world, which in turn was founded on the traditional Jewish division of humanity into Jews and Gentiles. On the other hand, in West Africa the Portuguese eventually came to categorize the native inhabitants as primarily practitioners of *feitiço* (witchcraft) rather than idolaters – a view that gave rise to the long-lasting, but now generally discredited, concept of West African fetishism.

After the Portuguese had made the great breakthrough to India, they spread extremely rapidly throughout most of maritime Asia by taking advantage of the established trading routes of the Indian Ocean and the China seas. Beyond Kerala, many of their pioneering voyages – and therefore first encounters – were made by obscure adventurers sailing aboard Asian interport vessels rather than by official crown expeditions. Consequently, the details of first encounters in this vast region are often obscure.

The earliest direct Portuguese contact with Chinese in China illustrates this uncertainty. The Portuguese had heard about China in India, and when

[9] Magalhães and Miranda, *Os primeiros 14 documentos*, p. 98.

[10] For Hindus as *gentios*, see Rubiés, *Travel and Ethnology in the Renaissance*, p.148.

Diogo Lopes de Sequeira was sent on an official reconnaissance mission to Malacca in 1509, he was instructed to seek information about the Chinese, including their military capacity, their religion, their trade, and their attitude toward Islam. The Portuguese indeed encountered expatriate Chinese at Malacca and learned much about them. Most of this information was accurate, but some of it was not – as indicated in the account of "The Very Great Kingdom of China" written in India by Duarte Barbosa, probably between 1511 and 1516, before any known Portuguese visit to China itself. Here Barbosa correctly reported that the Chinese made much excellent porcelain – but incorrectly thought that it was manufactured from a paste made of ground shells mixed with white-of-egg and buried for a long period in the ground.[11] He obviously had little understanding of the complexities of Chinese religious beliefs and customs, with their subtle mixture of Daoism, Buddhism, and Confucianism, merely referring to the people as *gentios* and the emperor as a heathen much addicted to idol worship. On the other hand, we know that some writers in sixteenth-century China described the Portuguese in terms that were fanciful to the point of grotesqueness, repeating rumors that they were goblins, descended from cannibals and barely human. They were also reputed to be violent, unpredictable, and highly dangerous – and to have kidnapped and eaten children. Their behavior made it impossible to incorporate them into the Chinese tribute system.[12]

Another people of whom the Portuguese initially became aware through indirect reports were the Sinhalese of Ceylon. It was on the basis of pre-contact information that the king of Portugal first decided that it would be advantageous to build a fortress on Ceylon. According to the Portuguese writer Fernão de Queiros, when D. Lourenço de Almeida finally reached the island in 1506, the king of Kotte offered friendship and vassalage to the king of Portugal. However, *Rajavaliya*, a Sinhalese chronicle, says the Portuguese were granted a *dâkum* – that is, an audience in a manner implying subordination. It appears this was an encounter the Portuguese had already evaluated before it took place – and that both sides subsequently interpreted to suit their respective interests.[13]

[11] M. L. Dames, ed., *The Book of Duarte Barbosa* (London, 1918–1921), vol. 2, pp. 213–214.

[12] For Chinese rumors that the Portuguese were goblins and so forth, see K. C. Fok, "Early Ming Images of the Portuguese," in R. Ptak, ed., *Portuguese Asia: Aspects in History and Economic History (Sixteenth and Seventeenth Centuries)* (Stuttgart, 1987), pp. 144–145. For the reputation of the Portuguese in Chinese eyes as violent and dangerous, see Jonathan Porter, "The Troublesome Feringhi: Late Ming Chinese Perceptions of the Portuguese and Macau," *Portuguese Studies Review* 7 (Spring–Summer, 1999), no. 2, pp. 14–16.

[13] Jorge Flores, *Os Portugueses e o Mar de Ceilão: Trato, diplomacia e guerra (1498–1543)* (Lisbon, 1998), pp. 124–125.

From the beginning, the Portuguese were aware of the urgent need to communicate more effectively with natives and developed procedures for this purpose. As early as the 1440s, it was standard practice to try to seize individuals and take them back to Portugal so they could learn Portuguese and also reveal something of their own ways. Later, they could serve as interpreters. Another common practice was to leave behind a young Portuguese or two at the conclusion of a first encounter. Their brief was to establish working relations with the natives, win their trust, and learn their language.[14]

Violence was never far below the surface at initial encounters, although its use as a first resort by the Portuguese was unusual. As already noted, on the coast of Saharan Africa in 1436, two mounted Portuguese had attacked the first natives they saw, without warning. But, as their voyaging extended, the Portuguese developed less confrontational approaches, preferring persuasion to force, where possible. First encounters, however they were managed, gave rise to images of others that were often lasting – both in Portuguese minds and in the minds of those they encountered. Such images could play a crucial role in the development of future relationships.

Frontier Encounters

By about the middle of the sixteenth century, the Portuguese were well entrenched in maritime Asia and at various points on the fringes of West and East Africa. They had also begun their occupation of coastal Brazil, and, for them, the making of first contacts with unfamiliar peoples by sea was virtually over. Portugal had acquired an almost global network of settlements, fortresses, and trading posts, scattered among three continents and numerous islands. With the framework of its maritime empire in place, Portugal was moving forward from an era of first encounters to one of frontier encounters – that is, encounters along the borders of what was by then Portuguese-controlled territory and increasingly also into interiors well beyond that territory.

Unlike initial encounters, which were sudden, unprecedented, but essentially fleeting occurrences at which each side learned about the existence of the other for the first time, most frontier encounters developed gradually and were often maintained over long periods. The Portuguese possessions in Asia adjoined an immense diversity of nations, kingdoms, and cities, many of them wealthy and highly sophisticated by contemporary European standards. In Brazil and Africa, Portuguese settlements adjoined regions and

[14] Russell, *Prince Henry*, p. 203.

societies hardly less complex, if more modest in material achievement. The Portuguese experience of frontier encounters was correspondingly rich and varied.

To many contemporaries, frontiers seemed first and foremost lines of defense in zones of confrontation. Across them clashes took place, and they had to be watched and guarded accordingly. Even from Goa itself, the seat of Portugal's viceroy in Asia, a Franciscan friar could remark in 1587 that this was a frontier land of conquest – without seeming to say anything particularly startling.[15] It is therefore hardly surprising that fortresses were among the most visible manifestations of the Portuguese presence overseas. Portugal itself had long experience with frontier fortresses, and the institutions that went with them, through the centuries of the Reconquest. The Portuguese intrusion into Morocco, which began with the capture of Ceuta in 1415, had likewise been sustained only by maintaining a defensive ring of fortresses. In Asia and tropical Africa, and to a lesser extent even in Brazil, virtually every official Portuguese settlement or possession came to include one or more fortresses. Many of these still exist today and impress the visitor with their awesome appearance and often massive dimensions. They include Fort Aguada in Goa, Fort Jesus in Mombasa, and the fortresses of São Jerónimo in Damão and São Miguel in Luanda, and the vast complex of fortifications that defended Diu. As these buildings suggest, in the sixteenth and seventeenth centuries a high proportion of the white population in Portugal's scattered overseas possessions were either soldiers or former soldiers.

The violence that actually took place on these frontiers varied much in kind and intensity over time. Early on it was often predatory and poorly controlled. Later it was better controlled, more institutionalized, and more truly defensive in nature – for, once the general pattern of their overseas interests and possessions had been settled, the Portuguese concentrated on protecting what they had gained. This meant manning the fortresses, maintaining fleets, and occasionally confronting major crises, such as the two celebrated sieges of Diu in 1538 and 1546 by Gujarati and Ottoman forces. It was in response to these sieges that the architect Francisco Pires designed the massive defenses of Diu, thereby introducing into the Portuguese defense system overseas, for the first time, military fortifications typical of the European Renaissance.

Life within a Portuguese frontier garrison could occasionally be dangerous, but it was usually just tedious. In 1630, Dom Fernando de Noronha, a young nobleman, was sent with a contingent of troops to reinforce the great São Jerónimo fortress at Damão in Gujarat. When he arrived, there was a

[15] Cited in C. R. Boxer, *The Portuguese Seaborne Empire, 1415–1825* (London, 1969), p. 208.

tense anticipation within the garrison, for rumor had it that a huge Moghul army was approaching. For three months, Dom Fernando alternated on and off guard duty – waiting for the enemy and the wet monsoon. Nothing eventuated, and routine and boredom slowly set in, which for Dom Fernando was only interrupted in the end by embarking on a predatory cruise.[16] In such monotonous situations, which probably prevailed in most Portuguese fortresses for most of the time, garrisons merged increasingly into the community where they were stationed. They mixed with native auxiliaries, they drew most of their supplies, their entertainment, and their women from what was available nearby, and – when opportunity offered – they participated in business ventures with local or visiting Asian traders. If they took the ultimate step and deserted, they disappeared, of course, into the nearby native interior.

While one form of military presence on the frontier was the sedentary fortress garrison, another was highly mobile expeditionary columns that penetrated into distant interiors. Until about the 1620s in Asia, and much later in Africa and Brazil, Portuguese columns often intruded deep into neighboring lands on plundering or slaving raids, punitive expeditions, or outright attempts at conquest.

In Brazil, the main objective of such incursions was to seize Amerindian men, women, and children and bring them back to the white settlements to provide labor. This process has been particularly well studied for the colonists of the São Paulo region, although it in fact occurred on the frontiers of most of Portuguese Brazil. In São Paulo, when by about 1580 the local native population had been eliminated or absorbed into settled society, the colonists turned increasingly to the inhabitants of more distant, unsubdued regions in their search for a workforce. Repeated expeditions were launched deep into the interior to seize and bring back captives. The most sought-after victims were the relatively numerous Guaraní, who were particularly valued because they already practiced agriculture. Bands of colonists known as *bandeirantes* (slave raiders), together with their native allies and dependents, raided the vast area south and southwest of São Paulo, attacking and destroying villages, seizing captives, and between 1628 and 1641 effectively destroying the recently founded Jesuit missions in Guairá and elsewhere on the ill-defined border with Spanish Peru. These predatory expeditions wrought widespread destruction on native society. Later, in the 1650s–1670s, because of their formidable reputation as Indian fighters, *bandeirantes* were called on by the authorities in Bahia to conduct a series of punitive expeditions

[16] Anthony Disney, "The Estado da Índia and the Young Nobleman Soldier: The Case of Dom Fernando de Noronha," *Mare Liberum* 5 (July 1993), pp. 66–70.

against unsubdued Amerindians in the northeastern backlands. The result was a virtual campaign of extermination.[17]

Meanwhile, in West Africa, in the mid-1570s King Sebastian had agreed to treat the kingdom of Ndongo as a *conquista* – a territory earmarked for conquest. Paulo Dias de Novais was licensed to invade Ndongo and was granted a *donatária* (seigneury) within its borders that stretched vaguely inland from the mouth of the Kwanza River for as far as he could conquer. This fateful decision, which set Portugal on a course of carving out for itself a territorial empire in West Africa and planting white settlements, would weigh heavily on both Portuguese and Africans for centuries to come. In 1576, Novais founded the city of Luanda, establishing there the characteristically Portuguese institutions of a fortress, churches, a *câmara* (town council), a *Misericórdia*, a hospital, and a jail. *Sesmarias* (land grants) were distributed to the north and south. From Luanda, Novais himself, and later his successors, gradually forced their way into the interior, spurred on by an increasingly desperate search for silver mines, which in reality did not exist. It was a bloody and prolonged struggle against fierce Mbundu resistance. Gradually, however, the Portuguese succeeded in establishing a series of fortified posts in the interior that formed the nucleus of what eventually became Portuguese Angola.[18] Comparable situations developed in some other parts of the Portuguese world, particularly in Mozambique and, for awhile, Ceylon.

In Asia, where opportunities for plunder tended to be greatest, short-term incursions were generally a more common feature of the military frontier than expeditions of conquest, especially during the early years. Such incursions were carried out in the tradition of the *razzia* (raid) common during the Iberian Reconquest. Many were the work of private adventurers, but some were official, or at least semiofficial. Albuquerque's famous capture and sack of Malacca, which yielded a huge booty (although most of it was subsequently lost in a shipwreck), was in part just a great *razzia*. In 1543, another governor of Goa, Martim Afonso de Sousa, mounted his ambitious "pagoda voyage" – a major plundering expedition aimed at looting various

[17] John Monteiro, *Negros da terra: Índios e bandeirantes nas origens de São Paulo* (São Paulo, 1994), pp. 55, 60–63, 68–75, 92–96.

[18] For the history of the Portuguese in Angola, see David Birmingham, *Trade and Conflict in Angola: The Mbundu and Their Neighbours under the Influence of the Portuguese, 1483–1790* (Oxford, 1966); and John K. Thornton, *The Kingdom of Kongo: Civil War and Transition, 1641–1718* (Madison, WI, 1983); Thornton, "The Development of an African Catholic Church in the Kingdom of Kongo," *Journal of African History* 25 (1984), pp. 147–167; and Thornton, *Africa and Africans in the Making of the Atlantic World, 1400–1800*, 2nd ed. (Cambridge, 1998).

southern Indian temples that achieved little success.[19] Another scheme, hatched in 1615 by a notorious Portuguese slave trader and piratical adventurer, Sebastião Gonçalves Tibau, involved attacking Mrauk-U in Arakan, with the aim of looting the imperial treasure of the ancient Mon kingdom. Although it won the support and participation of the viceroy at Goa, this enterprise also failed – and its failure helped bring an end to Portuguese military adventurism in the Bay of Bengal.[20]

Of course, not all Portuguese frontier encounters were military. Frontiers are transition zones across which all kinds of peaceful contacts may occur. At frontiers, cultures meet, learn about each other, exchange information, and form compromises with each other. This process took place wherever the Portuguese encountered other peoples, traditions, and ways of life. The Portuguese most deeply involved in such encounters were usually those who resided permanently or at least for long periods overseas and gradually accumulated personal experience of native peoples.

Peaceful frontier encounters were often by-products of either trade or religious proselytizing. One of the most important and famous instances of the former occurred between the Portuguese and the Chinese in South China. In about 1557, under circumstances that are still not entirely clear, Portuguese traders had been permitted to settle at Macao, a small peninsula near the mouth of the Pearl River.[21] But they were confined to Macao only, being forbidden by the Chinese authorities to visit anywhere on the mainland except under strictly controlled conditions. Representatives of the Portuguese were only allowed to enter nearby Canton to conduct business during the annual trade fairs, after which they had to return immediately to Macao. Despite these restrictions, the Macao Portuguese for three-quarters of a century drove an extraordinarily profitable trade with China, mostly exchanging Japanese and Spanish American silver for Chinese silk and porcelain. It seems much of this trade was clandestine, with Chinese smugglers bringing their wares secretly to Macao, even though they faced death under

19 Sanjay Subrahmanyam, *The Political Economy of Commerce: Southern India, 1500–1650* (Cambridge, 1990), p. 266. Compare the following accounts of this episode by the Portuguese chroniclers Correia and Couto: Gaspar Correia, *Lendas da Índia* (Oporto, 1975), vol. 4, pp. 299–305; Diogo do Couto, *Décadas da Ásia* (Lisbon, 1736), vol. 1, pp. 567–568 (Dec. 1, liv. 9, chap. 7).

20 On Tibau and his exploits, see Maria Ana Marques Guedes, *Interferência e Integração dos Portugueses na Birmânia ca. 1580–1630* (Lisbon, 1994), pp. 155–169.

21 The most authoritative recent review of the origins of Macao may be found in Rui Manuel Loureiro, *Fidalgos, Missionários e Mandarins: Portugal e a China no Século XVI* (Lisbon, 2000), Chap. 21. C. R. Boxer, *Fidalgos in the Far East, 1550–1770* (The Hague, 1948) also remains useful.

Chinese law if detected. It was thus to a degree a permeable frontier, which commercial enterprise found effective ways of circumventing.[22]

Missionaries likewise ventured across frontiers in their search for souls. China again was a major case in point. For years the Macao Jesuits were unable to gain leave to work in the Celestial Kingdom – until first Michele Ruggieri and then his colleague Matteo Ricci achieved the remarkable feat of learning sufficient Mandarin to communicate fluently with senior Chinese officials. This so impressed the officials that they granted the missionaries license to stay in Canton – a great frontier breakthrough that had taken nearly half a century to achieve. By 1595, Ricci, himself now dressed as a mandarin, had managed to reach Nanking. From there he went on to the court of the Wan Li emperor at Beijing, where in 1603 he converted Paul Hsu, the imperial chief minister.[23]

In Brazil also, the frontier fringing the Portuguese coastal settlements was frequently crossed by Franciscan, Jesuit, or other missionaries. But this was a different kind of missionary frontier beyond which lay not great exotic kingdoms but a seemingly lawless wilderness. In 1607–1608, the Jesuit Fathers Francisco Pinto and Luís Figueira made an epic journey into the backlands of Ceará, eventually reaching the remote Gê-speaking Tacarijú people beyond Ibiapaba. The Tacarijú trusted neither them nor their message, attacked their camp, and clubbed Pinto to death, forcing Figueira into shocked retreat.[24] Clearly, the risks involved in preaching to unfamiliar tribal peoples could not be taken lightly – especially where marauding slavers had already spread fear and suspicion.

Negotiations

Encounters between Portuguese and other peoples were very likely, sooner or later, to lead to negotiations – that is, discussions to clarify mutual expectations and determine the future direction of relationships. Often, negotiations were formal, with official representatives of the Portuguese crown meeting and negotiating with local leaders, who, in turn, sometimes sent envoys to Lisbon. However, Portuguese traders, adventurers, or churchmen at times also conducted negotiations at native courts, with their own private agendas quite distinct from those of the crown. There were many instances of both

[22] J. M. Flores, "Macau e o comércio da Baía de Cantão (séculos XVI e XVII)," in A. T. de Matos and L. F. F. R. Thomaz, eds., *As relações entre a Índia Portuguesa, a Ásia do Sueste e o Extremo Oriente* (Macao, 1993), p. 46.

[23] The best biography of Ricci, firmly based on the sources, remains Vincent Cronin, *The Wise Man from the West* (London, 1955).

[24] John Hemming, *Red Gold: The Conquest of the Brazilian Indians* (London, 1978), p. 209.

kinds of negotiations, beginning in West Africa in the fifteenth century but reaching their peak in the Asian phase of Portuguese expansion.

One part of West Africa that interested the Portuguese, mainly as a source of slaves and ivory, was the kingdom of Benin, located inland from the steamy, fever-ridden coast of the Niger Delta. Benin was inhabited mostly by Edo-speaking people, under a paramount chief called the *oba*. He and King João II exchanged envoys in 1486, resulting in the formation of a short-lived Portuguese trading post at Ughoton and expectations among the Portuguese that the *oba* would soon accept baptism. In 1514, the *oba* dispatched another ambassador to Lisbon, probably aiming to secure firearms, but the Portuguese responded by sending priests rather than guns. A few baptisms were secured, including that of one of the *oba*'s sons. But when a new *oba* took power in 1516, the flirtation with Christianity ceased, and King Manuel's priests had to leave.

In 1533, King João III sent Franciscans to Benin in yet another attempt to convert that kingdom, but they soon withdrew, deeply shocked by the *oba*'s refusal to abandon human sacrifice. Apparently, successive *obas* saw little advantage in the Portuguese connection, and it ultimately became clear that formal Christianization and Westernization in Benin were never likely to advance very far. High-level contacts with the kingdom accordingly petered out, although informal contacts – through the presence of private military advisers, traders, returned slaves, and a few local converts – proved more lasting and pervasive.[25]

Portuguese relations with another ruler – the king of Kotte in Ceylon – developed rather differently. Portugal sought to reduce Kotte to client status. The principal prize was control of the cinnamon for which lowland Ceylon was renowned, but accessing the gem and elephant trades and enabling the church to garner souls for Christ while ousting the Malabar Muslims from the area were also important objectives. Gradually the Portuguese got the upper hand in Kotte, mainly through diplomatic pressure backed, where necessary, by force. They built a fortress in Colombo in 1518 and secured an "alliance" with the king. When in 1521 Kotte was split among three rival brothers, the Portuguese threw their support behind the oldest, Bhuvanekabahu. He soon became dependent on Portuguese support and, as their influence grew, the Portuguese increased pressure on him to abandon Buddhism for Catholicism. This he did not do, but he allowed Portuguese missionaries to conduct a notably successful campaign of evangelization within his dominions. Eventually, frustrated by Bhuvanekabahu, the

[25] A. F. C. Ryder, *Benin and the Europeans* (London and Harlow, 1969), pp. 29–33, 45–52, and 70–72.

Portuguese had him murdered and replaced by his grandson, Dharmapala, who soon accepted baptism. Dharmapala died in 1597, having bequeathed Kotte to the king of Portugal.[26]

The bequest of Kotte, providing a substantial foothold from which to expand deep into Ceylon, seems at first sight a triumphant vindication of Portuguese diplomacy. Yet it also drew the Portuguese into a quagmire, for they had to make good their claim against determined Sinhalese opposition. A long, costly struggle, with many changes in fortune, ensued for three-quarters of a century. In the end, the Portuguese were forced out of Ceylon, although this might not have happened had the Dutch not intervened against them.

Most formal Portuguese negotiations with Asian courts were conducted less aggressively than those with Kotte, for the Portuguese were seldom in a position to challenge significant Asian rulers, except on the sea. Nevertheless, over time, they constructed a remarkably wide and complex network of overseas diplomatic relationships. Given the huge distances from the court in Lisbon, these relationships within maritime Asia were managed, in practice, by the viceroy at Goa. He occupied the center of a diplomatic web so extensive that it equaled or surpassed those maintained by many contemporary European monarchs.

The formation of Portugal's diplomatic network in the Indian Ocean received its first great impetus from the conquests of Afonso de Albuquerque. After his seizure of Goa, Albuquerque received delegations from some of the most powerful rulers of India, including the Hindu emperor Krishna Deva Raya of Vijayanagara and the Muslim raja Mahmoud Begarha of Gujarat. He also received an ambassador from Shah Ismael of Persia and in response proposed to Ismael in 1510 a Persian-Portuguese alliance against the Ottoman Turks. This amounted to an attempt to exploit sectarian differences within Islam, the Ottomans being Sunnis, whereas Ismael was an uncompromising Shiite. In 1512, Albuquerque also received an ambassador from the Coptic Christian emperor of Ethiopia, who requested a treaty of alliance.[27]

[26] On the history of Sri Lanka in this era, see Tikiri Abeyasinghe, *Portuguese Rule in Ceylon, 1594–1612* (Colombo, 1966); and "Portuguese Rule in the Kingdom of Kotte in Sri Lanka, 1594–1638," *The Sri Lanka Archives* 1 (1983), no. 1, pp. 1–14.

[27] Albuquerque's diplomacy may be followed in outline in Geneviève Bouchon, *Albuquerque: Le lion des Mers d'Asie* (Paris, 1992), especially pp. 191–192, 219–222, 227–229, and 238. Portuguese relations specifically with Vijayanagar are discussed in J. M. dos Santos Alves, "A cruz, os diamantes e os cavalos: Frei Luís do Salvador, primeiro missionário e embaixador Português em Vijayanagara (1500–1510)," *Mare Liberum* 5 (1993), pp. 9–20; and M. A. da Lima Cruz, "Notes on Portuguese Relations with Vijayanagara," *Santa Barbara Portuguese Studies* 2 (1995), pp. 13–39, but the most thorough and innovative

After Albuquerque, the Portuguese continued to extend their diplomatic contacts east of the Cape of Good Hope. Viceroys at Goa came to maintain diplomatic contacts with numerous states and provincial administrations in India, including Bijapur, Ahmadnagar, Golconda, Moghul Surat, Moghul Bengal, Madurai, and various princedoms on the Kanara and Malabar coasts. Spies and informers supplemented the network, and a viceroy could write to the king in 1632, "I have spies in all the courts of the kings of India."[28] Paying for envoys, for obligatory gifts, and for other costs related to all this activity became in time a significant strain on the resources of the viceroyalty.

East of India were many more powers with which negotiations were from time to time conducted, including Aceh and Pasai in Sumatra, Bantam and Mataram in Java, Johor on the Malay Peninsula, the kingdoms of Siam, Pegu, and Ava in mainland Southeast Asia, China, and Japan. Because of its vast size, prestige, and power, China was a special case. The Portuguese did not get leave to send an envoy to the Chinese court until 1520. When their ambassador, the celebrated pharmacist and writer Tomé Pires, finally reached Beijing, he waited in vain for an imperial audience and was then arrested. Finally, he either died in jail or suffered execution at the hands of his captors for violations of Chinese sovereignty committed by his fellow countrymen off the coast of Guangdong.[29] Meanwhile, King Manuel, who miscalculated the limits of the possible in China, ordered a Portuguese fort to be established on the Chinese coast. The commander charged with this task was soon driven off by Chinese coast guards, ending for the time being Portuguese attempts to establish a presence, diplomatic or otherwise, in the Celestial Kingdom.

The conduct of diplomatic negotiations, from Benin to Bantam and Kongo to Kyoto, involving so many unfamiliar peoples, languages, and cultures, presented the Portuguese with an unprecedented challenge. To communicate, the Portuguese and the myriad others obviously had to be mutually intelligible. This fundamental problem was tackled in some areas by employing or developing lingua francas. In the early years, basic Arabic often served this purpose, and most expeditions carried Arabic-speaking interpreters with them. But during the course of the sixteenth century, as the Portuguese established their presence throughout the port cities of Asia and

analysis of interactions between this South Indian polity and Europeans – including the Portuguese – is now that of Rubiés in *Travel and Ethnology in the Renaissance*.

[28] Panduronga S. S. Pissurlencar, ed., *Assentos do Conselho do Estado, vol. 1 (1618–1633)* (Goa, 1953), p. 335.

[29] For Tomé Pires's mission to China, see Loureiro, *Fidalgos, missionários e Mandarins*, pp. 265–288.

East Africa, Portuguese itself was increasingly adopted as an international medium of communication, albeit in a simplified form. Many Indians, Indonesians, and Africans, especially in coastal areas, acquired a certain competence in Portuguese, which they seem to have learned readily. Portuguese remained an international language of diplomacy in much of maritime Asia well into the eighteenth century, when it was gradually displaced by English.

The language barrier was also broken by Portuguese learning the local tongues of the regions into which they intruded. Although this was probably never done systematically by more than a handful of Portuguese, the process began early. During Vasco da Gama's first visit to India in 1498, an anonymous Portuguese carefully compiled a vocabulary of Malayalam words and phrases, which was appended to the account of the expedition supposedly written by Álvaro Velho.[30] Later, it was mostly the Catholic religious, particularly the Jesuits, who pioneered linguistic studies, compiling vocabularies, dictionaries, and grammars in Asian, African, and Amerindian languages. It was therefore often churchmen who acted as official interpreters on diplomatic missions or even served as the actual ambassadors at royal or viceregal request. This was particularly so at the courts of the great powers of South and East Asia, including the Moghuls in India, the Ming and early Qing in China, and the Tokugawa shoguns of Japan. However, while it was primarily the Jesuits who mastered such languages as Mandarin in a scholarly sense, some ordinary Portuguese also learned to converse in native languages at an everyday level. At the same time, Portuguese possessions and outposts quickly acquired their own native *linguas* (interpreters), who rapidly became indispensable.

In addition to the state, private Portuguese conducted negotiations with local peoples when it suited them. In delicate situations, especially if official and unofficial interests were in conflict, this could spell disaster. When in 1576 Paulo Dias de Novais established an officially authorized Portuguese settlement at Luanda in Angola, his presence was regarded as an unwelcome intrusion by the freelance Portuguese and São Toméan slave traders already operating in the area. One of them contrived to convince the paramount chief, Ngola Kiluanji, that Novais constituted a serious threat. His suspicions roused, Kiluanji ordered the killing of all Portuguese in or near his capital, Kabasa, and about thirty were massacred, together with their slaves. Kiluanji then moved against Novais himself, and the long sequence of Angolan wars, which lasted until 1683, thereupon commenced. A gradual extension of Portuguese-controlled territory from the coast into the interior followed.

[30] See Ravenstein, trans., *A Journal of the First Voyage of Vasco da Gama*, pp. 105–108.

Probably the most persistent private practitioners of Portuguese overseas diplomacy were the Macao merchants, who operated collectively through their *câmara*.[31] It was through the Macao *câmara* that routine negotiations with the nearby authorities in Guangdong were handled. The Macao *câmara* also conducted negotiations with the Japanese. It was responsible for the disastrous mission sent to Nagasaki in 1640, which tried to secure reversal of the shogun's edict of expulsion but ended in mass execution of the delegation.

Encounters between Portuguese and Amerindians in Brazil sometimes gave rise to negotiations, although not to formal diplomatic missions of the kind that occurred in Asia and Africa. In Brazil, negotiations were often conducted by Jesuit missionaries, who naturally gave prominence to evangelizing whenever opportunity offered. A celebrated exponent of the art of negotiating with Amerindians was the seventeenth-century missionary-priest, Father António Vieira. Arguably Vieira's greatest tour de force was his visit to the fierce and previously hostile Nheengaiba Amerindians of Marajó Island at the mouth of the Amazon in 1659, most of whom he persuaded to make peace with the Portuguese and to declare their loyalty to the king of Portugal.

Interactions

As the Portuguese consolidated their presence overseas, encounters and negotiations merged, almost imperceptibly, into interactions. Portuguese and various peoples of Asia, Africa, and Brazil increasingly associated together on a day-to-day basis. They learned about each other, exchanged ideas, and adapted to each other's ways – and their mutual acculturation led gradually toward more stable long-term relationships.

Most Portuguese interactions with native peoples arose in the first instance from what might be called professional or occupational contacts. In some instances, this led to a remarkable diffusion of specialist knowledge between cultures. The Portuguese were able to spread so rapidly throughout maritime Asia because they acquired pilots, sailing directions, and seafaring lore from Asians. In Asia, they also extended their scientific knowledge. This is well demonstrated in Garcia da Orta's seminal study of Indian botany and pharmacology, published at Goa in 1563 – a book that drew heavily on Indian informants and subsequently became one of the foundation

[31] C. R. Boxer, *Portuguese Society in the Tropics: The Municipal Councils of Goa, Macao, Bahia, and Luanda, 1510–1806* (Madison, WI, 1965), pp. 49–50.

stones of tropical medicine.[32] Conversely, Portuguese and Jesuit informants brought knowledge of European mathematics, cartography, painting styles, clockmaking, and even printing to various Asian courts.

With few exceptions, Portuguese first went overseas as young men engaged for military service. This meant they often first became acquainted with Africans, Asians, and Amerindians as either enemies or allies, or sometimes as military employers. Those Portuguese soldiers (*soldados*) who decided to sell their services to native leaders often ended up living among indigenous peoples for quite prolonged periods. As we now know, the defection of Portuguese renegades to the Muslim side had been a fairly common phenomenon during the Reconquest in Portugal. It occurred again in sixteenth-century Morocco, and it also appeared very early in maritime Asia. Of course, often such defections were more or less involuntary, as when men found themselves prisoners with little hope of release for many years, if ever. After the defeat of King Sebastian at the battle of Alcazarquibir in Morocco in 1578, many Portuguese, mostly from his army's rank and file but also including a number of noblemen, became incorporated into the Sa'adian sultan's desert army.[33]

In Asia, Portuguese renegades were soon being welcomed into the forces of the sultans of Bijapur and other local rulers, especially if they could offer expertise in gunnery. Renegades adopted the dress, lifestyle, and demeanor of those into whose society they had gravitated, and often embraced Islam, even undergoing the rite of circumcision. Among the earliest and best-known renegades in Asia was a group handed over to Albuquerque at Goa in 1512 as part of a peace agreement with the Bijapuri general, Rassul Khan. These unfortunates were punished with mutilation, their ears, noses, right hands, and left thumbs all severed.[34]

Rather than turning renegade, many Portuguese *soldados* simply hired themselves out. This they did, individually or in groups, to whichever Asian ruler offered them attractive pay and conditions. Such men integrated less thoroughly into their host societies than did renegades, remaining at least nominally Christian and sometimes accompanied by their own chaplains.

[32] Garcia da Orta, *Colóquios dos simples e drogas e cousas mediçinais da India* (Goa, 1563). (Alternatively, see the facsimile edition, Lisbon, 1963.)

[33] On renegades in North Africa, see Isabel M. R. Mendes Drumond Braga, *Entre a Cristandade e o Islão (séculos XV–XVII): Cativos e renegados nas Franjas de duas sociedades em confronto* (Ceuta, 1998), pp. 40–49. Defections in Asia are reviewed in Dejanirah Silva Couto, "Some Observations on Portuguese Renegades in Asia in the Sixteenth Century," in Anthony Disney and Emily Booth, eds., *Vasco da Gama and the Linking of Europe and Asia* (New Delhi, 2000), pp. 178–201.

[34] Castanheda, *História*, vol. 1, pp. 720–721; Correia, *Lendas*, vol. 2, pp. 316–318.

Most returned, in due course, to the Portuguese enclaves. In the late sixteenth and early seventeenth centuries, such adventurers were to be found particularly in the lands fringing the Bay of Bengal. One report of 1627 alleged that there were then 3,000 Portuguese in Muslim service in Bengal and another 500 with the sultan of Makassar.[35]

A few Portuguese military adventurers contrived to carve out for themselves spectacular careers in their adopted countries. One such was Filipe de Brito, an audacious mercenary, sometime pirate, and private conquistador. Brito was appointed captain of Syriam on the Irrawaddy Delta by the king of Arakan. He used Syriam as a base for a Portuguese-Asian private army through which he dominated all the ports on the northeastern shores of the Bay of Bengal, with their lucrative maritime trade. In the end, he was crushed by the Taung-ngu king of Ava in 1612, captured, and executed by impalement.[36]

A less ostentatious, but probably more representative, military adventurer was the unnamed Portuguese who in the late 1620s was serving as adviser and personal bodyguard to the ruler of Sada in northwest Madagascar.[37] Further west, on the African mainland, there were many Portuguese "frontiersmen" who became well acculturated into local societies, partly through military activity. In the Zambezi valley, from the late sixteenth century some enterprising local Portuguese boldly carved out for themselves large *prazos* (landed estates) with the aid of their African slaves and dependents. Called *muzungos* in local parlance, these men became in effect tribal chieftains. They intermarried or cohabited with Africans and spoke their languages, and within a generation or two came to resemble, in both physical appearance and lifestyle, the Bantu peoples among whom they lived. Eventually, many *muzungos* crossed completely to the other side of the cultural frontier, abandoning any pretense of loyalty to their Portuguese origins, thereby becoming "transfrontiersmen."[38]

Frontiersmen in colonial Brazil also interacted closely with indigenous peoples, although the circumstances – and the outcome – were rather

[35] Anthony Disney, *Twilight of the Pepper Empire: Portuguese Trade in Southwest India in the Early Seventeenth Century* (Cambridge, MA, 1978), p. 21.

[36] For Brito's remarkable career, see Sanjay Subrahmanyam, *The Portuguese Empire in Asia, 1500–1700: A Political and Economic History* (London, 1993), pp. 128–129, or, for a more detailed review, Guedes, *Interferência e integração*, pp. 134–138.

[37] Anthony Disney, "Jesuits Going East: The Experiences of Fathers Dominique le Jeunehomme, Agostino Tudeschini and Tranquillo Grassetti en Route to the China Mission in the Early Seventeenth Century," *Review of Culture*, 2nd ser. (1994), no. 21, pp. 238–239.

[38] Michael N. Pearson, *Port Cities and Intruders: The Swahili Coast, India, and Portugal in the Early Modern Era* (Baltimore, 1998), pp. 149–151.

different. The best known of the Brazilian frontiersmen were the *bandeirantes* of São Paulo, who in the late sixteenth and the seventeenth centuries made numerous expeditions into unsubdued Amerindian territory. During their time in the wilderness, these men became heavily dependent on their native guides and followings and adopted much of the Amerindian lifestyle. They dressed in part-Amerindian, part-European fashion and ate native foods. However, after participating in one or two such expeditions, most *bandeirantes* settled down quietly to farm, usually in the São Paulo area. Only a small minority went on to make repeated journeys, in due course becoming highly experienced backwoodsmen, fluent in native languages, and familiar with native cultures. The *bandeirantes* were therefore typically frontiersmen, not transfrontiersmen, and most of them remained firmly within a Portuguese colonial subculture. Of course, this did not inhibit extensive miscegenation. Ultimately, few families in colonial São Paulo did not have at least some trace of Amerindian blood.

The Portuguese expansion being an essentially maritime enterprise, interactions were also common at sea. Especially when voyaging east of the Cape of Good Hope, Portuguese often kept close company aboard ship with Asians and Africans, including local pilots, lascars, merchants, sepoys, slaves, and sometimes even Asian women. All this could happen on Portuguese ships, but even more on Asian-owned and manned country vessels, on which Portuguese often traveled as passengers or served as skippers and pilots. Living for days in cramped conditions with people of another culture inevitably increased mutual awareness. Usually, shipboard interactions were relatively tolerant and incident-free, although there were exceptions. The Florentine merchant Francesco Carletti, who traveled extensively aboard both Portuguese and Asian ships at the turn of the sixteenth century, thought it scandalous that Arab, Bengali, and Turkish sailors on a voyage to Malacca in 1599 were allowed by their *serang* (native bosun) to bring their wives and girlfriends with them. Carletti also recalled a frightening standoff aboard a Japanese junk en route from Nagasaki to Macao over a point of honor. Japanese sailors armed with bows and cutlasses confronted Portuguese passengers and their retinues, who brandished muzzle-loaders and swords. The situation was only diffused, with great difficulty, by the intervention of Jesuit missionaries.[39]

The world of commerce was also an important arena within which interactions took place. Engaging in trade cross-culturally required from those involved a considerable degree of mutual understanding and trust, as had

[39] Francesco Carletti, *My Voyage around the World*, ed. and trans. Herbert Weinstock (New York, 1964), pp. 136–139, 185–186.

been appreciated by Prince Henry in the 1440s when he prohibited slave raiding on the coast of West Africa in order to encourage slave trading. Within a few years, in various parts of West Africa, Portuguese traders were mingling freely with Africans and often acculturating into local society to a quite remarkable degree. One such area was Upper Guinea. Here free-lance Portuguese, and Portuguese Cape Verdeans, penetrated the interior via the Senegal, Gambia, and other rivers, fanning out in search of slaves and gold. In due course, many settled down in African villages, married local women, and fathered mixed-blood children. Within a generation or two, their descendants were thoroughly acclimatized, fluent in the native languages, and substantially Africanized – although they usually still clung proudly to their Portuguese identity. Though they were referred to somewhat despisingly as *lançados* (outcasts), their local knowledge and capacity to survive the rigors of West Africa, where many white newcomers succumbed so easily to tropical diseases, nevertheless gave them a decisive advantage.

Similar compromises occurred in Asia. Within a decade of Vasco da Gama's first visit to Calicut, there were Portuguese traders settled in various Malabar ports, especially Cochin. Many developed good business and domestic relationships with Indian and Arab traders, and personal links with the people among whom they now lived. There were also Portuguese traders on the Coromandel Coast, in Bengal, in Ceylon, in the coastal cities of East Africa, and in various other parts of South and Southeast Asia. Often these men put down local roots and became permanent or long-term residents. Whether they were *casados* (married settlers in Portuguese possessions) or *solteiros* (literally bachelors, but by extension settlers living in native territory), their support for formal Portuguese expansion was typically lukewarm, for an informal presence better suited their private interests. Their relationships with Asian trading partners were usually cordial and always crucial to business success. Carletti, who did much business through the Portuguese settlements in Asia, shared this cordiality. He praised the acumen and reliability of the Gujarati merchants with whom he dealt at Goa – and, given that he disposed there Chinese silk he had acquired in Macao, at over 70 percent profit, his satisfaction is understandable.[40]

Portuguese right across the social spectrum, from viceroy to apprentice seaman, did business with Asian traders, and many acquired local business partners, creditors, and agents. Viceroy Linhares (1629–1635) was closely associated with two Hindu brothers, Rama and Baba Keni, who acted on his behalf in many lucrative deals, particularly involving commodity foodstuffs and spices. A necessary by-product of such relationships was that even

[40] Ibid., pp. 202–206.

Portuguese at the highest level of the colonial administration to some extent got to know, and interact with, individual Asians. Conversely, some Asian businessmen found it in their interests to settle in or near Portuguese towns, where they learned much about Portuguese ways and in some cases came to speak Portuguese fluently.

Interactions between Portuguese and natives through sexual and domestic relationships also flourished and became a quintessential part of the expansion process. Until well into the eighteenth century, the Portuguese who went overseas were overwhelmingly men. Under the circumstances, they naturally sought out the company of native women. Because most such Portuguese, except for sailors, had little chance of ever returning to Portugal, the relationships they developed with local women were frequently long-term. Intermarriage and cohabitation between overseas Portuguese and Asian, African, or Amerindian women were the outcome. Interactions of this kind, and their consequences, have been well studied for northeastern Brazil. There, especially on the sugar plantations of colonial times, an ethnically and culturally hybrid society evolved from the intermixing of Portuguese, Africans, and Amerindians. Although developed within a broadly Portuguese framework, this society was strongly influenced by the traditions of Amerindian Brazil, and of West Africa, in many fundamental ways, including its speech, diet, styles of cooking, child-rearing methods, and folklore. Meanwhile, beyond the sugar zone, hybrid Portuguese-Amerindian societies and cultures evolved, including that of the São Paulo plateau, as native Brazilians underwent the traumatic experience of forced integration as a captive labor force.[41]

Of course, in Portugal's expansion, religion was at the heart of much interaction. In this regard, traditional Western historiography has always focused on the Portuguese Christian missions and their tenacious campaigns to convert non-European peoples to Catholicism – whether seen as selfless and heroic or as mere manifestations of European aggression and destructiveness.[42] However, in reality, religious interaction was always a two-way process. Apart from those Portuguese who in North Africa,

[41] Although the classic evocation of the society of the northeastern sugar zone remains Gilberto Freyre, *The Masters and the Slaves* (New York, 1946), the reader will find much more recent research reflected in works such as Stuart B. Schwartz, *Sugar Plantations in the Formation of Colonial Brazil: Bahia, 1550–1835* (Cambridge, 1985), especially chap. 3, and (within the context of the Brazil–Angola connection), Luiz Felipe de Alencastro, *O trato dos viventes: Formação do Brasil no Atlântico Sul* (São Paulo, 2000). On the Portuguese–Amerindian society of São Paulo, see Monteiro, *Negros da terra*.

[42] Another approach to the role of Catholic missionaries in these centuries has been to treat them as "cultural mediators." For an overview, see Rui Manuel Loureiro, "Religiosos

and later Asia, actually defected to Islam in quite significant numbers, there were others who were to a greater or lesser extent influenced by alien faiths. Many overseas Portuguese became less narrow and intolerant than their metropolitan brothers, and they were generally more inclusive in their beliefs than was the Portuguese church as a formal institution. In East Africa, the Afro-Portuguese showed a prudent respect for the local spirit world and the indigenous specialists who managed it, accepting many pagan beliefs and superstitions. In Brazil, the spirit realm of the New World Amerindians was a reality for many, and Afro-Brazilian voodoo rites, such as *candomblé*, were widely practiced. In Asia, too, syncretic practices formally unacceptable to the church authorities were nevertheless often present within settler and convert communities – as demonstrated by the concern of the Goa Inquisition for crypto-Hinduism among Indo-Portuguese Catholics.

Nevertheless, to Portuguese administrations from the sixteenth century to the late eighteenth, and also to many individual Portuguese on the ground, religious interaction essentially meant promoting and spreading the Catholic faith. Responsibility for indoctrinating and baptizing pagans was accepted by the crown from very early in the expansion – indeed, the chronicler Zurara claimed that to save souls was one of the five reasons why Prince Henry embarked on West African exploration. At the end of his account of the Henrican voyages, Zurara also wrote that by 1448 the prince's efforts had brought some 927 Africans to Portugal, the vast majority of whom received baptism.[43] Of course, most of them were also quickly sold into slavery.

By the late fifteenth century, Portuguese religious policy in Africa was focused on converting leaders. An early success was the baptism of Mwene Kongo Nzinga a Nkuwu (João I) in 1491, only a few years after the Portuguese had made contact with the kingdom of Kongo. Although João's espousal of Christianity appears later to have cooled considerably, his son – Mvemba Nzinga (Afonso I) – became firmly committed to the new faith, which he promoted vigorously throughout the Kongo kingdom, with Portuguese backing.[44] He adopted European dress, learned to speak, read, and write Portuguese, and became personally familiar with not only the

Ibéricos em Demanda das Índias," in *Viagens e viajantes no Atlântico quinhentista* (Lisbon, 1996), pp. 138–139, 146, 148, 153.

43 *The Chronicle of the Discovery and Conquest of Guinea*, vol. 2, p. 288.

44 For the Portuguese and Christianity in the Kongo kingdom, see Thornton, "The Development of an African Catholic Church," and Anne Hilton, *The Kingdom of Kongo* (Oxford, 1985), chap. 3.

Christian Scriptures but also the secular history of Portugal. Christianity took hold in Kongo, but in a syncretic form, blending with rather than displacing traditional beliefs and practices. The cult of ancestors was subsumed in that of the saints, and even the Portuguese themselves were classified as *simbi* (spirits) from the transoceanic land of the dead. Right down to the mid-nineteenth century, the Catholic sacraments were widely administered in Kongo, and Portuguese and mulatto chaplains, military advisers, and secretaries for many decades remained intermittently influential at court; but traditional Kongolese *ngangas* (mediums/religious practitioners) also continued to be consulted along with Catholic priests – despite the disapproval of the latter.

On the other side of Africa, early in the seventeenth century, Monomotapa Mavura, paramount chief of the Karanga in Mozambique, was baptized by Dominican missionaries in 1629. This had the immediate practical consequence of opening up large swathes of territory in the interior to Portuguese traders and prospectors, which in turn led to violent protests against their influence, only suppressed after considerable bloodshed.[45]

In Asia and Brazil, the outstanding missionary order was the Society of Jesus. The Jesuits arrived in monsoon Asia in 1542 and in Brazil in 1549, and they quickly made their influence felt. In Asia, first under the leadership of Francis Xavier and later that of Alessandro Valignano, they established a wide-flung network of Christian missions. Although the Jesuits were an international body with their headquarters in Rome, their Asian missions were manned mostly by Portuguese and were run within the organizational framework of the Portuguese empire. The advance bases of the Jesuits in Asia, and most of their personnel, were concentrated in Portuguese settlements, especially Goa and Macao. However, their most spectacular missions were planted well beyond the tiny Portuguese enclaves, in such places as the Moghul empire (Agra), Japan (Nagasaki), China (Beijing), and South India (Madurai). By the end of the sixteenth century, there were perhaps half a million Catholic converts in Asia. Several of the missions appeared to be on the verge of decisive breakthroughs, and the conversion of all Asia to the faith seemed, to some Jesuit optimists, a not unrealistic hope. But in the end there was no such denouement – the Moghul emperors toyed with Christianity but finally lost interest, the church in central South India remained marginal, and converts in China were never more than a tiny minority. In Japan, where the largest number of Christians had been baptized by the early seventeenth century, the entire mission crumbled when the Tokugawa shoguns turned against the faith, initiating one of the most

[45] Malyn Newitt, *A History of Mozambique* (London, 1995), pp. 88–97.

devastating and systematic persecutions the church has ever suffered. By 1640, Christianity had all but disappeared from Japan, and the Japanese government had adopted the *Sakoku* (closed country) policy, which deliberately kept Japan isolated from undesired outside influences until Commodore Perry's famous visit in 1852.[46]

It is apparent to us – although obviously it was not to most Portuguese in Asia in the sixteenth and seventeenth centuries – that genuine conversion to Western-style Christianity could seldom be achieved on a mass scale without so disrupting traditional cultures and societies that strong reaction, at some stage, was probably inevitable. However, where the Portuguese were in a position to back up their missionaries with political power, the long-term outcome was often different. In their own possessions, or even in places where they simply had strong influence, populations were sometimes converted en masse. The Goa territories, the Parava villages in southeast India, eventually much of coastal Ceylon, and Timor under the Dominicans were all cases in point. It was in these kinds of areas, rather than in the great empires and glittering courts on which so much of the Jesuit effort was concentrated, that the Portuguese had their most lasting religious impact, creating Catholic communities that have survived and flourished to this day.

To the first Portuguese who encountered them, the Tupinambá Amerindians of the coastal forest zone of Brazil seemed to have no religion at all and therefore to be potentially easy converts. The early Jesuits took a similar view, apparently thinking they could fill the minds of the Amerindians as they might write on a blank page. It soon proved otherwise, for, of course, the Amerindians had their own cosmological beliefs, their spirit world, and their shamans. They also had what to the Jesuits were some highly unacceptable customs, such as cannibalism, polygamy, and an addiction to a semiritualized form of warfare, which they did not easily abandon. The Jesuit interaction with Brazilian Amerindians soon became more draconian, and from the late 1550s the Society sought to concentrate its neophytes into mission villages called *aldeamentos*, where they could be closely supervised and more or less forcibly indoctrinated.[47] If the Amerindians survived – and many, struck down by smallpox, measles, and other imported diseases, or by the marauding raids of *bandeirantes* seeking forced labor, did not – they usually became, in time at least, nominally Christian. By the end of the

[46] See Dauril Alden, *The Making of an Enterprise: The Society of Jesus in Portugal, Its Empire, and Beyond, 1540–1750* (Stanford, CA, 1996), especially chaps. 3, 6, and 9; and C. R. Boxer, *The Christian Century in Japan, 1549–1650* (Berkeley, CA, 1951), chaps. 7 and 8.

[47] Monteiro, *Negros da terra*, pp. 42–51.

sixteenth century, *aldeamentos* were the key component in Amerindian evangelization, and Brazil contained in all perhaps 150 of them.

Conclusions

First encounters, characteristic of the early stages and extreme outer edges of Portuguese overseas expansion, were by their nature intense but fleeting experiences. By contrast, frontier encounters were more or less continuous during all phases of the expansion and presence overseas until 1800. They occurred typically in interiors beyond the rim of established Portuguese coastal settlements, took on a variety of forms, and gave rise to attitudes and stereotypes that had lasting influences. First encounters and frontier encounters both usually involved or led to dialogue through negotiations. Especially in Asia, negotiations were often conducted in the form of high diplomacy, which could be put in motion at an initial encounter if that encounter was of sufficient moment. A kind of advanced cell would then be established from which embassies would fan out to neighboring centers, where new cells would in turn be formed, from which further diplomatic contacts might be extended. At the same time as this high diplomacy was unfolding, a parallel development of more informal negotiations – low diplomacy – was also taking place as communications grew and strengthened between individual Portuguese merchants, adventurers, and others and indigenous rulers and communities.

Encounters and negotiations soon merged into interactions. The desire to make native peoples conform to Portuguese norms of belief and behavior, especially through conversion to Catholicism, was a powerful impulse encouraging one form of interaction. But it was counterbalanced by other, more informal kinds of interaction, as overseas Portuguese found themselves transplanted into host societies from which they drew their women, increasingly their domestic culture, and ultimately many of their values. These processes involved great progress in communicating cross-culturally, especially through the mastering of mutually comprehensible languages. The contrasting and in some respects conflicting trends of evangelization and Europeanization on the one hand and acculturation of Portuguese into local societies on the other – both trends pursued more strongly by the Portuguese than by any other expanding European people, except possibly the French – led to the blooming of a series of hybrid cultures, from Cape Verde to the Zambezi and from São Paulo to Macao, that were among the most striking by-products of Portugal's overseas expansion.

Anthony Disney

BIBLIOGRAPHICAL ESSAY

There is no general work in English that focuses on Portuguese encounters, negotiations, and interactions with other peoples as such, but a good deal of interesting material can be found in A. J. R. Russell-Wood's *A World on the Move: The Portuguese in Africa, Asia, and America, 1415–1805* (New York, 1992). There are also some excellent essays in Stuart B. Schwartz, ed., *Implicit Understandings: Observing, Reporting and Reflecting on the Encounters between Europeans and Other Peoples in the Early Modern Era* (Cambridge, 1994), especially those by Wyatt MacGaffey on West Africa and Chandra Richard de Silva on South Asia, together with Schwartz's introduction.

Gomes Eanes de Zurara, *The Chronicle of the Discovery and Conquest of Guinea*, translated and edited by C. R. Beazley and Edgar Prestage (London, 1896–1899), remains the only English translation of the prime source for the early West African voyages. A good general overview of these voyages, and of early Portuguese contacts with Africans, is to be found in A. H. de Oliveira Marques, ed., *Nova história da expansão Portuguesa, vol. 2: A expansão quatrocentista* (Lisbon, 1998), Part I, and Peter Russell's *Prince Henry 'the Navigator': A Life* (New Haven, CT, 2000) is an excellent biography based on a lifetime's scholarship. On Portuguese images of Africans in the late fifteenth century, see J. da Silva Horta, "A representação do Africano na literatura de Viagens, do Senegal à Serra Leoa (1453–1508)," *Mare Liberum* (1991), pp. 209–339.

There is a good range of reliable secondary works in English concerning Portuguese contacts with various parts of West Africa. Among them are David Birmingham's *Trade and Conflict in Angola: The Mbundu and Their Neighbours under the Influence of the Portuguese, 1483–1790* (Oxford, 1966), A. F. C. Ryder's *Benin and the Europeans* (London, 1969), Anne Hilton's *The Kingdom of Kongo* (Oxford, 1985), and various writings of John K. Thornton – *The Kingdom of Kongo: Civil War and Transition, 1641–1718* (Madison, WI, 1983), "The Development of an African Catholic Church in the Kingdom of Kongo," *Journal of African History* 25 (1984), pp. 147–167, and *Africa and Africans in the Making of the Atlantic World, 1400–1800*, 2nd ed. (Cambridge, 1998). P. E. H. Hair's "Discovery and Discoveries: The Portuguese in Guinea, 1444–1650," *Bulletin of Hispanic Studies* 69 (January 1992), no. 1, pp. 11–28, is suggestive. John Vogt's *Portuguese Rule on the Gold Coast, 1469–1682* (Athens, GA, 1979), and J. Bato' Ora Ballong-Wen-Mewuda's *São Jorge da Mina, 1482–1627* (Lisbon, 1993, in French), together give an extensive picture of Afro-Portuguese relationships in the El Mina region. East Africa is well served by Malyn Newitt's authoritative *A History of Mozambique* (London, 1995) and Michael Pearson's insightful overview *Port Cities and Intruders: The Swahili Coast, India, and Portugal in the Early Modern Era* (Baltimore, 1998).

The principal source for Vasco da Gama's first voyage is the journal, usually attributed to Álvaro Velho, translated into English in E. G. Ravenstein, ed., *A Journal of the First Voyage of Vasco da Gama, 1497–1499* (London, 1898), and Sanjay Subrahmanyam's *The Career and Legend of Vasco da Gama* (Cambridge, 1997) is a groundbreaking study as much about da Gama's subsequent image and reputation as about his life. Two early sixteenth-century Portuguese descriptive surveys of Asia and Asians that are available in English translation are M. L. Dames, ed., *The Book of Duarte Barbosa* (2 vols., London, 1918–1921), and A. Cortesão, trans. and ed., *The Suma Oriental of Tomé Pires and the Book of Francisco Rodrigues* (2 vols., London, 1944). There is also much fascinating detail concerning Portuguese–Asian interactions in various late sixteenth- and seventeenth-century accounts by foreign European residents and visitors in the region. One of the best informed is that of the Dutchman Linschoten, of which there is an archaic English translation – A. C. Burnell and P. A. Tiele, eds., *The Voyage of John Huyghen van Linschoten to the East Indies* (London, 1884) – and a much superior recent Portuguese edition: Arie Pos and Rui Manuel Loureiro, eds., *Itinerário, viagem ou navegação de Jan Huygen van Linschoten para as Índias Orientais ou Portuguesas* (Lisbon, 1997). An enlightening, often entertaining, but somewhat neglected travel narrative by a Florentine voyager who journeyed widely in the Portuguese world is Francesco Carletti's *My Voyage Around the World*, ed. and trans. Herbert Weinstock (New York, 1964).

The key Portuguese scholar writing on the Portuguese in Asia in the sixteenth century and their relationships with Asians has in recent years been Luís Filipe F. R. Thomaz. A selection of some of Thomaz's more important writings is gathered together in *De Ceuta a Timor* (Lisbon, 1994). See also his informative *Early Portuguese Malacca* (Macao, 2000). Another important historian with much to say about how the Portuguese related to Asia is Sanjay Subrahmanyam, particularly in the collection of his articles entitled *Improvising Empire: Portuguese Trade and Settlement in the Bay of Bengal, 1500–1700* (Delhi, 1990), and his general study *The Portuguese Empire in Asia, 1500–1700* (London, 1993). Joan-Pau Rubiés, in *Travel and Ethnology in the Renaissance: South India through European Eyes, 1250–1625* (Cambridge, 2000), has carefully reviewed and analyzed Portuguese and other European perceptions of Vijayanagara, concluding that much contemporary travel literature was in fact remarkably well informed rather than, as often supposed, merely projecting Orientalist assumptions. A significant development in recent years has been the appearance in Portugal of an increasing number of monographs on the Portuguese in Asia in the form of regional studies. Many of these monographs have a primarily economic or political focus, but most give at least some attention to social and cultural interactions. They include, for Thailand, Maria da Conceição Flores's *Os Portugueses e o Siâo no século XVI* (Lisbon, 1991); for Burma, Maria Ana Marques Guedes's *Interferência e integração dos Portugueses na Birmânia ca. 1580–1630* (Lisbon, 1994); for Portuguese India, Maria de Jesus dos Mártires Lopes's *Goa setecentista: Tradição e modernidade* (Lisbon, 1996) and Catarina Madeira Santos's *Goa é a Chave de Toda a Índia – Perfil político da capital do Estado da Índia (1505–1570)* (Lisbon, 1999); and for Ceylon and South India, Jorge Manuel Flores's *Os Portugueses e o Mar de Ceilão: Trato, diplomacia e guerra (1498–1543)* (Lisbon, 1998). On the Portuguese in East Asia, the classic, pioneering overviews of C. R. Boxer – especially *Fidalgos in the Far East, 1550–1770* (The Hague, 1948), and *The Christian Century in Japan, 1549–1650* (Berkeley, CA, 1951) – remain fruitful sources of both insight and information, but the major overview of early Portuguese relations with China, and analysis of Portuguese information gathering in the Celestial Kingdom, is now Rui Manuel Loureiro's *Fidalgos, missionários e mandarins: Portugal e a China no século XVI* (Lisbon, 2000). For later times, see George B. Souza's *The Survival of Empire: Portuguese Trade and Society in China and the South China Sea, 1630–1745* (Cambridge, 1986). Much useful material can also be found in *Review of Culture*, 2nd Ser., No. 21 (1994), which focuses on the Jesuits in Macao and China, and in Roberto Carneiro and A. Teodoro de Matos, eds., *O século Cristão do Japão* (Lisbon, 1994), in which several of the contributions are in English.

On formal diplomatic relations and treaties, the main study is Antonio de Vasconcelos de Saldanha, *Iustum imperium – Dos tratados como fundamento do império dos Portugueses no Oriente* (Lisbon, 1997). The literature on Christian missions is vast, especially on those of the Jesuits. Concerning this subject, in addition to the works mentioned earlier, the reader is directed to Dauril Alden's *The Making of an Enterprise: The Society of Jesus in Portugal, Its Empire, and Beyond, 1540–1750* (Stanford, CA, 1996), and to a suggestive short article by Rui Manuel Loureiro, entitled "Religiosos Ibéricos em Demanda das Índias," in Maria da Graça M. Ventura, ed., *Viagens e Viajantes no Atlãntico Quenhentista* (Lisbon, 1996).

For relations among Portuguese, Amerindians, and Africans in Brazil, Gilberto Freyre's *The Masters and the Slaves* (New York, 1946), although faulted and clearly outdated, remains an evocative, almost timeless classic. However, the most important recent study of Portuguese–Amerindian relations is John Manuel Monteiro's *Negros da terra: Índios e bandeirantes nas origens de São Paulo* (São Paulo, 1994). Monteiro has also written in English "The Crises and Transformations of Invaded Societies: Coastal Brazil in the Sixteenth Century," in *The Cambridge History of the Native Peoples of the Americas, vol. 3: South America* (Cambridge, 1999), Part I, pp. 973–1023. John Hemming's *Red Gold: The Conquest of the Brazilian Indians* (London, 1978) and *Amazon Frontier: The Defeat of the Brazilian Indians* (London, 1987) remain useful, especially as sources of information, and Dauril Alden's "Changing Jesuit Perceptions of the Brasis during the Sixteenth Century," *Journal of World History* 3 (1992), no. 2, pp. 205–218, is a thoughtful introduction. Jorge Couto's *A construção do Brasil: Ameríndios, Portugueses e Africanos do Início do povoamento a finais de quinhentos* (Lisbon, 1995), and Maria Beatriz Nissa da Silva, ed., *Cultura Portuguesa na terra de Santa Cruz* (Lisbon, 1995), Part I, "Portugueses e Índios," may also be consulted with profit. On the impact of Africa and Africans on Brazil, see Luiz Felipe de Alencastro's *O trato dos viventes: Formação do Brasil no Atlântico Sul* (São Paulo, 2000). Alencastro stresses the links between Brazil and Angola as twin poles of a single exploitative system.

10

PORTUGUESE IMPERIAL AND COLONIAL CULTURE

Diogo Ramada Curto

Among the new modes of analysis in historical studies, the concept of political culture opens a twofold possibility. On the one hand, it refers to the different and dynamic meanings ascribed to their own actions by the agents involved in the Portuguese expansion. On the other hand, it offers us the opportunity to examine in different ways the meanings associated with the creation or imposition of new forms of dominion within the Portuguese world. My emphasis on the meaning of actions is deliberately opposed to any form of political determinism based on the alleged influence of various discourses or political theories. However, both political theory and political culture do belong to a more general system based on channels of information and communication, on a canon of literary and historical texts, on a hierarchy of political values and forms of legitimization, and finally on a set of political attitudes and patterns of behavior. If this typology suggests an agenda for future research, for the moment the results I seek are limited to a revision of old topics or stereotypes usually projected inappropriately into the history of the Portuguese empire during the early modern period.

Any inventory of the stereotypes long associated with Portuguese overseas enterprise risks being incomplete. Such leading twentieth-century historians as Jaime Cortesão, Charles Boxer, and Vitorino Magalhães Godinho have already overturned some of the more persistent and incorrect ideas about Portuguese imperial culture. Cortesão challenged the supposed centralism and authoritarianism of the Portuguese imperial system by calling attention to the existence of Portuguese colonial communities, from Macao to São Paulo, that were in effect small and dynamic republics. Some of Boxer's main contributions concern the social history of power: He emphasized a local scale of analysis and paid attention to different processes of decision making and practices of communication between different authorities. If his way of understanding the process of European expansion sometimes overstressed the effect of individual values in the course of history, such as the "tenacity" of captains or military leaders, one must recognize at the same time his efforts to understand the concrete sources of conflict, the role of racial discrimination, and the abuses of power that appeared within the same process. Godinho reinforced our appreciation of the complexities of the Portuguese enterprise in the Indian and Pacific oceans, as well as in the Atlantic world. He compared the role of state institutions to the activities of private traders, who were particularly active during the second half of the sixteenth century in the East; criticized generalizations about a Portuguese monopoly of trade by closely examining the contracts between the state and merchants; and called attention to the hybrid social type of "warrior-merchant," whose actions and attitudes were central to the political culture of the Portuguese empire. These three authors have provided the basis for a profound revision of the periodization of Portuguese expansion by challenging a simplistic view of imperial decline.

Continuing the effort to unsettle old simplifications about the political, social, and economic character of the empire, this chapter will attempt to suggest what a newer cultural history, attentive to the strategies and resources of locally grounded authors, might look like. Through an analysis of texts produced in six different times and places, this chapter demonstrates how various actors relied on and used ideological constructions and cultural practices to defend economic self-interest, status, or larger projects of empire. The strategies they deployed ranged from evoking medieval ideas of fealty to the king, to developing antiquarian defenses of a classical heritage, to self-conscious mythmaking involving Catholic origins or noble values. Some demonstrated respect for the societies met by the Portuguese; others reinforced an imperial order by appealing legalistically to papal bulls or theories of representation. Some sought to renegotiate their roles advantageously within the colonial order, whereas others employed various forms of resistance. Of course, there is the risk that "an excessive stress on difference and complexity reduces analysis to mere description."[1] However, the wager of presenting six vignettes as the backbone of the analysis is worth making to reopen the field to new hypotheses after twenty-five years of an obsessive repetition of single-cause explanations. Religious motives, specifically a millenarian ideology attributed to a faction in the court of D. Manuel yet at the same time said to be the main feature of a supposed Portuguese worldview, have become for some recent historians the essential means of

[1] C. A. Bayly, "The First Age of Global Imperialism, c. 1760–1830," *The Journal of Imperial and Commonwealth History* 26 (1988), no. 2, p. 34.

understanding the Portuguese empire.[2] Against this reductive view – very similar to the spiritual claims emphasized by the official colonial ideology of the Salazar regime – the Portuguese empire during the early modern period needs to be understood from the point of view of multiple causes and as a result of complex interaction between culture, tradition, and political action.

A Slave-Interpreter Wins His Freedom

João Garrido was born in an unknown location on the Guinea Coast around the middle of the fifteenth century and was acquired either by sale or capture in one of the few slaving expeditions that the Portuguese and Genoese conducted together in this era. Brought to the city of Lagos, in southern Portugal, he was baptized and sold to Gonçalo Toscano, a member of the local gentry. We know that on a few occasions he returned to Guinea on Portuguese vessels as an interpreter and intermediary. In 1477, while in Guinea on one of those voyages, he was able to deliver a petition to an unknown emissary, who in turn carried it to the king in Portugal. The petition appears to have included a claim by Garrido for manumission and a request to be allowed to trade in gold and slaves on his own behalf. Although his master contested his claim, Prince D. João, the future King D. João II, received his petition favorably and granted him not only his freedom but also exemption from all taxes on all commodities. The sole document that informs us about this exchange, the official letter, or *carta de alforria*, granting Garrido his freedom, indicates that the king was pleased to honor his request because his services as an interpreter were considered by the crown to be of crucial importance to "the public good of the kingdom [and] because he is important to the trade in Guinea from which so many benefits are obtained."[3]

Although this first tale must be reconstructed from no more than a few lines in a single letter, it nonetheless illustrates a series of large points about royal power, the character of slavery, and channels of communication and information within the nascent empire. First, Garrido's situation and action illustrate points now much emphasized by historians of Africa and of cross-cultural trade more generally: the participation of local agents in the social and economic life of the European empires, and the active capacity of these

[2] Jean Aubin, "Duarte Galvão," *Arquivos do Centro Cultural Português* 9 (1975), pp. 43–85.

[3] Sousa Viterbo, *Noticia de alguns arabistas e interpretes de linguas Africanas e Orientaes* (Coimbra, 1905), pp. 32–33.

agents to perceive and represent the encounters using European cultural terms to their own advantage.[4] Middlemen, who knew the languages and customs of both parties in trading encounters, were essential to the functioning of cross-cultural trade. Indeed, Garrido's success in winning his freedom is literally incomprehensible without an understanding of the opportunities for Africans created by a system of communication based on slave-interpreters. The political leaders of the Guinea Coast sold numerous slaves to the first Portuguese with whom they came in contact. Once in Portugal, they learned the language and converted to Catholicism. According to the Venetian Alvise Ca' da Mosto, who participated in a voyage to Guinea in the mid-fifteenth century, each ship sent to the region contained such an interpreter. Ca' da Mosto further explained that the captains of these vessels recruited the interpreters from among the slaves who had been brought to Portugal and who had learned Portuguese. The slave's owner was compensated with the right to obtain another slave recently brought from the tropics. By custom, after a slave-interpreter had made four voyages and brought his master four new slaves in return, he could obtain his freedom. The entire system was a means of promoting the instruction of slaves in Portuguese.[5] If this description is correct, Garrido's submission of a petition for his freedom becomes an assertion of his claims to justice within a system whose rules he had come to understand. Indeed, his request to the king was perhaps only a reaction to a master who refused to accept the rules of the system. The happy ending of this story seems to have been the intervention of the king in protecting the African against his master.

Garrido's story represents a particular instance of a system for overcoming the language barrier that was widely used in the discovery period.[6]

4 Philip D. Curtin, *Cross-cultural Trade in World History* (Cambridge, 1984); John Thornton, *Africa and the Africans in the Making of the Atlantic World* (Cambridge, 1992); Suzanne Preston Blier, "Imaging Otherness in Ivory: African Portrayals of the Portuguese ca. 1492," *The Art Bulletin* 75 (1993), pp. 375–396; George E. Brooks, *Landlords and Strangers: Ecology, Society and Trade in Western Africa, 1000–1630* (Boulder, CO, 1993); and Wyatt MacGaffey, "Dialogues of the Deaf: Europeans on the Atlantic Coast," in Stuart B. Schwartz, ed., *Implicit Understandings: Observing, Reporting, and Reflecting on the Encounters between Europeans and Other Peoples in the Early Modern Era* (Cambridge, 1994), pp. 249–267.

5 Alvise de Cà da Mosto, *Navegações de Luís de Cadamosto*, ed. Giuseppe Carlo Rossi (Lisbon, 1944), p. 62.

6 Peter E. Russell, "*Veni, vidi, vici*: Some Fifteenth-Century Eyewitness Accounts of Travel in the African Atlantic before 1492," *Historical Research* 66 (June 1993), no. 160, pp. 115–128; Geneviève Bouchon, *L'Inde découverte, Inde retrouvé, 1498–1630: Études d'histoire Indo-Portugaise* (Lisbon and Paris, 1999), pp. 303–310; Anthony Disney, "The Portuguese Empire in India c. 1550–1650: Some Suggestions for a Less Seaborne, More Landbased

Columbus thought that the same should be implemented in the Caribbean islands. Vasco da Gama tried to use it, bringing home some natives of the Malabar Coast. But we should also note that since the fifteenth century alternative patterns of communication had also been created on the west coast of Africa. The establishment in those lands of groups of Portuguese *lançados*, those who went native and learned the local languages, created new opportunities for communication. Pedro Álvares Cabral used this system when he left behind some Portuguese on the coast of Brazil at the end of his first voyage. At the same time, and especially during the first half of the sixteenth century, we can see the institutionalization of the work of interpreters, with their inclusion on the payrolls of Portuguese factories. Later on, in the mid-sixteenth century, the creation of schools for the indoctrination of young boys by the Jesuits in India and Brazil represented a return to the use of local human resources in order to establish channels of communication. In comparison with other European powers, the Portuguese seem to have relied on local agents to an exceptional degree. Certainly, we need to recognize the capacities for learning local languages demonstrated by different groups of *lançados* in Africa or in the East, as well as by groups of *paulistas* (residents of São Paulo) or *bandeirantes* (slave raiders) in Brazil. The same can be said of the Jesuit priests who mastered local languages in Brazil, in India, and later on in China and Japan. However, one must note the massive involvement of non-Portuguese agents in the work of translating and establishing channels of communication between the different worlds opened up by Portuguese overseas expansion. These people were also central agents for the gathering and transmission to the Portuguese of many forms of local knowledge. The full extent of the information gathering that passed through such channels remains little explored, but it may not be excessive to suggest that it was at least as important as that chronicled in the conventional saga of navigators, pilots, and humanist intellectuals pushing back the frontiers of European knowledge.

There are also other ways of looking at the agency of the Africans and their descendants. From the moment the first African slaves were sold in Lagos in the 1440s, we know that they used Catholic confraternities to organize and regulate their own communities in the New World and elsewhere. The public appearance of these groups, with their own music and dances, is particularly evident during the cyclical or regular festivals controlled by the secular and sacred powers. The brotherhoods of Nossa Senhora do

Approach to Its Socio-economic History," in John Correia Afonso, ed., *Indo-Portuguese History: Sources and Problems* (Bombay, 1981), p. 156 (case of a *lingua* working as middleman).

Rosário assumed this purpose not only in Portugal but also in the Atlantic islands and in Brazil. In a word, Catholic institutions gave to the Africans and their descendants the opportunity of having a voice in a hierarchical society.[7] In Lisbon, in the mid-sixteenth century, at least 10 percent of the population was African, and in some areas such as the Ribeira their concentration was even greater. It was from there that 200 black people who sailed to India in 1513 with the fleet of Diogo Mendes de Vasconcelos were recruited.[8] It is difficult to say whether the involvement of these Africans in Portuguese Indian Ocean enterprises should be considered optional or a forced commitment, just as we face the same problems with other forms of ambiguous agency such as those concerning women or sexual relations. In 1546, for example, the municipal council (*câmara*) of Funchal, on Madeira Island, denounced recently arrived Portuguese men who were living in adultery with African slave women. According to the civic denunciation, the men were entirely under the thumb of these women, who stole their owners' money to buy their own liberty. This in turn produced a social situation that deeply concerned the conservative men who ruled the city: too many freed slaves. If the document's account of the situation is accurate, these slave women clearly had the capacity to invent new forms of social relations.[9]

Beyond the question of agency, the story of João Garrido suggests that the slave-interpreters drawn into the net of Portuguese culture deployed for their own purposes certain political values shared with the native-born Portuguese. As has been noted, it is difficult to reconstruct the exact dialogue between the slave and the prince. It is also impossible to know how many African slaves were thus able to address requests to the king in order to improve their condition, even if one suspects that few may have done so. However, the language used in the letter signed by the prince, addressing the request of one as humble as an African slave, reveals a ruler who wanted to show himself as compassionate, benevolent, and prompt to reward good service from whomever it might come. As with a father linked by affection to his son, the language promising a reward implies a hierarchical and paternalistic society where every person is linked to the head. In Portugal, the paternalism involved in such rewards from the crown – the so-called *mercês* or *benefícios* – was theorized in the beginning of the fifteenth century

[7] Patricia A. Mulvey, "Slave Confraternities in Brazil: Their Role in Colonial Society," *The Americas* 39 (1982), pp. 39–68.

[8] Afonso de Albuquerque, *Cartas*, ed. Raimundo António de Bulhão Pato, vol. 1 (Lisbon, 1884), p. 123.

[9] Alberto Vieira, *Os escravos no arquipélago da Madeira: Séculos XV a XVII* (Funchal, 1991), p. 496.

in the *Livro da virtuosa benfeitoria*, attributed to the collaboration between the Infante D. Pedro and Friar João de Verba.[10] Here the conception of political order was shaped by a vocabulary where affective expressions of obligation, obedience, and love coexisted with the demonstration of duties and services. This political language based on rewards was centered on the figure of the benevolent king, distributing honors or nominating people for different positions and through these acts receiving the love of all the members of society. In parallel with the distribution of those gifts, the king was also conceived as a paragon of virtues, receiving counsel or advice. The Infante D. Pedro made particularly explicit reference to the king's role as the distributor of benefits in some of his letters to his brother, the king D. Duarte, particularly when their youngest brother, D. Fernando, was in prison after the disaster at Tangier. The existence of this patrimonial and personal system of rewards is perhaps one of the most enduring elements of imperial political culture throughout the entire ancien régime, molding the actions and attitudes of all those involved in Portuguese enterprises overseas.[11] The cases of Vasco da Gama and Luís de Camões searching for rewards from their kings are particularly well known, and the same can be said about those who participated in the recovery of Bahia from the Dutch in 1625 or in gold prospecting in Brazil during the first half of the eighteenth century. The habits or titles of the military orders were among the most desirable rewards requested. It is difficult to know how and when this political culture based on rewards (*mercês*), personal ties, and affective vocabulary was displaced by another. In any case, it is better to conceive of a political culture as a structure defined primarily by its continuities rather than its discontinuities.

[10] Infante D. Pedro and Frei João de Verba, *Livro da vertuosa benfeytoria*, ed. Adelino de Almeida Calado (Coimbra, 1994); Colin M. MacLachlan, *Spain's Empire in the New World: The Role of Ideas in Institutional and Social Change* (Berkeley, CA, 1988), pp. 40–41.

[11] Anselmo Braamcamp Freire, *Emmenta da Casa da India de 1503 a 1583* (Lisbon, 1907); Luciano Ribeiro, *Registo da Casa da Índia* (2 vols., Lisbon, 1954); Luís de Albuquerque, *Um exemplo de "Cartas de serviços" da Índia* (Coimbra, 1979); Jean Aubin, "'Mercês' Manuélines de 1519–1520 pour l'Inde," in Aubin, *Le Latin et l'astrolabe: Recherches sur le Portugal de la Renaissance, son expansion en Asie et les relations internationales*, vol. 2 (Paris, 2000), pp. 563–577; Vítor Luís Gaspar Rodrigues, "Sebastião Lopes Lobato: Um exemplo de ascensão social na Índia Portuguesa de Quinhentos," *Revista da Universidade de Coimbra* 36 (1991), pp. 375–388; Ivana Elbl, "The Overseas Expansion, Nobility, and Social Mobility in the Age of Vasco da Gama," *Portuguese Studies Review*, vol. 6, Part II – *On the Age of Vasco da Gama*, ed. Timothy J. Coates (1997–1998), pp. 53–80; Fernanda Olival, "O Brasil, as companhias Pombalinas e a nobilitação no terceiro quartel de setecentos," in *Do Brasil à metrópole efeitos sociais (séculos XVII e XVIII)*, ed. Mafalda Soares da Cunha (Évora, 2001), pp. 73–97.

The Holy Cross of Goa

In 1551, forty-one years after the conquest of Goa, João de Barros brought out the first volume of his history of the Portuguese overseas, the *Décadas da Asia*. This vast compilation of information about lands from Africa to China still remains, of course, a fundamental source for historians interested in the conquest of Goa. Scholars today tend to highlight its evidence about rivalries within the empire, notably between the private interests trading with Cochin and the partisans of a strong imperial system centered in Goa,[12] and of the extent of intermarriage between Portuguese men and indigenous women.[13] Less noticed is the striking account of Goa's Christian origins provided by this humanist who also served as the crown's financial official. Soon after the conquest, he asserts, an old metal crucifix was discovered in the foundations of a building within the city. When the governor, Afonso de Albuquerque, was notified of this discovery, he immediately ordered a procession to bring the crucifix to a church. After this solemn act, the same crucifix was sent on to King D. Manuel. Not long thereafter, an old Christian will written in a Goan language, Canarim, was also found. Both artifacts – the crucifix and the letter in a local language – became proofs for Barros of a long tradition of Christianity in Goa. Using this evidence in the same manner that contemporary antiquarians used archaeology and inscriptions to prove the ancient origins of European cities, he went on to construct a sort of foundation myth for Goa "because at present, we do not have another memory of the founding of this city." Lacking firm knowledge of its founder, "we take as a basis the new light of faith that we have discovered here and the architecture and civility of Spain shall be raised upon this foundation." This myth of the founding of a new social order has one of its most important claims in the recognition that "this city, formerly a place of idolatry and blasphemy, is today not only magnificent in its buildings, well defended against attack, and great in commerce, but it is also a city that has been made sacred by the holy masses conducted by priests in the cathedral and by the prayers and observances of the Franciscans and Dominicans living in the convents." In other words, the new political order – identified by the buildings and maintained by the military, traders, and clergy – based itself above all on a Christian myth. It was a myth that provided the king of Portugal all the legitimacy he needed to justify

[12] Inácio Guerreiro and Vítor Luís Gaspar Rodrigues, "'O grupo de Cochim' e a oposição a Afonso de Albuquerque," *Studia* 51 (1992), pp. 119–144.

[13] Diogo Ramada Curto, "Descrições e representações de Goa," in *Histórias de Goa*, ed. Rosa Maria Perez (Lisbon, 1997), pp. 45–86.

his capture of the city from "those pagan masses and perfidious Moors." Finally, this conception of political and social order is distinct from another, which was based on the organization of indigenous villages surrounding Goa. They were separate from the powers that now dominated the city and had come together in the past to form the court and institutional power of political leaders before the arrival of the Portuguese.[14]

Whereas Garrido's story is one of a presumably illiterate cultural broker empowered by the demands of trade in lands distant from the imperial center, Barros's history introduces us to the world of court intellectuals building an understanding of empire within the framework of learned culture. In this effort, he had numerous models on which to draw. Emphasis on Christian origins would seem to fit with the current historiographic emphasis on empire as inspired by religious enthusiasm, but the range of different voices or rhetorical tropes that Barros uses leads us to wonder about the depth of his commitment to religion as the sole source of historical authority. The author proceeds as an antiquarian in the Renaissance and humanist tradition and searches for material proof and written documents. This scholarly procedure, usually applied to the study of classical heritage, is used by him to invent a foundation myth that justifies the conquest of Goa by the Portuguese. The very antiquarian searching for documents and material traces, the methodology, becomes the mythmaker. At the same time, the content of the myth, invented or forged, concerns a religious ideology inspired by the medieval themes of Crusade and just war against the infidel. As the Crusaders had fought to liberate the Holy Sepulcher in Jerusalem, so the Portuguese in the conquest of Goa rescued the supposed holy crucifix and then created a holy city. The complexity of Barros's thought is revealed by these contradictory terms: on the one hand, the modern criteria of proof created by antiquarians and humanists; on the other hand, the fabrication of a myth with medieval roots inspired by Crusader ideology. In the monumental *Décadas* and in other works, such as the *Ropica Pnefma*, the historian of the Portuguese empire – who also served as the main financial official of the Casa da Índia – developed other interesting themes, such as the geographical description of Asia, or an impressive conception of society as a mercantile system of exchange. The myth of Crusade coexists in Barros with these other more modern themes. If one accepts such a coexistence of themes, various ways of reading his work arise, and it becomes difficult to accept that Barros believed in the founding myth that he endorsed. The same cautious relation between, on the one side, the fabrication of myths

[14] João de Barros, *Ásia*, *Década II*, liv. V, caps. I, II, ed. António Baião and Luís F. Lindley Cintra (Lisbon, 1974), p. 189.

or symbols and, on the other, personal beliefs should also be applied to a series of generalizations concerning some forms of spirituality inside court circles.

The central preoccupation of Barros's *Décadas* is of course the glorification of the makers of the Portuguese empire. The acts, deeds, and careers of many captains, including Afonso de Albuquerque, are detailed with fond attention. By the middle of the sixteenth century, this sort of praise-singing to the great founders of the empire was becoming common. Fernão Lopes de Castanheda, Gaspar Correia, and other authors competed in the same field, writing texts that established hierarchies of heroes and events. The censorship that applied to the publication of these works of history meant that these authors frequently needed to be somewhat elliptical in their discussions. For instance, while defending the thesis that every nobleman had origins more humble than is recognized, João de Barros was indirectly participating in a discussion about the social basis of political power in the Estado da Índia.[15] Similarly, Castanheda was accused of defending certain factions organized around particular families in disregard of others. Correia's work remained unpublished for reasons that are still unknown, but they were perhaps related to his defense of Albuquerque. The national epic *Os Lusíadas* by Luís de Camões had already been conceived during the 1550s but was published in Lisbon in 1572. The desire to produce an epic poem celebrating the Portuguese expansion and conquests had been expressed since the age of D. João II, but only Camões was able to fulfill the expectation. However, glorifying and celebrating Portuguese actions and heroes did not mean forgetting criticism about the same empire. Although a spate of discourses, including a range of letters, reports, literary and dramatic pieces, histories, and finally the epic poem, celebrated the empire, simultaneously they also contained criticisms of the same enterprise. Famously, in *Os Lusíadas* we have the image of the old man on the beach at Restelo, from where Vasco da Gama sailed to India, denouncing the vanity and the ignoble ambitions of those who travel overseas.

The last context that must be evoked in order to arrive at an understanding of the moment when the *Décadas* and other books celebrating Portuguese expansion were published concerns Spain and Europe. In 1548, Gonzalo Fernandez de Oviedo published his *Historia general y natural de las Indias*, where the glory of the Portuguese was diminished in relation to that of the Spanish (Books XX and XXIII). The Castilian historian could not omit mention of the actions that took place in Southeast Asia and Rio de la

[15] António Alberto Banha de Andrade, *João de Barros historiador do pensamento humanista Português de quinhentos* (Lisbon, 1980), p. 46.

Plata, but his account of these encounters emphasizes local interests and local merchant communities and reduces the importance of central Portuguese actions. In the same period, the *Historia de las Indias* (History of the Indies) by Bartolomé de las Casas included an account of Portuguese expansion that highlighted many barbarous acts of looting and enslavement of Africans and criticized Zurara, Castanheda, and especially Barros for falsely glorifying Portuguese achievements.[16] The *Libro de las costumbres de todas las gentes del mundo* (Antwerp, 1556), originally written by Boemus in Latin and translated into Castilian by Francisco Tamara, was a classic compilation of information about the different peoples around the world. In the third part of his translation, Tamara added news about both Indias, including the territories discovered by the Portuguese in the East, which were discovered, he said, by "nuestros Españoles," a deliberate melting of Portuguese and Castilians into a single Hispanic vision that Tamara justified on the grounds that the Iberian Peninsula's languages were all virtually identical.[17] Between 1550 and 1559, Giovanni Battista Ramusio published the first monumental collection of travel accounts. The initial section devoted to India included some translations of Portuguese texts but challenged the idea created by contemporary Portuguese historians of a "Portuguese Asia."[18] André Thevet's *Les singularitez de la France antarctique* of 1557–1558 and Hans Staden's 1557 travel account of Brazil similarly cast the Portuguese settlement of Brazil in a negative light. Thus, it can probably be argued that the spate of Portuguese chronicles was a response to the proliferation of European histories and travel accounts that implicitly criticized and diminished the Portuguese conquerors.

In the Service of the Crown

In 1607, the registrar of the factory of Cochin sent a long report about the pepper trade to the king and the councils in Madrid.[19] In the first and longest part, Francisco da Costa recalled his experience of twenty-one years in the service of the crown and his direct responsibilities, within the administration of the trade by the crown officials, for the past ten years. He then offered a detailed description of the workings of the pepper trade under the control of the crown monopoly, providing information on the system of weights, the

[16] Fray Bartolomé de las Casas, *Historia de las Indias* (Madrid, 1994), vol. 1, pp. 459–493.

[17] Francisco Tamara, *El libro de las costumbres de todas las gentes del mundo y de las Indias* (Antwerp, 1556), pp. 28, 328.

[18] Antonio de Piero, "Della vita e degli studi di Gio. Battista Ramusio," *Archivio Veneto*, new series, 4 (1902), pp. 5–112.

[19] *Documentação ultramarina Portuguesa*, vol. 3 (Lisbon, 1963), pp. 293–361.

various prices, the different stages of negotiation, the forms of fiscal control, the accounting practices, and the manner of loading the boats with pepper. Costa's description of the geography of the trade circuits is particularly noteworthy. These included the Malabar Coast – wherein Cochin occupied a central place – and its relations with the Coromandel Coast and Bengali port cities. Portuguese pepper trade networks extended as far as Malacca in the east and Lisbon's Casa da Índia in the west. The scarcity of allusions to Goa, the capital of the Portuguese Estado da Índia, suggests that the idea of an articulated political system under a single hierarchy is in need of revision. Whereas Cochin was portrayed as almost an autonomous city directly dependent on the political decisions of Lisbon or Madrid, Goa seems to be outside the pepper trade. Costa's description of what was presented as an efficiently working system was also an implicit attack on an alternative contract system, that between the crown and rich New Christian bankers, who were represented in India by well-known merchants. To defend the monopoly of the crown against this alternative system was a personal choice, and Costa justified it with a detailed description of the pepper trade. His political program and his knowledge of economics were two sides of the same coin.

In the second and shorter part of his report, Costa dealt with the cultivation and production of pepper. His attention to botanical and agricultural matters had a double justification. First, he knew it would be of interest to a European audience of intellectuals. Second, an in-depth knowledge of the production of pepper was crucial for those crown officials who would be involved in the trade in the future. Knowledge is one of the tools necessary for the exercise of power, and we can see how the author had already established the link between the two. Francisco da Costa presented himself as the crown official able to transform experience – accumulated by himself and other crown officials before him – into a valuable legacy for future bureaucrats. The report was the most concrete form of this legacy, one that could be used by future crown officials, providing them with specific knowledge that would enable them to compete with other agents involved in the trade, notably the representatives of the crown's contractors.

The third and last part of the report described the funeral and coronation ceremonies of the rajas of Cochin. This, too, was a valuable form of information that made the person who commanded it useful to the crown. Just a few years earlier, in 1601, at the last change of a ruler in Cochin, the Portuguese captain Garcia de Melo had needed to procrastinate shamefully when the successor to the throne, Viragela, asked him to perform customary Portuguese ceremonies for the cremation of his just deceased predecessor. The last such ceremony had taken place almost fifty years earlier, so in order to perform it according to traditional customs, Garcia de Melo had to consult the oldest men of the city. In his text, Costa describes himself as the person charged with this investigation. After the funeral rites were completed, the same proceeding was used to organize the coronation. On the Portuguese side, the new captain, Cosme de la Fecta, led the public ceremonies, which included the reception of the new raja by the municipal authorities in front of the cathedral and the raja's coronation inside the church with the gold crown given to the rulers of Cochin one hundred years earlier by D. Manuel of Portugal. The registrar of the factory ascribed to himself the functions of antiquarian and master of ceremonies, referring to his decisive role in the organization of all these events. The oath taken by the raja of Cochin, invented by Francisco da Costa, was celebrated by the Portuguese as the establishment of a relation of subordination to the king of Portugal, Philip II (Philip III of Spain). Indeed, this ceremony marked the end of a period when the sovereign of Cochin considered himself a peer of the Portuguese king. Similarly, this new oath strengthened the credit and reputation of the Portuguese nation. In other words, implicit in Costa's report was the fact that in Cochin the empire was successfully imposed at last.

Costa's report, written in Cochin in 1607, is striking for two reasons: first, for the imposing picture it paints of Asian trade, in which the actions of the Portuguese appear relatively insignificant; second, the idea of a Portuguese empire was not only an expectation but a political project that Francisco da Costa and his captain were able to institute in 1601 through the invention of a new oath. Let us examine these two different and perhaps contradictory points. As an economic analyst, Francisco da Costa evaluated the 10 percent of the pepper trade controlled by the Portuguese crown and compared this Portuguese trade with Europe with the total amount of pepper actually produced in southern India, driven by the existing Asian country trade or by the old routes of the caravan trade. From the point of view of the defense of the *carreira da Índia*, the situation in Malacca was even worse. There, the official Portuguese trade from Asia to Europe was threatened by two kinds of competition. The fact that the Dutch were already able to compete with Malacca because of an alliance with the kingdom of Aceh undermined any hope of a Portuguese monopoly on the trade from that area. At the same time, the private Portuguese traders who were established in Malacca were transporting pepper from Southeast Asia to the Chinese markets, partly replacing a network of trade once controlled by the Chinese themselves. In fact, Francisco da Costa was well aware of the role private Portuguese merchants played in Asian country trade. These private traders, mostly those who were in the process of going native, were regarded as one of the main threats to the Estado da Índia, especially in Malacca. However, for the registrar of the factory at Cochin, the relations between all the agents or institutions competing for control over the pepper trade could not be reduced to a simple opposition between the interests of the crown and private traders. The game was much more complex, and Francisco da Costa knew it well.

According to the thesis suggested by Costa, it was the aims of the traders who represented the New Christian bankers in Cochin that were in much more real terms opposed to the interests of the crown. No one in the hierarchy of the Estado da Índia, examined at the level of the city and factory of Cochin, was completely impervious to this tension. Officials of the crown were particularly vulnerable at the time when the pepper contracts were distributed to the trade-merchants, as they repeatedly fended off the offers of bribes and other pressures from New Christian bankers. Here, the picture of what was going on in the ground gets mixed with the language of moral discourse about the characteristics of a good bureaucrat, as represented by the virtues of the registrar himself. In other words, Costa's report provides not only an analysis but also a personal testimony of his services and actions on behalf of the king and the councils. However, in spite of the various ways one might interpret the Portuguese presence in Cochin, Costa's report continually stresses the importance of local agents – rulers and merchants – in successful pepper trade. The different types of local merchants held center stage. They either established the prices or, if unable to do so, sold at whatever markets would bring them the highest price. They also extended credit, and all other agents involved in the pepper trade were dependent on them. The local rulers, including the sovereign of Cochin, were sometimes able, Costa alleged, to impose their wills on the merchants, but only on isolated occasions. The registrar believed that if the Portuguese could regularly distribute gifts among the political leaders, it might be possible to assure the supply of pepper by the merchants. His description of the gifts regularly given by the Portuguese to the raja of Cochin belongs to the same kind of political theory that states that the giving of gifts to the ruler leads to the acquisition of trade monopolies. However, Francisco da Costa also knew that any Portuguese gift could be outbid by the local merchants, and by doing so the merchants would be able to break the Portuguese monopoly and sell their pepper wherever they wished.

This picture of the local merchant and the local ruler has had two important historiographical repercussions. The first concerns the relations between merchants and states in the Indian Ocean. Recently, some historians have defined the merchant communities of the Indian Ocean in the early modern period as a free-market system independent of state intervention. Meanwhile, other historians have located the key to understanding trade and power dynamics in the Indian Ocean in the links established between the merchant communities and the different forms of political organization. In this case, temples, brotherhoods, or other corporations have been indicated as the main loci of interaction between trade and politics. Francisco da Costa's description suggests a third model, however, in which the merchants were free to act using the mechanisms of prices imposed by the market while at the same time the rulers could also intervene and impose their will on the merchants in defense of their own financial interests. This intermediate model for understanding the relations between merchants and states in the Indian Ocean leads to a second historiographical discussion. The theory of the costs of protection proposed a long time ago by Frederic C. Lane – relating the use of violence to economic interests, and war to merchandise – does not apply well to the description provided by Costa.[20] For the registrar of the factory of Cochin, the costs of protection were borne by the Portuguese, but the exercise of coercion was transferred, at least ideally, to the local or indigenous powers.

If Francisco da Costa was able to portray the different dimensions of the Asian pepper trade, including the small part played in it by the Portuguese, his political imagination created an imperial expectation. I would insist on mapping these two contradictory perspectives: On the one hand, the complete description of Asian trade diminishes relatively the importance of the Portuguese; on the other hand, certain signs or actions were perceived as an indication of the larger imperial project. For the registrar of the factory of Cochin, and perhaps in the intellectual world at the beginning of the seventeenth century, there was no contradiction between what we would today consider opposite perspectives. But what kind of political imagination did Francisco da Costa possess? The economic analysis in the first part of his report links the work to the genre of *arbitrios*, or works of advice, so common in the Iberian world in the Age of Quixote. The existence of an intellectual trend toward political advice can signify three things: an enlargement of the public sphere of political debate; a maturation of the political instruments of decision making; or simply a new and more elaborate form of petitioning for favors by the king. All three are found in the report. The report also illustrates the growing importance of writing practices in the early modern period. Francisco da Costa's defense of the pepper trade as administered specifically by crown officials was not accepted by Madrid. The new *Regimento* (rules) for the pepper trade, promulgated in 1612, moved in the opposite direction,

[20] Frederic C. Lane, "Force and Enterprise in the Creation of Oceanic Commerce," 1st ed. 1950, reprinted in Lane, *Venice and History: Collected Papers* (Baltimore, 1966), pp. 399–411.

toward the contract system. The court bankers won the day. Yet Costa's strategy of addressing a report to the king proved fruitful in another way. After Costa's death in 1612, his brother was able to ask for a reward from the king based on a citation of Francisco's services. The report was the best proof that Costa had been a model bureaucrat, totally dedicated to the service of the crown. If the personal strategy of creating a legacy for his family proved to be effective, the report included another strategy for the creation of an empire. The registrar of the factory of Cochin claimed that it was through his invention of a new kind of ritual that the raja of Cochin was subordinated to the king of Portugal. In his political imagination, the strategy for creating an empire was enmeshed in the reputation of his king and the personal interests of himself and his family.

The third part of the report speaks the language of antiquarians and masters of ceremonies. This language, too, was of growing importance. The strategy of inventing rites and rituals to symbolize the subordination of local rulers to European empires was used once again more than half a century later in 1663, when the Dutch took Cochin from the Portuguese. After expelling 4,000 members of the Portuguese families, Rijklof van Goes crowned a new raja using a chaplet with the Dutch company's coat of arms.[21] Thus, European imperial expectations were confirmed.

The Maranhão Rebellion

In 1684, the Jesuits were expelled for the second time from the region of Maranhão, a vast Amazonian territory that at this time housed no more than a thousand Portuguese attempting to control a large but elusive indigenous population. The Jesuits had already been expelled once, in 1661–1662, after their outspoken criticism of the enslavement of the Amerindians had aroused the antipathy of the settler population. Almost thirty years later, the antislavery "rhetoric" of the famous Jesuit António Vieira was still recalled by a historian of the rebellions of Maranhão for the anger it provoked among the settlers, for whom the main value of the Estado do Maranhão consisted of the work of enslaved Indians.[22] As was usual in the colonies, however, governmental decrees were rarely enduring. The Jesuits returned to the area soon after.

[21] Holden Furber, *Rival Empires of Trade in the Orient, 1600–1800* (Minneapolis, 1976), p. 90.

[22] For the manuscript tradition of criticisms of Vieira's sermons, see Lisbon, Biblioteca Nacional, cód. 589, fls. 82–83v: "Carta satyrica de D. Felicianna contra o sermão q o P. Antonio Vieira prégou em a capella real pelos annos da rainha n.s. no de 1668."

Their second expulsion from the region was the by-product of a far more complicated local struggle between different factions of settlers within Maranhão, a struggle whose complexities remind us that the politics of even this sparsely populated frontier region cannot be reduced to a simple opposition between missionaries concerned with protecting the Indians and settlers eager to exploit them. In 1684, with the provincial governor momentarily away from the capital city of São Luís, the local mixed-blood population of *mamelucos* and the municipal council (*câmara*) decided that they had had enough of both the Jesuits and a group of merchants in the city who possessed a royal monopoly on the trade in African slaves. Evidently led by the merchant Manuel Beckman, they seized the inhabitants of the local Jesuit house and placed them aboard a ship bound for Lisbon. A representative of the *câmara* accompanied them, carrying a petition to the king that urged him to repeal the privileges of the favored group of slave merchants, who were accused of attempting to engross all local trade and drive up prices unfairly. Monopolies, even royally granted ones, were prejudicial to the common good, the insurgents argued, adding that "the laws or orders of the Crown may be canceled when there are right reasons" recognized locally by "the people and heads of the Republic" – a claim for the rights of the people to have a say in verifying laws that is strikingly novel, or at least not very common, within a Portuguese context. When the governor sought to return to São Luís, the inhabitants of the town refused to let him enter. Only after a new governor, Gomes Freire de Andrada, was sent out from Lisbon to Maranhão did the inhabitants of the city recognize the authority of a royal lieutenant, after a year of de facto autonomy.

After ordering the execution of Beckman and pardoning the rest of the local population, Freire de Andrada set out both to reinforce his control over the region and to advance his own career by commissioning several histories in which his successful pacification of the region stands as the highlight of the story. Remarkable about these histories is the ambiguous stand they appear to take on the revolt of 1684–1685 and its theoretical justifications. The tendency in the accounts of the first expulsion, as noted, was to stress the opposition between the settlers and the Jesuits. The political values and conflicts suggested by the second expulsion cannot be similarly reduced to a single opposition between these two groups. Three main questions will be addressed in a discussion of these histories: What were the principal political languages used to defend the new governor and what was considered to be the new political order? How were the Amerindians perceived? And finally, what was the nature of the political dynamic at that moment, which consisted of conflicts among different social groups far more complicated than the discord between Jesuits and settlers?

The *América abreviada suas notícias e de seus naturais, em particular do Maranhão*, completed in Lisbon in 1693 by the secular priest João de Sousa Ferreira, draws from different political languages.[23] References to the papal bulls that conceded to the Portuguese kings the rights over the lands divided in the Treaty of Tordesillas (1494) suggest one kind of political theory. The authority of the pope is presented as being at the top of a territorial hierarchy with kingly authority at its second level. Thus, the legitimacy of the Portuguese kings in relation to their conquests did not derive from their negotiations with the Spanish kings but directly from the pope. By the same token, once the English had submitted to the pope at the end of the fifteenth and beginning of the sixteenth century, all the claims to the liberty of the seas developed from the age of Elizabeth I could no longer be considered valid. The existence of *padrões*, or marking stones, dividing the American lands of Portugal and Spain and symbolizing an Iberian way of taking possession is parallel to the discussion of the scientific calculations of leagues in order to locate the border. This was an ongoing discussion between Portuguese and Spanish authorities that had started over the Moluccas (1524–1525), had returned in the dispute over the colony of Sacramento (ca. 1680), and would continue during the discussions that led to the treaties of Madrid (1750) and Santo Ildefonso (1777). All these references suggest the existence of the static or invariable political theory based on papal bulls, but João de Sousa Ferreira suggests that their meaning at any given time was dependent on their use at that specific moment. For example, he refers to some legal documents about the border question that had been recently discovered in the royal archives by a certain Jesuit. The allusion to this new fact creates a sense of a political language at that time shared by the Jesuits and those who spoke against them.

Another kind of political language used both by Sousa Ferreira and by Francisco Teixeira de Morais in his *Relação histórica e política dos tumultos que sucederam na cidade de S. Luís do Maranhão* is based on the model of the virtuous prince.[24] The good prince, governor, or captain should value the common good over his own personal interests or individual passions. He should epitomize the virtues of justice and moderation and create an orderly polity, in contrast to the lies of the tyrant, who is represented by Machiavelli in the work of Sousa Ferreira and by Nero in the *Relação* of Teixeira

[23] P. João de Sousa Ferreira, "América abreviada," *Revista do Instituto Histórico Geográfico Brasileiro* 57, part I (1894), pp. 5–153.

[24] Francisco Teixeira de Morais, "Relação historica e politica dos tumultos que succederam na cidade de S. Luiz do Maranhão," *Revista do Instituto Histórico Geográfico Brasileiro* 40, part I (1877), pp. 68–155, 303–410.

de Morais. The image of the virtuous prince descends from a medieval tradition and was of course criticized explicitly by Machiavelli; it can also be interpreted as a moral idealization in opposition to the realism of Tacitus. In any case, the political language of virtue is reduced to simple moral oppositions between order and disorder, justice and tyranny, common good and individual passions, or the ultimate dramatic fight between truth and falsehood. Overlapping this kind of language are references to a variety of historical situations that are used as comparisons to make sense of the events that occurred in Maranhão. In the account of Teixeira de Morais, Tacitus's Rome is the main point of reference. In Sousa Ferreira's work, it is a succession of injustices that led to the decline of Portuguese power in Asia. He draws from the history of the Spanish in the Indies to suggest mechanisms, such as the power of the *audiências* (courts) over the governors and the trusteeships over the indigenous peoples in the *encomienda* system, which Ferreira believes should have been adopted in Maranhão. If discussions of these historical situations were introduced in order to bring about reforms or *alvitres*, they were also mostly means of reinforcing the model of the virtuous prince and defining what should be considered the correct political order. The description of the ceremony of entry performed in 1685 by the new governor in Maranhão, in opposition to the misuse of religious processions by the rebellious faction, was a way of using ritual to stress virtue. In this last case, virtue consisted of and was also promoted by the proper use of ritual.

Sousa Ferreira, the author of the *América abreviada*, also drew on a variant of the common mode of European historical explanation, a view that traced back the origins of the various people on Earth to Noah's three sons. This history, derived from Genesis, had already been suggested by the Jesuit Simão de Vasconcelos (based on the work of other Jesuits, such as José de Acosta). Sousa Ferreira's purpose was to appropriate older Jesuit writings against positions held by the Society of Jesus locally and thus defend the enslavement of the Amerindians. The same body of knowledge could be cited to defend opposite positions. In this particular interpretation, biblical texts validated a hierarchical conception of the world and justified the enslavement of the Amerindians. The descendants of Ham, after having populated Africa, migrated to America; this is the reason why "blacks and Indians are similar in their vices and faces, as they show in their noses and other grotesque features, as much as in their black color, since many Indians are black, and many people from Angola have a red skin as do the indigenous people from America." The Indians of Asia, descending from Shem, occupied a higher position because they had straight hair and were organized in political units, whereas the descendants of Ham, without any form of political organization and considered cannibals, fell much below. In this lowest level of hierarchy, based on the mythology of the Bible and on strong racist criteria, Sousa Ferreira placed the Amerindians. The European descendants of Japheth, with their white color and their Catholicism, were natural noblemen who could legitimately civilize and enslave their inferiors. Yet, hereditary inequalities of ancient origin were not the only justification for the enslavement of Indians advanced by Sousa Ferreira. He also resorted to ethnography and reported on local traditions passed from generation to generation, such as the *xeramunha ropi*, whereby enemies captured in war were enslaved. The citation of these indigenous traditions in turn allowed the application of the juridical tradition ascribed to the Roman law, which accepted the legitimacy of buying local slaves after at least seventy years of practice, as it was happening in the Maranhão at the end of the seventeenth century.

Were these colonial perceptions of the Amerindians mostly elaborate rationalizations for the purpose of justifying their enslavement? Sousa Ferreira and Teixeira de Morais dedicated particular attention to the history of the laws underlying the different types of enslavement, referring to the tensions among settlers, crown authorities, Jesuits, and other religious orders. In the shadow of the conflicts for the control of the Amerindians, Teixeira de Morais refers to the constant dangers posed by the Amerindian groups. However, discourses, including works of history, are speech acts, which do not summarize all sorts of actions and interactions. Yet references to the threat posed by the Amerindians occupy a marginal place in both the *América abreviada* and the *Relação histórica do Maranhão*, which reveals more about the strategies of the observers than about the reality observed. The strongest stereotype shaping the perception of the Indians was not their violence but their purported barbarism: They live "without law, faith, or any king" (*sem lei, fé, nem rei*). To this statement, obsessively repeated by both Sousa Ferreira and Teixeira de Morais, were added different judgments and examples with regard to their cannibalism, their alcoholic tendencies, and, in the case of women, their perverse sensuality. By repeating all these stereotypes about the primitives, pervasive in so many texts about Brazil and the New World from the sixteenth century onward, both authors intended to justify the civilizing mission of their masters, sometimes designated as conquerors and white noblemen. It is difficult to determine whether this set of stereotypes or judgments arose directly from the original sources, such as the Bible – postulating a world hierarchy or a chain of being and imposing a civilizing mission on the Europeans and their descendants – or if they were already part of a special language with its own autonomy. In any case, the religious frame of reference was so strong that the diseases decimating the Indians were perceived as God's punishment for the sins of the indigenous populations. In all of Sousa Ferreira's narrative, there is no mention of the biological exchanges that occurred with the arrival of the Europeans. Another example of the bias introduced by the author of the *América abreviada* concerns the practice of abortion. Cannibalism is the only explanation he gives of why Amerindian women aborted a pregnancy – never that it could possibly be understood as a form of resistance against the power of the settlers.[25]

In contradiction to the image of the Amerindians as barbaric and primitive, it is possible to find in the works of both historians elements promoting and even glorifying their skills. The support that native Americans offered to the Portuguese during the fight against the occupation of the Maranhão by the Dutch in 1641–1642 is one of the best examples of how warrior values were used this time to glorify the brave Amerindians. The same can be said of indigenous assistance during the *jornadas*, or explorations of the hinterlands, where the Europeans and their descendants even recognized that they were totally dependent on the local Indians for travel routes, the gathering of information, and food. In one of the most radical statements of the era, Sousa Ferreira argues that "for us [the Portuguese settlers] as for the Spanish and the English, it would be impossible to know the virtues of the things in America if the indigenous had not taught them to us." The dependence of the settlers on the enslaved Amerindians was also explained by other reasons. Because African slaves were expensive and the settlers were poor, the principal form of wealth consisted of the Amerindians. This argument implicitly recommended moderation in the treatment of slaves and a comparative assessment of costs and benefits. Sousa Ferreira suggested also, at a time of seemingly permanent rebellions by African slaves, that the Amerindians ought to be the principal source of slave labor. Even if this idea contradicts the belief that Africans had a higher potential for integration into Catholicism, the evidence of contemporary African rebellions is used to justify and to praise the Amerindian slaves. Finally, as for different ways of glorifying and praising the Amerindians, we can cite the parallel apology of the *mazombos* or *filhos do Brasil*, who were described as being more prepared to make war in Brazil than Europeans, precisely because they copied Amerindian habits for surviving in the hinterlands, most notably their nakedness. In short, the *mazombos* or *filhos do Brasil* went native, which becomes a virtue in this context.

The defense of the *mazombos* contained a series of contradictions, or at least ambiguities. It was explained, on the one hand, that the group went native because of mixed-blood marriages and, on the other hand, because

[25] About the relation between abortion and resistance to colonialism, see Natalie Z. Davis, *Women on the Margins: Three Seventeenth-Century Lives* (Cambridge, MA, 1995), pp. 186–187.

the values of the group were those of the nobility and white men. A second ambiguity concerns the political dynamism that developed in particular during the 1680s in São Luís do Maranhão in opposition to the governors. The main tendency of these texts is the representation of municipal power as the defender of local interests, which suggests almost a kind of republicanism adopted by those born in the colony and elected to the *câmara* who, with their families and properties, were well established. One of the strongest idealizations of a political order based on this implicit republicanism took place during the fight against the Dutch in 1641–1642, when the *câmara* elected as *capitão-mor* someone born in Maranhão. By the some token, this quasi-republican nativism includes a defense of the *mamelucos* against the Europeans, the last represented in particular by the governors, who held short commissions of three years that prevented them from establishing roots in the colony. In consequence, they tended to serve their own interests. This concession to the feelings against outsiders is paradoxically well represented in the way Manuel Beckman, the leader of the rebellious faction executed by the new governor, came to be portrayed: His erstwhile supporters were insistently reminded that he was born in Lisbon of a German father and a mother with Jewish blood.

In conclusion, where we find an opposition between the municipal power and the governor, in situations where the former is defending the common good and the latter his own private interests, an ideal of conciliation between them persists. Therefore, there is no contradiction between the defense of quasi-republicanism in Maranhão and the acceptance of a mythical political order led by a paternal king and his allegedly virtuous governors. In 1685, the ceremony of the entry into São Luís do Maranhão of the new governor, Gomes Freire de Andrada, is perhaps the best way of representing this articulation between the proto-republic and the authority of the king.

The Great Families of São Paulo

In the middle of the eighteenth century, Pedro Taques de Almeida Pais de Leme (1714–1777) compiled a vast history of a type very different from those discussed so far, an enormous genealogical manuscript called "Nobliarquia Paulistana: Genealogia das principais famílias de São Paulo." A growing interest in genealogy was visible across Brazil at the moment when Taques compiled his genealogies. Similar accounts of the ancestry and actions of the leading local families were also prepared in the same period in Bahia and Pernambuco. What is interesting about these genealogies is that they show us how a long-established genre in the metropole became in this era an instrument for the creation of local colonial identity. On the one hand, we can view Taques as a serious archival historian obsessed with assembling documentary proofs for his assertions. He exhaustively mined local archives for notarial and royal documents that would establish family connections or demonstrate the honors attained by the individuals about whom he wrote. He also criticized Sebastião da Rocha Pita, member of the Royal Academy of History, because his *América Portuguesa* (Portuguese America) (Lisbon, 1730) did not use enough documentary evidence. At a time when the philosophical historians of the Enlightenment, such as Voltaire or Montesquieu, were depicting the Iberian empires as models of political decay, this member of the local elite of São Paulo – who probably was not unaware of these books – pursued a form of erudite history that may perhaps have represented for him a response to such images. On the other hand, many of the stories Taques told within his genealogies apparently derived from nothing more than family legend or community reports. Some of the vignettes found in his accounts of São Paulo's leading families appear to have had little function other than to amuse the reader. Parts of the narrative recount actions of family members that serve primarily to enhance their honor, and Taques often told these stories in a manner that recalls the anecdotes and small stories of the era. The work also contains what seem to be moral tales, such as the anecdote of a São Paulo resident (*paulista*) who killed his daughter in 1721 because he suspected that she was carrying on an illicit romance. Certain individual biographies appear to be drawn from memoirs written by the individual in question and thus transport into the text the traditions of autobiography and personal writing of the time. Others are evidently drawn from funeral orations and echo the encomiastic qualities of these works. The rules and forms of erudite history, biography, memoirs, funeral orations, and the anecdote all mingle together within this genealogical compilation.

What qualities constituted honorability in this colonial setting? What kinds of actions did Taques particularly highlight among the families whose histories he wrote? The essence of the genealogy often lies in creating a direct connection between the living members of a family and a distant, illustrious ancestor. Taques's genealogies, however, portray a fairly open local elite. A few families are traced back to distant ancestors of renown. Most of the genealogies, however, highlight the alliances and actions of family members in the new land. The most important criterion for inclusion in the compilation appears simply to have been birth in São Paulo. This is not to say, however, that all local families were equally distinguished. Those who had participated in the conquest of the Indians received the strongest praise. Taques exults in the defeat of "barbarous" cannibals by *paulistas* or *sertanejos* (backwoodsmen). Beyond defending the violence exercised against the indigenous people, Taques also glorifies the control exercised over African slaves by the *paulistas*. The tale of a captain who in the middle of the eighteenth century killed 3,000 Maroons, in attacks on those fortified communities of escaped slaves (*quilombos*) so frequently organized in Brazil, and brought back their ears to prove it, is recounted with evident approval.

However, the warrior able to penetrate the backlands is not the single model of action. Another figure of virtue is the exemplary master of the *casa grande* (great house). Taques's genealogies, in fact, provide a model of the ideal Brazilian colonial household, a version of the Aristotelian *aeconomia*. In such a house, the slaves lived in quarters of their own, far from the space occupied by the master but close to the livestock. The master's table was well furnished with food and a complete set of silver objects. Baldachins decorated the beds. A chapel with a triptych stood at the center of the household, and the master displayed liberality and hospitality to all who entered his premises. Meanwhile, holding a royal office or membership in the *câmara* of São Paulo was still another source of family honor, and unpaid offices brought special prestige because they showed the family freely serving the crown, an old aristocratic virtue. Thus, beyond the models of honor based on the warrior and the master of the household, there is a third that concerns relations with the crown and assumed the form of a title or an official function. The latter were considered higher in status the less they depended on state finances, which reinforced the liberality of an idealized noble. In other words, the models shaping the individual lives selected and descriptions of those lives by Pedro Taques were based upon the political language of virtue. This was the case of the courage ascribed to the warrior and the liberality attributed to the master or to the king's servant.

Above all, one notes in Taques's manuscript a desire to distance the leading families of São Paulo from nonwhite blood. One of the most prominent early inhabitants of São Paulo was João Ramalho, who was believed by other authors to have reached Brazil even before Pedro Álvares Cabral. He is known to have founded an enduring dynasty with many branches after marrying the daughter of the chief of Piratininga. In Taques's genealogy, this marriage with a high-born Amerindian woman is no source of honor for Ramalho; instead Taques highlights the titles conferred on Ramalho by the crown. Likewise, in an anecdote about a fight between rebellious Indians and one *paulista* supported by his *mameluco* (mixed-blood) sons, the sons come to be classified as "white" by the end of the narration. Taques also treats as unproblematically white the members of the Pretos family, even though their family name (roughly, the Portuguese equivalent of "black") suggests that the family had African ancestors. What is the meaning of this strategy of portraying all the *paulistas* as white men? In Jesuit accounts of Brazil from the sixteenth through the eighteenth centuries, *paulista* and *mameluco* were virtually interchangeable terms. Therefore, the claim to whiteness used to define the *paulistas* by Pedro Taques is a kind of answer to the stereotype constructed by the Society of Jesus – implicitly stated, however, because the genealogy tries to avoid the conflicts between *paulistas* and Jesuits.

In recounting the lives and deeds of the *paulistas*, Taques stresses their accomplishments beyond the *patria* (for him, the São Paulo area) as well as within it. They helped to recover Bahia and Angola from the Dutch and to defend Rio de Janeiro from the French. They opened up the region of Ceará, or Maranhão, and played a central role in the discovery and exploitation of Minas Gerais. They become, in short, central agents in the larger history of Brazil and Maranhão. Their identity stands in sharp contrast with the settlers coming from the mother country, the so-called *emboabas*. This last opposition was not created by Pedro Taques, for at least since the beginning of the seventeenth century the *reinóis* (emigrants born in Portugal) were criticized as searching for quick profit in order to go back to Portugal. From then on, it was common practice to oppose the private interests of the *reinóis* to the common good of Brazil, which was defended only by those settlers establishing roots, and most especially by those who were born in the colony. Pedro Taques used the same antithesis to denounce the governors, who, after serving a commission of three years, went back to Portugal full of riches instead of working for the common good of the Estado do Brasil.

In Portugal, the drawing up of family trees or genealogical histories was an extremely common practice, promoted especially by royal and noble houses during the eighteenth century. Whereas in Europe this typically reinforced hierarchy and aristocracy, in Brazil, the genealogical genre was used to identify local groups, namely the *paulistas* searching for a larger territory in which to spread their influence and actions. It would be misleading to see the germs of a nascent Brazilian national identity in this account of the role of the *paulistas* on a wider Brazilian canvas. Taques's *patria* remains the region of São Paulo. His text nonetheless shows how regional identities were used to stake claims against rival contenders for the wealth of the larger area. Although he depicts an open elite, rather than one defined by descent from a small number of founding fathers or ancestors, Tacques was no egalitarian either. The main characteristic of genealogy as a genre, its traditional connection with the defense of the true nobility, strongly affected the image of the *paulistas*. Valorous deeds, selfless public service, outstanding management of a large household, perseverance in serving the crown abroad, and whiteness were the virtues of this group that achieved a form of nobility through its conduct. Therefore, the *paulista* is defined by his virtues, very far away from the political ideal in Spanish America of a *creole* or mixed-blood identity.[26] Such a picture expressed a colony's resistance to its mother country, or at least to its rapacious agents who travel overseas from the mother country to suck the colony dry (a process similar to the aristocratic reaction that happened in Europe during the same period). Such a work is not far removed from being a defense of the colony and its independence, but it was not necessarily disloyal to the crown.

Goa between Colonial Control and Local Resistance

In 1751, the Marquis of Alorna wrote an extended balance sheet of seven years of government for the benefit of the Marquis of Távora, his successor as viceroy of the Estado da Índia. His political discourse is divided into three parts. The first part deals with Portugal's local political allies and enemies. The second discusses the European rivals established in India. Finally, Alorna describes what he calls the internal organization of the Estado, informing his successor about the different political, financial, judicial, or religious institutions already in place. Even allowing for the expected attitudes of a gentleman-soldier, suspicion is the word that best describes the way in which the king's representative viewed the institutions surrounding him.[27] The state council was useless. The high court was potentially opposed to the viceroy. The archbishop constantly threatened the king's jurisdiction. What then were the main instruments of government available to the head of the

[26] If in Spanish America it is possible to trace a political imagination shaped by the identity of the *criollo* (creoles), based upon memories of an Amerindian past and creating patriotic feelings, in Brazil it seems the tendency of the Society of Jesus to monopolize the production of knowledge contributed to delaying the same kind of political imagination and perhaps led to the articulation of a radical attitude toward the Amerindians by intellectuals outside the church. Curiously, both the intellectuals protected by Pombal and the Jesuits expelled by the same enlightened minister disputed over very similar issues concerning the colonial treatment of the Indians: See Anthony Pagden, *Spanish Imperialism and the Political Imagination: Studies in European and Spanish-American Social and Political Theory, 1513–1830* (New Haven, CT, 1990); David A. Brading, *The First America: The Spanish Monarchy, Creole Patriots, and the Liberal State, 1492–1867* (Cambridge, 1991); and Lourenço Kaulen, S. J., *Resposta apologetica ao poema intitulado O Uruguay composto por José Basílio da Gama* (Lugano, 1786), reedited in *Revista do Instituto Historico Geographico e Ethnographico Brasileiro* 68 (1907), pp. 93–324. However, works such as "La nobiliarquia Paulistana," using a much more traditional political language, did not participate in the same kind of debate.

[27] On an attitude of gentleman-soldiery, see C. A. Bayly, "The First Age of Global Imperialism," pp. 28–47.

Estado? According to Alorna, the viceroy must secure the "affection" of all the army officers and soldiers and the "goodwill" of the common people. Then, the exercise of power by the use of "virtues" is emphasized in the memorandum, showing how a regime characterized by justice and rewards can be established between the viceroy – who is the mirror image of an idealized paternal king – and his subordinates, including the suffering widows and orphans. In accordance with this traditional political language, and in contrast with the accumulation of imperial knowledge related to political and military matters included in his report, Alorna denounces as unreliable all the information gathered from the testimony of the local Hindus, especially if they were Brahmins. Equally, he considers it absolutely necessary to protect his successor from an excess of zeal and from the illusory ideas proposed by all the local advisers on fiscal matters (*arbitristas*).[28]

In order to understand Alorna's political discourse in the context of the Estado da Índia as it really worked, it is necessary to turn to other archival documents. For instance, one of the most striking uses of an idealized vocabulary occurs not only in the written advice of the highest political representative but precisely when the different villages or rural communities – called *gancarias*, to which the juridical status of a municipal power is sometimes attributed – addressed the viceroy. In general, their complaints or petitions, such as when asking for the removal of new forms of taxation, tend to portray the community in a state of economic depression and poverty, unable to support a new contribution. Based on the traditional image of humble vassals asking for protection, the use of this artifice is part of the same political language, in which the king is portrayed as a paternal figure, distributing rewards and practicing a direct or personal form of justice in order to win the love of his people. During the first half of the eighteenth century, the political system of the Estado da Índia continued to be shaped by this kind of language. Therefore, this idealized language of virtues could not be reduced to an intellectual construction, available only in theoretical works, but was used for practical reasons even in the lower channels of communication between the viceroy and the *gancarias*, in common with so many petitions addressed by individuals or by municipal *câmaras* inside the Portuguese world.

In contrast with the idea of virtuous harmony and peaceful integration depicted in idealized form in so many treatises, Alorna's description of the full range of governing institutions takes us inside a world of conflicts among institutions, which is also evident in other archival sources. Some of these

[28] Felipe Nery Xavier, ed., *Instrucção do Ex.mo Vice-Rei Marquez de Alorna ao seu successor o Ex.mo Vice-Rei Marquez de Tavora*, 3rd ed. (Nova Goa, 1903).

conflicts arose from the nomination to the same institution of people with different backgrounds; others arose from battles over jurisdiction between two or more institutions. If his successor wanted to escape from a permanent scenario of conflicts, the Marquis of Alorna warned, he would have to develop a militarized and populist political program. Although this advice had the potential to spark a kind of modern Caesarism, the existence of multiple conflicts between and inside so many institutions reminds us that the ongoing process of building and controlling an empire created no panoptical system, no unified mechanism of political control to be exercised over colonized and unprotected people, but a system that presented many alternatives and choices. At the same time, it is necessary to distinguish between the imperial projects and discourses that attempted to establish a normative frame and their practical accomplishment at the institutional level. For example, when the Marquis de Alorna dismisses as unfaithful the information provided by Hindus, especially Brahmins, he is dreaming about a political order very far from the one that he actually encountered in Goa, and curiously, the political projects of some *arbitristas* often contain the most dramatically totalitarian systems of social control over the colonized.

Therefore, one can argue that the set of institutions created by the Estado da Índia intended to create an imperial political order marked by the effective social control of the colonized. Some projects advocated almost totalitarian forms of control and demanded the exclusion of local or Hindu informers. However, the level of conflicts across the same institutions shows the weakness of the same imperial system. The analysis of how those institutions worked (based upon archival sources from the last quarter of the seventeenth century until the mid-eighteenth century) can also show the continuous negotiations between their agents and the populations they sought to dominate, including the different forms of knowledge created by the latter and used by the former. Four different types of institutions exemplify this process. First, the *relação* (high court) records contain many complaints by its magistrates about the high level of local litigation. For the judges, the only way to answer the judicial demands of the local population – identified by their castes or communities – was through rapid oral trials. Clearly, a judicial institution based on a metropolitan model had to adapt its functions to the nature of local demand; the constant denunciations of this situation reveal how enmeshed the high court was in a local context of negotiation. Second, the case of the army exemplifies another way of adapting a European institution to local needs and demands. The different plans for creating a native army, developed from the end of the seventeenth century onward, included proposals for the rapid rotation of leadership among the upper castes, especially the Brahmins and Chardos. The control of military forces had to be adapted to a local context of negotiation between different social groups. The municipal powers (*câmaras*) constitute a third institutional area where it is possible to see how control of the local population necessitated negotiation. This is particularly evident in the fiscal contributions of the local communities (*gancarias*), where the central authorities were totally dependent on local leaders for information and required their collaboration, first of all to organize a census.

The manner in which church institutions had to adapt to local circumstances is particularly complex and revealing. Putting aside for the moment the case of convents and monasteries related to the work of specific religious orders (and the particular case of convents that were directly involved with the question of matrimonial strategies), we need to consider the work of different types of church institutions. The functioning of the Inquisition of Goa offers, perhaps, one of the best models of social or religious control at-large, but it also included microconflicts and internal denunciations within Hindu groups and indications of persecution against merchant groups. The Inquisition's efforts to eradicate Hindu ceremonies and ritual practices were not a simple linear process of religious and social control. For example, the defense of *bôtos*, who were regarded as Hindu priests, and the necessity of authorizing their presence among the Hindus were justified before the Inquisition by a practical argument: Since they taught how to write, they could not be expelled from the area of jurisdiction because without writing merchant activities would be impossible.[29] Other examples reveal that even an institution as dedicated to orthodox control as the Inquisition was compelled to adapt its work to a local context of knowledge and to forms of negotiation. One need only look at various authorizations conceded to local communities that allowed them to practice Hindu rituals and ceremonies. As a matter of fact, in the church accounts of these Hindu rituals and ceremonies – which were related to the life cycle and particularly to wedding celebrations or to other annual festivities – the women are obsessively portrayed as dancers or as being naked as they performed their rituals of purification involving water. In the Inquisition records, but mostly in the records of the archbishop, the repetition of the same rules forbidding those rituals can be taken as a sign of their constant presence, which sometimes was directly authorized by church authorities (specifying that the Portuguese could not attend those ceremonies).

A last example deserves more attention. The institution of the Father of Christians (Pai dos Cristãos) was created in the sixteenth century. Controlled

[29] Joaquim Heliodoro da Cunha Rivara, ed., *Archivo Portuguez-Oriental, vol. 6 – supplement* (New Delhi, 1992, 1st ed, Nova Goa, 1857–1877), p. 295.

by the Jesuits and responsible for the recruitment of a growing number of indigenous priests, this institution intended to control the raising of local orphans, giving them a Catholic education in a specific house (Casa dos Catecúmenos). Following their rules, it is possible to notice that one of the arguments used in the Casa's defense was that when the father died, the widowed mother – generally assumed to be a prostitute – was unable to provide a proper education to her child. This forced enrollment is a good example of how a colonial institution imposed its power over the destiny of a clearly voiceless group by the force of law. From the last quarter of the seventeenth century onward, however, a debate ensued about the legitimacy of this institution and especially about its right to take charge of orphans without the family's consent. Once more, colonial authority turns out to have been strongly contested. The extended families of those who were taken in by the order of the Father of Christians, led most often by the grandparents, consistently fought for the right to keep the children with them. A particularly important form of resistance was flight into the backlands, beyond the frontiers of Goan territory – a technique of resistance also used to counter increased taxation, army mobilization, or persecution of merchant groups by the Inquisition. In 1715, the activities of persecution of an unusually aggressive Father of Christians prompted so much flight that the entire economy of the city of Goa was reportedly threatened. The Portuguese authorities quickly realized that "without Indians it was impossible to live in this Estado da Índia."[30] In short, if it is necessary to start insisting on the development of a set of institutions of social control (although those institutions were crossed by various conflicts), it is also crucial to notice the different forms of local negotiation and resistance that were developed even by the most voiceless groups, as happened in the case of orphans and their families. Therefore, only in the discourse of the Marquis de Alorna was it possible to conceive of an ideal political and social order excluding the Hindus (mostly the Brahmin informers) and reducing the people to a single category.

Conclusion

The six episodes presented here offer enough evidence for a general argument, one that from the beginning has been conceived as multifaceted. The explication of that argument supposes different levels of abstraction. First of all, different meanings – recognized as ideas, beliefs, ideology, languages, or culture – are part and parcel of the actions performed by concrete agents.

[30] Ibid., p. 88.

Therefore, the events and texts analyzed reveal the importance of those more stable forms of culture and simultaneously their uses in particular situations where different people interact. The middle-range position defended here rejects, on the one hand, the notion that ideas and theories operate in some kind of spatial separation from social and political circumstances, and on the other hand, the belief that political behavior is shaped solely by contingent circumstances that appear in specific moments and spaces. The evocation of the king's paternalism by an entrepreneurial African slave in the fifteenth century; the invention of a foundation myth articulating Christian and humanist ideas by a court historian of the sixteenth century; the political projects (*arbítrios*) proposed by the registrar of the factory of Cochin in the beginning of the seventeenth century; the republican ideas that circulated in the organization of the local power of Maranhão at the end of the seventeenth century; the predisposition to reinforce traditional, noble, and racist values by a genealogist in São Paulo writing during the second half of the eighteenth century; and the idealization of an imperial order based on a political language of virtues, which only existed outside of specific situations of institutions at work and negotiation with locals, are all representative of this middle-range position.

A second set of conclusions concerns an understanding of the continuities and changes that characterize Portuguese political cultures and imperial ideologies. This is a complex problem that deserves attention. At the macro level of analysis, which takes as units of study the dynamism of the oceans, the six episodes fit neatly into the general trends attributed to Portuguese activities overseas: the step-by-step establishment of a presence on the African coast during the fifteenth century, particularly the participation in the African slave trade and the development of the plantation system; the actions in the East during the sixteenth century, exemplified by the conquest of Goa, imagined as the Rome of the Orient; the debate surrounding the decline of trade and the rise of competition from other Europeans in Asia, which threatened the Portuguese Estado da Índia; the occupation and settlement of Maranhão in the seventeenth century, usually told from the point of view of Father António Vieira; the penetration and occupation of the backlands of Brazil by the *paulistas* in the second half of the eighteenth century; and finally the continuation of the Portuguese empire in the East during the eighteenth century. Although brief, the episodes all fall within the great process by which the Atlantic displaced the Indian Ocean during the seventeenth century as the main theater of Portuguese expansion (although they do not touch on the Portuguese presence in North Africa).

However, my decision to concentrate on a micro scale of analysis excluded some other macro questions that have large implications for the shaping of

Portuguese political cultures. One of these questions has been how the Portuguese or their descendants who lived outside of the Portuguese imperial structures were able to maintain their own identity. Future research should return to this question, looking at the role of Portuguese groups and individuals, such as the Portuguese living on the Coromandel Coast, the Bay of Bengal, or the Guinea Coast, or in Potosí or Buenos Aires. Another question concerns the rivalry, or in some cases collaboration, between the Portuguese and other European nations overseas. Occasionally, this rivalry took form as books and had a major impact. The publication by the Dutchman Jan Huygen van Linschoten in 1596 of his *Itinerario naer cost ofte Portugaels Indien* and by Charles Dellon in 1688 of the *Relation de l'Inquisition de Goa*, both appearing in various editions and translations, diffused the image of an intolerant Portuguese Estado da Índia, bloated with conspicuous consumption or sunk in corruption that was implicitly contrasted with the dynamic merchant companies and relative tolerance that was believed to mark the overseas activities of the North European nations. These and other printed works – never published in Portuguese – created a stereotype of the Portuguese presence in the East. Curiously, we do not find the same kind of construction and diffusion of stereotypes by foreigners concerning Portuguese America until the beginning of the nineteenth century, when travelers and historians such as Henry Koster and Robert Southey defined the main features of Brazil.

Even if microanalysis does not illuminate some of the general trends, the method has advantages when the main purpose is to understand both continuities and the processes of change. Enlarging on these six episodes, it is possible to challenge some of the most common ideas about cultural and political change during the early modern period. For instance, the first case, concerning João Garrido and his correspondence with the crown, challenges the meaning of slavery since the fifteenth century and the meaning of political representation in the same period. The possibility of an African slave addressing a letter to the king at the beginning of the early modern period – like the forms of public representation of groups of slaves and their descendants in feasts and ceremonies – contrasts with the top-down view of racism and social control over the Africans, which increased during the following centuries (as is evident in the vignettes about the Maranhão and the *paulistas*).

The second case, based on the description of Goa by João de Barros, shows that in the mid-sixteenth century an individual could make use of the humanist and antiquarian criteria of proof without any sense of inconsistency and simultaneously contribute to the invention of a Christian myth. This fact challenges several presumptions. On the one hand, it shows the vitality of religious or, more precisely, Catholic thought, even in the work of an author influenced by the classics and by the actions of warriors and nobles, as well as by the new forms of knowledge based on experience and the wheels of commerce. On the other hand, the small myth of the foundation of Goa created by Barros is in itself a good example of an idealization. It is difficult to know whether this idealized construction or literary invention was actually believed by this author and his court circle. However, as with other ideological constructions – such as the one fabricated by Francisco da Costa about the coronation of the "king" of Cochin as vassal of the Portuguese king, or the one by Pedro Taques, author of a noble and white image of the *paulistas*, or even the one by the Marquis of Távora in Goa based upon the political language of virtues – the creation of a myth does not necessarily imply a system of belief shared by its author and his circle. An idealization can be considered simply an alternative to another order, the one that really existed, at least in the observer's mind. This conclusion should be emphasized at a moment when some historians tend to project into the past as leading factors determining the actions of the Portuguese overseas, religious beliefs, particularly of forms of mysticism and millenarianism, developed by court circles.

The report of the registrar of the factory at Cochin, containing descriptions of the Asian trade and political projects to promote the Portuguese empire, raises questions about a linear understanding of the most crucial processes of change. On the one hand, the discourse of Francisco da Costa, written at the beginning of the seventeenth century, relativizes the impact of the Portuguese on maritime trade in the Indian Ocean. More than a century after the arrival of Vasco da Gama at Calicut, local merchant communities and their trade still remained dominant. On the other hand, the advice of Costa to the factory and his way of imposing Portuguese sovereignty locally maintain a clear relation of continuity with the practices followed by the Dutch East India Company. The evidence of this continuity supplants simplistic readings based on the contrast between alleged Catholic warrior countries and Protestant capitalist ones, readings that are inspired by propaganda such as the works by Linschoten and Dellon already noted. Inside the Portuguese empire, the precocious interest in trade, like the defense of self-interest based on the acquisition of riches, disturbs the historiographical perspectives that exaggerate the contrast between early Portuguese enterprises and the creation of merchant companies by the English and the Dutch.

The vignettes related to the exercise of local power in Maranhão and to the constructed genealogical image of the *paulistas* introduce another kind of problem. These few examples hardly represent an inventory of all the political languages available in the territories of Portuguese America, but they show the coexistence of different languages, each inscribed in different traditions of thought and connected with specific political agendas. The political discourses on Maranhão, written in 1692, incorporate the realism of Tacitus with the political language of virtues, the defense of a native and local form of republicanism with references to the authority of papal bulls and the histories written by Jesuits. The disparity of these languages as they emerge at specific moments is one of the best examples of the tension between the existence of a cultural tradition and its contingent use. The same disparity reveals also a tension between what derives from tradition and what is related to the ongoing processes projected into the future. The genealogy of Pedro Taques is a particularly illuminating example of this way of conceiving the relation between continuity and change. The text shows how the mixed group of *paulistas* – perhaps one of the first to claim autonomy for Brazilians – is identified by the use of one of the most traditional languages of the eighteenth century, that based upon the stereotypes of the noble and white man, which was well preserved by the genealogical discourse. Even if it remains difficult to generalize from a necessarily limited number of specific cases, a micro-level analysis of these cases captures many of the tensions and ambiguities between these forms of continuity and change.

The last situation stresses the differences between the discourse of the viceroy of the Estado da Índia in 1751, a set of institutions for political, religious, and social control, and the various forms of local resistance. The Marquis de Távora's example shows how the idealization of a political order based on the language of virtues may coexist with a realistic description of imperial institutions and international relations. The conflicts and rivalries that characterized the work of the same institutions bring into question the idea of a unified mechanism of imperial control and suggest not only a sort of indigenous assistance but also a continuous negotiation between colonial agents and the populations under domination. Moreover, any imperial or colonial order includes a range of forms of resistance, labeled either commotion or rebellion by the Portuguese authorities. In Goa, during the first half of the eighteenth century, for instance, local communities and Hindu families could appropriate for their own purposes the language of virtues in order to address petitions to the viceroy. They also participated in the work of colonial institutions, reflecting an image of continuous litigation, but their most striking attitudes consist in their open resistance to colonial violence. Historians should recognize this kind of local dynamism as a permanent feature of any imperial power. In spite of the claims for an idealized political order, Portuguese authorities at that time were forced to accept the force of that kind of local dynamism.

Finally, it is necessary to review the most common interpretations of the Portuguese empire. In very general terms, it seems that they have been profoundly shaped by a sense of space, by the awareness of geography, and by the use of spatial metaphors. A complex vocabulary has been adopted in order to make sense of the Portuguese world during the early modern period, shaping the historiographical debate in spatial terms: seaborne versus land-based empire, center versus periphery, networks of trade and communication, and stability versus movement. The six cases illustrated here can be read as a series of examples that fit in this spatial frame of analysis because they all demonstrate the existence of a variety of geographical situations, which is difficult to reduce to a single perspective. However, one can also argue that the same six vignettes – dealing with the meanings ascribed by the agents to their actions and relations – cannot be reduced to this traditional vocabulary. The channels of communication and forms of gathering information used by the Portuguese and their descendants – mostly their way of relying on and adapting the social practices and knowledge already in place – depend more on the concrete work of agents and social groups than on any abstract network. The same can be said about the various textual and symbolic forms – based on diplomatic documents (such as the papal bulls), juridical claims for local republics, histories, descriptions, or literary texts, such as rituals or ceremonies – used by different agents. If there is a hierarchy of political values and forms of legitimization incorporated by those agents throughout their careers, it needs to be understood in terms of their language and symbolic forms, which cannot be reduced to any spatial discipline.

It is not surprising, therefore, that the image of a paternal and accessible king can be used by an African slave of the fifteenth century, traveling between the Guinea Coast and Portugal; by the registrar of the factory of Cochin and his brother asking for price guarantees in exchange for political advice; by *maranhenses* (residents of Maranhão) and *paulistas* at the end of the seventeenth and throughout the eighteenth century; or simultaneously by the viceroy and the population of Goa asking for protection. The conception of a sacred order is defended in order to impose Catholicism on a city like Goa, to sustain it in the chapel of a household in Brazil, or to justify missionary activities, including the education of orphans taken under the control of the Father of Christians in Goa. The ideals of rationality and the common good are attributed to institutions as different as the factory of Cochin, the *câmara* of São Luís do Maranhão, or the viceroyalty of Goa. Finally, the central values of an old European nobility are used to identify a mixed group in the periphery of Brazil and to define the ideal of an open elite. In all cases, the social habits and the use of incorporated languages or symbolic forms determine the actions and decisions of groups or individuals, which is a context somewhat different from a spatial frame or geographical determinism.

Generalizations, however, are difficult to make when one intends to understand political culture as a set of political attitudes and patterns of behavior. The simple topdown view of social control or the debate between those advocating social forms of integration and those defending social forms of discrimination (including racial discrimination) belong to an analytical vocabulary with too many limitations, which is moreover full of the marks of a present-day ideological debate, and of little use in the consideration of the six episodes. The same can be said when we try to apply to our six cases – presented as fragments of a series arranged chronologically, starting in the fifteenth century and ending at the second half of the eighteenth century – the idea of a process of civilization. Then, the micro-historian smiles, imagining himself as another João Garrido using another language to defend his own particular interests.

BIBLIOGRAPHICAL ESSAY

This chapter follows the same lines of inquiry initiated by the author in his collaborations in the following volumes: "Descrições e representações de Goa," in Rosa Maria Perez, ed., *Histórias de Goa* (Lisbon, 1997), pp. 45–86; "A visão Europeia do mundo em finais do século XV: Continuidades, rupturas e resistências," in Joaquim Oliveira Caetano, ed., *Gravura e conhecimento do mundo* (Lisbon, 1998), pp. 23–50; "A língua e o império" and "A literatura e o império: Entre o espírito cavaleiroso, as trocas da corte e o humanismo cívico," in Francisco Bethencourt and Kirti Chaudhuri, eds., *História da expansão Portuguesa, vol. 1 – A formação do império (1415–1570)* (Lisbon, 1998), pp. 414–454; "Cultura escrita e práticas de identidade," in Bethencourt and Chaudhuri, *História da expansão Portuguesa, vol. 2 – Do Índico ao Atlântico (1570–1697)* (Lisbon, 1998), pp. 458–531; "As práticas de escrita," in Bethencourt and Chaudhuri, *História da expansão Portuguesa vol. 3 – O Brasil na balança do império (1697–1808)* (Lisbon, 1998), pp. 421–462; "As expansões no Oriente," in Diogo Ramada Curto, ed., *O tempo de Vasco da Gama* (Lisbon, 1998), pp. 59–85; and Curto, guest-editor, *European Empires in the East during the Early Modern Period*, special issue of *Portuguese Studies* (2000). In these contributions, I have tried to discuss concrete forms of Portuguese imperial and colonial culture during the early modern period, articulating different dimensions.

The first dimension concerns a variety of forms of communication, notably based upon written practices, distributed by genres and involving different forms of perception. Readers interested in the subject should take into consideration the following classic studies: Charles R. Boxer's "Three Historians of Portuguese Asia (Barros, Couto and Bocarro)," *Boletim do Instituto Português de Hong-Kong* 1 (1948), pp. 3–32; Sérgio Buarque de Holanda's *Visão do Paraíso: Os motivos Edênicos no descobrimento e colonização do Brasil* (Rio de Janeiro, 1959); Philip D. Curtin's *The Image of Africa: British Ideas and Action, 1780–1850* (Madison, WI, 1964); Margaret T. Hodgen's *Early Anthropology in the Sixteenth and Seventeenth Centuries* (Philadelphia, 1964); Donald Lach and Edwin J. Van Kley's *Asia in the Making of Europe* (3 vols., Chicago, 1965–1993) (a monumental work that should be read taking into consideration the criticisms raised by M. N. Pearson's "Objects Ridiculous and August: Early Modern Perceptions of Asia," *The Journal of Modern History* 68 (1996), pp. 382–397); Jaime Cortesão's *História do Brasil nos velhos mapas* (2 vols., Rio de Janeiro, 1965–1971); and John Elliott's *The Old World and the New, 1492–1650* (Cambridge, 1970). A shift toward a more anthropological perspective about encounters can be followed through the consultation of more recent works.[31]

There are some solid studies analyzing Portuguese sources of the fifteenth and sixteenth centuries: António Alberto Banha de Andrade's *Mundos novos do mundo: Panorama da difusão, pela Europa, de notícias dos descobrimentos geográficos Portugueses* (2 vols., Lisbon,1972); José Sebastião da Silva Dias's *Os descobrimentos e a problemática cultural do século XVI* (Coimbra, 1973); Joaquim

[31] Nathan Wachtel, *La vision des vsaincus: Les Indiens du Pérou devant la conquête Espagnole, 1530–1570* (Paris, 1971); Anthony Pagden, *The Fall of Natural Man: The American Indian and the Origins of Comparative Ethnology* (Cambridge, 1982); Serge Gruzinski, *La colonisation de l'imaginaire: Sociétes indigènes et occidentalisation dans le Mexique Espagnol XVIe–XVIIIe siècle* (Paris, 1988); Frank Lestringant, *Le Huguenot et le sauvage: L'Amérique et la controverse coloniale en France, au temps des Guerres de Religion (1555–1589)* (Paris, 1990); James Lockhart, *The Nahuas after the Conquest: A Social and Cultural History of the Indians of Central Mexico, Sixteenth through Eighteenth Centuries* (Stanford, CA, 1992), chaps. 7–9; Vicente L. Rafael, *Contracting Colonialism: Translation and Christian Conversion in Tagalog Society under Early Spanish Rule* (Durham, NC, 1993); Stuart B. Schwartz, ed., *Implicit Understandings: Observing, Reporting and Reflecting on the Encounters between Europeans and Other Peoples in the Early Modern Era* (Cambridge, 1994); Karen Ordhal Kupperman, ed., *America in European Consciousness, 1493–1750* (Chapel Hill, NC, 1995); Walter D. Mignolo, *The Darker Side of the Renaissance: Literacy, Territoriality, and Colonization* (Ann Arbor, MI, 1995). The same anthropological perspective reached a climax in the debate between Gananath Obeyesekere, *The Apotheosis of Captain Cook: European Mythmaking in the Pacific* (Princeton, NJ, 1992), and Marshal Sahlins, *How "Natives" Think: About Captain Cook, for Example* (Chicago, 1995). A challenging study of the relation between imperial or colonial structures and forms of knowledge or networks of communication deals with the British Empire in India: C. A. Bayly, *Empire and Information: Intelligence Gathering and Social Communication in India, 1780–1870* (Cambridge, 1997).

Barradas de Carvalho's *À la recherche de la spécificité de la Renaissance Portugaise* (2 vols., Paris, 1983); José V. de Pina Martins's *Humanisme et Renaissance de l'Italie au Portugal: Les deux regards de Janus* (2 vols., Paris, 1989); Vitorino Magalhães Godinho's *Mito e Mercadoria, Utopia e prática de navegar: Séculos XIII–XVIII* (Lisbon, 1990); Luís de Matos's *L'expansion Portugaise dans la littérature Latine de la Renaissance* (Lisbon, 1991); Sylvie Deswarte-Rosa's *Ideias e imagens em Portugal na época dos descobrimentos: Francisco de Holanda e a teoria da arte* (Lisbon, 1992); and Luciana Stegagno Picchio's *Mar Aberto: Viagens dos Portugueses* (Lisbon, 1999). Studies about literature in Colonial Brazil should start with António Candido's *Formação da literatura Brasileira: Momentos decisivos* (2 vols., São Paulo, 1959); Sérgio Buarque de Holanda's *Capítulos de literatura colonial*, ed. António Cândido (São Paulo, 1991); Alfredo Bosi's *Dialéctica da colonização* (São Paulo, 1992); João Adolfo Hansen's *A sátira e o Engenho: Gregório de Matos e a Bahia do século XVII* (São Paulo, 1989); Alcir Pécora's *Teatro do Sacramento: A unidade teológico-retórica-política dos sermões de António Vieira* (São Paulo, 1994); and Ivan Teixeira's *Mecenato Pombalino e poesia neoclássica* (São Paulo, 1999). Other recent and innovative studies inspired by an anthropological perspective deserve particular attention: Laura de Mello e Souza's *Inferno Atlântico: Demonologia e colonização séculos XVI–XVIII* (São Paulo, 1993); Ronaldo Vainfas's *Ideologia e escravidão: OS letrados e a sociedade escravista no Brasil colonial* (Petrópolis, 1998) and *A Heresia dos Índios: Catolicismo e rebeldia no Brasil colonial* (São Paulo, 1995); Inès G. Zupanov's *Disputed Mission: Jesuit Experiments and Brahmanical Knowledge in Seventeenth Century India* (New Delhi, 1999); and Joan-Pau Rubiés's *Travel and Ethnology in the Renaissance: South India through European Eyes, 1250–1625* (Cambridge, 2000).

Another dimension concerns the relation between politics and ideology, including the role of individuals, specific social groups, and institutions.[32]

[32] Studies in this field are particularly developed in relation to Spanish America and they should be used as a pattern of comparison. Readers should take into consideration the following studies: J. H. Parry, *The Spanish Theory of Empire in the Sixteenth Century* (Cambridge, 1940); C. H. Haring, *The Spanish Empire in America* (New York, 1947); Luis Weckmann, *Constantino el Grande y Cristóbal Colón: Estudio de la supremacia papal sobre las islas (1091–1493)*, introduction by Ernst H. Kantorowicz (Mexico, 1992; 1st ed., 1949); Lewis Hanke, *The Spanish Struggle for Justice in the Conquest of America* (Philadelphia, 1949); Marcel Bataillon, *Études sur Bartolomé de las Casas* (Paris, 1966); Irving A. Leonard, *Books of the Brave: Being an Account of Books and of Men in the Spanish Conquest and Settlement of the Sixteenth-Century New World*, introduction by Rolena Adorno (Berkeley, CA, 1992; 1st ed., 1949). The reading of these classics should be followed by more recent studies in the domain of political ideas: Colin M. MacLachlan, *Spain's Empire in the New World: The Role of Ideas in Institutional and Social Change* (Berkeley, CA, 1988); Anthony Pagden,

Studies in this field in the context of the Portuguese empire belong to different traditions. Unifying perspectives should be found in the general tendency to focus on the work of specific institutions or to follow political events.

The financial organization of the state, including mercantilism, state monopolies, the role of contractors (*asientistas*), and the creation of companies, has been studied in João Lúcio de Azevedo's *Épocas de Portugal económico* (Lisbon, 1929); Vitorino Magalhães Godinho's *Os descobrimentos e a economia mundial* (4 vols., Lisbon, 1981–1983; 1st ed., 2 vols., 1963–1971) and *Les finances de l'état Portugais des Indes Orientales* (Paris, 1982); Manuel Nunes Dias's *O capitalismo monárquico Português (1415–1549): Contribuição para o estudo das origens do capitalismo moderno* (2 vols., Coimbra, 1963–1964) and *Fomento e mercantilismo: A companhia geral do Grão Pará e Maranhão (1755–1779)* (2 vols., Pará, 1970); Anthony Disney's *Twilight of the Pepper Trade: Portuguese Trade in Southwest India in the Early Seventeenth Century* (Cambridge, MA, 1978); James C. Boyajian's *Portuguese Trade in Asia under the Habsburgs, 1580–1640* (Baltimore, 1993); Evaldo Cabral de Mello's *Olinda Restaurada: Guerra*

Spanish Imperialism and the Political Imagination: Studies in European and Spanish-American Social and Political Theory, 1513–1830 (New Haven, CT, 1990); and James Muldoon, *The Americas in the Spanish World Order: The Justification for Conquest in the Seventeenth Century* (Philadelphia, 1994).

The emphasis on the domain of political ideas should be balanced by the reading of analyses of imperial institutions, local answers, and forms of resistance. See Charles Gibson, *The Aztecs under Spanish Rule: A History of the Indians of the Valley of Mexico, 1519–1810* (Stanford, CA, 1991; 1st ed., 1964); Steven J. Stern, *Peru's Indian Peoples and the Challenge of Spanish Conquest: Huamanga to 1640* (Madison, WI, 1982); Karen Spalding, *Huarochirí: An Andean Society under Inca and Spanish Rule* (Stanford, CA, 1984); Nancy M. Farriss, *Maya Society under Colonial Rule: The Collective Enterprise of Survival* (Princeton, NJ, 1984); and Steven J. Stern, ed., *Resistance, Rebellion, and Consciousness in the Andean Peasant World 18th to 20th Centuries* (Madison, WI, 1987). Perhaps the most balanced synthesis of ideology and political action concerning Spanish America is in Brading, *The First America: The Spanish Monarchy, Creole Patriots and the Liberal State, 1492–1866* (Cambridge, 1991). Niels Steensgaard's *The Asian Trade Revolution of the Seventeenth Century: The East India Companies and the Decline of the Caravan Trade* (Chicago, 1974) and Om Prakash's *European Commercial Enterprise in Pre-colonial India*, in *The New Cambridge History of India*, vol. 2, Part V (Cambridge, 1998), are the best introductions to a comparison between the Portuguese Estado da Índia and other European trading companies. Batavia offers an interesting comparative example of a Dutch colonial city. See Jean Gelman Taylor, *The Social World of Batavia: European and Eurasian in Dutch Asia* (Madison, WI, 1983); Leonard Blussé, *Strange Company: Chinese Settlers, Mestizo Women, and the Dutch in VOC Batavia* (Providence, 1988). The British empire has been the object of new and very challenging studies. See C. A. Bayly, *Imperial Meridian: The British Empire and the World, 1780–1830* (Essex, 1989); Thomas R. Metcalf, *The Ideologies of the Raj*, in *The New Cambridge History of India*, vol. 3, Part IV (Cambridge, 1995); and David Armitage, *The Ideological Origins of the British Empire* (Cambridge. 2000).

e Açúcar no nordeste, 1630–1654 (Rio de Janeiro, 1975), pp. 103–189; Carl A. Hanson's *Economy and Society in Baroque Portugal, 1668–1703* (Minneapolis, 1981); Dorival Teixeira Vieira's "Política financeira," in *Historia geral da civilização Brasileira*, ed. Sérgio Buarque de Holanda, vol. 1, Part II (São Paulo, 1960), pp. 340–351; Arthur Cézar Ferreira Reis's "O comércio colonial e as companhias privilegiadas," in Buarque de Holanda, *História geral da civilização Brasiliera*, vol. 1, Part II, pp. 311–339; António Carreira's *As companhias Pombalinas de Grão Pará e Maranhão e Pernambuco e Paraíba*, 2nd ed. (Lisbon, 1983); and Jorge Pedreira's *Estrutura industrial e mercado colonial: Portugal e Brasil, 1780–1830* (Linda a Velha, 1994).

Institutions such as factories, captaincies, and fortresses have been analyzed in Capistrano de Abreu's *Chapters of Brazil's Colonial History, 1500–1800*, with an introduction by Stuart B. Schwartz (New York, 1997); Panduronga S. S. Pissurlencar's *Regimentos das fortalezas da Índia* (Bastorá-Goa, 1951); Alexandre Lobato's *Estudos Moçambicanos: Evolução administrativa e económica de Moçambique, 1752–1763, vol. 1 – Fundamentos da criação do governo geral em 1752* (Lisbon, 1957); Charles R. Boxer and Carlos de Azevedo's *A fortaleza de Jesus e os Portugueses de Mombaça* (Lisbon, 1960); Virgínia Rau's *Feitores e feitorias "Instrumentos" do comércio internacional Português no século XVI* (Lisbon, 1966); Luís Filipe Thomaz's *De Ceuta a Timor* (Carnaxide, 1994), pp. 291–402, chap. 8 – "De Malaca a Pegu" (reedition of two studies first published in 1966 and 1976); Maria Emília Madeira Santos's "Afonso de Albuquerque e os feitores," in Luís de Albuquerque and Inácio Guerreiro, eds., *II Seminário Internacional de História Indo-Portuguesa: Actas* (Lisbon, 1985), pp. 201–226; J. Bato'ora Ballong-Wen-Mewuda's *São Jorge da Mina, 1482–1637* (Lisbon, 1993); António Vasconcelos Saldanha's *As capitanias do Brasil: Antecedentes, desenvolvimento e extinção de um fenómeno Atlântico* (Lisbon, 2001; 1st ed., 1992); and José Manuel Correia's *Os Portugueses no Malabar (1498–1580)* (Lisbon, 1997).

Portuguese colonial cities offer another field of studies. Charles R. Boxer's *Portuguese Society in the Tropics: The Municipal Councils of Goa, Macao, Bahia, and Luanda, 1510–1800* (Madison, WI, 1965) remains a masterpiece. However, it would be necessary to integrate this book in a longer and complex tradition emphasizing the importance of local structures of power, well represented by the works of João Lúcio de Azevedo, *Os Jesuítas no Grão-Pará: Suas missões e a colonização*, 2nd ed. (Coimbra, 1930), pp. 149–185, Jaime Cortesão, *História dos descobrimentos Portugueses*, vol. 1 (Lisbon, 1975), pp. 218–237, and "Goa nos princípios do século XVII, como criação urbana mais típica do império Português," in Cortesão, *O império Português no Oriente* (Lisbon, 1968), pp. 241–278. Goa and its territory have been studied in Felipe Nery Xavier's *Bosquejo historico das communidades das aldeias dos concelhos das Ilhas, salsete e bardez*, ed. José Maria de Sá and J. B. Amâncio Gracias (Bastorá, 1903); J. H. da Cunha Rivara's *Brados a favor das comunidades das aldeias do Estado da Índia* (Nova-Goa, 1870); P. S. S. Pissurlencar's *Tombo da ilha de Goa e das terras de salcete e bardes* (Bastorá, 1952); Teotónio R. de Souza's *Medieval Goa: A Socio-economic History* (New Delhi, 1979); Thomaz's *De Ceuta a Timor*, pp. 245–289; Michael Pearson's "The Portuguese in India," in *New Cambridge History of India*, vol. 1, Part 1 (Cambridge, 1987), pp. 87–115; Maria de Jesus dos Mártires Lopes's *Goa setecentista: Tradição e modernidade (1750–1800)* (Lisbon, 1996); and Catarina Madeira Santos's *"Goa é a chave de toda a Índia" perfil político da capital do Estado da Índia (1505–1570)* (Lisbon, 1999). The history of Macao has been traced in George Bryan de Souza's *The Survival of Empire: Portuguese Trade and Society in China and the South China Sea, 1630–1754* (Cambridge, 1986); Pierre–Yves Manguin's *Os Nguyen Macau e Portugal: Aspectos políticos e comerciais de uma relação privilegada no Mar da China, 1773–1802* (Macao, 1999); and António H. de Oliveira Marques, ed., *História dos Portugueses no Extremo Oriente*, vol. 1, Parts I and II; vol. 2; vol. 3 (Lisbon, 1998–2001). For Malacca, see Paulo Jorge de Sousa Pinto's *Portugueses e Malaios: Malaca e os sultanatos de Johor e Achém, 1575–1619* (Lisbon, 1997). With regard to Portuguese colonial cities within the Estado da Índia, one should take into consideration two small articles by Anthony Disney: "The Portuguese Empire in India c. 1550–1650: Some Suggestions for a Less Seaborne, More Landbased Approach to Its Socio-economic History," in John Correia Afonso, ed., *Indo-Portuguese History: Sources and Problems* (Bombay, 1981), pp. 148–162; and "Contrasting Models of Empire: The *Estado da Índia* in South Asia and East Asia in the Sixteenth and Early Seventeenth Centuries," in Francis Dutra and João Camilo dos Santos, eds., *The Portuguese in the Pacific* (Santa Barbara, CA, 1995), pp. 26–37. The relation between cities (or fortresses) and their hinterland and the configurations of power between social groups guided by commercial interests or factional divisions are brilliantly analyzed for Mozambique in Allen Isaacman's *Mozambique: The Africanisation of a European Institution, the Zambezi Prazos, 1750–1902* (Madison, WI, 1972); and Malyn Newitt's *A History of Mozambique* (Bloomington, IN, 1995).

Studies of colonial cities of Brazil can be read in a comparative frame, for which see Gilbert M. Joseph and Mark D. Szuchman's *I Saw a City Invincible: Urban Portraits of Latin America* (Wilmington, DE, 1996). A selection should start with John Monteiro's *Negros da terra: Índios e bandeirantes nas origens de São Paulo* (São Paulo, 1994). For Bahia, See John Russell-Wood's *Fidalgos and Philanthropists: The Santa Casa da Misericórdia of Bahia, 1550–1755* (Berkeley, CA, 1968); and Stuart B. Schwartz's *Sovereignty and Society in Colonial Brazil: The High Court of Bahia and Its Judges, 1609–1751* (Berkeley,

CA, 1973) and *Sugar Plantations in the Formation of Brazilian Society: Bahia, 1550–1835* (Cambridge, 1985). For Minas Gerais, see Laura de Mello e Souza's *Desclassificados do ouro: A pobreza mineira no século XVIII*, 3rd ed. (Rio de Janeiro, 1990); Luciano Figueiredo's *O avesso da memória: Cotidiano e trabalho da Mulher em Minas Gerais no século XVIII* (Rio de Janeiro, 1993); and John Russell-Wood's "Local Government in Portuguese America: A Study in Cultural Divergence," in his *Society and Government in Colonial Brazil, 1500–1822* (Aldershot, 1992), pp. 187–231. For Pernambuco, see Evaldo Cabral de Mello's *A Fronda dos Mazombos: Nobres conta mascates, Pernambuco, 1666–1715* (São Paulo, 1995).

Analyses of political events involving the Portuguese empire tend to concentrate on internal debates regarding different projects of reform as much as on diplomatic relations or military actions. Portuguese historian Jorge Borges de Macedo offers particularly good examples of this type of analysis. From his vast bibliography full of ideological projections and manipulations, two books are particularly important: *Um Caso de Luta pelo Poder e a sua interpretação "Os Lusíadas"* (Lisbon, 1976); and *História diplomática Portuguesa: Constantes e linhas de força* (Lisbon, 1982). Panduronga S. S. Pissurlencar's *Agentes da diplomacia Portuguesa na Índia (Hindus, Muçulmanos, Judeus e Parses)* (Bastorá-Goa, 1952) remains a masterpiece. Jean Aubin's interest in political history has had a tremendous impact by his insistence on a return to chronology based on kingdoms, the study of diplomatic relations, and establishing relations between court factions and ideologies. See the compilation of his articles in *Le Latin et L'Astrolabe: Recherches sur le Portugal de la Renaissance, son expansion en Asie et les relations internationales* (2 vols., Paris, 1996–2000). The fact that Aubin came to the Estado da Índia as a former student of the Safavid empire enabled him to emphasize a non-Eurocentric perspective as well as a philological approach toward documents in a variety of languages. But this point of view was perhaps more coherently developed in Denys Lombard's masterpiece *Le carrefour Javanais: Essais d'histoire globale* (3 vols., Paris, 1990). Following similar lines of inquiry, Luís Filipe Thomaz is the most dynamic of the students of Aubin and Lombard and the author of many important works, including *De Ceuta a Timor*, especially pp. 1–244; *A questão da Pimenta em meados do século XVI: Um debate político do governo de D. João de Castro* (Lisbon, 1998); and as coauthor with Geneviève Bouchon, *Voyage dans les Deltas du Gange et de l'Irraouaddy: Relation Portugaise anonyme (1521)* (Paris, 1988). Thomaz's article "Estrutura política e administrativa do Estado da Índia no século XVI," originally published in 1985, was adapted, translated, and coedited into English by Sanjay Subrahmanyam as "Evolution of Empire: The Portuguese in the Indian Ocean during the Sixteenth Century," in James Tracy, ed., *The Political Economy of Merchant Empires: State*

Power and World Trade, 1350–1750 (Cambridge, 1991), pp. 298–331. Over the years, Subrahmanyam has translated into English the ideas of Aubin and Thomaz and has tried to use them to write larger syntheses, as in his *The Portuguese Empire in Asia, 1500–1700: A Political and Economic History* (London, 1993); see also his edited volume *Sinners and Saints: The Successors of Vasco da Gama* (New Delhi, 2000; 1st ed., 1995). Interesting examples of studies under the supervision of Thomaz are: Maria Ana Marques Guedes, *Integração e Interferência dos Portugueses na Birmânia ca. 1580–1630* (Lisbon, 1994); Jorge Flores, *Os Portugueses e o Mar de Ceilão: Trato, diplomacia e guerra (1498–1543)* (Lisbon, 1998); Jorge Manuel dos Santos Alves, *O domínio do norte de Samatra: A história dos sultanatos de Samudera – Pacém e de Achém, e das suas relações com os Portugueses (1500–1580)* (Lisbon, 1999); and Manuel Lobato, *Política e comércio dos Portugueses na Insulíndia: Malaca e as Molucas de 1575 a 1605* (Macao, 1999).

Another selection of biographies, analyses of political events, or studies of diplomatic relations should take into consideration the early modern period. Peter Russell has published an interesting biography: *Prince Henry "the Navigator": A Life* (New Haven, CT, 2001). Charles Boxer's biographies provide interesting models, as we can see in his *Salvador de Sá and the Struggle for Brazil and Angola, 1602–1686* (London, 1952) or *Francisco Vieira de Figueiredo: A Portuguese Merchant-Adventurer in South East Asia, 1624–1667* (The Hague, 1967). The same can be said about J. A. Gonsalves de Mello's *João Fernandes Vieira* (2 vols., Recife, 1956); Dauril Alden's *Royal Government in Colonial Brazil, with Special Reference to the Administration of the Marquis of Lavradio, Viceroy 1769–1779* (Berkeley, CA, 1968); and Francis Dutra's *Matias de Albuquerque: A Seventeeth Century Capitão-Mor of Pernambuco and Governor General of Brazil* (Ann Arbor, MI, 1969). Treaties and diplomatic relations have been treated in a series of collective volumes and in specific books: Luis Antonio Ribot Garcia, ed., *Congresso Internacional de Historia El Tratado de Tordesillas y su Epoca* (3 vols., Madrid, 1995); Avelino Teixeira da Mota, ed., *A viagem de Fernão de Magalhães e a questão das Molucas: Actas do II Congresso Luso-Espanhol de História Luso-Ultramarina* (Lisbon, 1975); Charles Martial de Witte, *La correspondance des premiers nonces permanentes au Portugal, 1532–1553* (2 vols., Lisbon, 1980–1986); Geoffrey Parker, "David or Goliath? Philip II and His World in the 1580s," in Richard Kagan and Geoffrey Parker, eds., *Spain, Europe and the Atlantic World: Essays in Honour of John H. Elliott* (Cambridge, 1995), pp. 245–266; António Vasconcelos de Saldanha, *Iustum imperium: Dos tratados como fundamento do império dos Portugueses no Oriente: Estudo de história do direito internacional e do direito Português* (Lisbon, 1997); Evaldo Cabral de Mello, *O negócio do Brasil: Portugal, os países baixos e o nordeste, 1641–1669* (Rio de Janeiro, 1998); Luís Ferrand de Almeida, *A colónia do Sacramento na época da sucessão de Espanha* (Coimbra, 1973); André Ferrand de Almeida,

A formação do espaço Brasileiro e o projecto do novo atlas da América Portuguesa (1713–1748) (Lisbon, 2001); Jaime Cortesão, *Alexandre de Gusmão e o tratado de Madrid* (9 vols., Rio de Janeiro, 1950–1963); and Charles R. Boxer, ed., *A Descriptive List of the State Papers of Portugal, 1661–1780, in the Public Record Office, London* (3 vols., Lisbon and London, 1979–1983).

Efforts to discuss and define what is a colonial identity have been made mostly in Brazil. A selection of the more important studies should include Oliveira Viana's *Populações meridionais do Brasil* (2 vols., Rio de Janeiro, 1952; 1st ed., vol. 1, 1918); Gilberto Freyre's *Casa Grande e Senzala: Formação da famiglia Brasileira sob o regimen de economia patriarchal* (Rio de Janeiro, 1933); Sérgio Buarque de Holanda's *Raizes do Brasil* (Rio de Janeiro, 1936); Caio Prado Júnior's *Evolução política do Brasil e outros estudos* (São Paulo, 1953); Fernando A. Novais's *Portugal e Brasil na Crise do antigo sistema colonial*, 2nd ed. (São Paulo, 1979); Evaldo Cabral de Mello's *Rubro Veio: O imaginário da Restauração Pernambucana* (Rio de Janeiro, 1997) and *O nome e o sangue: Uma parábola familiar no Pernambuco colonial* (São Paulo, 1989); F. J. C. Falcon's *A época Pombalina: Politica, economia e monarquia ilustrada* (São Paulo, 1982); Carlos Guilherme Mota's *Atitudes de inovação no Brasil, 1789–1801* (Lisbon, 1967); Kenneth R. Maxwell's "The Generation of the 1790s and the Idea of Luso-Brazilian Empire," in Dauril Alden, ed., *Colonial Roots of Modern Brazil* (Berkeley, CA, 1973), pp. 107–144, and Maxwell's *Conflicts and Conspiracies: Brazil and Portugal, 1750–1808* (Cambridge, 1973); John Russell-Wood, ed., *From Colony to Nation: Essays on the Independence of Brazil* (Baltimore, 1975); and Stuart B. Schwartz's "The Formation of a Colonial Identity in Brazil," in Nicholas Canny and Anthony Pagden, eds., *Colonial Identity in the Atlantic World, 1500–1800* (Princeton, NJ, 1987), pp. 15–50. To this list must be added three collective volumes: João José Reis and Flávio dos Santos Gomes, eds., *Liberdade por um fio: História dos quilombos no Brasil* (São Paulo, 1996); Fernando A. Novais, gen. ed., *História da vida privada no Brasil, vol. 1* – Laura de Mello e Souza, ed., *Cotidiano e vida privada na América Portuguesa* (São Paulo, 1997); and Ronaldo Vainfas, ed., *Dicionário do Brasil colonial, 1500–1808* (Rio de Janeiro, 2000).

11

LANGUAGE AND LITERATURE IN THE PORTUGUESE EMPIRE

Luís de Sousa Rebelo

The capture of Ceuta in Morocco signaled the beginning of Portuguese expansion overseas. The reporting of this and similar events was made possible by the decision of the court to appoint an official chronicler. The conditions under which the dynasty of Avis had emerged required an explanation and a full account of its foundation, for the mechanisms of succession had been altered by the ascent of Dom João I (1385–1433). He was an illegitimate son and the most unlikely successor to Dom Fernando, his half-brother, when Dom Fernando died in 1383. The appointment of a chronicler carried forward an old tradition of court scribes that went back to Alfonso the Wise, king of Léon and Castile (1221–1284). Alfonso was the author of the *General Estoria* (General History), a work that served throughout the Iberian Peninsula as a source of information on the histories of its kings and the peoples under their rule.

The traditional importance of historiography in Portuguese letters was enhanced by the new need to report on the events of oceanic expansion and on the contacts established with new peoples. Portuguese prose was thus faced with the challenge of describing new things and new customs. On the other hand, Portuguese chroniclers also developed a discourse on the legitimacy of political power. This makes historiography a good subject with which to start the study of the language in its informative and creative expression.

The court chronicler of Dom João I, Fernão Lopes (ca. 1380–1459), relied on this tradition when he produced the chronicles of three kings, covering the period that led up to Dom João's succession. Being a writer of genius, his chronicles are literary masterpieces. With remarkable realism and psychological insight he describes palace intrigues and the agitation of the people in the streets during the political crisis that occurred between

1383 and 1385. He develops the argument that the choice of the new king was providential, endowing the king with a charisma that reflected divine approval. The overseas policy of the dynasty of Avis becomes in his hands a kind of mission that would be embraced by the whole country.

Gomes Eanes de Zurara (ca. 1410–1470), who succeeded Fernão Lopes as chronicler, continued to stress this effect in his *Crónica da Tomada de Ceuta* (Chronicle of the Seizure of Ceuta). The concern with prophecy as a rhetorical and ideological device to keep the logic of the narrative focused on the messianic figure of the new king is in evidence in this chronicle. Unlike Fernão Lopes, Zurara was not a gifted writer and his style is at times rather heavy, overlaid with a disconcerting erudition that has little to do with his subject. But he included in his narrative an episode that sealed the destiny of Portuguese expansion.

To prepare the assault on the city and study its defenses, Dom João I had sent a delegation to the court of Sicily with the apparent intention of marrying one of his sons to the queen, knowing she would not accept him since he was not the heir to the throne. On his return with the delegation, one of the ambassadors told the king he knew that Ceuta would soon be Portuguese. He told the king of an earlier encounter in North Africa, near Ceuta, with an old Moor, who had asked him how many sons King Dom Pedro had. When the Moor was reminded of Dom João, the master of Avis, he cried, for he knew the city would fall to the Christians the day the master became king.

The link between this chronicle and the chronicle of Dom Pedro by Fernão Lopes may have been provided by Fernão Lopes himself when he was preparing the sequel to his work. Zurara probably used his drafts, thus retaining a coherence of discourse that announced the future of Portuguese expansion. At the same time, the reader is often reminded by the author that Dom João I himself did not pay any attention to prophecies or omens. This paradox had the effect of reiterating the charismatic character of the new dynasty while putting an end to further Messianic expectations.

Zurara also wrote the chronicle of Guiné (*Crónica dos Feitos da Guiné*). Based on a former chronicle of the deeds of Prince Henry, erroneously known as the "Navigator," which he had finished in 1453, this chronicle describes the exploration of the West African coast and the first contacts of the Portuguese with the local population. Moved by the spirit of the Crusade against Islam, Zurara is nevertheless sensitive to the suffering of the first black slaves arriving in Lagos, Portugal. When they were divided into small groups, and the husbands separated from their wives, he was moved by their tears of despair. Zurara gives us the earliest picture of the destruction of the family by the slave trade. Although he shared the view, common at the time, that Gentiles could be made slaves because their souls were the prey of false religion, he is touched by the scene and understands the humanity of people who, he reckoned, had the same feelings Christians did.

The problem of how the Portuguese saw the Africans in the early stages of their discoveries is rather complex. Originally there was a negative reaction, derived from the color of their skin, which identified them with the devil. Descriptions in medieval literature systematically conveyed this meaning, but the religious idea behind this concept was going to change in tone. The African was originally presented as the Moor, a term that covered both the Negro and the white Muslim. The Moor was the well-known enemy from the days of the reconquest of the Iberian Peninsula. This stereotypical notion of the Moor as opposed to the Christian faithful was no longer applicable to define all Africans, however. In the texts of fifteenth-century travelers or in Zurara's chronicles of Guiné, closer contact with Africans leads to their being presented with different shades of Muslim religion and different attitudes regarding their relations with Christians.

The idea of a continuous Islamic power stretching from the Western Sahara to Sierra Leone was not confirmed by the exploration of the African coast. The African was seen in the context of his environment and in a more anthropological perspective. The way people dressed, how they worked, what they cultivated, and how they traded became capital items in the description of the communities encountered by the Portuguese. These peoples are referred to as Gentiles. The term still has a religious connotation. It covers non-Christians who are not yet the enemies of the Christian faith and are therefore capable of conversion to Christianity. Being initially unable to qualify many of the people they came across, the Portuguese defined them as "wild men," which makes them capable of conversion.

At the request of King Afonso V (1438–1481), the grandson of Dom João I, Zurara wrote chronicles on the Meneses family, which are rather monotonous pieces on aristocratic life. In this work, frequent raids by the Portuguese into the territory outside their conquest reveal no interest on their part in knowing the population they assaulted.

In his florid style, Zurara reflects the aesthetic tastes of the court of Dom Afonso V. He prefers long sentences, often getting confused by subordinate clauses and becoming rather mixed up in the use of tenses. Portuguese prose was adapting itself to new ideas and new values, as well as to aristocratic aspirations that were trying to find their own expression.

A clear contrast to Zurara is provided by Rui de Pina (1440–1522), who succeeded to the official post. He is a matter-of-fact narrator, a simple reporter of events, dry and concise in his writing. His career was different from that of his predecessors. Pina had the trust of Prince Dom João, who was to become King Dom João II (1455–1495) upon his father's death in 1481. Afonso V frequently left the country on his travels abroad and, in his absence, the prince was left in charge of the affairs of the state. Since 1474, he had been involved with the policy of the Atlantic discoveries. Dom João needed good collaborators and found a reliable one in Rui de Pina, who was entrusted with diplomatic missions.

In 1482 and 1483, Dom João II sent him to the court of Castile. He was also the secretary of an embassy sent to Pope Innocent VIII in 1484–1485. On his return, he was invited to write the biography of Dom João II. In 1493, he was chosen as envoy to the court of the Catholic king in Castile to settle the dispute between the two countries after the discovery of America by Christopher Columbus. He was instrumental in the signing of the Treaty of Tordesillas (1494), which divided the world, known and to be known, between Castile and Portugal. Dom Manuel I (1469–1521), the successor to Dom João II, appointed him court chronicler and keeper of the national archives in 1497. Rui de Pina was a productive author. He wrote the chronicles of six kings belonging to the dynasty of Burgundy and three chronicles of the dynasty of Avis: on Dom Duarte, Dom Afonso, and Dom João II.

The most interesting evidence showing how the Portuguese fared in their contacts with the peoples they were encountering in West Africa appears in the chronicle of Dom João II (Chapters 57 to 63). This section concerns the kingdom of Kongo and how the African king, the *manikongo*, was converted to Christianity. The Portuguese had direct experience with Islamic civilization in their own country, and it was not difficult for them to find people at home who knew Arabic. Traders or others with business connections would be easily available. In some circumstances, when an interpreter was not present, sign language would inevitably be resorted to by soldiers and sailors, as we find in Zurara's chronicle of Guiné (*Crónica dos feitos da Guiné*). As they moved along the West African coast, the Portuguese realized that Arabic was not understood by the peoples they came across and that other languages were spoken by the natives of the lands they discovered.

One of the most important agents in spreading the knowledge of Portuguese in those distant countries was the church, whose missionary work of conversion requires the use of language not only for communication on ordinary affairs but also for the purpose of religious instruction. At the same time, many of the religious orders were committed to the study of native languages, and it was their work that produced the first grammar books of these languages.

A good example of the nature of these contacts is provided by Rui de Pina's account of the arrival of the Portuguese in the kingdom of Kongo, as noted. The conversion of the *manikongo*, or king of the Kongo, to the Christian faith is reported in detail. There is also an Italian version of this episode, which is a translation of the Latin from an original text in Portuguese by the hand of Rui de Pina. The collation of the two texts shows some discrepancies in the narrative, but both reveal the problem of communication between the Portuguese and the people of Kongo.

When Diogo Cão discovered the Kongo, he could not understand its people. Although he was well provided with interpreters of different languages, Bantu, the language spoken by the natives, was not among them. Christian messengers were dispatched to the *manikongo*, titular chief at M'banza Congo in what is now northern Angola, taking him presents from the king of Portugal. The Portuguese emissaries were detained for so long that the Portuguese captain, who had initially received the Kongolese envoys from the African court, decided to take some of the Africans back to Portugal with him. Since the Africans were noblemen in their own society, they were presented at the court and instructed in the Portuguese language and matters of faith. The king of Kongo was furious when he learned that his countrymen had been taken to Portugal, but he spared the lives of the messengers. One year later (1485), when the Kongolese were returned, the *manikongo* was delighted and asked for further help from Portugal.

By training in the Portuguese language a few people from the communities they had encountered, the invaders established the necessary channels for communication, even if their methods appeared to be unscrupulous. To gather information about the places they had discovered along the West African coast, they used *lançados*, banished men who were landed at a particular spot from which they were to be picked up a few months later by the captain of the ship. But the friars and the priests, who went to Africa, Asia, and South America for the purpose of converting the peoples of those continents, were the real agents of communication between Portugal and the new worlds.

Rui de Pina is often accused of paying little attention to the Portuguese expansion overseas. The fact is that he lived in an era when the crown was trying to assert itself as the central power in governing the country, and Pina was more involved with this matter than with the navigations. His viewpoint in the historical narrative was conditioned by the king's struggle, and he tried to understand it within the framework of the operations taking place overseas. In the chronicle of Dom Duarte, the son and successor (1438) of King Dom João I (1391–1438), Rui de Pina assessed the Portuguese policy in Morocco. He reviewed the disaster of the Portuguese assault on Tangier (1437) and the responsibility that Dom Henrique had in it. By neglecting to adhere to the instructions of the military council, Dom Henrique had put the whole operation in jeopardy. So dismayed was he with his own failure that he withdrew to Sagres in southern Portugal and never left the place, devoting all of his efforts to the exploration of the African coast, gathering information and organizing expeditions. Far more than a personal failure, the disaster was seen by Rui de Pina as the result of disobedience and a breach of discipline in the chain of command.

Rui de Pina's chronicle of Dom Afonso V gives a good factual account of the conflicts that divided the aristocracy and, together with the chronicle of Dom Duarte, shows Henry "the Navigator" in a critical light, praising the role of the regent Dom Pedro. In his biography of Dom João II, Pina had the opportunity to convey to his readers his own experience of life at court, for he knew the monarch well and was well acquainted with the documentation of the period. But he decided to present the facts in the version that Dom João II had chosen to offer his contemporaries, which earned him the epithet of "Perfect Prince." Unlike Fernão Lopes, Pina was not a gifted writer, but he was capable of acute psychological insight. His description of the encounter between Afonso V and Louis XI of France in the chronicle of Afonso V is a literary gem, reflecting the author's wit and subtle observation.

Chronicles were not the only literary genre favored by the court. The court of Avis was a center of flourishing literary activity. Books and reading were a common interest of the royal family. Dom João I produced a treatise on the art of hunting, *Livro da montaria*, written after 1415 and before 1433, which reveals his concern with exercising the body by devising strategies that were equally effective in war. His son Dom Duarte wrote a book on horseback riding where he makes some penetrating observations on the psychology of fear. Objectivity and pragmatism, the value of experience, and attention to the subjective world are the main features of the new mind emerging in Portugal in the 1400s. This pragmatism extended to questions of faith. Nonbelievers, said Dom Duarte in his *Leal conselheiro* (Loyal Counselor), compiled in 1437 or 1438, should behave in a moral and Christian fashion to be on the safe side regarding the salvation of their own souls.

The experiences of the voyages overseas and the consequences of the contact with new civilizations and cultures appear in the morality plays (*autos*) of Gil Vicente (1460/70–1536?). He provided the entertainment at the courts of Dom Manuel (1495–1521) and Dom João III (1521–1557) at a time when the Portuguese seaborne empire was already well defined. He introduces African characters in his plays (*Fragoa d'amor*, 1525; *Clérigo da Beira*, 1526; *Nau d'amores*, 1527) and shows them speaking Portuguese in their own fashion. He called it the "guinéu," or the language of Guiné.

By showing the difference in speech from the accepted linguistic norm, not only did he provoke the laughter of his public but he was also attuning their ears to Portuguese creoles. The creole of Cape Verde and the Bantu, following the Portuguese contact with the *manikongo*, are not present in Gil Vicente's plays, but he is the first to be aware of the importance of the "new languages" and their use for literary purposes.

The Portuguese elite and the crown were sensitive to the fact that they were in a country that was culturally on the periphery of Europe, and they tried to overcome this problem. Gil Vicente shared the apprehension of the religious movements in Europe that questioned the policy of Rome regarding spiritual matters and material interests, as he showed in his *Auto da Feira*, the name of a big market where stallholders trade spiritual values and the name also of Vicente's allegorical play.

The crown acted in a direct and more systematic way, seeking to bridge the gap between Portugal and the rest of Europe. Aware of the marginal position of the country in relation to Italy and France, in 1485 Dom João II invited an Italian humanist of Sicilian origin, Cataldo Parísio, to teach Latin to his illegitimate son, Dom Jorge. Soon Cataldo had a small coterie around him attending his lectures. The crown understood the need to have civil servants who were well trained in the humanities if Portugal was to be effective in maintaining chancelleries and courts. At the same time, many members of the nobility and the church visited Italy, mainly Florence, to hear the great humanist Angelo Poliziano. Gifted young men were also sent by the crown to the University of Salamanca in Spain before they moved to the universities of Italy and France.

Having succeeded in strengthening the power of the crown over that of the nobility, Dom João II advanced his plans for the expedition that would discover the sea route to India. He died in 1495, but two years later, Vasco da Gama sailed from Lisbon, returning in 1499 with the news that he had reached the subcontinent by sea. The interest in the humanities had not diminished inside the country, and the crown was frequently approached by foreign humanists who offered their services to celebrate the Portuguese voyages in Latin, the international language of the day.

Curiously, Portuguese humanists appeared initially to be more interested in producing a work of merit in one of the better-known literary genres in Latin than in composing an account of the great deeds of their countrymen. The sea voyage of Vasco da Gama changed that attitude. But it was under the pressure of foreign humanists that the first account was written. At the request of a colleague, a brief narrative of the events was published in 1573 by André de Resende (1500–1573). This apparent indifference reflects the effects of a mentality on the periphery that above all sought integration into the European mainstream. The number of Portuguese scholars studying in Italy and other countries was significant and was made possible by the cultural policy pursued by Dom Manuel during his reign (1495–1521). He supported more than fifty scholarships for Portuguese students in the college of Sainte Barbe in Paris.

Later, Dom João III (1502–1557) reversed the trend when he invited André de Gouveia, a Portuguese scholar who was the best educational administrator in France, to found a humanist college in Coimbra (1547). Dom João's goal was to attract the intellectual diaspora back to Portugal in an effort to overcome the sense of cultural marginality that had affected Portuguese intellectuals. Dom Manuel and Dom João III developed an intensive cultural policy aimed at increasing the level of literacy in the country. Grammars and textbooks were published to teach young boys the rudiments of Latin and the structure of their own language. Women at court were driven by the same enthusiasm and love of learning. Princess Dona Maria, the daughter of Dom Manuel, had a small circle of woman friends who excelled in the humanities.

The sense of being on the European periphery was balanced by a growing sense of the dimensions of the Portuguese expansion overseas. The territories of the empire were the peripheral areas in relation to metropolitan Portugal. This led the intellectual elite to act as if Portugal were a cultural center. Meanwhile, literary tradition and innovation entered into conflict with each other as new genres and literary forms were adopted.

The traditional meters common on the Iberian Peninsula were cultivated by poets who were already attracted to the new Italian forms that heralded the poetic revolution of the Renaissance. Francisco Sá de Miranda (1487–1558) had perceived the great changes that were taking place outside the country. In 1521, Sá de Miranda left for Italy, where he saw Rome, Venice, and Milan, not returning home until 1526. This long stay abroad had a lasting influence on his literary tastes. He was a personal friend of King Dom João III, who had plans for him in his administration. But Sá de Miranda disliked life at court and withdrew to his estate in northern Portugal. There he became a solitary and independent voice who observed the changes happening to his country following the discoveries and the first Portuguese settlements overseas. His letters or satires, addressed to the king or to his own friends, are vigorous pieces of social criticism, molded in traditional meter, in which he exposes the behavior of the courtiers who disguised their real intentions. Their dissembling gave them an apparent credibility at the court, which was questioned by Sá de Miranda. Many were the evils the poet saw emerging from the overseas expansion. One of them was slavery, which he condemned in unambiguous terms. On the other hand, new knowledge was a positive result of the discoveries. The need for a new poetic discourse, capable of dealing with the questions of the day, led Sá de Miranda to treat social reform in his bucolic poems, reviving an old tradition of this genre.

Shifting from the social to the lyric mode, Sá de Miranda was equally competent in handling the traditional meters as well as the new ones. He adopted new genres to express his thoughts and convey his emotions. He introduced the Italian meter, chose the tercet of Dante, and cultivated the *canção*, or canzone, in the Petrarchean style. He was an innovator and a traditionalist who balanced the tendency toward the satirical and toward social criticism with lyric expression and the effusion of sentiment, controlled by the rigorous discipline of the literary genre. His sonnets, the first to be written in Portuguese, are remarkable for their purity of form and the adequacy of their language. Ariosto's Ottava rima was another novelty in Portugal, and many were the poets who followed Sá de Miranda's example in the 1500s. The pastoral genre attains its highest achievement in the eclogue *Basto* composed by Sá de Miranda at the time he renounced the court in 1526. The melancholy for what he was leaving behind pervades the poem and is only compensated for by the intense life of contemplation he finds in the peace of the countryside.

Sá de Miranda's poems should be esteemed not only for the high moral tone of his thinking but also for the aesthetic quality of his verse. He uses language in a concise way in his search for expression. His syntax seems at times to be rather clipped and terse, capturing the beauty of the image in a combination of sounds, rhythm, and color that shows the inner tension of the subject. His friend Bernardim Ribeiro (1480?–?) used bucolic poetry to express a refined feeling of love with metaphysical connotations. He published a sentimental novel, *Menina e Moça* (Ferrara, 1554), that captured the tone of a woman's emotions in the framework of a complex allegory.

The treatment of wealth and power in different literary genres that took into account the new views of the Renaissance was a way for Portugal to enter into the mainstream of the European imagination. António Ferreira (1529–1569) expressed in his poems the new fear that pervaded Portuguese society, caused by the introduction of literary censorship as one of the functions of the Inquisition, launched in 1536. He tried also to look at Portuguese history from a broader perspective, choosing an episode of real history that might serve his purpose of producing a tragedy of national stature. His play *A Castro*, published posthumously by his son in 1598, was based on actual fact. The love of Prince Dom Pedro of Portugal for Dona Inês de Castro, the lady-in-waiting of his wife, is the subject of the work. Aware of the danger that Prince Dom Pedro might give the crown to one of the sons he had by Inês de Castro, to the detriment of his legitimate heir, his father,

King Dom Afonso IV, conferred with his counselors about the best way of avoiding this. Reason of state prevailed over any other consideration. Dona Inês de Castro would have to be executed, argued the king's advisers. The scenes between the king and Castro herself, who tried to make him change his mind by appealing to his feelings as a grandfather, are intensely dramatic, making the work essentially a drama of choice. Castro chooses to face the king, when she could have run away. The king might have overruled his counselors on compassionate grounds but decides to leave the decision to them, choosing not to choose.

By setting the problem within the context of contemporary political theory, António Ferreira was moving from an intellectually peripheral position to the cultural center. His classicism, tempered in the case of *A Castro* by his own reading of Machiavelli, expressed his desire to participate in a cultural movement of wide implications – the Renaissance. But Ferreira was still an isolated case.

Integration in the European tradition through literary achievement was concurrent with the discovery of the sea route to India and with the spirit of the discoveries, born out of the opening of the European continent to a planetary dimension. Portugal was seen then by Portuguese intellectuals as the cultural center or, at least, as a country that was no longer on the periphery. However, the distinction between Portuguese pragmatism, or practical experience, which had led to the successful outcome of the voyages of discovery, and the scientific theory that was developing in the rest of Europe, was emerging, leaving open the question of Lisbon's centrality.

The new currents of thought, or rather the new spirit that lent credence to such aspirations among the national elite, leading up to the epic impulse in prose and poetry, was conveyed by the Portuguese chronicles responding to the achievement in navigation and expansion in the first half of the sixteenth century. They cover the period that extends from 1497 to the 1590s. Not all of them, however, cover this period as a whole. Fernão Lopes de Castanheda (ca. 1500–1559) planned to write the *History of the Discovery and Conquest of India* by the Portuguese in ten volumes. Gaspar Correia (1495?–1565?), in his *Lendas da Índia*, covers the same period, giving a detailed account of what happened between 1497 and 1542. João de Barros (1496?–1570/71), in his *Décadas da Ásia*, stops in 1540. Diogo do Couto (1542–1616), who intended to continue Barros's work, goes as far as the year 1600 in his own *Décadas*. Of all these authors, the first one to publish was Fernão Lopes de Castanheda, who had lived for ten years in the East and had visited some of the places he described. The divisions into periods of ten years (*décadas*) followed the pattern of the Roman historian Livy in his *History of Rome,* revealing a Portuguese sense of continuity with a glorious past.

The first book of Castanheda's *History of the Discovery and Conquest of India* was published in 1551. It covered the sea voyage of Vasco da Gama and the first contacts of the Portuguese with the East up until the war with the *zamorin*, the ruler of Calicut, in 1504. It was the first account published on the subject and enjoyed great success, with translations into French, Castilian, Italian, and English. But the publication encountered some difficulties. Castanheda told the truth, and the truth displeased a few noblemen whose conduct at the siege of Diu (1538) had been less than exemplary. This group brought pressure to bear on the regent, Dona Catarina, who put a stop to the circulation of the book. These incidents are important if one wants to understand how the historical discourse and the mythology of the discoveries took shape and developed.

In 1554, Castanheda's history was reprinted, and a comparison between this edition and the first one (1551) is revealing. The edition of 1554 was changed and revised by the author. In the 1551 version, the honor of the preparation of the sea voyage was rightly attributed to Dom João II. In the 1554 version, credit for the whole project is given to King Dom Manuel, known as "the Fortunate." Moreover, a new emphasis appears in the account of the events. The voyage of Vasco da Gama is now attributed to providential design, not mere accident or human intention. This shift reflected the views of a small circle at court, which had Dom Manuel at its center. These ideas were not accepted by the entire court, but they influenced the monarch at a time when the idea of the empire was taking shape and gaining substance in his mind.

One of the most active promoters of the exceptional role of the king and the providential character he was destined to have in world history was Duarte Galvão (1445?–1517). He was a close adviser to Dom Manuel and in a position to guide his decisions. He wrote many letters and official documents and was no doubt privileged to speak his own views as well as those of his sovereign, once they had agreed on what was to be said in general terms. Of Galvão's many letters, there is one that is transcribed by Castanheda in his *History* of 1554. It is a letter addressed by Dom Manuel to the *zamorin*, which was to be delivered to him in an Arabic version. The letter referred to the unique character of that encounter, which was taking place under the protection of the Holy Ghost and was an encounter that had always been in the mind of God. That moment became the foundation of the historical epoch of Portugal. Everything that had happened before acquired a new meaning and, considered in retrospect, revealed the fulfillment of a plan of providential design. The navigations carried out along the Atlantic coast of Africa in a piecemeal fashion by order of Prince Henry were now seen as having been guided by a divine hand that had the discovery of the sea route to India as its ultimate goal. Prince Henry was Dom Manuel's uncle and, according to this version of events, both were engaged in the execution of the project.

This view was embraced despite the lack of any documentary evidence that Prince Henry had ever made any plans to reach India. Such a unique encounter was the work of God, and the linking of East and West could not be resisted. This vision entailed also the idea that all mankind was to be united in the same Christian faith. The policy of expansion announced by Dom Manuel and Duarte Galvão in their letter of March 1, 1500, addressed to the *zamorin* of Calicut and delivered to him by Pedro Álvares Cabral, signaled a moment of great political significance in the political ideas of the Portuguese court. Dom Manuel became the center of messianic expectations. At the request of the king, Duarte Galvão revised the history of his predecessors, going back to the foundation of the monarchy. He traced the continuity of a process but also claimed that in one single voyage Dom Manuel had done what had not been accomplished in the prior sixty years. When he describes the discoveries, his language takes on an epic tone that foreshadows the discourse of Camões in *The Lusiads* (1572). His interpretation of history followed the pattern of biblical interpretation by trying to decipher mysteries and prophecies in the accounts of the past. For this reason, the humanist historian João de Barros considered Duarte Galvão more of an ideologue than a chronicler.

Dom Manuel, however, tried to live up to the messianic expectations he had generated and at one time cherished the idea of a great assault on Mecca, relying on his great commander Afonso de Albuquerque for the execution of this project. Other ideas ultimately prevailed at the court, and these wild fantasies of world domination gave way to more pragmatic goals. Garcia de Resende (1470–1536) described the conflicts at court in his biography of Dom João II (1545) and compiled a *cancioneiro geral* (General Song Book) (1516) with interesting information on the period and subtle poetical debate.

In the 1554 second edition of his *History of India*, Castanheda added a new chapter to his work. In Chapter 28, he linked the discovery of the sea route to India not only with all the explorations that preceded it, which is quite logical, but also with the first person who had the idea of exploring the African Atlantic coast. "It seems," he said, "that Prince Henry had started these navigations by divine inspiration." This is a cautious assertion, and the ambiguity of the statement leaves sufficient doubt as to Prince Henry's actual intentions. In the same way that he had eliminated from the 1554 edition the description of the confusion of the Portuguese at the reception they were given at the court of Calicut, Castanheda was trying to make his work acceptable to the Portuguese establishment, giving in to the mythology created around "Henry the Navigator" and to the dignified picture Lisbon wanted to project of a historic encounter.

João de Barros was well prepared for continuing this line. Being of noble origin, he entered the king's service through his father's recommendation. In 1525, Dom João III appointed him treasurer of the House of India. Hence, he was in an excellent position to assess the state of Portuguese affairs. His *Décadas da Ásia* showed acute awareness of the importance of the discoveries, mainly of the first two voyages by sea from Lisbon to India, which anchored Portuguese power in Asia. His style has an epic tone and was originally shaped in a narrative of fantasy and chivalry entitled *Chronicle of Emperor Clarimundo* – a totally imaginary tale that is a representation of Portugal.

In his *Décadas*, taking two voyages as the pinnacle of Portuguese achievement (the second had also opened the route to Brazil), Barros places the 120 years he intends to cover on a planetary stage. The great conflict in this drama is between Islam, identified with the Antichrist, and Christianity. The power of Islam was extended to the Iberian Peninsula as a punishment inflicted on the Christians for their heresies. Gradually, the Christians recover their land, and when Dom João I captures Ceuta, one may say that God has been reconciled with His people in the spreading of the Gospel and in the punishment of Islam.

João de Barros offers a historical foundation for the idea of the Crusade against the infidel and accepts it as a justifiable political doctrine. He is more subtle and far more complex when he deals with the question of providential aid. He embeds it at a deep level of the narrative. He looks at the present and gives meaning to times past by valuing those times in retrospect, placing prophecy that anticipates the present in the individual consciousness of the actors of his historical drama. But no one character has a prophetic function in his tale. When Prince Henry orders his expeditions to go beyond Cape Nam, Barros claims that there were many who said he did it because he was inspired by a divine oracle. By attributing the interpretation of the prince's decision to a small group, the chronicler avoid expressing his own reservations yet at the same time makes Henry the instrument of God's will. Consequently, all the navigations that took place before da Gama's voyage to India have a theological character, and that voyage is described in an epic tone reminiscent of the many narratives of shipwrecks and sufferings that were to come after the discovery of the sea route to India. The narrative transcends the events and gains in literary quality without losing the accuracy of its reporting.

João de Barros was a solid historian who also had great literary talent. He based his work on documents, searched for the truth in archives, and employed translators who knew Oriental languages to provide reliable versions of the events. He did not conceive of history in a narrow, national sense, whatever his ideological views might have been, but on a planetary scale. By then, the Portuguese language had acquired more flexibility of expression and a syntactic subtlety based on the readings of the Latin classics. The contacts with the outside world and new continents and civilizations had enlarged the Portuguese lexicon. The humanists had imposed a grammatical discipline that did not constrain verbal inventiveness and generally encouraged the search for new words and semantic accuracy.

Because of its overseas expansion, Portugal had become, in the mind of the national elite, the center of European culture. Literary nationalism and a sense of successful rivalry with ancient Rome, and antiquity in general, pervaded the writings of the period. João de Barros had based his *History of Asia* on the model of the Roman historian Livy, producing a work that vied with the past in the excellence of style and the importance of the events reported. Like the Roman historian, he invented as necessary the speech of the main actors of the historical drama. In these speeches, political policies were formulated and personal motivations made clear. For a brief period, Portugal seemed to share a new cultural prestige in Europe. Literary celebrations aside, however, it must be noted that Portuguese supremacy, achieved in the techniques of navigation and shipbuilding, excluded to a large extent the speculative side of science, which was emerging elsewhere in Europe and was required for the progress and development of society.

Barros was also concerned with the Jewish question inside Portugal. He wanted to bring the Jewish communities, who were important for national and international trade, inside the fold of the Christian religion by persuasion and not by coercive measures. His work *Ropica pnefma* (Spiritual Merchandise) is an Erasmian dialogue in tone and language, written for this purpose.

The apparent success of the voyage to India seen from one perspective did not correspond to the actual reception the Portuguese had in Calicut. In general, the Portuguese were unwelcome in the city. Their arrival in the East disturbed the long-standing trade circuits of the Indian Ocean, and the Muslim traders were not pleased with the Portuguese presence. Their exchange products had small value and their ceremonial gifts were of low quality. Álvaro Velho, the presumed author of the report of the first voyage to India, noted that the Portuguese gifts for the *zamorin* made his ministers laugh. It is clear from the reading of the report that the Portuguese were ill informed about the situation in India and were unprepared to face Indian civilization. They had only the vaguest notions about it. The social and religious practices of the Hindus were assimilated to European patterns. When Vasco da Gama and his men, for example, entered a Hindu temple, although they found it a bit odd, they believed it to be a Christian church. The praying Brahmin, wearing white clothes and fingering his beads, was identified with a Christian priest. The Indian goddess Durga was assumed to be the Virgin Mary. Álvaro Velho paid attention only to those aspects of Asian civilization that could be associated with Portuguese experience. In general, it could be said that the first voyage, the first direct contact between East and West by sea, turned out to be a great failure. The Portuguese took account only of the same, of what they could identify with in their own culture, and failed to understand a rich and complex civilization such as the one they found in Asia. Moreover, as noted, Arab traders of spices, who exerted a strong pressure on the sultan of Calicut, were hostile to the newcomers because they were likely to interfere with the traders' interests.

In 1500, Pedro Álvares Cabral was the commander of the second fleet sailing to India. Of the thirteen ships in the fleet, only about half reached their destination. This time the Portuguese were better equipped militarily. For over three months, they were stationed off the port of Calicut, learning about Indian society and trying to obtain the coveted spices. They spent their time among the local population, observing their habits and manners. In the *Report of an Anonymous Pilot*, observation is far wider and more complex than in the report attributed to Álvaro Velho. The character of Indian society is described in more detail and with a better understanding of its structure. In the description of the Gujarat merchants and their different groupings, the anonymous author uses the word "caste," assigning the meaning that it has retained since. It is the oldest example of its usage in a Portuguese text. Gradually, the Portuguese began to note the differences within Indian society itself and also realized that there was great hostility toward themselves. In the end, they chose the military solution and imposed themselves with brute force.

From the fifteenth century, in the wake of the navigations, the Portuguese language was spoken in wider and wider areas and was a means of communication with diverse peoples in Asia, Africa, and America. Spoken initially, if sparsely, along the African coast, the use of the language extended to the populations stationed on the border of the Indian Ocean. By means of political domination, the Portuguese succeeded in establishing trade relations, creating conditions for the convenience of using the language in their small settlements. Afonso de Albuquerque in India (from 1510 to 1515) effectively promoted a policy of mixed marriages, and these communities used the Portuguese language and favored its expansion. In Goa and in other areas where the Portuguese established themselves, the administration used the Portuguese language, which became obligatory for everyone. Consequently, schools were set up to teach Portuguese. The first school was established at Cochin by Afonso de Albuquerque; in Goa, elementary schools were founded in rural areas when Dom João de Castro became viceroy (1545–1548).

After military intervention, the second factor explaining the expansion of the Portuguese language in Asia was trade. With the conquests of Afonso de Albuquerque, new outposts for trading were made possible for the crown and for private individuals. When Afonso de Albuquerque captured Malacca (1511), he opened up the doors to Portuguese merchants and encouraged the development of an extensive network that was supported by Portuguese-speaking peoples stationed on the Asian rim of the Pacific Ocean. For three hundred years, Portuguese was the vehicle of communication. It was usually a language grammatically simplified, or a creole, which would be the basis of all creoles still in existence or that have already disappeared in that part of the world.

The sources of these comments are the references of foreign travelers who visited those places at the time; official documents of a special character; Portuguese vocabulary to be found in the local languages; works of a didactic character published for the teaching of Portuguese; many books printed in Portuguese by the missionary Protestants from Batavia, Colombo, Trangambar, and Veprey to present their religious doctrine; and the formation of Portuguese creole languages.

A third factor in the expansion of the Portuguese language was missionary work. In 1545, the Spanish Jesuit Francis Xavier asked for missionaries who could speak Portuguese. In 1600, at a time when Portuguese power was waning in the East, an English merchant, who met a Japanese lord, was able to make himself understood in Portuguese. Between 1602 and 1633, the Dutch took Portuguese interpreters aboard their ships. In 1646 and 1656, the kings of Ceylon used the Portuguese language in their communication with the Dutch. But in the seventeenth century, Portuguese had to face other competitors in Asia. The Dutch, the English, the Danes, the French, and the Spaniards vied to break up the monopoly of Portuguese trade. During the period when Portugal was associated with Spain under the dual monarchy (1580–1640), it was attacked by the enemies of Spain. This circumstance contributed to the decline of its power. By the 1800s, the influence of the Portuguese language in Asia disappeared in the face of the political and trade supremacy of Britain. The language was spoken and used officially only in the territories under Portuguese administration – Goa, Damão, and Diu in India; Macao in China; and Timor. We leave aside here Africa, the Atlantic islands, and Brazil.

The Indo-Portuguese creole languages in Asia were the creole of Malacca, known as the Christian *papiá*, spoken in western Malaysia; the creole of Macao, which was no longer spoken after 1800; and the creole of Sri Lanka (Ceylon). The creoles of Chaul, Tellicherry, Cannanore, and the Cochin fortress were all spoken in India by small communities and began to lose their importance by the end of the nineteenth century.

The pastoral needs of the missionaries were another important factor in the promotion of the Portuguese language. Missionaries taught the language to the peoples they encountered in order to instruct them in the Christian faith. On the other hand, they also produced grammars of the new languages they came across, with the intention of doing their pastoral work in the native language of the peoples they wanted to convert. An interesting case is the relationship of the Portuguese with Japan. The Portuguese arrived in Japan in 1543, and the action of the Jesuits was particularly remarkable. The trade between Japan and the Portuguese favored the contacts between the two countries. The ships of the "barbarians of the South" brought in huge profits to the rulers of Kagoshima and Nagasaki. At the same time, trade with China prospered and provided information about that ancient country. In 1549, the Jesuits first set foot in Kagoshima. Relations were established with the local ruler, and pastoral work started soon after. Saint Francis Xavier and his companions sought to convert the ruler under the assumption that, once he was converted, his people would follow suit. The conversions in Kagoshima and Yagamushi were quite promising. In 1639, when the Portuguese were forced to leave, although trade between Macao and Nagasaki was over, 200,000 Christians were left behind.

The Portuguese language was the first instrument of communication between Japan and the West. Other foreigners were obliged to use it in their relations with the Japanese. The missionaries brought into Japan a press with movable metallic characters, which was used to spread knowledge of the Japanese language. Father João Rodrigues, S. J., was the author of the first grammar of the Japanese language, *Arte da Lingoa de Iapan* (Nagasaki, 1604–1608), which is consulted to this day by Japanese experts who want to know the history of their language. We owe to the Jesuits the transcription of Japanese into the Roman alphabet. This enables us to know the pronunciation of Japanese in the sixteenth century. The Christian books published during that period are useful for the same purpose. Important also is the Latin-Portuguese and Japanese dictionary printed in Amacura, Japan, in 1595. The vocabulary of the Japanese language, *Vocabulário da Lingoa de Iapan com a declaração em Português, feito por alguns Padres e Irmãos da Companhia de Jesus* (Nagasaki, 1603), is essential for the study of the lexicon at the time.

Concern with the study and the teaching of the Portuguese language started early with the discoveries, as evidenced by the remark of the chronicler João de Barros, in 1540, that the stone *padrões* (pillars) the Portuguese erected on the places they had reached would pass with time but not the language they left behind. The language had its day as a vehicle of general communication. There are many borrowings in Portuguese from other Oriental languages besides Japanese. The Portuguese words one finds in Japanese and the Japanese words found in Portuguese testify to the close relationship that existed between these cultures. In spite of the differences, the first contacts between the Christian Portuguese and Hinduism were favored by certain cultural ambiguities. Catholicism had a figurative art that could be made to correspond in the Indian imagination with the representations of the Hindu religion. This gave the Portuguese an advantage over the Dutch, whose Calvinism was less congenial to the character of Oriental faith. The resistance or persistence of the Portuguese language over 300 years owes much to such factors. That the Portuguese were the first in the region also gave their language an advantage. The economic supremacy of Great Britain supplanted its use in trade relations with the adoption of English, as noted. By 1800, the situation had changed, although there were pockets, as we have seen, where Portuguese survived in reduced form.

Expansion opened up new fields to Portugal that gained the country a central position in Europe. Luís de Camões (ca. 1531–1580) chose to celebrate in the discovery of the sea route to India all the earlier voyages that culminated in the success of Vasco da Gama's expedition. In his epic *The Lusiads* (1572), Camões sings of the people and the heroes of his own country; he sings of the people of Portugal rather than of a single individual.

Written in the Italian ottava rhyme cultivated by Ariosto, the epic is not simply a poem of praise and exaltation of national deeds. It is a poem of serious reflections on history and society that reveals a grave preoccupation with the state of the Portuguese empire and the future of the nation. In an original way, uncommon in an epic poem, Camões makes his personal voice heard more than once and harbors no illusions about the difficulties that threaten to undermine the fabric of the empire. As a reader of the *Décadas* by João de Barros and other chronicles, Camões turned to a poetic historical discourse to which he gave new life, adopting a style shaped by the tradition of grand rhetoric. In his tale, in which the discovery of the sea route to India by Vasco da Gama is the central subject, he comes to a high point in the narrative that enables him to see Portuguese history in retrospect. On their return voyage, the navigators are guided by Venus to the Island of Love (cantos 9 and 10). The goddess has prepared a special reception for da Gama and his men as a reward for their labors. In the banquet that followed, a complete portrait of the solar system was given in detail, and a nymph foretells the coming exploits of the Portuguese in a future that is the present in which Camões was writing. The dimensions of the planet and its riches for mankind are revealed in this vision that encompasses also the relationship between the physical and the intellectual, the sensual and the philosophical, the imaginative and the moral, the "Roman" and Christian versions of the world. The Island of Love may be to a certain extent an allegory in which carnal pleasures have their place, but it also reflects desires and utopian ideals that are suggested by its own pastoral setting.

The criticism leveled by Camões at the bad counselors of the king, his condemnation of corruption, and other evils he detected in colonial administration are already a warning that this state of affairs could not go on for much longer without serious consequences for the empire and for the nation itself. This is an original characteristic of *The Lusiads*, where disapproval is often substituted for praise. Camões had the sharp eye of the humanist whose concern must be voiced to prevent or avoid major disasters. Persuasion could change people's minds, even those who were deeply steeped in the convictions of their own faith. João de Barros tried to argue with Jews, seeking their conversion to the Christian faith. In one of his works, *Ropica pnefma* (1532), discussed earlier, he went so far as to uphold the virtues of a Christianity purged of fanaticism and freed from mundane interests, a Christianity that came close to the spirit and the word of the New Testament. Camões did not share this vision, but he was receptive, to a certain extent, to its ideals. Yet Camões's commitment to the idea of the empire and the sense of Crusade that sustained it made him an enemy of Islam.

This hostility must be understood in its context. The fall of Constantinople in 1453 and the occupation of the Balkans by the Turks had spread the fear of a Muslim invasion of Europe. The Christian victory at the battle of Lepanto, one year before the publication of *The Lusiads* (1572), brought great relief to Europe, but the fear persisted. Camões breathed the air of his time. He had been a soldier in Africa and Asia and could not separate the idea of European security from that of the threat of Islam. For this reason, *The Lusiads* became the poem of the moment in Christian Europe. Translated into Castilian in 1580, it became the epic of the Iberian peoples in the mind of Spanish intellectuals. The epic expressed a collective feeling and opinion that belonged to the Christian community in general. The curious paradox was that at the time of this recognition, the intellectual elite were acutely aware of the symptoms of decline that were undermining Portuguese society.

The contradictions of this conflict are present in the lyric poetry of Camões and are made visible, among other themes and subjects, in the vagaries of fortune, time, and chance. Camões searches for the inner truth of the self through many experiences that provide the substance of his lyric. He used the traditional verse meters but soon followed the Italian style by writing sonnets, *canções* (canzoni), eclogues, and all the other genres favored by the Renaissance, continuing the trend initiated by Sá de Miranda. The vicissitudes of his life and the history of his time are intrinsically linked, and this unity of experience is a feature of his originality as a poet. His poetic apprenticeship was under Petrarch, and he found in Dante the symbol of the woman-angel. But he transformed the notion of love that was the guide of these poets into a form of knowledge that embraced the "various flames" that consumed his soul. Unlike Petrarch and Dante, he never tried to produce a sentimental biography focused on the beloved. For him there was no Laura and no Beatrice; there was no one pivotal figure but instead many who were the subject and object of his poetry in a quest of the spiritual in bodily reality.

Camões traveled widely, living for seventeen years away from his country. He returned to die in poverty after completing his epic poem. In many respects, his personal experience was the same as that of his countrymen. Nomadism had become a way of life for the Portuguese, especially when the lure of riches drew them to the East and later to Brazil in the 1700s. The travel literature of the 1500s records these movements of population, and if a significant part of it has only scholarly interest and no literary value, the other part reveals qualities of observation that made this literature both scientifically and aesthetically valid. The travels of the Venetian Marco Polo, among other texts, revealed extraordinary places, strange habits, religions, customs, and marvels of nature that had never been seen before. The book was printed in 1502 in Portuguese and provided a model for the literature of exploration. Foreign travel books were read in the circle of the princes of Avis and were gradually superseded in their importance by direct accounts of Portuguese travelers and explorers. Remarkable for the detail of his description was the letter addressed to Dom Manuel by Pêro Vaz de Caminha telling the king about the finding of Brazil and the first encounter with the Amerindians.

Portuguese travel books can be divided into two distinct groups. The first group consisted of the works of travelers who wanted to know the geography of the places they had visited and the best routes of access to them. The *True Information about the Lands of Prester John* (1540), by Father Francisco Álvares, who had lived in Ethiopia, was an interesting and reliable account of a figure that had fascinated Europe. Prince Henry never ceased looking for Prester John in the explorations of the western African coast that he promoted. Finding this priest-king, a Christian, would provide an ally for the Portuguese in their ventures into the lands of the infidel. Later, when Prester John was identified as a ruler of Ethiopia and direct contact was established with his court, the chronicler Damião de Góis (1502–1574) showed a remarkable tolerance and understanding of the religious practices of the Ethiopian church, which were different from the Roman practices adopted in the West. Damião de Góis wrote two books in Latin (in 1532 and 1540) on the subject to draw the attention of the church to the convenience of accepting such differences.

It is often claimed that one of the characteristics of the Portuguese is their universalism in view of the different peoples and civilizations they had met in their voyages. But this claim is often disproved by experience. Góis believed, as did many theologians in his day, that the same God could be worshipped in different forms. He was shocked when he received the news that his book *Fides, Religio, Moresque Aethiopium* (1540) had been prohibited by the Inquisition. His belief in a universal faith was not shared by the church of Rome. As a historian, he had been superseded by his contemporaries in his approach to the subject. Góis was moved by moral questions. In his chronicle of Dom Manuel (1566–1567), he exposed the false miracle that led to a pogrom in Lisbon, and he had no hesitation in pointing out the misdemeanors of some clergymen. His descriptions of Lisbon and its opulence in the reign of Dom Manuel, when trade with the East began to flourish, give us an impressive picture of the riches that flooded the ports and the importance of European trade.

The second group of travel books comes under the specific designation of narratives of shipwrecks. They report disasters at sea and were written shortly after the event, collecting the testimony of the victims and their suffering. They were published as small pamphlets with loose pages, sold in any shop and eagerly bought by the public. The account of the shipwreck of *Sepúlveda* (first edition ca. 1554), which Camões included in *The Lusiads*, and of the *Nau São Bento* (1564) and a few others, were collected into two volumes in the eighteenth century under the title *História trágico-marítima* (The Tragic History of the Sea). These accounts were written in a colloquial style that retained the oral quality of reporting, and some of them were composed by authors of distinction such as Diogo do Couto (1542–1616).

The Tragic History of the Sea is one of the most impressive literary genres emanating from Portugal, not only for the dramatic and human quality of the narrative but also for what it reveals about the causes of the shipwrecks. The regulations laid down in the royal instructions (*regimentos*) were often ignored, and captains were easily bribed into allowing excessive cargo on board. These transgressions had dire consequences in a storm or when there was an error of navigation, especially because the pilots engaged were less and less experienced. The sheer bulk of the carracks, built to carry more and more goods, made them difficult to maneuver, a problem that was especially dangerous when they were attacked by Dutch ships. The demand for trade called for a larger fleet, a need that was not satisfied simply by building larger ships. This failure was seen as one of the factors that contributed to the decline of the empire.

It is ironic that when Portugal had become the center of the world (in the eyes of a major part of its elite), the signs of its contraction into the margins of Europe were already becoming visible. The brilliant period that lasted from 1500 to 1536 had been short-lived. The country was unable to consolidate a policy that would maintain its monopoly on navigation, which was being destroyed on the high seas by competing European powers. The epic of Camões, as we have remarked, shows he was aware of these dangers and reflected the poet's apprehensions.

Fears, shipwrecks, disasters, and adventures, which are the main features of the Portuguese destiny overseas, are admirably reported in a matter-of-fact style in the *Peregrinação* (Peregrination) by Fernão Mendes Pinto (1510?–1583). The book has always been difficult to classify as to its literary genre. There are voyages, descriptions of battles, and shipwrecks, but they are all centered on one particular character, the narrator, making the book a kind of autobiographical romance. More or less finished by 1569, the *Peregrinação* was posthumously published in Lisbon in 1614. Fact and fiction are intertwined in Mendes Pinto's story, but we know enough about Pinto himself to affirm his real existence. He corresponded with Jesuit missionaries and knew one of the most distinguished of them, Father Francis Xavier, the saint, whose mass conversions in the East became famous. Religious orders were important not only for their commitment to the expansion of the Christian faith but also for their exploration of unknown lands in order to find peoples who needed their missionary work. The Jesuits were intensely active in this respect and distinguished themselves in their study of foreign languages as a vehicle for their work on Christianization. In 1564, Mendes Pinto became a wealthy merchant and gave Francis Xavier a substantial sum of money to build a church in Japan. Mendes Pinto had met Xavier in 1547 and was so impressed by his personality that he joined the Jesuit Order in 1554. Later, he left of his own accord, but he kept up good relations with the fathers, which would indicate that his departure from the order did not incur their disapproval.

This is the objective information we have about the author of the *Peregrinação*, information that is not to be found in his book. We need not doubt, however, the account Mendes Pinto gives of his boyhood and his reasons for leaving home. Fernão Mendes Pinto was the son of poor parents who could not provide their family with adequate opportunities locally, so when an uncle took him to Lisbon in 1521, Mendes Pinto seized the opportunity to flee twelve years of abject poverty in his father's house and run to the Alfama district, where he took passage on a caravel bound for Setúbal. This was the beginning of a life of adventure, full of fears and risks, that took him to the East in 1537, after a short period of service in a powerful family who held important posts in India. The *Peregrinação* tells of the wanderings of its narrator, including, for the first time in Portuguese literature, stories of pirates. The long, explanatory title of the book says it all. Mendes Pinto was a soldier of fortune, trader, pirate, agent, and ambassador during twenty-one years in Ethiopia, Persia, Malaya, India, Burma, Siam, Cochin China, East India, China, and Japan, sailing uncharted Oriental seas. He was shipwrecked five times, captured thirteen times, and enslaved sixteen times. He met a saint, repented his ways, returned home, and wrote his story for his children and posterity.

Mendes Pinto's story cannot be separated from *The Lusiads* of Camões. *The Lusiads* tells the epic tale of the discoveries and the achievements of the Portuguese in founding a seaborne empire. The *Peregrinação* shows the other side of the coin, the misery and pain of many Portuguese, whose destinies appear conflated into a single life as an example of the ordinary man's vicissitudes. This anti-epic character of the book reveals a self-irony and self-criticism that, although not altogether uncommon in the writings of the period, were never pushed as far as in the *Peregrinação*.

Equally remarkable is the light in which China is shown. It is described very often as an ideal society – the Celestial City set against the Condemned City. It is not simply a country of wonders but a painful standard against which to measure the vicious character of the society created in the East by merchants, soldiers, pirates, and others. The economic, social, and administrative organization of Chinese society is presented as a model. The plan of the cities, the order of the streets, the markets, and the number of bridges and waterways reveal an organization that is matched by an equal preoccupation with the social "welfare" of the people who inhabit the urban space. Mendes Pinto describes hostels for the poor and for prostitutes, as well as various other elements of social assistance that make it a blueprint for a caring state. This is obviously an exaggerated picture of Chinese reality, which was conveyed to him by the records of Portuguese travelers. Curiously, these favorable views were confirmed by his own observations, which contrasted social life at home with the Oriental model. Mendes Pinto's judgments were conditioned by his time. He saw life in the same light as many of his contemporaries, but his vision encompassed not only the experience of his adventures but a desire for moral change, which is also present in *The Lusiads*.

The prominent position Portugal had attained in Europe was short-lived. It was undermined by the corruption of the empire and by a collective greed that promoted a fragile trade at the expense of the development of the country at home. Moral concern about the situation was expressed in the vague utopian ideals in the work of Mendes Pinto modeled on Chinese society, pictured as the perfect commonwealth. When he returned to Portugal, the country was ruled by the regent, Dona Catarina of Austria, the widowed queen of Dom João III. Dom Sebastião came of age in 1568 and embraced the project of an empire in North Africa, spurred on by acts of piracy committed by Arab ships along the Portuguese coast. Against the better judgment of his advisers, he prepared an expedition into North Africa and was defeated and killed during the battle of Alcazarquibir. With the loss of the king, Portugal came to be ruled by Philip II of Spain under the dual monarchy. It lasted from 1580 until 1640, when finally the Portuguese monarchy was restored.

For a sixty-year period, while Portugal was under Spanish domination, the belief was widespread among the people that King Sebastian was alive and would come and liberate them from captivity. This was a potent messianic myth that occasionally sustained the elite through the years of Spanish rule. By agreement, not always in practice, the Portuguese were left in command of their own administration at home and overseas. They were aware of their loss of prestige and the effects it had on their culture. They were becoming peripheral in Europe. Writers and intellectuals struggled to continue the national tradition. Their sense of the importance of their own history remained undiminished.

Diogo de Couto (1542–1616), appointed by the Spanish king as the keeper of Goa's archives, took upon himself the task of continuing the work of João de Barros, choosing for this purpose a similar chronological system. Couto's *Décadas* focused mainly on the Portuguese administration in Asia, showing how the administrators cared more about their private interests than the crown's. Couto's bitterness arose out of the indifference with which his denunciations were received and because of the successive obstacles that were put in the way of the publication of his work. Some of his *Décadas* were lost in a shipwreck, manuscripts were purloined, and one full printed edition was destroyed in a fire at his printer's premises. These disasters were perceived by Couto not as accidents but as intentional acts to silence him. For this reason, his *Practical Soldier* (there are three versions of this text) is a systematic and thorough exposure of the Portuguese colonial system. The fear of the imminent collapse of the Portuguese empire of the East haunted the minds of many Portuguese, and measures to arrest its decline were suggested – measures that implied an institutional reform according to traditional codes as well as a change in moral attitudes. If the loss of political autonomy were to be coupled with the loss of the empire as well, that would mean the end of national identity. Hence the anxiety one finds in the writings of many Portuguese intellectuals of the late sixteenth and early seventeenth centuries.

Francisco Rodrigues Lobo (1573/74?–1621), who cultivated in his poetry many of the themes favored by Camões and employed them in the mannerist and baroque styles with remarkable success and originality, was particularly concerned with the state of the Portuguese language and developed his own theory on the baroque in his *Corte na Aldeia* (Court in the Village) (1619). More than a small treatise on aesthetics, this book, divided into sixteen dialogues, dealt with fashion, etiquette, and social manners, establishing a pattern of social civility that could be used as a model in the small courts that proliferated in the noble mansions throughout the country. By giving them a consistency and harmony of purpose, Lobo created a model that could be adopted in general. He examined not only the importance of style as literary expression but also its influence in the civility of manners according to status and station in society. This nationalism preserved the artistic cult of the language in the face of the splendor of Castilian.

Some Portuguese authors, such as Dom Francisco Manuel de Melo (1608–1666), were bilingual and equally distinguished as writers in both Portuguese and Spanish. His Spanish poetry was sensitive and good, competing with the great names of the century. But Melo's attraction to Spanish literature did not in any way affect his nationalism. When the Duke of Bragança headed the movement for Portuguese independence in 1640, Dom Francisco Manuel de Melo joined his cause, although he had frequented the court in Madrid.

The most eminent figure of the century was António Vieira, S. J. (1608–1697), who claimed with rare dialectical boldness a central position for Portugal in the world. A man of action, he was also a man of vision. Vieira became famous when, at the age of sixteen, he penned the annual letter from Brazil, a common practice of the Society of Jesus. He did not write about the missionary church but about the invasion of Bahia by the Dutch in 1624 and their expulsion the following year.

Vieira chose a political event to heighten awareness of a resistance movement against the occupation of Pernambuco by the Dutch between 1630 and 1654. The opposition to the Dutch occupation was extended to the domination of Portugal by the Spanish Hapsburgs. From the periphery of the empire, Vieira expressed a nationalist ideal that included a colonial policy. The Jesuit effort to enforce crown legislation that restricted enslavement of indigenous peoples in Brazil found in Vieira a vigorous agent and an eloquent supporter. The Jesuits had devised certain strategies to persuade the settlers to stop holding Amerindian slaves illegally. Refusing to offer auricular confession was one of them. But these were extremely unpopular measures. In 1640, the settlers succeeded in having the Jesuits expelled from São Paulo and Santos because of their attitude.

The great vision of Vieira follows the line of Sebastianism – the return of the dead king to liberate Portugal from Spanish control. Sebastianism had its predecessor in the messianic ideas of a popular poet. They fueled a spirit of independence that found its fulfillment in the choice of the Duke of Bragança as the new king. Vieira managed this doctrinal transference from Sebastian to Dom João de Bragança, adapting the prophecy to the needs of the new times. Vieira came from Brazil in 1641 to offer the allegiance of the colony to Dom João IV, as he was to be known. In the difficulties of the war with Castile that followed, Vieira proved himself as a diplomat, an economist, and a political and social innovator who created new business companies with New Christian money and fought the Inquisition over its persecution of the Jews. He campaigned with his fellow Jesuits to liberate the Amerindians, who were to be integrated in the social project of the Society of Jesus.

Wherever he went, Vieira showed an intense energy and asserted himself as a prodigious orator who knew how to persuade and dramatically convince his audiences. He rallied the resistance of Brazil against the Dutch in fiery sermons built on arguments that gained the support of the wavering population. Yet this man, who had an eminently practical mind, developed a new prophetic vision of the world and the central role to be played in it by Portugal. The new king, later identified with Dom João IV, would come to lead a victorious army against the Turks, inaugurating the fifth empire of the world. The power of Portugal in the world would be the fulfillment of this utopian ideal. Vieira's views led to trouble with his fellow Jesuits, however. His contacts with the Portuguese Jewish community in Holland, the capitalist companies he promoted, and his vision of Portugal's fifth empire set him on a collision course with the tribunal of the Holy Office, whose repressive character was clearly exposed in the debate that followed.

On the whole, the works of Padre António Vieira, published in over fifteen volumes of sermons and letters, cover almost all the important features of Portuguese life in the seventeenth century. Remarkable for their ideological importance are his essays on the "history of the future." We know already of the polemics of Vieira with the Holy Office. But the situation worsened in the 1700s. The ideas of the Enlightenment and the consequent hostility toward the Society of Jesus combined to repudiate the Sebastianism of Vieira, adding the claim that the Bandarra prophecies were his own invention. The enlightened despotism of Sebastião José de Carvalho e Melo, Marques de Pombal (1699–1782) and minister of Dom José I (1714–1777), supported a rationalism that had no truck with flights of imagination and was indifferent to messianic theories.

The leading role that Vieira had assigned to Portugal as the head of the fifth empire, in keeping with the book of Revelation, was going to reappear in Pombal's rethinking of the national question but from a totally different perspective. Curiously, this awareness of the past of a "great nation" reemerged in the 1750s, when Brazilian gold was being unloaded in Lisbon and Pombal had been particularly successful in challenging British commercial hegemony in Portugal. At one stage of his thinking, Pombal, who had been the Portuguese envoy in London and had studied the achievements of the British economy closely, conceived a grand design that would make Brazil as part of the Portuguese empire more autonomous and free of dependence on the British. The solution he envisaged was totally political and never materialized, but it shows how the idea of being in the center and in the mainstream of Europe, either as a great power based on the importance of its empire or as a distinct culture among other European cultures, continued to be present in the minds of Portuguese intellectuals.

The Marquis de Pombal was not only a great reformer of education but also a man of vision regarding the choice of a national language in Brazil. It had become clear to the Portuguese that the natives in Brazil used one language all along the coast, despite the multiplicity of indigenous Amerindian languages. Certain words might differ in some places, but this did not prevent the natives from understanding one another. In 1531, there were already some Portuguese who had learned the Tupi language of the Indians.

The Jesuits, following a dominant concern of the Society of Jesus, tried to learn the language. Father João Azpilcueta Navarro (d. 1557) translated into the Tupi language the *Suma da Doutrina Cristã*, an instruction book on Christian doctrine. José de Anchieta, S. J., who replaced Navarro, went even further. He wrote the *Arte da Gramática da língua mais usada na costa do Brasil*, a grammar of the Tupi language. He was learned in the most widespread indigenous languages and knew there were many tribal groups who differed in their speech. His work became a major contribution to the endeavors of future missionaries. Published in Coimbra in 1595, the text was used in manuscript in the college of Bahia in 1560 to teach the language of Brazil. Vieira praised Anchieta's work as a grammarian. But Fernão Cardim (1540?–1625) produced the best description of the diversity of nations and languages in Brazil, making a clear distinction between the languages and nations of the interior and those he found along the seacoast. This situation was seen by Vieira as a special difficulty for missionary work in Brazil. He claimed that, whereas the missionaries in China and Japan had only one language to learn in each country, in the region of the Amazon, they had to cope with 150 of them.

The complex linguistic mosaic of the country was made more difficult by the African languages spoken by the slaves. The Tupi language had become the *língua geral* (common language) of the natives on the coast, with the diversity of languages spoken by the Amerindians throughout Brazil as its competitors. The colonialist policy of diversifying the tribal and geographic origins of the African peoples that the settlers imported to Brazil was designed to prevent the slaves from unifying and to keep them submissive. It also had the advantage of making the Portuguese language the most convenient common tongue. But the new settlers who arrived from Portugal had great difficulty in understanding the Amerindians. If any pressure was put on the indigenous people to learn Portuguese, they could always fall back on the policy of the Jesuits, who spoke the Tupi *língua geral* and received the Amerindians in their villages and compounds.

The Marquis de Pombal changed this situation radically. In a directive of 1757, he made Portuguese the official language in the Amerindian settlements of Pará and Maranhão. Boys and girls attending school, and natives capable of instruction, were not allowed to use the language of their nations. An important piece of legislation defined the status of the natives. By the royal letter of January 15, 1754, the difference between natives and whites had been abolished, and a writ of April 4, 1755, had established that Amerindians could marry whites. The writ of May 8, 1758, confirmed that the Amerindians were the masters of their freedom and their property. Any native who had a knowledge of the Portuguese language and the necessary qualifications could have access to a post in public administration.

This was one of the most remarkable acts of Pombal's administration. The imposition of one language over all the others caused many problems and could not be implemented peacefully. In the provinces of the north, Maranhão and Pará, Portuguese had come into wider use since 1755. But for over three centuries, Portuguese and Tupi were used side by side. Boys and girls spoke the *língua geral* at home with their parents, relatives, and friends but spoke Portuguese at school. Gradually, the European language gained ground. Many were those who objected to the imposition of a single language by a colonial power. The harsh treatment given to the Indians and blacks by the Portuguese and the bloody battles they had with them created a climate hostile to linguistic acceptance. Those opposed to the law had it abolished by the royal letter of May 12, 1798. The national language remained an open question and had not been settled by 1803. The differences between the Portuguese language of Brazil and that of Portugal tended to create uncertainty about language and national identity. But none of the alternatives was easy, and Portuguese spread widely with a rich variety of linguistic invention that revealed the strands of Brazilian society and the composition of its identity.

BIBLIOGRAPHICAL ESSAY

There is no satisfactory history of Portuguese literature in English. Aubrey F. G. Bell's history of Portuguese literature (Oxford, 1922) is totally inadequate, finishing near the end of the nineteenth century. Under the circumstances, it cannot be recommended. The best work on the subject is *História da literatura Portuguesa*, by António José Saraiva and Óscar Lopes (Oporto, 1989, or any later edition). Essential for the knowledge of Portuguese literature is the yearly journal *Portuguese Studies*, edited by the Department of Portuguese, King's College London, published since 1985.

The best works for studying the Portuguese language in relation to the development of Portuguese culture are Edwin B. Williams's *From Latin to Portuguese* (Philadelphia, 1938); Paul Teyssier's *Histoire de la langue Portugaise* (Paris, 1980); João de Barros's *Diálogo em louvor da nossa linguagem*, edited by Luciana Stegagno Picchio (Modena, 1959); David Lopes's *Expansão da língua Portuguesa no Oriente nos séculos XVI, XVII e XVIII*, a new edition brought up-to-date by Luís de Matos (Oporto, 1969); and Alfred Hower and Richard A. Preto-Rodas's *The Portuguese World in the Times of Camões* (Gainesville, FL, 1985).

The study of the Portuguese language is clearly linked in the period 1400–1800 with the literature of oceanic expansion, as it had to face the challenge of describing unknown lands and peoples. The concept of "discovery" continues to be valid when applied, for example, to a sea route that has been found and is regularly used in relation to a point of return. For ideas on the concept of "discovery" and "discovering," see António Galvão's *Tratado dos descobrimentos antigos e modernos* (Lisbon, 1563), translated into English by Hakluyt in 1603. A luminous essay on the subject is Vitorino Magalhães Godinho's "A ideia de descobrimento e os descobrimentos e expansão," *Anais do Clube Militar Naval* 120 (October–December 1990), pp. 627–642.

Language and Literature

The historical and cultural background, the encounters with new peoples, and the observation of the other in the context of maritime expansion are well covered in Bailey W. Diffie and George D. Winius's *Foundations of the Portuguese Empire, 1415–1580* (Minneapolis, 1977; 2nd ed. 1985); Sanjay Subrahmanyam's *The Portuguese Empire in Asia, 1500–1700: A Political and Economic History* (London, 1993); Michael N. Pearson's "The Portuguese in India," in *The New Cambridge History of India* (Cambridge, 1987); and Francisco Bethencourt and Kirti Chauduri, eds., *História da expansão Portuguesa* (5 vols., Lisbon, 1998–1999).

For the political and religious ideas that form the cultural background of the period, see Jean Aubin's *Le Latin et l'astrolabe* (2 vols., Lisbon and Paris, 1996, 2000). The mental process of changing ideas and interpreting the results of observation is analyzed in *Viagens do Olhar* (Oporto, 1998) by Fernando Gil and Helder Macedo, with a contribution by Luís de Sousa Rebelo.

The attempt by the Portuguese intellectual elite to bring Portugal into the cultural center of Europe, especially through Latin as the general language of communication, is assessed in *A tradição clássica na literatura Portuguesa* (Lisbon, 1982) by Luís de Sousa Rebelo, as well as in his "Literatura, intelectuais e humanismo cívico," in Diogo Ramada Curto, ed., *O tempo de Vasco da Gama* (Lisbon, 1988). See also Amadeu Torres, *Noese e crise na epistolografia goesiana* (Paris, 1982).

In order to follow the path of oceanic expansion and linguistic contact, see Peter Russell's *Prince Henry 'the Navigator': A Life* (London, 2000); Paul Teyssier's *La langue de Gil Vicente* (Paris, 1959); and Luís de Sousa Rebelo's introduction to *The Peregrination of Fernão Mendes Pinto*, abridged and translated by Michael Lowery (Manchester, 1992), pp. xi–xxxi. For the complete work in English, see Fernão Mendes Pinto, *The Travels of Mendes Pinto,* edited and translated by Rebecca D. Catz (Chicago, 1989).

There are also some texts of Fernão Lopes available in English versions, such as *The English in Portugal, 1367–87*, with extracts from the chronicles of Dom Fernando and Dom João, with an introduction, translation, and notes by Derek W. Lomax and R. J. Oakley (Warminster, 1988). The intellectual history of the period helps in the understanding of the literary background. For this purpose, see *Portuguese, Brazilian and African Studies: Studies Presented to Clive Willis on His Retirement*, edited by T. F. Earle and Nigel Griffin (Warminster, 1995).

For the reader with no knowledge of Portuguese, there are a small number of English translations of the basic texts from the period covered by this volume. Stephen Reckert's *From the Resende Song Book* (London, 1998) provides a good introduction to the *cancioneiro geral* of Garcia de Resende.

Reckert is mainly concerned with the literary and aesthetic qualities of the poems, leaving aside any references to the social background of the time. *Luís de Camões: Epic and Lyric* (Manchester, 1990) offers a good approach to the subject, with translations and essays by Maurice Bowra, Helder Macedo, and Luís de Sousa Rebelo. A new translation of *The Lusiads* by Landeg White is available (Oxford, 1997). Essential documentation has been collected and edited in English translation by Charles David Ley in *Portuguese Voyages, 1498–1663* (London, 1947, last reprint 1960).

On culture and history, the best works are Luís de Albuquerque, *O confronto do Olhar* (Lisbon, 1991); Francisco Bethencourt and Diogo Ramada Curto, *Memoria da Nação* (Lisbon, 1991); and a series of works by Charles R. Boxer: *The Portuguese Seaborne Empire, 1415–1825* (London, 1969); *The Dutch Seaborne Empire, 1600–1800* (London, 1973); *The Christian Century in Japan, 1549–1650*, 2nd ed. (Manchester, 1993); *The Golden Age of Brazil: The Growing Pains of a Colonial Society, 1695–1750*, 2nd ed. (Manchester, 1995); *João de Barros: Portuguese Humanist and Historian of Asia* (New Delhi, 1981); and "Three Historians of Portuguese Asia: João de Barros, Diogo do Couto and António Bocarro," *Boletim do Instituto Português de Hong Kong* 1 (July 1948), pp. 15–44.

Interesting also are the studies by C. R. Boxer on cultural and ideological aspects of the period: *Mary and Misogyny: Women in Iberian Expansion Overseas, 1415–1815. Some Facts, Fancies and Personalities* (London, 1975); and *The Church Militant and Iberian Expansion, 1440–1770* (Baltimore, 1978).

The following works provide good insights into the life and attitudes of the Portuguese overseas: Carl A. Hanson's *Economy and Society in Baroque Portugal, 1669–1703* (Minneapolis, 1981); George D. Winius's *The Black Legend of Portuguese India: Diogo do Couto, His Contemporaries and the 'Soldado Prático'* (New Delhi, 1985); and Carmen M. Radulet's *O cronista Rui de Pina e a "Relação do Reino do Congo": Manuscrito inédito do "Códice Riccardiano de 1910"* (Lisbon, 1992).

Comprehensive studies on specific topics of sixteenth-century literature are the works of T. F. Earle: *Theme and Image in the Poetry of Sá de Miranda* (Oxford, 1980); *The Muse Reborn: The Poetry of António Ferreira* (Oxford, 1988); and *The Comedy of the Foreigners* (Oxford, 1997), an interesting essay on a much neglected play. T. F. Earle has also published a critical edition of António Ferreira's *Poemas Lusitanos* (1598) (Lisbon, 2000), which includes the tragedy *A Castro*. The same scholar found, in the library of an Oxford college, *O Livro de Ecclesiastes* (Venice, 1538), by Damião de Góis, which he reproduced with an introduction and commentaries (Lisbon, 2002).

A reliable work on the humanist Damião de Góis continues to be Elizabeth Feist Hirsch's intellectual biography *Damião de Góis: The Life and*

Thought of a Portuguese Humanist (The Hague, 1967). This text was written over thirty years ago and since then many scholars have added to her research.. The Portuguese translation *Damião de Góis* (Lisbon, 2002) is to be recommended for the preface by J. V. de Pina Martins, who redresses the critical balance. See also J. V. de Pina Martins, Amadeu Torres, and L. Sousa Rebelo, *Damião de Góis: Humanista Português na Europa do Renascimento* (Lisbon, 2002).

For a new assessment of the role of science and humanism in Renaissance Europe, the reader can look at *Pedro Nunes e Damião de Góis, dois rostos do humanismo Português* (Lisbon, 2002), coordinated by Aires A. Nascimento. It deals mainly with the reception of humanist thought by Pedro Nunes.

For an understanding of the missionary work of António Vieira, S. J., in Brazil, the reader has a sound work in Thomas M. Cohen's *The Fire of Tongues* (Stanford, CA, 1971). A good study on the rhetorical importance of literary genres and their influence on the contemporary reader is Richard A. Preto-Rodas's *Francisco Rodrigues Lobo – Dialogue and Courtly Love in Renaissance Portugal* (Charleston, SC, 1971). For the development of Brazil, Kenneth Maxwell's *Pombal: Paradox of the Enlightenment* (Cambridge, MA, 1995) is recommended.

12

THE EXPANSION AND THE ARTS: TRANSFERS, CONTAMINATIONS, INNOVATIONS

Luís de Moura Sobral

Whoever approaches the arts related to or resulting from the Portuguese expansion is confronted with some serious difficulties. If the student is familiar with the history of Spanish American art, the situation can even appear a little odd. Studies of the arts in Spanish Latin America and the Philippines have been systematically pursued for at least the past fifty years, and the reader will easily find today an impressive series of excellent general surveys and monographic studies in different languages. Hispanic American arts and architecture can indeed be understood within the logic of their continuous historical evolution from around 1500 until the period of independence.

In the case of the Portuguese, however, nothing of the kind occurs. First of all, the arts of the Portuguese expansion, with the notable exceptions of the Brazilian and, to a lesser degree, the Goese cases, appear as an irregular sequence of separate episodes. These episodes have very little or nothing in common in terms of commission modalities, production, and consumption, or in terms of aesthetic values. To be sure, the arts and architecture of the Portuguese expansion reflect the very unsystematic, scattered nature of the so-called Portuguese empire, a characteristic that is pointed out in several chapters of the present volume. This is a situation hardly suitable for standard monographical treatment.[1]

There are also difficulties of a methodological type. Following Sousa Viterbo, who coined, more than a century ago, the label "Indo-Portuguese" apropos an exhibition of decorative arts (*Arte ornamental*) in Lisbon in

[1] See in Francisco Bethencourt and Kirti Chaudhuri, eds., *História da expansão Portuguesa* (Lisbon, 1998–1999), the chapters by Rafael Moreira in vol. 1, pp. 455–489 and vol. 3, pp. 463–493, and by Moreira and Alexandra Curvelo in vol. 2, pp. 532–570; see also Pedro Dias, *História da arte Portuguesa no mundo (1415–1822)* (Lisbon, 1998–1999).

1882, the arts of the Portuguese expansion toward the East have been labeled Afro-Portuguese, Sinhalese-Portuguese, Sino-Portuguese, Nippo-Portuguese, and Moghul-Portuguese, according to the areas of provenance of the pieces. However, these categories hardly fit the complex, varied historical reality. Indeed, African ivories with Portuguese themes can only be fully understood if studied within the contex of African art. Namban art is nothing but a very small chapter in the history of Japanese art. How then should one define or consider the Luso, or Portuguese, component of the above-mentioned labels?

Inversely, there is nothing "Oriental" in the Garcia Fernandes (fl. 1514–1565) paintings of the history of Saint Catherine that have been in the Goa cathedral since the middle of the sixteenth century, and there is nothing Oriental or Portuguese in the majestic Divine Providence church in the same city (1656–1672), designed by the Italian architect Carlo Ferrarini. Similarly, there is nothing particularly American about the churches carved in Portugal and shipped to Brazil to be mounted there (e.g., the College of the Jesuits and Nossa Senhora da Conceição da Praia, both in Salvador). The only common denominator in all these works is, somehow, the pivotal presence of the Portuguese and the resulting confrontation (contamination, integration) of different cultural and aesthetic realities and attitudes.

In fact, the arts of the Portuguese expansion were produced during a period of 400 years under diverse physical, historical, and political circumstances. They served different functions within the religious and the civil spheres. The Portuguese settled in uninhabited lands (the Atlantic islands), in areas with scarce or no urban traditions (Brazil), and in regions with high degrees of cultural development (Africa and Asia). The periods of time they would stay in those regions varied from a few months to several centuries. They built fortresses, designed or reorganized towns, traded objects, ordered hybrid artifacts for European or local functions, and imported from Portugal and other European countries artists, sculptures, paintings, tile panels (*azulejos*), and even entire churches. Portuguese or Portuguese-trained architects and artists produced buildings and works of art related, in different degrees, to both European and local traditions. Eventually, new functional and formal responses and solutions were put forward.

On the other hand, Portuguese trade brought from Africa, the East, and the Americas huge quantities of exotic products and luxury artifacts that eventually found their way to European collections and *Kunstkammern* (cabinets of curiosities) from the fifteenth century on. These objects were collected in their original form, but some of them were modified by European artists and artisans, with the consequence that they then took on new practical or symbolic functions. This important aspect of the arts of the expansion should not be underestimated. Non-European artists had also worked in Portugal since the beginning of the process. Portuguese workshops copied and reproduced in their turn African and Oriental techniques; hence the difficulty of dealing in a synthetic way with such a gigantic amount of material. Fortunately, there are the monuments, the works of art, and the artifacts, some of which are technically and aesthetically superb. This chapter will focus on a limited number of works, among the most symbolic and aesthetically meaningful, with regard to the three categories presented in the chapter's title. We will see examples of pure artistic transfers from Europe to other regions and from overseas to Europe; we will investigate cases of aesthetic and technical contamination; and, finally, we will discover some innovations. The discussion will follow the historical development of the expansion process from Africa and the Atlantic islands, to the Far Eastern regions, especially during the fifteenth and sixteenth centuries, and finally to Brazil in the seventeenth and eighteenth centuries.

Castles, Fortresses, and Cities

The castle of the Middle Ages underwent a series of radical transformations at the beginning of the sixteenth century caused by developments in the use of artillery.[2] A fortress would no longer have a keep or tower at its center and would present instead lower walls arranged in huge polygonal forms with bastions at the angles. These bastions were equipped with cannons that were positioned to completely cover, through a system of cross-fire shootings, the entire perimeter of the structure.

After some experiments and adaptations in North Africa, in around 1460 the Portuguese built their first castle overseas on the island of Arguim, on today's Mauritania coast, which would become the prototype for their fortified factories in Africa and Asia.[3] Arguim was a typical medieval castle, as would be other fortifications on the coasts of East Africa, Arabia, and India. However, even before the close of the fifteenth century, a new type of defensive structure was put forward.

Some improvements were introduced in the legendary São Jorge da Mina (El Mina, Ghana), which, for the next century and a half, would play a central role in the organization of Portuguese trade. Using local materials, the fortress was built in 1481 by the sea captain Diogo de Azambuja (1432–1518)

[2] I will follow Rafael Moreira, ed., *História das fortificações Portuguesas no mundo* (Lisbon, 1989).

[3] C. R. Boxer, *The Portuguese Seaborne Empire: 1415–1825* (London [1969], 1991), p. 25.

in a very short period of time under the technical supervision of the little-known master mason Luís Afonso. The most important wood and stone pieces were carved in Portugal. The El Mina fortress was a squared structure with towers at its corners. One of these was strong and rectangular, obviously designed to defend the drawbridge placed in the center of the nearby wall. The structure presented therefore some modern characteristics (towers for cross firing) and exerted a strong influence on subsequent military architecure, both in Portugal and overseas. The buildings were augmented in 1596 with two powerful bastions before the place was captured by the Dutch in 1637.

In the intricate history of the conquest and defense of coastal towns in Africa, Arabia, and Asia during the first decades of the sixteenth century, several castles and fortresses were built either by professional architects or by the military. Most of them continued the medieval tradition, although some presented the new features related to the particularities of fire armament. Around 1530, however, things changed with the introduction in Portugal of the fully developed bastion system.

The turning point in the history of Portuguese military architecture came in the 1540s with the reconstruction of Mazagão (El Jadida) in southern Morocco. Mazagão had to be impregnable in order to secure logistic support for the Portuguese fleets on their way to the East. It proved to be so, and it would not be abandoned until 1769, by decision of the Marquis de Pombal, under geopolitical considerations and after a siege by Moroccan troops. When the Portuguese first conquered the place in 1514, a small castle was built by Diogo de Arruda. In 1541, under the pressure of political events, an impressive technical committee was sent to the African coast. It consisted of Benedetto da Ravenna, an Italian engineer in the service of Emperor Charles V, and the architects Miguel de Arruda (1500?–1563, nephew of Diogo) and Diogo de Torralva (1500–1566). New plans were drawn by Ravenna and modified by the two other architects. João de Castilho (1480?–1552) arrived in the same year from the Tomar ateliers, in Portugal, with 1,500 masons. The huge building was completed within one year. It presents an irregular square shape with thick defensive walls and gigantic bastions at the corners. The original Diogo de Arruda building was transformed by Castilho into a cistern (completed by Lourenço Franco in 1547) that still exists. The new type of fortress with bastions would henceforth be the rule in all the Portuguese territories. In India, the bastions were for the first time used in 1546, by Francisco Pires, in the spectacular reconstruction of the Diu fortress.

By the middle of the sixteenth century, new theoretical interests centered on the study of mathematics radically changed the very nature of the architectural milieu. Miguel de Arruda, one of the architects of Mazagão, is the key figure in establishing a Portuguese tradition (indeed a true "school," after recent scholarship) of military architecture and city planning. He prepared the ground for the "bastion revolution," and plans elaborated by him or by his students were to be executed in Africa, Asia, and Brazil. Important for the next period was the foundation in 1647 in Lisbon of the School of Fortification and Military Architecture (Aula de Fortificação), which was expected to cope with urgent defensive tasks during the troubled Restoration period (1640–1668). Similar schools were then opened in other parts of the Portuguese territories and especially in Brazil (Salvador, 1696; Rio, 1698; São Luís do Maranhão, 1699; Recife, 1701). Luís Serrão Pimentel (1613–1679), the founder of a "Portuguese school of city-planning," was the first teacher of the Aula de Fortificação. In his *Método Lusitânico de desenhar as fortificações das praças regulares e irregulares* (Portuguese Method for the Design of Fortifications for Regular and Irregular Settlements) (1680), Serrão Pimentel acknowledges what appears to be a typical Portuguese preference for gradual transformation of spaces, as opposed to the creation ex nihilo of a definite and closed structure. Serrão Pimentel stresses the necessity of adapting to concrete situations instead of using a purely intellectual or theoretical model. Echoing no doubt the main defensive concerns of his time, Serrão Pimentel views the city as intimately related, if not confined, to the ramparts of a fortified place. This pragmatic approach appears for the first time to have provided theoretical grounds to a well-established tradition.[4]

In North Africa, for instance, at the beginning of the expansion process, elements of Portuguese urban tradition such as *rossios* (*largos*, or public squares) and *ruas direitas* (main streets), as well as Portuguese institutions such as town halls, *Misericórdias* (charitable institutions), parish churches, and monasteries, were integrated into the conquered cities. New towns, on the other hand, followed the Continental preference for coastal, riverside emplacements or for the tops of hills for either practical (e.g., proximity to harbors and water supplies) or defense reasons. Most of the time, in Madeira and the Azores, towns faced the south, as at home in Portugal. Organic, therefore, rather than rectilinear, some early foundations nevertheless present evidence of tentative orthogonality for ordering the urban

[4] On Portuguese urbanism, see Walter Rossa, "A cidade portuguesa," in Paulo Pereira, ed., *História da arte Portuguesa* (Lisbon, 1995), vol. 3, pp. 233–323; *Cidades Indo-Portuguesas/Indo-Portuguese Cities: A Contribution to the Study of Portuguese Urbanisn in the Western Hindustan* (Lisbon, 1997), and several essays in Walter Rossa, ed., *Colectânea de estudos: Universo urbanístico Português, 1415–1822* (Lisbon, 1998). See also Nestor Goulart Reis, *Imagens de vilas e cidades do Brasil colonial* (São Paulo, 2000); and José Manuel Fernandes, *Sínteses da cultura Portuguesa: A arquitectura* (Lisbon, 1991).

fabric – Ribeira Grande and Ponta Delgada in São Miguel; Praia and Angra in Terceira; Horta in Faial, Azores; and Funchal in Madeira.

It is now generally accepted that the urban evolution of Goa was shaped by traditional Portuguese constants and was not geometrically regulated ab initio (as Tavares Chicó had suggested); so was Salvador on the American continent, the first Brazilian capital. In the light of today's knowledge, Daman, in India, appears to be the only case of a regulated town plan in the Renaissance conception. Daman was designed by Giovanni Battista Cairati, the first chief engineer of India (between 1583 and 1596), taking as a module the quarter of the small castle built around 1560, after the conquest of the town. In Brazil, the chief engineer, Francisco Frias de Mesquita, designed at the beginning of the seventeenth century a very regular grid structure for São Luís do Maranhão. This regularized pattern would become the rule for the design of new cities, especially during the eighteenth century. This was not so, however, in the Minas Gerais district, where Ouro Preto, Sabará, São João d'El-Rei, and Serro, among others, were shaped by the very movement of openings, displacements, and closings of gold and precious stone mines, creating a type of organic city that was in fact similar to old Continental ones. That is why the Minas Gerais cities resemble the Mexican mining cities of Taxco and Guanajato, or the Peruvian (today's Bolivia) Potosí. Mariana, also in Minas Gerais, formally designed in 1745 by José Pinto de Alpoim, professor at the Rio School of Fortification, presents the only important exception to this state of things. After the reconstruction of Lisbon following the 1755 earthquake, however, several proposals were offered to regularize the plan of the city of Goa. In 1774, plans were sent to India to that effect but were not executed because the city had been progressively abandoned in favor of the more wholesome Panjim.

Scholars of colonial urbanism have in the past opposed the Portuguese tradition in favor of the Spanish one. The latter, typical of Renaissance idealism, was in a sense more sophisticated or more advanced. After recent studies, this opposition no longer stands. On the one hand, it is now accepted that a "good deal of the urban reality in America was not generated by the projected and organized action of the conquistadors."[5] On the other hand, as has been said, the Portuguese school of city planning recommended a more pragmatic approach to the site and to specific situations. Furthermore, one should not forget that Mexico City and Cuzco, the most obvious and monumental examples of orthogonal design, were built over the ruins of previous Aztec and Inca towns that were already geometrically regulated in pre-Hispanic times.

[5] Ramón Gutiérrez, *Arquitectura y urbanismo en Iberoamérica* (Madrid, 1983), p. 85.

Import and Export: Africa and Asia

As is well known, trade and religion were intimately associated during the Portuguese (and the Spanish) expansion. Moreover, the total adherence of Portugal to the Counter-Reformation in the second half of the sixteenth century opened new and rich perspectives for artistic activities. Indeed, more than ever before, religion became the central motor for the development of architecture and the visual arts. Present from the beginning of the process, missionary activity increased strongly during the sixteenth century, when the Society of Jesus practically had a monopoly. Needless to say, Catholic proselytism was the main means of cultural penetration.

Missionary as well as secular cult practices required appropriate buildings; huge amounts of carved, painted, or printed images; liturgical furniture; objects; books; and vestments. These accompanied the Portuguese in their first travels. Hundreds, if not thousands, of European works of art (and especially engravings) were therefore exported to Africa, Asia, and America from the very beginning of the expansion process. A Jesuit source of 1584, for instance, mentions a request from Japan alone to Rome for 50,000 pictures, most of them, no doubt, engravings.[6] Very few of these works are still extant, and others are known to us solely through archival documents or literary evidence.

Contemporary chronicles describe the strong impression some of these images exerted on Asian populations. Father Fernão Guerreiro reported in 1603–1611 the emotion caused by a copy of the *Madonna del Populo* in the Jesuit mission in Agra.[7] No doubt, the image of a gentle mother with her child, presented as the Mother of God, would have a strong appeal to the "poor women," who, according to Guerreiro, first saw it. Like all court art, Moghul imperial art was a refined one, conceived for the consumption of a restricted group of people. Moghul figurative arts represented reality in a highly idealized way, very different indeed from the more realistic Western tradition. Under these circumstances, we can easily conceive that the *Madonna del Populo* would appear to the "poor women" in a much more familiar, direct way. Similar reasons, of both an artistic and religious character, can explain the reactions to the painting of the Virgin Mary first brought by Francis Xavier to Japan in 1549. The enthusiasm toward that new form of painting was such that Shimazu Takahisa

[6] Yoshitomo Okamoto, *The Namban Art of Japan* (New York, 1972), p. 97.

[7] Kirti Chaudhuri, "O Impacte da expansão Portuguesa no Oriente," in Bethencourt and Chaudhuri, *História da expansão Portuguesa*, vol. 1, p. 504.

(1514–1571, the lord of Shimazu) and his mother ordered copies of it for themselves.[8]

We know of several first-quality works of art sent overseas from Europe. I have already mentioned the seven panels with the story of Saint Catherine (ca. 1538–1540) by Garcia Fernandes, formerly in the main altarpiece of the Goa cathedral and today in the sacristy. Fernandes (fl. 1514–1541) was one of the most celebrated Lisbon artists of the period, and the Goa series indicates the importance given, at such an early date, to the artistic programs of the new capital of the Estado da Índia. Likewise, the Jesuit fathers of Salvador, Brazil, ordered from Rome in the mid-1690s sixteen oils on copper with stories of the life of the Virgin. Intended to decorate the chest of drawers in the sacristy of their church, today's cathedral, the paintings are in the classic baroque manner typical of the Roman art of the period. In both cases, the paintings proposed to artists and amateurs in the Brazilian and Goese capitals were first-rate examples of the newest artistic tendencies being practiced in the West.

All these works exerted immediate influence. Garcia Fernandes's, for instance, were copied in different media and would inspire local artists for generations to come. Luxury artifacts imported from Africa and India to Europe are other examples of simple transfers of cultural products. Likewise, artists and specialized craftsmen and craftswomen from the colonial territories arrived in Europe to work there. Rauluchantim, for instance, was a famous Indian goldsmith, who first worked for the governor Afonso de Albuquerque in Goa and then, between 1518 and 1520, for the court of King Manuel in Lisbon. There he was employed in the execution of pieces "in the manner and tradition of India," although no extant work can now be attributed to him.[9]

Ivories and Bronzes

Chronologically, the so-called Afro-Portuguese or Luso-African ivories appear as one of the first artistic consequences of the encounter and contamination of distinct cultural realities.[10] They are also superb works of art that

[8] Tamon Miki, "The Influence of Western Culture on Japanese Art," *Monumenta Nipponica* 19 (1964), nos. 3–4, p. 146.

[9] Nuno Vassallo e Silva, ed., *A herança de Rauluchantim/The Heritage of Rauluchantim* (Lisbon, 1996), p. 15.

[10] William B. Fagg, *Afro-Portuguese Ivories* (London, n.d.); Ezio Bassani and William B. Fagg, eds., *Africa and the Renaissance: Art in Ivory* (New York, 1988); Maria Helena Mendes Pinto, ed., *Marfins d'além-mar no Museu de Arte Antiga/Overseas Ivory in the Museu de Arte Antiga* (Lisbon, 1988); Francisco Hipólito Raposo, ed., *A expansão Portuguesa e a arte do Marfim*

belong, from an artistic as well as a technical point of view, entirely to the sphere of African art. They were avidly collected in Renaissance Europe, and several pieces reached Central European *Kunstkammern* through the actions of Catherine of Portugal (1507–1578), sister of Emperor Charles V and wife of King João III. These pieces are typical export art objects. Their skilled makers simply complied with the specific needs of their new clientele. This eventually provided new models. A great deal of these objects were in fact for European functions, either profane or religious. Eventually, the new forms were adopted by local artists and workshops, and, indeed, some of the new characteristics can be found in works as late as the eighteenth century.

African ivories are mentioned in Portuguese royal collections from the time of King João II (reigned 1481–1495), but they must have been circulating in Portugal before those dates. Today, some 200 ivory pieces are extant, the remnants of a production of hundreds of works: saltcellars, pyxides, spoons and forks, knives and dagger handles, oliphants (hunting horns), crucifixes, and small statuettes. These pieces were produced in workshops in the areas of present-day Sierra Leone, Benin, and perhaps Congo (Zaire) from the end of the fifteenth to the mid-sixteenth century. These were places with long traditions of carving ivory, a precious material prized in Europe since antiquity. It was then only natural that the Portuguese started using African know-how for a lucrative trade. Ivory-carving techniques were not practiced in Portugal before the expansion era, whereas they had an ancient tradition elsewhere in Europe. However, the rarity of ivory brought about a general decline of this luxury art form in Europe in the fifteenth century. Significantly, interest in ivory carving revived with the expansion and with access to new stocks of raw material.

More than half of the total extant pieces come from Sierra Leone workshops. Kathy Curnow divides the pieces into two groups, according to their more or less close dependence on Portuguese models or iconography.[11] In the first group, she was able to distinguish four workshops. One fork and one spoon in the British Museum are good examples of the extraordinary virtuosity of Sapi (the inhabitants of coastal Sierra Leone, as the Portuguese called them) artists. The handles writhe themselves into knots and are decorated with local motifs (pythons and crocodiles) together with Manueline devices (Figure 12.1). An oliphant, or hunting horn, in the Armeria Reale of Turin

(Lisbon, 1991); and Kathy Curnow, "Africa, VI, 2(ii): Ivory," in *The Dictionary of Art* (1996), vol. 1, pp. 325–328.

[11] Curnow, "Africa, VI, 2(ii): Ivory," pp. 325–328; see also Suzanne Preston Blier, "Imagining Otherness in Ivory: African Portraits of the Portuguese ca. 1492," *The Art Bulletin* 75 (1993), pp. 375–396.

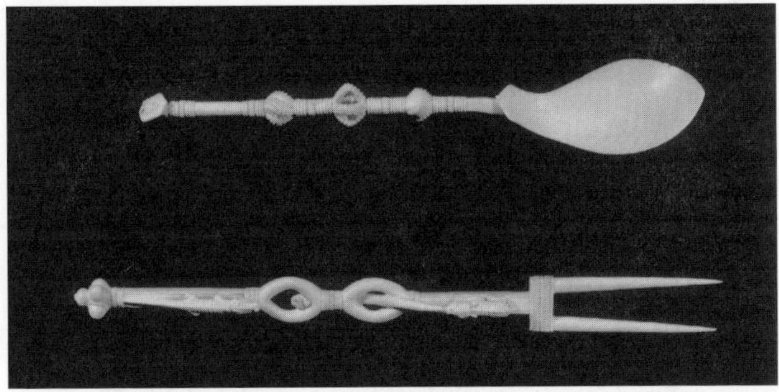

Figure 12.1. Spoon and *fork*, late fifteenth–early sixteenth century, ivory, Sierra Leone. The British Museum, London. (© Copyright the British Museum.)

is also typical of this group. It presents the mouthpiece on the extremity and not on the side, as was common in African horns, and its surface is covered with series of heraldic or figured reliefs divided by parallel rings. The reliefs represent huntings scenes, coats of arms of the Portuguese ruling house of Avis, and the emblem of King Manuel (the armillary sphere).

To the second Sierra Leone group belongs the absolute masterpiece of the series, the saltcellar in the Museo Nazionale Preistorico e Etnografico Luigi Pigorini in Rome (Figure 12.2). Ivory saltcellars were inspired, so it seems, by European metal cups with a convex cover or lid. Both the base and the cup of the Rome saltcellar are decorated with human figures and other elements of European and African origin. The Rome piece is extremely elegant, avoiding overdecoration. Slender human figures are seated on the base, two male Portuguese alternating with African women, separated by vertical elements with crocodiles. The most spectacular and unexpected scene appears on the top of the lid. A crouching Portuguese with an axe in his right hand is about to execute a prisoner while six trophy heads lie in front of him. This has been convincingly interpreted by Curnow as a ritual representation of the tribal leader in the Sierra Leonean tradition. The figure on the lid would then be a *lançado*, a Portuguese renegade or outlaw who escaped from the control of his superiors and melded into the African human and cultural landscape, speaking native languages, marrying local women, and acting as a direct, if more or less illegal, link between the Africans and the Europeans.

Ivories from Benin rely more deeply on local artistic tradition. When the Portuguese reached the region in the 1470s, Benin was a powerful centralized state, with a rich court art tradition that included specialists in brass casting. Benin ivories present typical African animals and motifs, and also

Figure 12.2. Sapi-Portuguese saltcellar, late fifteenth–early sixteenth century, ivory, Sierra Leone. (Rome-EUR, Museo Nazionale Preistorico/Etnografico Luigi Pigorini. No. Inv. MPE 104079. By concession of the Ministerio per i Beni e le Attività Culturali.)

Portuguese figures, these being more stylized than those from Sierra Leone, with strong heads and short and heavy bodies. Benin spoons, common in European Renaissance *Kunstkammern*, where they were often mistaken for Turkish, are very different from Sierra Leone's. They have a small handle, often with short zoomorphic themes. Hunting horns, decorated either with Manueline or geometric motifs, are also closer to the African tradition because they present the mouthpiece on the side.

Benin brass (or, as they are frequently if incorrectly called, bronze) reliefs are even more distantly related to European culture.[12] Metal artistic techniques were introduced in Benin as early as the twelfth century. Brass was employed in the fabrication of statuettes and relief plaques to decorate pillars in palaces and houses. During the period of the contacts with the Portuguese, the second period of the development of Benin brass art according to Felix

[12] Alain Jacob, *Bronzes de l'Afrique noire* (Paris, 1974).

Figure 12.3. Portuguese captain and his black retainer, sixteenth–seventeenth-century, brass. (Museum of Mankind, Dept. of Ethnography, the British Museum, London. © Copyright the British Museum.)

von Lushan, figures of Portuguese soldiers with firearms were often included in these decorative reliefs.[13] They were therefore intended for Beninese local use and were known to the West only after the sack and destruction of Benin City (in present-day Nigeria) in 1897 by the British (Figure 12.3).

Brass and ivory works of art were also sent to Portugal from the Christianized kingdom of Kongo during the first half of the sixteenth century, although none or almost none of these are extant today. There is therefore an early Afro-Christian art dating from the beginning of the sixteenth century, represented by brass statuettes of the Virgin and Child and crucifixes, where the figures present visible African facial characteristics. The African tendency toward idealization is evident in a seventeenth-century figure of

[13] Felix von Lushan, *Die Altertümer von Benin* (Berlin, 1919), as reported by Jacob, *Bronzes de l'Afrique noire*, p. 25.

Figure 12.4. Nkangi crucifixe, seventeenth century, bronze, Ba-Kongo. (Città del Vaticano, Museo Missionario Etnologico, Rome.)

Christ with thin elongated arms nailed to the cross and a flat, geometrically decorated body (private collection) (Figure 12.4). It must be noted that some of these pieces, the so-called *nkangi* crucifixes and *kuluzu* crosses, were integrated into local magical traditions, their former religious function being therefore extended in a typical process of cultural contamination.

By the mid-sixteenth century, the Portuguese had established solid trade mechanisms in the East. They quickly took advantage of the variety of technical expertise in different luxury industries that was now accessible to them. Imports of African ivories therefore decreased, to be ultimately replaced by products from the East. Other artifacts, of both religious and profane character, also joined the flux of exportation, which included furniture, jewelery, porcelains, textiles, and other items. This diverse production has been called Indo-Portuguese in a general way, as we have seen.

Ivory began to be employed in a systematic way in the making of religious imagery.[14] The majority of extant Eastern ivory work is indeed of a

[14] Bernardo Ferrão de Tavares e Távora, *Imaginária Luso-Oriental* (Lisbon, 1983); and Margarita Mercedes Estella Marcos and Lydia Sada de González, *Ivories from Far Eastern Provinces of Spain and Portugal* (Monterrey, 1997).

religious character, typical of the Counter-Reformation and the baroque periods. The production of such works started in the sixteenth century and increased dramatically in the next two centuries. Of small dimensions and sometimes polychromed and gilded, ivory religious imagery was well suited for private worship and piety and also as collecting items. Indeed, a considerable number of these pieces continue to circulate today in the art market. When compared with the Hispano-Philippine pieces produced at the same time and representing the same themes, Luso-Oriental ivories are more distant from European prototypes.[15] They are less expressive, more dependent on the form of the tusk, and the carving is also less subtle. From an iconographical point of view, the themes represented are the ones recommended by the Council of Trent: Jesus Christ, the Virgin Mary, and the saints.

Among the most interesting Luso-Oriental ivory sculptures, the series of the Infant Jesus deserve special attention. The figure of the young Jesus occupied a very special position in post-tridentine popular piety and was often represented by seventeenth-century Iberian artists. One of the most frequent themes is the infant Jesus *Salvator Mundi* (Savior of the World), standing naked on a rectangular base or over the terrestrial globe. In one instance (Oporto, private collection), he sits on the globe and is asleep, resting his head on his left hand. In other examples, he wears a tunic and holds the instruments of the Passion, poses and themes frequently found in sixteenth-century engravings.

Sometimes the figure of the Infant Jesus asleep is merged with the theme of the Good Shepherd, and the composition as a result is more complex and monumental. The young Jesus now sits on the top of a conic construction closely dependent on the form of the elephant tusk. The base is divided into superposed levels (two, three, or four) heavily carved, with settings or grottoes with evangelical or hagiographic figurations and decorative elements derived from Indian flora and fauna. Constant, under the figure of the sleeping infant, is a fountain, obviously the eucharistic *fons vitae* (fountain of life). Often, in the grottoes of the base, are found representations of penitent saints (Mary Magdalene, Jerome, and Peter), whose meaning is directly connected with the Good Shepherd: They will be saved as was the stray sheep (Figure 12.5). Other common depictions are the Nativity, the Annunciation, and the Evangelists. The general disposition of these works has been related to Buddhist or Hindu traditions, and the figure of the sleeping infant was said to derive from the First Meditation of the Buddha as bodhisattva.[16]

[15] Bernardo Ferrão de Tavares e Távora, "Imaginária Hispano-Filipina e Indo-Portuguesa," *Gil Vicente* 25 (1974), nos. 3–4, pp. 49–58.

[16] Távora, *Imaginária Luso-Oriental*, pp. xlviii, 86, etc.

Figure 12.5. Good Shepherd, seventeenth century, ivory. (Palácio do Correio Velho, Carlos Vasconcelos e Sá, Lisbon.)

However, this interpretation is hardly acceptable. The pose of the sleeping Infant is indeed common in Christian iconography, and it could very well have been taken from one of the engravings by the Wierix family in the late sixteenth century on the general subject of the *cor Iesu* (heart of Jesus).[17] The ivory pieces, carved as it seems during the seventeenth century alone, reflect, as a matter of fact, a kind of popular devotional syncretism frequently found in provincial areas in Europe, Ibero-America, and elsewhere. In any case, the Good Shepherds are among the most peculiar creations of the so-called Indo-Portuguese art in ivory.

Caskets and Furniture

Ceylon (present-day Sri Lanka) produced many ivory objects after European models, especially during the sixteenth century. These pieces, both in form and in iconography, are often closer to local spirit and artistic traditions than

[17] Marie Mauquoy-Hendrikx, *Les Estampes des Wierix* (Brussels, 1978), vol. 1, nos. 438, 479–480; vol. 2 (Brussels, 1979), no. 1443.

Figure 12.6. Ivory casket, c. 1543, Kotte. (Schatzkammer Residenz, Bayerische Verwaltung der staatlichen Schlösser, Gärten und Seen, Munich.)

their Indian counterparts. A group of ivory caskets, done in Kotte in the mid-sixteenth century, have long attracted attention and have been recently reexamined.[18] Their shape follows contemporary Portuguese traveling boxes or trunks, with their rectangular form and a three-part, roof-like cover. The surfaces offer ample room for decoration, which is usually in the form of narrative reliefs. Several of these caskets were collected by Queen Catherine of Portugal, who had some of them sent to members of her Hapsburg family all over Europe in the sixteenth century. In fact, none are found in Portuguese collections today.

One of these caskets, now in the Munich Schatzkammer Residenz, is intimately related to events in the history of Ceylon (Figure 12.6). The story it tells is about the political struggle for dynastic legitimacy. Bhuvaneka Bahu, king of Kotte (reigned 1521–1551), sought the support of the king of Portugal in order to secure the throne of the Ceylon empire for his grandson Dharmapala. In 1542–1543, an embassy was therefore sent to distant Lisbon

[18] Amin Jaffer and Melanie Anne Schwabe, "A Group of Sixteenth-Century Ivory Caskets from Ceylon," *Apollo Magazine* 149 (1999), no. 445, pp. 3–14.

carrying a sculpted effigy of Dharmapala, which was eventually crowned by João III of Portugal. This extraordinary scene is represented on the front side of the casket, together with the oath of loyalty of the prince to the Portuguese king. In both reliefs, Dharmapala is accompanied by his grandfather, who actually did not make the trip to Lisbon. Another casket, also in Munich, represents episodes of the liberation of Diu by João de Castro (1546), inspired, like a famous series of tapestries now in the Vienna Museum, by Gaspar Correia's *Lendas da Índia* (Legends of India) (at the time not yet published) or by other accounts of the events, some of which were soon to be published in Europe.[19]

Ivory was also lavishly used by Indian cabinet makers together with different varieties of precious woods (especially teak and ebony), tortoiseshell, mother-of-pearl, metalwork, and even gems. These cabinets were very popular in Portugal, particularly during the late seventeenth century after Queen Catherine of Bragança, wife of Charles II, introduced them to the English court. They were made by Indian and Portuguese artisans alike, either on the Malabar Coast or in Portugal. There are two different types: a simple chest of drawers, or the trunk proper with a base. An example of the first type (without a base), in the Lisbon Museu de Arte Antiga, is typically Moghul, with inlaid floral and figurative elements on ivory, flat and idealized as usual. These include Indians and Europeans, hunting scenes, peacocks, and even double symmetrical representations of Hercules and the Nemean lion (Figure 12.7).

Cabinet bases can be more or less elaborate, with drawers and zoomorphic carved legs, sometimes in the form of the Indian divinities Nagini, Naga, or Garudas. A teak cabinet, also in the Lisbon Museum, supported by four Indian mermaids, the Nagini, holding their breasts, has very linear designs of inlaid ebony representing curious lion-like animals. The eyes of the funny little beasts are made out of small round pieces of ivory, which gives the curious impression that the cabinet is staring at the visitor (Figure 12.8). The most sumptuous Moghul cabinet in the Lisbon Museum, supported by four ebony lions, is divided into two parts: the upper chest of drawers and an imposing base, almost a cabinet on its own. The inlaid ivory decoration of this piece, some of which has been painted in green and brown, is of great density. The representation includes Indian women and men, hunting scenes, elephant parades, pairs of lions and birds, and, on the doors of the

[19] Maria Antónia Gentil Quina mentions, among others, Diogo de Teive, *Commentarius a Lusitanis in India apud Dium gestis anno Salutatis nostrae MDXLVI* (Coimbra, 1548); Damião de Góis, *De Bello Cambaico* (Louvain, 1549); and *Nouvelles des Indes* (Paris, 1549). *Tapeçarias de D. João de Castro* (Lisbon, 1995), pp. 113–114, 119–120.

Figure 12.7. Moghul cabinet, seventeenth century, teak, ebony, and ivory. (Reboredo Madeira collection, Lisbon. Photo: José Pessoa, Divisão de Documentação Fotográfica, Instituto Português de Museus.)

lower part, the giant *simurgue*, the mythical bird of Sindbad the Sailor's *Voyages*, holding two elephants in its claws (Figure 12.9).

As has been said, Indian goldsmiths had worked for Europeans since the time of the first contacts. Indeed, using materials not known before in Portuguese art (tortoiseshell, mother-of-pearl, and polished rhinoceros horn), together with precious metals and gems, these artists produced some of the most sumptuous pieces of the period.[20] Outstanding are the works given in 1597 to the Carmo Monastery of Vidigueira, Portugal, by Father André Coutinho, born in Oporto and the first priest to be ordained in China.

A Goese, late sixteenth-century casket was presented in 1591–1597 to the Augustinian Graça Monastery in Lisbon by Filipa de Vilhena, widow of Matias de Albuquerque, the fifteenth viceroy of India. Made entirely in gold filigree, the casket was integrated into the monumental tabernacle of the church and served to keep the Eucharist (Figure 12.10). Whatever

[20] Vassallo e Silva, *The Heritage of Rauluchantim* (1996); and Maria Helena Mendes Pinto, ed., *Van Goa naar Lisboa: Indo-Portuguese Kunst 16e–18e Eeuw* (Brussels, 1991).

Figure 12.8. Indo-Portuguese cabinet, seventeenth century, teak, ebony, and ivory. (Museu Nacional de Arte Antiga, Lisbon. Photo: José Pessoa, Divisão de Documentação Fotográfica, Instituto Português de Museus.)

its original function, no doubt profane, the Goese casket after arriving in Lisbon acquired a new sacred status, which it would maintain for centuries to come.

Other objects of non-European origin were modified to be able to perform specific liturgical Catholic functions. A coconut bowl with a rhinoceros handle and gilt silver mounts, once in the *Kunstkammer* of Rudolph II in Prague and dating from the second half of the sixteenth century (now in the Kunsthistorisches Museum in Vienna), used to contain holy water, is a superb example of this cultural and formal hybridism.[21] These occurrences of religious contaminations can be compared to the Kongo *Nkangi* crucifixes mentioned earlier. Moghul craftsmen produced in

[21] Fernando Checa Cremades, ed., *Felipe II: Un Monarca y su Época. Un Príncipe del Renacimiento* (Madrid, 1999), no. 279, p. 662.

Figure 12.9. Moghul cabinet, seventeenth century, sisso, ebony, and ivory. (Museu Nacional de Arte Antiga, Lisbon. Photo: Luís Pavão, Divisão de Documentação Fotográfica, Instituto Português de Museus.)

Figure 12.10. Casket, late sixteenth century, gold and enamel, Goa. (Museu Nacional de Arte Antiga, Lisbon. Photo: José Pessoa, Divisão de Documentação Fotográfica, Instituto Português de Museus.)

Figure 12.11. Casket, late sixteenth century, tortoiseshell and silver, Goa. (Museu Nacional de Machado de Castro, Coimbra. Photo: José Pessoa, Divisão de Documentação Fotográfica, Instituto Português de Museus.)

the late sixteenth century a series of tortoiseshell and silver caskets of the most refined kind. The one in the Machado de Castro Museum in Coimbra is one of the finest, combining Moghul vegetal and animal motifs with typical Renaissance scrolls (Figure 12.11).

Textiles, Paintings, and Porcelain

Transfers of materials, technical skills, and iconographic motifs also occur in the textile domain. Persian tapestries, quite common in Portugal during the sixteenth and seventeenth centuries, were instrumental in the development of the so-called Arraiolos "tapestries" industry in Portugal. On the other hand, Guimarães linen was exported to India, while Indian woman embroiderers had been working in Portugal since the beginning of the sixteenth century. Silk came, of course, from China. The result of all this is a fascinating group of embroidered coverlets aesthetically related to Asian art but decorated with Western themes, either religious, mythological, or historical.[22]

One of the most unexpected examples of the latter, dating from the late seventeenth century, is now in the Caramulo Museum in Portugal.

[22] *Colchas bordadas no Museu Nacional de Arte Antiga: India, Portugal, China, séculos XVII–XVIII* (Lisbon, 1978); *Portugal and the East through Embroidery: 16th to 18th Century Coverlets from the Museu Nacional De Arte Antiga, Lisbon* (Washington, DC, 1981).

It represents in a central medallion a rather comic episode in the history of Venus and Mars. The two lovers are caught in bed by Vulcan, Venus's husband, who imprisons them in a net while in the upper part of the composition the Olympian gods laugh (Figure 12.12). The story was told by Ovid (*Metamorphoses*, IV, 171–189), and the embroiderers could have taken as a model one of the engravings or woodcuts used to illustrate an edition of the popular book. To my knowledge, no other representation of this episode was produced during the seventeenth century in Portugal in any medium because in fact mythological painting is virtually absent there. The main male actors on the embroidered scene present typical Indian traits, with fine mustaches that make them look like today's popular Indian movie heroes.

I have already mentioned the exportation of paintings from Europe to the East. Most of the paintings done for the Portuguese-controlled territories, however, were the responsibility of local artists, either Europeans or locally trained natives. With a few exceptions, the extant examples do not show the same quality as works in other media and techniques that we have reviewed so far. Painting indeed has special characteristics. One must not forget that Eastern artistic conceptions were different from those of the West. Modern European naturalism or realism, a notion central to European culture, no doubt presented particular challenges for artists educated under different traditions. Indeed, this naturalism was essential for the figurative religious art of the Counter-Reformation and the baroque. In order to touch and move the heart, images had to resemble reality as much as possible; they had to show convincingly the sufferings of the Savior, of the martyrs, and so forth. This required particular techniques (perspective, anatomy, and physiognomy) not needed elsewhere. These considerations help to explain, at least in part, the differences in quality of the different media I have mentioned. Because the decorative arts were not based on representation but rather on the meticulous control of the materials, they were not affected by the difficulties of the modern European mimesis.

Series of paintings, on wood panels, on canvas, or as murals, are found all over Goese territory and await scholarly attention.[23] Of special interest is the Franciscan series on the lateral walls of the sanctuary in the St. Francis church in Old Goa. Invariably, these works follow, with greater or less liberty, European engravings, as is the case with an oil painting on wood, with a nice oblong wooden and ivory frame, in the Xavier Centre of Historical Research

[23] Matthew Lederle, *Christian Painting in India* (Bombay, n.d.); Vitor Serrão, "A pintura na antiga India Portuguesa nos séculos XVI e XVII," *Oceanos* (1994), nos. 19–20, pp. 102–112.

Figure 12.12. Coverlet with Venus, Mars, and Vulcan, late seventeenth century, embroidered silk, Goa. (Museu do Caramulo, Caramulo. Fundação Abel de Lacerda. Gift of José Silveira Machado. Photo: Museu do Caramulo.)

(Alto Porvorim, Goa), recently published.[24] It is entitled the *Adoration of the Infant and the Virgin* but represents in fact the *Mystical Marriage of St. Catherine* and was painted in imitation of the original composition by Veronese (1575, in the Museum of the Accademia in Venice), which was engraved in 1582 by Agostino Carracci.

The porcelain trade was virtually a Portuguese monopoly during the sixteenth century.[25] Exported to the East and to the West through Macao, the porcelain came from different production centers in China but, as a general rule, was decorated in nearby Canton. In Lisbon, around 1580, it could easily be purchased in the six specialized shops on the Rua Nova dos Mercadores. The creation at the beginning of the seventeenth century of the Dutch and English East India companies introduced a dramatic change in the import–export situation in the East. The Dutch, followed by the British, soon supplanted the Portuguese in the porcelain trade. During the seventeenth, eighteenth, and nineteenth centuries, porcelain sent to the West was generally referred to as Compagnie des Indes. Expressly made for the export market, this porcelain was inferior in quality to the pieces reserved for internal consumption and especially for the imperial court.

One of the earliest examples of Chinese porcelain made for a Portuguese patron is the ewer from about 1519 in the Medeiros e Almeida Foundation, Lisbon. It presents the typical white and blue Ming decoration, featuring the armillary sphere, the emblem of King Manuel I (Figure 12.13). Other Portuguese officials in the East ordered pieces for personal use and had their names painted on them. The *Bottle of Jorge Alvares*, dated 1552, in the Caramulo Museum, is an example of this practice. The white and blue decoration is richer than in the previous example, with a midsection nicely covered with swimming fish amid aquatic vegetation. Powerful Portuguese families started a practice long followed of ordering from Canton ateliers porcelain services with a coat of arms, for which they provided designs. This massive importation stimulated the imitation of Chinese models in Portuguese, French, German, and Dutch ateliers in Europe.

Needless to say, the religious orders also commissioned porcelain pieces, duly identified with their emblems. From the first half of the sixteenth century on, there appeared plates, bowls, and vases decorated with Christian

[24] Charles J. Borges, "Questões em torno das formas de representação na arte religiosa Indo-Portuguesa," *Oceanos* (1994), nos. 19–20, p. 81.

[25] Artur Teodoro de Matos, ed., *A influência Oriental na cerâmica Portuguesa do século XVII* (Lisbon, 1994); and Pedro Dias, ed., *Reflexos: Símbolos e imagens do Cristianismo na porcelana Chinesa/Reflections: Symbols and Images of Christianity on Chinese Porcelain* (Lisbon, 1997).

Figure 12.13. Ewer, Ming dynasty, c. 1519, porcelain, China. (Fundação Medeiros e Almeida, Lisbon. Photo: Casa-Museu da Fundação Medeiros e Almeida.)

symbols. Some of them feature scenes from Christian history, but the actors have Chinese faces, such as *Crucifixion with the Virgin and St. John* (ca. 1700, Lisbon, private collection) or *Baptism of Christ* (ca. 1735, Coimbra, private collection).

A bottle from about 1620–1630, now in the Lisbon Museum, shows on one of its sides a peculiar form of cross with three crossbars, one at its base, one at the center, and the last one at the top (Figure 12.14). Furthermore, it is flanked by two banana trees, while four dragonflies are seen on the upper part of the composition, surrounding the cross like angels. At the base of the bottle are two other Passion attributes, or *arma Christi*, the cock and the scourge, and, at the left corner, a dog with a torch in its mouth (the *Domini canis*), which identifies the piece as a Dominican commission.

This complete Sinolization of the Gospel recalls the missionary activities of the Society of Jesus and its problematic and controversial effort to adapt to Chinese culture. As is well known, Michele Ruggieri (who arrived in Macao in 1579) adopted Chinese words to mention Christian divinities, and Matteo Ricci (who arrived in 1582), the architect of the Jesuit strategy in

Figure 12.14. Bottle, Ming dynasty, ca. 1620–1630. (Museu Nacional de Arte Antiga, Lisbon.)

China, used the word *Shangdi* (Lord of the Highs) to signify God.[26] European prints and engravings were likewise used as models by Chinese porcelain painters. A nice covered cup from around 1750, with the figure of St. Ignatius Loyola (Lisbon, Ricardo Espírito Santo Silva Foundation), for instance, repeats an engraving by Schelte A. Bolswert after Rubens dated 1622.

Two exceptional monuments in Lisbon bear witness to the taste for collections of Chinese porcelain among the Portuguese high nobility in the last quarter of the seventeenth century. The Porcelain Room in the Santos Palace, presently the embassy of France, was, most likely, the work of José Luís de Lancastre (1639–1687), the third Count of Figueiró. The walls and the pyramidal ceiling of the room were then covered by more than 450 pieces, dishes and plates, dating from the 1520s to the 1620s. Today only the ceiling (263 pieces) is extant. The second example, like the Porcelain Room also dating from around 1670, is quite different in nature. Fragments of china as well as entire plates were used together with pebbles and shells to decorate the walls of a grotto in the gardens of the Fronteira Palace on

[26] Wang Bin, "Deus e Tian: Paradoxo de representação do que está para além da representação," *Revista de Cultura Instituto Cultural de Macau* (1994), no. 21, pp. 93–106. (There are English editions of this journal.)

the outskirts of Lisbon. In quite an extraordinary gesture of magnificence, its builder, João de Mascarenhas (1632–1681), the first Marquis of Fronteira, after a banquet offered to the future King Pedro II, had the plates broken and the pieces installed in the grotto in order to preserve the memory of the princely visit.

The Southern Barbarians in Japan: Namban Art

One of the most fascinating episodes of Portuguese-related art in the East is so-called *namban* art, or the art of the "southern barbarians," an expression, so it seems, without negative connotations.[27] *Namban* art was produced during a very short period of time from the mid-sixteenth century to about 1650, ten years or so after the Japanese harbors were closed to the Portuguese. Epiphenomenal to the history of Japanese art, namban art products are of the utmost interest for the history of the Portuguese in Japan.

Together with paintings, engravings, and books, the Jesuits brought to Japan European artists to teach at art schools and at printing ateliers they established in some of their colleges and seminaries. The painter Giovanni Nicolao, S. J., for instance, who arrived in Japan in 1583, had to escape to Macao in 1614 after the Japanese banishment of the Christians.[28] The painting school he had opened in Arima, Japan, was then transferred to Macao, where it continued to operate until his death there in 1626. Between 1591 and 1611, Jesuit presses published in Japan more than thirty books, some of them illustrated with engravings or etchings.[29]

At the same time, baptized daimyos (Japanese nobles) built chapels in their castles and had them decorated by Japanese artists, such as the one at Usukine Castle, decorated by Kano Eitoku (1543–1590) in 1562. Twenty years later, Japanese envoys traveled to Europe, from where they brought, in 1590, new artworks, books, and musical instruments. The consequence of all this activity was a curious Western mania in the Nagasaki region, the apogee of which was between 1591 and 1614.[30]

[27] Miki, "The Influence of Western Culture," pp. 146–185; Okamoto, *The Namban Art of Japan*; *Exposição de Arte Nambam* (1981); *Arte Namban: Influencia Española y Portuguesa en el arte Japonés, siglos XVI y XVII* (Madrid, 1981); Muno Vassallo e Silva, ed., *No caminho do Japão: Arte Oriental nas colecções da Santa Casa da Misericórdia de Lisboa* (Lisbon, 1993).

[28] Miki, "The Influence of Western Culture," p. 148.

[29] Kiichi Matsuda, *The Relations between Portugal and Japan* (Lisbon, 1965), pp. 81–84; see also J. M. Braga, "The Beginnings of Printing at Macao," *Studia* 12 (1963), pp. 29–137.

[30] On the second Japanese embassy to Europe (1613–1620), see *Da Sendai a Roma: Un' ambasceria giapponese a Paolo V* (Rome, 1990).

Artworks and artifacts produced in this context have been divided into two broad categories: the religious ones are called *kirishitan* art; the profane or industrial, *namban* art. Lacquer boxes, lacquer flasks, lacquer furniture, and lacquer Christian liturgical objects were particularly praised because this technique was not known in the West. However, the most spectacular *namban* artworks are the celebrated *namban byobu,* or screens (hence the Portuguese and Spanish words *biombo*).[31] Painted paper screens belong to an ancient Japanese tradition and are counted among the most prestigious forms of art in that country. They were commissioned for members of local ruling classes or for rich merchants and never, as far as we know, for export. Usually, *namban* screens were made in pairs, and each one was divided into six panels, only one side of which was painted.

The first *namban* screens can be dated very precisely from 1593. They are related to a celebrated reunion at Toyotomi Hideyoshi's (1535–1598) Nagoya Castle in the province of Hizen, Kyushu, to which the captain of the Portuguese *nao* (ship) and his retinue were invited. The Portuguese parading in Nagasaki harbor were observed with sympathetic curiosity and amazement by the painter Kano Mitsunobu (1560–1605), who had been working at Nagoya Castle. Back in Kyoto, Kano Mitsunobu painted the first *namban byobu*, using the drawings he had made in Nagasaki.[32] His works were so successful they started a tradition. Following his example, artists would represent the Portuguese disembarking and parading in Nagasaki harbor, while a boat can be seen at the left, with sometimes, at the far left, an imaginary view of Goa, from which the *nao* prepares to leave.

Namban screens have been divided into five groups.[33] The first includes the works done between 1593 and 1605, after the drawings made at Nagasaki by the Kano painters. Screens of group 2 were designed by Kano Naizen (five known examples) and by artists of the Tohoku (more than ten known examples) and Hasegawa schools between 1606 and 1615. Group 3 includes six screens designed by Kano Sanraku and Tomonobu between 1616 and 1660. To group 4 are ascribed five examples of lesser quality by Machi-eshi artists (1661–1673), who actually had never seen the Portuguese. The last group includes seven screens of the school of Hanabusa, known as *Kaiko-kei* (1673–1687).

The Lisbon Museu de Arte Antiga owns outstanding examples of the first two groups. The pair attributed to Kano Domi and dated around 1593–1600,

[31] Mendes Pinto, *Biombos Namban/Namban Screens* (Lisbon, 1988).

[32] Okamoto, *The Namban Art of Japan*, pp. 71–72; Tadao Takamizawa, "Biombos namban," in *Arte Namban*, pp. 9–10.

[33] After Takamizawa, "Biombos namban."

when the Portuguese were accepted and influential in Nagasaki, divides the story into two parts: the arrival of the black *nao* and the parade of the Portuguese. The scenes are extremely vivid and colorful, giving a detailed account of the goods being disembarked and transported and the persons involved in the activities (captain, sailors, servants, and black slaves). Products brought by the Portuguese and represented by the painters include tobacco, Persian horses, Portuguese wine, olive oil, olives, capers, almonds, jams, and even Alentejo cheeses (Figures 12.15 and 12.16). The second pair is signed with the seal of the painter Kano Naizen (1570–1616) and is dated around 1603–1610. This time the *nao* appears in both screens. In the first, it leaves the city of Goa, symbolized by a pagoda-like viceroy palace at the left. In the second, we can see members of the religious orders, carefully identified by the colors of their habits: Jesuits in black, Franciscans in brown, Dominicans in white and dark blue, and Augustinians in grey.

Namban screens record the first, if brief, episode of the fascination of the Japanese with the West. This fascination was real and sympathetic, not tainted with any negative overtones whatsoever. The screens constitute, furthermore, the most detailed and accurate visual record of the Portuguese in the East at that time. This result was achieved by great masters in the most sophisticated art forms and techniques at their disposal. There are no Portuguese or European equivalents to these first-rate works of art. The reason for this is obvious. Human or ordinary reality was not a primary concern of painters in Portugal, as was the case similarly in the great majority of other European countries. During the sixteenth, seventeenth, and eighteenth centuries, Portuguese painters depicted supernatural beings and events almost exclusively, although in a more or less "naturalistic" way, depending upon the stylistic or formal options of the moment. To gain an accurate idea of the inhabitants of non-European places of the time, painters from a different cultural tradition were needed. Dutch painters Frans Post (1612–1680) and Albert Eckhout (ca. 1610–1665), for example, represented people, landscapes, and the flora of Brazil in the mid-seventeenth century, but they were trained in a Calvinist country, where religious imagery had been largely abolished and where other genres of painting had been put forward. Still, Eckhout's and Post's innumerable Brazilian women, men, and fruits do not escape the rules of Dutch contemporary still lifes and portrait genres.

Other themes appear in other Western-related screens: European social customs, world maps, the four great cities of the West (Lisbon, Madrid, Rome, and Constantinople), or series of warriors on horseback, taken from old European prints.

Figure 12.15. Namban screen, attr. Kano Domi, 1593–1602. (Museu Nacional de Arte Antiga, Lisbon. Photo: Francisco Matias, Divisão de Documentação Fotográfica, Instituto Português de Museus.)

Figure 12.16. Namban screen, attr. Kano Domi, ca. 1593–1602. (Museu Nacional de Arte Antiga, Lisbon. Photo: Francisco Matias, Divisão de Documentação Fotográfica, Instituto Português de Museus.)

Religious Architecture: Atlantic Islands and Asia

Little has been said so far about the arts in the Atlantic islands, Madeira, and the Azores. The culture of the islands, uninhabited before Portuguese settlement during the fifteenth century, is indeed a consequence of simple transfers from the European continent. The arts there evolved within Portuguese frames of reference, presenting here and there some regional variants. One of the most obvious of these consists in the use of local basalt

Figure 12.17. Manueline portal, parish church, Ponta Delgada, São Miguel Island, Azores. (Photo: Victor Melo, "O Retrato.")

stone, which confers on the buildings a distinctive appearance, different indeed from the architecture on the Continent.[34]

In the Madeira Islands, some gothic elements still remain, both in civil and religious buildings, dating from the mid-fifteenth century. Late gothic or Manueline architecture is better represented, however, in the archipelagos. The Funchal Cathedral (Madeira), two portals of the parish church of Saint Sebastian (1533–1545), Ponta Delgada (São Miguel Island, Azores), and the parish church of Saint Sebastian (Terceira Island, also in the Azores) are the most interesting examples of the series (Figure 12.17).

Manueline elements are also evident in India, the most well known of which is the main portal of the Church of St. Francis in Old Goa.[35] This

[34] Francisco Ernesto de Oliveira Martins, *Subsídios para o inventário artístico dos Açores* (Angra do Heroísmo, 1980); Nestor de Sousa, *A arquitectura religiosa de Ponta Delgada nos séculos XVI a XVIII* (Ponta Delgada, 1986); Rui Carita, *História da Madeira* (Funchal, 1989–1992).

[35] Carlos de Azevedo, *Arte Cristã na India Portuguesa* (Lisbon, 1959); Azevedo, *A Arte de Goa, Damão e Diu* (Lisbon, 1992); José Pereira, *Baroque Goa* (New Delhi, 1995); see also Sebastian Elavathingal, *Inculturation & Christian Art: An Indian Perspective* (Rome, 1990).

Figure 12.18. Manueline portal, Church of St. Francis, 1527, Old Goa. (Photo: Architect José Manuel Fernandes collection.)

elegant doorway shows a trefoil arch at the top, crowned with the Portuguese blazon and armillary spheres (Figure 12.18). The portal is a remnant of the first church, built in 1527 but replaced in 1661 by the present one. Manueline forms must have been naturally associated, so to speak, with Catholicism because similar portals continued to be built during the seventeenth century in Protestant-controlled areas, such as, for instance, the Church of Our Lady of Hope on Vypeen Island, in front of Fort Cochin.[36]

In Old Goa, the novelties introduced in Portugal were copied there practically at the same time. The portals of Our Lady of Rosary (ca. 1543) are classic in form, proportions, and vocabulary, and the church itself still follows a Manueline typology. The turning point toward classicism will happen a little later, in the Goa Cathedral. Started in 1562, after plans by Miguel de

[36] José Manuel Fernandes, "Vestígios do Manuelino na arquitectura religiosa de influência Portuguesa na India: Malabar, Coromandel, Goa," *Oceanos* (1994), nos. 19–20, pp. 136–154.

Arruda, the Cathedral belongs to a series of similar contemporary buildings in Portugal (Leiria, Mirando do Douro, Portalegre) and the Atlantic islands (Angra, Azores) built to accommodate the creation of new dioceses. The Goa church is the largest of the group. It follows the common *Hallenkirche* type and presents a three-story façade structured in classic motifs taken from Serlio's *Architettura* (1537–1575). A similar phenomenon occurs in the Spanish Americas, more or less at the same time, where the great cathedrals (Mexico, Puebla, Lima, Cuzco) were built after the classic model of Jaén, Spain, by Andrés de Vandelvira (1509–1575).

Among the Jesuit examples, the Bom Jesus Basilica (1594–1605) in Goa was one of the most influential. With a four-story façade (one more than the Goa Cathedral), and Corinthian columns at the base, it uses triangular fanlike spandrels, instead of the canonical Giacomo della Porta volutes, to mark the transition, in the upper level, between the central axis and the lateral ones (Figure 12.19). This motif will later be used in different buildings in Goa. Maybe the most spectacular case of direct transfer in Old Goa, as far as architecture is concerned, is the Church of St. Cajetan, or of the Divine Providence, designed by Father Carlo Ferrarini (1656–1672), an Italian architect. It is a superb building with colossal Corinthian columns and pilasters set against a three-story façade, and an extra fourth story set behind and above the triangular pediment. With a cupola at the crossing that can be seen above the façade, it is obvious that St. Cajetan (Figure 12.20) echoes St. Peter's Basilica in the Vatican.

Another outstanding Jesuit monument, St. Paul's Church, designed by Father Carlo Spinola, S. J., was built in Macao.[37] Formerly dedicated to the Assumption of the Virgin, it was started in 1602, but the façade was not completed until 1644. Four years before, the church had been consecrated to the Immaculate Conception, at a time when this devotion was being strongly advocated in Portugal. In the Cortes of 1646, Mary was declared the patron saint of the country. Standing at the top of a hill, with a staircase of sixty-eight steps in front of it, the church was a magnificent building, with its interior richly decorated with gilt sculpture and paintings (Figure 12.21). Unfortunately, it was completely destroyed by fire in 1835. Today, only the façade remains. The Jesuit college in Macao was an important education and learning center. Considered to be the first university of the Western type in Asia, it operated the first printing press with metal movable type in the East.

[37] Gonçalo Couceiro, *A Igreja de S. Paulo de Macau* (Lisbon, 1997); Juan Ruiz-de-Medina, "Un Jesuita de Madrid arquitecto de la Iglesia de São Paulo, Macao," *Revista de Cultura, Instituto Cultural de Macau* (1994), no. 21, pp. 37–50.

Figure 12.19. Bom Jesus Basilica, 1594–1605, Old Goa. (Photo: Architect José Manuel Fernandes collection.)

The façade, the only extant part of the building, is an impressive piece of architecture, two stories high with a two-story crowning section and a triangular pediment at the top. The stories are separated by entablatures with Ionic and Composite columns. With its complex iconographic program, as far as I know not yet fully explained, the façade unfolds like an engraved front page of one of the Jesuits' contemporary propaganda books. The statue of the Immaculate Conception, to which the temple is dedicated, stands in the center, adored by six angels in stone relief. Above it stands the statue of infant Jesus surrounded by symbols of the Passion, likewise in stone relief. In the middle story, in four niches, are the statues of Jesuit saints: Francis Borgia, Ignatius Loyola, Francis Xavier, and Aloysius Gonzaga. Traditional Immaculate and Marian symbols were distributed along the frieze of the

Figure 12.20. Church of the Divine Providence or of St. Cajetan, 1656–1672, Old Goa. (Photo: Architect José Manuel Fernandes collection.)

second entablature: the tabernacle, the *speculum sine macula* (mirror without stain), the *porta clausa* (closed door), and the chandelier with seven branches. In the compartments between the columns around the Virgin, there are other Immaculate attributes: the *fons hortorum* (fountain of the gardens), the cedar of Lebanon, the olive tree, and the palm tree.

Figure 12.21. Façade of St. Paul's Church, ca. 1644, Macao. (Photo: Instituto Cultural da Região Administrativa Especial de Macau.)

From an iconographic point of view, the reliefs in the third story are the most interesting. To the left of the *fons hortorum* stands a big *navis ecclesiae* (or Noah's Ark), another symbol of the Virgin. Parallel to this, to the right, stands the apocalyptical beast vanquished by the small figure of Mary. The motif was copied from a well-known engraved Immaculate Conception by Cornelis Cort, dated 1567, and it therefore does not represent, as has been strangely enough suggested, the Lernaen hydra, the seven-headed hydra of the Hercules legend. At the top, in the pediment, other Immaculate attributes are to be found, the sun and the moon (*pulchra ut luna, electa ut sol*). The most intriguing reliefs, however, are the ones on the lateral scrolls of the same story. They are accompanied by Chinese inscriptions and represent, to the right, a reclining skeleton and, to the left, a prostrate winged devil, whose chest is pierced by an arrow (Figures 12.22 and 12.23). The Chinese ideograms near the last one say that "the memory of the dead ancestors must

Figure 12.22. Façade of St. Paul's Church, detail of the death, ca. 1644, Macao. (Photo: Instituto Cultural da Região Administrativa Especial de Macau.)

Figure 12.23. Façade of St. Paul's Church, detail of the devil, ca. 1644, Macao. (Photo: Instituto Cultural da Região Administrativa Especial de Macau.)

arouse our moral sense."[38] The chrysanthemum, a well-known Japanese symbol, is one of the main motifs of the façade. No doubt, the plastic

[38] I am grateful to Prof. Wang Zeng Yang, President of the Macao Cultural Institute, for the kind translation of the inscriptions.

sermon in the façade proclaims the triumph of the Immaculate Conception over death and evil, and I feel that it is, in symbolic and propagandistic terms, a response to Japanese religious persecutions at the time. We know in fact that several exiled Japanese Christian painters worked on the church after they had fled from their homeland. Under these circumstances, it is not impossible that the dead devil evokes the frightening statues of the Ni-o, the traditional guardians in Japanese temples.

Depicting the imaginary triumph of a foreign religion in contrast with the very real and cruel Japanese repression, the façade of St. Paul symbolizes the limits of Portuguese expansion toward the East.

Brazil

In Brazil, the Portuguese did not find huge centralized states with highly developed forms of urban culture as had been the case with the Spaniards in Mexico or Peru. On the contrary, because the area lacked the attraction of immediate riches (such as spices, gold, or luxury manufactured goods) still easily available in the East, it would take more than three decades after the Alvares Cabral voyage for the Portuguese to found their first towns on the American continent (Olinda, 1535; Recife, 1540; and Salvador, 1549). These settlements naturally followed familiar European prototypes in structuring urban spaces and functions, as well as in the use of architectural typologies. The domination of cultural transfer from Europe was therefore almost absolute during the first two centuries of Portuguese America, whereas the presence of aboriginal traditions can be discerned in the arts of Hispanic America from the very beginning of the sixteenth century. Nevertheless, given the importance this American country was to have in Portuguese history and the continuous presence of the Portuguese there for such a long period of time, Brazil constitutes the most important chapter in the history of the arts of the Portuguese expansion.[39]

For an art history student arriving from other American places – Mexico City, Quito, or Cuzco, for instance – the distinctive character of the Brazilian colonial past is striking. The difference is first apparent in the urban morphology of the historical towns (which are generally organic as opposed to

[39] Carlos Lemos, José Roberto Teixeira Leite, and Pedro Manuel Gismonti, *The Art of Brazil* (New York, 1983); Damián Bayón and Murillo Marx, *L'art colonial sud-américain: domaine espagnol et Brésil* (Paris, 1990); Gutiérrez, *Arquitectura y urbanismo en Iberoamérica*; and the chapter on Brazil by Myriam Ribeiro de Oliveira, "La Pintura y la Escultura en Brasil," in Ramón Gutiérrez, ed., *Pintura, escultura y artes utiles en Iberoamérica, 1500–1825* (Madrid, 1995), pp. 283–304.

the orthogonal Hispanic *damero*, or checkerboard pattern, disposition) and by the prevalence of a certain number of traits that originated in the Portuguese classic architectural tradition: simple volumes; white, plain surfaces circumscribed by stone architectural frames; and limited façade ornaments. Nowhere in Brazil can we find the equivalent of the imperial monumentality of the main Mexican cities, with their huge *plazas mayores* (central squares), parallel streets and regular *manzanas* (house blocks), massive cathedrals, and rich private palaces. The façade-retable, a church façade ornamented like an altarpiece, so typically Hispanic and so important for the theatricalization of the urban reality, is virtually unknown on the Lusitanian side. Rather, decoration is reserved for the interior of the religious buildings, and then painting, sculpture, and the decorative arts will completely modify the plasticity and symbolism of the space.

For the sake of simplicity, the arts of colonial Brazil will be studied under two main divisions: the coastal area and Minas Gerais province. In the principal centers of the first, Salvador, Recife (and Olinda), and Rio de Janeiro, we can easily follow the development of the arts from the end of the sixteenth century forward. Minas Gerais only entered the history of art in the eighteenth century. It was there, however, that some of the most audacious architectural experiments ever tried in the Americas were to take place.

Transfers to the Coast

In contrast with Goa or even, curiously enough, with Mexico, where a portal in the Huejotzingo Franciscan monastery seems to echo Manueline morphology, there are no signs of Gothic or Manueline architecture in Brazil. The most ancient architectural remain here is the Garcia de Avila Tower Palace (Casa da Torre) in the Tatuapara harbor, near Salvador, Bahia. Built around 1570, the Avila Palace had a celebrated hexagonal chapel with a cupola, and rich stucco decoration in the interior, perhaps Mudéjar, in the typical Renaissance taste.

The cathedral of Salvador, Bahia, the first capital of Brazil, is a remarkable monument and a repository of the arts of all the periods of the colony.[40] It was built between 1657 and 1672 for the Jesuits, following the typology of the Society of Jesus: one single large nave, interconnected side chapels, and no transept. The stone façade was carved piece by piece in Lisbon, shipped to Salvador, and remounted there (Figure 12.24). For a long time to come, given the lack of good local building stone and also, one suspects, for protectionist reasons, important stone architectural pieces were sent from

[40] Germain Bazin, *L'architecture religieuse baroque au Brésil* (Paris, 1956–1958).

Figure 12.24. Cathedral (formerly Jesuit College), 1657–1672, Salvador, Bahia. (Photo: author.)

Portugal. The wooden ceiling of the nave follows a pattern published in Serlio's *L'Architettura* (IV, fol. 69). The altarpieces in the lateral chapels illustrate the different phases in the history of this liturgical piece of furniture.

In the sanctuary, the Portuguese-born painter Domingos Rodrigues, S. J. (ca. 1632–1706), left a series of eighteen scenes of the life of Jesus, using eclectic engraved sources as models (Veronese, Zuccaro, Maarten de Vos, Goltzius, and Rubens) (Figures 12.25 and 12.26). The paintings were done between 1665 and 1670 and illustrate the meditation themes for the Second Week of the *Spiritual Exercises* of St. Ignatius Loyola and therefore had an obvious pedagogical character. I know of no other example of the kind in any other Jesuit church.[41] Behind the sanctuary stands the monumental sacristy, richly decorated in the late seventeenth century with Portuguese marbles, by then a fashionable technique in Lisbon (Figure 12.27). The decoration includes also *azulejos*, a long chest of drawers for the liturgical vestments,

[41] The cycle by Domingos Rodrigues has been studied by Luís de Moura Sobral, "Pintura e composição de lugar: Un ciclo Jesuítico na Bahia do Padre António Vieira," *Oceanos* (1997), nos. 30–31, pp. 218–230.

Figure 12.25. Christ and the Woman Taken in Adultery, by Domingos Rodrigues, 1665–1670, oil on wood panel. Salvador Cathedral. (Photo: author.)

Figure 12.26. Christ and the Woman Taken in Adultery, by Adriaen Collaert (1560–1618) after Maarten de Vos, engraving, late sixteenth century. (Photo: Acervo da Fundação Biblioteca Nacional, Brazil.)

Figure 12.27. Sacristy, Salvador Cathedral, late seventeenth century, Salvador, Bahia. (Photo: author.)

and paintings. Besides the oils on copper already mentioned, ordered in Rome at the very end of the seventeenth century, there are stories of the Old Testament of the same date but of a much lesser quality. They stress, through the use of typological correspondences, the essential role of the Virgin in the salvation process of humankind. In the *cassoni* (coffers) of the ceiling there are twenty-one portraits of saints, martyrs, and distinguished members of the Society, a real gallery of the *uomini famosi* (famous men) of the Jesuit Order, among which is included Carlo Spinola, the builder of Macao's Church of St. Paul, who was martyred in Japan in 1622. The martyrs are divided into two groups separated by the founders of the Society. The crucified martyrs of Japan face the Crucifixion altar at the north side, while the stabbed Brazilian martyrs face the Virgin of Sorrows altar at the opposite side. (The original statue of the Virgin has been removed.) This is a grandiose piece of Jesuit propaganda, claiming superior recognition (beatification or canonization) for those who followed the suffering examples of Mary and her Son.[42] Above the sacristy was located the library of the College, the ceiling of which is decorated with one of the most spectacular *quadratura* of the city, painted around 1735–1736 by the Portuguese specialist António Simões Ribeiro (fl. 1700–1745), painter of the ceilings of the Royal Library in Coimbra (Figure 12.28).

Painting on canvas is far less frequent, and of a lesser quality, in Brazil than in Hispanic America. Domingos Rodrigues's paintings in Salvador are supposed to be among the earliest there, and they are dated in the 1660s. Of course, paintings were also imported from Portugal, although this is a problem still demanding research. Around 1700, for instance, Bento Coelho (ca. 1620–1708) sent from Lisbon to the sugar mill church (or chapel) of Paripe, Bahia, twenty-five paintings, but all have vanished.[43] Less than ten years later, the same painter's atelier shipped to the new See of São Luís do Maranhão seven (or eight) paintings on copper that represent the Stations of the Cross (five are extant in loco).[44]

In Salvador there is an important tradition of painted *cassoni* ceiling decorations which, for the most part, still wait to be studied. The one in the St. Francis convent church, done between 1736 and 1738, consists of a series of twenty-eight paintings with typical Immaculist themes, using the old system

[42] Luís de Moura Sobral, "*Ut Pictura Poesis*: José de Anchieta e as pinturas da sacristia da Catedral de Salvador," *Barroco* 18 (1997–2000), pp. 209–246.

[43] Carlos Ott, *História das artes plásticas da Bahia (1550–1900), vol. III: Pintura* (Salvador, 1993), p. 21.

[44] Rafael Moreira, "Uma *Via Crucis* da oficina de Bento Coelho no norte do Brasil," in Luís de Moura Sobral, ed., *Bento Coelho (1620–1708) e a cultura do seu tempo* (Lisbon, 1998), pp. 67–83.

Figure 12.28. Allegory of the Sapientia, attr. António Simões Ribeiro, ceiling of the former library of the Jesuit College, ca. 1735–1736. Salvador Cathedral, Bahia. (Photo: author.)

of correspondences between the Old Testment and the New Testament.[45] In the parish church of São João D'El-Rei, Minas Gerais, there are two paintings by another important artist from Lisbon, André Gonçalves (1685–1762).

[45] Luís de Moura Sobral, "Eva-Maria, *Tota Pulchra*: Narração e alegoria nas pinturas do tecto de S. Francisco de Salvador" (Salvador, 2001).

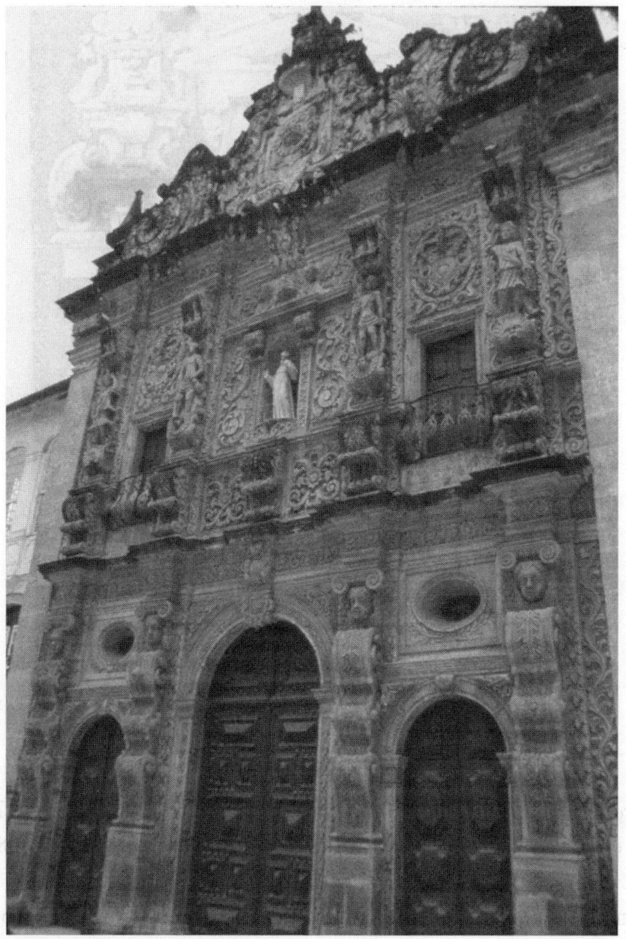

Figure 12.29. Church of the Third Order of St. Francis, attr. Gabriel Ribeiro, façade, 1702–1703, Salvador, Bahia. (Photo: author.)

In the St. Anthony Chapel in São Roque, São Paulo, a small painting representing the *Infant Jesus with the Jesuit Dress* was found some years ago, but its whereabouts is now unknown.[46] It shows all the characteristics of the celebrated Portuguese woman painter Josefa de Obidos (1630–1684). The canvas must date from the very last years of her activity because the chapel was inaugurated in 1682.

The church of the Third Order of St. Francis has the most surprising façade in Salvador (Figure 12.29). Attributed to Gabriel Ribeiro (1702–1703)

[46] Reproduced in Aracy Amaral, *A Hispanidade em São Paulo: Da casa rural à capela de Santo António* (São Paulo, 1981), p. 103, fig. 138.

Figure 12.30. Wendel Ditterlin, *Architectura*, 1598, Plate 102. (Photo: *The Fantastic Engravings of Wendel Ditterlin*, New York, Dover Publications, Inc., 1968.)

and constructed in local stone, it has been frequently related to Hispanic American art. Indeed, this is the only façade of its kind in Brazil, decorated like a wooden retable, or like a piece of ephemeral architecture. It is a two-story structure crowned by an elaborate, fancy scroll pediment. The two entablatures are supported by anthropomorphic Ionic pilasters taken from Wendel Ditterlin's *Architectura* of 1598 and by heavy *quartelões* (console pilasters used by cabinetmakers) with the statues of four human figures, hitherto not convincingly interpreted (Figure 12.30). Rather than being the reflection of some Hispanic prototype, however, the façade of the Third Order is related to the Flemish mannerist tradition and particularly to the ephemeral architecture of the, also Flemish, *joyeuses entrées*. Indeed, a plausible model for it could be the Arch of the Flemish Nation, one of the triumphal arches erected in Lisbon to honor Philip II (Philip III of Spain), as shown in the Juan Schorkens engraving of 1622 (Figure 12.31).

Figure 12.31. Juan Schorkens, *Arch of the Flemish Nation*, engraving from J. B. Lavanha, *Viagem da Catholica Real Magestade del Rey D. Filipe II*, Madrid, 1622. (Biblioteca Nacional Madrid.)

Quadratura painting (oil on wood, and never *a fresco*) is another characteristic of the baroque arts in Brazil. It was little used in the Hispanic Americas.[47] Introduced in Rio de Janeiro by Caetano da Costa Coelho (fl. 1706–1749) in the Penitência Chapel (1737–1742), it would be continued especially in Salvador and in Minas Gerais. In Salvador, the great *quadratura* artist is José Joaquim da Rocha (1737–1807), the author of the ceiling of Our Lady of the

[47] Magno Moraes Mello, *A pintura de tectos em perspectiva no Portugal de D. João V* (Lisbon, 1998).

Conception on the Beach, Salvador (1772–1774). This monumental decoration features the apotheotical Virgin Mary with the four continents at her feet, adoring the Holy Lamb (Figure 12.32). Present still are God the Father at the top, the two St. Johns, and, distributed around in the faint architecture base, the four doctors of the church, four virtues, and four prophets of the Old Testament. Another specialist in *quadratura*, the more provincial José Soares de Araújo (fl. 1765–1799), was active in Diamantina, Minas Gerais, until the end of the eighteenth century.

Quadratura consists usually of two parts: an architectural foreshortened setting and a central scene, often a glorification or an apotheosis of a saint. The composition has to be arranged in such a way that it accentuates the illusion of infinite space. This does not happen, however, in Brazilian *quadratura* because the central composition is presented like a frontal view, as if it was intended to be hung on a vertical wall. Foreshortening human figures in dynamic attitudes required specialized training that the artistic education system of the time obviously was not yet able to provide.

There are in Brazil several examples of the typical baroque "total work of art," or the *bel composti*, to employ the apt Berninesque expression.[48] As in Portugal, these festive interiors, whether responding to a single decorative theme or resulting from a coherent juxtaposition of elements during a certain period of time, combine different artistic techniques: gilt *talha* (wood carvings), sculpture, painting, and *azulejos*.

In the Hispanic and Portuguese world, particularly during the baroque period, wood carving was a major artistic activity, and some of the most meaningful artworks of the period were done in this technique. As far as interior church decoration is concerned, the altarpiece (*retábulo*), now devoted exclusively to the Eucharist and therefore with few or any paintings and sculptures, became the central focus and the most important symbolic piece of the entire ensemble. The central part of the piece was transformed into a tribune (a huge niche) where a pyramidal throne is placed. This typical Lusitanian feature was developed around 1670 to honor the Eucharist.

At the same time, there appeared in Portugal the so-called Salomonic column, which very quickly would become the most important structural element of the altarpiece. Indeed, the presence of the Salomonic column became so overwhelming in the architecture of the period that it alone defines a phase in the development of the Hispanic, Portuguese, and Ibero-American baroque. Although in Mexico and Central America the "Salomonic baroque" was replaced around 1730 by what has been called

[48] See the material published in Luís de Moura Sobral, ed., *Struggle for Synthesis: The Total Work of Art in the 17th and 18th Centuries* (Lisbon, 1999).

Figure 12.32. Triumph of the Immaculate Conception by José Joaquim da Rocha. Ceiling of the church of Nossa Senhora da Conceição da Praia, 1772–1774, Salvador, Bahia. (Photo: author.)

the "estípite baroque," the Salomonic column would continue to be used in Portugal and Brazil during the entire baroque cycle.

The evolution of this Portuguese "Salomonic baroque" altarpiece can be divided into two slightly different periods: the first (in Brazil, around 1690–1730) is defined by a portal-like type, with Salomonic columns and Salomonic archivolts; the second (1730–1760) features Salomonic columns but a different, composite upper section, with broken pediments and canopies, more directly dependent on the Andrea Pozzo models. The first period has been, inaccurately and abusively, named the "national style," while the second was called the "joanino style."

As is well known, the "Salomonic column" derives from antique prototypes (second and third centuries B.C.), originally from the eastern part of the Roman Empire, existing in the Vatican Basilica from the fourth century. After the Middle Ages, they were believed to have come from the Jerusalem Temple. These columns always played important architectural and symbolic functions in St. Peter's, before and after the new Basilica was built and decorated in the sixteenth century. Of course, Bernini's monumental Baldaquino (1627–1633) would transform the motif into the quintessential paradigm of the new aesthetics, although interest in the Salomonic column among artists and architects continued to increase during the sixteenth century. Rubens's paintings, tapestry cartoons, and book illustrations particularly would be of paramount importance for the popularity of the theme. Whatever the reason, nowhere would the Salomonic column play such an important part in the definition of a baroque style and mentality as in the Iberian and Ibero-American arts of the baroque. Needless to say, the theme also reached the Orient, where it was employed in *talha* work and in interior stucco decoration. A silver processional baldacchino in the church of São Domingos in Macao was inspired directly by the Bernini model (even including the typical Berninesque column divided into three tiers).

In Brazil, Salomonic columns were used until the very end of the eighteenth century – for instance, in the São Bento Monastery, Rio de Janeiro, by Inácio Ferreira Pinto (ca. 1760–1828). Although present everywhere in *talha* altarpieces (and even in an uncommon stone altarpiece in Nossa Senhora da Guia, Paraíba, of ca. 1763–1778), curiously enough, the Salomonic column never appears in the exterior of the buildings, contrary to what happened in Portugal and Spanish America.

A rococo phase in architectural decoration occurred in Brazil after 1760 and, in some places, continued well into the nineteenth century. Other types of support would then be used (console pilasters, columns with straight shafts), painted in white with gilt fillets. A good example of this new type of altarpiece can be seen in Mariana, Minas Gerais, in the three main altars

Figure 12.33. Interior of the church of the Monastery of St. Francis, started in 1723, Salvador, Bahia. (Photo: author.)

of the church of Nossa Senhora do Rosário, from about 1790, by Francisco Vieira Servas. António Francisco Lisboa, the "Aleijadinho" (1730–1814), is the author of the main altar of the Chapel of the Third Order of Saint Francis, Ouro Preto, Minas Gerais, done in 1790–1794. Here, however, the altar, with straight shaft columns, sprinkled with sculpted motifs, is integrated into the ensemble of the decoration of the sanctuary. The "Aleijadinho" put at the top of the arch of the altarpiece a sculpted and relief group of the Trinity, which marks the continuity between the different artworks present in the sanctuary.

Sometimes, the gilt *talha* overflows from the sanctuaries or from the lateral chapels and invades and covers all the available surfaces in the temple. There are in Brazil several types of these "gilt grottoes," as they were once called. In Salvador, the most spectacular *talha* interior is in the church of the Monastery of St. Francis, started in 1723 (Figure 12.33). The temple, from the ceiling to the walls and to the side chapels, is entirely covered with gilt wood carvings. The ceiling, divided into compartments of different forms (octagons, stars, and hexagons), contains a most unusual series of Old Testament paintings (oil on wood panels) arranged in a complex allegory of the Immaculate Conception.[49]

[49] Moura Sobral, "Eva-Maria, *Tota Pulchra.*"

Figure 12.34. Façade of the church of the Monastery of São Bento, Francisco Frias de Mesquita, 1617–1633, Rio de Janeiro. (Photo: author.)

Whereas in São Francisco in Salvador the white walls are visible under the *talha* level, in the chapel of the Third Order of Penitência in Rio, the impression is that the beholder finds himself inside a gigantic gold reliquary. In Rio, the walls were changed into sheets of gold. This impressive interior, one of the most stylistically homogeneous of its kind in the Lusitanian world, is the work of the Portuguese artists Manuel de Brito and Francisco Xavier de Brito and was done between 1726 and 1743.

Another outstanding example of a *talha* interior in Rio is in the São Bento Monastery, the oldest remaining monument in the town. The church was designed around 1617 by Francisco Frias de Mesquita, Brazil's chief engineer between 1603 and 1640. However, its construction did not begin until 1633, and the contrast between the functional and cold exterior and the inside space could not be more striking (Figure 12.34). The interior is in fact completely covered by *talha*, in a laudatory program centered on a number of important Benedictine figures: four popes, four bishops, and four saint kings (Figure 12.35). This vast ensemble occupied artists from the mid-seventeenth century (Alexandre Machado Pereira) almost to the end of the eighteenth (José da Conceição and Simão da Cunha).[50]

[50] Mateus Ramalho Rocha, *A Igreja do Mosteiro de São Bento do Rio de Janeiro* (Rio de Janeiro, 1991).

Figure 12.35. Interior of the church of the Monastery of São Bento, seventeenth–eighteenth centuries, Rio de Janeiro. (Photo: author.)

Azulejos of blue and white, typical colors of the eighteenth century, were also used in São Francisco in Salvador in the church and other parts of the monastery.[51] They were manufactured in Portugal in the atelier of Bartolomeu Antunes (1688–1753). Those in the sanctuary are dated 1737. The series in the cloister was placed there between 1746 and 1748. Thirty-eight panels of them copy the engravings of Otto van Veen's *Théâtre moral de toute la philosophie des Anciens et des Modernes* (Brussels, 1669). These complex allegories would provide endless meditation themes for the Franciscan friars and also for their visitors. On the upper floor of the cloister, other

[51] For the *azulejos* in Brazil, see José Manuel dos Santos Simões, *Azulejaria Portuguesa no Brasil, 1500–1822* (Lisbon, 1965).

Figure 12.36. December, by Bartolomeu Antunes, *azulejo* in cloister of the Monastery of St. Francis, 1746–1748, Salvador, Bahia. (Photo: author.)

azulejos represent the five senses, the continents, and the months of the year. Their European authors did not bother, however, to present the correct sequence of the seasons on the southern continent. In tropical Brazil, December or January continue to be represented as chilly months, and the first is represented by an old man selling roasted chestnuts on the streets (Figure 12.36).

Sometimes *azulejos* panels are the most important decorative elements of church interiors. This happens, for instance, in the chapel of Nossa Senhora da Glória do Outeiro in Rio (stories of the Song of Songs by Valentim de

Figure 12.37. Song of Songs, by Valentim de Almeida, *azulejos*, ca. 1735, Nossa Senhora da Glória do Outeiro, Rio de Janeiro. (Photo: author.)

Almeida, around 1735) and in the St. Anthony Monastery in Recife (life of St. Anthony, around 1730–1740). The Song of Songs was also illustrated in the sacristy of the Parish church of Santo Amaro, Bahia, in the second half of the eighteenth century (Figures 12.37 and 12.38).

As is well known, ephemeral celebrations were an important element of baroque life and art. They were organized for special occasions such as the acclamation of kings, the arrival of new governors or bishops, royal exequies, and religious and popular feasts. Architects, sculptors, and painters worked together with poets and scholars in the design of imposing ephemeral monuments, triumphal arches, and cars. Some of these constructions were recorded in drawings, but most of them are known to us only through literary descriptions. Some feasts could last for several weeks, or even months, and could include processions and parades with cars and allegorical figures of both religious and mythological characters, series of emblems, paintings accompanied by Latin inscriptions, musicians and dancers, fireworks, literary contests, theatrical representations, and so forth.

The acclamation of João IV, the new Bragança monarch, was celebrated in Rio in March 1641, a few months after the Lisbon coup of December 1, 1640. Macao celebrated the event during two months in 1642. The feasts included spectacular representations staged at the then unfinished façade of

Figure 12.38. Song of Songs, azulejos, second half of the eighteenth century, parish church of Santo Amaro, Bahia. (Photo: author.)

St. Paul's church, processions, dances, and triumphal cars with allegorical figures.[52]

In Brazil, one of the most celebrated feasts of the baroque period was the Ouro Preto "Eucharist Triumph" of 1733, on the occasion of the inauguration of the Parish Church of Nossa Senhora do Pilar (the solemn transfer of the Holy Sacrament to the new temple). The program of this feast would later serve as the model for the sumptuous reception of the new bishop of Mariana, Frei Manuel da Cruz, in 1748. Both events were recorded in literary form.[53]

Royal exequies were also the occasion for ceremonies of a particular kind. The exequies of Pedro II, celebrated in Rome in 1707 in the church of Saint-Antony of the Portuguese, exerted great influence. They had been designed by the Roman architect Carlo Fontana (1634–1714), whose drawings were engraved and published in 1707. They would serve as models for the exequies in honor of João V (he died in 1750), the most important ceremonies of

[52] Diogo Ramada Curto, "O questionamento da identidade," in Bethencourt and Chaudhuri, *História da expansão Portuguesa*, vol. 2, pp. 477–480.

[53] Simão Ferreira Machado, *Triunfo Eucharistico* (Lisbon, 1734); anonymous, *Aureo throno Episcopal* (Lisbon, 1749); see Affonso Avila, *O lúdico e as projeções do mundo barroco* (São Paulo, 1980), pp. 113–133.

their kind in the Portuguese world during the baroque period. They were celebrated in Madeira, the Azores, Brazil (Olinda, Recife, Salvador, Ouro Preto, São João D'El-Rei, Sabará, Rio, and Belém), and Angola.[54] In the old Salvador cathedral (demolished in 1933), the catafalque erected in 1750 was decorated with painted clothes, wooden statues, and stucco.

The discovery of new architecture, new works of art, and new artistic techniques in Africa, Asia, and the Americas was echoed by Portuguese writers of the sixteenth century. Furthermore, these authors admired the antiquity of these arts and sometimes related them to European classic antiquity. The historian João de Barros (ca. 1496–1570) describes the ruins of the ancient city of Zimbabwe. Fernão Mendes Pinto (1510–1583) admires the city of Peking – greater, he says, than any other he knows in Europe, Africa, or Asia. João de Castro (1500–1548) speaks about pagodas in India, which he describes with great accuracy. After the relief of the siege of the Indian city of Diu in 1546, he will send two stone steles to his villa in Sintra, near Lisbon, to be put in the entrance of a commemorative chapel. Francisco de Holanda (1517–1584) was the first theoretician of the Renaissance to include Africa, Asia, and the Americas in a universal reflection about the arts.[55]

Innovations in Minas Gerais

One of the most fascinating topics in the history of the arts of the Americas is the creation of a school of late baroque architecture in the hinterland of Minas Gerais. For the first time, as a matter of fact, American architects would systematically challenge the well-established Iberian tradition of straight walls joined at right angles in church architecture. The spatial animation would no longer be the consequence of glittering, rich materials put on the walls, combined in a *bel composto*; it would result from the walls themselves, from the way they are able to model the space. The plan of the building would therefore be elongated, polygonal, oval, or would result from a combination of ellipses. Examples of the same kind are extremly rare and isolated in the Spanish Americas (Saint Theresa in Cochabamba, Bolivia,

[54] João Manuel Tedim, "Morte, poder e espectáculo barroco nas exéquias de D. João V no espaço atlântico português," in José Alberto Gomes Machado, ed., *A Arte no Espaço Atlântico do Império Português, III Colóquio Luso-Brasileiro de História da Arte* (Évora, 1997), pp. 71–77.

[55] Sylvie Deswarte-Rosa, "Antiquité et nouveaux-mondes: À propos de Francisco de Holanda," *Revue de l'Art* (1985), no. 68, pp. 55–72, reprinted (and translated into Portuguese) in Sylvie Deswarte, *Ideias e imagens em Portugal na época dos descobrimentos* (Lisbon, 1992), pp. 9–54.

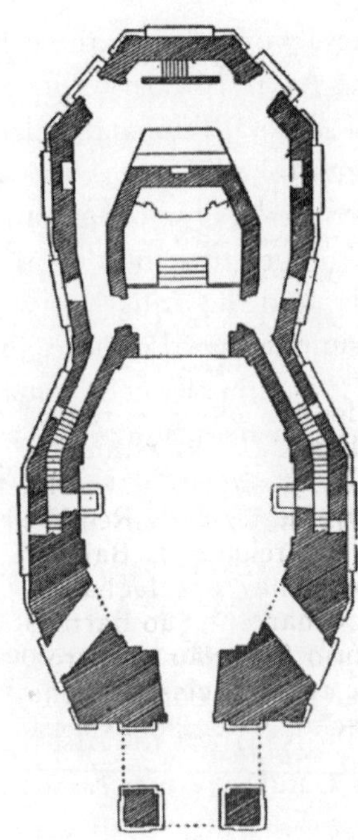

Figure 12.39. Church of Nossa Senhora da Glória do Outeiro, plan, 1714–1739, Rio de Janeiro. (Photo: Instituto de Património Histórico e Artístico Nacional, Rio de Janeiro.)

1753; Huérfanas in Lima, 1742–1766; and Pocito in Mexico, 1771–1791), and they do not assume the systematic character of the Brazilian case.

The discovery at the end of the seventeenth century of gold and diamond mines in the Minas Gerais district had caused a gold rush into the area. Towns appeared overnight, replacing mining camps but keeping for the most part much of their casual and loose structure. Since the crown had prohibited the establishment of religious orders in the area, lay brotherhoods took a very important place in shaping the social and religious life of these places. On the other hand, not restrained by conservative monastic patterns, patrons were more receptive to novelties; indeed, novelties were required by the dynamics of rival brotherhoods.

The genealogy of Minas Gerais's new architecture can be traced back to the small pilgrimage church in Rio de Janeiro, Our Lady of the Gloria do Outeiro (1714–1739), designed by José Cardoso Ramalho and decorated with Song of Songs *azulejos* (Figure 12.39). The chapel is formed by two oblong, irregular ovals, the larger for the nave and the other for the sanctuary and the sacristy behind. Lateral corridors embedded in the walls lead to the pulpits in the middle of the nave and, in the opposite direction, to the sacristy.

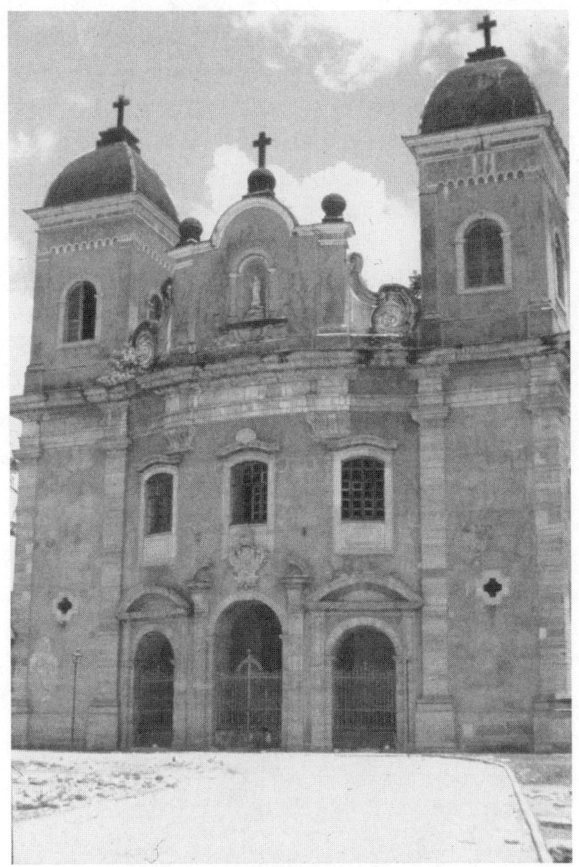

Figure 12.40. São Pedro dos Clérigos, António de Sousa Calheiros, ca. 1753, Mariana, Minas Gerais. (Photo: author.)

If the dates given are exact (they are in fact controversial), the Rio building antedates the closest Portuguese example, São Pedro dos Clérigos in Oporto (1732–1748). Two churches in Minas Gerais come next: São Pedro dos Clérigos in Mariana (ca. 1753) and Our Lady of the Rosary in Ouro Preto (1757), both attributed to António de Sousa Calheiros (fl. 1736–1760) and resulting from the intersection of two ellipses (Figures 12.40–12.43). They present a protuberant façade with a portico and lateral cylindrical towers. Resemblances to Fischer von Erlach's Salzbourg Collegiate and other Central European buildings are obvious. Although this question is still open to debate, these Minas Gerais works are somehow related to a series of chapels and small churches in northern Portugal with similar spatial characteristics: Bom Jesus da Cruz in Barcelos (ca. 1704), São Sebastião das Carvalheiras (1715–1717) and Guadalupe (ca. 1718–1719) in Braga, Senhor

Figure 12.41. São Pedro dos Clérigos, António de Sousa Calheiros, southern elevation, ca. 1753, Mariana, Minas Gerais. (Photo: author.)

Figure 12.42. Nossa Senhora do Rosário, António de Sousa Calheiros, 1757, Ouro Preto, Minas Gerais. (Photo: author.)

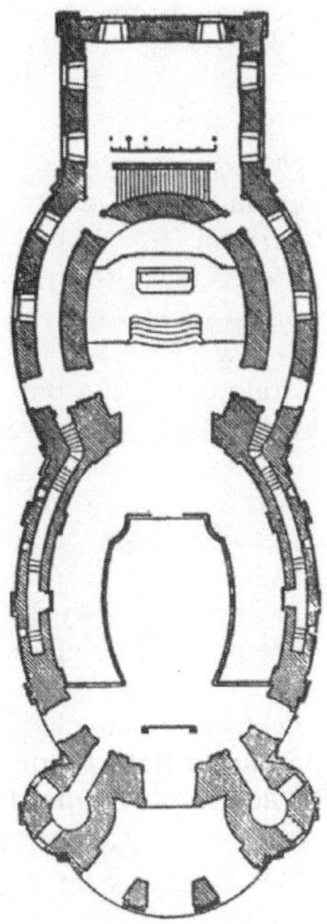

Figure 12.43. Nossa Senhora do Rosário, António de Sousa Calheiros, plan, 1757, Ouro Preto, Minas Gerais. (Photo: from Paulo F. Santos, *A Arquitetura Religiosa em Ouro Preto,* Rio, 1949.)

Jesus das Barrocas in Aveiro (ca. 1722), and others. In terms of freedom of conception and variety in the plastic treatment, however, the Brazilian examples are far richer and more innovative.

António Francisco Lisboa, the "Aleijadinho" (1735–1814), has been canonized as the absolute artist-hero of baroque Minas Gerais or rather of all Brazil. The son of a Portuguese man and a black slave woman, he was a learned man and a gifted sculptor and architect, indeed, a typical baroque *maître d'oeuvre.* Aleijadinho appears to be the creator of the church of the Third Order of St. Francis in Ouro Preto, a masterpiece of late baroque architecture (started 1766) (Figures 12.44–12.47). In the façade, he handles materials, colors, and all the architectural elements with sensuality and extreme elegance, graduating the reliefs and volumes from the Ionic columns of the first plan to the cylindrical towers behind. He emphasizes the entrance axis by displaying above the portal a lacelike sculpture he carved himself in beautiful green soapstone, a local material. This includes cherubs, garlands of flowers, fragmented canopies, angels, and a three-part medallion with the emblems of the Franciscan Order and, supported by these, a relief with the

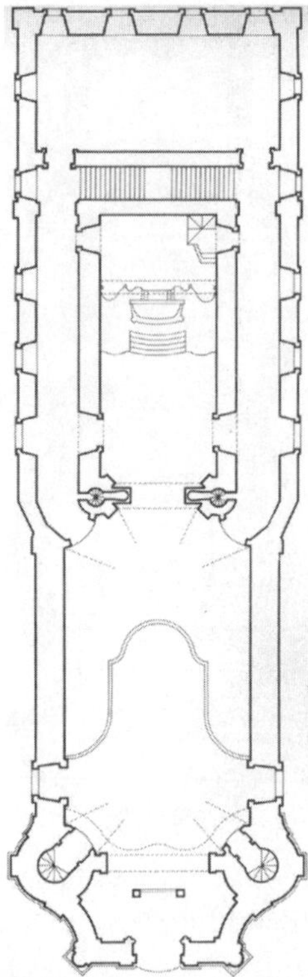

Figure 12.44. Chapel of the Ordem Terceira de São Francisco, plan, Ouro Preto, Minas Gerais. (Photo: from Yves Bottineau, *Baroque ibérique*, Fribourg, Switzerland: 1969.)

Virgin. Her crown links this composition with the round medallion in the upper part of the façade, where Aleijadinho sculpted *Saint Francis Receiving the Stigmata*. In 1774, Aleijadinho designed another church for the same brotherhood in São João D'El-Rei. It has protuberant lateral cylindrical towers in the façade, convex nave walls, and a rectangular sanctuary. The decoration of the main portal, also in soapstone, uses composite pilasters of the *quartelão* type (Figure 12.48).

In the open-air sanctuary of Congonhas do Campo (second half of the eighteenth century), the Aleijadinho would likewise display his talents as sculptor and art director, or *metteur en scène*, in dealing with monumental groups of sculptures. The sanctuary consists of a church on the top of a hill (finished ca. 1771), a terrace with a theatrical staircase, and six chapels with the Stations of the Cross (1802–1818). The stone statues of the twelve prophets of the Old Testament were distributed over the balustrades of the

Figure 12.45. Ordem Terceira de São Francisco, António Francisco Lisboa ("Aleijadinho"), started 1766, Ouro Preto, Minas Gerais. (Photo: author.)

stairs. They were done by Aleijadinho and his assistants between 1800 and 1805, and their completion marks the end of the artist's brilliant career.

The architectural experiments and achievements of Minas Gerais would not be possible in any other part of the Portuguese territories, and certainly not in continental Portugal. They are a consequence of a long process of maturation, where artistic traditions, technical skills, and personal talent were combined. The place and times were no doubt favorable to new syntheses, innovative responses, and fresh starts.

Art and architecture produced during the three centuries of the colonial period in Brazil are no doubt the most meaningful of the entire Portuguese expansion not only for, say, their intrinsic plastic values, but foremost because those works of art and architecture never ceased to live; they stand there and still contribute to the ongoing and never-ending process of building a living culture.

Figure 12.46. Ordem Terceira de São Francisco, António Francisco Lisboa ("Aleijadinho"), detail of the façade, Ouro Preto, Minas Gerais. (Photo: author.)

Figure 12.47. Ordem Terceira de São Francisco, António Francisco Lisboa ("Aleijadinho"), main entrance, Ouro Preto, Minas Gerais. (Photo: author.)

Figure 12.48. Ordem Terceira de São Francisco, António Francisco Lisboa ("Aleijadinho"), main entrance, São João D'El-Rei, 1774, Minas Gerais. (Photo: author.)

BIBLIOGRAPHICAL ESSAY

The first survey of the material covered by this chapter was published only recently, in the form of chapters included in the first three volumes of Francisco Bethencourt and Kirti Chaudhuri, eds., *História da expansão Portuguesa* (5 vols., Lisbon, 1998–1999). They were written by Rafael Moreira (vol. 1, pp. 455–489, and vol. 3, pp. 463–493) and by Moreira and Alexandra Curvelo (vol. 2, pp. 532–570). These were followed by Pedro Dias's two-volume *História da arte Portuguesa no mundo (1415–1822)* (Lisbon, 1998–1999), now the standard reference work on the subject. It continues to be the case, as for other related areas, that most literature on this subject is in Portuguese.

The catalogue of *Circa 1492: Art in the Age of Exploration*, edited by Jay A. Levenson (Washington, DC, 1991) provides synthetic essays and entries on the arts of Africa (by Ezio Bassani, pp. 63–68, 182–191), Japan and China (by Sherman E. Lee, pp. 315–327, 351–362), and India (by Stuart Cary Welch, pp. 363–366) about the time of the first contacts with the Portuguese. A recent exhibition catalogue, *Cultures of the Indian Ocean* (Lisbon, 1998), following identical methodology, supplements the Washington book.

On military architecture, the best reference work is Rafael Moreira, ed., *História das fortificações Portuguesas no mundo* (Lisbon, 1989); a small essay by the same author on related matters should also be consulted: "A escola de arquitectura do Paço da Ribeira e a Academia de Matemáticas de Madrid," in Pedro Dias, ed., *As relações artísticas entre Portugal e Espanha na época dos descobrimentos* (Coimbra, 1987), pp. 65–77. On Portuguese urbanism, see the synthesis by Walter Rossa, "A cidade Portuguesa," in Paulo Pereira, ed., *História da arte Portuguesa* (Lisbon, 1995), vol. 3, pp. 233–323, and by the same author *Indo-Portuguese Cities* (Lisbon, 1997) and *Colectânea de estudos: Universo urbanístico Português, 1415–1822* (Lisbon, 1998). There is also a separate bilingual publication with abstracts of the papers presented at an international conference held at Coimbra University in March 1999, *Universo urbanístico Português/The Portuguese Urbanistic Universe: 1415–1822* (Lisbon, 1998). See also José Manuel Fernandes's *Sínteses da cultura Portuguesa: A arquitectura* (Lisbon, 1991).

Ivories have been extensively studied and exhibited. See the exhibition catalogues by Francisco Hipólito Raposo, ed., *A expansão Portuguesa e a arte do Marfim* (Lisbon, 1991), and by Maria Helena Mendes Pinto, ed., *Marfins d'além-mar no Museu de Arte Antiga/ Overseas Ivory in the Museu de Arte Antiga* (Lisbon, 1988) and *Arte do Marfim* (Porto, 1998), with English translation.

Since the pioneering studies by William B. Fagg at the beginning of the twentieth century (William B. Fagg, *Afro-Portuguese Ivories*, London, n.d.), African ivories have been studied by Ezio Bassani and William B. Fagg, eds., *Africa and the Renaissance: Art in Ivory* (New York, 1988).

On Indo-Portuguese ivories, see the rich material collected by Bernardo Ferrão de Tavares e Távora and illustrated in *Imaginária Luso-Oriental* (Lisbon, 1983). For a comparative study with Hispano-Philippine ivories, see also by Bernardo Ferrão de Tavares e Távora "Imaginária Hispano-Filipina e Indo-Portuguesa," *Gil Vicente* 25 (1974), nos. 3–4, pp. 49–58, and especially Margarita Mercedes Estella Marcos and Lydia Sada de González's *Ivories from Far Eastern Provinces of Spain and Portugal* (Monterrey, 1997).

An introduction to African brass art can be found in Alain Jacob's *Bronzes de l'Afrique noire* (Paris, 1974).

On Indo-Portuguese jewelry and furniture, see the catalogue edited by Nuno Vassallo e Silva, *A Herança de Rauluchantim/The Heritage of Rauluchantim* (Lisbon, 1996), with essays by Vassallo e Silva, Pedro Dias,

Susan Stronge, Annemarie Jordan Gschwend, José Jordão Felgueiras, and Leonor d'Orey. All the known caskets from Ceylon were recently reviewed by Amin Jaffer and Melanie Anne Schwabe, "A Group of Sixteenth-Century Ivory Caskets from Ceylon," *Apollo Magazine* 149 (1999), no. 445, pp. 3–14.

For textiles, see the catalogues *Colchas bordadas no Museu Nacional de Arte Antiga: India, Portugal, China, séculos XVII–XVIII* (Lisbon, 1978) and *Portugal and the East through Embroidery* (Washington, DC, 1981). The study of paintings has been generally overlooked. Painting in the Estado da Índia was very briefly surveyed in Vitor Serrão's "A Pintura na Antiga India Portuguesa nos séculos XVI e XVII," *Oceanos* (1994), nos. 19–20, pp. 102–112. See also Matthew Lederle's, *Christian Painting in India* (Bombay, n.d.). On Christian painting in China, see Michel Beurdeley's *Peintres Jésuites en Chine au XVIIIe siècle* (Paris, 1997). A good introduction to Chinese porcelain and the West is Pedro Dias, ed., *Reflexos: Símbolos e imagens do Cristianismo na porcelana Chinesa/Reflections: Symbols and Images of Christianity on Chinese Porcelain* (Lisbon, 1997).

In the issue numbered 19–20 of *Oceanos* (1994), there is ample material on Indo-Portuguese art and culture. For this vast theme, Carlos de Azevedo's *Arte Cristã na India Portuguesa* (Lisbon, 1959) and *A Arte de Goa, Damão e Diu* ([1970] Lisbon, 1992) are still useful introductory readings. See also José Pereira's *Baroque Goa* (New Dehli, 1995) and Maria Helena Mendes Pinto, ed., *Van Goa naar Lisboa. Indo-Portuguese Kunst 16e–18e Eeuw* (Brussels, 1991). Other essays on the architecture in Goa by Helder Carita, José Manuel Fernandes, and Rafael Moreira were published in *Oceanos* (1994), nos. 19–20. Judilia Nunes's *The Monuments in Old Goa* (Delhi, 1979) should be read with some caution. For St. Paul's Church in Macao, see Gonçalo Couceiro, *Igreja de S. Paulo – Fortaleza do Monte/St. Paul's Church – Fortress of the Monte* (Macao, 1990), and Fernando António Baptista Pereira, ed., *As ruínas de S. Paulo: Um monumento para o futuro/St. Paul's Ruins: A Monument towards the Future* (Lisbon and Macao, 1994).

Christian art in India, within an intercultural context, was discussed by Sebastian Elavathingal, *Inculturation & Christian Art: An Indian Perspective* (Rome, 1990), and by Teotónio R. de Sousa in "A Arte Cristã de Goa: Uma Introdução Histórica para a Dialética da sua Evolução," *Oceanos* (1994), nos. 19–20, pp. 8–14.

A good general history of *namban* art is still Yoshitomo Okamoto's *The Namban Art of Japan* ([1965], English ed., New York and Tokyo, 1972). On the same subject, see Tamon Miki, "The Influence of Western Culture on Japanese Art," *Monumenta Nipponica* 19 (1964), nos. 3–4, pp. 146–185, and several recent exhibition catalogues: *Exposição de arte namban* (Lisbon, 1981); *Arte namban: Influencia Española y Portuguesa en el arte Japonés, siglos XVI y XVII* (Madrid, 1981); and *No caminho do Japão: Arte Oriental nas colecções da Santa Casa da Misericórdia de Lisboa* (Lisbon, 1993). A good, brief presentation of *namban* screens is Maria Helena Mendes Pinto's *Biombos namban/Namban Screens*, 2nd ed. (Lisbon, 1988). *Namban* art has been systematically cataloged in Mitsura Sakamoto, Ide Yoichiro, Yujiro Ochi, and Hidaka Kaori's *An Essay of Catalogue Raisonné of Namban Art. I: Japanese Early European-Style Painting* (Tokyo, 1997).

Several general histories of the arts in Brazil are available. The following can be used: Carlos Lemos, José Roberto Teixeira Leite, and Pedro Manuel Gismonti's *The Art of Brazil* (New York, 1983); and Damián Bayón and Murillo Marx's *L'art colonial Sud-américain: Domaine Espagnol et Brésil* (Paris, 1990). For comparison with the arts of Hispanic America, see Ramón Gutiérrez's *Arquitectura y urbanismo en Iberoamérica* (Madrid, 1983), and, edited by the same writer, *Pintura, escultura y artes utiles en Iberoamérica, 1500–1825* (Madrid, 1995). The chapter on Brazil is by Myriam Ribeiro de Oliveira and appears on pp. 283–304.

The standard survey of Brazilian religious architecture is still Germain Bazin's *L'architecture religieuse baroque au Brésil* (2 vols., Paris, 1956–1958). The same author wrote the classic monograph on the Aleijadinho, *Aleijadinho et la sculpture baroque au Brésil* (Paris, 1963). Myriam Ribeiro de Oliveira defines a roccoco variant of the baroque in *O rococó religioso no Brasil e seus antecedentes Europeus* (São Paulo, 2003). A recent catalogue in French is also useful: *Brésil baroque, entre ciel et terre* (Paris, 1999). Several essays on different aspects of the baroque in Brazil by Cristina Ávila, Maria Helena Flexor, Eduardo França Paiva, Myriam Ribeiro de Oliveira, and Sônia Gomes Pereira were included in Luís de Moura Sobral, ed., *Struggle for Synthesis: The Total Work of Art in the 17th and 18th Centuries* (Lisbon, 1999).

There is a monograph on the São Bento Monastery in Rio by Mateus Ramalho Rocha, *A Igreja do Mosteiro de São Bento do Rio de Janeiro* (Rio de Janeiro, 1991), and another on the São Francisco Convent in Salvador, Bahía, is forthcoming. On tiles (*azulejos*), see J. M. dos Santos Simões's *Azulejaria Portuguesa no Brasil, 1500–1822* (Lisbon, 1965).

There is not yet a reliable general study of painting in colonial Brazil. After the pioneering studies by Joaquim Cardoso, Nair Batista, Hannah Levy, and Luiz Jardim in the 1930s and 1940s (in *Revista do Patrimônio Histórico e Artístico Nacional*), Carlos Ott produced a series of texts that need to be used with the utmost care. For the study of several iconographical cycles in Salvador, Bahía, see the studies by Luís de Moura Sobral, "Pintura e composição de lugar: Un ciclo Jesuítico na Bahia do Padre António Vieira," *Oceanos* (1997), nos. 30–31, pp. 218–230; "*Ut Pictura Poesis*: José de Anchieta e as pinturas da sacristia da Catedral de Salvador," *Barroco* 18 (1997–2000), pp. 209–246; and "Eva-Maria, *Tota Pulchra*: Narração e alegoria nas pinturas do tecto de S. Francisco de Salvador," in *Anais do IV Congresso de História da Bahia* (Salvador, 2001), vol. 1, pp. 175–187.

13

SCIENCE AND TECHNOLOGY IN PORTUGUESE NAVIGATION: THE IDEA OF EXPERIENCE IN THE SIXTEENTH CENTURY

Francisco Contente Domingues

Translated by Neil Safier

In the early years of the European expansion, Portuguese mariners and those who pondered the impact of their circumnavigations came to affirm the value of experience as a criterion of scientific truth. Both as a criterion established through practice and as a value in observation, experience was tremendously important in dismantling the structures of knowledge inherited from classical antiquity. This was particularly true in fields such as the physical geography of the oceans and coasts, the celestial configuration of stars and constellations, and the existence of previously unknown and unsuspected human, plant, and animal populations, fields in which the Portuguese expeditions were to have a major impact.

These new realities were absorbed over the course of a slow and empirical process that lasted more than a century. But the plodding pace in no way precluded this process from taking advantage of an emerging opportunity to produce a new architecture of knowledge. In most cases, the observation of novel circumstances did not mesh with classical knowledge, in spite of the fact that this legacy was constantly used and consulted as a body of reference. The process was long and, in certain aspects, tedious, even on an individual level: How does one begin to describe the experience of those men who witnessed with their own eyes the enfeeblement of their inherited worldview, or who learned from others about the weaknesses of its foundations?

As Reyer Hooykaas has stated so well, "The inner conflict in the minds of people who, as a consequence of the discoveries, were witnessing the beginning of a new epoch in the history of mankind, is nowhere more clearly revealed than in the writings of the Portuguese of the sixteenth century."[1]

The notion of "experience" in the Portuguese Renaissance played a decisive role in the creation of a new critical mentality. It made possible, when it did not explicitly forge, the formation of what today's historians call the scientific mentality. Nonetheless, scholars have often reduced the knowledge acquired by Portuguese navigators and writers merely to the sensory and empirical levels, which are often, but not uniquely, representative of what they gained.

The accepted idea that there is some kind of "scientific experience" that characterizes the Scientific Revolution in the seventeenth century presupposes the existence of a "prescientific experience" that precedes it. The notion of a linear progression in the construction of an edifice of knowledge, which only became complete in the seventeenth century, follows from this concept. The validity of the idea of linear progress is, however, universally acknowledged to be epistemologically inadequate.

The extensive and rigorous study of the idea of experience in the Portuguese Renaissance requires us to make certain preliminary observations that it is hoped will be deducible from the examples that follow. In the first place, in contradistinction to the motivating spirit behind the works of Galileo, for example, the idea that lived experience is merely "prescientific" or "nonscientific" is correct to the extent that sensory experience cannot be placed at the same level as rational thought. It is the balanced counterpoint of sensory and rational observations that characterizes the underlying theoretical foundations of the use of experience as a criterion for ordered and methodical knowledge of physical reality, and it is precisely this idea that distinguishes from Galilean physics Duarte Pacheco Pereira's perception that the waters of the globe are surrounded by land, affirmed as this belief was by Pereira's own experience.

On the other hand, the nature of this differentiation leaves no question as to the restricted and well-delineated extent of its application. Some of the most notable intellectual achievements of the Portuguese navigations, including the recognition of wind and current patterns or the coastal hydrography of Africa, or even the understanding of the various constellations of the Southern Hemisphere, could have been accomplished only through direct observation on the spot; that is, through practical experience. No research project based upon the formulation of any kind of hypotheses would have been able to produce the genuine "geographic revolution" that took place

[1] Reyer Hooykaas, *Humanism and the Voyages of Discovery in Sixteenth Century Portuguese Science and Letters* (Amsterdam, 1979), p. 99.

during the fifteenth and sixteenth centuries and was accomplished uniquely through the medium of direct observation. Ultimately, following this line of reasoning, Henricus Martellus Germanus's map of circa 1489, which shows the direct connection between the Indian and Atlantic oceans, experimentally proven by Bartolomeu Dias in 1487–1488, is as valuable for the history of geography as Galileo's experiments are for the history of physics. As such, the meaning of "scientific experience" as it is commonly understood seems highly reductive, failing to take into account the disparate realities of the scientific corpus, broadly imagined to be the central core of the so-called Scientific Revolution.[2]

What has been written regarding the geographic revolution that took place in the period of the great navigations could also be applied independently to the fields of medicine and botany, to take only two examples of disciplines where direct observation carried with it decisive results. However, the geographic revolution should be distinguished from these other areas for its preponderant role in the formation of new worldviews during the Renaissance.

Other decisive aspects of this transformation have to do with questions of temporality and attitude. The three case studies to which we will refer in the pages that follow illustrate clearly an obvious point that nonetheless deserves reconsideration: that there are no successive chronological stages in the Scientific Revolution, let alone periods that are hermetically sealed from one another. Dom João de Castro appears unquestionably "modern" in relation to Fernando Oliveira, who was writing nearly a half-century later, and this element brings up the important question of "scientific attitude," which is perfectly evident in the works of D. João. Why he has not been recognized as a "precursor" of modem science is a false problem on many levels, beginning with the notion of a precursor itself. Dom João de Castro is a scientist, even in the most conservative sense of the word, because he thought and conducted himself as such: What limited his work was merely what was available to him and the precarious methods accorded to him by the period in which he lived. As Luís de Albuquerque so aptly observed, D. João de Castro went as far as he was able with the instruments he possessed – those that could be produced in his time. There is often a decisive technological dimension to the scientific process, and it is this dimension that often inhibits decisive innovation. But this limitation does not interfere with the fundamental question of whether a scientific attitude is exemplified.

[2] This concept seems, justifiably, to elicit more and more reservations from contemporary historiography. See Steven Shapin, *The Scientific Revolution* (Chicago, 1998).

The Portuguese maritime discoveries did not lack one of the defining features of scientific innovation: the publication of results. News of the maritime discoveries traversed all of Europe. The problem is not one of primacy, or of who may have been the first (a question that is normally irrelevant, in fact), but rather how a given piece of news was incorporated within a common intellectual framework and the consciousness on the part of the actual protagonists of the importance of the process in which they were involved. In the case of the Portuguese, this consciousness was not at all lacking.

These maritime discoveries did not bring about a scientific revolution (or prescientific revolution, as the case may be), at least not in the sense that is normally attributed to these terms. One finds, however, that the existing attitudes fulfilled these requirements, taking them as far as they possibly could go. In this sense, even though the other authors on maritime topics did not rise to the level of a D. João de Castro, the concept of experience that emerged from their navigations was profoundly revolutionary for several areas of human understanding. This idea served not only as the tool for the disassembly of inherited knowledge but also for the construction of a new geographical image of the physical world.

Duarte Pacheco Pereira's Idea of Experience

Born around 1460, Duarte Pacheco Pereira was one of the most fascinating figures of the period of the great Portuguese navigations. Emerging from noble lineage, he stood out as an expert in maritime navigation, becoming a navigator, military hero, and author of one of the sixteenth century's most important works, the *Esmeraldo de Situ Orbis,* a book that the author may have intended merely to serve as a navigation log for the route between Lisbon and India. However, the book is much more than a mere *roteiro* (directions for sea travel), because it contains observations of numerous kinds, including those describing the native groups that inhabited the coasts of Africa in addition to other topics.[3]

We say that the author may have intended his *Esmeraldo* to be a navigation log because we are uncertain of the author's true intentions: The work exists in only two copies, both from the eighteenth century and both incomplete.

[3] For more details on Duarte Pacheco Pereira, see the most extensive study on his life and works: Joaquim Barradas de Carvalho, *A la recherche de la spécificité de la renaissance Portugaise: l' "Esmeraldo de situ orbis" de Duarte Pacheco Pereira et la littérature Portugaise de voyages à l'époque des grandes découvertes* (2 vols., Paris, 1983).

Did Duarte Pacheco complete his work? It is impossible to say, but what is certain is that if one day the original (or a complete copy) is discovered and it includes the drawings that are missing from the extant copies, we would find ourselves in front of a work of unprecedented amplitude, especially given the period in which it was written.

The author of the *Esmeraldo* was also renowned for other reasons, as a short side trip through certain essential elements of his biography will make clear. Toward the end of the 1480s, when he was still less than thirty years old, Pereira was known to have been performing cosmographical observations along the coast of Africa. He may have been adding new details to nautical charts, whose constant updating was essential for Portuguese navigators of the day. Even at this early date, Pereira was acknowledged as an expert in his field, and in 1494 he was assigned to a mission of great importance. He was asked to take part in the commission that would discuss the Treaty of Tordesillas with the kings of Castile and Aragon. The technical aspects of this treaty were of crucial importance, and there is no question that Pereira's expertise was put to good use in the discussions that ensued.

In 1503, he departed for the East with two cousins, Francisco and Afonso de Albuquerque, the latter of whom would become governor and chief architect of the Portuguese empire in Asia. Pereira earned his fame as a great hero in defending Cochin against the *zamorin* of Calicut. Left at the Cochin fortress with a small contingent of troops, he and his men resisted for three months against the *zamorin* and his much larger army. When Pereira returned to Lisbon in 1505, he was received by the king as a true hero.

Pereira most likely composed the *Esmeraldo* in the years following his return to Portugal, and certainly no later than 1509. In that year, he was sent to participate in an urgent mission to intercept the French corsair *Mondragon,* which had attacked a Portuguese ship. In the aftermath, one French ship was sunk and three others were taken over. Other biographical details of Pereira's life in the years following this attack are available but are not germane to the current discussion, with the possible exception of one particularly obscure event. In 1519, he was named to the military command of the fortress of São Jorge da Mina on the coast of Africa, from which he returned in shackles for reasons that have yet to come to light. It seems that he may have offered his services to the Castilian king, who was involved at the time in a dispute with Portugal over technical matters with vital commercial repercussions. The meridian agreed upon during the Treaty of Tordesillas was to be extended to the east, but it remained unclear who would control the Moluccas archipelago, the center for clove production. João III of Portugal and Charles V each disputed the other's claim to these islands, and the issue was never resolved to the satisfaction of either party. The Moluccas were, in fact, located entirely within the Portuguese hemisphere, but there is every reason to believe that even the Portuguese cosmographers believed differently. Among them was Duarte Pacheco, who may have demonstrated all too well the logic of the Castilian claims. Nevertheless, in later years, he was forgiven for these errors and spent his final days in Portugal, reconciled with King João.[4]

Many aspects of the *Esmeraldo* give the impression that it is a unique work, even though the circumstances just described certainly may influence this perception. One of its most notable features is precisely the affirmation of focused experience as a criterion of knowledge. In historiographical terms, Duarte Pacheco has been pointed to as an example of someone who lived in a period of transition. Tied down to the medieval conceptions under which he grew up and was educated, he was nonetheless able to assimilate modern ideas and show himself capable of understanding the novelty of the times in which he lived precisely because he took part in these explorations himself.[5] Pacheco's use of the term "experience" allows for this kind of reading, as well as other more extreme historiographical interpretations based on the literal meanings of the word.[6] The most celebrated phrase of the *Esmeraldo* is an excellent starting point for us to understand what Duarte Pacheco meant when he referred to "experience, which is the mother of all things." But exactly what kind of experience is Pacheco talking about?[7]

The *Esmeraldo* contains two passages that have been cited ad nauseum, the one just quoted and another that refers to the alleged journey of Duarte Pacheco to Brazil in 1498, two years prior to Pedro Álvares Cabral's transatlantic voyage. In spite of the fact that it takes us away from the purpose of this chapter (although much less so than it seems, as I will make clear),

4 Avelino Teixeira da Mota, "Duarte Pacheco Pereira Capitão e Governador de S. Jorge da Mina," *Mare Liberum* 1 (1992), pp. 1–27.

5 This is the overall idea of Joaquim Barradas de Carvalho's work, cited earlier. Another example that subscribes to the same perspective is Margarida Barradas de Carvalho, "Nature et naturalisme dans *l'Esmeraldo de Situ Orbis* de Duarte Pacheco Pereira," *História e Sociedade*, nos. 8/9 (1981), pp. 65–69.

6 An example is João de Castro Osório, *A revolução da experiência: Duarte Pacheco Pereira, D. João de Castro* (Lisbon, 1947), a useful book only for the historiographical study of the subject.

7 For an analysis of the concepts of experience and nature in the works of Duarte Pacheco, see Luís Filipe Barreto, *Descobrimentos e ranscimento: Formas de ser e pensar nos séculos XV e XVI* (Lisbon, 1983), pp. 242–253.

we should recall the citation that has been held up as proof that Brazil was already known prior to Cabral's journey in 1500:

> . . . and for this reason, blessed Prince [he is writing to Manuel I], we have known and seen that in the third year of your Reign, the one thousand four hundred and ninety-eighth year of our lord, when your highness ordered us to discover the western parts, passing beyond the great ocean, where there is to be found and navigated a vast continent [*tão grande terra firme*], with many large islands adjacent to it.[8]

This would be an unequivocal statement had we cited it in its entirety. We can thus conclude from this text that Duarte Pacheco traversed the Atlantic in 1498 and discovered a continental landmass (*terra firme*) on the other side – that is, the American continent. Did he arrive in Brazil? Almost certainly, but he covered an extensive swath of coastline, and we do not know precisely where he may have been or how far he actually went.

More important than these questions, however, are the circumstances that led the author to refer to this journey. Was it in order to claim to have discovered this region first, since the work was written in 1505–1508 and Cabral had been recognized since 1500 as the one who discovered Brazil? In no way does this hypothesis seem appropriate. What was truly at stake is quite different. For the expert navigator recognized by the king, for the diplomat who served in Tordesillas, and, when seen through the lens of the values of the time, above all else for the hero of Cochin, who was received with pomp and circumstance by the king in Lisbon, the voyage at hand was of small matter and would never even have deserved mention had there not been another underlying question altogether.

The citation regarding his journey appears shortly after a segment referring to a completely different discussion: Is the Earth's land surrounded by water, or is the water surrounded by land? This problem was of great import for human understanding at the time, and there had been no definitive answer to date.[9] Duarte Pacheco, in fact, thought that the continents surrounded a great body of water, which took the form of a large lake. That

[8] Duarte Pacheco Pereira, *Esmeraldo de Situ Orbis,* Book I, Chapter 1. The reference edition of this manuscript is Joaquim Barradas de Carvalho, *Esmeraldo de Situ Orbis de Duarte Pacheco Pereira* (Lisbon, 1991).

[9] To understand the importance of this question, see W. G. L. Randles, "Classical Models of World Geography and Their Transformation Following the Discovery of America," in W. Haase and M. Reinhold, eds., *The Classical Tradition and the Americas, vol. 1: European Images of the Americas and the Classical Tradition* (Berlin, 1994), pp. 5–76. See also W. G. L. Randles, *Geography, Cartography and Nautical Science in the Renaissance: The Impact of the Great Discoveries* (Ashgate, 2000).

is, when traveling by water, one would always come upon land because the Earth's oceans were surrounded by land on all sides. It was an incorrect notion, of course, but one that many of the most learned individuals of the day believed and a question the truth of which could not be easily ascertained one way or the other.

How is it, then, that Duarte Pacheco convinces his readers to accept his point of view? How is he able to affirm that his interpretation is the correct one? He does this in two ways. First, he summons the opinions of classical authors, an essential criterion although not necessarily a decisive one, given that some authors affirmed the opposite even though they, too, were cited in the text of the *Esmeraldo.* What tips the scale is the second criterion, which employs Duarte Pacheco's own experience; that is to say, what he saw objectively: "It follows that the land has water within it and the ocean does not fence in the land . . . but rather, the land, which because of its size encloses within its center all the Earth's waters. And beyond all that is said, experience, which is the mother of all things, sets the record straight and removes us from our doubts." There is no doubt that Duarte Pacheco discusses his journey not in order to proclaim that he was the first to arrive at wherever his destination might actually have been but merely to guarantee his assertion that land surrounds the oceans on all sides.

What Duarte Pacheco's voyage validates for us is this context of affirmation, even though it is beyond our purpose here to discuss the plausibility of the supposed distances traveled as expressed in the two known copies of the *Esmeraldo.* What makes no sense whatsoever is to discuss whether he discovered Brazil in 1498. In the first place, "to discover" never means "to arrive for the first time." In the second place, and most importantly, Duarte Pacheco's point was to inform the reader that the ocean was no bigger than a large lagoon that one crossed to reach land on the other side.[10] It is this that is proven by the navigator's experience, by the lived sensory experience that is foreign to any later notion of scientific experience. Nonetheless, this kind of sensory experience was a decisive means for obtaining new forms of knowledge. Through this process, Duarte Pacheco was led into error as to

[10] Few today doubt the veracity of Duarte Pacheco's 1498 voyage. Jorge Couto's documentary analysis, by which he explained the circumstances of Duarte Pacheco's expedition with reference to the internal politics of the Iberian Peninsula, seems to reinforce this hypothesis. Unlike many others before him, Couto did not fall into the trap of discussing the verisimilitude of Duarte Pacheco's testimony based on noncredible handwritten instances of which only later copies are known. See J. Couto, *A construção do Brasil: Ameríndios, Portugueses e Africanos no início do povoamento a finais de quinhentos* (Lisbon, 1995), pp. 149–160. Any remaining doubts are clarified by analyzing the context in which the author of the *Esmeraldo* recounts his voyage in 1498.

the true form of the Earth, but it was precisely in this way that Bartolomeu Dias brought the Ptolemaic worldview to its ruin.

Dom João de Castro's Idea of Experience

In an article published in 1995, Onésimo Teotónio Almeida enumerated the innovations brought about by the works of four authors of the Portuguese Renaissance (Duarte Pacheco Pereira, Pedro Nunes, D. João de Castro, and Garcia da Orta):

(a) rejection of the authority of the ancients per se;
(b) acceptance of experience as the key criterion of truth;
(c) development of a scientific outlook and methodology;
(d) interface of theory and practice, and of scholars and artisans;
(e) overall awareness of the importance of the new knowledge acquired by the Portuguese navigators in the opening of new frontiers.[11]

Do these authors truly represent the Portuguese Renaissance, or are they isolated cases? Are they merely random names in a group of notable men, or do they constitute an elite that was entirely foreign to the characteristic features of their age?

These are important questions, especially because we know that there was a notoriously large gap between the academic knowledge in the universities and the world of navigation, as demonstrated by Luís de Albuquerque in one of the most remarkable of his last articles.[12] On the other hand, the navigations were far from the only activities of the Portuguese Renaissance. Nonetheless, it is unquestionable that this maritime experience provided the

[11] Onésimo Teotónio Almeida, "Portugal and the Dawn of Modern Science," in George D. Winius, ed., *Portugal, the Pathfinder: Journeys from the Medieval toward the Modern World, 1300–ca. 1600* (Madison, WI, 1995), pp. 343–344.

[12] Luís de Albuquerque, "Náutica e cartografia em Portugal nos séculos XV e XVI," in his *A Universidade e os descobrimentos* (Lisbon, 1993), pp. 91–101. This article attempts to emphasize the gap that existed between the practice of navigating and the theoretical instruction in the university. The material on this subject runs large and is treated almost incontestably in Albuquerque's bibliography. For a more substantial articulation of the same thesis, with more erudite argumentation, see Albuquerque, *Ciência e experiência nos descobrimentos Portugueses* (Lisbon, 1983). The positions laid out in this article often represent points of view that are historiographically out of date. Of the many myths related to the history of the Portuguese discoveries that have proved themselves perennial, the link between the university and the practice of navigation has been one of those that has persisted the longest.

navigators, and those who reflected upon their activities, with new visions of the world on many levels.

This new way of seeing the world was burdened, to a large extent, by the weight of description, as we see from the oft-cited observations of Pedro Nunes:

> There is no question that this Kingdom's navigations of the last hundred years are among the greatest, most marvelous, and most impressive single feats of any other people in the world. The Portuguese dared to confront the great Ocean-Sea. They plunged in without hesitation. They discovered new islands, new lands, new seas, new peoples, and what is even more, a new sky and new stars.[13]

The existence of this disagreement, if not outright confrontation, between theoreticians and practitioners of the navigational sciences is also unquestionable. The latter accused the former of not resolving adequately the practical problems that arose at sea; the theoreticians retorted that their concerns did not embrace how things actually worked in practice.

The work of Pedro Nunes may have served as the focal point around which this conflict revolved, as is evidenced by the example of Fernando Oliveira, the author whose work will be discussed in the subsequent section and who offered copious and virulent criticisms of Nunes's work in his *Ars Nautica*.[14] Indeed, Pedro Nunes himself assumes a particularly defensive posture in the opening of his *Tratado em defensão da carta de marear* (Treatise in Defense of the Sea Chart), the text from which the preceding citation was drawn. This posture is evident from the work's very first lines:

> A while back, my lord, I wrote up a short treatise relating to several doubts which Martim Afonso de Sousa brought back with him when returning from Brazil. In order to satisfy these doubts, I brought to the task not only practical aspects of the arts of navigation, but also elements of geometry and navigational theory. I have scrupulously brought together common rules of this art [of navigation] with terms and elements of science, which the pilots ridicule.[15]

The pilots may have laughed, but Martim Afonso de Sousa did not. He was one of the few ship captains who knew the art of navigation and had brought problems to Nunes to solve. The identical situation arose with

[13] Pedro Nunes,"Tratado em defensão da carta de marear," in Pedro Nunes, *Obras,* vol. 1 (Lisbon, 1940), p. 175.

[14] Fernando Oliveira, *Ars nautica,* Library of the University of Leiden, Manuscripts, Cod. VOSS. LAT. F. 41, Part I passim.

[15] Nunes, "Tratado em defensão da carta de marear," p. 175.

D. João de Castro. Contrary to what is often thought, fleet and ship captains were not required to have nautical knowledge. This task was the exclusive purview of the pilots, who excelled in everything related to navigation. There were few sea captains who knew about these areas in the sixteenth century, the two cases cited being exceptions.

It remains curious, however, that in both cases where Pedro Nunes was sought out to resolve nautical problems, these requests came from individuals who were not professionals of the sea (i.e., pilots or other mariners) and, furthermore, who had an entirely different kind of contact with him than they otherwise could have had. This contact may have taken place in the circle of D. Luís, the king's brother and disciple of Nunes, where D. João might have even learned mathematics with the cosmographer (as the prince himself did, alongside Martim Afonso and other noblemen of the prince's circle). Certain authors have surmised this connection from a passage in the *Roteiro de Goa a Diu.* But none of this makes D. João de Castro's case any less exceptional.

Later on, "Castro forte" (1500–1548), as Luís de Camões referred to him in *The Lusiads,* was celebrated primarily as governor and viceroy of India. At this stage in his career, D. João de Castro was recognized not only as honest and upstanding but also as a military hero for his defense at the second siege of Diu, a feat for which his fame made the rounds in Europe.[16] Parallel to these accomplishments, he is reputed to have written a treatise on the sphere, a noteworthy text in the field of sea routes, and to have left an exceedingly valuable collection of letters.[17]

It may seem paradoxical, but we will not reflect at greater length on the career of D. João de Castro, in spite of his being an outstanding example not only of a scientifically inquisitive spirit in sixteenth-century Europe but also of the intersection between theory and practice to which Onésimo Almeida referred earlier. Even though a satisfactory and updated biography of D. João has yet to be written, two studies, one by Luís de Albuquerque

[16] "Reflexos do segundo cerco de Diu na Europa," in Armando Cortesão and Luís de Albuquerque, eds., *Obras completas de D. João de Castro,* vol. 4 (Coimbra, 1981), pp. 147–173.

[17] "Tratado da sphaera, por perguntas e respostas a modo de dialogo," in Cortesão and Albuquerque, *Obras completas de D. João de Castro,* vol. 1, pp. 15–114. This attribution of authorship had never been seriously challenged until the publication of an article by Suzanne Daveau that, without explicitly denying his authorship, requires a certain degree of caution in identifying the author of this treatise. See "Qui est l'auteur du Tratado da Esfera attribué à D. João de Castro?" in *Mare Liberum* 10 (1995), pp. 33–54. The letters have been published in Cortesão and Albuquerque, *Obras completas de D. João de Castro,* vols. 1 and 2 (sea routes) and 4 (letters).

and another by Reyer Hooykaas, have already laid out the essential aspects of this important work.[18]

It is worth calling attention to the story of a scientific investigation made in response to a veritable research program that achieved concrete results through a process whose most minute details can be followed and dated. We know the precise year, month, and day on which the solution to the problem was found.

Dom João de Castro solved various problems related to terrestrial magnetism, an important field with respect to navigation, whether directly or indirectly. When leaving for Goa in 1538, he carried several instruments that had been given to him by D. Luís and had been made by an artisan named João Gonçalves. The goal was to prove a rule put forward by Pedro Nunes,[19] and the result consisted of the fifty-six observations of magnetic declination that are found within the route narrative (*roteiro*), accompanied by their respective explanations.

This was in every sense a research program. It begins with the formulation of a hypothesis, followed by contracting with an artisan to produce the appropriate instruments, which are later tested systematically in the field. This entire process is organized through the mediation, energy, and interest of D. Luís, who, like D. João, also happened to be a student of Pedro Nunes, as mentioned.

These conclusions can be seen as extremely important for the history of science, even though it is true that European historiography has not recognized them as such, mostly because their circumstances are largely unknown. Yet, they are clearly documented.

Dom João rejected the idea that there was a direct relationship between the direction of the compass and the determination of longitude, an idea that at the time had currency among pilots. Although the problem of determining longitude at sea was solved when John Harrison's fourth prototype chronometer was successfully tested in the second half of the eighteenth century, we know the problem had particularly preoccupied pilots from the time that navigation on the high seas became routine.[20]

[18] Luís de Albuquerque, *Ciência e experiência*; and Reyer Hooykaas, "Science in Manueline Style," in Cortesão and Albuquerque, *Obras completas de D. João de Castro,* vol. 4, pp. 231–426.

[19] D. João de Castro, "Roteiro de Lisboa a Goa [Roteiro da viagem que Dom João fez a primeira vez que foy a India no anno de 1538]," in Cortesão and Albuquerque, *Obras completas de D. João de Castro*, vol. 1, pp. 127–128.

[20] For a general overview on longitude and navigation, see William J. H. Andrews, ed., *The Quest for Longitude: The Proceedings of the Longitude Symposium* (Cambridge, MA, 1993).

Another notable aspect of D. João's work is the discovery of compass variation, which took place on August 5, 1538, and merits citing at length the entry from the *roteiro:*

> Monday, August the 5th, I turned directly toward the sun in Mozambique. . . . On this day, I wanted to work with the shadow instruments to calibrate the compass variation, and since it was not yet 11 A.M., the shadow of the needle was already far beyond the line of noon; at which time, having asked for some compasses to put alongside the instrument, I found them so far out of alignment that I was shocked. While one pointed east, the other pointed north. I was held in great suspense, until I understood the cause. It was a bed that was in the same place that I wanted to carry out my experiment, and the iron from this structure pulled the compasses and caused them to vary in this way. From these observations, I gathered that an operation I had done on the thirtieth of June at the meridian, which according to the compasses was East of the Cape by 5 1/2 degrees, a position I felt was highly irregular, as well as others I had done during the stop in Brazil and for which I had found notable differences, had been thrown off for having taken these observations near some piece of artillery, or anchors, or some other piece of iron.[21]

If, through his observations, D. João de Castro was able to set aside definitively the erroneous correlation that had been established between magnetic declination and the calculation of longitude (although pilots continued to use the values of magnetic declination as points of reference for their navigations), as was said before, his contributions to the study of terrestrial magnetism did not receive the same acclaim. He still deserves to be recognized as having been the first observer of the phenomenon that would later come to be called local attraction.[22]

Fernando Oliveira's Idea of Experience

Father Fernando Oliveira's story is entirely different from the two preceding cases. Although he did not have the same kind of maritime experience as Duarte Pacheco or D. João de Castro, this did not prevent him from leading an adventurous life, full of surprising incidents that are outside the scope of this study. Nonetheless, he has received far less attention than either of the two others.[23]

[21] D. João de Castro, "Roteiro de Lisboa a Goa," pp. 243–244.

[22] Luís de Albuquerque, *Ciencia e experiência,* p. 115.

[23] Francisco Contente Domingues, *Experiência e conhecimento na construção naval Portuguesa: Os tratados de Fernando Oliveira* (Lisbon, 1985), pp. 339–364.

Oliveira's oeuvre is extremely multifaceted and includes two printed books, both pioneering in their respective areas: *Gramática da linguagem Portuguesa* (1536) (Grammar of the Portuguese Language) and *Arte da guerra do mar* (1555) (The Art of War at Sea). Many of his works remained in manuscript during his life, which explains in large part why Oliveira was known above all else as a grammarian. Only recently has he begun to be recognized for his work on maritime topics. Although his *Livro da fábrica das naus* (Book on the Construction of Ships) was finally published in 1898,[24] the *Ars nautica*, a veritable naval encyclopedia without equal in its genre, still remains in manuscript form,[25] although a printed edition is currently in preparation under the sponsorship of the Naval Academy in Lisbon. Only recently has this work been the object of a significant study, in particular the section dealing with naval architecture.[26] Without question, Oliveira's work deserves more extensive treatment than it has received.

Aside from the interest that the *Arte da guerra* has elicited among specialists of naval strategy and warfare, it should be said that the *Livro* remains to be fully explored, and this is even more true for the *Ars nautica*. A published author is not necessarily a known author.

The *Livro da fábrica das naus* (ca. 1580) was the first treatise on naval architecture written in Portuguese, even though it was Oliveira's second text on the topic, because the second section of the *Ars nautica* (about naval architecture) was written by him prior to the composition of the *Livro da fábrica das naus.* Rather than merely translating into Portuguese from its original Latin that part of the earlier work, which is the way the production of the *Livro* has been portrayed, Oliveira in fact fundamentally

[24] Henrique Lopes de Mendonça, *O Padre Fernando Oliveira e a sua obra nautica: Memoria, comprehendendo um estudo biographico sobre o afamado grammatico e nautographo, e a primeira reproducção typographica do seu tratado inedito Livro da Fabrica das Naos* (Lisbon, 1898). Republished with essays by Francisco Contente Domingues, Richard Barker, and Maria Teresa Duarte (Lisbon, 1989).

[25] Alonso de Chaves wrote his well-known *Qvatri Partitv En Cosmographia* about thirty years before Oliveira, but it is not comparable in any sense either for the length of the book or the depth of analysis. Chaves gives a very short and merely descriptive list of ships' names, whereas Oliveira wrote a treatise on the same subject in Part II of his *Ars nautica*, for instance. Chaves's manuscript is in Madrid at the Biblioteca de la Real Academia de la Historia, colleción Salazar y Castro, Cod. 9/2791). See also Paulino Castañeda Delgado, Mariano Cuesta Domingo, and Pilar Hernandez Aparicio, eds., *Quatri partitu en cosmographia practica, y por otro nombre espejo de navegantes* (Madrid, 1983).

[26] João da Gama Pimental Barata, "A 'Ars Nautica' do Pe. Fernando Oliveira: Enciclopédia de conhecimentos marítimos e primeiro tratado científico de construção naval (1570)," *Memórias do Centro de Estudos de Marinha* 2 (1972), pp. 183–197, republished in *Estudos de Arqueologia Naval* 2 (1989), pp. 129–149.

rewrote the second part of the *Ars nautica* for the *Livro,* moving away from the predominantly theoretical tone that characterizes the earlier work. But he does manage to maintain the particular kind of thinking characteristic of the *Ars nautica,* even though the precise way in which he depicts the practice of the shipyards, and the specificity of the architectural solutions he proposes, still need further examination.[27]

The novelty of the *Livro* is its thematic unity, since most European technical literature on naval architecture at the time appeared as miscellanies as opposed to works specifically dedicated to this single topic. An excellent example of this difference is the oft-cited book by Diego Garcia de Palacio, *Instrvcion navtica,*[28] a text far more interesting for its having been published at all than for what is actually contained within its pages. Contrary to the *Instrvcion,* Oliveira's *Livro* is the only text of the entire range of fifteenth- and sixteenth-century works that is dedicated extensively to an analysis of the conditions of knowledge beyond strictly technical contents, making it also important for the study of the Renaissance "philosophy of knowledge" and a landmark on this specific genre of literature. Of course, similar works also occasionally consider the same questions: It is sufficient to recall the Portuguese treatise that follows the *Livro* chronologically, João Baptista Lavanha's *Livro primeiro da architectura naval* (First Book of Naval Architecture).[29] Oliveira's epistemological approach is not only more extended than usual, but what is more, it is coherent with its technical approach. For Fernando Oliveira, knowledge exists to the extent that its roots are explained. He considers it essential, for example, to discuss the origin and formation of the technical lexicon he employs.

In proposing to regularize naval architecture according to clear and general precepts – after having recognized that the arts were subject to the particular judgment of each individual and that no order or criterion would be universally accepted or recognized – Oliveira places before the reader in hierarchical order the sources on which the process of knowing must

[27] Although he was recognized for a long time as an author with a theoretical approach, it is today understood that Oliveira was in fact closer to the actual practice of the dockyards than was thought before. See Francisco Alves, Paulo Rodrigues, and Filipe Castro, "Aproximação arqueológica às fontes escritas da arquitectura naval Portuguesa," in Francisco Contente Domingues and Inácio Guerreiro, eds., *Fernando Oliveira e o seu tempo: Fernando Oliveira and His Era* (Cascais, 2000), pp. 227–256.

[28] Diego Garcia de Palacio, *Instrvcion navthica, para el bven vso, y regimiento de Ias Naos, su traça, y gouierno conforme à Ia altura de Mexico* (Mexico, 1587).

[29] Initially published in 1965; a new edition has recently been released. See João Baptista Lavanha, *Livro primeiro da architectura naval* (Lisbon, 1996).

be constituted. They are, in this exact order, the classical authors, his own experience, and contemporary authors. The first group is the principal source, and in the course of the entire work, only once does Oliveira contradict one of these authors (Pliny). The work refers very little to contemporary authors, certainly much less than one might imagine would be the case. The *Livro* makes reference solely to Guillaume Budé and, even as Oliveira invokes the common precepts of civil architecture (because there were no classical authors who wrote on naval architecture, Renaissance writers turned to the precepts of civil architecture), he makes no direct reference to any contemporary authorities on the subject. The Palladio to whom he refers is not the renowned Italian architect Andrea Palladio, author of one of the most famous works of the Renaissance, but rather the author of a treatise on agriculture from the second century A.D.[30] Nonetheless, we find in Fernando Oliveira's work a consciousness of novelty that Onésimo Almeida noted was an outstanding attribute of the period, if not one of its most authentic features: "In this we owe more praise to ourselves than to the Greeks or the Latins: for more has been done for navigation in 80 years, than was accomplished during the 2,000 in which they reigned."[31]

Affirming the novelty of the period is on a par with affirming the criterion of experience as a necessary element for the validation of knowledge. But there are two unavoidable obstacles in Oliveira's language: the inheritance from classical antiquity and the primacy of nature. His rationale is straightforward: If perfection is a divine attribute, and nature is a divine creation, then man has no choice but to imitate nature. Guided by the lessons of the ancients, men of Oliveira's time had only to imitate nature with their ingenuity and validate what they did through experimentation. It is for this reason that the hulls of ships mimicked so closely the anatomy of fish, the creatures that God created to travel through water. The fact that Fernando Oliveira wrote this at the same time that Mathew Baker, the master shipbuilder of Henry VIII, designed a ship's hull on the design of a fish in England – without any explanation of why he did it[32] – may indicate that the two knew one another (from the time that Oliveira was imprisoned by the English, only to later gain the personal confidence of Henry VIII), or that the two shared the same epistemological presuppositions.

[30] *The Fourteen Books of Palladius Rutilius Taurus Aemilianus on Agriculture,* trans. T. Owen (London, 1807).

[31] Lopes de Mendonça, *O Padre Fernando Oliveira,* p. 154.

[32] Mathew Baker (and others), *Fragments of Ancient English Shipwrightry,* Cambridge University, Magdalene College, Pepysian Library, Ms. 2820.

In the end, a single citation may serve as the best summary:

> I say that art is the doctrine of the word or the example, founded upon solid reasoning, and confirmed through experience. Or, as others have said, it consists of copying materials taken from good writers. And whether you believe in the first path or the second, art will always depend on the doctrine that is learned and put into practice, without which what we know or do is devoid of art. What we understand or imagine without experiencing or putting into practice is called science [i.e., theory], an unfinished form of knowledge. For what qualifies as the peak of human knowledge is experience.[33]

As we can see from these three examples, for Portuguese authors of the sixteenth century the notion of experience was complex and diversified. But for those directly or indirectly involved in the navigations, experience was at the foundation of the process of acquiring knowledge that, for the most part, could only be obtained in this way.

In the particular case of D. João de Castro, the change went far beyond practical necessity. His example serves to show that the authority of the classics could fail and that direct observation of reality was the best means of making contact with other worlds. Specific errors became apparent in the work of classical authors ("Pliny made a mistake," as the mathematician Pedro Nunes wrote). The clear perception already existed that the new understanding afforded by the navigations superseded the learned inheritance from the past. In the eyes of those who have reflected on the impact of the navigations, this destructive effect of the new knowledge acquired by experience was one of the greatest conquests of the time. With the realization that new seas, lands, stars, and also new peoples, plants, and animals had been discovered, based on direct observation, there also arose the notion that a new world was beginning, a world that until then mankind had not seen in all its enormous wealth and diversity.

BIBLIOGRAPHICAL ESSAY

Portuguese historiography has always paid a great deal of attention to the great maritime navigations of the fifteenth and sixteenth centuries and, in particular, to their technical aspects: nautical sciences, cartography, and ship construction. In the first two of these categories, Portuguese scholars

[33] Lopes de Mendonça, *O Padre Fernando Oliveira,* p. 172.

attained positions of wide acclaim and worldwide recognition for their historiographical contributions, to the point that it would be impossible to study these subjects without knowing their work: Armando Cortesão, for the history of cartography; and Luís de Albuquerque, for the history of the nautical sciences. Albuquerque, in fact, received one of the highest forms of international recognition available to a historian when in 1991 he was awarded the status of "honorary member" of the American Historical Association, proposed by Wilcomb Washburn and Ursula Lamb.

In general, however, it is rare that Portuguese historians are recognized by their non-Portuguese colleagues, in large part because few publish regularly in languages other than Portuguese. It is not surprising, therefore, that in a country with such a long historiographical tradition relating to the history of maritime travel, it is possible to count on one hand those historians whose work has been published in the most important specialist journals on the subject, such as the *Mariner's Mirror* or the *American Neptune.*

On the other hand, it should be recognized that too often international scholars reciprocate by treating these topics without any knowledge either of the primary sources or of the historiographical work of Portuguese scholars. It follows naturally that there is a visible lag between the general synthetic works and the results of more recent studies by specialists on these topics.

The relationship between the history of scientific thought and the history of maritime discoveries has generally suffered from a certain lack of attention, and even more from the relative lack of knowledge of the relevance of maritime history to the general study of the history of science. While Portuguese historians do not normally put their utmost energy into the history of science, European and North American scholars ponder the history of scientific thought without considering sufficiently its connection with the history of maritime discoveries. The exceptions to the rule, in both groups, are few and far between.

For those who are interested in the kind of analysis presented in this chapter, two types of readings may be suggested. The first consists of the work of well-established authors who have set out the terms of the larger debate relating to these issues; and the second includes those who have more recently treated these topics and who have indicated new areas of potential inquiry.

Of the first group, Luís de Albuquerque should be mentioned foremost. He is the author of numerous texts, including significant and essential studies that treat the relationship between science and the overseas expeditions. One book in particular stands out among the rest: *Ciência e experiência nos descobrimentos Portugueses* (Science and Experience in the Portuguese Discoveries) (Lisbon, 1983). It is a short but excellent synthesis that has been out of print for quite some time and was never translated into English. Albuquerque's last published work, *Historia de la navigación Portuguesa* (History of Portuguese Navigation) (Madrid, 1992), available only in Spanish, returned to the same topic, although it tended to focus more on the nautical sciences per se. Among his list of published works (which include more than 1,000 items), the few that are in English unfortunately do not give an adequate picture of the importance of his work. The list of his most important studies can be found in Francisco Contente Domingues, "Ricordo di Luis de Albuquerque," *Notiziario* 2 (1994), pp. 13–27.

It was through Luís de Albuquerque that one of the most important contemporary historians of science became interested in the Portuguese maritime discoveries and their relationship to science and the arts. Reyer Hooykaas's most prominent work in this field is entitled *Humanism and the Voyages of Discovery in Sixteenth Century Portuguese Science and Letters* (Amsterdam, 1979), but he also wrote a highly important study that should be required reading: "Science in Manueline Style," in Armando Cortesão and Luís de Albuquerque, eds., *Obras completas de D. João de Castro,* vol. 4 (Coimbra, 1981), pp. 231–426.

A basic reference in the field is the work of William G. L. Randles, a historian of science whose profound erudition and command of numerous languages has allowed him to produce a series of studies unequaled in their rigor. His broad knowledge of sources and secondary bibliography allows him to transcend microanalysis and offer larger, more comprehensive overviews with an expansive reach. Some of his more important articles have just been reissued in *Geography, Cartography and Nautical Science in the Renaissance* (Aldershot, 2000), among others the one cited in the footnotes, a quite remarkable and impressive tour de force of scholarship and erudition: "Classical Models of World Geography and Their Transformation Following the Discovery of America." The author returned to a favorite theme, the subject of a previous book, *De la terre plate au globe terrestre: Une mutation épistémologique rapide, 1480–1520* (Paris, 1980), but the reader should prefer the Portuguese version, *Da terra plana ao globo terrestre* (Lisbon, 1990), because the author corrected some misprints in the original French version.

On the second group, A. A. Marques de Almeida was one of the first Portuguese historians to study in theory what the history of science, and the practice of it, is in the period considered ("Sobre a História da Ciência," *Clio,* n.s. 2 [1997], pp. 7–29). A major work was devoted to economic thought, *Aritmética como descrição do real (1519–1679): Contributos para a formação da idade moderna em Portugal* (2 vols., Lisbon, 1994), with important references for the history of science and the navigations. Two articles are closely related: "Inovação e resistência na prática científica no Portugal das descobertas," in João Medina, ed., *História de Portugal*, vol. 4 (Lisbon, 1994), pp. 157–168, and "A formação do discurso científico no Portugal das descobertas entre fins do século XV e meados de Quinhentos," *Mare Liberum* 13 (1997), pp. 11–39.

Luís Filipe Barreto, already cited in the footnotes, with his *Descobrimentos e ranscimento: Formas de ser e pensar nos séculos XV e XVI* (Lisbon, 1983), should be consulted. Later, he published *Os descobrimentos e a ordem do saber: Uma análise sociocultural* (Lisbon, 1987), but his larger work, the Ph.D. thesis entitled "A Ordem do Saber no universo cultural dos descobrimentos Portugueses" (2 vols., Lisbon, 1990), is only available in a typed version.

The numerous writings of Onésimo Teotónio Almeida deserve careful reading, since he is an author with full control of the sources in both Portuguese and English. Almeida analyzes the perception of the Portuguese contribution to science and technology in books published in English and concludes that almost all (with a very few exceptions) simply ignore both the sources and the bibliography of the Portuguese historians. His article cited is a major contribution to our understanding of the subject. See "Portugal and the Dawn of Modern Science," in George Winius, ed., *Portugal, the Pathfinder* (Madison, WI, 1995), pp. 341–361, and also *Oceanos*, no. 49 (2002), pp. 9–17.

In this last issue of *Oceanos* (no. 49), the journal of the National Commission for the Commemoration of the Portuguese Discoveries, can be found a series of important articles, namely the one by Henrique Leitão: "Sobre a difusão Europeia da obra de Pedro Nunes," *Oceanos*, no. 49 (2002), pp. 111–128.

Part IV: The Comparative Dimension

14

PORTUGUESE EXPANSION IN A GLOBAL CONTEXT

Felipe Fernández-Armesto

Portugal's early modern empire was unique, but its uniqueness can only be appreciated against the background of the history of other empires. The framework has to be global – not confined, as it commonly is, to European imperialism. And it has to encompass land empires along with the "seaborne empires" that have traditionally been selected for comparative purposes. There are two reasons for this.

First, Portugal's empire, although often correctly described as a "seaborne" and even a "seaboard" affair, experienced a transition common to most European imperialism of the period: Late in the day, it became more and more committed to landward expansion.[1] This made it typical in a broad sense, for although our historical tradition has concentrated on the study of maritime empires of European origin, most early modern imperialism was of the kind that has prevailed throughout history: It was territorial and based on expansion into areas contiguous by land with those already occupied by the imperial power.

Secondly, for something like half the period from 1400 to 1800, in areas where Portuguese activity was most intense, European imperialism played a relatively small part in shaping the societies it encountered. Throughout the sixteenth century, and for most of the seventeenth, the Portuguese imperial commitment was greatest in Asia – where Europeans crawled like lice on the hide of the continent – and on the imperial route that led there. Portugal's New World outpost in Brazil was of interest initially only as an offshoot of

[1] Anthony Disney, "The Portuguese Empire in India, c. 1550–1650: Some Suggestions for a Less Seaborne, More Landbound Approach to Its Socio-economic History,' in John Correia-Afonso, ed., *Indo-Portuguese History: Sources and Problems* (Bombay, 1981), pp. 148–162.

that same route, discovered in the course of an excursion into the Atlantic in search of the winds that led eastward;[2] and although African products – especially slaves and, where available, gold – should not be underestimated, they played only an ancillary role in Portugal's imperial economy once access to the Indian Ocean had been opened. The prospects for participation in intra-Asian shipping and the intercontinental spice trade then became, for most participants, the areas of greatest opportunity. Portuguese imperialism therefore operated mainly in theaters dominated by indigenous states and empires: Interference was modest, disruption only intermittent and limited in scale and scope. Even in the eighteenth century, the "equality of civilizations" was little compromised by Western intrusions into Asia.[3] In some respects, and in some places, effects received by the Portuguese exceeded those inflicted by them – especially where they were defeated or "went native," or where hybrid cultures evolved.

Nonetheless, the emphasis historians usually place on European maritime imperialism is justified. Long-range maritime imperialism was genuinely one of the original features of the early modern period in world history.

[2] Luís de Albuquerque, *Os descobrimentos Portugueses* (Lisbon, 1983), pp. 149–174; Damião Peres, *História dos descobrimentos* (Oporto, 1983), pp. 327–349.

[3] For a conspectus of the scholarship that has led to this conclusion, see A. Disney, ed., *Historiography of Europeans in Africa and Asia, 1450–1800* (Aldershot, 1995), pp. xii–xvi; and J. R. Wills, "Was There a Vasco da Gama Epoch?" in A. Disney and E. Booth, eds., *Vasco da Gama and the Linking of Europe and Asia* (New Delhi, 2000), pp. 350–360. The tradition began with Jacob C. van Leur, "On the Eighteenth Century as a Category in Indonesian History,' in *Indonesian Trade and Society: Essays in Asian Social and Economic History* (The Hague, 1955), pp. 268–289 – an essay first published during the Second World War. Works important in relating it to the history of Portuguese imperialism are Blair B. Kling and Michael N. Pearson, eds., *The Age of Partnership: Europeans in Asia before Dominion* (Honoloulu, 1979); M. N. Pearson, *Coastal Western India: Studies from the Portuguese Records* (New Delhi, 1981); George Winius, "The Shadow Empire of Goa in the Bay of Bengal," *Itinerario* 7 (1983), pp. 83–101; M. N. Pearson, "India and the Indian Ocean in the Sixteenth Century,' in A. Das Gupta and M. N. Pearson, eds., *India and the Indian Ocean, 1500–1800* (Calcutta, 1987), pp. 71–93; Sanjay Subrahmanyam, *Improvising Empire: Portuguese Trade and Settlement in the Bay of Bengal, 1500–1700* (Delhi, 1990); K. McPherson, "Chulias and Klings: Indigenous Trade Diasporas and European Penetration of the Indian Ocean Littoral," in Giorgio Borsa, ed., *Trade and Politics in the Indian Ocean: Historical and Contemporary Perspectives* (New Delhi, 1990), pp. 33–46; L. F. F. R. Thomaz, "The Portuguese in the Seas of the Archipel during the Sixteenth Century," in *Trade and Shipping in the Southern Seas: Selected Readings from Archipel, xviii, 1979* (Paris, 1984), pp. 75–92; M. N. Pearson, ed., *The Portuguese in India*, The New Cambridge History of India, vol. 1 (Cambridge, 1987); and S. Subrahmanyam and L. F. F. R. Thomaz, "Evolution of Empire: The Portuguese in the Indian Ocean during the Sixteenth Century," in James D. Tracy, ed., *The Political Economy of Merchant Empires: State Power and World Trade, 1350–1750* (Cambridge, 1991), pp. 298–331.

Seaborne empires, forged around seas, adhering to their rims and dependent on maritime communications, had been known in antiquity and the Middle Ages in the Mediterranean. The Knytlinga empire around the North Sea in the eleventh century has been put in this category, as has the trans-Channel "Norman empire" that succeeded it.[4] The Chola empire of the same period, although evidence about it is elusive, probably qualifies for admission in the same category.[5] Networks of commercial communities or colonies and, to some extent, of political allegiance, were spread around monsoonal seas in what we think of as the Middle Ages from centers in southern Arabia, the Persian Gulf, India, and China. For a moment in the fifteenth century, Chinese flag-waving along commercial routes in monsoonal seas seemed about to acquire an imperial character, with large-scale naval expeditions, which reached Arabia and East Africa, and spasmodic political interventions as far afield as Java, Ceylon, and Malacca. For adventurers from Western Europe in the same period, the African Atlantic, encompassing the Canary Islands, the Azores, and some stations on the African coast, became an arena of conquest and colonization. Never before, however, as far as we know, had maritime imperialism on the scale of the early modern period been attempted, let alone achieved.

Moreover, while European impact varied considerably and was almost negligible in some areas, there were two contexts in which its effects were tremendous. Contact, conflict, and contagion overhauled parts of the New World where white colonization penetrated: New diseases killed millions and recarved the demographic profile, while new biota stripped and reclothed vast environments. Meanwhile, with increasing intensity in the seventeenth and eighteenth centuries, parts of Africa experienced challenges arising from the slave trade. Warfare was encouraged, raptor-states emerged, and in some places the depredations of slavers had distorting demographic effects.[6] The extent of these changes, in both Africa and the Americas, is much disputed and cannot be quantified with anything like exactitude. But in the American case, even the most modest estimates are formidable.[7]

[4] John Le Patourel, *The Norman Empire* (Oxford, 1978).

[5] Kenneth R. Hall, *Trade and Statecraft in the Age of the Colas* (New Delhi, 1980).

[6] David Birmingham, *Trade and Conflict in Angola: The Mbundu and Their Neighbours under the Influence of the Portuguese, 1483–1790* (Oxford, 1966); Patrick Manning, *Slavery and African Life: Occidental, Oriental and African Slave Trades* (Cambridge, 1990); and John K. Thornton, *Africa and the Africans in the Making of the Atlantic World, 1400–1680* (Cambridge, 1992).

[7] See David Henige, *Numbers from Nowhere: The American Indian Contact Population Debate* (Norman, OK, 1998), for a critique of the literature on New World demography, and Joseph Inikori and Stanley Engerman, eds., *The Atlantic Slave Trade: Effects on Economic*

Portuguese imperialism played a role of unquestionable significance in effecting these transformations. The transplantation of sugar to America, for which Portuguese colonists were largely responsible in Brazil, was the most thoroughgoing new influence on the ecology of the region between the ranchlands of northern New Spain and the Brazilian *sertão* in the sixteenth century. Portuguese agents, moreover, played a major role in the slave trade: They controlled key emporia, supplied more shipping than competitors of any other nation, and dominated contacts with some of the indigenous states that were the most prolific suppliers of slaves in Africa.

Furthermore, the facts remain that modern world history has been dominated by initiatives from Western Europe and that Portugal was in the vanguard of them, especially in long-range navigation, commerce, and colonization; maritime exploration and the science associated with it; the transplantation of culture over vast distances; and the worldwide exchange of biota, which wrought changes in the environments touched by the unprecedentedly far-reaching communications of the period. An account of the global context of Portuguese expansion must therefore tackle the big question of modern world history: Why the West? Why did the region to which Portugal clings and the civilization to which it belongs play an unprecedented role in our period and register achievements so disproportionate to their apparent potential?

The best course through the world context of Portugal's imperial history is outward, following that of the Portuguese empire-builders: beginning in Portugal itself with "the problem of Portugal" – how such a small home country mothered such a big empire; then broadening to maritime Western Europe; next, heading out into the trade-wind environment of the Atlantic; crossing to the monsoon system of maritime Asia; and ending with the great land empires of the period, which Portugal's increasingly resembled. To some extent, this pathway through the material also traces a route through time from the local and regional beginnings of Portuguese expansion, through its Atlantic and Asian phases, to its landward culmination in the phase dominated by Brazil.

The Problem of Portugal: Small Starting Place

"Portugal: not a small country" was a slogan of the Salazar years. Even the dictator, however, was willing to acknowledge that before imperial

Society and Peoples in Africa, the Americas and Europe (Durham, NC, 1997), for a recent appraisal of effects on tropical Africa.

expansion Portugal was small. The contrast between the breadth of Portuguese imperialism and the modest dimensions of the home country is the most conspicuous mystery of Portuguese history and one of the most puzzling contrasts in the history of the world. The state of the statistics allows only very rough computations, but in the early sixteenth century Portugal's population was probably little more than half of England's and one-quarter of Castile's, probably about one-tenth that of France, and much smaller even than that of the Low Countries.[8] Few other resources were available to make up for the lack of land and people. The salt pans of Setúbal were the only form of abundance conferred by nature. Poverty and famine were commonplace afflictions.[9]

The resource base seemed inadequate even for the maritime outlook that Portugal's position encouraged. Of its potential rivals in overseas empire-seeking, only the Netherlands had less access to timber and iron for shipbuilding. Even the paucity at Portugal's command seemed vulnerable, with a long, awkward land frontier, unprotected by any easily defensible barrier and patrolled by a dauntingly powerful neighbor. In this respect, Portugal was far worse-off than the Netherlands, where Spanish armies had to operate at a double disadvantage, far from home and restrained by intractable geography. The one advantage historians sometimes ascribe to Portugal – internal peace after the dynastic settlement of 1385, while much of the rest of Western Europe was convulsed by fifteenth-century civil wars – was equivocal

[8] The current consensus favors about 15 million for France at the end of the fifteenth century. See Christopher Allmand, ed., *The New Cambridge Medieval History*, vol. 7 (Cambridge, 1998), p. 421. Compare, however, J.-F. Sirinelli and Daniel Couty, eds., *Dictionnaire de l'histoire de France* (2 vols., Paris, 1999), vol. 2, pp. 1238–1239, where a well-supported figure of 21 million for 1582 is estimated at double or triple the level of a hundred years previously. A million and a half is a reasonable estimate for Portugal in the early to mid sixteenth century (Allmand, *New Cambridge Medieval History*, vol. 7, p. 627). Pierre Chaunu, *L'Espagne de Charles Quint* (2 vols., Paris, 1973), vol. 1, pp. 76–98, 125–132, reckons nearly 7 million for Castile in the early sixteenth century. J. A. van Houtte, *Economische en sociale geschiedenis van de Lage Lande* (Antwerp, 1964), pp. 130–131, indicates over 2,600,000 for the Low Countries in the early sixteenth century, although it should be borne in mind that the Dutch Republic at the time of the great expansion of the seventeenth century is generally said to have had under 2 million inhabitants. England's population is universally acknowledged to have grown rapidly in the late sixteenth century, but the figure for the early part of the century is much disputed and is not now generally put at above 3 million (2.8 million in 1547 according to Penry Williams, *The Later Tudors: England, 1547–1603*, Oxford, 1995, p. 1).

[9] Virginia Rau, *Estudos sobre a história do sal Português* (Lisbon, 1984); A. H. Oliveira Marques, *Introdução a história da agricultura em Portugal: A questão cerealifera durante a idade media* (Lisbon, 1978); and A. de Castro, *A evolução económica de Portugal dos seculos XII a XV*, vol. 11 (Lisbon, 1980).

in its effects. Civil wars are often preludes to empire because they create aggressive elites for whom employment must be found and because they set off scrambles for resources that can lead peoples far afield.

As a place from which to found a great empire, Portugal therefore invites the response of the yokel who, when asked to direct a passing motorist, replied, "If I was you, I wouldn't start from here." Imperialism is sometimes the result of overflowing resources, superabundance of power, or spillage of surplus population. Portugal's belongs in a less privileged category. Its seaward turn resembled that of a third-world country today, desperately drilling for offshore resources in initial reliance on foreign capital and savoir-faire: particularly that of the Italian, especially Genoese, entrepreneurs and technicians who played a major part in the seaward ventures of the fourteenth and fifteenth centuries.[10] Portugal's sustained quest for empire was a response to poverty and insecurity and a case of what might be called "small-country psychosis": the need to grow by conquest. Together, these circumstances help to explain the first problem of the history of the Portuguese empire, how it happened at all, and they suggest an approach to understanding the next-strangest feature of the story: the tenacity that made the earliest European seaborne empire one of the longest-enduring.[11]

Nothing can make Portugal's imperial career unsurprising, but the broader the framework of comparison in which it is beheld, the easier it is to understand. Far-flung seaborne enterprises often start from a home base that is poor or of limited exploitability, with restricted opportunities to landward. Marginal peoples, on or beyond the edges of great civilizations, are often tempted into colonial or commercial adventures. The locus classicus, in every sense of the term, is that of ancient Greece – "the sister of poverty," according to Hesiod, a skeleton-land, in Plato's perceptions, where the bones of rock poked through the thin flesh of soil.[12] The Greeks' great rivals in long-range colonization, the Phoenicians, started from a narrow coast. Southern Arabia, Gujerat, and Fukien have housed great ocean-going civilizations in similarly situated home bases. Japan is not often thought of as home to long-range maritime imperialism, but it occupies a position comparable to Portugal's at the opposite extremity of Eurasia. In key respects Japan has experienced a history comparable to Portugal's, for the conditions

[10] Charles Verlinden, "European Participation in the Portuguese Discovery Era," in George Winius, ed., *Portugal the Pathfinder* (Madison, WI, 1995), pp. 71–80.

[11] I should make clear that I refer to tenacity purely descriptively and do not intend it to be understood as a means of explanation of Portuguese imperial successes along the lines, for example, of Charles R. Boxer's use of the concept of "rootedness," especially in his *The Portuguese Seaborne Empire, 1415–1825* (London, 1991), p. 120.

[12] *Works and Days,* 392, trans. A. W. Mair (Oxford, 1908), p. 11; *Critias,* 111B.

of navigation in its home waters make the scale of Japanese empire building impressive, just within what we have come to think of as its own islands.[13] Japan's two spells of wider-reaching seaborne imperialism are suggestive: In the late sixteenth century, it was foiled by the insufficiency of the available technology, and in the twentieth, when steamships could break out of the restraining meshwork of the winds, it was defeated by insuperable odds.

In Western Europe, too, until the late Middle Ages, the only long-distance, ocean-going initiatives we know began in relatively poor and peripheral places: the seaborne pilgrimages of hermits from Ireland and the ventures of raiders, pirates, and colonists from Scandinavia. The seaborne empires of the medieval Mediterranean were founded from narrow rivieras, in the Genoese and Catalan cases, or from the unpromisingly salty, marshy islands of the Venetian lagoon. The empire that in its day successfully imitated, challenged, and outplayed Portugal's was the most similarly situated – that of the Netherlands, also a marginal and naturally ill-favored place. Castilian imperialism, despite its many distinctive features, also belongs, broadly speaking, in this category. France and England – places better equipped or more lavishly resourced, and apparently well positioned – were long dogged by ill success. In the "space race" for early modern seaborne empires, it helped to come from behind.

Rimland: Portugal in Maritime Western Europe

Portugal's imperial experience is only fully intelligible in the context of histories of outreach by other small, peripheral maritime communities. More particularly, it is part of a uniquely Western European and maritime story. It is usual to speak loosely – and misleadingly – of "European" seaborne imperialism in the early modern and modern periods. Virtually the only European seaborne empires, however, were founded, more locally, from Western Europe's Atlantic-side rimland. At first glance, it looks like an incoherent place.[14] It stretches from the Arctic to the Mediterranean, across contrasting climates, ecozones, menus, churches, folklores, musical traditions, historical memories, and ways of getting drunk. Languages become

[13] F. Fernández-Armesto, "The Indian Ocean in World History," in A. Disney and E. Booth, eds., *Vasco da Gama and the Linking of Europe and Asia* (New Delhi, 2000), pp. 11–29 at pp. 19–21.

[14] For a recent defense of the coherence of the concept, see Barry Cunliffe, *Facing the Ocean: The Atlantic and Its Peoples* (Oxford, 2001).

mutually unintelligible with unshared roots in the last four thousand years or so. Norwegians have a naturalized national dish called *bacalau*, after a Spanish or Portuguese prototype, and the recipe, at its best, calls for olive oil. But there are few such traces of shared experience. As you follow the coast from north to south, everything seems to change, except the presence of the sea.

That sea has given Europe's Atlantic-side peoples a singular and terrible role in world history. Virtually all the large-scale maritime world empires of modern history were founded from this fringe. There were, at most, three possible exceptions. Italy had a brief and modest little empire, built up at intervals between the 1880s and 1930s, in Libya, the Dodecanese, and the Horn of Africa, which could be reached through the Mediterranean and the Suez Canal without imposing on the Atlantic. Russia had a Pacific empire of sorts in the Aleutian Islands, with outposts on the west coast of North America, until Alaska was sold to the United States in 1867. Finally, there were the short-lived networks of slave stations and sugar islands founded from Baltic ports, in Courland and Brandenburg, in the seventeenth century.[15]

Not only were virtually all maritime empires founded by Atlantic-side states, there was, effectively, no Atlantic-side state that did not have one. The only possible exceptions are Norway, Ireland, and Iceland, but these states did not achieve sovereignty themselves until the twentieth century and therefore missed the great ages of oceanic empire building. Iceland is anomalous in almost every way. The Irish, although they had no empire of their own, were participants as well as victims in that of Britain. With a certain delicious schadenfreude, Norwegians are rediscovering the guilt of their ancestors' own quasi-imperial past as participants in Danish and Swedish slaving ventures.[16] Every other European state with an Atlantic seaboard

[15] A. V. Berkis, *The History of the Duchy of Courland, 1561–1765* (Towson, MD, 1969), pp. 75–79, 144–157, 191–195. Sweden is not an exception to the rule that links European maritime imperialism with an Atlantic-side position. Gothenburg, opening onto the North Sea, which is an arm of the Atlantic Ocean, makes Sweden an Atlantic-side power and, for much of the period in which its own colonial expansion via the Atlantic was concentrated, it controlled or had privileged access to Norwegian ports and to Bremen.

[16] It is worth recalling, too, how important a contribution the ubiquitous Norwegian seaman and skipper made to European shipping around the world in the nineteenth century and how disproportionately Irish and Norwegians were represented in what was certainly the greatest colonial phenomenon of the era (although it is not often classed as such): the imperial expansion of the United States across and beyond America, mainly at the expense of Mexico, Canada, and Red Indian polities. See Ingrid Semmingsen, *Norway to America: A History of the Migration* (Minneapolis, 1980), pp. 121–131; and Arnold Schrier, *Ireland and the American Migration* (Minneapolis, 1958).

has in the course of modern history taken to the ocean with prows set on empire. This applies to relatively tiny and peripheral communities, such as Portugal and the Netherlands, and even Scotland briefly while it was still a sovereign country,[17] as well as to others, such as Spain, Germany, and Sweden, which have relatively short Atlantic-side coasts and large hinterlands pulling their interests in other directions.

When receiving an honorary doctorate in his eighties, Salvador de Madariaga said it was a case of unusual precocity; the same can be said of the maritime imperial career of Europe's Atlantic rim. In this respect, the miraculous thing about "the European miracle" is that for so long there was no miracle. Western Europeans – and few Europeans are more western than the Portuguese – like to congratulate themselves on the way they have shaped the past and present of their continent. Yet, considered from one point of view, Westerners are the dregs of Eurasian history and the salient they inhabit is the sump into which Eurasian history has drained. A renaissance or three, the medieval expansion of Latin Christendom, the scientific revolution, the Enlightenment, the French Revolution, and industrialization can all be fairly represented as formative movements that started in the west and spread eastward. In a genuinely long-term perspective, however, Europe's west has been at the receiving end of great transmissions of culture. The spread of farming and mining, the arrival of Indo-European languages, the colonizations of Phoenicians, Jews, and Greeks, the coming of Christianity, the migrations of Germans, Slavs, and steppelanders, and the receptions of learning, taste, technology, and science from Asia have all been influences exerted from east to west. Many of these movements have left refugees at the Atlantic end of Europe, occupying what, for most of history, have been inhospitable and unpromising shores. There, for hundreds, or perhaps in some cases thousands, of years, they remained, without exercising much in the way of seaward initiative.

Overwhelmingly, Europe's Atlantic-side peoples are classifiable today, in the light of their modern history, as maritime peoples. The Atlantic provided them with vocations for fishers and seafarers and regional traders. Once nautical technology permitted, the ocean offered highways of seaborne migration and empire building. Yet the unexplained paradox of Western European history is that the call of the sea was long unheard. When they reached the sea, most of these peoples were stuck there, as if pinioned by the prevailing westerlies that blow onto all their shores. Coastwise shipping kept their communities in touch with one another; pelagic hermits contributed to the mystique of the sea; and some places developed deep-sea

17 O. H. K. Spate, *Monopolists and Freebooters* (London, 1983), p. 180.

fisheries at unrecorded dates. But, except in Scandinavia, the achievements of civilization in Western Europe owed little or nothing to the maritime horizon until what we think of as the late Middle Ages.

Meanwhile, Western Europe occupied the outer edge of world maps of the time. Scholars in Persia or China, confident in the superiority of their own civilized traditions, thought Christendom hardly worth a mention in their studies of the world. Efforts to expand east and south from Latin Christendom – landward into Eastern Europe or via the Mediterranean into Asia and Africa – made some progress but were generally repulsed or compelled to retreat by plagues and great freezes.[18] Even when the continuous history of the recorded exploration of the Atlantic began, in the late thirteenth century, none of Europe's Atlantic seaboard peoples took a leading part in it. The European discovery of the Atlantic was an enterprise launched from deep in the Mediterranean, chiefly by Genoese and Majorcan navigators who unstoppered their sea by forcing their way, against the race of the current, through the Strait of Gibraltar. From there, some turned to exploit the familiar commerce of the north; others turned south into waters unsailed – as far as we know – for centuries, toward the African Atlantic and the islands of the Madeira group and the Canaries. Portugal, with Castile, was a privileged part of rimland because it lay on the route from the Mediterranean to the Atlantic.[19]

The Uniqueness of Rimland: Why the West?

Culture is part of an unholy trinity – culture, chaos, and cock-up – that roams through our versions of history, substituting for traditional theories of causation. It has the power to explain everything and nothing: the "rise of the west," "the European miracle," and the elevation of Western societies to paramountcy in the modern history of the world. Thanks to the displacement of traditional concentrations of power and sources of initiative in the last two centuries, the former centers, such as China, India, and the

[18] See F. Fernández-Armesto, *Before Columbus: Exploration and Colonization from the Mediterranean to the Atlantic* (Philadelphia, 1987); Fernández-Armesto, *Millennium* (London, 1999), pp. 162–163; J. R. S. Phillips, *European Expansion in the Middle Ages* (Oxford, 1988); and P. Chaunu, *L'Expansion Européenne du xiiie au xve siècles* (Paris, 1969), pp. 93–97.

[19] F. Fernández-Armesto, "Spanish Atlantic Voyages and Conquests before Columbus," in John B. Hattendorf, ed., *Maritime History, vol. 1: The Age of Discovery* (Malabar, FL, 1996), p. 138. For the notion – well developed in Portuguese historiography – of Portugal as a frontier zone between the Mediterranean and the Atlantic, see, for example, O. Ribeiro, *Portugal: O Mediterrâneo e o Atlântico* (Lisbon, 1986).

Islamic world, became peripheral, and the former peripheries, in Western Europe and the New World, became central. Capitalism, imperialism, modern science, industrialization, individualism, and democracy – all the great world-shaping initiatives of recent history – are supposed, in various ways, to be peculiar inventions of societies founded in or from Europe. In part, this is because counterinitiatives from elsewhere have not yet been given due attention. In part, however, it is simply true. It is tempting, therefore, to attribute the Western European outreach, with all its consequences, to something special about the culture of Western Europe.[20]

Most of the cultural features commonly adduced are unhelpful, either because they were not unique to Europe; or because they were not specially concentrated in the maritime regions of Western Europe from where the Atlantic breakthrough was projected; or because they are phony; or because they were not around at the right time. The political culture of a competitive state system was shared with Southeast Asia. In any case, the role of the state in early modern empire building was generally small in the early stages. As a religion conducive to commerce, Christianity was equaled or excelled by Jainism, some Buddhist traditions, Islam, and Judaism, among others. Missionary zeal is a widespread vice or virtue and – although most of our histories ignore the fact – Islam and Buddhism both experienced extraordinary expansion into new territories and among new congregations at the same time as Christianity in what we think of as the late Middle Ages and the early modern period.[21] The tradition of scientific curiosity and empirical method was at least as strong in Islam and China as in the West, although it is true that a distinctive scientific culture did become discernible later in Europe and in parts of the Americas settled from Europe.[22] Imperialism and aggression are not white men's vices: The European empires of the modern world, and their continuators in areas settled from Europe, were made in an expanding world, full of emulous competitors.

Nevertheless, a peculiar culture of exploration and adventure did exist in Western Europe at the material time. In late medieval Western Christendom,

[20] The literature is too vast for convenience of citation, but among works on the uniqueness of the West, those that have been most conspicuous in recent years have been Eric L. Jones, *The European Miracle* (London, 1963), and David Landes, *The Wealth and Poverty of Nations: Why Some Are So Rich and Others So Poor* (London, 1998). On the other side of the question, see Jack Goody, *The East in the West* (Cambridge, 1996), and Kenneth Pomeranz, *The Great Divergence: China, Europe and the Making of the Modern World Economy* (Princeton, NJ, 2000).

[21] Fernández-Armesto, *Millennium*, pp. 283–308.

[22] A. W. Crosby, *The Measure of Reality: Quantification and Western Society, 1250–1600* (Cambridge, 1997); F. Fernández-Armesto, *Truth: A History* (London, 1997), pp. 120–160.

explorers were steeped in the idealization of adventure. Many of them shared or strove to embody the great aristocratic ethos of the late Middle Ages, the "code" of chivalry, which shaped everything done by elites – or those who aspired to join them – in Western Europe.[23] Their ships were gaily caparisoned steeds and rode the waves like jennets. Their role models were the footloose princes who won themselves kingdoms by deeds of derring-do in popular romances of chivalry – the "pulp fiction" of the time – that often had a seaborne setting: figures such as the medieval Brutus, who, when Troy was lost, found a realm in Albion; or Prince Amadis of Gaul, who battled giants and won an enchanted island; or Prince Turián, who found his fortune aboard a ship and his love across an ocean.[24]

The "squires" who surrounded the Infante Dom Henrique and who captained his seafaring ventures included thugs and pirates, but they gave themselves storybook names and chivalric airs. Columbus, whose life's trajectory startlingly resembled the plot of a chivalric romance of the sea, probably had such role models in mind.[25] Despite the maddening reticence that makes Vasco da Gama so unapproachable, we can be sure that he took seriously his own chivalric obligations as a knight successively of the orders of Santiago and of Christ. John Cabot has left even fewer sources than Vasco da Gama with which to construct his mental world, but the Bristol from which he launched his voyage was familiar with the English romances of seaborne chivalry of the time, including the *Gesta Arthuri*, which ascribed to the mythic king the conquests of Greenland and the North Pole, among others. Henry VII, that staid monarch with a businessman's reputation, was not unsusceptible to such romance himself and called his heir Arthur, after Britain's Charlemagne or Alexander, the once and future king who would return to redeem his claims.[26] This messianic touch links the chivalric tradition with the millenarian sentiments rife in the courts where Columbus and Vasco da Gama were commissioned. Ferdinand the Catholic allowed himself

[23] Maurice H. Keen, *Chivalry* (New Haven, CT, 1984), pp. 1–43.

[24] F. Fernández-Armesto, "The Sea and Chivalry in Late Medieval Spain," in J. B. Hattendorf, ed., *Maritime History, vol. 1: The Age of Discovery* (Malabar, FL, 1996), pp. 137–148; Fernández-Armesto, "Exploration and Discovery," in Allmand, *New Cambridge Medieval History*, vol. 7, pp. 175–201; J. Goodman, *Chivalry and Exploration, 1298–1630* (Woodbridge, 1998).

[25] F. Fernández-Armesto, "The Contexts of Columbus: Myth, Reality and Self-Perception," in A. Disney, ed., *Columbus and the Consequences of 1492* (Melbourne, 1994), pp. 7–19 at p. 10.

[26] F. Fernández-Armesto, "Inglaterra y el Atlántico en la baja edad media," in A. Béthencourt Massieu et al., eds., *Canarias e Inglaterra a través de la historia* (Las Palmas, 1995), pp. 11–28.

to be represented in a tradition – strong for generations at the Aragonese court – that represented the king as the "last world emperor" prophesied since the twelfth century. Millenarian fantasies may have been part of the Reconquest heritage in Portugal. The first king of the Avis dynasty was actually called "Messiah of Portugal."[27] Millenarian tradition, kept alive in spiritual Franciscan traditions popular with observant Franciscans, resurfaced at court in the reign of Manuel I.[28] Part of Afonso de Albuquerque's inspiration for his attempted conquest of Mecca was a hope of liberating Jerusalem and precipitating the end of the world.[29]

Although it is mischievous to accuse other cultures of hostility or indifference to trade and seafaring, the cult of seaborne chivalry did have the effect of ennobling in Europe activities that elsewhere had a derogating drag on rank or a depressant effect on social mobility. Landlubbers' complacency induced contempt for the maritime life among elites that did not read maritime romantic fiction. The Chinese naval effort of the early fifteenth century was undermined by mandarin opposition which reflected the priorities of a landlubber class.[30] In fifteenth-century Malacca, Muslim traders used titles of nobility and Hindu merchants used the lesser, Sanskrit-derived style of *nina*; but they could not attain the highest ranks.[31] Rulers in that region had hands permanently sullied with traffic, but none dared style himself, like the Portuguese king, "Lord of Commerce and Navigation." It would be a mistake, however, to suppose that maritime Asia was hobbled by prejudices or that its potential long-range trades and empires were lamed and limited by cultural deficiencies. On the contrary, many Asian states were run by sultans and *zamorins* with something like entrepreneurial flair; the suitability of traditional societies in the region to be homes of empires and

27 L. de Sousa Rebelo, "Millénarisme et historiographie dans les chroniques de Fernão Lopes," *Arquivs do Centro Cultural Portugues* 26 (1989), pp. 97–120; M. Garcez Ventura, *O Messias de Lisboa: Um estudo de mitologia política (1383–1415)* (Lisbon, 1992).

28 A. Milhou, *Colón y su mentalidad mesiánica en el ambiente Franciscanista Español* (Valladolid, 1983). J. Aubin drew attention to exalted religious language at Dom Manuel's court in "Duarte Galvão," *Arquivos do Centro Cultural Português* 9 (1975), pp. 43–85, reprinted in *Le Latin et l'astrolabe: Recherches sur le Portugal de la Renaissance, son expansion en Asie et les relations internationales* (Lisbon and Paris, 1996), pp. 11–48 (see especially pp. 30–33). S. Subrahmanyam, *The Career and Legend of Vasco da Gama* (Cambridge, 1997), pp. 54–57, calls this "messianism."

29 Antonio Baião, ed., *Comentarios do grande Afonso de Albuquerque* (2 vols., Coimbra, 1922–1925), bk. IV, Chap. 7.

30 Edward L. Dreyer, *Early Ming China* (Stanford, CA, 1982), p. 120.

31 L. F. F. R. Thomaz, "The Economic Policy of the Sultanate of Malacca (XVth–XVIth centuries)," *Moyen-orient et Océan Indien* 7, pp. 1–12, especially p. 8.

springboards of capitalism is demonstrated by the eventful mercantile and imperial histories of so many of them.[32]

The Atlantic: Portugal in the Trade-Wind System

Rimland was distinguished less, however, at the material time by its culture than by its geographical situation and by the problems and opportunities of the Atlantic-side environment. To master an ocean, you have to penetrate the secrets of its winds and currents. Throughout the age of sail – that is, for almost the whole of history – geography had absolute power to determine the limits of what man could do at sea. By comparison, culture, ideas, individual genius or charisma, economic forces, and all the other motors of history meant little. In most of our traditional explanations of what has happened in history, there is too much hot air and not enough wind.

The Atlantic is dominated by a trade-wind system; that is, by a regular pattern of prevailing winds that blow in the same direction regardless of the season. From around the northwest corner of Africa, all year round, trade winds curl across the ocean to within a few degrees above the equator; in the summer, these winds spring even further north and can be felt fairly constantly on the southwest shores of the Iberian Peninsula. Thanks to the northeast trade winds, the maritime communities around the mouths of the Tagus and Guadalquivir rivers had privileged access, by comparison with other parts of maritime Europe, to much of the rest of the world. The prodigious reach of the Spanish and Portuguese empires in the age of sail was in part the result of this good fortune. Except for certain Maghribi communities, which remained surprisingly indifferent to seaward enterprise in this period,[33] no other Atlantic-side peoples enjoyed a position near the outward path of the northeast trades and none had the maritime technology and traditions that Western Europeans were able to exploit. The trading peoples of the circum-Caribbean region did not develop means of long-range navigation by sea; the commercial vocation of cities and kingdoms in West Africa was oriented toward river traffic and coastal cabotage.[34] In the Southern Hemisphere, the same pattern is roughly mirrored by winds that link the latitudes of southern Africa to Brazil. Like the northeast trades,

[32] K. R. Hall, *Mandarin Trade and State Development in Early South-east Asia* (Honolulu, 1985); S. Subrahmanyam, *The Portuguese Empire in Asia, 1500–1700: A Political and Economic History* (London, 1993), pp. 9–29.

[33] C. Picard, *L'océan Atlantique musulman au moyen age* (Paris, 1997), pp. 31–32, 393–458.

[34] A. Szászdy-Nagy, *Un mundo que descubrió Colón* (Valladolid, 1979); Szászdy-Nagy, *Los guías de Guanahani y la llegada de Pinzón a Puerto Rico* (Valladolid, 1995).

these winds become more directly easterly, swinging as they approach the equator. Between the two systems, around or just north of the equator, are the almost windless latitudes called the Doldrums. Beyond the latitudes of the trade winds, in both hemispheres, westerlies blow. In the Southern Hemisphere, they are remarkably strong and constant.

The wind system resembles a code of interlocking ciphers. Once part of it was cracked, by a concentrated spell of tenacious exploration in the 1490s, the solution of the rest followed rapidly. The preliminary effort was long and laborious because early explorers, with their vision limited to small patches of the ocean dominated by apparently unremitting winds, were like codebreakers denied a sufficient sample with which to work. Only the long accumulation of information and experience could make a breakthrough possible. Even then, a sudden and almost visionary inspiration was necessary to unlock the system and start the rapid phase of decipherment. In the course of return voyages against the wind, navigators, who had absolutely no means of keeping track of their longitude, increasingly made huge deep-sea detours in search of westerlies that would take them home. This risky enterprise was rewarded with the discovery of the Azores – a mid-ocean archipelago more than 700 miles from any other land. All but two islands of the group appear recognizably on marine charts not later than the 1380s. This was a stage undervalued in existing literature but of enormous significance: Open-sea voyages of a length unprecedented in European experience were now being undertaken; from the 1430s, when Portuguese way stations, sown with wheat or stocked with wild sheep, were established in the Azores, they became almost routine.[35]

Several attempts were made during the fifteenth century to explore Atlantic space, but most doomed themselves to failure by setting out in the belt of westerly winds, presumably because explorers were keen to be sure of a guaranteed route of return. You can still follow the tiny gains in the slowly unfolding record on rare maps and stray documents. In 1427, an otherwise unknown voyage by a Portuguese pilot called Diogo de Silves was recorded on a map.[36] Silves established for the first time the approximate relationship of the islands of the Azores to one another. Shortly after mid-century, the westernmost islands of that archipelago were reached. Over the next three decades, voyages of exploration farther into the Atlantic were often commissioned by the Portuguese crown, but none is known to have

[35] F. Fernández-Armesto, "Atlantic Exploration before Columbus,' in Winius, *Portugal the Pathfinder*, pp. 41–70.

[36] A. Cortesão, *História da cartografia Portuguesa* (2 vols., Coimbra, 1969–1970), vol. 2, pp. 150–152.

made any further progress – perhaps because they departed from the Azores, where the westerlies beat them back to base. Only an observer of unusual powers could have detected in these tentative efforts the background of the breakthrough of the 1490s. In some ways, it was like falling over a threshold: There was no need for a particular innovation because the savoir-faire and practical experience of European sailors simply accumulated bit by bit until the makers of the Atlantic breakthrough found themselves stumbling on the far side of a critical gap. Certainly the Atlantic breakthrough was preceded by a long period of unspectacular change in which, little by little, navigators got ever farther out to sea.

The great Atlantic breakthrough can be identified precisely with three voyages (if we leave out suppositious earlier journeys for which the evidence is nonexistent or inadequate). Columbus's Atlantic crossing of 1493 established viable, exploitable routes across the Central Atlantic and back – routes that would hardly be bettered throughout the rest of the age of sail. (I relegate Columbus's earlier crossing in 1492 to a place of secondary importance because the outward route discovered on that occasion was unsatisfactory and was never tried again.) John Cabot's voyage from Bristol to Newfoundland in 1496 created an open-sea approach to North America using the easterly winds available in a brief season of spring variables. This route was of little short-term value but ultimately proved to be an avenue to an enormously influential imperial terrain and to the most exploitable of the "new Europes" created across the world by early modern colonizing movements. In 1497, Vasco da Gama's first voyage to India discovered a route across the path of the Southeast Atlantic trade winds to meet the westerlies of the far south. At the end of the decade, Pedro Alvares Cabral retraced da Gama's route and reached the meridian of the Brazil current, which diminished the danger of navigation on a lee shore and made possible a Portuguese coastal empire in South America. Little in the subsequent history of the world can be properly understood except in this context, peculiar to a single decade of achievement, of the power of projection of Western European seafaring.

The effect of the three voyages in combination was to crack the code of the Atlantic wind system. Instead of an obstacle to the expansion of European peoples along its seaboard, the ocean became a means of access to previously unimaginable empires and trades. The European West was thrust beyond its historic confines. The Portuguese contribution was to unlock the southeast trades, which provided ways to South America and Asia, while the westerlies of the far south really did put a girdle around the Earth; they squeezed and shaped some of the world's most lucrative trade routes for the rest of the age of sail. The Atlantic, which had been a barrier for the whole of recorded history, now became a link.

The Indian Ocean: Portugal in the Monsoon System

In 1617, students of rhetoric in the Jesuit college at Goa performed a remarkable pageant entitled "The Tragicomedy of the Discovery and Conquest of the Orient." One of the highlights of the drama was the appearance of a chorus of Brazilian Indians, parrots, and monkeys, including one parrot who claimed a starring role, engaging in a dialogue, in the Brazilian Indian language, Tupi, with a performer in the role of the king.[37] Apart perhaps from the famous painting of the Magi, attributed to Grão Vasco, in which a Brazilian Indian joins the kings from the East, there could be no more striking feature of the unique virtue of the Portuguese empire at its height. It linked the West to the East, the Atlantic to the Indian Ocean (the newest ocean of long-range exchange to the oldest), and a trade-wind system to the seas of the monsoon. This dual character – partly monsoonal, partly reliant on fixed winds – remained characteristic of the Portuguese system. The Spanish empire relied on fixed winds; it grew up around the wind system of the Atlantic and Pacific, joined by an overland link across Central America. Spanish shipping hardly had to venture into monsoonal seas. The main axes of the Dutch empire similarly were fixed wind systems. From the second decade of the seventeenth century, the favored Dutch route across the Indian Ocean was with the "roaring forties" and the southeast trades, although they also used monsoons for return journeys and intra-Asian shuttles.

The monsoon system works like a reversible escalator. Above the equator, northeasterlies prevail in winter. For most of the rest of the year, the winds blow steadily from the south and west. In summer, hot air over the land rises and cool air streams in from the sea, equalizing the pressure. The aerial currents flow laden with rain, which falls over the land, cooling it and simultaneously generating energy, which makes the air even warmer. The wind drives the zone of upward convection ever deeper into the continent, sucking in more ocean air. By timing voyages to take advantage of the monsoon, navigators under sail could set off confident of a fair wind out and a fair wind home.

It is a fact not often appreciated that, overwhelmingly, the history of maritime exploration has been made by voyagers who headed into the wind,

[37] J. Sardina Mimoso, *Relación de la Real Tragicomedia con que los Padres de la Compañía de Jesús en su Colegio de San Antón de Lisboa recibieron a la Magestad Católica de Felipe II de Portugal y de su entrada en este Reino* (Lisbon, 1620). For an inportant study that explains the context of the transmission of knowledge of Tupi in the Jesuit Order, see M. C. D. M. Barros, "The Office of *Lingua:* A Portrait of the Religious Tupi Interpreter in Brazil in the Sixteenth Century," *Itinerario* 25 (2001), no. 2, pp. 110–140.

presumably because it was at least as important to get home as to get to anywhere new. Spectacular exceptions, such as Columbus's crossing of the Atlantic or the early Spanish trans-Pacific navigations, registered as extraordinary achievements precisely because their protagonists had the boldness to sail with the wind at their backs. Conditions in the Indian Ocean liberated navigators from any such constraints. One must try to imagine what it would be like to feel the wind, year after year, alternately in one's face and at one's back and gradually come to realize that a venture with an outward wind will not necessarily deprive one of the means of returning home. The predictability of a homeward wind made the Indian Ocean environment the most benign in the world for long-range voyaging.

The sailors who actually experienced this environment did not, of course, always express appreciation of their luck. All seafarers are alert to the dangers and difficulties of their own seas, and the indigenous literature of the ocean is full of scary stories calculated to inhibit competitors or inspire fear of God. To storytellers, seas are irresistible moral environments where storms are shafts from the quivers of meddlesome deities; most cultures regard freak winds as phenomena peculiarly manipulable by God or the gods. Those accustomed to the Indian Ocean in the age of sail shared, along with these traditions, a heightened perception of its obstacles.[38] There was poetic truth in the old maps that showed the Indian Ocean landlocked,[39] for it was a hard sea to get out of. The lost but much-cited sailing directions known as the Rahnama, which go back at least to the twelfth century, warned of the "circumambient sea, whence all return was impossible" and where Alexander was said to have set up "a magical image, with its hand upraised as a warning: 'This is the ne plus ultra of navigation, and of what lies beyond in the sea no man has knowledge.' "[40] Hard to get out of, the ocean was correspondingly hard to get into. Access from the east was barely possible in summer, when typhoons tear into lee shores. Until the sixteenth century, the vast, empty expanse of the neighboring Pacific preserved the ocean against approaches from beyond the China seas. Shipping from the west could enter only by way of an arduous detour through the South Atlantic and around Africa, while stores wasted and fresh water spoiled. The southern approaches, which then had to be crossed, were guarded in summer by fierce storms. No one who knew the reputation of these waters would venture between about ten and thirty degrees south or sixty and ninety degrees east

[38] See K. Chaudhuri, *Trade and Civilisation in the Indian Ocean* (Cambridge, 1985), p. 15.

[39] See, for example, Kenneth Nebenzahl, *Atlas of Columbus and the Great Discoveries* (Chicago, 1970), pp. 4–5.

[40] Hadi Hasan, *A History of Persian Navigation* (London: Methuen, 1928), pp. 129–30.

without urgent reason in the season of hurricanes. The lee shores toward the tip of Africa were greedy for wreckage at the best of times. From al-Masudi in the tenth century to Duarte Barbosa in the sixteenth, writers of guides to the ocean noted that the practical limit of navigation was to the north of the bone-strewn coasts of Natal and Transkei, where survivors of Portuguese ships wrote *The Tragic History of the Sea*.[41]

The ocean therefore remained chiefly the preserve of peoples whose homes bordered it or who traveled overland – such as some European and Armenian traders – to become part of its world. The breakthrough that brought Atlantic navigators directly into this zone, in their own ships, was genuinely one of the great formative moments of world history, for although the impact on indigenous trade and states in Asia was small, the effect on the Atlantic world was immeasurably enriching: An arena of commerce that in the early sixteenth century was only just beginning to experience the effects of transoceanic trade was brought into contact with the world's richest, oldest, and most extensive zone of long-range commerce. For a hundred years this role of link between the oceans was discharged almost exclusively by Portuguese.

The Landward Turn: Portugal and the Early Modern Land Empires

Although Portugal's empire began as a seaboard affair of forts, trading places, coastal settlements, merchant diaspora, and "shadow imperialism," and although it remained throughout its history a maritime structure of long-range communications maintained by sea, it also became a land empire. In the eighteenth century, landward expansion attained vast proportions in Brazil and was undertaken, on a less ambitious scale, in the hinterland of Goa. Landward imperialism in the early modern period was rife with problems and opportunities recognizable to the student of seaborne empires: the cant of holy war, the reliance on the technology of victory, and the puzzles of incommensurable cultures and alien environments. The two greatest examples of the period – those of Russian and Chinese imperialism – can stand for the rest.

Muscovite imperialism gleams from the *Icon of the Hosts of the Heavenly King*, made in the third quarter of the sixteenth century. Led by Solomon

[41] Al-Masudi, *Les Prairies d'or*, ed. B. Meynard and P. Courteille (9 vols., Paris, 1861–1914), vol. 3 (1897), p. 6; Al-Masudi, *The Book of Duarte Barbosa*, ed. M. Longworth Dames (2 vols., London, 1898), vol. 1, p. 4; C. R. Boxer, ed., *The Tragic History of the Sea, 1589–1622* (London, 1959).

and David, Russians march across a fantastic landscape of mountains and rivers, with saints Boris and Gleb guarding the rear, from a city of infidels, ringed by fire, toward a shrine of the Virgin. The earthly army is flanked by heavenly hosts, ghostly cavalry, and the Orthodox founder-emperors of the Russian Orthodox tradition, Volodomir and Constantine. "Although the martyrs were born on earth," reads the commentary, "they succeeded in attaining the rank of angels."[42] Two real leaps of Russian imperialism inspired this art. First, the conquest of Kazan gave the tsars command of the entire length of the Volga River – the corridor of commerce at the western edge of Asia – and eliminated Russia's great rival for control of Siberia's fur trade. Furs summoned Russians to conquest and colonization as gold lured Spaniards and spices captivated the Portuguese. The tsars' next task was to conquer Siberia itself and control the production as well as the trade. In 1555, Ivan IV began to call himself "Lord of Siberia." Three years later, he cut a deal with a big dynasty of fur dealers, the Stroganoffs, who were prepared to pay to turn that titular Siberian lordship into reality. The language of a chronicler's account reflects the typical mindset of European conquistadores in new worlds: the assertion that pagans have no rights; that their lands are "empty"; that they are subhuman – bestial or monstrous; that colonization can be promoted by fiscal privileges; and that the work is holy.[43]

From the 1570s, the "protection" of Russian armies "against the fighting men of Siberia" was proclaimed for indigenous peoples who submitted and paid tribute in furs.[44] Characteristic of European military operations on remote frontiers, the Russians ascribed their success to technology: firearms mounted on river barges, from which the water-borne conquerors exchanged bullets for bowshots with defenders on the banks. The Siberian khan was said to be dismayed to hear that "when they shoot from their bows, then there is a flash of fire and a great smoke issues and there is a loud report like thunder in the sky . . . and it is impossible to shield oneself from them by any trappings of war."[45]

Native peoples were subjected to tribute and controlled by oaths. Ostyaks were made to swear on a bearskin on which a knife, an axe, and a loaf were spread: The oathbreaker would choke to death or be cut to pieces in battle with men or bears. The Yakuts had to pass between the quarters of a

42 Robin Cormack and D. Glaser, eds., *Art of Holy Russia* (London, 1998), p. 180.

43 Terence Armstrong, ed., *Yermak's Campaigns in Siberia* (London, 1975), pp. 38, 41, 43–44, 49–50, 60, 65, 69.

44 Ibid., pp. 40, 138, 290–293; R. H. Fisher, *The Russian Fur Trade, 1550–1700* (Berkeley, CA, 1943), p. 21.

45 Armstrong, *Yermak's Campaigns*, pp. 46, 108; compare p. 59, where the Ostyaks' intimidation by gunfire that shatters their sacred tree is described.

dismembered dog.[46] The first object of the conquest, however, was not to vanquish these "savages" who ranged the taiga and tundra but to eliminate the only state capable of challenging Russia in the region, the Tatar khanate of Sibir, which dominated the eastern tributaries of the Irtysh River. Thus the conquest was sold as a crusade and depicted symbolically by representations of gospel rays spread from the eyes of Christ between colonists' cities. Russians credited Khan Kuchum with a prophetic vision in October 1581: "The skies burst open and terrifying warriors with shining wings appeared.... [T]hey encircled Kuchum's army and cried to him, 'Depart from this land, you infidel son of the dark demon, Muhammad, because now it belongs to the Almighty.' "[47]

By the late seventeenth century, Russian expansion in eastern Siberia met China's, where the Manchus were preempting or pursuing Russian rivals in a war zone along the Amur River. The road that led here was kept smoother, according to Ferdinand Verbiest, "than Catholics in Europe keep the road on which the Sacrament is to be conveyed."[48] The Treaty of Nerchinsk of 1689 formalized Ch'ing claims to vast unexplored lands of doubtful extent in the northeast of Asia, where some cartographers imagined a huge proboscis pointing to or even joining America. Much of this territory was effectively beyond any practical frontier of settlement; generally, however, Ch'ing imperialism was of an intensive kind compared with Russia's. It was dedicated not merely to economic exploitation and trade but also to colonization and the acculturation and assimilation of indigenous peoples. Before the century, outer Mongolia had been crudely incorporated into the empire, and more than 1.5 million settlers had been lured into Szechwan by the promise of fiscal immunities. The Sinkiang frontier was peopled next, more thinly, by a mixture of enforced deportation and inducements to voluntary settlers; 200,000 migrants had settled by the end of the century. Manchuria, homeland of the Ching dynasty, was normally closed to settlers, but its rich soils drew them unofficially in the hundreds of thousands until officialdom was obliged to recognize a fait accompli. Meanwhile, the Manchus, despite imperial efforts to preserve their identity, were progressively Sinicized. On all fronts, the pressure of intensive new settlement provoked a cycle of conflicts and solutions ominously familiar to students of European colonialism:

[46] Ibid., p. 61; B. Bobrick, *East of the Sun: The Conquest and Settlement of Siberia* (London, 1993), p. 70.

[47] Bobrick, *East of the Sun*, p. 43; compare the version in Armstrong, *Yermack's Campaigns*, p. 163: "Unclean son of the dark demon, Bakhunet, leave this land, for the land and its fulness is the Lord's."

[48] P. J. D'Orleans, *History of the Tartar Conquerors of China*, ed. The Earl of Ellesmere (London, 1854), p. 132.

tribal peoples reshuffled or penned in reservations; militarized agricultural colonies growing wheat, barley, peas, and corn while keeping the natives compliant; and schools erected to spread the Chinese language and values.[49]

Similarly, European maritime empires were bound, sooner or later, to lumber onto land, where traditional imperialism led, for the difference between a sea empire and a land empire is more than a mere matter of location or of geographical characterization or classification. Sea empires are empires of trade, which they seek always to channel and sometimes to control. Land empires attempt additionally or instead to control production. Columbus envisaged a trading setup when he first encountered Hispaniola, imagining a European merchant colony under a Castilian aegis trading in cotton, mastic, and slaves.[50] Really, none of these products were available in large quantities. Instead, the economic policy underlying the Spanish presence came to be the discovery and direct exploitation of the gold mines of the island. Columbus's war of conquest of 1495–1496 can be represented, albeit on a small scale, as the first step toward the creation of a Spanish territorial empire. This trend was consolidated by the conquests of Mexico and Peru, as a result of which Spaniards found themselves obeyed, with remarkable docility, over huge tracts of the most densely populated territory in the Americas. Indeed, Spain had acquired, within the space of a few years and in their entirety, two of the fastest-growing and most environmentally diverse empires of the age.

Other European empires in the Americas, without the advantage of exploitable local labor sources on the scale of the Spanish lands, tended at first to expand to landward on only a very modest scale, to increase the areas of cultivation of the crops they introduced, such as sugar in the Caribbean, West Indian tobacco in Virginia, rice in the Carolinas, and wheat almost everywhere. Sometimes spectacular effects could be achieved in a small space: France's colony of Saint-Domingue in the eighteenth century occupied only half the island of Hispaniola, hardly much of a land empire in terms of size but an island of *Wirtschaftswunder* (economic miracles) that became for a while the world's major producer of coffee and sugar.[51] The local product of Brazil that first attracted commercial attention on a fairly large scale was logwood. Sugar soon replaced it, but it was a laborious crop

[49] Joanna Waley-Cohen, *Exile in Mid-Qing China* (New Haven, CT, 1991); R. H. G. Lee, *The Manchurian Frontier in Ch'ing History* (Cambridge, MA, 1970).

[50] Consuelo Varela, ed., *Cristóbal Colón: Textos y documentos* (Madrid, 1984), pp. 142, 145.

[51] M. Begouen Demeux, *Mémorial d'une famille du Havre: Stanislas Föache, 1737–1806* (Paris, 1931), pp. 18–24; J. P. Poussou, "L'age Atlantique de l'économie Française," *L'information historique,* lox (1997), no. 1, pp. 21–33.

to plant, harvest, and refine, greedy of capital and demanding lots of specialized labor.[52] It was suitable only to coastal enclaves where it could be successfully grown and easily shipped, and it would never on its own have induced planters to create a large territorial domain in Brazil's hinterland.

In the course of their efforts in Asia, the Portuguese also did not attempt to add direct control of production to their interests in trade. The only significant exceptions to this rule were the "Northern Province" of Portuguese India, between Chaul and Damian, where palms and rice were grown under Portuguese supervision to provide provisions for garrisons, crews, and workers, and Ceylon, where Portuguese garrisons were able to enforce, for awhile, a monopoly of the cinnamon trade so thorough as to give them effective control of production. In the early seventeenth century, the total number of indigenous people living under Portuguese rule in India was under half a million.[53] The leap into what might be called production imperialism was made by the Dutch conquerors of the clove-, nutmeg-, and mace-producing islands of the East in the 1660s.[54] Even then, European-controlled territory in Asia was modest, and it was only in the eighteenth century that a Dutch land empire of substantial proportions gradually took shape in Java. This was the only European land empire in the East until the British East India Company acquired direct rule over Bengal by an adventure in opportunism in the late 1750s.

By then, the landward temptation had seduced Britain and France into attempts to imitate Spain's New World mainland empire. Britain's American land empire wore a substantial look because of its large immigrant population and the enthusiasm with which, from the 1760s, settlers moved to open up the interior.[55] France's empire in Louisiana was little more than an outline on the map. Frenchmen, despite the density of their home population, were reluctant emigrants in the eighteenth century.[56] Still, both states claimed, if they did not effectively exercise, control of great swaths of the North American hinterland prior to French withdrawal in 1763. In part, these were preemptive and speculative ventures, designed to exclude Spain from areas of as yet largely unknown potential.

Portugal's early interest in the interior of Brazil was of a similar character, provoked by Spanish interest in the navigation of the Amazon in the early

[52] F. Mauro, *Le Portugal et l'Atlantique au XVIIe siècle, 1570–1670* (Paris, 1960), pp. 113–257.

[53] Disney, "The Portuguese Empire in India," p. 151.

[54] A. Reid, *Southeast Asia in the Age of Commerce* (2 vols., New Haven, CT, 1988–1993), vol. 2, pp. 277–303.

[55] Bernard Bailyn, *Voyagers to the West: Emigration from Britain to America on the Eve of the Revolution* (New York, 1987), pp. 8–20.

[56] Silvia Marzagalli, "The French Atlantic," *Itinerario* 23 (1999), no. 2, pp. 70–83, at p. 73.

seventeenth century.[57] Portuguese attention, however, became increasingly focused on Brazil as the century wore on and the empire was restructured. Strained by long wars with the Netherlands and Spain, and – more significantly – pressured and overawed by the rise of such dauntingly powerful indigenous Asian states as those of the Moghuls, the Tokugawa shoguns, and the Safavids in the time of Shah Abbas, Portugal withdrew from most of its sovereign outposts in the East.[58] Brazil became, faute de mieux, the jewel in the crown of a now compact empire. Most of the Brazilian coast was less than two months' sail from Lisbon or the African slave ports. Even so, the state was slow to undertake the risks and costs of landward imperialism. The hinterland empire remained largely an affair of private slavers and ranchers until the 1680s, when reports of gold and diamond finds deep in the interior began to accumulate. By early in the second half of the century, aggressive activity had pushed Spanish outposts back roughly to the line of the present linguistic boundary. Although Spain's New World land empire was much greater in extent, Portugal's was in some ways more impressive: carved out of hostile environments, where there was little useful manpower and where most of what there was had to be enslaved (when the Portuguese could catch it) and forcibly redistributed.

What Difference Did It Make?

Early modern Portuguese imperialism, unlike nineteenth-century industrializing empires, was not based on crushing technical superiority. Swagger, sleight-of-hand, terror tactics, and intimidation all played a part in making it work. In some places, it worked by bluff. In others, it was kept going by narcotics or drink. Mostly, like all large-scale imperialism in the period, it relied on deals with local and regional elites. For all the trouble Portuguese intruders caused to host communities when they arrived as merchants or soldiers of fortune, or when they came in force demanding trading enclaves, their usefulness generally outweighed their nuisance value. They brought firearms and missionaries, for instance, to Kongo and Japan, and astronomical instruments and ideas for garden-design to China.[59]

[57] J. Carvajal et al., *La aventura de Amazonas* (Madrid, 1992); Mauro, *Le Portugal et l'Atlantique*, pp. 139–40.

[58] Ernst van Veen, *Decay or Defeat? An Inquiry into the Portuguese Decline in Asia, 1580–1645* (Leiden, 2000).

[59] Jonathan Spence, *The Search for Modern China* (London, 1990), p. 100, and photograph of the ruins of the Summer Palace Gardens opposite p. 133 and in J. Turner, ed., *The Dictionary of Art* (39 vols., London, 1996), vol. 3, p. 517. G. A. Bailey, "'Le style Jésuite

They also gratified many of their African hosts by buying slaves. They had expertise, especially in war, that made them employable almost everywhere. They were of value in Asia because they vastly extended the spice market and brought much-needed new shipping into the "country" trades. They were allies or mercenaries against Muslims in Ethiopia and Vijayanagara, against Spaniards in Ternate and Tidore, against Burmese in Bengal, and against Thai in Cambodia. In Cannanore, they reputedly obtained a right of hereditary deference as a result of a duel won by a champion, although they forwent the corresponding right of sexual hospitality.[60]

The Portuguese empire was too big and too environmentally diverse to be consistent. The bureaucratically policed royal spice-trade monopoly made it resemble, in one respect, Venice's medieval "*étatiste*" empire, but most imperial structures associated with Portuguese expansion were much looser and locally sui generis. Western imperialism in Vasco da Gama's wake is now seen as a feeble affair, and Asia's "Vasco da Gama era" is regarded as not much different from the period that preceded it. Indigenous states remained largely intact, with European sovereignty confined – at least until well into the seventeenth century – to spots that hardly modify the overall picture and outside which colonization was a mere "shadow" presence or "improvised" at private initiative.[61] The European merchants who penetrated the ocean in the meantime by way of the Cape of Good Hope are now seen as similar in character to their ancient and medieval predecessors, who usually came by way of the Nile River and the Red Sea. They fitted into the existing framework of trade and served regional markets and suppliers. Only in the seventeenth century did the situation change radically because the Dutch East India Company pioneered a new, fast route across the ocean, enforced monopolies of key products, and, late in the century, moved directly to selective control of production as well as trade routes.

The Portuguese arrived in the East as impoverished barbarians, agape at the natives' plenty. An early window-shopper in China was Fernão Mendes

n'existe pas': Jesuit Corporate Culture and the Visual Arts," in J. W. O'Malley et al., eds., *The Jesuits: Cultures, Sciences and the Arts, 1540–1773* (Toronto, 1999), pp. 38–39, gives bibliographical indications I have been unable to trace: *Le Yuanming, jeux d'eau et palais Eeuropéens du XVIIIe siècle à la cour du Chine* (Paris, 1987); A. Durand and R. Thiriez, *The Delights of Harmony: The European Palaces of the Yuanmingyuan and the Jesuits at the XVIIIth-Century Court of Beijing* (Worcester, MA, 1994); and Craig Clunas, *Pictures and Visuality in Early Modern China* (Princeton, NJ, 1997).

60 *Voyages célèbres et remarquables faits de Perse aux Indes orientales par le Sr Jean-Albert de Mandelslo, considérablement augmentez en cette dernière édition et divisez en deux parties*... (2 vols., Amsterdam, 1727), pp. 265–266.

61 Winius, "Shadow Empire"; Subrahmanyam, *Improvising Empire.*

Pinto, the Portuguese Sinbad, who from 1521 to 1558 claimed to have sailed the East as a soldier of fortune, penetrating every cranny of the accessible Orient, surviving more shipwrecks, enslavements, slaughters, storms, and changes of wind and fortune than any reader could reasonably believe. His travelogue is a masterpiece of picaresque literature, with many delicious asides, both sententious and satirical. Although his description of China is no more verifiable than the rest of his book, it fairly reflects the country's image with his contemporaries. In the tingle excited by the excess of everything, it rings true. The author walks around the markets of Peking, for example, "as if in a daze" at the quantities of "silk, lace, canvas, clothes of cotton and linen, marten and musk and ermines, delicate porcelain, gold- and silver-plate, seed-pearls and pearls, gold-dust and gold-bullion," and as for the base metals, gems, ivory, spices, condiments, and foods: "Well, all these things were to be had in such abundance that I feel as if there were not enough words in the dictionary to name them all." Mendes Pinto, who could never forgo irony for long, felt obliged to excuse himself from cataloging the riches of China "so that everyone will see with what generosity the Lord our God has shared out with these benighted people the fruits of the earth he created."[62]

Yet transmissions of culture usually happen under the skin of empire and do not have to be politically inoculated. Junior partners in economic relationships can be sources of innovation. Travelers from afar are often tenacious custodians of their own cultural baggage. In culture, the sorcerer's apprentice can work alchemical transmutations. Like so many barbarian interlopers in advanced civilizations, the Portuguese had daunting strengths and transforming powers. Now, romantic nostalgia tempts the beholder of the ruins of the Portuguese East: the smooth-faced redoubts in Mombasa; the crumbling fortifications in Laristan, where caravan routes reached the coast; the scutcheons carved in red stone over the doors of merchant palaces in Cambay; the ruined gate of the fort of A Famosa in Malacca; the backless façade of São Paulo in Macao, where the Catholic, Lusophone community has not yet been swamped; the lavish churches, Portuguese sign boards, and architectural echoes in Goa; a few words of Portuguese origin in modern Japanese; and a few Japanese valleys where Christianity survived in secret for two-and-a-quarter centuries. But these are shoals of an eroded past. Except as a forerunner of later, larger-scale imperialisms, it is not around the Indian Ocean that Portuguese imperialism achieved its greatest impact.

[62] Fernão Mendes Pinto, *The Peregrination of Fernão Mendes Pinto,* trans. M. Lowery (London, 1920), pp. 156–157.

First, it influenced rimland by way of example. It is doubtful whether Castilian expansion would have gotten under way in the Atlantic without the stimulus of Portuguese competition. Castilian commitment to the conquest of the Canary Islands was feeble until the opportunity emerged to forestall the Infante Dom Henrique.[63] Castilian trading licenses to Guinea in the 1470s were issued in the course of war with Portugal, and it was here that Andalusian navigators acquired much of their mastery of the Atlantic.[64] The Castilian royal commission to Columbus was in part the result of envy at the profitability of Portugal's African trade; Magellan's was a response to Portuguese prominence in the trade of the spice islands. The Dutch were drawn to the Indian Ocean in emulation of the Portuguese example. The methods and nature of the Atlantic trades in sugar and slaves in the seventeenth century were borrowed, by almost all the European states and businesses that took part in it, from the Portuguese and Spanish models in Brazil and the Caribbean.

Secondly, Portugal played a vital role – or, for its black and native Brazilian victims a lethal one – in creating the Atlantic networks around which modern Western civilization took shape: revealing the South Atlantic wind system and linking it with the Indian Ocean; and pioneering transfusions of blood and culture across the ocean. The Portuguese example taught the potential of the transatlantic slave trade to other Europeans who engaged in it. The Atlantic is, in a sense, a Portuguese sea, with Portuguese-speaking communities dotted around its shores. But the African tints and flavors in much New World Atlantic-side culture, especially in Brazil, were transmitted in the early modern period in Portuguese slave ships.

Portuguese imperialism probably played a role in one of the great themes of the economic history of the early modern world: the altered balance of trade and wealth between "East" and "West"; that is, between the hitherto rich and industrially advanced economies of South and East Asia and the previously impoverished economies of Europe, which had long labored under the burden of an adverse trading account with partners at the other end of Eurasia. This adverse balance did not swing decisively in Europe's favor until the early nineteenth century for India and not until well into the second half of the same century for China. The relationship in the interim between European imperialism and Western economic growth is obscure, problematic, and fiercely debated. Nevertheless, the great extension of European economic activity into new markets and zones of production in the sixteenth, seventeenth, and eighteenth centuries evidently enriched

[63] P. E. Russell, *O Infante Dom Henrique e as Ilhas Canarias* (Lisbon, 1979), p. 19.

[64] J. W. Blake, *Europeans in West Africa* (2 vols., New York, 1967).

some parts of Europe, and it is generally presumed to have contributed toward the rapid growth that began in some Western economies in the late eighteenth century and led to industrialization in the nineteenth. In particular, thanks to new mining enterprises on colonial frontiers, profits of trade with previously unexploited markets, and fees earned by European carriers in the "country trades" of maritime Asia and the Indian Ocean, the expansion generated quantities of specie that European economies, compared with those in Eastern Asia, had generally lacked until this time. These new resources could, in turn, fuel expanding trade around Eurasia along the *carreira da Índia* and on the other routes opened by European navigators.[65]

At intervals during the history of Portuguese expansion, the Portuguese economy enjoyed privileged access to new sources of liquidity, especially gold and cowrie shells (which were highly prized by some of the slave-supplying societies of West Africa).[66] The story began with marginal Portuguese participation in the Saharan gold trade, especially from the factory of Arguim, from the 1440s. It continued at an accelerated rate with the establishment of the factory of São Jorge da Mina in 1482 and with the establishment of trading relations with the gold-rich empire of Mwene Mutapa in East Africa. These were opened, indirectly, in 1501 and yielded significant amounts of the precious metal at intervals until late in the seventeenth century. The gold and diamonds of late seventeenth- and eighteenth-century Brazil were a significant element in this increasing liquidity in the hundred years or so up to 1780, and especially in the period of high gold production in Brazil in the first half of the eighteenth century.[67] Meanwhile, Portuguese trade in the Atlantic grew relatively cash-rich, thanks to

[65] See H. E. Cross, "South American Bullion Production and Export, 1550–1750," in J. F. Richards, ed., *Precious Metals in the Later Medieval and Early Modern Worlds* (Durham, NC, 1983), pp. 397–423; A. Attman, *American Bullion in the European World Trade, 1600–1800* (Gotheburg, 1986); the summary in A. Gunder Frank, *ReOrient: Global Economy in the Asian Age* (Berkeley, CA, 1998), pp. 131–164, 278–283. Although insufficiently recognized in the subsequent literature, L. Dermigny's *La Chine et l'occident: Le commerce à Canton au XVIIIe siècle* (3 vols., Paris, 1964), made a contribution of fundamental importance. K. Pomeranz's *The Great Divergence: China, Europe and the Making of the Modern World Economy* (Princeton, NJ, 2000) takes a commendably larger view, looking at the distribution of resources in general and stressing the dynamic consequences of imperialism in the New World, on which see also Fernández-Armesto, *Millennium*, pp. 345–363.

[66] V. Magalhães Godinho, *Os descobrimentos e a economia mundial* (2 vols., Lisbon, 1963–1965), vol. 1 160–233, 327–347, 379–389. On diamond production, see C. R. Boxer, *The Golden Age of Brazil* (Manchester, 1995), pp. 205–225.

[67] Attman, *American Bullion,* pp. 27–29; C. R. Phillips, 'Trade in the Iberian Empires," in Tracy, *Rise of Merchant Empires: Long-Distance Trade in the Early Modern World, 1350–1750* (Cambridge, 1991), pp. 34–101 at p. 65.

the premium yielded by the slave trade and the leeching of precious metals from the Spanish empire.

Where – apart from the lavish gilding that makes some eighteenth-century Portuguese churches seem like temples of mammon, and the "braids, ornaments and other fripperies"[68] denounced by moralists – did the gold go? And the silver, which Portuguese slave merchants acquired from their customers – especially those in the silver-rich economy of the Spanish empire? The only prudent answer, given the present state of knowledge, is that, although much of it was diffused through Portuguese trade with Northern Europe and especially with England,[69] we do not know its final destination. It should not be assumed that silver "flocked" to China and gold to India to pay for Europe's abiding trade deficit. The Dutch experience in the seventeenth century suggests that increased trade with China and India could be financed from profits, which the Portuguese also made in abundance as carriers of intra-Asian trade. After redistribution in Europe, the total amount of increase in liquidity in Europe and America seems to have exceeded the increase in the value of trade in Asia.[70] In any case, historians' obsessions with commercial and monetary matters should probably be reined in: They are a *mal de siècle* of the modern, capitalist, industrialized economic era, with its huge volumes of trade and its preoccupation with cash computations of value. The stuff of world history is not primarily economic but cultural. In exchanges of culture, trade played only a small part in the early modern period, when volumes of trade were still relatively small and when other vectors of culture – such as migration, war, pilgrimage, exploration, and religious, scientific, and diplomatic missions – were all still of relatively great importance.

Finally, in the most fully global context, Portuguese expansion helped to carry the "seeds of change" that transformed so many environments and reversed the age-old pattern of evolution. Until the sixteenth century, evolution was on a divergent course, as the biota of mutually isolated or barely accessible continents grew increasingly distinct. Since then, as a result of the long-range shipping that spanned oceans and linked continents, evolution

[68] Giovanni Antonio "Antonil" Andreoni, quoted in C. R. Boxer, *The Golden Age of Brazil* p. 55.

[69] Even here, caution is advisable: Although gold remittances from Portugal to Britain continued throughout the eighteenth century, they declined in the second half and even experienced a brief reversal in 1790–1791. The overall balance of trade favored Portugal from 1787. See J. Ehrman, *The British Government and Commercial Negotiations with Europe, 1783–1793* (Cambridge, 1962), especially pp. 4–16, 205.

[70] W. Barrett, "World Bullion Flows, 1450–1800," in J. D. Tracy, ed., *The Rise of Merchant Empires*, pp. 224–254.

has been in a convergent phase where the same crops and livestock – and even the same diseases and human types – tend to recur all over the world. The state of the sources does not make the apportionment of responsibility easy: In most cases, the evidence about the chronology of the transmission of particular life forms cannot be matched with particular voyages or documented experiments in acclimatization. It is certain, however, that Portuguese experiments introduced the pepper and spices of India and the Moluccas into the soil of the New World and took chilies and Brazilian nuts and pulses, such as cashews and peanuts, to new homes in the cuisines of parts of East, South, and Southeast Asia.[71]

Broadly speaking, there were three types of long-range outreach available to imperial societies in the early modern period. They could follow trade winds (or all-year prevailing systems) like the Spanish and Dutch; monsoonal systems, like those that inflated far-reaching ambitions in maritime Asia; or they could expand to landward, like Russia in Siberia or China in Central Asia. The Portuguese did all three. Considered as an empire in the strict sense – a power structure that spreads political allegiance by conquest – the result was tentative and unsystematic. Readers of this book may feel that it has deconstructed its own subject: Earlier chapters have emphasized indigenous initiatives to such an extent that the "Portuguese empire" seems neither particularly imperial nor altogether Portuguese. Yet the Portuguese early modern outreach looks most impressive, paradoxically, in the broadest possible context. If we ask what difference it made to this place or that, the answer will, in most cases outside Portugal and Brazil, be modest. If we ask how big was its effect on the world, the answer is: huge. Today's world would be unrecognizable without it.

BIBLIOGRAPHICAL ESSAY

The best short introduction to the global-historical context of the European, and therefore a fortiori Portuguese, expansion in the "early modern" period is now David R. Ringrose's *Expansion and Global Interaction, 1200–1700* (New York, 2001). In recent years, the subject has been approached from five distinct and, in some respects, contrasting perspectives. First, a search for the origins of a new political "world order" or economic "world system" that distinguishes "modernity" from the era presumed to have preceded it has been represented magnificently by the work of Fernand Braudel, *Civilisation*

[71] A. J. R. Russell-Wood, *A World on the Move: The Portuguese in Africa, Asia and America, 1415–1808* (Manchester, 1992), pp. 153–180; V. Magalhães Godinho, *Os descobrimentos e a economia mundial* (4 vols., Lisbon, 1980–1983), vol., 4, pp. 23–50.

matérielle: économie et capitalisme, xve–xviiie siècles (3 vols., Paris, 1979), and Immanuel Wallerstein, *The Modern World-System* (3 vols. so far, New York, 1974–1989). In this tradition, "the rise of the West" seems the dominant and decisive theme of the period, and a vast amount of work has been devoted to exploring the nature and origins of this supposed phenomenon, notably, in recent years, William McNeill's *The Rise of the West* (New York, 1972), Eric L. Jones's *The European Miracle: Environments, Economies and Geopolitics in the History of Europe and Asia* (Cambridge, 1981), John M. Roberts's *The Triumph of the West* (London, 1985), Geoffrey Barraclough ed., *The Times Atlas of World History,* 4th ed. (London, 1993), and David Landes's *The Wealth and Poverty of Nations* (New York, 1998). Meanwhile, a more recent and radical tradition in global history has attempted to transcend Eurocentrism and assign the "rise of the West" a less prominent place. Two of the great monumental works of modern historiography helped to lay the groundwork for this revisionist enterprise by suggesting the extent of the West's cultural and technological indebtedness to Asian cultures: Joseph Needham's *Science and Civilisation in China* (12 vols. so far, Cambridge, 1956–); and Donald F. Lach's *Asia in the Making of Europe* (9 vols. so far, Chicago, 1965–). Joseph R. Levenson's *European Expansion and the Counter-example of Asia* (Englewood Cliffs, NJ, 1967) and Marshall G. S. Hodgson's *The Venture of Islam* (3 vols., Chicago, 1974) were of enormous importance in inspiring the effort that in the 1990s generated a number of attempts to write global history on new lines, including Felipe Fernández-Armesto's *Millennium: A History of the Last Thousand Years* (New York, 1995, latest ed. *Millennium: A History of Our Last Thousand Years* [London, 1999]), which pioneered an attempt at an approach from multiple perspectives, and Jack Goody's *The East in the West* (Cambridge, 1996), a superb essay that, proceeding by case studies, identified a number of Eurocentric myths, while A. Gunder Frank's *ReOrient: Global Economy in the Asian Age* (Berkeley, CA, 1998) made a powerful case for reorientation within the traditional trajectory of economic history. Frank wrote with the fervor of conversion from a previously opposed point of view that can also be detected in Eric L. Jones's *Growth Recurring: Economic Change in World History* (Ann Arbor, MI, 2000). Kenneth Pomeranz's *The Great Divergence: China, Europe and the Making of the Modern World Economy* (Princeton, NJ, 2000) represents a systematic attempt to identify the role of European expansion in the adjustment of the global balance. A fourth type of approach has been by way of comparative case studies in the method known as "comparative world history," so far with modest results represented, for instance, among recent work, by Philip D. Curtin's *The World and the West: The European Challenge and the Overseas Response in the Age of Empire* (Cambridge, 2000). Finally, the importance of the environmental perspective has been demonstrated by William McNeill's *Plagues and Peoples* (New York, 1976) and Alfred W. Crosby's *Ecological Imperialism: The Biological Expansion of Europe, 900–1900* (Cambridge, 1986) for microbiota and macrobiota, respectively. Henry Hobhouse's *Seeds of Change: Six Plants that Transformed Mankind* (London, 1999) made an important contribution, as did the exhibition catalogue edited by Herman J. Viola and Carolyn Margolis, *Seeds of Change* (Washington, DC, 1991). Felipe Fernández-Armesto's *Civilizations: Culture, Ambition and the Transformation of Nature* (New York, 2001) attempts to classify global history into environmental categories.

Recent histories of the Portuguese empire that help to set it in global context include Joel Serrão and A. H. de Oliveira Marques's *Nova história da expansão Portuguesa* (11 vols., Lisbon, 1992–1998), which concentrates on political and social history. V. Magalhães Godinho's *Os descobrimentos e a economia mundial* (4 vols., Lisbon, 1991), which is in effect a new edition of the important work cited in footnotes 66 and 71, is confined to economic matters – interpreted somewhat narrowly as mainly concerned with commercial and monetary matters. A. de Oliveira et al., *História dos descobrimentos e expansão Portuguesa* (Lisbon, 1990), is a consciously introductory work that does not extend beyond the sixteenth century.

INDEX

Index

Index

Index

Index

Index

Index

Index

Index

Index

Index

Index

Index

Index

Index

Index

Index

Index

Index

Index

Index

Index

Index

Index